Conversation Analysis

We live our lives in conversation, building families, societies and civilisations. In over seven thousand languages across the world, the basic infrastructure by which we communicate remains the same. This is the first ever book-length linguistic introduction to conversation analysis (CA), the field that has done more than any other to illuminate the mechanics of interaction. Starting by locating CA by reference to a number of cognate disciplines investigating language in use, it provides an overview of the origins and methodology of CA. By using conversational data from a range of languages, it examines the basic apparatus of sequence organisation: turn-taking, preference, identity construction and repair. As the basis for these investigations, the book uses the twin analytic resources of action and sequence to throw new light on the origins and nature of language use.

REBECCA CLIFT is Senior Lecturer in the Department of Language and Linguistics, University of Essex. She is co-editor of *Reporting Talk* (Cambridge, 2006).

CAMBRIDGE TEXTBOOKS IN LINGUISTICS

General editors: P. AUSTIN, J. BRESNAN, B. COMRIE, S. CRAIN, W. DRESSLER, C. EWEN, R. LASS, D. LIGHTFOOT, K. RICE, I. ROBERTS, S. ROMAINE, N.V. SMITH.

Conversation Analysis

CONVERSATION ANALYSIS

REBECCA CLIFT

University of Essex

CAMBRIDGE
UNIVERSITY PRESS

CAMBRIDGE
UNIVERSITY PRESS

University Printing House, Cambridge CB2 8BS, United Kingdom

Cambridge University Press is part of the University of Cambridge.

It furthers the University's mission by disseminating knowledge in the pursuit of education, learning and research at the highest international levels of excellence.

www.cambridge.org
Information on this title: www.cambridge.org/9780521198509

© Rebecca Clift 2016

First published 2016
Reprinted 2017

Printed in the United Kingdom by Clays, St Ives plc

A catalogue record for this publication is available from the British Library

Library of Congress Cataloging-in-Publication Data
Clift, Rebecca author.
Conversation analysis / Rebecca Clift, University of Essex.
Cambridge, United Kingdom ; New York : Cambridge University Press, 2016. | Includes bibliographical references.
LCCN 2016012971
LCSH: Conversation analysis.
LCC P95.45 .C63 2016 | DDC 302.34/6–dc23
LC record available at https://lccn.loc.gov/2016012971

ISBN 978-0-521-19850-9 Hardback
ISBN 978-0-521-15719-3 Paperback

Imagination is not, as is sometimes thought, the ability to invent; it is the ability to disclose that which exists.

John Berger

Contents

Figures

Tables

Preface

As I write, conversation analysis (CA) has just marked the first half-century of its existence as an established domain of research since the first of Harvey Sacks's *Lectures on Conversation* in 1964. While CA emerged through sociology, it has a reach that goes far beyond, into anthropology, psychology, communication, cognitive science, evolutionary theory, education, clinical research and practice, and electrical engineering.

In particular, however, this book is for linguists: students of language who may be familiar with some approaches to the study of language, but less so with investigating its use in interaction. However, it is a testament to both the centrality of language in interaction and the growing influence of CA in linguistics that the groundbreaking paper of Sacks et al. (1974) on turn-taking is 'by far the most cited' paper to have appeared in *Language*, the journal of the Linguistic Society of America since 1924 (Joseph, 2003:463).

The disciplinary scope of the book

As an overview of the methods and findings of CA, the format of the book may be unfamiliar to those expecting a textbook organised along traditional linguistic lines. So those areas within the standard linguistic compass, such as phonetics, morphosyntax and semantics, are not represented here in familiar guise, as subjects of 'top-down' investigation. Rather, in accordance with the 'bottom-up' methods of CA, interactional phenomena usually investigated within such domains are the focus insofar as they are implicated in the construction of *action*. Moreover, while the concern with action may be familiar to linguists, it is in the bottom-up methods of investigating action – in *sequences* rather than as discrete acts – that CA diverges from much familiar linguistic inquiry. A orientational overview with respect to the central concerns of CA, and its relationship to work in relevant linguistic territory, is provided in the first chapter. This makes it clear that, while CA's investigation of 'language in context' announces its obvious pertinence to semantics and pragmatics, its focus on the construction and recognition of action makes it relevant far beyond these domains. So, as we shall see in the chapters that follow, the concern with the construction of action is germane to investigations of its phonetic, prosodic and morphosyntactic resources; and the focus on how action is recognised speaks to central questions in both psycholinguistics and sociolinguistics.

Linguistic data

The vast majority of work in CA to date has been conducted on the data of English, and so the foundational expositions inevitably, and regrettably, reflect this linguistic bias. There is now a growing body of CA work on languages other than English, and many of the foundational arguments here could be exemplified in data from a variety of languages; however, in keeping with the primary expository function of the book, I have, for the sake of clarity, kept in the main to English exemplars. Where possible, however, cross-linguistic data are included to illuminate how linguistic variation is accommodated in the universal principles of interactional organisation. So in keeping with the design of the volume as an overview, the number of exemplars of each analytic point are here limited. This, it should be stressed, goes against usual CA conventions, which standardly require at least three exemplars to show that a practice is not idiosyncratic to a particular episode of interaction. Only one or two are generally used in this book for illustrative purposes, to keep the size of the volume under control. The excerpts themselves are transcribed according to the conventions developed by Gail Jefferson, and described in Chapter 2. In a few cases, where the source uses slightly different notation, the reader is referred to the source material for detailed information on conventions.

With respect to coverage of linguistic resources, the skewing towards morphosyntactic phenomena is representative of the research in the discipline as a whole. Sustained conversation-analytic engagement with phonetic and prosodic features of interaction has come late, relative to the development of the field. I have, where possible, included some of this work to indicate the scope of investigation in this field, aware that for some it will be nowhere near enough.

It should also be noted that, while work on phenomena such as eye-gaze and embodiment are increasingly the subject of analytic attention, consideration of those domains is here restricted, in keeping with the linguistic focus of the book. The same applies to a stream of work that has been termed 'Applied CA': that is, the examination of interaction in work or institutional settings, such as the clinical environment, courtroom interaction or broadcast interviews. Certainly, data from these contexts are employed in what follows, but their institutionality is not necessarily germane to the points they are illustrating.

These caveats are offered on the premise that the reader will be guided by the references and further reading suggestions below.

A note on how to use this book

In aiming to introduce some of the foundational work in CA and present an overview of its core working methods, this book aims for a logical progression and coherence, such that each chapter presupposes familiarity with concepts introduced in earlier ones. Chapter 1 is an orientational overview for those who have some background in linguistics and approaches to language use. It aims to show how the 'bottom-up' analytic focus of CA has yielded insights inaccessible to top-down methods. It is not intended to be an overview of various approaches, but rather assumes some knowledge of them in order to stake out the distinctive territory of CA. Chapter 2, on the origins of CA, and the rationale for CA transcription conventions, is relatively self-contained, so readers wishing to move straight to findings may wish to go straight from the Introduction to Chapter 3 and pick up Chapter 2 later. However, like the Introduction, Chapter 2 unavoidably – and designedly – looks ahead to material in other Chapters. Chapters 3, 4, 5 and 6 do, in particular, nevertheless, assume progression; Chapter 7 less so. In some places, it is inevitable that examination of the data in an earlier chapter makes reference to phenomena in a later chapter. This is particularly the case for Chapter 7, on repair. In the same way that repair is potentially relevant at any moment – it occurs in the course of many exchanges throughout the book – so Chapter 7 may be potentially relevant at any moment. It is thus relatively independent and can be read for clarification regarding repair at any earlier stage. Chapter 8, the Conclusion, returns to the issues raised in the Introduction, Chapter 1. There is a certain amount of cross-referencing between chapters – data excerpts being examined in one chapter may include phenomena pertinent to discussion in another, and so in some cases, an excerpt in one chapter is re-examined with a different lens in another.

As an introduction to CA, this book does not aim to be comprehensive and has had to be selective. The references should provide a guide for further reading. The most useful collections of primary sources are Atkinson and Heritage (1984), Lerner (2004), Drew and Heritage (2006, 2013). Sidnell and Stivers (2013) is a collection of specialist overviews. With respect to specific topics, Schegloff (2007a) is the baseline resource for sequence organisation, and Hayashi et al. (2013) is a cross-linguistic collection of work on repair. Sidnell (2009) is a cross-linguistic collection on a variety of topics. Linguistically informed collections include Ochs et al. (1996), Selting and Couper-Kuhlen (2001), Ford et al. (2002), Hakulinen and Selting (2005), Szczepek Reed and Raymond (2013) and Thompson et al. (2015). Couper-Kuhlen and Selting (1996) and Barth-Weingarten et al. (2010) focus on prosody and Couper-Kuhlen and Ford (2004) on phonetics. For CA in institutional settings, Drew and Heritage (1992) and Heritage and Clayman (2010) are the places to start.

CA work appears in a number of journals, including *Language in Society*, *Journal of Pragmatics*, *Discourse and Society*, *Discourse Studies* and *Text and*

Talk, but its home base has become *Research on Language and Social Interaction*. There are two main international conferences where CA work is prominent: the International Conference on Conversation Analysis (ICCA), once every four years, and the biennial International Pragmatics Association Conference (IPRA), where CA represents a significant stream of work.

The International Society for Conversation Analysis (ISCA) is at: isca .clubexpress.com. ISCA is a professional association designed to serve the needs of researchers, both faculty and student, of language and social interaction across a variety of disciplines. In its own words, a major aim is to 'encourage and enhance interdisciplinary research into the structure and dynamics of social interaction through the creation of a multi-disciplinary community of scholars'. The ISCA website contains useful links to other relevant professional associations, and to the academic journal *Research on Language and Social Interaction*. With respect to other online resources, there is a helpful CA tutorial established by Charles Antaki at http://homepages.lboro.ac.uk/~sscal/sitemenu.htm.

The research materials databases originally set up by Paul ten Have have been an invaluable resource over many years and are continuously updated. These are the main page and bibliography pages for materials in ethnomethodology and conversation analysis: http://emcawiki.net/Main_Page; http://emcawiki.net /EMCA_bibliography_database.

Acknowledgements

I have benefited enormously along the way from the generosity of many. Paul Drew, David Good, Rachael Harris, the late Gail Jefferson and John Local have, at various times and in various places, been wise and inspiring teachers. Paul read an early draft and provided invaluable guidance. The LSA Summer Institute at UCSB 2001 and the term I spent at UCLA in 2002 were the most intense and intellectually stimulating times of my academic life; for them, I am hugely indebted to Manny Schegloff, Steve Clayman, John Heritage, Gene Lerner, Sandy Thompson and Don Zimmerman. Over the years – and in many a data session – I have found in Charles Antaki, Liz Holt, Celia Kitzinger, Irene Koshik, John Rae, Hiroko Tanaka, Ray Wilkinson and Sue Wilkinson sources of insight and support. I have also very much appreciated the support of Steve Levinson and his group, especially Nick Enfield and Tanya Stivers, formerly at the MPI, Nijmegen; subsequent MPI researchers Joe Blythe, Simeon Floyd, Elliott Hoey, Elizabeth Manrique and Giovanni Rossi gave generously of their material, some still in press. A number of people – Charles Antaki, Liz Holt, Leendert Plug and Ray Wilkinson – read drafts and provided very helpful observations and nudged me in the direction of clarification. I owe a particular debt to John Heritage, Chase Raymond and Kobin Kendrick for extremely detailed and constructive comments on the entire manuscript. They gave my first draft more care than I had a right to expect. What improvements resulted are due to all of these people. I also pay tribute, with gratitude for his unfailing forbearance, to my editor, Andrew Winnard, who kicked the whole thing off, and Bethany Gaunt, Christina Sarigiannidou and my hugely conscientious copy-editor Jacqueline French, and the rest of the team at Cambridge University Press.

Closer to (my) home, colleagues, current and former, provided welcome support in ways too numerous to mention (usually over meals too numerous to mention): Doug Arnold, Bob Borsley, Dave Britain, Sonja Eisenbeiss, Adela Ganem, Wyn Johnson, Florence Myles, Beatriz de Paiva, Andrew Radford, Louisa Sadler and Andrew Spencer. My students over the last twenty years have taught me more than I have taught them, but I must single out Faye Abu Abah, Angeliki Balantani, Ariel Vazquez Carranza and Caroline Dunmore for their thoughtful comments on various drafts. Those anonymised in the pages to come, whose interactions we are privileged to witness, deserve the thanks of us all.

Closer still, I am deeply thankful for the wisdom and guidance of Kathryn Burton at a vital time. I'm also very grateful to my sister Naomi; my brother-in-law Jonathan Seglow and my dear friend James Allen were also a source of encouragement from other corners of the academic world.

All of these people, directly or indirectly, had some positive influence on the production of this book.

My debt to four people goes beyond words: my parents, Jean and Marc, whom I miss every day; and at home, Graeme and Esme. Together, over the years, they have kept 'My suspect edifice upright in Air/As Atlas did the sky', and it is to them that this volume, and its author, are dedicated.

1   Introduction: why study conversation?

This chapter shows the importance of studying conversation as a route into understanding language in social life. As an introduction to the chapters that follow, it establishes the 'Two Things': the two fundamental things at the core of conversation analysis (CA): action and sequence. We examine some basic linguistic conceptions of the purpose of language, the often indirect relationships between grammatical forms and functions, and the role that 'meaning' and 'context' have played in the investigation of language, within the domains of semantics and pragmatics. Understanding how actions are accomplished collaboratively across sequences of talk provides insights into the basic infrastucture of interaction that may be overlooked in the face of the structural diversity of, and constant evolution in, the languages of the world. We explore areas of commonality and difference between CA and other domains of work within linguistics. This is done initially through an overview of three dominant theories within pragmatics, Speech Act Theory, Gricean implicature, and Relevance Theory, showing something of how some of the phenomena examined in these approaches are treated in the data of CA. We then examine more overtly observational approaches, such as sociolinguistics, interactional linguistics, anthropology and discourse analysis, to show the distinctive contribution CA brings to work on language in interaction: one that goes far beyond the traditional domains of linguistic study. This Introduction ends with an overview of the chapters to follow.

We live our lives in conversation; between the first 'hello' and the last 'goodbye', conversation is where the world's business gets done. Each of us owes our very existence, at least in part, to conversation; we conduct our lives through it, building families, societies and civilisations. Yet the means by which this is done is anything but obvious. This book is an introduction to the study of conversation through the methods and findings of conversation analysis (CA), the domain that has done more than any other to examine interaction, that is, action between people.

Language – at the meeting point of biology and culture – has been the object of intellectual inquiry for centuries, and long regarded as the core of what it is to be human; the investigation of language structure is a basic project in the cognitive sciences. However, only in the last half-century has systematic attention been given to the domain of interaction – where language may be the central component, but not the exclusive one.

In taking interaction as its focus, this book seeks to investigate the communicative and cultural constraints shaping language as they intersect with the cognitive. It takes the stance that, to establish what it is to be human, what happens *between* minds – the visible work done by participants in interaction – is fundamental to finding out what is *in* them. We start by establishing the twin foundations of CA: **action** and **sequence**, and how they promise to illuminate some of the central concerns in linguistics. Through the lens of these, we examine a number of traditional linguistic domains to offer some of the insights CA has made into some long-standing linguistic conundrums concerning the meaning of utterances. In doing so, we not only show what linguistics has to gain from an apprehension of both action and sequence, but also introduce the analytic themes to be pursued in the following chapters.

1.1   The basics: the 'Two Things'

The 'Two Things' game invites us to identify the two fundamental things about any domain.[1] For CA, the two things from which all else follows are *action* – broadly, the things we do with words[2] – and *sequence* – 'a course of action implemented through talk' (Schegloff, 2007a:9). For those more used to dealing with sentences, utterances, meaning and grammar, the terms represent a wholesale methodological tilt of a familiar planet, linguistics, on its axis, and it may not be immediately apparent how either figures in language use. However, the importance of both goes back to the very origins of human evolution.

While the dating of the origins of language is a matter of some dispute (see Dediu and Levinson, 2013, for a reassessment of the usually quoted 50,000–100,000 years to half a million years), what is beyond doubt is that there is evidence of cooperation among our earliest human ancestors, *Homo habilis*, around 2 million years ago. In other words, joint action in the form of cooperation and coordination has been central in the development of humankind. In addition, around seven thousand languages, at a rough estimate, have evolved and are in present-day use; and the study of this diversity and its origins provides linguistics with some of its fundamental and motivating questions regarding the basis for linguistic structure and the nature of its biological and cultural underpinnings.

In seeking to understand this diversity, many have recognised the origins of language change in language use (see, e.g., Hopper, 1987; Lehmann, [1982]1995; Croft, 2000; Coussé and Mengden, 2014; Bybee, 2015). As Evans and Levinson put it: 'most linguistic diversity is the product of historical cultural evolution operating on relatively independent traits' (2009:444). Thus, the examination of linguistic structure reveals 'general cognitive abilities: the importance of repetition in the entrenchment of neuromotor patterns, the use of similarity in categorization, and the construction of generalizations across similar patterns' (Bybee, 2006:730; see also Edelman, 1992, and Hurford, 2007).

There are, of course, uses of language that are not embodied in interaction – jotting down a shopping list, reading a novel or working on a computer – but overwhelmingly, we encounter language, and are socialised, in interaction, and specifically in that particular form of interaction that we recognise as ordinary

---

[1] This proposes that for any subject, 'there are only two things you need to know. Everything else is the application of those two things, or just not important', e.g. trading in stocks and shares: '1. Buy low 2. Sell high'; acting on stage: 1.'Don't forget your lines' 2. 'Don't run into the set.' See Glen Whitman, 'The Two Things' website, currently at: www.csun.edu/~dgw61315/thetwothings.html.

[2] To paraphrase Austin (1962).

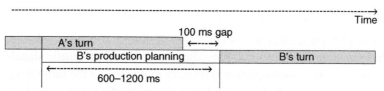

Figure 1.1 *Overlap of comprehension and production processes in conversation (based on Levinson, 2013a:104)*

conversation.[3] This is equally the case in the phylogenetic development of language down the ages as in the ontogenetic development of the individual. A major contribution to work on the emergence of linguistic structures has been that which examines the discourse basis of various grammaticalisation traits, whether features such as grammatical transitivity (Hopper and Thompson, 1980), lexical categories (Hopper and Thompson, 1984), syntactic change (Givón, 2008, Traugott, 2010) and phonology (Bybee, 2001).

Alongside the interest in the interactional foundations of language evolution and structural diversity, work in psycholinguistics (Clark, 1996) and formal linguistics (e.g. Traum, 1994; Ginzburg, 2012; Ginzburg and Poesio, 2015) has also sought to ground investigation of language in its interactional home base. As such work has recognised, actions – and specifically linguistic actions, such as requesting, inviting, complimenting, complaining, agreeing, disagreeing and so forth – are not unilateral, but jointly and collaboratively achieved. Moreover, as we shall see in the course of this book, this applies as much to actions that, on the face of it, appear to be unilateral, such as referring or informing.

While the value of investigating language as action is thus recognised in many domains of linguistic research, less so is the means by which action is implemented: the sequence. In its focus on how actions are implemented across sequences, CA is committed to studying the spontaneous online production and understanding of language *in time*. One of the most striking facts about the temporal production of turns-at-talk is that while it takes over 600 milliseconds to plan and produce the shortest turn in conversation (Levelt, 1989), on average, and depending on the particular language, gaps between conversational turns are around 200 milliseconds (de Ruiter et al., 2006, Stivers et al., 2009); see Figure 1.1.

There thus has to be an element of linguistic 'double-tasking' in comprehension and production processes. As Levinson notes, conversational participants

> must have parsed what they have heard and understood its grammar well enough to predict both the content and its structure, so that they can predict when it will come to an end (otherwise their response may come too early or too late) . . . action ascription involves numerous dimensions . . . so it would seem to

---

[3] For talk that is not conversational, and a product of specific, standardly work-based, contexts, such as the medical encounter or courtroom exchanges – so-called institutional talk – see Drew and Heritage (1992) and Heritage and Clayman (2010). See also Chapter 4 for how the turn-taking system for ordinary conversation constitutes the baseline for such institutional talk.

be a much more complex and indeterminate process than decoding the structure
and content of the turn. That is the miracle ...   (2013a:103–4)

The implications for interaction across languages of diverse structures, whether
left- or right-branching, are profound. Prosodic, syntactic and pragmatic signalling of turn completion or incompletion is directly motivated by the turn-taking
system, so that, for example, the English relative clause structure in the turn 'I am
reading the book which I gave you' is potentially more vulnerable to overlap than
the equivalent clause in the comparable Dravidian or Japanese turn, glossable as
'The I to-you given book I am reading' (Levinson, 1983:365). In the development
of the discipline, and in the body of research to date, the CA focus has been just
this miracle: how actions are implemented and recognised in talk-in-interaction –
or, in its abbreviated form, 'talk'[4] – a term now preferred over 'conversation' as
the more general designation for our interactions through language.

The cross-linguistic study of coordinated action is in its early days relative to the
long-established research programme in modern linguistics. Moreover, evidently
the bottom-up, rigorously empirical working methods of CA are not conducive to
making top-down generalisations. However, the search for universals initiated by
Chomsky (1957, 1965) and, from another perspective, by Greenberg (1963, 1966),
and still subject to vigorous debate (see Evans and Levinson, 2009; and Levinson
and Evans, 2010) resulting in the more recent proposal that recursion is 'the only
uniquely human component of the faculty of language' (Hauser et al., 2002:1569)[5]
focuses in no small part on issues of methodology, interpretation and standards of
evidence in linguistics (see, e.g., Everett, 2005, 2009; Jackendoff and Pinker, 2005,
and the responses in Nevins et al., 2009). In contrast, the conversation-analytic focus
on participants' own displayed understandings has delivered incrementally.
However, as we shall see, these bottom-up methods have already yielded enough
evidence to suggest that in the face of all the structural variation and diversity across
the languages of the world, elements of the procedural infrastructure of interaction
(Schegloff, 1992b:1338) studied by CA are indeed universal. So turn-taking, the
organisation of sequences, the conversational preference for particular actions and
the organisation of repair mechanisms in talk – all part of that procedural infrastructure – are proving to be empirically robust across languages and language
groups. As Levinson observes:

> language is held to be essentially universal, whereas language use is thought
> to be more open to cultural influences. But the reverse may in fact be far more
> plausible: there is obvious cultural codification of many aspects of language
> from phoneme to syntactic construction, whereas the uncodified, low-level
> background of usage principles or strategies may be fundamentally culture-
> independent ... Underlying presumptions, heuristics and principles of usage
> may be more immune to cultural influence simply because they are

[4] Schegloff notes that none of the research on embodiment and bodily conduct has undermined any
of the findings established on the basis of talk alone (2009:360).
[5] We return to this issue in Chapter 3.

prerequisites for the system to work at all, preconditions even for learning language.   (2000:xiv)

The chapters that follow explore the implications of the methodological tilt towards 'action' in 'sequence', starting in this Introduction by examining some of the foundational work in CA and what it has to offer linguistics. It first examines some approaches to language use and the search for meaning within semantics, pragmatics and sociolinguistics, and then briefly examines the domains of interactional linguistics, linguistic anthropology and discourse analysis as the areas of investigation with the greatest perceived overlap with CA. However, despite areas of common interest, there are also areas that are methodologically and perspectively distinct; this stakes out the basic territory.

1.2   The view from linguistics

1.2.1   The search for meaning

All sciences search for underlying regularities – that's the game, and there is no branch of linguistics . . . that is not a player . . . The art is to find the highest level generalization that still has empirical 'bite'.   (Evans and Levinson, 2009:475)

The paper in the *Proceedings of the National Academy of Sciences* puts it crisply: 'language has two functions: to convey information and to negotiate the type of relationship holding between speaker and hearer' (Pinker et al., 2008:833).[6] In this, it virtually echoes the perspective of Malinowski a century ago, who in coining the phrase 'phatic communion'[7] thereby gave students of language licence to dismiss certain things done in interaction as essentially social and so unworthy of consideration by students of language:

Are words in Phatic Communion used primarily to convey meaning, the meaning which is symbolically theirs? Certainly not! They fulfil a social function and that is their principal aim, but they are neither the result of intellectual reflection, nor do they necessarily arouse reflection in the listener . . . we may say that language does not function here as a means of transmission of thought.   (1923:315)

This emphasis on language as essentially 'transmission of thought', its object 'to convey meaning', is preserved in the traditional division of labour within linguistic study.[8] Here, in very broad terms, the study of word and sentence meaning,

---

[6] In his best-selling popular linguistics book, Pinker puts it even more simply: 'This is the essence of the language instinct: language conveys news' (1994: 83).

[7] 'phatic communion . . . a type of speech in which ties of union are created by a mere exchange of words' (Malinowski, 1923:315).

[8] One prominent pragmatic approach, namely Relevance Theory, does consider so-called phatic communication within the scope of cogntive pragmatic theory (see Žegarac and Clark, 1999) but does not question the essential distinction between the so-called phatic and non-phatic.

largely the preserve of semantics, overlaps with the domain of pragmatics. This takes utterance meaning – that is, the meaning of a sentence in its context (Bar-Hillel, 1970; see also Levinson, 1983: 18–19) as the object of investigation. Within the study of pragmatics, three theoretical perspectives in particular have focused on utterance meaning: Speech Act Theory, Grice's theory of implicature, and Relevance Theory. The last – and indeed most recent – of these three, Relevance Theory, has, of all pragmatic approaches, attempted to address the issue of context and how it figures in utterance interpretation. In its concern with context, it shares a focus, if not a methodology, with sociolinguistics, the empirical orientation of which would suggest it has common cause with CA. Moreover, both interactional linguistics and discourse analysis share some, but not all, of the aims and methods of CA. The following sections briefly examine each of these domains of study in turn to establish the similarities and differences between these approaches and CA; they show why, when it comes to interaction, CA puts action and sequence at the heart of its investigations.

On semantic meaning: stability in action

The linguistic emphasis on language as information transfer, embodied in what Reddy (1979) identifies as a conduit metaphor (cf. Malinowski's 'words ... to convey meaning'), suggests that meaning – encoded and then decoded in the act of communication – is linguistic 'cargo'. However, it is evident that as soon as we examine interaction, a conception of 'meaning' may be enriched by a consideration of both action and sequence. Take, in the first instance, a simple example, grounded firmly in the realm of the so-called phatic: *thank you.*

The fact that meaning does not necessarily map straightforwardly onto use is evident when we consider the meaning of *thank you* in French. Standardly, this is taken to be *merci* – and, indeed, in the context of, for example, accepting a gift, this equivalence holds. However, in one everyday context, it is clear that, in actual fact, *thank you* in English is used in just the opposite way to *merci* in French, and that is in response to an offer. Where a standalone *thank you* accepts an offer, a standalone *merci* rejects one: the actions implemented by these apparent semantic equivalents are thus here entirely contrastive. Here, a search for meaning turns up apparent equivalents, whereas an investigation of action reveals them, in this interactional context, to be sharply divergent.

So understanding that *thank you* might be appropriate to accept a gift, but not, in English, to refuse a drink, depends upon our recognition of what the prior turn was doing. Moreover, with its interactional production, the sequential properties of *thank you* become evident, in that the prosody of *thank you* intrinsically anchors it in a specific sequential position. That is, while stress on *thank* announces this action as initiating thanks, stress on *you* announces it as *reciprocating* thanks. *Thank **you*** implicitly proposes itself as responsive to a prior expression of thanks.

Action, then, is implemented across sequences. Furthermore, if an example such as *thank you* appears mundane and inconsequential – indeed, to be dismissed as merely phatic – consider this: one contributing factor in the world's biggest airline disaster to date, at Tenerife airport in 1977, was a misunderstanding of what the apparently mundane word *Okay* was doing (Roitsch et al., 1977). The message from the cockpit of a KLM plane to the control tower, 'we are now uh-takin' off' or 'at take-off' (the recording is unclear) is met by 'Okay' and then a pause of nearly two seconds. The next portion of the utterance is obscured for the KLM pilot because of radio interference. Here, it subsequently emerged that the control tower was using 'Okay' to acknowledge the prior talk – as a receipt token (on which, see Schegloff, 1982). The pilot, however, taking 'Okay' not simply as a receipt but to authorise take-off duly did so, unable, in thick fog, to see the Pan Am plane in his path. Five hundred and eighty-three people lost their lives in the ensuing collision.[9]

We use the same resources to implement actions across sequences, whether apparently insignificant or hugely momentous – and it is this consequentiality (or, rather, con-sequentiality) of such communicative actions that an appeal to meaning does not wholly capture, even in the case where the meanings of *thank you* or *OK* are intuitively accessible. For many lexical items, intuitions with respect to meaning are reasonably straightforwardly accessed, and indeed fairly malleable; so, as Heritage notes, 'the typification "drink" may be revised towards a more 'fringe' meaning, if when offered "a drink", your host is boiling a kettle' (2011:264).[10] In this instance, context clearly picks out the typification, just as a head nod might either be – according to context – accepting an offer of a drink or buying a Ming vase worth millions (on the latter, see Heath, 2013). But how to understand context when, in the case of linguistic objects (in the most general sense of the term), the semantic core itself may not be easily accessible? The meaning of *drink* or, for that matter, *thank you* or *okay* may be straightforwardly and readily available to intuition, but this is by no means always the case. It is at this point that the analytic relevance, not only of action, but of sequences of action, becomes apparent, for the apprehension of both meaning and context.

There are clearly cases where specifying the meaning of a linguistic object is not straightforward. Take, for example, the commonly used English particle *actually*. A search for 'high level generalisation', as noted by Evans and Levinson, clearly needs to account for something so recurrently used in conversation; and yet, it does not follow that recurrent use can necessarily lead a

---

[9] *Okay* was, as a consequence, dropped from the authorised standard phrases used in air traffic communications. For conversational uses of *okay*, see Beach (1993).

[10] As Johnson-Laird observes, nouns are in fact more like pronouns than is commonly recognised. As with Heritage's example of *drink*, Johnson-Laird illustrates how, at utterance level, context picks out salient aspects of any given object on the example of the lexical item *tomato* where different features are selected by utterance context – in (a) its spherical shape, (b) its colour and (c) its squishiness:
(a) The tomato rolled across the floor
(b) The sun was a ripe tomato
(c) He accidentally sat on a tomato   (1987:197)

native speaker to formulate what *actually* means.[11] However, it is here that starting, not from the generalisation but from the 'empirical bite' – examining a linguistic object on various occasions of its interactional use – may provide some analytic yield. Of course, 'bite' had been effectively ruled out of the game by Chomsky in setting out the main aims of linguistics in his distinction between 'competence' and 'performance':

> A record of natural speech will show numerous false starts, deviations from rules, changes of plan in mid-course, and so on. The problem for the linguist, as well as for the child learning the language, is to determine from the data of performance the underlying system of rules that has been mastered by the speaker-hearer that he puts to use in actual performance.   (1965:4)

However, excluding any investigation of 'the data of performance' because of its apparently 'degenerate quality and narrowly limited extent' (p. 58), and seeking underlying regularities from idealised and abstracted linguistic data risks ruling out of the game just the 'record of natural speech', in Chomsky's words, which may be necessary to the investigation – material such as the following:[12]

(1) (Clift, 2001:277; H88:U:2:2)
      (L=Lesley, K=Kevin. Gordon is L's son, who has just done a driving test (l. 2); Katherine her daughter, who is currently away at university.)

```
 1L   [hYe:s. Oh: shame.h.hhhh Gordon didn't pass his
 2      test I'm afraid,h=
 3K    =Oh dear
 4L    .k.tch He's goin- (.) Well.hh u-he was hoping tih get
 5      it (0.2) in: uh in the summer but u (.) they're getting
 6      very booked up so I don't know if he'll even: get it in
 7      the:n.h
 8      (1.1)
 9K    Yes I: ah: no doubt he's back e(.)t uh
10      (0.5)
11L    .hhhh Yes. We're going up- (.) we:ll- (.) we're get(0.2)
12→    actually it's g'nna be a rather busy Ju:ne, Kathrine's
13      home f'three weeke:n:ds. As it happens people're coming
14      do:wn'n c'n bring'er down which is rather nice,
15      (1.2)
16L    which e-aa::: so we're rather looking forward t'that,hh
17      (1.5)
18L    hA[n:
19K      [Yes indee:[d (--------)
```

---

[11] In current dictionary definitions, the prime emphasis is laid on its function as a marker of fact and truth, 'as opposed to *possibly, potentially, theoretically, ideally*; really, in reality' (*Oxford English Dictionary*, 1933), and its sense is also paraphrased as 'strange as it may seem' (*Longman Dictionary of Contemporary English*, 1984). The *OED* states that it is 'not said of the objective reality of the thing asserted, but as the truthfulness of the assertion and its correspondence with the thing; hence added to vouch for statements which seem surprising, incredible, or exaggerated'.

[12] The transcription conventions for CA are discussed in Chapter 2.

(2) (Clift, 2001:274; H:1:1)
    (L=Lesley, F=Foster. L has rung up F to check that there will be no Sunday school that week.)

```
1F    T's a group service'n the evening whi[ch is very suitable=
2L                                         [Yes.
3F    =f'youngsters.
4     (.)
5L    Yes.=I js s-u thought I'd che:ck=
6F    =M[m:.
7L      [I:n case there wz a: misprin:[t.°(Again.)°
8F                                    [Yes no no we're havin:g
9→    ehm:(0.4) w'l I'm away actually b't uh: it's just a group
10    Sundee,
11L   Yes.
```

Here is ample evidence of the 'numerous false starts,[13] deviations from rules, changes of plan in mid-course' that, if our search is solely for meaning, threatens to obscure the objects of investigation. However, if instead of treating such data as 'degraded', we start from the premise that there might be phenomena to be discovered in them – that we focus on the actions being done in the talk – we can start, at the very least, by making observations. So, for example, attention to what are known as repairs and their environment (adjustments or alterations in the talk directed to problems of hearing, producing or understanding – an issue to which we return in Chapter 7) reveals that the particle *actually* is implicated in different ways in the trajectory of the talk. So in (1), 'actually it's g'nna be a rather busy June' (l. 12) serves to redirect the subsequent trajectory of the talk, where the lead-up to it, replete with so-called false starts, in the wake of bad news, had been decidedly delicate. However, in (2), 'w'l I'm away actually' (l. 9), 'actually' serves to mark the end of a parenthetical insert, after which the talk resumes its prior topical line 'but uh: it's just a group Sundee'. These two observations offer only a glimpse of the more extended analysis in Clift (2001), in which, at one point, we see a single speaker, over a sequence of seventy-eight lines, producing 'actually' in four different positions in the turn: placements that, on each occasion, are seen to be wholly systematic, given the actions being implemented at that given moment (249–51). Thus it is proposed that what *actually* does in a stretch of interaction is systematically linked to (a) its position in a turn, or its component turn-constructional units,[14] and (b) the action launched by that turn, whether self-repair (as in (1) and (2)), informing, or topic shift. So in this case the syntactic possibilities exemplified through flexibility of placement are seen to be selected on the basis of interactional exigencies, revealing something of the reflexive relationship between grammatical and interactional competence.

---

[13] We examine what such 'false starts' can be used to do in Chapter 7.
[14] Turns and turn-constructional units (TCUs) are discussed in Chapter 4.

So, then, when it comes to interaction, it would appear to make as much sense to talk of what *actually* does as what it means. The stable semantic core of contrast and revision (Clift, 2001:286) has its particular sense on each occasion selected by its sequential context, just as the proximity of a boiling kettle selects the type of *drink* being offered.[15] Heritage proposes one possible conceptualisation of this action implication of language in the following terms:

> the appropriate image of a word or a symbol is perhaps that of a large complex organic molecule such as a protein or amino acid existing in three dimensions, in which a variegated profusion of structural configurations and protrusions stand ready to lock into the empirical world of the here and now, stabilizing in the moment (and often for longer) both word and world.   (2011:268)

Examining these moments of stability has much to offer the linguistic attempt to understand the underlying mechanisms of language change and diversity. Heritage, in this connection, invokes the 'philosopher's axe' whose blade and handle have been replaced many times – so it is with language and its components, subject to subtle and imperceptible shifts over generations through myriad interactions between cognitive and communicative constraints. So we would not necessarily recognise the language of our distant ancestors, yet at any moment in time we assume we are speaking the same language: as Sleeth (1982, quoted in Heritage, 2011:67) points out, the Romance languages are the divergent end-products of the gradual, 'imperceptible' change of Latin across time – a temporal shift that has its spatial correlate in the Romance dialect continuum from northern France to southern Portugal, between the far extremes of which there is no mutual comprehension. In this respect, the linguistic work on grammaticalisation mentioned earlier has been critical in tracing how elements of grammar embody a process whereby recurrent formats become sedimented (Bybee, 2001, 2010; Fox, 2007). As Blythe (2013:883), working on Aboriginal languages, notes, repeated selection of particular linguistic structures by reference to interactional and cultural constraints, ultimately leads language down the path to grammaticalisation. Structuration is thus driven by the interactional preference for particular constructions (a topic to which we return in Chapter 5), showing how culture in effect selects for the emergence of structure. How exactly such structures are tailored to the doing of particular actions might suggest that the natural home for such investigation is pragmatic approaches to language use, and in particular those concerned with the distinction between the form and function of utterances: Speech Act Theory, the Gricean theory of utterance interpretation and Relevance Theory.

Pragmatic meaning: three perspectives
(a) Speech Act Theory

Of course, 'doing things with words' has been an object of inquiry in pragmatic approaches to language since Austin's (1962) observations regarding

---

[15] See Clift et al. (2013:210–11) for discussion of an exemplar in the field of colour perception.

speech acts, and Searle's subsequent programme of Speech Act Theory (1965, 1969, 1975). This recognises the apparent conundrum that, for example, *Is that your coat on the floor?*, said by parent to child, is not the yes/no question that its form suggests, but rather a directive to pick the coat up (such that a child responding only with *yes*, say, risks being sanctioned for cheek).[16] The conundrum for pragmatics, of course, rests in the distinction between the form of the utterance and the action it implements. Or take the following recorded occurrence, in which an utterance with the structural form of a question (l. 1) and an answer (l. 2) are simultaneously also an invitation that is accepted:

(3) (From Schegloff, 1972:107)

```
1  B   Why don't you come and see me some[times
2  A                                      [I would like to
3  B   I would like you to...
```

In this case, a question and its answer are clearly vehicles for other actions.

What is evident from the 'coat on the floor' example – that an interrogative form may not, in fact, launch a question – is noted by Bolinger (1957) in his general study of questions, and indeed Stivers (2010) found that requests for information comprised only 43 per cent of all question forms in a videoed corpus of American English interaction.[17] To give some sense of this problem, here is a selection of utterances, all in interrogative form, but which, as we shall see, in the course of this book, implement very different actions in their contexts.

Utterance	Action
For whom.	Agreement
What are you doing.	Invitation
What am I doing?	Repair initiation
What are you doing?	Complaint
Have you got Embassy Gold please?	Request
Are you going into town?	Offer
What did she say about talking with her mouth full?	Directive

This problem is not, of course, restricted to interrogatives. Take the following utterance, which appears straightforwardly, from its imperative form, to be a directive:

Don't.

While intuitively this appears to be produced by one speaker seeking to restrain another from doing something, returning it to the context from which it came invests it with a wholly different kind of force:

---

[16] We shall see in Chapter 5 what might motivate such an exchange in these terms.

[17] Dryer (2008) notes of 842 languages that a full 16 per cent do not use interrogative morphosyntax in information requests.

(4) (Clift, 2005:1644; from Parker, 2001)
     (D=David, adolescent client; T=Therapist)
```
1    D    I always behave in all of them but (0.3) in=English and
2         Maths and Science and French (.) I can't.
3         (1.3)
4    T→   Don't.
5         (0.8)
6    D    Mm.
7         (0.5)
8    T    Say to yourself (0.8) [It's not that I can't, it's that=
9    D                          [Mm.
10   T    =I don't.
11        (0.9)
12   D    Mmm
13        (0.5)
14   T    °Oka:y°,
15        (1.8)
16   T    If you can't (0.8) you lose control, if you don't you're
17        in control.
```

It is clear from David's 'Mm' in line 6 that what he understands the therapist to be doing is not issuing a directive, but rather proposing that he substitute his assertion that he 'can't' (l. 2). The therapist's lines 8 and 10 incorporate both what David had said ('can't') and her own proposed substitute ('don't'), explicitly counterposing the two formulations. David's 'Mmm' (l. 12) reiterates his earlier assent. The understanding of 'Don't' at line 4 is of course here highly dependent on the postpositioning of David's 'can't' in the prior turn; the therapist uses it as a resource with which to build, in a form of syntactic parasitism (Heritage and Sorjonen, 1994), her own turn (see Rae, 2008, for lexical substitution as a therapeutic resource).

What such exemplars show with great clarity is that the form of an utterance alone cannot necessarily be relied upon to deliver how it is understood by its recipient, and this is the case no less for prosody than syntax. So, for example, there have been recurrent claims about the meanings associated with particular prosodic patterns. One common assumption is that rising prosody is standardly used in the delivery of questions (Bolinger, 1957; Ladd, 1980; Pierrehumbert, 1980). In fact Stenström (1984), using a corpus of spoken English, shows that at least 50 per cent of yes/no questions are in declarative form and finds that 75 per cent of those are on falling intonation (see also Geluykens, 1988; Weber, 1993). In the following excerpt, it is quite clear that Lesley (at ll. 10–11) is informing her daughter Katherine, rather than asking her, for all that her informing is done on rising prosody:

(5) (Heritage, 2012a:12–13; Field X(C):2:1:4)
```
1    Les    Anyway when d'you think you'd like to come home ↓love.
2           (.)
```

```
 3    Kat    Uh:m (.) we:ll Brad's goin' down on Monday.
 4           (0.7)
 5    Les    Monday we:ll ah-:hh.hh w: ↑Monday we can't manage
 6           because (.) Granny's ↓coming Monday↓
 7           (0.4)
 8    Kat    Oh:,
             (13 lines of transcript omitted)
10    Les→   .hhh Yes alri:ght..hh The -thing is (.) u-we're all
11      →    meeting Granny off the bus: on Monday eve↓ni:ng?
12    Kat    ehYeah,
13    Les    .hhhh But -then Dad could come: back 'n hhhave iz ↓tea
14           'n then go on: to Glastonbur[y
15    Kat                                [Ye:s well if I'm at the
16           Kidwell's house it dzn't matter (.) I mean he c'n come:
17           pick me up whenever 'e wants to °can't h[e°
```

We shall return to this exchange in Chapter 6 and see in some detail how Lesley comes to be heard as informing, rather than asking, Katherine. However, what the wider sequence immediately shows us is that, for example, at line 6 Lesley is clearly taken by Katherine to be informing her about future plans involving Granny, as indicated by Katherine's 'oh' at line 8, a receipt token shown in Heritage (1984a) to display a 'change of state' from not-knowing to knowing.[18] There is thus a sequential basis for understanding lines 10–11 to be an informing rather than a question.

This sequential basis for understanding actions is explored further in Chapter 6. As such, it sheds important light on a recurrent problem: how to map linguistic forms onto functions (see Levinson, 1983, for a detailed analysis of the problems within Speech Act Theory). These problems have, in linguistics, been treated under the rubric of indirectness (Pinker et al., 2008, has an account grounded in logic). However, the examination of actions in sequence promises, as we shall see, to yield more in the way of social and developmental motivations for such structures. Levinson has an illuminating reanalysis of so-called indirect requests (1983:356–64) in which an ostensible information question such as 'Do you have Marlboros?' (Merritt, 1976:325) is understood to be a request by dint of its recurrent position as a preface to a request in a sequence. Levinson's reanalysis of requests is evidently based on an understanding of actions as sequentially grounded. Chapter 6 examines other indirect actions and proposes a more general account across categories of action.

It is, of course, necessary at this point to check bathwater for babies; claiming that a relationship between the elements of linguistic construction such as prosody or morphosyntax might be more complex than originally conceived is not, of

---

[18] Local dismantles some of the claims about meanings mapping straightforwardly on to prosody in his analysis of the prosodic features of *oh*, warning against 'a simplistic assigning of meaning to pitch contours independently of the interactional, lexical and grammatical environments in which they occur' (1996:202).

course, suggesting that the contribution of linguistic form is necessarily out-weighed by sequential position to the understanding of the action an utterance is implementing. In the domain of prosody, a quantitative survey by Sicoli et al. (2014) on a cross-linguistic sample of ten languages varying widely in structure[19] suggests that the initial pitch of a question that significantly deviates from a speaker's median pitch, in the top 10 per cent of that speaker's range, is associated with questions designed to solicit agreement with an evaluation rather than infor-mation. Thus, in these contexts, marked pitch appears to correlate with marked social action. That the gap between one turn and its next is, on average, only 200 milliseconds, requiring, as noted earlier, an element of linguistic double-tasking is thus in part accounted for by such recognisable cues. Furthermore, experimental work by Gisladottir et al. (2015) suggests that 200 milliseconds into an incoming turn, recipients can identify the action being projected when the utterance has only been partially processed. A qualitative study by Couper-Kuhlen (2001) shows how, in a corpus of phone calls, the 'reason for call' turn may be marked with a high pitch offset at the beginning of the turn, which distinguishes it from other preliminary business early in the call. Other work by Couper-Kuhlen has examined the morphosyntax of particular action formats; in that connection, she notes that such formats provide a basis 'on which recipients form working hypotheses about what action a co-participant is initiating. And it does this relatively early in the turn, thus enabling recipients (i) to determine an appropriate responsive action and (ii) to implement it in a timely fashion' (2014:645).

Couper-Kuhlen's work on offers, proposals, requests and suggestions has estab-lished by means of frequency relations that participants deploy specific linguistic forms to frame their directive-commissive actions as one type or another and recipients rely on these same linguistic forms to recognise these, and to respond accordingly (2014:636). She shows how participants clearly differentiate between, for example, actions undertaken jointly where costs and benefits are shared (pro-posals) from actions undertaken unilaterally where one party is the beneficiary of some action at cost to the other (offers). In the following extract, the particpants can be seen to be working towards establishing what is a proposal and what is an offer. So Edna, phoning Margy to thank her for a recent lunch party, launches a plan (ll. 35–6) to take Margy and her mother to a restaurant ('Coco's', l. 36) for lunch – one that is positively assessed at lines 38 and 40 by Margy:

```
(6)  (Couper-Kuhlen, 2014:626)
34   Mar   =We'll have to do tha[t more] o[:ften.]
35   Edn→                       [.hhhhh] [Well w]hy don't we: uh-m:=
36      →  =Why don't I take you and Mo:m up there to: Coco's. someday
37         for lu:nch. We'll go, buzz up there to[h,
38   Mar                                         [k, Goo:d.
39   Edn   Ha:h?
```

<hr>

[19] The languages surveyed were: ǂĀkhoe Haiǁom (Namibia), Danish, Dutch, American English, Italian, Japanese, Korean, Lao, Tzeltal (Mexico) and Yélî Dnye (Papua New Guinea).

```
40  Mar    That's a good deal..hh- .hh=
41  Edn→   =Eh I'll take you bo:th [up
42  Mar                          [No::::: we'll all go Dutch.=
43  Mar    =But [let's do that.]
44  Edn         [N o : we wo:n']t.
```

In response to this apparent acceptance (l. 40), however, Edna reiterates her earlier
position at line 41 ('I'll take you both up', although Margy knows she does not drive),
perhaps to pursue a more embracing response. This is now met by a refusal from
Margy (l. 42) whose response indicates that she takes the prior turn to be an invitation
to pay for her and her mother. So while there is joint commitment to an upcoming
outing, there is dispute concerning the terms on which it will take place. Couper-
Kuhlen's study of how actions are implemented examines how relative costs and
benefits to speakers are embodied in their syntactic forms. So Edna repairs her initial
format 'why don't we' (l. 35) to 'Why don't I' (l. 36) – that is, moving from a
'proposal' format, with its implication of shared costs and benefits, to an 'offer'
format, the switch to 'I' implying she will unilaterally bear the costs of the outing. Yet
in line 37, she continues with 'we' – apparently reverting to a 'proposal', which is
what Margy greets with a positive response, in line 38, and reiterates in line 40.
Indeed, the form of that response, 'that's a good deal', itself suggests that Margy
hears this as an enterprise where the costs are shared. However, when Edna thereupon reverts to 'I' in what is hearably[20] a clarification – 'I'll take you up' – the 'offer'
format embodied in the switch of pronoun prompts a vehement rejection.

The form of the utterance is thus seen to be criterial to the action it prosecutes.
Nevertheless, here we have an analysis where the categories of action are
warranted by being grounded in the participants' *own* displayed understandings
of the kind of project in which they are jointly engaged – understandings that are
only visible by examining the interactional sequences in which the actions are
embedded. As Drew and Holt remark:

> the components of a turn's construction – at whatever level of linguistic
> production – are connected with the activity which the turn is being designed
> to perform in the unfolding interactional sequence of which it is a part, and to
> the further development of which it contributes.   (1998:497)

Furthermore, 'whatever level' of linguistic construction includes those levels
which might not, on the face of it, be salient or easily recognisable as consequential. So, as we shall see in Chapter 4, examination of the phonetic design of talk
has revealed the extent to which articulatory detail is implicated in projecting turn
continuation versus the relevance of speaker transition.

---

[20] The term 'hearably (an x)' perhaps requires some clarification, if only because it (and similar
phrases such as 'a hearable x') are recurrently used in CA, in favour of perhaps more accessible or
elegant phrases such as 'interpretable' or 'understandable' '(as an x)'. It is not here simply as an
unwieldy substitute but makes a specific claim about the public availability of an utterance to be
recognised to be doing a particular action through a specific interactional practice, while the
processes of interpretation, and what is understood, remain inscrutable.

It is only, then, in such sequences of talk that *courses* of action are made visible. While Speech Act Theory captures the action orientation of language in interaction, its focus on speech *acts* fails to recognise the sequential nature of action beyond the utterance or utterance pair. Moreover, getting analytic traction on any component of a turn's construction is only possible by examining where it is placed in a turn, and where its turn is itself placed within a sequence of turns. This analytic principle that 'position' – the placement of a turn in a sequence – is as important as 'composition' – its form – in establishing what a turn is understood to be doing (Schegloff, 1993:121) because it is emic, a resource *for participants*, will be discussed further in Chapter 3.

Examination of languages other than English shows the orientation to actions across sequences, rather than single acts as such, particularly clearly. So, for example, interactional norms for English suggest that an action such as an offer might consist of a two-utterance sequence: the offer and its acceptance or rejection. However, as we shall see in Chapter 5, norms for offers in Arabic, to take but one example, involve a complex sequence of negotiation, involving multiple refusals, before their eventual resolution. It is also quite clear that actions may themselves be the culmination of complex sequences of action. Take the situation in which you approach a closed door with a cup of coffee in each hand. I, approaching the door at the same time, might standardly be expected to recognise your need and so come to your aid by opening it for you; indeed, doing so would be a mark of interactional competence. In such a circumstance, a verbalised request from you to me to open the door might represent a relative failure of such competence on my part; clearly, a whole complex of embodied and multimodal semiotic resources are marshalled in the coordination of actions.

In thus identifying action as inextricable from sequence, CA aims to achieve the 'empirical bite' that Speech Act Theory has found elusive – and we shall see, in Chapter 5, how it has captured some of the very generalisations sought by both.

(b) Gricean implicature

If Speech Act Theory's central focus is the action orientation of language, Grice's theory of implicature (1975, 1978) is concerned with the logical inferencing procedures of utterance interpretation. Its working assumptions, however, have much in common with Speech Act Theory, in its focus on the utterance pair. While a theory of utterance interpretation by definition abstracts away from the temporal production of utterances, it therefore inevitably overlooks inferences such as the following, at line 4:

```
(7) (Drew, 1990:28)
1  A:    This- chemotherapy (0.2) it won't have any lasting effects
2        on having kids will it?
3        (2.2)
4  A:→   It will?
5  B:    I'm afraid so
```

In lines 1–2, the patient asks the doctor a question, and then at line 4, in the absence of a response, displays her own conclusion ('It will?') as to what the answer will be – as it turns out, correctly. As we shall see in Chapter 3, the inference drawn by the patient here is not derived from what is said, but rather, what is not: it is grounded in an orientation to displayed, publically accountable norms, and located in the absence of an immediate response by the doctor. Moreover, it is in attending to the absence of something that CA methodology, with its focus on the online, incremental production of utterances in time, is unique. From this perspective, the silence at line 3 is, as we shall see, as much an interactional object as the utterances preceding and following it.

That the non-occurrence of something may be an analytic resource is, of course, only possible by reference to possible contexts of occurrence. In this respect, the CA focus on sequences of action makes visible just those contingencies. So, as we saw in extract (5), 'oh' marks a change of state from unknowing to knowing. Such an analysis is no mere assertion, but emerges from observation of just those contexts of non-occurrence. In his foundational study, Heritage (1984a) presents the following, particularly revealing, exchange. *Oh* appears initially straightforwardly to receipt the answer to a question. Three sequences of Question–Answer-*Oh* (with occurrences of 'oh' marked (a)–(c) at ll. 3, 8 and 14) run their course. However, at arrow (d) at line 19 we see that another question receiving its answer is receipted, not with 'oh', but with 'of course':

```
(8)   (Heritage, 1984a:310)
      (Nancy is questioning Hyla about a possibly-prospective boyfriend, 'he', l. 1.)
1     N      .hhh dz he 'av 'iz own apa:rt [mint?
2     H                                    [.hhhh Yea:h,=
3     N a→   Oh:,
4            (1.0)
5     N      How didju git 'iz number,
6            (.)
7     H      I(h) (.) c(h)alled infermation'n San Fr'ncissc(h) [uh!
8     N b→                                                      [Oh::::.
9            (.)
10    N      Very cleve:r, hh=
11    H      =Thank you [: I-.hh-.hhhhhhhh hh=
12    N                 [W'ts 'iz last name,
13    H      =Uh:: Freedla:nd..hh [hh
14    N c→                        [Oh [:,
15    H                               [('r) Freedlind.=
16    N      =Nice Jewish bo:y?
17           (.)
18    H      O:f cou:rse,=
19    N d→   ='v [cou:rse,
20    H          [hh-hh-hh hnh.hhhh=
21    N      =Nice Jewish boy who doesn' like tih write letters?
```

As Heritage observes: 'In effect, the recipient withholds a change-of-state proposal and thus retrospectively proposes that her previous, question intoned inference ['Nice Jewish boy?' . . .] is to be heard as having been a comment on something self-evident rather than an inference concerning something still in doubt' (1984a:311). So it is the *non*-production of a particular linguistic object here in a sequential environment where one might initially assume that it was relevant which leads the analyst to inspect what it is that makes this the exception – so-called deviant-case analysis.[21] The analysis of *oh* as a change-of-state token is thus grounded in sequential evidence in environments of both occurrence and non-occurrence. Indeed, this analysis is further underwritten by the attested non-occurrence of *oh* in certain non-conversational contexts, for example its withholding by doctors in the consultation part of a medical encounter, where the production of a change-of state-token at a vulnerable juncture might have 'dire consequences for patient peace of mind' (Heritage and Clayman, 2010:32).[22] This is not, then, implicature in the Gricean sense, but the implication, in the general, pre-theoretical sense, derived from the normative use of *oh* as displaying a change of state.

Further compelling evidence of the action orientation of implication is demonstrated in Goodwin's remarkable (1995) study of someone who, having had a stroke, is left able to produce only three words: *yes, no* and *and*.[23] Once again, we see the synergy between a linguistic object and its sequential environment. Goodwin remarks that, given that these all presuppose links to other talk, and tie units of talk, such as clauses, to each other

> this vocabulary set presupposes that its user is embedded within a community of other speakers. His talk does not stand alone as a self-contained entity, but emerges from, and is situated within, the talk of others, to which it is inextricably linked. This raises the possibility that despite the extraordinary sparseness of this system, its speaker might nonetheless be able to engage in complicated language games, to say a wide range of different things while performing diverse kinds of action, by making use of resources provided by the speech of others.   (1995:234)

So, for example, the following shows how the husband's limited vocabulary is accommodated in guessing sequences:

```
(9)  (Goodwin, 1995:239-40)
31   Nurse      English muffin?
32              (3.4)
33   Husband→   Ye:s.
```

---

[21] For the most significant early instance of this in CA, see Chapter 3 on the discussion of Schegloff (1968).

[22] Other such contexts, discussed in Heritage and Clayman (2010:29–33), include classroom interaction, broadcast news interviews and courtroom interaction.

[23] There is now a growing CA literature on interactions involving atypical populations, and, in particular, social interactions involving people with brain damage (see, e.g., the collection in Goodwin, 2003a). For an overview, see Antaki and Wilkinson (2013).

```
34   Nurse      A:[nd what would you like on it.
35   Wife          [Just one.
37                 (0.8)
38   Nurse      Jelly?
39                 (1.0)
40   Husband→   No:
41                 (0.8)
42   Wife       Butt[er?
43   Nurse          [Butter?
44                 (0.3)
45   Husband→   Yes.
46                 (0.6)
47   Nurse      Okay.
```

While, in Chapter 3, we shall see further how this sequence is organised, it is evident here that the 'Okay' (l. 47) brings to a close an extraordinary demonstration of the capacity for joint action. Here the full linguistic competencies of co-participants are mobilised by the husband's production of the contrastive *yes* and *no*. So *yes* proposes an exit from the guessing (the 'yes' at l. 33 provides for the nurse to move on, in the next turn, from the category of 'breakfast items' to introduce the issue of 'spreadables', first itemised at l. 38) and *no* proposes a continuation of the guessing – the 'No' at line 40 prompts another guess at lines 42 and 43, and one which is met by 'Yes' at line 45, which provides for the termination of the sequence at line 47.

In jointly mobilising the sequential possibilities of *yes, no* and *and,* the two parties to interaction reveal the irredeemably context-bound nature of understanding. As such, they provide striking demonstrations of Hutchins's (1995) 'cognition in the wild' – cognition as a public and socially distributed process,[24] embedded in the material environment, and of Livingston's (2008) studies of 'reasoning in the wild'. Livingston, examining reasoning across a number of domains, notes of reasoning in checkers: 'reasoning in checkers isn't a form of universal reasoning that's applied to the play of checkers; it's a type of reasoning *indigenous to, living within, and sustained by the practices of,* crossboard play' (2008:8; italics added). The understanding of *yes, no* and *and* is similarly 'indigenous to, living, within, and sustained by the practices of' talk-in-interaction. Such an exchange undermines a view that there is 'no-escape-from-syntax' (Piatelli-Palmarini, 2010:161). However, if it seems an isolated and extreme case, consider Enfield's observations regarding so-called normal language development:

> normal human infants achieve rich communication without syntax when they are at the one-word stage of language acquisition (around age 12 to 18 months). Moreover, before this stage, infants can communicate without any language at all. How do they do it? By recourse to bodily forms of signaling (e.g., pointing,

---

[24] Extract (39) in Chapter 3 examines a case of linguistic embedding distributed over two parties.

gestures and gaze) riding on a chassis of elite human capacities for cooperation, prosociality, and naïve psychology ... We can communicate without syntax. What we can't do is communicate without a cognitive and bodily infrastructure for social interaction.   (2010a:1601)

With such exemplars we have come about as far from the Chomskyan abstraction of the 'ideal speaker-listener, in a completely homogenous speech-community' (1965:3) as it is possible to come.[25] It is the outcome of starting, not with hypotheses, but with Evans and Levinson's 'bite': in the temporal contingencies and interactional exigencies of shared, and collaborative, action.

(c) Relevance Theory

Relevance Theory, of all pragmatic approaches to utterance interpretation, has attempted to address the issue of context. It recognises the inherent problems with the code-conduit model of communication and argues against simplistic notions of information transfer, going beyond the purely linguistic. So an utterance such as *You've had your hair cut!* would not, in Relevance Theory, be dismissed as purely relational, and so beyond the scope of pragmatic theory. It recognises that context shapes interpretation;[26] but context is, for Relevance Theory, a set of assumptions used in the process of utterance interpretation. In this respect, despite drawing on a wide range of data sources, Relevance Theory has similar working methods to other pragmatic approaches in its focus on utterances and utterance pairs. So its discussion of the structural ambiguity inherent in, for example, *My son has grown another foot* (Sperber and Wilson, 1982:83) concentrates on how one interpretation (a growth spurt) may be selected over the other (the sprouting of an additional limb). Clearly, no-one would claim that such an ambiguity is likely to arise for participants to interaction; the value of such utterances lies in their use as heuristic devices. However, conceiving of context exclusively in terms of interpretive assumptions, grounded in a presumption of optimal Relevance (Sperber and Wilson, 1995:270) is to ignore what, for participants to interaction, is the central component of context, and that is, as we have seen, sequence in which the utterance is embedded. Indeed, examining empirically occurring, attested ambiguities only reinforces the importance of action and sequences of action in the interpretation of utterances. So, for example, the following extract demonstrates just such an instance of an actually occurring ambiguity. The utterance at issue – 'For whom' at line 12 – is initially taken by B to be the question that its form suggests, and he duly launches an answer to that question, 'Well he says-' (l. 13). However, A, hearing from the

---

[25] For an arresting example of collaborative interaction with no shared linguistic resources, see Levinson's (2006) account of his interaction with a deaf home-signer on Rossel Island, Papua New Guinea.

[26] As Foer also notes of the process of remembering: 'We don't remember isolated facts, we remember things in context' (2011:58). Foer examines a number of domains (including chess, and – in an example much beloved of philosophers – chicken sexing) in which 'skill' is often attributed by practitioners to intuition, but is, in fact, a combination of pattern recognition and memory. See, for a general account of skill and expertise, also Gladwell (2005).

beginning of line 13 that B is producing an answer, intervenes at line 14 – 'By what standard' – with a clarification. Despite this clarification taking the form, once again, of a question, it is clear from line 15 that B now takes the prior turn to be an assessment to be agreed with, 'That's exactly what I mean' (l. 15). The excerpt is taken from a radio call-in show where B has called the host, A, to report a disagreement that he, B, has had with his high-school history teacher ('he', l. 2) over the morality of US foreign policy:

```
(10)   (Schegloff, 1984a:28)
1    B    An's- an (      ) we were discussing, it tur-
2          it comes down, he s- he says, I-I-you've talked
3          with thi- si- i- about this many times. I said,
4          it come down t'this:=
5    B    =Our main difference: I feel that a government,
6          i- the main thing, is- th-the purpose a'the
7          government, is, what is best for the country.
8    A    Mmhmm
9    B    He says, governments, an' you know he keeps- he
10         talks about governments, they sh- the thing
11         they sh'd do is what's right or wrong.
12   A→   For whom.
13   B    Well he says- [he-
14   A                  [By what standard
15   B    That's what- that's exactly what I mean. he s-
16         but he says ...
```

The crux of the ambiguity – and the misunderstanding by B – lies in the *action* being performed at line 12, and it goes to the very heart of the relationship between utterance form and function. As we have seen, questions (e.g. *Is that your coat on the floor? Why don't you come and see me sometimes?*) can be used to implement a variety of actions. In the following extract, taken from earlier in the conversation from which the extract above comes, there is another case in point at lines 7–8. Once again, B is talking about his history teacher ('he', l. 1), and that teacher's stance on US foreign policy since the time of George Washington:

```
(11)   (Schegloff, 1984a:35–6)
1    B    Because- an'he did the same thing, in
2          War of- The War of Eighteen Twelve, he said
3          the fact that we were interested in expansion,
4          t'carrying farther, was (  ) something against.
5          Y'know a-argument t'use against. But see the
6          whole thing is he's against, he's [very- he's (  )
7    A→                                      [Is he teaching
8    →    History or Divinity
9    B    I don'kno(h)w. But he's very anti-imperialistic.
```

On the face of it, lines 7–9 have the form of a question and its answer, a confession of ignorance. However, against a background where it has already been established that they are talking about a history teacher, 'Is he teaching History or Divinity' cannot be a genuine enquiry – and 'I don'kno(h)w' not (as the laugh token in the course of its production suggests) a claim of ignorance.[27] In the same vein, in extract (10) 'For whom' at first is taken to be a question, requesting a clarification of the history teacher's perspective of which B has just given ('he says', l. 9) a summary. However, just as 'Is he teaching History or Divinity' may not (and is, indeed, not, in this case) heard as a genuine question, but as a means of showing understanding of, and agreement with, B, 'For whom' can similarly be taken to be a display of agreement with B. Schegloff (1984a) provides an extraordinarily detailed analysis of the extract, but for current purposes it may suffice to note the following. In the first place, this display of agreement by A with B is grounded in his showing that he can voice a part of B's possible argument, and that he is, in doing so, sympathetic. As Schegloff observes, 'Regularly recipients side with tellers, I suppose because that is in part how tellers choose recipients for stories' (p. 47). So here it is clear that B is reporting a conversation with alternate positions ('he says', l. 2; 'I said', l. 3; 'he says', l. 9), representable schematically (with the history teacher as C), as BCBC – with the teacher, C's, position, 'the thing they sh'd do is what's right or wrong' (ll. 10–11) occupying the last turn in B's reporting of the exchange. As Schegloff notes of the utterance at line 12, 'For whom', it

> is then, by an extension, produced in a slot *in that conversation* (i.e., the one being reported on) that the formula assigns to B, or if you like B's side, and there is a basis then for hearing it as a contribution to, and thereby an understanding of and agreement with, that side, or with B. It is thus that it can come off as a proposed piece of B's argument, for B eventually to appreciate it as 'exactly what I mean'.   (1984a:47)

Moreover, that eventual appreciation is produced as a response to A's intervention at line 14 – 'By what standard' – which syntactically, prosodically, in its stress placement and in the way it builds off line 11 is, Schegloff notes 'as close to an equivalent for 12 – "For whom" – as I can imagine' (p. 40). In both its placement and form, it thus invites a reanalysis of line 12, with a wholly different outcome.

Instead of a theoretically conceivable ambiguity, then, we have one encountered and managed in real time by the parties involved. Furthermore, both possible analyses of the same utterance are grounded in an identification of the *action* it is doing in the *sequence* in which it is embedded. Once again, we see, too, that the identification of the action itself depends upon an apprehension of not only the composition of the utterance in question but also its position in its sequence: the central resource for participants in establishing the salient components of context.

---

[27] We return to this issue in section 6.2.1, under 'Epistemic domains, mobilising response and the epistemic engine'.

1.2.2   Observational approaches

With the exception of Relevance Theory, work in pragmatics does not, in the main, take naturally occurring data as the topic of investigation, and so the distinctness of conversation-analytic data from this kind of work should in this respect already be clear. However, in its use of recorded materials, CA is similar to a number of other disciplines investigating language use. In what follows, we examine the areas of commonality and difference between some of these observational approaches to language.

(a) Sociolinguistics

Sociolinguistics, the study of linguistic variation, lodges context above all in aspects of identity, taking speaker variables – of geography, ethnicity, gender and class, among others – as determining factors in language use. Two classic studies – one on phonological variation, and one on grammatical variation – here show something of how aspects of context are captured in sociolinguistics.

In his groundbreaking experiment on the phonology of New Yorkers, Labov prompts a redoing of the utterance involving the phrase *fourth floor* in department stores of varying social cachet (1972) to focus on the variation in the pronunciation of post-vocalic /r/ – variation that is linked ultimately to language change. There are two main divergences here from CA work. In the first instance, Drew (2013) shows that what Labov categorises as 'repeats' would in fact be partial repeats; thus an utterance being redone for this purpose, in a different sequential position, would have components entirely omitted (for a discussion of what components get omitted, see Schegloff, 2004a; for a more general discussion of these 'other-initiated repairs', see Chapter 7). So, for example:

```
(12)   (From Drew, 2013:232)
1   Jean:    Well I mean I won't be where she c'n get me honey
2   Ans.:    Pardon?
3   Jean:→   I won't be where she c'n get me.

(13)   (From Drew, 2013:232)
1   Ava:     Yeh w'll I'll give you a call then tomorrow. when I
2            get in 'r sumn.
3            (0.5)
4   Bee:     Wha:t,
5   Ava:→    <I'll give yih call tomo[rrow.]
6   Bee:                             [Yeh: ] 'n I'll be ho:me
7            t'morrow.
```

As Drew remarks:

> Here then are the diverging paths of sociolinguistics and CA; sociolinguistic analysis focuses on variation and difference between speakers, whilst CA focuses on common, shared practices for talk-in-interaction, practices that underlie and are central to what we do when we use language in social interaction.   (2013:286)

The other important divergence from CA resides in the external features of contextual identity which constitute the variationist's points of reference: the so-called bucket model of context where some pre-established social framework is viewed as 'containing' participants' speech behaviour (Drew and Heritage, 1992:19). A classic study of grammatical variation by Brown and Gilman (1960) shows how the so-called T/V distinction (denoting, loosely speaking, an informal and formal term of address, respectively, to a recipient) in European languages is implemented by reference to social relationships. English, of course, now lacks such a distinction in its second-person singular reference form and is preserved in any substantial form only in literary texts such as Shakespeare.[28] It nonetheless displays distinctions by means of other linguistic resources (see, e.g., Ervin-Tripp, 1972, on the rules of address for American English). So, for example, one striking vignette that shows how contextual considerations shape usage comes from James Gregory, the white prison warder responsible for Nelson Mandela during some of his twenty-seven years of incarceration.[29] Mandela addressed Gregory during that time as 'Mr Gregory', but received 'Nelson' in return – a usage highlighting the asymmetry of their institutional relationship. However, over the years the two men became friends, and when Mandela became President of South Africa, the two adopted a dual system for their terms of address: in public, reciprocal title + last name ('Mr Mandela' – 'Mr Gregory'); in private, reciprocal first names ('Nelson' – 'James') – the dual system showing due attention to certain dimensions of context.

So, clearly, variations in usage point to certain dimensions of context, such as power or intimacy, as shaping speakers' choices of one variant over another. However, it is equally clear that usage, far from being invariantly tied to status, as a bucket model of context suggests, can vary even within the scope of a single exchange. With respect to T/V usage in English, only literary exemplars remain, but in the famous opening act of *King Lear*, there is frequent alternation between *thou* and *you* by the king in address to his daughters. In a linguistic analysis, Fowler (1986) discusses how switching between these variants would have had an emotional impact lost on modern audiences.[30] Furthermore, while modern English interaction has lost such possibilities in its second-person pronoun, such variation with respect to other features is just as evident. In the following

---

[28] Now only preserved in familiar contemporary form in, for example, Christmas carols (e.g. 'God Rest Ye, Merry Gentlemen').

[29] Related by James Gregory on BBC Radio 4, *Midweek*, 1994.

[30] In modern English, shifts in status are achieved (or attempted) through other means. Cherie Blair, the wife of the former British Prime Minister Tony Blair, reports a failed attempt of hers to challenge her proposed status vis-à-vis her recipient, and its consequences: "'At one point in that first year [of Tony Blair's premiership], Princess Anne came over and said something that included 'Mrs Blair'. 'Oh. Please call me Cherie', I said. 'I'd rather not', she replied. 'It's not the way I've been brought up.' 'What a shame,' I said." Her relationship with the princess "went rapidly downhill and never recovered'" (Rosalind Ryan 'Cherie Blair: What She Said', *The Guardian*, 12 May 2008).

exchange, a speaker switches from 'ain't' (l. 6) to, in his very next turn, 'It's not' (l. 8):

(14)   (Jefferson, 2003:234)
        (Senior attending physician Slater is commenting on intern Fitch's suggestion that
        a patient be scheduled for a 'psych consult'. S=Slater; F=Fitch)

```
1    S    It ↑might be worth it 'cause..it might be
2         Y'know kind of [an unstable mo[ment where
3    F                    [°Mm°              [Mhm
4    S    .hhh Just getting on a waiting list'n having an:
5         (0.7).hhh (.) something happen in a couple
6    →    months just (.) ain't gonna do the jo:[b.
7    F                                          [Yeah.
8    S→   .hhh It's not that she's got a crisis it's just
9         this is the m- the right ti:me
10        (.)
11   F    M[hm
12   S     [period in which something ought to happe[n.
13   F                                              [Mhm.
```

In a discussion of *ain't* usage in contexts where the same speaker also uses the more standard *I'm*/*it's*/*that's not* ..., Jefferson shows how *ain't* in such cases is deployed as what she calls 'an idiomatic resource' in environments of 'persistent ambiguity' (2003:234).[31] Examples such as this suggest that, while it is relatively straightforward to see that (although less so to explain how) speakers' linguistic behaviour may be tied to *status*, it is less easy to capture the momentary and dynamic adjustments made by speakers to their interactional *stance* from one moment to the next. In grounding analyses in the detail of how actions are built through the design of turns, CA can show how aspects of identity are oriented to, and endogenously generated in, the incremental progression of the talk itself. So, for example, in the following exchange, the mother (M) and father (F) of a baby, separately and distinctly, respond to the Health Visitor's (HV) observation in line 1:

(15)   (Drew and Heritage, 1992:33)
        ('He' is a newborn baby, who is chewing on something.)

```
1    HV   He's enjoying that [isn't he.
2    F →                     [°Yes, he certainly is=°
3    M →  =He's not hungry 'cuz (he) he's ju(h)st (h) had
4    →    'iz bo:ttle.hhh
5         (0.5)
6    HV   You're feeding him on (.) Cow and Gate
7         Premium.
```

In their responses the mother and father display very different understandings of the Health Visitor's first turn. The father, in doing an emphatic agreement, treats it

---

[31] See also the discussion of *thee*/*thuh* alternation in section 6.1.1.

as an observation; the mother, by contrast, produces a defensive account in the face of what might have been hearable as a challenge to her competence as a mother. In the two sharply distinct responsive turns here we can see not only that two different actions are implemented, but also how, in effect, two distinct contexts are being constructed in the talk: one conversational, the other, alert in its orientation to parental competence, institutional.

Orientations to context, and thus identity, are thereby seen to emerge from action, rather than context providing fixed parameters somehow containing action. So while the analytic paths of CA and sociolinguistics might initially seem divergent, it is clear that work in CA is able to shed a different light on the sorts of phenomena that sociolinguistic methods are examining, through orientations to stance as well as status. Chapters 5 and 6 in particular show how such orientations emerge from the CA treatment of context. Such diverse phenomena as the origins of grammaticalisation and the construction of identity in talk can trace their ultimate source to the selection of one interactional resource over another in the implementation of actions.

(b) Interactional linguistics

As we shall see in Chapter 2, the emergence of CA within sociology, and its concern with the organisation of interaction, has meant that it has traditionally declined to accord any primacy to language per se, except and insofar as it constitutes a vehicle for social action. At the same time, within linguistics, pioneering work on grammaticalisation has long recognised interaction as the crucible for language use and thus language change, whether in functional syntax (e.g. Givón, 1979; Chafe, 1980; Du Bois, 1980; Hopper and Thompson, 1984) or work in cognitive linguistics on embodiment and gesture in communication (e.g. Kita, 2003; Sweetser, 1990, 2006; Futrell et al., 2015). Using interactional data, work by Auer (1984) on problematic reference in conversation and Houtkoop and Mazeland (1985), on turns and discourse units is distinctive for its early use of CA in its approach to linguistic phenomena. Interactional linguistics (IL), a term heralded by the arrival of Couper-Kuhlen and Selting (2001), formalised the linguistic status of work in this domain, work that shares the methods of CA, while retaining, as its primary investigative focus, language and linguistic form. The emphasis on the observation of *grammar* reflects IL's baseline concern with the units and structures of linguistic inquiry, with CA methods as the tools of investigation. In this respect, work in IL has led the way in the investigation of the phonetic and prosodic resources used in interaction, which, aside from Schegloff (1998b), had been relatively unexplored. So, for example, Couper-Kuhlen (1992) examines the prosody and speech rhythms of repair, Ford (1993) is a study of adverbial clauses and recipiency and Fox and Thompson (2010) examine responses to *wh*-questions. The collection edited by Couper-Kuhlen and Selting (1996) addresses prosody, that by Fox (1996) examines anaphora, and Ochs et al. (1996) focus primarily on morphosyntax. However, Ford et al. state:

we understand the linguistic unit-types and categories such as 'apposition', 'tag question', and 'left-embedded structure' as inherited from methods that are either introspective or aimed at cognitive explanations (or both), rather than derived from a commitment to understanding forms of social action ... Our interest, then, is in holding ourselves and others more accountable to a social action-based grounding for turn-construction.   (2013:17–18)

In some cases, the convergence of linguistic concerns with CA methods reveals the limits of linguistic categories as descriptively adequate for interaction; so, for example, Curl et al., investigating the phonetic properties of utterance repetitions in interaction, state flatly that

we have found no evidence that 'prosody,' as commonly conceived, is relevant or useful in explaining participants' understandings of utterances. That is, the separate and individuated treatment of phonetic resources which are typically dubbed 'prosodic' does not seem to be warranted by the observable behaviour of participants. This is not to say that resources which might fall under the rubric of 'prosody' are not at work here: they plainly are. However, we have shown that these resources only form a part of the practice, which incorporates features of lexis, articulatory details, loudness, duration, syllabic make-up, and a variety of pitch characteristics. Furthermore, the part played by 'prosodic' resources seems no greater than that played by others.   (2006:1748)

Such a finding is only made possible by treating linguistic categories themselves as matters to be empirically established.

Early collections of work in IL were innovative in the diversity of languages brought to the enterprise. While the overwhelming majority of early work in CA was on English, the increasing body of work on other languages – and much of that presented here – is in large part attributable to linguists seeking to establish how specific languages are shaped in their interactional implementations.

All in all, it would be fair to say that the boundary between IL and CA is now extremely fuzzy and primarily a reflection of original disciplinary training in linguistics or sociology, respectively; researchers in both publish in the same journals and attend the same conferences (see the Preface).

(c) Interactional sociolinguistics and linguistic anthropology

In this respect there is a convergence of focus, if not method, with pioneering work gathered under the general umbrella of interactional socio-linguistics. Hymes's notion of 'communicative competence' (1966), introduced in the wake of Chomsky's notion of linguistic competence, and dedicated to the empirical examination of cultural variation where Chomskyan models assumed structural universality, ushered in a whole stream of work on different speech communities, known as the ethnography of communication. With their origins in linguistic anthropology, two landmark collections of ethnographic work,

Gumperz and Hymes (1972) and Bauman and Sherzer (1974),[32] set the agenda for sociocultural research in linguistics. The former includes work on speech patterns in Burundi (Albert), American–English address forms (Ervin-Tripp), Yakan litigation (Frake), and African-American speech acts (Mitchell-Kernan); the latter, pragmatic norms in a Malagasy speech community (Keenan), the regulation of speech among the Warm Springs Indians (Philips), greetings and status in Wolof (Irvine) and conversations in an Antiguan village (Reisman). Indeed, it was in ethnography that universals of language use subsequently emerged as an empirical possibility, with the proposal of Brown and Levinson (1978, 1987) of an orientation to politeness as the foundation of cooperative behaviour across cultures and communities.

Current work in CA has all of this antecedent research as its comparative touchstone. As we see in the next chapter, the origins of CA lie in sociology, and specifically in ethnomethodology; however, the presence of Garfinkel's 'Remarks on Ethnomethodology' and the work of Sacks on the analysability of children's stories in Gumperz and Hymes (1972) and Sacks's chapter on the telling of a dirty joke by American teenagers in Bauman and Sherzer (1974) show the extent of the convergence between sociological work in CA and ethnographic work in linguistics. Moreover, in subsequent years, as much anthropological-ethnographic work has increasingly dovetailed with CA, for example, in work on Kilivila of the Trobriand Islands (Senft, 2010), on Tzotzil (Haviland, 1998) and Yucatec Maya (Hanks, 1990) of Mexico, Guyanese Creole (Sidnell, 2001) and Lao (Enfield, 2007a), it has continued to contribute to findings in CA. With respect to methodology, the increasing use of video data which originated in such work as, for example, examining the embodied language practices of children (Goodwin, 1990, 2006; Goodwin and Cekaite, 2012) and socialisation (see, e.g., Duranti et al., 2011) is now at the leading edge of work in CA.

As is no doubt evident, the overlap in both working methods and basic assumptions between IL, interactional sociolinguistics, linguistic anthropology and CA is often such as to make the utility of distinct labels, beyond their institutional value, somewhat moot; as a domain *sui generis*, CA has attracted researchers from sociology, anthropology, psychology, as well as linguistics – and indeed the authors cited in this book may claim affiliation with any of these disciplines, or none. An author's affiliation may thus often be as much a reflection of their disciplinary origins as a commitment to a stream of work distinct from CA.

1.3   Beyond language: discourse analysis and CA

Of all the approaches to naturally occurring interaction, it is discourse analysis (DA) that is most vulnerable to terminological confusion with CA, if only

---

[32] The title of Bauman and Sherzer (1974) is *Explorations in the Ethnography of Speaking*, which adds yet another possibility – but without, apparently, more scope – to the terminological profusion.

because DA, in all of its incarnations, takes as its object of investigation language displaying coherence beyond the single utterance, often conceptualised as the 'text' or 'discourse'. However, from then on, the forms of DA are variegated indeed, from the study of multi-sentence texts, which may be spoken or written (see Brown and Yule, 1983), to critical discourse analysis (CDA), which seeks to reveal the underlying ideologies presumed to reinforce and perpetuate social and political inequalities through language use (see, e.g., van Dijk, 2007; Wodak, 2013). The perspective of these forms of DA – which include explicit ideological commitments such as Foucauldian discourse analysis (FDA), inspired by the work of Foucault and Derrida – are encapsulated in Mayr's statement that 'As a practice of power, hegemony operates largely through language' (2008:14). So it is much less language here, and still less interaction, that is the focus. Moreover, as top-down forms of analysis, they are informed and characterised by the analyst's ideological positioning. As a rigorously bottom-up form of analysis, CA, in contrast, and as we have seen, puts participants' own displayed orientations at the centre of the analysis. To the criticism that this method makes CA unnecessarily restrictive and conservative, ignoring more self-evidently urgent and pressing social issues such as oppression and violence, Schegloff responds that

> Rape, abuse, battering . . . do not exist in some other world, or in some special sector of this world. They are intricated into the texture of everyday life for those who live with them. How else are we to understand their explosive emergence where they happen if not by examining ordinary interaction with tools appropriate to it, and seeing how they can lead to such outcomes . . . If interaction is produced within a matrix of turns organized into sequences, etc., and if it is from these that motives and intentions are inferred, identities made relevant, stances embodied and interpreted, etc., how else – when confronted by the record of singular episodes – are we to understand their genesis and course, how else try to understand what unwilling participants can do to manage that course to safer outcomes, how else try to understand how others might intervene to detoxify those settings?   (1999:561–2)

So the singular episode, in its concrete particulars, is the starting point for CA. The ambiguity of 'For whom' in extract (10) is a matter of empirical fact, not theoretical construct; and whether Edna is making a proposal or an offer in (6) is one that is a matter for her and her co-participant to resolve in and through their talk. Moreover, an exchange that may, on the face of it, involve a man and a woman and may appear to show one interrupting the other does not *ipso facto* mean either that gender is a determinate factor in that interaction or that 'interruption' was indeed involved (see, for a case in point, Schegloff, 1997a).[33] As Heritage puts it, 'both the turn-taking procedures and the associated recognizability of interruptive departures from them are anterior to, and independent of, empirical distributions and interruptions as between males and females or

---

[33] In Chapter 6 we examine how such sociological or psychological characteristics may be oriented to through the practices of interaction.

between powerful and powerless individuals' (2008:303–4). It is thus only *after* such structural features of, say, turn-taking and interruption have been identified that it might make sense to examine how demographic characteristics (e.g. gender, ethnicity, class) or what we understand to be personality traits (e.g. sociability, introversion) might be manifested in interaction. As Schegloff notes, quantitative analysis – often regarded as the only means of access to such features – should not, then, be regarded as an alternative to single case analysis (of which the data of, e.g., 'For whom' (extract (10)) was an instance), but rather, built on its back (1993:102).

In CA, discourse-oriented social psychologists have thus found an alternative to the assumption in mainstream psychology that discourse is a direct and unmediated reflection of mental states, motives and intentions. Discursive psychology, emerging in the late 1980s, is, as a form of DA, perhaps closest to CA in its methodology and assumptions, although its specific interest in the psychological has meant that its data has tended to be less conversational and more explicitly task-oriented, such as focus groups (Edwards and Stokoe, 2004) or counselling (Edwards, 1995). It uses the methods of CA to examine the linguistic practices through which such mental states are invoked and made relevant by participants to discourse (see Potter and Wetherell, 1987; Edwards and Potter, 1992; Antaki et al., 2003; Potter, 2012), considering psychology 'as an object *in* and *for* interaction' (Potter and te Molder, 2005:2).[34] In some ways, the evolution of discursive psychology has paralleled that of interactional linguistics; like many linguists who originally deployed CA methods in an examination of language structure, many of the social-psychologists who originally saw in such methods ways of investigating psychology are now motivated by examining the practices of interaction itself. Responding to a proposal that analysts take into account speakers' retrospective accounts of what they were up to, Antaki captures the conversation-analytic recognition that 'there is ... a profound difference between individuals' undemonstrated inner feelings, hopes and intentions ... and the visible "participants' concerns" which are available for public consumption' (2012:493). Indeed, in seeking to understand interactional practices and the ways in which they intersect with human agency in shaping conduct, CA finds common cause, if not common methods, with psychology itself; as Enfield puts it: 'when we study human interaction, we are studying the mind, in the real sense of that word: an interpretive system that is distributed through and across people, places, and times' (2013:xviii).[35]

---

[34] But see Schegloff (1997a, 1998a, 1999) for discussions of the distinctions between DA and CA.
[35] Schegloff notes with approval John Jones's argument in the highly influential 'On Aristotle and Greek Tragedy' (1962):

> that it is mistaken, or simply a subsequent cultural imposition, to treat the Oedipus myth as involving a tragic hero. That grows out of a tacit ontology in the Judeo-Christian stream of Western culture that it is the single 'minded' and embodied individual that is the locus of social reality – here realised in the notion that the person named Oedipus is the locus of the play's action and import, and its 'tragic hero'. The

1.4   Action and sequence: the implications

For linguistics, there are both practical and theoretical implications. As Borsley and Ingham (2002:5) note, if one wants to know if a language allows parasitic gaps within subjects, nothing is to be gained by attempting to search for naturally occurring examples when one can more easily and fruitfully simply elicit acceptability judgements from a native speaker. In contrast, CA starts from specific observations in the data – from the 'empirical bite'. While such a stance is clearly not, of course, devoid of its own analytic assumptions or unconstrained by guiding intuition regarding the value of particular phenomena, it seeks to discover phenomena in the data, rather than test specific hypotheses about them. So an initial observation that, for example, in extract (8), three sequences of *Question – Answer – Oh* are followed by a sequence where a question and an answer are not followed by *Oh*, prompts the analyst to investigate the properties of *oh*. Analyses are warrantable and transparent,[36] and their grounding in the data of interactional sequences has opened up whole new and unforeseen seams of investigation into what, on the face of it, are unrelated phenomena. To take but one example, the whole research domain of epistemics, initiated by Heritage and Raymond (2005), owes its origins to the analysis, twenty years previously, of *oh* (Heritage, 1984a, 1998, 2002a), and subsequent work on yes/no interrogatives (Raymond, 2003) – all of which we discuss in the following pages; the merging of two initially independent streams of investigation has resulted in work which itself has extensive reach. So work on epistemics, as we see in Chapter 6, sheds light on, among other issues, identity construction in interaction and also on some of the form–function conundrums mentioned earlier.

The profound theoretical and methodological implications for linguistics should become ever clearer. In claiming that it might make as much sense to talk of what *oh* (or *actually*, or *yes* or *no*) *does* as what it *means* is to recognise that what we understand to be meaning is not embodied in an abstraction away from moments of production and interpretation, but rather is an emergent, sequential property. Furthermore, focusing on action and the resources for constructing action, rather than language per se, has made it more, not less, possible to recognise what connects us to our forbears; as Heritage observes:

> It is instructive, when reading the plays of Shakespeare, to recognize that while the language of the plays maybe somewhat arcane at times, the actions are not. The language, it is clear, has undergone numerous shifts in meaning and some of it has decayed out of usage altogether. The actions, by contrast, are stunningly recognizable and meaningful.   (2011:268)

alternative view is that there are certain sorts of recurrent situation that are the locus of tragedy ... it is the situation which is the relevant reality, the effective source of Oedipus' – and any person's – story and fate. The individuals who are caught up in it at any given moment are what is transient.   (Schegloff, 2003a:38)

[36] This is discussed further in Chapter 2 on transcription.

1.5   The organisation of this volume and overview of chapters

As an introduction to CA primarily for linguists, the chapters in this volume are not organised along traditional linguistic lines for the simple reason that CA findings do not, as we have seen, necessarily directly or straightforwardly map on to linguistic domains. CA methods identify linguistic and other resources implicated in the building of actions by bringing specific types of linguistic expertise to bear on the phenomena in the data, rather than problematising specific linguistic categories as such, a perspective that will be discussed further in the next chapter.

This volume accordingly seeks to discover phenomena – to borrow a phrase from Curl et al. (2006) – typically dubbed prosodic, morphosyntactic and pragmatic insofar as they serve the actions which CA takes as its focus. As we shall see, actions are constructed out of particular combinations of morphosyntax and sequential position, prosody (or, rather, 'prosodies', as Ogden (2012) has it), embodiments and gaze – and so we consider all of these resources.

Chapter 2 sketches in the origins and intellectual perspectives of CA and is orientational and methodological in nature. It shows how the work of Harvey Sacks's investigations into the social and moral order of interaction were indebted, in different ways, to the work of Erving Goffman and Harold Garfinkel. It then examines the ways in which analysis is dependent upon the specific conventions developed to capture the temporal production of utterances in talk. It includes a detailed list of conventions, with notes linking the analysis with the transcription conventions making it possible.

Chapters 3 to 7 collectively address different elements of the 'procedural infrastructure' – the physics – of interaction. Chapter 3, on sequences in interaction, starts by exploring the foundational concept of 'position and composition'. As we have seen, the objects of linguistic analysis have tended to be the lexical, morphological, syntactic, phonological and phonetic composition of phrases and sentences. In this chapter we outline in more detail how the understanding or perception of turns at talk is shaped by their sequential position. In doing so, it introduces a basic, and apparently universal, resource in interaction, the adjacency pair: an elemental building block for many interactional sequences. We show how the adjacency pair can be expanded, both before and after, into larger sequences of talk, before considering what this reveals about the human capacity for joint action across the languages of the world.

Chapter 4 examines the fundamental organisation of talk in turns as investigated in the classic paper by Sacks et al. (1974) on turn-taking – work that was revolutionary in its examination of the online, temporal and interactional production of utterances. The turn-taking model is a universal system implemented with the local resources of a given language. The syntactic, prosodic, phonetic and pragmatic resources of particular languages, alongside features such as gaze and embodiments, are marshalled and implemented by means of this system: the self-administered organisation of participation in turns. After an overview of the basic model, where participants standardly attempt to achieve one speaker talking at a time, with no gap, and no overlap between speakers, we examine the implications when this is not achieved, in overlap and silence.

Chapter 5 is the first of two chapters on the structure of longer sequences of action. It builds on preliminary observations regarding adjacency pairs and examines the relationship between actions across sequences through what is known as preference organisation – broadly speaking, observed biases towards the use of particular structures. In identifying the role of culture in shaping and selecting particular structures on the path to grammaticalisation, preference organisation is the meeting point of the social and the linguistic. We examine how speakers build their turns to either conform or resist in the face of constraints proposed by an initial turn. These range from actions which appear to be clearly collaborative, such as requests, to those which, on the face of it, are not, such as reference to persons in interaction.

Chapter 6 investigates another aspect of how sequences are constructed through the examination of identity in interaction. While standardly, linguistics has examined identity through appeal to categories external to the talk, the CA focus on participants' own orientations as revealed endogenously through their interactions has uncovered a number of analytic resources for the interpretation of utterances that go beyond the construction of identity as such. The chapter first examines the work of Harvey Sacks in investigating the 'apparatus' by which recognisable common-sense understandings are generated and related to the sequential construction of identity. It then investigates two domains that are shown to figure in the understanding of action: knowledge and authority. In examining participants' orientations to these, CA has discovered that, alongside relatively stable attributions of status, we can identify moment-by-moment interactional adjustments available by reference to participant stance. CA work on these, in the areas of epistemic rights and deontic authority, has given us the means of understanding phenomena that have been long-standing linguistic conundrums. One is the frequent mismatch between the form of an utterance and the action it implements. The other is the motivation for indirect utterances. Both issues here are illuminated by reference to actions in sequence.

Chapter 7 is devoted to the organisation of repair, the final element in our overview of the infrastructure of interaction. Repair is the means by which interactants maintain a shared world-view, defending intersubjectivity, and so deals with the exigencies of the real-time, online production of utterances. We also see how the hesitations, dysfluencies and false starts that characterise repair can be vehicles for actions in themselves. Repair can be initiated by either the current speaker ('self') or the recipient ('other'). Here we provide taxonomy of self- and other-initiations of repair and show how resources for repair may go beyond the linguistic, into implicit forms of repair implemented by forms of gaze and embodiment.

Chapter 8, the Conclusion, draws together some of the prominent themes of the volume as a whole in reflecting on the legacy for linguistics of a half-century of conversation-analytic research.

2 Towards an understanding of action: origins and perspectives

This chapter has two main aims: to examine the origins of CA in the work of Harvey Sacks, and to provide some methodological perspective that informs the CA treatment of data. It starts by tracing the influence on Sacks of Erving Goffman, who conceived of interaction as an autonomous domain of study, and Harold Garfinkel, whose central legacy was how members of a society reason beyond what is said, and how they share that reasoning to achieve intersubjectivity. It examines Sacks's early observations as he worked on recorded data, and how he worked with collections to show the systematicity of interactional practices. Key to his unmotivated examination of data was the development of a transcription system by Gail Jefferson that captured talk in its temporal, online production. We examine some of the practices that would not be captured by transcription systems that focused only on the linguistic content of what was said. The final section of the chapter is an overview of the transcription conventions linked to analytic sketches of the phenomena discoverable through them.

> The aspects of things that are most important for us are hidden because of their simplicity and familiarity. (Wittgenstein, 1953: para.129)

Pioneering work in CA has its origins in the highly empirical sociological investigations of Harvey Sacks at the University of California, Los Angeles, in the early 1960s. Sacks's concerns were not specifically linguistic, let alone conversational, at all; what we would recognise as the first conversation-analytic observations were made on the materials available to him at the time: a corpus of phone calls to a helpline operated by the Los Angeles Suicide Prevention Center. Sacks approached this corpus influenced by two early associations: one with Harold Garfinkel, whose concern with members' methods of practical reasoning formed the basis of ethnomethodology (see, e.g., Garfinkel, 1967), and also with Erving Goffman, who was establishing the study of face-to-face interaction as an object of inquiry in its own right (see, e.g., Goffman, 1959, 1961, 1963, 1964).[1]

In dissenting from the view that the details of everyday life are 'an inherently disorderly and unresearchable mess' (Heritage and Clayman, 2010:8), both Goffman and Garfinkel, in different ways, made such details the object of systematic inquiry. The personal engagement of Sacks with both Garfinkel and Goffman originating in Sacks's graduate studies, and the intellectual context of his work, is recounted in Schegloff (1992a:xii–xxxi): the introduction to the extraordinary collection of Sacks's lectures by Emanuel Schegloff, Sacks's principal collaborator within CA. What follows are brief sketches of the streams

---

[1] In an early lecture, Sacks positions himself vis-à-vis Wittgenstein, Freud and others (1992a: 26–8).

of work represented by each, and of some of the ways in which their influence is manifest in Sacks's observations.

2.1   On Goffman and Garfinkel

> I assume that the proper study of interaction is not the individual and his psychology, but rather the syntactical relations among the acts of different persons mutually present to one another ... Not then, men and their moments. Rather moments and their men.   (Goffman, [1967] 2005:2–3)

Goffman's insistence that the study of face-to-face interaction – 'the interaction order' (1983) – could be an independent domain of analytic investigation, and not a reflection of psychology, sociology or linguistics, is key in the development of CA as an autonomous domain of inquiry. In the face of a prevailing assumption in mid-twentieth-century sociology that interaction is too disorderly to yield to systematic analysis, he insisted that the interaction order is a visible insitution in its own right, like the family, education or the legal system. Moreover, this particular institution is the medium through which the business of these others is transacted. In this respect, Goffman figures in the development of CA in much the same way as Durkheim in sociology[2] and Saussure in linguistics.[3] His reference to 'syntactical relations' identifies the essentially structural character of the interaction order where the individual is morally and publicly accountable within a framework of social logic, and where interactants deploy such syntax, which provides for the ordering of actions, in the analysis of one another's motives and identities. As he notes: 'The general capacity to be bound by moral rules may well belong to the individual, but the particular set of rules which transforms him into a human being derives from requirements established in the ritual organization of social encounters' ([1967] 2005:45). Those requirements consist of a complex set of rights and obligations linked to aspects of identity and to large-scale social institutions, but, with respect to interaction, centrally to a conception of 'face': 'the positive social value a person effectively claims for himself ... an image of self delineated in terms of approved social attributes' (p. 5). However, Goffman proposed that, alongside a 'rule of self-respect', there is a 'rule of considerateness' so that members of a group in social encounters tend to conduct themselves in such a way as to

---

[2] 'My main influences were [Lloyd] Warner and [A. R.] Radcliffe-Brown, [Emile] Durkheim, and [Everett] Hughes. Maybe [Max] Weber also' (Goffman, in Verhoeven, 1993:321).

[3] Indeed, one of Saussure's translators characterises Saussure's contribution to the study of language in terms which are strikingly resonant of Goffman's perspective:

'Language is no longer regarded as peripheral to our grasp of the world we live in, but as central to it. Words are not mere vocal labels or communicational adjuncts superimposed upon an already given order of things. They are collective products of social interaction, essential instruments through which human beings constitute and articulate their world' (Harris, 1988:ix).

maintain their own face and those of the other participants, and notes that this kind of mutual acceptance appears to be a basic structural feature of interaction (p. 11). So, in proposing to study the normative organisation of practices and processes that constitute the interaction order, Goffman opened up a whole new domain of work and initiated the systematic investigation of the micromoments of social interaction. As he observed:

> The human tendency to use signs and symbols means that evidence of social worth and of mutual evaluations will be conveyed by very minor things, and these things will be witnessed, as will the fact that they have been witnessed. An unguarded glance, a momentary change in tone of voice, an ecological position taken or not taken, can drench a talk with judgemental significance. Therefore, just as there is no occasion of talk in which improper impressions could not intentionally or unintentionally arise, so there is no occasion of talk so trivial as not to require in each participant to show serious concern with the way in which he handles himself and the others present. (Goffman, [1967] 2005:33)

As we shall see in the course of this book, the possibility that there could be a systematic study of these 'signs and symbols' and that they could lead to the discovery of universals of social interaction was to prove prescient.

If Goffman was interested in how face considerations shape action, and how moral inferences may drive interaction, the work of Harold Garfinkel was concerned with the means by which actions are produced and recognised. Garfinkel had studied with Talcott Parsons, and saw in Parsons's conceptualisation of action as *the* structure of social action (1937) a failure to engage with processes of mutual understanding in the context of action. Garfinkel's concern came to be the shared methods ('members' methods' or 'ethnomethodology') of practical reasoning informing both the production and the recognition of actions. He introduces his *Studies in Ethnomethodology* by stating that they 'seek to treat practical activities, practical circumstances, and practical sociological reasoning as topics of empirical study, and by paying to the most commonplace activities of daily life the attention usually accorded extraordinary events, seek to learn about them as phenomena in their own right' (1967:1). He asserts that a world shared in common is, in fact, 'a set of practices by which actions and stances could be composed in a fashion which displayed grounding in, and orientation to what Schegloff calls "knowledge held in common"' (1992b:1298):

> 'Shared agreement' refers to various social methods for accomplishing the members' recognition that something was said-according-to-a-rule and not the demonstrable matching of substantive matters. The appropriate image of common understanding is therefore *an operation rather than a common intersection of overlapping sets*. (Garfinkel, 1967:30; italics added)

Garfinkel's commitment to investigating the commonsense knowledge and practical reasoning informing language use led him to undertake what have become known since as his 'breaching experiments'. Seeking to identify the unspoken, underlying assumptions, presuppositions and methods of inference normally supporting a world shared in common, Garfinkel asked his students 'to engage an acquaintance or a friend in an ordinary conversation and, without indicating that what the experimenter was asking was in any way unusual, to insist that the person clarify the sense of his commonplace remarks' (p. 42). Some of the results were reported thus, where S is the subject and E the experimenter:

(1) (Garfinkel, 1967:43)
(On Friday night my husband and I were watching television. My husband remarked that he was tired. I asked, 'How are you tired? Physically, mentally, or just bored?')
S   I don't know, I guess physically, mainly.
E   You mean that your muscles ache or your bones?
S   I guess so. Don't be so technical.
     (*After more watching*)
S   All these movies have the same kind of old iron bedstead in
     them.
E   What do you mean? Do you mean all old movies, or some of them,
     or just the ones you have seen?
S   What's the matter with you? You know what I mean.
E   I wish you would be more specific.
S   You know what I mean! Drop dead!

(2) (Garfinkel, 1967:44)
(The victim waved his hand cheerily.)
S   How are you?
E   How am I in regard to what? My health, my finances, my school work,
     my peace of mind, my ... ?
S   (*Red in the face and suddenly out of control*) Look! I was just
     trying to be polite. Frankly I don't give a damn how you are.

It becomes quite evident that, often by the end of the first request for clarification, interactional – if not relational – breakdown is in progress. As Heritage (1984b) remarks on these findings, Garfinkel integrates the moral with the cognitive: 'In each case, the S treated the intelligible character of his own talk as something to which he was morally entitled and, correspondingly, treated the breaching move as illegitimate, deserving of sanction and requiring explanation' (1984b:81–2). Thus *How are you?* standardly gets the response *Fine* (even if, as Sacks, 1975, later points out, being 'fine' may be far from the case): to receive, instead of this standard response, *How am I in regard to my what ...?* – a challenge – is to call into question a world shared in common. In this respect the world of common understandings and the taken-for-granted has much in common with Grice's (1975) proposal of an assumed 'Co-operative Principle' in conversation that is the interpretive default for our understanding of utterances. In the chapters that follow, we examine in detail the expectations and assumptions that connect sequences of utterances like *How are you?* – *Fine* and examine precisely how the adjacent positioning of utterances is a fundamental resource for participants in building intersubjectivity. Thus, 'next turn' is the position in which a speaker displays an understanding of a prior turn, and if that understanding turns out to be mistaken, it can be repaired in the turn after that – so-called 'third position repair' (Schegloff, 1992b), which we discuss in Chapter 7, but which is exemplified in the extract below. This is taken from a conversation between sisters in their fifties, which began with a comment from Portia regarding their failure to get together recently. At line 3, Portia seemingly initiates the close of the conversation (Schegloff and Sacks, 1973), which is, however, taken by Agnes to reprise the earlier complaint about not getting together, as evidenced by her account at line 8:

```
(3)   (Schegloff, 1992b:1306)
1    Agnes     I love it.
2              (0.2)
3    Portia    Well, honey? I'll pob'ly see yuh one a' these
4              day:s.
5    Agnes     Oh:: God yeah,
6    Portia    [Uhh huh!
7    Agnes     [We-
8    Agnes     B't I c- I jis' [couldn' git down [there.
9    Portia→                   [Oh-           [Oh I know.
10             I'm not askin [yuh tuh [com dow-
11   Agnes                   [Jesus. [I mean I jis'- I didn' have
12             five minutes yesterday.
```

At line 9, 'Oh' initiates repair, and at line 10 Portia accepts Agnes's excuse for not visiting. It is the practices by which these common understandings are managed – the 'ethnomethods' of interaction – that constitute the resources used in the production and recognition of accountable action. In an early statement of CA method, Schegloff and Sacks state:

> We have proceeded under the assumption . . . that in so far as the materials we worked with exhibited orderliness, they did so not only for us, indeed not in the first place for us, but for the co-participants who had produced them. If the materials (records of natural conversation) were orderly, they were so because they had been methodically produced by members of society for one another.   (1973:290)

Sacks thus drew on two significant legacies: from Goffman he took the recognition of interaction as a domain of study in its own right, and from Garfinkel, the notion of reasoning beyond what is said, and the sharing of that reasoning to achieve intersubjectivity. It is, however, immediately clear that Sacks's working methods, with their detailed attention to recorded data, are distinct from both (for an extended consideration of the convergences, divergences and, at times, conflicts of Goffman's work and CA, see Schegloff, 1988a; and for a comprehensive account of CA's origins in the work of Garfinkel, see Heritage, 1984b).

2.2   Harvey Sacks: from ethnomethodology to conversation analysis

The ethnomethodological underpinnings of CA, and thus the immediate influence of Garfinkel on Sacks, can be seen very clearly in an early essay by Sacks that provides a dazzling informing perspective on his work.[4] In it, he asserts that

> Whatever you may think about what it is to be an ordinary person in the world, an initial shift is not to think of 'an ordinary person' as some person, but as somebody having as one's job, as one's constant preoccupation, doing 'being ordinary'. It is not that somebody *is* ordinary; it is perhaps that that is what one's business is, and it takes work, as any other business does ... So I am not ... talking about an ordinary person as this or that person, or some average; that is, as a non-exceptional person on some statistical basis, *but as something that is the way somebody constitutes oneself, and in effect, a job that persons ... may be cooperatively engaged in to achieve that each of them ... are ordinary persons.*   (Sacks, 1984a:414–15; italics added)

He further notes that, given 'that it is almost everybody's business to be occupationally ordinary' (p. 419), it is remarkable to see how, when people report something out of the ordinary, they make a concerted effort to 'achieve the "nothing happened" sense of really catastrophic events ... A classically dramatic instance is, almost universally, that the initial report of the assassination of President Kennedy was of having heard backfires' (*ibid.*).[5] Gail Jefferson, subsequently examining the material Sacks collected, elaborates on this observation where she notes that reports in such cases, constructed to show that their producers essentially have the same response as anyone else might have, are recurrently formatted as 'At first I thought ... and then I realised': what Jefferson calls 'a device for normalizing extraordinary events' (2004a).[6] By the same token, a witness to Kennedy's shooting who reports as his first thought the catastrophic version of the event takes care to give an account of why he does:

> As the motorcade went down the side of Elm Street toward the railroad underpass, a rifle shot was heard by me; a loud blast, close by. I have handled firearms for fifty years, and thought immediately that it was a rifle shot.   (Jefferson, 2004a:147)

With both the account, 'I have handled firearms for fifty years', and construction of the thought as 'immediate' and, so to speak, unbidden, the speaker grounds his

---

[4] Compiled from lecture notes by Gail Jefferson after Sacks's death in a car accident in 1975.

[5] Or in more recent years, one might add, the first reports of the 9/11 attacks on the World Trade Center, where recurrently the reports from people hearing the news that a plane had flown into one of the twin towers was that their first thought was that it had to be a light aircraft (Jefferson, 2004a:163).

[6] A student moving to the UK mainland from Northern Ireland during the late twentieth-century conflict known as 'The Troubles' reported, on hearing fireworks explode on Bonfire Night, that his first thought was that a bomb had exploded, and so he dived behind a car; clearly, what counts as 'normal' is relative to context (my thanks to Elizabeth Holt for this report).

reasoning;[7] thus is response defensible, and his status as essentially 'ordinary' preserved. Sacks's insight, that 'being ordinary' takes work and is an accomplishment, clearly shows the ethnomethodological foundations of all subsequent work in the discipline.[8]

In one of his most striking observations, Sacks notes of a recent Californian earthquake that people who had house-guests at the time may well have found themselves apologising for the earthquake, because they were at the time in a relationship of responsibility towards them (1992a:296), and so accountable to them. One may find oneself 'host' in a number of contexts and get the credit for someone else's achievement (your guests at a restaurant congratulate you, not the chef); but correspondingly:

> you feel a need to apologize, and they know that you have to apologize and they hold you responsible when it turns out that the earthquake, the lousy movie, the fire, the rain, the automobile accident, whatever else, happened while you and they were together and you were in the position of being 'host'.   (Sacks, 1992a:296)

So in the position of being 'host', Sacks argues, one sees the world by reference to that responsibility (that, e.g., in the restaurant, the music is rather too loud, the table is by an open door or the glasses are smeary). So in such instances, Sacks sees that how members of a community themselves describe or explain the properties of any given situation – how they account for it – affords an insight into the organisation of their practical reasoning. In the earliest of his collected lectures, asserting that 'Accounts are most extraordinary' (1992a:4), Sacks argues that 'The fact that you could use questions – like 'Why?' – to generate accounts, and then use accounts to control activities, can be marked down as, I think, one of the greatest discoveries in Western civilization' (p. 5). The investigation of how people in any society account for events in the course of everyday activities is one route into establishing the foundations of their social organisation; as Sacks put it, 'culture is an apparatus for generating recognizable actions' (p. 226), or an 'inference-making machine' (p. 119) that is exposed in the ways in which descriptions are implemented in particular contexts. So, for example, Sacks invokes the classic study by Evans-Pritchard (1937) of witchcraft among the Azande to show how the Azande have no institutionalised notion of chance, but instead a notion of natural causes – which may, ultimately, be embedded in witchcraft. For Sacks, the accounts of the format *At first I thought . . .*

---

[7] The reporter for ABC news at the scene of the 9/11 attacks, Don Dahler, ventures to suggest, on personal experience, that the 'first thought' that a plane crashing into one of the twin towers was a light aircraft could not, in fact, be the case: 'Well, I have flown. I do not have a pilot's license, but I–I grew up on military bases. And I know the sounds of jets. And–and I've been in war zones and–and heard those kinds of different sounds. So, again, not to cause any kind of undue speculation but the sound itself was not of a prop plane. It was perhaps a jet, but it could have been a missile as well' ('WTC-2 Missile Strike on 9/11: Eyewitness Saw a Missile', www.youtube .com/watch?v=hq8eiNxKFXI).

[8] This assumption is explicitly captured in the title of Schegloff (1986): 'The Routine as Achievement'.

then I realised . . . provided just the sort of data that may be examined to see how they shape, and indeed are shaped by, the contexts in which they are embedded; such descriptive accounts, dependent for their sense on the contexts of their production, are thus irredeemably indexical (Bar-Hillel, 1954:359–79). It was with this perspective on the context-boundedness of descriptive accounts that Sacks approached his corpus of suicide helpline calls.

The primary attraction of the corpus of calls to the Suicide Prevention Center lay in the fact that it was naturally occurring, recorded interaction, which made it 'repeatably inspectable' (Schegloff, 2003b:39) for transcription, analysis and, potentially, reanalysis.[9] This, in itself, would not distinguish him from any other researcher investigating a recorded corpus of spoken material. The distinctiveness of Sacks's treatment was his observation that

> Recurrently, what stands as a solution to some problem emerges from unmotivated examination of some piece of data, where, had we started out with a specific interest in the problem, it would not have been supposed, in the first instance that this piece of data was a resource with which to consider, and come up with a solution for, that particular problem.   (1984a:27)

'Unmotivated looking' was thus the guiding principle of Sacks's examination of the data, and the view that the analyst was identifying speakers' solutions to interactional problems. It is a perspective which starts from 'the bite': identifying the solutions in the data, working back from them to discover what the problems are, rather than an assumption of what the problems are in the first place. The analysis is overwhelmingly data-driven, rather than analyst-driven – the analyst's guiding concerns, shaped by assumptions about the data or ideology, are here set aside. This bottom-up, data-driven approach is, more than anything else, what sets CA methods apart from other treatments of interactional data, as we saw in Chapter 1. In this context, Heritage and Stivers draw a pertinent analogy from the history of sociological analysis:

> Durkheim argued that suicide was to be analysed exclusively in terms of correlations between suicide rates, measures of social isolation, the business cycle and so on . . . the cumulative significance of this perspective was its delimitation of sociological inquiry to social behaviour in the aggregate, thus excluding all micro-level analyses of social behaviour and any aspect of the reasoning that might inform it. Yet suicide, and indeed other social conduct is not done 'in the aggregate'. It is done by particular persons and particular circumstances with particular underlying reasons . . . aggregate analyses of conduct could hardly be offered when the conduct in question was not considered in its concrete particulars.   (2013:660–1)

---

[9] 'It wasn't from any large interest in language, or from some theoretical formulation of what should be studied, but simply by virtue of [the fact that] I could get my hands on it, and I could study it again and again. And also, consequentially, others could look at what I had studied, and make of it what they could, if they wanted to be able to disagree with me' (Sacks, 1992a:622).

So it was in the 'concrete particulars' of his data that Sacks identified solutions to interactional problems.[10] An early instance was his observation regarding a phone call in his helpline corpus which, as Schegloff notes:

> ... began something like this:
>
> A: This is Mr. Smith, may I help you.
> B: I can't hear you.
> A: This is Mr. <u>Smith</u>.
> B: S<u>m</u>ith.
>
> After which Mr. Smith goes on, without getting the caller's name. And later, when Mr. Smith asks for the caller's name, the caller resists giving it. On the one hand, Sacks noted, it appears that if the name is not forthcoming at the start it may prove problematic to get. On the other hand, overt requests for it may be resisted. Then he remarked: Is it possible that the caller's declared problem in hearing is a methodical way of avoiding giving one's name in response to the other's having done so? Could talk be organized at that level of detail? And in so designed a manner?   (Schegloff, 1992a:xvi–xvii)

Sacks's 'unmotivated looking' had thus led to his intial observation about 'the caller's declared problem in hearing' (we return to the technical specification of this, and this sequence, as 'other-initiated repair' in Chapter 7). To regard *I can't hear you* as a solution led him to speculate about what the problem might be. The common-sense observation that there are places where things get done (such as giving one's name at the beginning of a conversation) and that, beyond these places, 'it may prove problematic' in turn led him to the possibility that in fact *I can't hear you* was the deft solution to the problem of having to avoid giving one's name in response to the proferring of another's while not being seen to avoid doing so.

The possibility that *I can't hear you* in such contexts is a methodical practice – a systematic solution to an interactional problem, irrespective of the personal characteristics, desires or beliefs of the participants involved – can only be established empirically, and from an assumption that, as Sacks famously stated: 'whatever humans do can be examined to discover some way they do it, and that way will be stably describable. That is, we may alternatively take it that there is *order at all points*' (Sacks, 1984b:22; italics added). This starting assumption[11] and

---

[10] In Chapter 6 there is further discussion of Sacks's work on the helpline calls with respect to the construction of identity.

[11] A starting assumption being distinct from the belief that such order at all points is a fact; as Schegloff subsequently clarifies:

> I do not myself believe that there is order at *all* points, nor do I think that Sacks believed this. If it were so, there would be no need to show that some particular manner of speaking was a 'locus of order,' that it was oriented to by participants, etc. If there was order at *all* points, social life – and talk-in-interaction in particular – could always be examined productively at *any* point and in *any* respect. In that case, there would be no need for new initiatives. The stance being put forward might instead better be put as 'order *possible* at any point'; that is, *no aspect of talk-in-interaction can be excluded a priori as a locus of order.*   (2004b:17)

its empirical exploration is a central component of CA method: the assembling of collections of similar cases across varieties of interactional data. For subsequently, Sacks supplemented the original corpus with calls of so-called 'mundane conversation'. It is this – the identification of recurrent instances – which ultimately makes possible the identification of generic practices and which is one source of CA's analytic strength. Another was the transcription system devised by Gail Jefferson, originally a student of Sacks's at UCLA, and later a collaborator, who transcribed some of his earliest materials and thus made the discovery of interactional phenomena possible.

2.3   Jefferson's transcription system

Jefferson's transcription system is to CA what the electron microscope is to the sub-cellular structure of matter: it is simply what makes observations possible. Some years after her development of the transcription system, and reflecting on transcription, Jefferson (2004b) shows us the following 'succinct and readable' transcript from the Watergate Tapes from Kutler (1997:253):

> (John Dean, White House Counsel, and President Nixon)
>
> DEAN I don't know the full extent of it,
> NIXON I don't know about anything else.
> DEAN I don't know either, and I [*laughs*] almost
>   hate to learn some of these things.

Kutler notes that, in his transcriptions

> I have edited the conversations with an eye toward eliminating what I believe insignificant, trivial, or repetitious . . . and often have omitted dutiful choruses of agreement by those present unless I believed them particularly important. The dialogue of innumerable uses of 'right', 'yeah', 'okay' often has been dropped . . . The 'uhs' and 'ahs' usually have been eliminated.   (1997:vii)

Jefferson undertakes to transcribe the same exchange thus:

```
(4)   (Jefferson, 2004b:15; line numbers added)
1     Dean       I ↑don't' kno:w the (.) full extent ↓'v it.↓
2                (0.7)
3     Dean       ↓Uh:::eh°
4                (0.9)
5     Nixon      °I don'noo° 'bout anything else exchhe[pt
6     Dean                                            [I don't either
7          →     in I:°w'd (h)als(h)o hhate tuh learn
8          →     [some a'] these thi]ngs..hh.hh.hh.hh
9                [W e l l] y a : h  ]
10               (0.2)
11    Dean       So ↑That's,hhhh that's that situation.
```

In a detailed exegesis of her transcription, Jefferson extracts some of the observations facilitated by its detail. Focusing on Nixon's 'exc^{hh}e[pt', she notes that it

> suggests that Nixon is going on to mention something else he knows about, i.e., we now have the word 'except'. And we have Dean starting up within that word, at 'exce ...', where after, Nixon stops. One thing that might be happening here is that Dean hears, in 'exce ... ', the word 'except' forming up, and starts to talk at that point. This 'recognitional-response' is a not-uncommon phenomenon ... Similarly, with 'exce ... ', Dean may hear the word 'except' forming up. Hearing that, he may hear that Nixon is starting to mention something else, knowledge of which Dean doesn't want to be burdened with. It may be that Dean moves then and there to stop any possible revelations by cutting in on the alerting word 'except', prior to its completion, with an agreement that specifically ignores its projection of further things (i.e., his 'I don't either' targets Nixon's initial proposal, 'I don't know about anything else'), and then goes on to announce his unwillingness to know any more. Then there is the laughter ...   (Jefferson, 2004b:17–18)

Jefferson's reflections here stand as testament to what her own transcription makes possible. The mention of laughter here is particularly striking because it was the transcription of laughter which opened up a whole new domain of study. Encountering the methodological problem in the helpline calls of transcribing what she heard as laughter, Jefferson notes of the transcriptions of the time[12] that 'laughter appears to be among the activity types that do not require, nor lend themselves to reporting of their particulars ... laughter is named, not quoted ...' (1985:27–8). It is possible to trace the transition from 'naming' to 'quoting' in the two versions of a transcript made by Jefferson ((5) and (6) respectively), twelve years apart; note, in particular, the distinct versions of the arrowed turns:

---

[12] George Orwell, in his essay 'Propaganda and Demotic Speech' ([1944] 1998), had envisaged the possibility of a transcription system along the following lines:

> What is wanted, evidently, is some way of getting ordinary, slipshod, colloquial English on to paper. But is this possible? I think it is, and by a quite simple method which so far as I know has never been tried. It is this: Set a fairly ready speaker down at the microphone and let him just talk, either continuously or intermittently, on any subject he chooses. Do this with a dozen different speakers, recording it every time. Vary it with a few dialogues or conversations between three or four people. Then play your recordings back and let a stenographer reduce them to writing: not in the shortened, rationalized version that stenographers usually produce, but word for word, with such punctuation as seems appropriate. You would then – for the first time, I believe – have on paper some authentic specimens of spoken English. Probably they would not be readable as a book or a newspaper article is readable, but then spoken English is not meant to be read, it is meant to be listened to. From these specimens you could, I believe, formulate the rules of spoken English and find out how it differs from the written language. And when writing in spoken English had become practicable, the average speaker or lecturer who has to write his material down beforehand could bring it far closer to his natural dictation, make it more essentially speakable, than he can at present.

(5) (Jefferson, 1985:28; GTS:I:1:14, 1965)

```
1    Ken        And he came home and decided he was gonna play with his
2               orchids from then on in.
3    Roger      With his what?
4    Louise     heh heh heh heh
5    Ken        With his orchids. [He has an orchid-
6    Roger →                     [Oh heh hehheh
7    Louise→    ((through bubbling laughter)) Playing with his organ yeah
8               I thought the same thing!
9    Ken        No he's got a great big [glass house-
10   Roger                              [I can see him playing with his
11              organ hehh hhhh
```

(6) (Jefferson, 1985:29; GTS:I:2:33:R2, 1977)

```
1    Ken        An' e came home'n decided'e wz gonna play with iz o:rchids.
2               from then on i:n.
3    Roger      With iz what?
4    Louise     mh hih hih[huh
5    Ken                  [With iz orchids.==
6    Ken        =Ee[z got an orchi[id-
7    Roger→        [Oh:.          [hehh[h a h.he:h].heh
8→   Louise                            [heh huh.hh] PLAYN(h)W(h)IZ O(h)RN
9               ya:h I[thought the [same
10   Roger            [.uh::        [.hunhh.hh.hh
11   Ken                            [Cz eez gotta great big[gla:ss house]=
12   Roger                                                 [I c'n s(h)ee ]
13   Ken        =[(           )
14   Roger      =[im pl(h)ay with iz o(h)r(h)g.(h)n.uh
```

Treating laughter, a non-linguistic phenomenon, as worthy of investigation in the first place, and trying to capture how and where the laughter occurred – quoting it, rather than naming it – had had, as we shall see, an extraordinary analytic yield. Because, as Jefferson observes: 'Once we have the specific "placement" of laughter as a possible phenomenon, we can begin to examine it as a methodic device' (1985:30). Of the above transcripts, Jefferson notes that, while the early transcript proposes that the entire utterance is produced 'through bubbling laughter', the later one captures the presence of laughter in, and only in, a discrete portion of the utterance: in the saying of an obscenity. Her meticulous attention to the placement of the laughter in the utterance leads her ultimately to propose that

> It may, then, be no happenstance occurrence that the explicit obscenity is slurred, and accountably slurred with the presence of laughter, and that the complex and delicate proposal about the authorship of the obscenity is produced with utter felicity, free of the laughter which can make an utterance difficult to 'hear.   (Jefferson, 1985:33)

As Jefferson shows across a range of exemplars, both presence *and* absence of laughter are salient; for the first time, laughter is not treated as an uncontrolled 'flooding out' (Goffman, 1961) but rather revealed as a methodical device to obscure the delicate component of an utterance, so implicating a recipient in its authorship.

Jefferson's subsequent work on laughter (1979, 1984a, 1985, 2004b, 2004c) and with Sacks and Schegloff (1987), stands as a testament to her design of a transcription system which, in her words, 'warrants and rewards more than a naming of (laughter's) occurrence' (1985:34). In a letter written to recommend Gail Jefferson for an academic post, Harvey Sacks pays tribute to Jefferson's papers on laughter:

> These need to be understood from the perspective of the appreciation of the potential interest laughter's examination has for social science as it is reflected in the great researchers who have tried to deal with it, e.g. Darwin, Freud, Huizinga, Simmel, etc. and from that perspective what she has done that is without precedent is to find ways of technically trapping that laughter examined in terms of the various units in which laughs can be placed, and the variable sizes the laugh units can have is actually very sharply coordinated and coordinative.[13]

Jefferson's transcription system has made it possible for others to set about 'technically trapping' laughter and has opened up a whole vein of research into laughter in interaction (see, e.g., Holt, 2010, 2011, 2012; Glenn, 2003, 2010; Haakana, 2001, 2010, 2012; Clift, 2012a, 2014; and the collection in Glenn and Holt, 2013).[14] As we can see, the transcription and analysis of laughter evolved in tandem with the very development of CA itself. Jefferson's initial methodological decision to capture exactly where laughter occurs, and what it sounds like, shows how Sacks's 'unmotivated examination' of data is neither atheoretical nor unintuitive (see Clift, 2005, on the role of intuition in such work).

2.4   Capturing phenomena

While the two versions of the same transcript in (5) and (6) are most vividly distinct in their representation of laughter, there are other differences in the later version which may be analytically consequential. Perhaps the most striking across the transcript as a whole is that of the orthography. Compare, for example, the alternative treatments of Ken's first turn. In the following it is rendered in normalised, familiar orthography:

---

[13] 'Order At All Points: The Work of Harvey Sacks', Exhibition at the Young Research Library, UCLA, June 2014 (Harvey Sacks to Paul M. Siegel, Department of Sociology, Ann Arbor, Michigan, 13 February 1975).
[14] The second of Harvey Sacks's topics in his collected lectures, from Fall 1964–Spring 1965, is 'On Suicide Threats Getting Laughed Off' (1992a:12–20): an indication of how early on laughter was treated as a topic of investigation.

(From (5) GTS:I:1:14, 1965)
```
1  Ken   And he came home and decided he was gonna play with his
2        orchids from then on in.
```

However, in the rendering below, Jefferson adopts what she calls 'modified standard orthography', designed to look to the eye as it sounds to the ear (Schenkein, 1978:xi).[15]

(From (6) GTS:I:2:33:R2, 1977)
```
1  Ken   An'e came home'n decided'e wz gonna play with iz o:rchids.
2        from then on i:n.
```

Inevitably, this form of orthography has to find a compromise between general accessibility, on the one hand, unlike, say, phonetic transcription (but see Walker, 2013, for some of the limitations from the perspective of phonetic detail), and access to information on the other (which represents the distinction in articulation between, e.g., *And he* and *An'e*). Jefferson (1983), recognising the perils of caricature in the latter, shows just how consequential the representation of ostensibly the 'same' turn may be. So, registering that a speaker, while being advised how to make tacos, maintains her pronunciation of the word *sauce* as 'sawss' in the face of her adviser's pronunciation, Jefferson notes that 'it may not be incidental, but may be part and parcel of her preserving non-subordinate status' (p. 12):

---

[15] Indeed, the fine orthographical distinctions made in Jefferson's transcripts extend to laughter, too; so, for example, in the 1977 GTS transcript, Roger's laughter in l. 7 is represented as:

```
[hehh[h a h he:h]  heh
```

In Sacks's observations on the telling of a dirty joke (1992b:471), the laughter is represented in a variety of ways in the wake of the joke's punchline:

```
K:     Next morning she talks t'the firs' daughter en' she s'z-- uh how
       come yuh- how come y'went YAAA::: las' night'n daughter siz
       well it tickled Mommy - second gi:rl, - How come yuh
       screa:med. Oh: Mommy it hu:rts. - Third girl, walks up t'her.
       (0.7) Why didn' y'say anything las'night. - W'you tol'me it wz
       always impolite t'talk with my mouth full,
       (1.5)
K:→    hh hyok hyok.
       (0.5)
K:→    hyok.
       (2.5)
A:→    HA-HA-HA-HA!
K:→    ehh heh heh // hehhh
(A)→   hehhhehhheh hhh
R:     Delayed rea:c//tio(h)n.
```

(7) (Jefferson, 1983:12; NB:II:2:R:1–2; line numbers added)
```
1  Gladys:→  you need uh hhamburger don't ↑chu.
2  Emma:      .hh Ye:u::s? e[n y]uh need [some: u]h:   ]
3  Gladys:→              [En ]        [s- .hh]sh:r]edded lettuce?
4  Emma:      Shredded lettuce en CHEE::SE?
               .
5  Gladys:→  Dih you need a hot sawss:?
6  Emma:      .t.hhh A TA↑: CO↑sah*:ss.
7  Gladys:→  A ta:co ↓s*aw:ss.
```

There are other indications in the data that the speaker may be preserving her non-subordinate status – Jefferson notes her naming of the ingredients, for example. However, her holding fast to 'sawss' (l. 7) in the face of her adviser's 'sahss' (l. 6) may be one element – the marshalling of phonetic resources – of a resistance with respect to relative status.[16] This possibility, with its potential analytic rewards, is what makes the risks of caricature ultimately worth running. As Jefferson says:

> once we begin to find possible phenomena in pronunciational details which are not in the first place obviously relevant … then we are either committed to transcribing all the talk in its pronunciational particulars, or to accepting the obliteration of a potentially fruitful data base.   (1983:12)

However, it is not only in the pronunciational details where the distinctness of CA transcription methods is evident. The analytic pay-off of representing non-linguistic action, so visible in the treatment of laughter, extends to a multitude of embodied phenomena. Hepburn (2004) discusses the transcription of crying and its features (e.g. sniffling, wobbly voice, sobbing, etc.). Or consider the use of throat-clearing (at least, in the UK), to alert a potential queue-jumper to the sanctionable nature of such conduct. Anyone wondering whether the effort of transcribing, for instance, inbreaths is analytically repaid might find the answer in data such as the following, where an absent father calling home is rebuked by the child's mother:

(8) (Schegloff, 2000:50; David and Robin, 1:1–29)
```
1            Ring rin-
2  Robin:   Hello.-
3  David:   Ro:bin?
4            (.)
5  Robin:   Yeah.
6  David:   Hi:.
7            (0.8)
8  Robin:   You have one hell of a nerve.
9            (0.2)
10 David:   (.hhhh)/(hhhh)
11           (0.8)
```

---

[16] See Chapter 6 for a general discussion of how orientations to status and relationships are embodied sequentially.

```
12   Robin:     Now listen ta me.=I jus' wanna tell you one thing.
13              (.)
14   David:     Yeah? ((Weakly; without lower registers of voice))
15              (0.8)
16   Robin:     Y'to:ld me on Sunday, (.) that you were coming home on
17              Thursday.
18   David:→    pt..hhhhh=
19   Robin:     =Y'didn't t- wait don't: (.) [inte]rrupt me.
20   David:                                  [OK-]
21   David:     O:okay,=
22   Robin:     =Y'didn' tell me how: you were coming, (1.0) y'could've come
23              by pla:ne, y'could've come by ca:r,=y'could've been
24              hitchhiking.
```

As Ogden observes, inbreaths, or more precisely, 'audible ingressive airflow' (2009:8–9) serve to mark iconically that the speaker is preparing to speak. Schegloff notes of this exchange that David's inbreath at line 18 'is apparently heard by Robin as a pre-talk inbreath, and hence as potentially pre-onset to overlapping (and interruptive) talk' (2000:51): interruptive, because Robin's own (l. 12) had served to project an extended telling, a 'pre-pre' (Schegloff, 1980; we discuss this further in section 4.2.3), in which what is to follow is itself a preliminary to a projected action. It is thus only possible to make sense of Robin's self-interruption at line 19, and her subsequent admonishment to see off the potential clash, because line 18 – a lip-smack followed by an inbreath – is captured in the transcription (see also Jefferson, 1993, on inbreath-initial topic shifts; and Walker, 2013:463–4, on how an inbreath can be used to interdict a next speaker starting up by being produced as close as possible to the end of that participant's TCU and the beginning of the next). As we shall see in Chapter 4, work on the correlation of pre-turn inbreath and response turns has been revealing about early response planning in turn-taking.

In the same vein, it is important to note, too, how the very first line of the transcription above is also a non-linguistic action: the ringing of the phone, so instrumental in the early groundbreaking CA work on phone call openings (Schegloff, 1968). It is not only inbreaths that may be interactionally implicative; Local and Walker's (2012) study of the phonetics of turn and talk projection[17] shows how 'audible outbreaths routinely follow words at the end of (points of possible syntactic completion) which are followed by turn-transition' (p. 270; see also Walker, 2004). In the following, Leslie produces an audible outbreath at the end of 'Saturday':[18]

(9)   (Local and Walker, 2012:270)
```
11   Les:   .hhh Uh:m (.) Hal is ↑it (.) da:ncing this
```

---

[17] We examine turn projection more extensively in Chapter 4.
[18] Local and Walker note that this is irrespective of whether turns end in voiceless plosives (2012:270).

```
12      →   Saturday, hhh
13          (0.6)
14  Hal:    Ah:::m
```

The prosody at the end of 'Saturday' is equivocal with respect to turn continuation, but syntactically the turn is possibly[19] complete, and the audible outbreath is thus one element that indicates the relevance of turn transition at this point.

In its transcriptional particulars, CA thus shows how phenomena clearly beyond the focus of linguistic attention, such as inbreaths and outbreaths, may have interactional import. However, it also examines phenomena that may not be part of a language's morphosyntax but may nonetheless be conventionalised. Thus clicks, phonemic in many southern and some East African languages, are in English 'in speech, but not of it', as Ogden puts it (2013:299). In English, represented usually as 'tsk tsk', and conventionalised as 'tutting' in disapproval (see, e.g., Reber, 2012), they have been revealed to have a regular distribution in English conversation. They may mark incipient speakership in pre-turn position as in (10) or in mid-turn position in word searches (Wright, 2011) as in (11) below (with clicks marked thus:!)

```
(10)    (Ogden, 2013:307; transcription as in original)
1   P     ↑whAt's on Offer at the mArket then to 'DAY.
2   I→    !h↓ ↑-wE:ll- we've gOt lots of -CHEEses-=
3         =we've got h↓ -PANcfAkes-=
4         =very h↓ traditional cOntinEntal -DISHes-
```

```
(11)    (Ogden, 2013:307; transcription as in original)
        ( M=Marjorie; D=Diane)
1   M     because there were One or 'TWO big 'Houses,
2   D     <<C> yeah>
3   M→    my (0.2) -?uhm- (0.4) ! 'SECondary 'schOOl,
4         the gIrls' 'HIGH school;= ↑'thAt had been a bIg'hOUse,
```

---

[19] On the use of the words *possibly* and *possible* in the book, which has come to be standard in conversation-analytic work, and which otherwise may be subject to confusion, Schegloff offers clarification:

> The usage is not meant as a token of analytic uncertainty or hedging. Its analytic locus is not in the first instance the world of the author and reader, but the world of the parties to the interaction. To describe some utterance, for example, as a 'possible invitation' (Sacks, 1992a:I:300–2) ... is to claim that there is a describable practice of talk-in-interaction which is usable to do recognizable invitations ... and that the utterance now being described can be understood to have been produced by such a practice, and is thus analysable as an invitation ... This claim is made, and can be defended, independent of whether the actual recipient on this occasion has treated it as an invitation or not, and independent of whether the speaker can be shown to have produced it for recognition as such on this occasion. Such an analytic stance is required to provide resources for accounts of 'failures' to recognize an utterance as an invitation ... for in order to claim that a recipient failed to recognize it as such or to respond to it as such, one must be able to show that it was *recognizable* as such, i.e. that it was 'a possible x' – for the participants. (1996a:116–17)

Thus 'possibly complete' here is used to indicate that the speaker has used the interactional resources available to bring the talk to a recognisable completion.

In (11) above, there are signs of trouble at line 3, where Marjorie pauses after 'my' – the beginning of a syntactic phrase, projecting more to come – and then the particle 'uhm' and a further pause. The click that is produced thereafter adumbrates the solution to the word search. As Ogden observes: 'Clicks, pauses and particles like "uhm" (with level pitch near the middle of the speaker's range) are very common markers of word search. In this context, clicks are part of a set of practices used to mark trouble finding words' (2013:308). Such sounds which, in English at least, are not part of the phonemic repertoire, thus reveal in the regularity of their distribution that they may be considered part of speakers' interactional competence (p. 316). Ogden's study of clicks and percussives (such as so-called lip-smacks and glottal closure) shows how these sounds are intricated into, and associated with, other behaviours, such as breathing and swallowing, which can also display highly systematic organisation.

2.4.1   Developments of the Jefferson system

Jefferson developed a set of transcription conventions on the audio data of English conversation. The set of conventions has accordingly widened to accommodate the demands of video data and data across a range of languages. Goodwin's (1981) conventions for gaze notation are used in this book (see, e.g., Chapter 4, extract (31)). For more focused work on gaze, Rossano (2013) has developed an explicit schema with respect to gaze orientation. Mondada (2007) uses a set of conventions for pointing inspired by Goodwin's gaze conventions and those of Schegloff (1984b) for gestures. Heath (1986, 2013) and Streeck (1993) have also developed systems for capturing gesture. Hepburn and Bolden (2013) provide a systematic overview of the CA transcription system, including a discussion of transcription in languages other than English. Researchers have developed their own system as a modification of the original Jefferson conventions. Standardly, transcriptions are in three lines: a transliteration into Roman orthography (if necessary) as the first line, a morpheme-by-morpheme English gloss, plus grammatical information, and finally a line of idiomatic English which tries as much as possible to capture the sense of the original turn (although Li, 2014, on Mandarin uses a four-line transcription, with the first line in the Chinese writing system, and Floyd, 2015, also uses a four-line system for the Ecuadorean language Cha'palaa). See conventions developed for Arabic (Clift and Helani, 2010), Korean (Lee, 2006), Mandarin (Wu, 2004) and Russian (Bolden, 2008), among others. So, for example, for Arabic:

```
(12)   (Abu Abah, 2015)
1  L:   (      ) ʔruːḥ ʔjybešš↑ahy
        (      ) (I) go get the te↑a
        (      ) (Shall I) go get the t↑ea
2  N:   >la la< tejyby:n              šay    tak[fe:n
        >no no< bring you (sing.fem) thing ple[ase
        >no no< (don't)   bring    anything ple[ase
```

With respect to tone languages, conventions are varied. Moerman (1988), one of the earliest researchers to apply CA extensively to a language other than English, uses diacritics for Thai, as does Hanks (2007) for Yucatec Maya. Enfield (2007a:35–6) uses a number system for Lao, with its five distinct lexical tones, such that 1=mid level, 2=high rising, 3=low rising or low level, 4=high falling and 5=mid-falling:

(13)   (Enfield, 2010b:2651)

```
dek2-nòòj4 khaw3  siØ bòØ paj3 cak2              khon2      lèØ
child          3PL.B IRR NEG go  INDEF.AMOUNT    person     PRF
(Of) the children,  they won't go,              none of    them.
```

In this book, excerpts will be transcribed as in the source material, which sometimes involves modifications to the Jefferson conventions (so, for example, work focusing on aspects of articulation and voice quality will have particular information marked that is not standardly transcribed). GAT2, the transcription system developed by Selting et al. (2011), is a modified Jeffersonian system with particular conventions for marking prosodic phenomena, and this is adopted where it is in the source material. Another modified system is CHAT-CA-lite, developed by Albert (2015) with the aim of producing machine-readable transcripts for the purposes of initial searches. This transcription format sticks as closely as possible to the visual appearance and widespread conventions of the Jefferson system.

If a transcription, then, opens up analytic possibilities, the process of transcription is logically the starting point of analysis. Some guiding principles with respect to transcription might be formulated thus:

- Transcription is a guide to the data, not a substitute for it.
- Transcription tries best to represent what the transcriber hears and/or sees (this involves two trade-offs: caricature vs. normalisation; readability vs. accessibility).
- Transcription and analysis have a reflexive relationship.
- Transcription is always provisional: it will mutate and evolve.
- Transcription is often a collective endeavour, a series of laminations over time.

The transcriptions of the data are available for inspection alongside their analysis, so that the means by which the analytic results are achieved are available to be either challenged or endorsed. In this way CA achieves the descriptive rigour and transparency to which experimental methods aspire.

2.5   CA transcription conventions: an overview

The following is a list of commonly used transcription conventions for audio data, taking Ochs et al. (1996) as a point of departure, and with brief notes, where deemed necessary, to show something of the analytic relevance of capturing such detail. In the data exemplars, excerpted below from fragments in the chapters to come, phenomena under discussion are marked in bold for ease of reference.

1.   Preliminaries [C]

A.   Transcriptions are standardly in the font Courier or Courier New, which are monospaced fonts, facilitating alignment of characters.

B.   Line numbers are indicated for each line (not each turn) down the left-hand side of the transcript for reference purposes. Non-linguistic actions are included. E.g.

```
1              Ring rin-
2      Robin:  Hello.-
```

As we shall see further in Chapter 3, the 'Hello' in line 2 is responding to the summons of the ringing phone. However, even if it is not immediately clear to the transcriber whether a non-linguistic action is salient to the interactants, the action should be included, as whatever salience it may have to participants may only become evident upon repeated inspection of the materials. See also section 4, paragraph A, below.

C.   Speakers in the data and names of places and institutions are given pseudonyms, usually with names fitting the syllable structure of the original.

D.   Arrows (→) beside speaker names indicate lines of analytic focus.

E.   Data source is given above the transcript; for short excerpts where data are not captured by audio/visual recording, the abbreviation FN (field-note) is standardly used.

F.   Transcriptions are in Jefferson's 'modified standard orthography' (see discussion in section 2.4 above)

2.   Temporal and sequential relationships

A.   Overlapping or simultaneous talk is indicated in a variety of ways.

[Separate left square brackets, one above the other on two successive
[lines with utterances by different speakers, indicates a point of overlap onset, whether at the start of an utterance or later.

]   Separate right square brackets, one above the other on two successive
]   lines with utterances by different speakers indicates a point at which two overlapping utterances both end, where one ends while the other continues, or simultaneous moments in overlaps which continue. E.g.

```
1      Caller   Downton, though, she worked fer::I dunno
2               if you know Russ Ogle[thorpe,
3      Desk                          [Yeah, I know'm. Mm hm,
4      Caller   She works fer him,
```

Here, the point at which Desk comes in at line 3 to overlap Caller's talk underlines the action being done: claiming recognition at the earliest opportunity.

All of the research into turn-taking organisation is dependent on marking areas of overlap where they occur. Centrally, these show a next speaker judging, by reference to a constellation of linguistic and interactional cues, when to start speaking during a current speaker's turn. See Chapter 4 on turn-taking.

// In some older transcripts, a double slash is used to indicate the point at which a current speaker's talk is overlapped by another. E.g.

```
K:      ehh heh heh // hehhh
(A)     hehhhehhheh hhh
R:      Delayed rea:c//tio(h)n.
```

An alternative way of capturing the overlap above would be:

```
K:      ehh heh heh    [hehhh
(A)     hehhhehhheh hhh
R:      Delayed rea:c[tio(h)n.
```

B.   Equal signs

=   Equal signs may come **in pairs**: one at the end of a line and another at the start of the next line. They are used to indicate two things:

1. If the two lines connected by the equal signs are by the same speaker, then there was a single, continuous utterance with no break or pause, which was broken up in order to accommodate the placement of the overlapping talk. E.g.

```
4    Joh   Oh, I was just gonna say come out and come over
5          here and talk this evening, [but if you're going=
6    Jud                               ["Talk", you mean get
7          [drunk, don't you?]
8    Joh   =[out you can't very] well do that.
```

2. If the lines connected by two equal signs are by different speakers, then the second followed the first with no discernible silence between them, or was 'latched' to it. E.g.

```
1    Lottie   Ah wouldn'ev'n le-e- tell Bud I:'d jis go ahead'n
2             have the party.
3    Emma     .t Yah,=
4    Lottie   =Tuh hell with im.
```

When there is a **single equal sign** in the course of one turn-at-talk it shows that the speaker is circumventing turn transition by compressing the space in which transition to a next speaker may occur. E.g.

```
12   Robin:   Now listen ta me.=I jus' wanna tell you one thing.
```

This phenomenon has been called the 'rush-through' (Schegloff, 1982, 1987c; Walker, 2010) and the 'abrupt-join' (Local and Walker, 2004). As suggested by these terms, a speaker may speed up on approaching the

transition space, and this may be captured, alternatively, by the following. E.g.

```
<   Joh:    Ha you doin-<say what 'r you doing.
```

This device has clear relevance to turn-taking issues, discussed in
Chapter 4.

C.   Numbers in parentheses indicate silence.

(0.5)   Silence is standardly represented in tenths of a second, so (0.5)
indicates half a second's silence. Because speakers have differing
speech rates, the interactional pause between speakers with fast
speech rates (e.g. the stereotypical New Yorker) clearly has a different interactional implication from that between speakers where the
speech rate is much slower (although see Chapter 3 for quantitative
evidence regarding this) – and there is some evidence that speakers
accommodate to each other with respect to speech rate (see Kendall,
2013, and, for rhythm beyond speech, McNeill, 1997). In order to try
and capture this interactional sense of what a silence implicates, CA
has standardly measured silences manually relative to speech tempo.
So the transcriber listens to a portion of the talk approaching the
silence, calibrating the counting of the silence to the speech rate.
The counting phrase is then produced at the rate of the preceding
talk (Auer et al., 1999; Wilson and Zimmerman, 1986). The counting
phrase might be something like 'Mississippi One, Mississippi Two,
Mississippi Three . . . ' where each syllable of the phrase marks two-
tenths of a second pause, and each complete phrase a whole second.
Thus, the silence ending at 'Mi-' is a (0.2) pause, 'Missi-' a (0.4)
pause, and the silence ending between 'Missi-' and 'Mississi-' is a
(0.5) pause. Note that when a pause occurs after a speaker has come
to a point at which the talk is possibly complete, the pause is
transcribed on a separate line. E.g.

```
9    D    .hh My ca:r is sta::lled.
10        (0.2)
11   D    ('n) I'm up here in the Glen?
```

We discuss the above excerpt further in Chapter 5, but see Schegloff
(1995a) for a detailed discussion of how the two-tenths of a second
pause at line 10 is 'as fully fledged an event in the conversation as any
utterance' (p. 198). Clearly, as shown in Chapter 1, silence at certain
places in talk is implicative (see, in particular, Chapters 3, 4 and 5) and
turn-taking and preference (to name but two orders of organization)
would not have been discoverable without making the silence available
to see.

(.)   A micropause of less than one-tenth of a second.

Note that some early transcripts have untimed silences simply marked (pause).

It should be noted that such artisanal measurements may then be subject to more objective examination. So Stivers et al. (2009) uses machine-read pauses across a ten-language sample to establish the robustness of Sacks et al.'s claims of universality for the turn-taking model (see Chapters 3 and 4). There is an extensive discussion of timings in Kendrick and Torreira (2014) who investigate CA claims, made on the basis of artisanal measures, regarding the timing of preference (discussed here in Chapter 5). On the basis of their sample of preferred and dispreferred actions, they suggest that 'Jefferson's timing undershoots objectively measured time by roughly 120 ms and that there is an additional undershoot of approximately 15% for each 1,000 ms' (p. 28). To put this in some kind of context, Greenberg, on a four-hour phonetically transcribed sample of spontaneous talk, finds that the mean average time to produce a syllable of spoken English is 200 ms. (1999:170).

3.   Aspects of speech delivery

A.   Punctuation marks are not used in their usual sense to mark aspects of grammar, but indicate intonation contours.

.   The period indicates a falling, or final, intonation contour, not necessarily at
?   the end of a sentence. Similarly, a question mark indicates rising intonation,
,   not necessarily a question. A comma indicates 'continuing' intonation, not
¿   necessarily a clause boundary. An upside-down question mark indicates a low rise, i.e. stronger than 'comma' intonation, but weaker than that indicated by a question mark. All of these possibilities are indicated in the excerpt below.

```
5     E    [PA:R:T of ut.w:Wuddiyuh -DOin.
6          (0.9)
7     N    What'm I do[in¿
8     E                [Cleani:ng?=
9     N    =hh.hh I'm ironing wouldju belie:ve tha:t.
10    E    Oh: bless it[s hea:rt.]
11    N                [In f a :c]t I: ire I start'd ironing en I:
12         d-I:(.)Somehow er another ir'ning js kind of lea:ve me: co:[ld]
13    E                                                            [Ye]ah,
14         (.)
15    N    [Yihknow,  ]
```

Note that at the end of line 12, there is no intonational marking, which indicates that the prosody here is level.

:   Colons are used to indicate the prolongation or stretching of the sound
      just preceding them. The more colons, the longer the stretch. E.g.

```
1   B   I: uh::: I did wanna tell you en I didn' wanna tell you
2       uh:::::: uh:: las' night. Uh::: because you had entuht-
3       uh:: company I, I-I had something (.) terrible t' tell you.
```

We examine this extract in Chapter 3, but this fragment clearly shows
a speaker having to impart difficult news. Hesitation, dysfluency and
a displayed reluctance to do so are all components of doing something –
here an announcement – with delicacy. In addition, Schegloff (1984b)
notes that so-called sound stretches may adumbrate self-repairs (on
which, see Chapter 7).

Note that graphically stretching a word on the page by inserting blank
spaces between the letters is not intended to indicate how it was
articulated, but rather is used to align with overlapping talk. E.g.

```
10  E   Oh: bless it[s hea:rt.]
11  N               [In f a :c ]t I: ire I start'd ironing
```

B.   A hyphen after a word or part of a word indicates a cut-off or
-      self-interruption, often done with a glottal stop. E.g.

```
Uh::: because you had entuht- uh:: company
```

The cut-off here is used to implement a self-repair (see Chapter 7), in
this case, substituting something that was starting to be produced
(arguably, here, *entertainment*) for something else. Jefferson (1986)
notes that such repairs may be an interactional resource in, for example, the construction of identity (discussed in Chapter 6).

C.   Underlining is used to indicate some form of stress or emphasis,
word either by increased loudness or by higher pitch. E.g.

```
1   J:  Anyway ah'll see you on Sunday[Ahnn.
2   A:                               [Yes.
```

Orthography may also indicate marked production in particular cases.
Schegloff (1989:144) transcribes a meal-time exchange between Rob
(R), about six years old, and his mother (M) with doubled letters in line 4
to indicate what Schegloff describes as 'clearly enunciated consonants':

```
1   M   Cut that (up)/(out) Rob
2       (0.2)
3   R   Hm?
4   M→  I saidd, 'Cutt itt'
5   R   ((Transfers fork from right to left hand))
```

WORD Particularly increased loudness relative to surrounding talk is indicated
by capital letters. E.g.

```
1    Tom:     Em
2             (2.0)
3    Tom:     ↓Em
4             (3.0)
5    Tom:→    EMiLY:
6    Em:      What.
```

So in the exchange above, Tom's first two attempts to summon Emily meet
with no response. It is only on his third summons, using the full form of the
name at line 5, with increased loudness, stress and the sound stretch at the
end of the name that Emily responds. The transcription of these features of
production thus gives us access to how phonetic and lexico-syntactic
resources combine to bring off recognisable actions.

D.   The degree sign indicates that the talk following it is markedly quiet or soft.
o   When there are two degree signs, the talk between them is softer than the
o o   talk around it. Producing talk softer or less loud relative to one's own talk
      may be a device for the doing of delicacy. So in the extract from the
      Australian language Murrinh-Patha below, when Mona, having been
      pressed to produce the name of someone whose name is subject to
      a naming taboo, does so, at line 8, she produces it *sotto voce*, thus display-
      ing the delicacy attending its production (see Chapter 5):
      (Blythe, 2013:900; lines of grammatical notation omitted here for clarity
      but supplied in Chapter 5)

```
6    Edna     Nanggalyu;
              Who was it?
7             (1.3)
8    Mona→    °Birrarriya.°=
              Birrarri.
```

Schegloff also discusses an American English instance from the mid-1960s
where a speaker, on the phone to her friend about a recent holiday trip to
Lake Tahoe in California, lowers her voice to deliver, *sotto voce*, 'what
could be reckoned to be prejudiced comments about various so called
"minority groups". Although she has little reason to believe she can be
overheard, she nonetheless lowers her voice to register an awareness of, and
orientation to, the impropriety of what she is doing' (2003c:34):

```
7    Bev                  And I don' know, Ann, but I think –
8             they're stealing a lotta Los Vegas.
9    Ann     I wouldn't be surprized.
10   Bev     The other thing that we noticed, ((voice drops in
11           volume)) You know, we didn't see any Jews, – you know
12           in Las Vegas, you [know how you see those greasy old=
13   Ann                       [Uh huh,
14   Bev     =women an' [men, but at-
15   Ann                [Uh huh,
```

```
16   Bev   And very few Negroes. ((voice moves to low-normal))
17         But we saw lots of Orientals.
18   Ann   [Mm hm,
19   Bev   [You see, I think they come in from San Francisco.
20   Ann   Mm hm,
21   Bev   ((voice returns to normal)) And the Orientals, you
22         know, always very well dressed,
23   Ann   Mm hm,
24   Bev   And they're tremendous gamblers.
25   Ann   Mm hm,
26   Ann   I think that's (      )
27   Bev   So uhm uh:: they have a grand time at the crap games.
28   Ann   Mm[hm,
29   Bev      [They-
30   Bev   They really at uh- it's a something to see, and I'm
31         glad I saw it, 'n I had a wonderful time doin' it.
```

E.   Combinations of underlining and colons are used to indicate intonation
     contours as follows:

_: If the letter(s) preceding a colon is underlined, then there is an 'inflected'
     falling intonation contour. E.g.

```
1   A   th'fuhrst bit'v (.) income isn'tax[ed.
2   B                                      [No: that's right, mm:
```

:   If a colon is itself underlined, then there is an inflected rising intonation
    contour. E.g. in 'fi:ne' here at line 3:

```
1   Vicki    How are ↓you all. [Yer a l]ittle ti:red] °nah°
2   Doreen                     [Oh wir]all fi:ne,]Yes I'm jus:
3            sohrta clearing up a bi[t nah,]
4   Vicki                           [°Ohhhh] deah, °
```

F.   The up and down arrows mark sharper rises or falls in pitch than
↑↓   would be indicated by combinations of colons and underlining, or may
     mark a whole shift, or resetting, of the pitch register at which the talk is
     being produced. E.g.

```
11   Les:   .hhh Uh:m (.) Hal is ↑it (.) da:ncing this
12          Saturday, hhh
```

and:

```
1   Vicki   How are ↓you all.
```

G.   The combination of 'more than' and 'less than' symbols indicates that
> < the talk between them is compressed or rushed. E.g.

```
1   A:   Good luck. Nice to [↑s e e:: y o u::      ]
2   B:                      [>Nice to< ↑ see:: you::]
```

Work on 'rush-throughs' and 'abrupt-joins' (see above) is a focused examination of speeded-up talk.

< >   Used in the reverse order, the 'more than' and 'less than' symbols can
indicate that a stretch of talk is markedly slowed or drawn out.

```
10    Mum   No::w, would you phlea:se <finish your ↑soup>
```

While there has been some work on slowed speech rate with respect to turn-
taking (see Local et al., 1986 on Tyneside English), there appears to be little
examination of this marked speech rate in the implementation of actions as
such. The slowed speech in the directive above is, however, surely implicated
in the constellation of features delivering the action. Here is an exemplar from
Murrinh-Patha, taken from just before the extract cited in section E above.
On first being asked to identify someone whose name is subject to a naming
taboo, Mona instead delivers a description which may enable Edna to identify
him for herself. The description is produced on markedly slower pace:
(Blythe, 2013)

```
1    E       ↑Nanggalardu, (.) ↓dannyiyerr↓ngime¿
             Who was it that told us that story?
2            (0.15)
3    Mona    <MaKA[:RDU]warda>;
             He isn't around any more.
```

H.   Hearable aspiration is shown where it occurs in the talk; the more hh's, the
hh   more aspiration. The aspiration may represent breathing or laughter (but
(hh) see Potter and Hepburn, 2010, on an alternative characterisation of laugh
particles as 'interpolated particles of aspiration' or IPAs). If it occurs inside
the boundaries of a word, it may be enclosed in parentheses in order to set it
apart from the sounds of the word (as shown in the turn below). E.g.

```
4    Bee:          [Ba::]sk(h)etb(h)a(h)ll?
5                  (h)[(Whe(h)re.)
```

See the discussion earlier in this chapter regarding laughter in interaction.

£ £   Talk enclosed within pound sterling signs is done in an auditorily recognisable 'smiling' voice:

```
4    Pat   [£I'm seventy-fi[:ve.£]
5    Meg                   [G  o:]shh!
```

Haakana (2010) discusses the distinct sequential contexts of laughter and
smiling. Clift (2012a) examines speakers' fine calibration of the delivery of
their turns with respect to laughter and 'smile voice' in the doing of
complaints.

.hh   Inbreaths are shown as 'hh's with a dot before it (sometimes raised)
˙hh   E.g.

```
1    Jessie   ..cuz she's nevuh been cah[mpin[g.]
2    Ann                                [.hhh[I ]t's smashing...
```

The marked overlap here shows Ann preparing to speak as Jessie comes to the end of her turn. See the discussion earlier in this chapter about the deployment of inbreaths in a range of interactional activities.

4.   Other markings

A.
(())

Double parentheses are used to mark the transcriber's description of events. Thus ((sniff)), ((sigh)), ((cough)), etc. E.g.

```
16   J   [and I don't know why:: love you think you can just go out
         [all
17   J   thuh ti:me pay
18       ((E wipes eyes with left hand))
19       [get taxis all thuh time and not pay (.) fer your living.
20   E   [((sniff))
```

These should be transcribed as we cannot know their analytic relevance in advance. So, for example, Hoey shows how sighing accomplishes specific work in interaction and that 'the variable positioning and delivery of sighs were responsive to and relevant for ongoing, incipient, and concluding units of action' (2014:196). Moreover, Jefferson raises the possibility that someone might hear 'laughter' when what has been done is 'coughing', and might then 'join in' that laughter by himself laughing (Jefferson, 1972:448–9). Twenty years later she discovers, in the course of transcription, a recorded case of someone laughing to another's possibly laughter-relevant but non-laughter noises (e.g. 'a frog in the throat', detailed in Jefferson, 2010). Jefferson captures the CA orientation to the possibilities of analysis thus: 'as Sacks said when a student asked, re. some remarks Sacks had made about Poetics in ordinary talk, "Couldn't that be carried too far?" Sacks responded: "The whole problem is that it's nowhere in the first instance. The issue is to pull it out and raise the possibility of its operation" [1995: 325] (2010:1484).

Aspects of voice quality may also be glossed in brackets:

```
5   CINZIA:   >gli gnocchi!< ((constricted))
              gnocchi
```

B.
(Mm)
(up)/
(out)

When all or part of an utterance is in parentheses, or the speaker identification is, it indicates uncertainty on the transcriber's part. Alternate hearings are given when it it not possible to distinguish between them. E.g.

```
1   M   Cut that (up)/(out) Rob
```

(–)   Sometimes transcribers designate the number of syllables heard with dashes; these indicators of what might have been said are particularly useful in joint or group collaboration over transcripts. It is quite possible to return to data after many years to hear something clearly which was once obscure or ambiguous.

( )   Empty parentheses show no hearing was possible of what was being said.

3   Why that, now? Position and composition in interaction

This chapter focuses on the sequence as an essential element of the procedural infrastructure of interaction. It starts by examining the the sequential placement of one utterance: *What are you doing?* **This shows that our understanding of the action implemented by an utterance is informed by not only the composition of an utterance but also its position in a sequence. It then introduces the adjacency relationship, and specifically the adjacency pair: the minimal interactional sequence. The relationship between the two parts of an adjacency pair – that of conditional relevance – is such that it allows us to specify the absence of a second pair part as the absence of something specific, and accountable. Conditional relevance – a fundamental source of coherence in interaction – is what provides for sequences to be constructed with reference to a base adjacency pair. We provide an overview of the possible expansions to an adjacency pair, both before and after. We then examine the increasing cross-linguistic evidence that sequences are a universal phenomenon. They not only afford us insight into forms of distributed cognition – the ways in which speakers collaborate in the accomplishment of actions – but also show us that context is, in the first place, for both participant and analyst, a sequential matter.**

Greeting somebody in the street proves no esteem whatever, but failure to do so conclusively proves the opposite.   (Simmel, 1959:400)

3.1   On position and composition

As we saw in Chapter 1, the conversation-analytic concern with trajectories of action, rather than individual utterances, takes us a long way from the traditional linguistic focus on the *composition* of phrases and sentences, abstracted away from their occurrences in sequences of interaction. Such abstractions are like photographs which fix a moment in a trajectory of action; the viewer is left to reconstruct the whole trajectory and so invest the action with meaning. However, the lived experience of the moment may be very different for those involved.[1] CA, in contrast, by putting the participants' displayed understandings at the centre of the analysis, makes the whole arc available for inspection by grounding the moment both *before* and *after* something else. This chapter examines what that 'something else' is by exploring further how the *position* of

---

[1] Take, for example, the controversy of Thomas Hoepker's iconic photo from 9/11 of New Yorkers sitting and relaxing in the sun while the twin towers smoulder in the background, deemed so sensitive it was only released five years later. Commentators duly invested this apparent display of callous disregard with allegorical import. One of the participants responded subsequently that they were actually in a 'profound state of shock and disbelief' (Jonathan Jones, 'The Meaning of 9/11's Most Controversial Photo', *The Guardian*, 2 September 2011).

an utterance in a sequence is criterial to understanding what a turn-at-talk is doing. As Schegloff notes: '*both position and composition* are ordinarily constitutive of the sense and import of an element of conduct that embodies some phenomenon or practice' (1993:121; emphasis in original). This chapter, accordingly, shows how what is being done at any moment in interaction is based as much on the sequential position of a turn as its intrinsic linguistic properties. We first consider what difference the position of ostensibly the 'same' utterance compositionally makes to how it is understood. We then start to explore the basic conversation analytic concept of adjacent positioning – a prime resource for participants in talk. In the first instance, we examine the adjacency pair, a – indeed, probably *the* – fundamental structure in the organisation of talk, in investigating how one turn may shape the production of what comes next. There is increasing evidence, as we shall see, of the existence of such an organisation across languages, in the face of structural diversity – the compositional particulars of each language. After showing the various possible expansions to an adjacency pair, we investigate an extended spate of talk to see how the property of coherence – hitherto considered primarily as an issue of 'topicality' in linguistics – derives from the sequence.

3.1.1   How position matters: *What are you doing?*

In exploring how the position of an utterance contributes to what a recipient makes of it, it is instructive to see how ostensibly the same utterance may be variously understood in different positions in a stretch of talk.

Take the utterance *What are you doing?* – on the face of it, a straightforward enquiry, as in the exchange at line 5 below. Nancy has been taking a class at a local university and, being much older than the other students, is finding them somewhat immature. Emma does a display of sympathy with Nancy's predicament with her idiom in lines 1–5, thus bringing her topic to a close (Drew and Holt, 1998); her 'Wuddiyuh –DOin' directly thereafter is evidently a separate unit, and one that moves onward to new business:

```
(1)   (Clift et al., 2013:217; NB:II:2:8/9)
1     Emm:    ... some a' that stuff hits yuh pretty ha:rd'n then: °yuh
2             thin:k we:ll d'you wanna be°
3             (0.7)
4     Nan:    hhhhhh[hh
5     Emm:→         [PA:R:T of ut.w:Wuddiyuh –DOin.
6             (0.9)
7     Nan:    What'm I do[in¿
8     Emm:               [Cleani:ng?=
9     Nan:    =hh.hh I'm ironing wouldju belie:ve tha:t.
10    Emm:    Oh: bless it[s hea:rt.]
11    Nan:                [In f a :c ]  t I: ire I start'd ironing en I:
```

```
12              d-I:(.)Somehow er another ir'ning js kind of lea:ve me: co:[ld]
13   Emm:                                                                   [Ye]ah,
14         (.)
15   Nan:   [Yihknow,]
16   Emm:   [Wanna c'm] do:wn 'av a bi:te'a lu:nch with me? I got s'm beer'n
17          stu:ff,
```

Emma's utterance in line 5 is immediately met by a pause of nearly a second, before Nancy then repeats the enquiry (transposing the pronoun) in line 7, which is a form of repair initiation (we discuss these forms of initiation in Chapter 7). Emma's proposal in line 8, 'Cleani:ng?', gives Nancy the ballpark for her response, which is another household chore ('ironing', l. 9). Only in line 16 does Emma reveal that her purpose in asking 'What are you doing?' is to invite Nancy over for a casual, impromptu lunch.

Compare that exemplar with the one below in which Emma is now the recipient (l. 3). It becomes quite evident to her that Margy asked this in the service of making a request – that Emma come over to help her with some (financial) bookwork ('calling back numbers') (see ll. 14–15); though it is likely that Margy's manifest disappointment in line 11 (<u>Oh::::</u>. Oh.) (see Couper-Kuhlen, 2009, for an investigation of some of the phonetic features of 'disappointment') contributed to Emma's recognition that Margy is not making a disinterested enquiry, but one that is motivated to lead up to something else:

(2) (Clift et al., 2013:218; NB:IV:9)
     (Margy is the caller; Emma's opening turn is unrecorded, so that we have only Margy's presumably reciprocal *Hello*.)

```
1    Mar:   ...lo:, °hhuh°
2    Emm:   How'r you:.=
3    Mar:   =Well wuhdiyuh doin. hh hnh
4           (0.5)
5    Emm:   .hhh (hhOh:) Margy?=
6    Mar:   =eeYeehuh. [a-
7    Emm:              [Oh: I'm jis sittin here with Bill'n Gladys'n
8           haa:eh* fixin'm a drink they're goin out tih ↓dinner:
9           (.)
10   Emm:   H[e's-
11   Mar:    [Oh:::::. Oh.
12   Emm:   Why: whiddiyih waant.
13          (1.0)
14   Mar:   hhuhh** Well?h I wunnid um come down en I wannidju tuh
15          (2) call some numbers back to me <b't it's not import'n
```

*'haa:eh' may be an abort of 'having a drink'
**'hhuhh' is a sigh, not a laugh

In each of these extracts, the enquiry *What are you doing?* turns out to have been preliminary to or leading to another action, an invitation and a request respectively. They are what are known as 'pres' (Sacks, 1992a:685–92;

Schegloff, 2007a), which we shall go on to examine in more detail later in this chapter, but what is relevant here is that such enquiries are made in the service of some other action, for which it might be advantageous to know whether, if an invitation or request were made, it is likely that the recipient would accept the invitation or grant the request (we pursue this in Chapter 5).

Compare those instances with a similar enquiry in Italian data.[2] Cinzia describes what she is doing as she cuts the dough for the gnocchi they are making, when her sister Lina asks 'beh:: no- (.) ma cosa ↑fa:i?' (*well no-, but what are you doing?*).[3]

(3) (Clift et al., 2013:219; CMM:TR28–8–98(gnocchi):-00:13:05-:artigianali)

```
1  Cinzia:   ora noi li facciamo un pochino:: *(0.8) ar**tigianali.
             now we make them a bit (0.8) amateurishly/free-style
2            (0.4)
3  Lina: →   beh:: no- (.) ma cosa ↑fa:i? (looking down at the dough)
             well no- (.) but what are you doing***
4            (0.4)
5  Cinzia:   >gli gnocchi!< ((constricted))
             gnocchi
6            (0.6)
7  Lina:     ↑ma ascolta! (.) ma- gua-=guarda che vanno la metà di=
             but listen (.) but loo- look they must be the half of =
8            que::lle::!=
             those!
9  Cinzia:   =no::::::!
*Cinzia takes a knife
**Cinzia starts cutting dough
***Cinzia puts knife down
```

In making this enquiry in line 3, Lina is plainly remonstrating with her sister, or complaining about the way she is cutting the gnocchi dough. They get into something of a stand-off about how best to prepare these gnocchi; Cinzia first holds her ground by stating the obvious (l. 5), Lina instructs her about how they should be made (l. 7), which then Cinzia disputes (l. 9).

So in extracts (1) and (2) *What are you doing?* is a pre-enquiry, made in the service (1) of setting up a subsequent invitation to come down for lunch, and (2) a request to come over to help out with some bookkeeping. In extract (3), by contrast, the ostensibly same enquiry does something quite different; Lina challenges her sister with regard to why she is making the gnocchi in that way and thereby remonstrates with her about her cooking techniques.

It is clear, then, that the different work or actions that these enquiries perform derives from or is associated with their immediate, contiguous sequential context.

---

[2] I am grateful to Chiara Monzoni for permission to use this data excerpt.
[3] The verb here – *fare* – is potentially ambiguous between 'make' and 'do' but is disambiguated to the 'do' hearing in sequential context.

In this last example, Lina asks Cinzia what she's doing, immediately after Cinzia has just described what she's doing (l. 1); this is also a context in which Lina can perfectly well see what Cinzia is doing: looking at dough that Cinzia is cutting up. There are a couple of linguistic features of the design of Lina's enquiry that contribute to its character as remonstrating; first, it is prefaced by 'beh:: no-' (*well no-*), and second, her prosody gives the enquiry a sceptical character, which is captured by the raised pitch and upward intonation in "↑fa:i?" (see Sicoli et al., 2014). The enquiries in the previous examples, by contrast, are made in a quite different sequential environment. They are both topic initial; they are unconnected with any on-going action sequence. This is most clearly the case in extract (1), in which Emma has summarised an aspect of their conversation about Nancy's fellow students, and then moves – abruptly – to an enquiry about Nancy. In extract (2) the enquiry comes right at the beginning of a telephone call. There has therefore been no prior conversation before Margy's enquiry about what Emma is doing; there has been only the opening 'hellos', then Emma's standard opening 'How are you' (Schegloff, 1986). So Margy is making her enquiry (l. 3) in first topic position, a position or slot in which the reason for calling might generally be announced; and though Margy's enquiry might compositionally be disguised as a form of reciprocal greeting, it is, as Emma comes to realise (in l. 12), nevertheless done in the service of a request (note that, as in Lina's enquiry in (3), Margy's turn in l. 14 is also 'well'-prefaced). So unlike Lina's enquiry in (3), these are both sequence- and topic-initial enquiries. Moreover, whereas Lina's purpose in asking 'What are you doing?' is pretty transparent to Cinzia, it is not so transparent to Nancy and Emma, respectively. In each case there is a similar sequential pattern – a pause (ll. 6 and 4, respectively), followed by a repair initiation (ll. 7 and 5, respectively) – manifesting some problem that the recipients have in responding to such a topic-initial enquiry.

To summarise then, what is ostensibly the same enquiry, *What are you doing?*, does something quite different when it is in topic-initial position, when it precedes and is made in the service of an upcoming action (invitation, request), than when it is in next position to the turn in which Cinzia tells Lina what she is doing. The action that a turn construction or *composition* – this same enquiry – performs derives from its contiguous sequential environment.

3.2   Adjacency and the adjacency pair

In this section we start to explore this concept of sequential position by examining how sequences may be constructed. The minimal sequence in interaction consists of two paired utterances: the **adjacency pair**. We only have to consider how many of our daily interactions are initiated (e.g. A: *Hi!* – B: *Hi!*) and terminated (A: *Bye!* – B: *Bye!*) by such pairs, or to consider a parent's first greeting to a newborn, to recognise how fundamental they might be. Indeed, as Stivers et al. (2009) point out, there is evidence for a human ethological basis for adjacent sequences of action and response, for example in early 'proto-conversation' between newborns and caregivers (see, e.g., Murray and Trevarthen, 1986; Striano et al., 2006). These paired actions have particular characteristics, and, as we shall see, sequences of talk may, by reference to them, also be expanded both before and after.

Fundamental to the notion of the adjacency pair is the notion of adjacency itself. In his lectures, Sacks notes the particular relationship that certain utterances have to each other:

> one relationship between utterances [is] a central one, and that is the adjacency relationship ... One of the most immediately observable ways in which the adjacency relationship matters is this sort of thing: A has talked at some point and he's selected B to do something. Now the way B has of showing, among other things, that he sees that he's been chosen, and chosen to do something, is to do that right then and there. And that is analytically a great resource for us ...   (1992b:43)

Sacks's observation – that the basic structural position is the relationship of adjacency between utterances, whereby a speaker's current turn displays his or her analysis of the immediately prior turn – provides some basic traction on the notion of sequential position. In sum:

1. In doing an action by means of a turn-at-talk (e.g. *it's a lovely day/you've had your hair cut!/you're standing on my foot!*) a speaker standardly projects the relevance of a particular (range of) 'next' actions to be done by a subsequent speaker.
2. In producing a next action, a speaker normally addresses the immediately preceding talk (Sacks, 1987).
3. In doing so, that speaker shows a number of understandings with respect to the prior action – that, for example, it was possibly complete, that it was addressed to them, and what type of action it was (e.g. *Yes, it's gorgeous/ Yeah, I thought it was getting a bit long/Oh, sorry*). These understandings are implicitly endorsed or, alternatively, may prompt repair in third position (e.g. *I didn't mean x, I meant y*; see Schegloff, 1992b, and for cases in point, Chapter 7, extracts (16) and (17).

So a sequence of adjacent utterances constitutes a mechanism whereby intersubjective understandings of particular actions can be displayed, checked and, if necessary, repaired (Schegloff, 1992b, 2007a). Now while adjacent positioning is the basic resource for participants in maintaining intersubjectivity, certain adjacent actions in interaction have a particularly strong cohesive relationship. So *Hi!* makes a particular type of response – a return greeting – relevant, such that the absence of one is particularly noticeable, accountable and sanctionable, in a way that the response to, for example, *It's a lovely day* is not.[4] Such an utterance pair

---

[4] While conditional relevance is a particularly strong constraint operating between the parts of an adjacency pair, it is clear that first pair parts of actions project differing degrees of constraint with

(*Hi – Hi*) is an instance of the minimal sequence in interaction, and the most powerful embodiment of the adjacency relationship: the adjacency pair. This is

(a) composed of two turns
(b) by different speakers
(c) adjacently placed; that is, one after the other
(d) ordered relative to one another; that is, they are differentiated into 'first pair parts' (FPPs) and 'second pair parts' (SPPs). First pair parts *initiate* some exchange, e.g. question, request, invitation. Second pair parts are *responsive* to the action of a prior turn, e.g. answer, grant/refuse, accept/decline.

Furthermore, adjacency pairs are

(e) pair-type related: types are exchanges such as greeting–greeting, question–answer and the like. To compose an adjacency pair, the FPP and the SPP come from the same pair type; so a greeting is responded to by a greeting (not, e.g., a refusal), and an offer is responded to by an acceptance or declination (and not, e.g., a greeting).

Figure 3.1 illustrates some examples of adjacency pair types.

Given the production of a first pair part by a speaker, the second pair part from a next speaker is immediately relevant and expectable, or, in other words, conditionally relevant. The notion of **conditional relevance** is what renders the absence of such a second pair part so salient and is captured by Simmel's epigraph at the beginning of this chapter: that, just as familiarity can render

	Exemplars		Pair type
1	A	Hi	*Greeting*
2	B	Hi	*Greeting*
1	A	What time is it?	*Question*
2	B	Half-past nine	*Answer*
1	A	Would you like a coffee?	*Offer*
2	B	Yes please/No thanks	*Acceptance/Declination*
1	A	Have you got a light?	*Request*
2	B	Yes, here you are/No, sorry	*Grant/Refuse*

Figure 3.1 *Examples of adjacency pairs*

respect to their responses. With Schegloff's canonical example of a summons, the absence of a second pair part is both accountable and sanctionable; and a cross-linguistic study of ten languages examining requests for information showed that approximately 90 per cent received responses either answering the question or displaying an inability to do so (Stivers et al., 2009). However, with some other actions, such as assessments, this is not the case; as Stivers and Rossano report, 'it is not difficult to find (a) instances without response where (b) this is treated by both participants as unproblematic' (2010:10). Stivers and Rossano (2010) duly go on to investigate the components of initiating actions involved in mobilising responses, reported in Chapter 6.

something invisible, it is *failure* to do something that is both observable and accountable.

Some of the earliest published conversation-analytic work, a distillation of Schegloff's doctoral research (published as Schegloff, 1968), is testament to the power of conditional relevance. Schegloff observes that in a corpus of roughly 500 phone conversations, all but one proceeds the same way in the opening turns; the exception is the following:

(4) (Schegloff, 1968:1079)
(Police make call)
Receiver is lifted, and there is a one-second pause

```
Police:   Hello.
Other:    American Red Cross.
Police:   Hello, this is Police Headquarters ...
          er, Officer Stratton [etc.]
```

The unique aspect of this call is that the caller speaks first; in all the other calls in this particular corpus, it is the called party – the answerer – who speaks first. This apparently simple observation has profound analytic implications. In the first place, if the answerer is answering, *what* is he or she answering? It would seem that the answerer is responding to the ringing of the phone – which is, then, an action requiring an answer. As for what kind of action it might be, Schegloff considers a number of items that could be answered, before noting that 'it seems that we could well regard the telephone ring as a summons' (1968:1080) to which *Hello* is the answer. A summons, followed by an answer, is an utterance pair; indeed, a summons without an answer is observably incomplete. Think of the compulsion we have to respond to summonses in a variety of forms: how difficult it is to resist an immediate response to the ringing of a phone, the knock at the door[5] or the arrival of an email in the inbox. As Schegloff notes, 'if ... a second pair part is not produced next, its non-occurrence is as much an event as its occurrence would have been. It is, so to speak, noticeably, officially, consequentially, absent' (2007a:20). Not all silence, then, is the same: the one-second silence after an invitation has been proffered has interactional meaning that a one-second silence in the course of one speaker's turn may not. One is reminded of Debussy's assertion that music is the space between the notes: positioning matters.[6]

---

[5] During the period of political turbulence in Northern Ireland known as The Troubles, 'persons still open the door and get shot – despite their knowledge that such things happen' (Cuff and Payne, 1979:151, cited in Silverman, 1998:106).

[6] Indeed, the transformative effect of context on music is encapsulated by Huron's observation that: 'In a given context, a tone will sound stable, complete, and pleasant. In another context, that exact same sound will feel unstable, incomplete, and irritating' (2006:173). So a 'B', for example, at the end of one musical sequence may sound like the final resting point for that melody, the note that completes it; at the end of another, it may sound unresolved and continuative. For a demonstration, see the neuroscientist Aniruddh Patel's (2008) lecture, 'The Music of Language and the Language of Music'.

The morally loaded word *failure* in Simmel's epigraph is thus all the more resonant in the context where a greeting has been proffered, but is not reciprocated. For the adjacency pair is where morality meets interactional structure: the conditional relevance of a reciprocal greeting is what makes its absence morally accountable, and an action – a snub – in itself. Accounts such as non-recognition (*I didn't recognise you with your new haircut*), non-hearing (*I didn't hear you across the road*), disapproval, and so forth – both imagined (on the part of the greeter) or actual (on the part of the greeted) – may thus be occasioned, and warranted, by such failure.

Given that conditional relevance pertains to *whatever* does (or does not) come next after the first part of some adjacency pair, when talk is produced, it is monitored for how it relates to that first part. So *Oh, look, it's beginning to rain* as a response to *How do you like my new glasses?* will be hearable insofar as it answers the question – or not. As Schegloff notes: 'Just as the questioner presents a puzzle of sorts to its recipient, so does the one who responds: that challenge is, "how is this an answer?" and "what answer is it?"' (2007a:21). Take, as an illustration, the following exchange:

(5)   (Sacks, [1973] 1987:58)
1   A: Yuh comin down early?
2   B: Well, I got a lot of things to do before getting cleared up
3   tomorrow. I don't know. I w- probably won't be too early.

The immediate response in line 2 is thus inspectable for how it constitutes an answer to the yes/no question in line 1. We shall, in Chapter 5, examine in more detail the observed interactional bias towards *yes* and agreeing answers, in an exploration of the notion of preference. However, here it will suffice to register Sacks's observation about the contiguity holding between the question in one turn and its response in the next: 'it takes independent activity of a questioner (to put the question at the end) and an answerer (to put the answer at the beginning) to get a contiguity of question and answer across their respective turns' ([1973] 1987: 57–8). So the observed preference for agreement interacts with the preference for contiguity, such that if an agreeing answer occurs it occurs contiguously, whereas a disagreeing answer – a so-called dispreferred response – such as in (5) above, is not only made as weak as possible but also occurs deep into its turn. This preference for contiguity is also revealed when there are two questions in a turn, as in the following:

(6) (Sacks, [1973] 1987:58)
1   A   Well that's good uh how is yer arthritis. Yuh still taking
2   shots?
3   B   Yeah. Well it's, it's awright I mean it's uh, it hurts once
4   'n a while but it's okay.

Note that the first answer (l. 3) is an answer to the second question, and the second answer (l. 4) is an answer to the first question. As Sacks notes:

it's a rather general rule that where two questions are produced, and you are going to have two answers, then the order of the answers is the reverse of the order of the questions. Notice that this preserves contiguity as much as possible; the only way to get contiguity at all, once two questions are in the one turn, is by having the answer to the second question go first.   ([1973] 1987:60)

As we shall see, the constraint to produce an immediate second pair part may be temporarily suspended while other elements intervene. However, there are also deflections such as 're-routes' (e.g. *I'm not the one to ask*), protestations of ignorance (e.g. *I've no idea*), challenges (e.g. *You're kidding!*) (see Levinson, 1983:307), and 'counters' that reverse the direction of constraint, as in the following:

(7) (Schegloff, 2007a:17; Tarplee, 1991:1)
```
1  Chi:  F→     What's this
2  Mom:  F_cnt→ er::m (.) yo[u  t]ell me: what is it
3  Chi:                      [° () °]
4                (1)
5  Chi:  S→     z:e:bra
6  Mom:          zebra:: ye:s
```

Here, the child's first pair part, a question, is redirected back by the mother ('you tell me', l. 2) – and the child produces the second pair part, which is endorsed by the mother (Schegloff, 2007a:17).

These exceptions aside, it is normatively the case that the relevance of a second pair part is on-going, until such time as it is (eventually) produced – as we shall see later in this chapter – or its absence accounted for (*I can't tell you right now*). The constraint to respond to a first pair part question is such that Stivers et al. (2010), surveying questions and answers across a sample of ten languages, found that less than 20 per cent of responses were non-answers, typically a claim of inability to answer, either through forgetting or, as in (8) below, not knowing:

(8) (Heritage, 1984b:250)
```
1  J   But the train goes. Does th'train go o:n th'boa:t?
2  M→  .h.h Ooh I've no idea. She ha:sn't sai:d.
```

Here, M's claim to ignorance is further buttressed by an account for it ('She ha:sn't sai:d') which also deflects responsibility for knowing.

3.2.1   Adjacency and cross-linguistic validity

The fact that the pioneering work on adjacency pairs and sequence organisation was conducted exclusively on the data of English clearly raises the issue of cross-linguistic validity. The composition of turns-at-talk will inevitably show wide-ranging structural variation across languages. So, to take the paradigm case of an adjacency pair, the polar (yes/no) question and its response, there are three different types of response systems across languages as identified by Sadock and Zwicky (1985; see also Morris-Jones, 1999). One group, including English, uses particles (*yes*/*no*) for positive and negative responses (in Chapter 5, we discuss *yes*/*no* further as 'type-conforming' responses). Another, including Korean and Japanese, are 'agree/disagree' languages, in which a positive particle affirms the proposition and a negative particle denies it, regardless of the question's polarity (Lee, 2013:431). Yélî Dnye, the language of Rossel Island, off Papua New Guinea, is of this type:

(9) (Levinson, 2010:2743)

```
1   A   doo            u     ntââ,     daa nye    lê
        NEG_Equative 3POSS sufficient NEG  2sFUTPI go
        It's not enough, you're not going? (the sea is too rough)
2   B   nyââ
        Yes (I am not going)
```

As Levinson notes, one way to think about these sorts of questions is 'Do you agree to the proposition that you are not going?' and their answers as 'Yes, I agree' (2010:2743). The third group of languages are 'echo' languages such as Welsh, where the repetition of the verb of a question serves as a basic form of positive and negative response, sometimes with other elements:

(10) (Morris-Jones, 1999:150)

```
1   A   alli          di   symud?
        can + FUT+2sg you  move
2   B   gallaf
        can + FUT + 1sg
        I can
```

Languages may also show evidence of more than one responsive resource. In a study of responses to polar questions in Finnish, Sorjonen shows that, contrary to standard assumptions, Finnish makes use of both echo responses and particles (2001:426) and is thus a mixed system.

In the face of such structural variety, a study by Stivers et al. (2009), examining video data of polar questions and their responses in ten languages, suggests that there is clear evidence that the obligation to produce a timely second pair part to a first holds across languages. The languages examined, showing wide variation in word order and sound structure, are the Khoisan language of Namibia, ǂĀkhoe Haiǁom, and the Mayan language of Mexico, Tzeltal; Italian, Korean and Lao, which belong to the Romance, Ural-Altaic and Tai language groups respectively; the language isolates Yélî Dnye, and Japanese; and the West Germanic languages Danish, Dutch and (American) English.

Within this structural variegation, those languages that have turn-final marking for questions, such as Japanese, Korean and Lao, might be predicted to generate slower responses to questions because the action delivered by the utterance only becomes apparent at the end of the turn. So in Japanese, the turn-final particle *ka* marks an interrogative when the predicate (e.g. verb) is in the polite form, as in the following:

(11) (Hayashi, 2010:2686)
```
teeketsuatsu        desu   ka
low.blood.pressure  CP:POL Q
Do (you) have low blood pressure?
```

Similarly, in the following example from Lao, the independent indefinite pronoun *ñang3* ('what', 'anything', 'something'), turn-finally, is interpreted as a question word:

(12) (Enfield, 2010b:2650)
```
qanø-nii4     méén1 ñang3
MC.INAN-DEM COP INDEF.INAN
What is this (thing)?
```

Contrast this with the Germanic languages in the survey, where interrogative marking is apparent from the start of the turn (e.g. *Who/What/Did*, etc.), and so the action is identifiable early on, such as in this instance from Danish:

(13) (Heinemann, 2010:2705)
```
Har du   fundet ud a' hvordan du aflytter en besked¿
Have you found out how you    of-listen   a message¿
Have  you  figured out how to listen to your messages¿
```

However, there is found to be a striking uniformity of median response latency across languages, irrespective of structure, ranging from 0 ms (English, Japanese, Tzeltal and Yélî-Dnye) to +300 ms (Danish, ǂĀkhoe Haiǁom, Lao) (overall cross-linguistic median +100 ms) (Stivers et al., 2009:10588; see Figure 3.2). So both English and Japanese, despite their very differing structures, pattern similarly; indeed, Japanese, of all the languages, has the fastest response time on average and Danish the slowest.[7] Stivers et al. note further that lack of clustering of the Germanic languages within the range of mean turn offsets is also evidence that interactional tempo is not grounded in linguistic and cultural kinship (2009:10590).

Levinson (2013a), musing on the problem of action recognition, notes that despite the existence of sentence-final particles in many languages, in actual practice many question-words in these languages are fronted (see Hayashi, 2010 on Japanese; Yoon, 2010 on Korean; and Enfield, 2010b on Lao) and concludes that 'there is some evidence for "front-loading", or at least omission

---

[7] Ethnographic reports on the Nordic languages would seem to suggest a high tolerance for silence, e.g. Reisman's claim that 'Some Danes appear to "nourish" a silence as one might appreciate a cozy fire' (1974:110), and his account of hosting visitors in Northern Sweden: 'We would offer coffee. After several minutes of silence the offer would be accepted. We would tentatively ask a question. More silence, then a "yes" or "no". Then a long wait' (p. 110). However, despite the fact that Stivers et al. report Danish as having the longest mean response time in their study, the mean offset is still less than a half-second – a quarter-second deviation from the cross-linguistic average, and thus far from the lengthy pauses suggested in ethnographic observation (2009:10591).

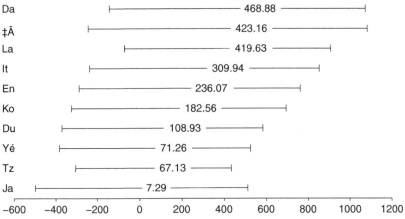

Figure 3.2 *Turn transitions: mean time across 10 languages. The mean time (in ms) of turn transitions for each language (±1 SD) in the 10 sample languages shows that speakers of all languages have an average offset time that is within 500 ms. However, there is a continuum of faster to slower averages across the sample. Milliseconds are shown on the x axis. Languages are arrayed along the y axis. ǂĀ, ǂĀkhoe Haiǁom; Da, Danish; La, Lao; It, Italian; En, English; Ko, Korean; Du, Dutch; Yé, Yélî Dnye; Tz, Tzeltal; Ja, Japanese. (Stivers et al., 2009:10589)*

of "back-loading'" with respect to linguistic action cues and concludes that it is 'a likely universal bias given the nature of the turn-taking system and the vulnerability to overlap' (p. 112).

With respect to the nature of the responses themselves, speakers of all languages provide answers significantly faster than non-answer responses, and a greater proportion of answers than non-answer responses (from 64% of all responses in Korean to 87% in Dutch and Yélî Dnye). Both findings underwrite Sacks's original observations for English and do, despite local structural variations, strongly suggest human universals in operation. We shall return to this study in the next two chapters, on turn-taking and preference; however, for current purposes, we note the robustness of the adjacency pair relationship as manifested across languages of widely varying structure in a diversity of cultural contexts.

3.3   Expansion beyond the adjacency pair

The adjacency pair thus constitutes a basic sequence, and is notable not just for its presence in most interactions but also for the fact that many other sequences are built around it. What Schegloff (2007a:27) calls a 'base pair' may be expanded before the first pair part, after the second pair part, and between the first and second pair parts (see Figure 3.3).

```
                              ← Pre-expansion
A       First pair part
                              ← Insert expansion
B       Second pair part
                              ← Post-expansion
```

Figure 3.3 *Expansions of a base adjacency pair (from Schegloff, 2007a:26)*

We now proceed to examine each of these expansions in turn, but do no more here than give an overview of the possibilities. For a more detailed, comprehensive account of sequence organisation, the reader is referred to Schegloff (2007a), to which the following sections on sequence expansion are indebted.

3.3.1   Pre-expansion

In the second extract in this chapter, we saw Margy phoning Emma to ask 'wuhdiyuh doin'. As we have seen, it is clear, subsequently, that Emma's 'why ...' in line 12 shows an orientation to Margy's question not as enquiring literally what she is doing at that precise moment (which may be self-evident), but as adumbrating a request of some kind:[8] 'whiddiyih waant' – correctly, as is revealed subsequently. The information question 'wuhdiyuh doin' and its response, which establish the conditions for proceeding – or not – with the request itself, thus here has the status of what is generically called a **presequence.** The summons–answer adjacency pair, also discussed earlier, is a generic presequence, whereby one speaker recruits another to interact by securing their attention. In the following, Tom, aged twelve, summons his nineteen-year-old sister Emily (l. 1); only upon securing her attention (l. 6) after three attempts does he proceed to business (the extracts are annotated with the base adjacency pair marked as F(irst) and S(econd) respectively, with the form of expansion marked in subscript):

```
(14)  (Clift, Family 1:5:6:49)
1    Tom:   F_pre→  Em
2                   (2.0)
3    Tom:   F_pre→  ↓Em
4                   (3.0)
5    Tom:   F_pre→  EMiLY:
6    Em:    S_pre→  What.
7    Tom:   F_b  →  ↑Why have you got the playstation in your
8                   room?=
9    Em:    S_b  →  =Because I'(h)m using it.
```

However, while the summons–answer sequence can be preliminary to any episode of interaction, there are a number of presequences which are type-

---

[8] That is not necessarily a request per se, but potentially, say, an invitation; 'whiddiyih waant' could be responded to by, say, 'I wanted to see if you were free.'

specific, that is, they standardly take their specific form from the first pair part to which they are preliminaries. In his discussion of these so-called pre-expansion sequences, Schegloff notes: 'The parties to pre-expansion exchanges display an orientation in them to a base adjacency pair which may subsequently develop' (2007a:28). We can see this subsequent development of a base adjacency pair from another presequence below. Here in (15) the pre-invitation at line 4 adumbrates the invitation itself at line 6:

```
(15)  (Schegloff, 2007a:30; JG 3:1)
1   Cla:          Hello
2   Nel:          Hi.
3   Cla:          Hi.
4   Nel: F_pre→   Whatcha doin'.
5   Cla: S_pre→   Not much.
6   Nel: F  →     Y'wanna drink?
7   Cla: S  →     Yeah.
8   Nel:          Okay.
```

Here, the response 'Not much' (l. 5) rules out a range of possible reasons for potential rejection, and so the invitation at line 6 can be issued in the likelihood that it will indeed be accepted, as, in line 7, it duly is.[9] Again in (16) below, the pre-invitation at line 2 is, at line 3, correctly recognised as a potential invitation – but one, this time, that is merely reported (ll. 4–5) once it is established (l. 3) that it will not be viable:

```
(16)  (Schegloff, 2007a:31; SB1)
1   Jud            Hi John.
2   Joh F_pre →    Ha you doin-<say what 'r you doing.
3   Jud S_pre →    Well, we're going out. Why.
4   Joh (F_b)→     Oh, I was just gonna say come out and come over
5                  here and talk this evening, [but if you're going=
6   Jud                                        ["Talk", you mean get
7                  [drunk, don't you?]
8   Joh            =[out you can't very] well do that.
```

So it is evident that the pres here are delivered to establish the conditions for proceeding – 'we're going out' in line 3 above effectively rules out compliance with the invitation about to be issued, as John observes in lines 5 and 8, and, as in (2), the request itself need not be issued and a subsequent declination never produced (for all that the requests themselves are, on these occasions, pursued by their recipients).

The response to the first pair part pres is therefore critical in establishing whether to proceed with action or not. As such, it constitutes either a 'go-ahead'

---

[9] Note in this connection that in extract (1), we see Emma's 'Wuddiyuh –DOin' receipted initially by nearly a second's pause (a clear indication of dispreference, on which see Chapter 5) and a next-turn repair initiator (on which, see Chapter 7 on repair); she issues the invitation nevertheless, with the outcome visible in Chapter 5, extract (14).

(as in 'What' in (14), l. 6, and 'Not much' in extract (15), l. 5), and so advances the action initiated in the sequence, or a 'blocking' response (as in 'Oh: I'm jis sittin' here with Bill'n Gladys'[10] in (2)) to which Margy's hearably deflated 'Oh::::. Oh.' at line 11 is testament.[11] That is why the preferred response to 'guess what' – a pre-announcement – is the go-ahead 'What' (Sacks, [1973] 1987):

(17) (Terasaki, 1976:36; 2004:195)
```
1  D F_pre→   .hh Oh guess what.
2  R S_pre→   What.
3  D F_b  →   Professor Deelies came in, 'n he- put another book on
4             'is order
```

And similarly, as variants:

(18) (Terasaki, 1976:53; 2004:195)
```
1  J F_pre→   Y'wanna know who I got stoned with a few (hh) weeks
2             ago?hh!
3  G S_pre→   Who.
4  J F_b  →   Mary Carter 'n her boy (hh) frie (hh) nd. hh.
```

(19) (Schegloff, 1988b: 451; HG:22–23)
```
1  H F_pre→   Y'know w't I did las'ni:[ght?
2  N S_pre→                          [Wha:t,=
```

Pre-announcements may be produced standardly in the formats *Guess/Y'know/ Remember* ..., plus *What/Who/Where/When* ... plus detail (Schegloff, 2007a:38); like other pres, they check out the basis for proceeding, in this case, with the announcement itself. However, the kinds of demands made on the recipient by announcements are somewhat different from those of invitations and requests, and so correspondingly are the interactional motivations for their production. The central motivation for pre-announcements is, of course, ensuring that the news about to be announced is not something already known by the recipient, in which case, the telling can be aborted:

(20) (Schegloff, 2007a:40)
```
1  F F_pre→   Didju hear about thee, pottery and lead poisoning
2             [(       )
3  L S_pre→   [Yeah Ethie wz just telling us [(       )
4  F                                         [I read an article
5             en I ca- in a the- I 'nno whether it was Newsweek
6             'r Time 'r what ...
```

---

[10] Note how the self-repair from 'haa:eh*' (what is hearably about to be 'having') to 'fixin'm a drink' introduces an extra element here whereby she is host: this is further discussed in section 6.1.2.

[11] Note in this connection that it looks as if Judy's 'Well, we're going out' in (16) is a blocking response, but Schegloff identifies this as a third possibility, embodied in Judy's subsequent 'Why': a hedging response, 'which can make a full response contingent on what the invitation is going to be' (2007a:31). In sequence-organisational terms, Schegloff terms *Why* in this position a 'post-pre', as it indicates that 'the speaker has understood something another has said as preliminary to something else' (p. 31, fn. 3).

However, in addition to the norms against telling people what they already know – an issue we explore in Chapter 6 – there is another rationale for proceeding cautiously which has to do with the character of the announcement itself. The pre-announcements themselves, if done with assessments, can indicate what sort of news is in the offing:

(21) (Terasaki, 1976:33; 2004:181)

```
1   D F_pre→   Hey we got good news
2   R S_pre→   What's the good news.
```

(22) (Terasaki, 1976:28; 2004:184)

```
1   D F_pre→   Didju hear the terrible news?
2   R S_pre→   No. What.
```

In the case of telling bad news, the pre-announcements can thus act as an alert to the gravity of what is to come; following the exchange above, a subsequent pre-announcement – an attempt at identification through recognitional reference (l. 3) (to which we return in Chapter 5) – prompts the recipient to guess the news:

(23) (Terasaki, 1976:28; 2004:190)

```
1   D F_pre→   Didju hear the terrible news?
2   R S_pre→   No. What.
3   D F_b  →   Y'know your Grandpa Bill's brother Dan?
4   R S_b  →   He died.
5   D          Yeah.
```

Indeed, it turns out that, as Sacks (reported in Schegloff, 1988b) first observed, in the case of bad news, getting the recipient to guess and formulate the news themselves is one systematic practice for avoiding having to tell the news altogether:

(24) (Schegloff, 1988b:443; DA:210)

```
1    B F_pre→   I: uh::: I did wanna tell you en I didn' wanna tell you
2      F_pre →  uh::::::uh:: las' night. Uh::: because you had entuht-
3      F_pre →  uh:: company I, I-I had something (.) terrible t' tell you.
4      F_pre →  So [uh:
5    F             [How terrible [is it.
6    B                           [.hhhhhh
7             (.)
8    B        Uh: ez worse it could be:.
9             (0.7)
10   F        W'y'mean Eva?
11            (.)
12   B        Uh yah.hh=
13   F F_b →  =wud she do die:?=
14   B        =Mm:hm,
```

So just as pre-invitations are directed to minimising the possibility of a declination being produced – the prospective inviter can bail out of the prospective invitation before producing it – pre-announcements here are similarly directed to avoiding having to announce grave news. However, with pre-announcements it is the producer of the prospective announcement who can devolve the responsibility for bearing bad tidings, by prompting a guess. The recipient is thus effectively implicated in the delivery of the bad news.[12]

Pre-announcements and pre-invitations are, of course, only a couple of instances of the wide range of possible pres (see, e.g., Schegloff, 2005, on *Did I wake you up?* as a possible pre-apology[13]). In Chapter 5 we examine some more pres – many of which have standardly, in linguistics, been treated as 'indirect' utterances (e.g. *Can you pass the salt?*) – in order to explore further how such pres are often recognised as the actions they foreshadow.

---

[12] The 'perspective display sequence', first described by Maynard (1989), whereby a speaker elicits a recipient's perspective before committing to his or her own assessment, is another such practice where the recipient is implicated in the perspective delivered. Here is an exemplar from ordinary conversation (Maynard, 1989:92):

```
1   B   Have you ever heard anything about wire wheels? [h h:h]
2   A                                                   [They can be a]
3       real pai:n. They- you know- they go outta lI::Ne a[n'-]
4   B                                                   [Yeah]
5       (0.3)
6   B   (Like) if you get a flat you 'afta take it to a special place ta get the
7       fat- fla- flat repaired?
```

Maynard (1992:336) shows how this conversational practice is deployed particularly in medical encounters whereby doctors implicate their patients in the delivery of bad news. In such encounters, the medical professional may elicit a patient's perspective before offering a diagnosis; note that in line 6 the doctor adopts an epistemically weak stance despite an epistemically stronger status (see section 6.2.1, under 'Epistemic domains'):

```
1    D   What do you see? as- as his difficulty
2    M   Mainly his uhm- the fact that he doesn't understand
3        everything and also the fact that his speech is very hard to
4        understand what he's saying, lots of time
5    D   Right.
6    D   Do you have any ideas WHY it is? Are you- do you?
7    M   No.
8    D   Okay I you know I think we BASICALLY in some ways agree
9        with you, insofar as we think that D's MAIN problem, you know
10       DOES involve you know LANGuage,
11   M   Mm hmm
12   D   you know both you know his- being able to underSTAND, and know
13       what is said to him, and also certainly also to be able to
14       express, you know his uh thoughts
15       (1)
16       Uh, in general his development
```

[13] Schegloff (2005) also provides an alternative, but not inconsistent, account of *Did I wake you up?* as a complaint pre-emption.

3.3.2   Insert expansion

A base first pair part having been produced, whatever comes next does not suspend the continuing relevance of its base second pair part. This encapsulates an important feature of adjacency: that this relationship of 'nextness' specifies a default contiguity that may be obstructed, so that seconds may not necessarily directly follow firsts. So while pre-expansions are initiated by the prospective speaker of a first pair part, insert expansions are, in contrast, standardly initiated by the prospective producer of a second pair part. Insert expansions may be either *post-first* or *pre-second* in character; we now examine each of these in turn.

A *post-first* insert (Schegloff, 2007a:100) appears to be dedicated to one task: repair. We shall examine the domain of repair in some detail in Chapter 7, but broadly, repair sequences are addressed to problems in hearing or understanding the preceding talk. For that reason, a post-first insert sequence addresses a problem with the prior first pair part which may 'interfere with the production of an appropriate response to it, or even grasping what an appropriate type of response would be' (Schegloff, 2007a:102), displacing the second pair part which is due, until that problem is resolved. Standardly, the prospective speaker of the second pair part initiates repair on the first pair part, from the more specific, as with the exemplar encountered earlier in this chapter, Nancy's 'What'm I doin' (from (1)), reproduced here as (25), to the general (e.g. *Huh?/What?/Sorry?*) as in line 5 of (26) below:

```
(25)   (Extract 1, fragment)
5      Emm:   Fpre→        [PA:R:T of ut.w:Wuddiyuh -DOin.
6                          (0.9)
7      Nan:   Fins→        What'm I do[in¿
8      Emm:   Sins→                   [Cleani:ng?=
9      Nan:   Spre→        =hh.hh I'm ironing wouldju belie:ve tha:t.
10     Emm:                Oh: bless it[s hea:rt.]
...
16     Emm:   Fb  →        [Wanna c'm] do:wn 'av a bi:te'a lu:nch with me?
```

```
(26)   (Schegloff et al., 1977:367)
1      A:             Were you uh you were in therapy with a private
2                     doctor?
3      B:             Yah.
4      A: Fb   →      Have you ever tried a clinic?
5      B: Fins→       What?
6      A: Sins→       Have you ever tried a clinic?
7      B: Sb   →      ((sigh)) No, I don't want to go to a clinic.
```

Furthermore, as (26) above makes clear, other-initiated repair sequences may, on occasion, be disagreement-implicative, that is, act as *pre-rejections* or *pre-disagreements* (Schegloff, 2007a:102) (see also extract (34), l. 5). In part this may be due to the fact that an other-initated repair violates the preference for contiguity obtaining between the parts of an adjacency pair; however, as

Schegloff notes: 'by not quite "getting" what was said, [such sequences] raise the possibility that it was "not quite right" . . . they provide a place in the very next turn in which the prior speaker can make some adjustment in what was said – to make it more accessible, and perhaps more "acceptable"' (2007a:151). (See also Schegloff, 2007a:151–3, for other-initiated repair as disagreement-implicated in other sequential positions.)

Pre-second insert expansions (Schegloff, 2007a:109) address the range of contingencies attendant on the production of a second pair part. One such contingency – where what follows the first pair part is itself a first pair part whose second is also immediately due – is displayed in the unparalleled concision of this exemplar cited in Levinson (1983:304):

(27)   (Merritt, 1976:333)
```
1   A: F_b   →   May I have a bottle of Mich?
2   B: F_ins →   Are you twenty one?
3   A: S_ins →   No
4   B: S_b   →   No
```

Here, one question–answer adjacency pair is embedded within another base pair, in this case, request–response. So although lines 2–3 show an adjacency pair where the second part immediately follows its corresponding first, lines 1 and 4 show the first and second parts separated. The production of a particular second pair part (l. 4) – here, the granting of a request with either 'yes' or 'no' – to the first (l. 1) is contingent on the satisfaction of a particular condition, itself established by a question–answer adjacency pair.

Contingencies related to the production of a second pair part can take a variety of forms. So, for example, in the following US emergency call, the request is produced at line 2, and its response at line 11; in between the two, there is what Zimmerman (1984) calls the 'interrogative series', a series of question–answer adjacency pairs in the service of establishing informational particulars that will assist in the dispatch of assistance:

(28)   (Zimmerman, 1984:214)
```
1    D            Mid-City emergency.
2    C F_b    →   Um yeah (.) somebody jus' vandalized my car,
3    D F_ins1 →   What's your address.
4    C S_ins1 →   Thirty three twenty two: Elm.
5    D F_ins2 →   Is this a house or an apartment.
6    C S_ins2 →   It's a house.
7    D F_ins3 →   Uh- your las' name.
8    C S_ins3 →   Minsky.
9    D F_ins4 →   How do you spell it.
10   C S_ins4 →   M.I.N.S.K.Y
11   D S_b    →   We'll sen' somebody out to see you.
12   C            Thank you.
13   D            Umhm bye.
14   C            Bye.
```

In section 3.4, extract (39), we see another instance of an adjacency pair where the first and second pair parts – at lines 1 and 92, respectively – are separated by a number of insert expansions.

3.3.3   Post-expansions

(a) Minimal post-expansions

Some sequence types, such as greetings and farewells, are recognisably complete after the second pair part. Moreover, in general, sequences involving preferred, or agreeing, second pair parts are closure-relevant, and sequences involving dispreferred, or disagreeing, second pair parts are expansion relevant (Schegloff, 2007a:117). In Chapter 1, we saw the following exchange, now below with turns labelled. This sequence in fact shows the three possible options with respect to sequence expansion and closure: 'yes' (l. 33) as sequence closing, 'no' (l. 40) as sequence expanding, and then 'yes' (l. 45) as prompting a minimal sequence expansion at line 47:

```
(29)  (Goodwin, 1995:239–40)
31  Nurse     F_b1  →  English muffin?
32                      (3.4)
33  Husband   S_b1  →  Ye:s.
34  Nurse     F_b2  →  A:[nd what would you like on it.
35  Wife               [Just one.
37                      (0.8)
38  Nurse     F_b2  →  Jelly?
39                      (1.0)
40  Husband   S_b3  →  No:
41                      (0.8)
42  Wife      F_b3  →  Butt[er?
43  Nurse     F_b3  →      [Butter?
44                      (0.3)
45  Husband   S_b3  →  Yes.
46                      (0.6)
47  Nurse     SCT   →  Okay.
```

After the nurse's first pair part in line 31 receives a 'yes' in line 33 from the husband, so closing that adjacency pair, the nurse proceeds to another first pair part at line 34: 'And what would you like on it'. She expands this turn with a candidate: 'Jelly?' (l. 38). The husband's 'No' at line 40 thus provides for an expansion of the sequence – and at lines 42–3 the wife, and then, in overlap, the nurse, propose another option: 'Butter?'. The husband's 'Yes', at line 45, might have closed the sequence, but the nurse's 'Okay' at line 47, accepting the prior action, minimally expands the sequence – that is to say, the sequence-expanding turn is itself closing implicative (Schegloff, 2007a:118), with a 'sequence-closing third' (p. 118) (compare also 'Okay' at l. 8 in (15)).

Other sequence types also display variation with respect to sequence closure after the second pair part, so, for example, other-initiated repair sequences may be taken to be complete after the adjacency pair. In the following, after repair is initiated by Fran at line 11 and completed by Ted at line 12, Fran takes up a new line of talk within the larger on-going sequence:

```
(30)  (Schegloff, 2007a:116)
1    Fra:     Whad'r y'guys doin et the bea::ch.
2    Ted:     n:No:thin,hh
3             (.)
4    Fra:     NO:the::[:n,
5    Ted:             [No::,
6             (0.2)
7    Fra:     Oh: good he[av'n.]
8    Ted:                [Get'n] ↑pi:nk,
9             (.)
10   Ted:     hh[hn,hn-hn] =
11   Fra: F→    [Hu:h?  ]
12   Ted: S→   =.hh Gitt'n pi:nk,
13   Fra:     Wah thoughtchu wren't goin' down tel nex' she-u-
14            th'weekeh:- ah mean the end a'the mo:nth.
```

Note that lines 11–12 are not a base adjacency pair, but a common type of adjacency pair sequence nonetheless; and the sequence is here treated as complete by the participants after the second pair part (Schegloff, 2007a:117). In contrast, in the following, repair is initiated by Lesley (l. 4) on Mum's question at line 2; upon Mum's repair (l. 5) and Lesley's response, Mum produces an additional turn (l. 8), to the sequence after the second pair part. This minimal post-expansion by means of the sequence-closing third is accomplished by the change-of-state token 'Oh' (Heritage, 1984a) combined with the assessment, 'good':

```
(31)  (Enfield et al., 2013:349)
1    Les          m-[Jem's
2    Mum Fb  →      [Are the family o:ff?
3                 (0.5)
4    Les Fins→   SORRY?
5    Mum Sins→   'Av your family gone o:ff?
6                 (.)
7    Les Sb  →   Ye:s,
8    Mum SCT→    Oh ↓goo:d.
```

The sequence-closing third here is, in fact, a composite of two common embodiments of third position objects: 'oh' and an assessment (see also Emma's 'Oh bless its heart' at line 10 in extract (1)). We saw the following exchange in Chapter 1. At lines 3 and 14 'Oh' is free-standing. At line 8, 'oh' is similarly produced to be free-standing, but after a subsequent brief pause, Nancy produces another move to close, with an assessment at line 10, 'Very clever':

(32) (Heritage, 1984a:310)

```
1    N Fb1 →   .hhh dz he 'av 'iz own apa:rt[mint?
2    H Sb1 →                              [.hhhh Yea:h,=
3    N SCT→    Oh:,
4              (1.0)
5    N Fb2 →   How didju git 'iz number,
6              (.)
7    H Sb2 →   I(h) (.) c(h)alled infermation'n San Fr'ncissc(h)[uh!
8    N SCT→                                                     [Oh::::.
9              (.)
10   N SCT→    Very cleve:r, hh=
11   H         =Thank you[: I-.hh-.hhhhhhhh hh=
12   N Fb3→                [W'ts 'iz last name,
13   H Sb3→    =Uh:: Freedla:nd..hh[hh
14   N SCT→                        [Oh[:,
```

An assessment may also constitute a sequence-closing third on its own, as occurs
in (33) at line 4:

(33) (Schegloff, 2007a:125)
('it' refers to the camera recording a meal-time exchange)

```
1    Don: Fb  →  I:s this ai:med accurate enou:gh?
2                (0.5)
3    Joh: Sb  →  Yes it's aimed at the table.
4    Don: SCT→   Grea:t.
5                (1.0)
```

In the following, we see both a composite sequence-closing third and what
Schegloff (2007a:142–8) calls a post-completion musing, or post-mortem,
whereby a sequence that has apparently been brought to a close is subsequently
revised. In the following, the composite sequence-closing third 'Oh. Okay' at line
11 appears to bring the sequence to a close, whereupon there is what Jefferson
(1981) calls topic attrition/topic hold, during which neither party contributes to
the sequence. However, with a softly delivered assessment, 'Gee I feel like a real
nerd' (l. 17), Karen proceeds to reciprocate the invitation earlier extended to her,
which is then itself declined:

(34) (Schegloff, 2007a:144)

```
1    Vic:  Fb   →  =I ca:lled um to see if you want to uh (0.4) c'm over
2                  en watch the Classics Theater.
3                  (0.3)
4    Vic:  Fb   →  Sandy'n Tom'n I,=
5    Kar:  Fins→   =She Sto[ops t'Conquer?
6    Vic:          [(     )-
7                  (0.4)
8    Vic:  Sins→   Yeh.
9                  (0.3)
10   Kar:  Sb   →  Mom js asked me t'watch it with her.h=
```

```
11   Vic:   SCT→   =Oh. Okay,
12                 (0.3)
13   Kar:          ihhh
14                 (0.2)
15   Kar:          ↑.hu:h.hh-hhh
16                 (0.3)
17   Kar:   PCM→   °Gee I feel like a real nerd° you c'n ahl come up here.
18                 (0.3)
19   Vic:          Nah, that's alright wil stay down here,
```

So *oh, okay,* assessments and composites thereof, as well as such post-completion musings, all constitute minimal post-expansions in that they are designed to possibly complete the sequence.

(b) Non-minimal post-expansions

In contrast to minimal post-expansions, non-minimal post-expansions are designed to occupy more than a turn. There exists a wide variety of sequence types constituting non-minimal post-expansions, many yet to be described; here we can mention only a few of the possible types of which Schegloff (2007a) has a more extensive account.

It was noted earlier that other-initiated repair may be disagreement-implicated; such disagreement-implicated repair sequences may constitute post-expansions. Extract (35) below shows repair initiated, at line 4, on an assessment ('She wouldn't behave for anything' (ll. 2–3)), but once this is repaired, the assessment is disagreed with. This in turn has disagreement-adumbrated repair initiated on it in line 7, in the face of which the speaker initially holds firm, only to produce a partial back down 'She could've been a lot worse' (l. 8):

(35)   (Schegloff, 2007a:154; Schegloff et. al., 1977:368)
```
1   Sta:            That's all. But you know what happened that night
2          F_b   →  we went to camp. Forget it. She wouldn't behave for
3                   anything.
4   Ala:   F_ins →  W-when.
5   Sta:   S_ins →  When we went to camp.
6   Ala:   S_b   →  She behaved okay.
7   Sta:   F_post→  She did?
8   Ala:   S_post→  Yeah. She could've been a lot worse.
```

However, while the sequence above displays a disagreeing second pair part ('she behaved okay') to a first, the one below shows that post-expansion of an agreeing second pair part may also take place. Here, Ken's question gets a positive response (l. 2), and the pause that follows suggests that the sequence is thereby, in accordance with the norms for such responses, complete; but then Roger revives the issue at line 4, and Dan backs down from his former display of certainty:

(36) (From Schegloff et al., 1977:364)

```
1   Ken   Fb     →   Is Al here today?
2   Dan   Sb     →   Yeah.
3                     (2.0)
4   Rog   Fpost  →   He is? hh eh heh
5   Dan   Spost  →   Well he was.
```

The pro-repeat 'He is?' at line 4 is one form of what Jefferson (1981a) calls
a 'news mark' which can prompt further topical talk. Such news marks include
'Really?' or 'Oh really?' So in the extract below, Mark questions Sherrie about
her upcoming wedding:

(37) (Schegloff et al., 1977:156–7)
      (Mar=Mark; She=Sherrie; Kar=Karen)

```
1    Mar:   Fb1     →   .hh What about the outside candlelight routine izzat
2                        still gonna go on?
3    She:   Sb1     →   No yih can't have outside candlelight it's a fi:re
4                        hazard.
5                        (0.5)
6    Mar:   Fpost1  →   Oh really?
7                        (.)
8    She:   Spost1  →   Yes[::.     ]
9    Kar:   Fpost2  →      [C'n have] it insi:de,
10                        (0.8)
11   Mar:   Fpost2  →   You c'd have 'm inside though?
12   Kar:   Spost2  →   Yeah
13                        (0.4)
14   She:   Fpost3  →   Yeh but who wants t'get married inside in the
15                        middle a' the summer when it's still light till
16                        n[ine o'clock. ]
17   Mar:   Spost3  →    [Gunna be beau]tiful outsi:de.
18                        (0.2)
19   She:              Ye:ah.
20   Mar:              E'll (jat'll) jus' be fanta:stic.
```

Mark's 'Oh really?' (l. 6) topicalises Sherrie's disaligning second pair part at
lines 3–4. However, as Sherrie confirms, Karen intervenes by rejecting the
grounds for Sherrie's dispreferred response. As Schegloff notes 'If "oh really?"
is the expansionary alternative to the sequence-closing "oh" with respect to
information, then Karen's rejection is the expansionary alternative to "okay"
with respect to acceptance or not of the action being done in the second pair part
turn' (1977:159). Mark assumes Karen's intervention as his own in line 11,
differentiating his turn from hers in lexicalising ('though') rather than stress
marking ('insi:de') the contrast between their position and Sherrie's.
In response, Sherrie defends her account for cancelling the 'outside candlelight
routine' (ll. 1–2) and Mark appears to accept this in his assessment. While the
other-initiated repairs in extracts (35) and (36) are vehicles for disagreements

		Sequence types *e.g.* (extract nos. for reference) *Summons–answer* (14)
	← **Pre-expansion**	*Pre-invitation* (15–16) *Pre-announcement* (17–24)
A **First pair part**		
	← **Insert expansion**	**Post-first inserts** *repair* (25–6) **Pre-second inserts** *adjacency pair(s)* (27–8)
B **Second pair part**		
	← **Post-expansion**	**Minimal post-expansions** *sequence-closing third* (1, 15, 29, 31–4) *post-completion musing* (34) **Non-minimal post-expansions** *repair* (35–7)

Figure 3.4 *Expansions of a base adjacency pair, with example sequence types*

approached tentatively, the forthrightness of the challenges to the second pair part at line 3 display a distinct form that post-expansion can take.

Figure 3.4 is a diagrammatic summary of the expansion possibilities of a base adjacency pair.

3.4 The sequence: coherence and distributed cognition

The preceding sections have shown how the adjacency pair may be expanded in various ways. The question of cross-cultural validity, addressed in section 3.2.1 above, also applies to expansion beyond the adjacency pair. Moreover, there does appear to be evidence to suggest that sequence organisation as described for English by Schegloff (2007a) is indeed universal. Kendrick et al. (2014) examine the adjacency pair and its systematic expansion in a sample of twelve structurally very distinct languages: ǂĀkhoe Haiǁom, Tzeltal, Yélî Dnye, English, Italian, Japanese, the Mandarin Chinese of Taiwan, Cha'palaa (Barbacoan; Ecuador), Siwu (Kwa; Ghana), Turkmen (Turkic; Turkmenistan), the language isolate Yurakaré, of Bolivia, and LSA (*Lengua de Señas Argentina*), the sign language of Argentina.

In all of these languages, expansions of adjacency pairs have been found. So, for example, all languages, with one exception, were found to use pre-expansions. The exception was Cha'palaa, where there appears to be an absence of pre-sequences, such that proceeding straight to the base request without a presequence is normative, giving interactions in Cha'palaa a character of direct forthrightness relative to the other languages in the sample (see also extract (46), Chapter 6, and extract (34), Chapter 7, for other instances). So, for example, while there is an initial summons in what follows, there is no pre-request:

```
(38)  (Floyd, 2015:11)
1  A    vieja
        old lady
2  B    aa
        huh?
3  A→   inu chuwa manka' kuka junu jee
        i-nu chuwa ma-n-ka-tu ku-ka junu jee
        1SG-ACC vine again-N-grab-SR give-IMP1 there yes
        give me the string there hey ((finger and lip point))
4  B    ((brings string))
```

However, all of the languages surveyed use insert expansions of the post-first, other-initiation of repair variety (we return to this as a possible universal in Chapter 7), and most appear to deploy pre-second inserts. All of the languages make use of post-expansions, both minimal and non-minimal. Furthermore, while Kendrick et al.'s survey examined twelve languages systematically, the fragments in this book testify also to the presence of the same basic organisation of sequences in, among others, Arabic, Bequian Creole, Danish, Finnish, French, German, Hebrew, Korean, Murrinh-Patha, Russian, Spanish, Swedish and Thai.

The survey by Kendrick et al. leads them to suggest that the formal organisation of the adjacency pair and its expansion is a translinguistic and transcultural phenomenon:

> an organization that belongs not to 'languages' or 'cultures' per se, but which is part of the infrastructure of interaction, 'an "interaction engine"' (Levinson, 2006), that all humans and human societies have in common. In agreement with Schegloff (2006), we propose that these structures emerge as solutions to recurrent socio-interactional problems, which are themselves basic to human sociality.   (Kendrick et al., 2014)

So far, then, we have examined fairly concise sequences in the interests of demonstrating forms of expansion. However, it is perhaps only in examining a more extended sequence that we can appreciate the extent to which the adjacency pair is a resource for coherence in interaction. Moreover, because expansions of a basic sequence are naturally occurring instances of linguistic embedding, they also afford us an insight into one of the most vigorously debated properties of language.

The following exchange between Bonnie, aged 14, and her on-off boyfriend, Jim, aged 15, may at first blush seem unremarkable. However, it is an extraordinary demonstration of the criterion of conditional relevance, where the first part of an adjacency pair – in this case, a request – posed in line 1 receives its second pair part nearly ninety transcript lines later. Between the two turns, all sorts of other business is conducted – but the conditional relevance of an appropriate response to line 1 is on-going until it is finally met at line 92:

(39)   (Adapted from Schegloff, 1990, 2007a:111–13, and Levinson, 2013b)
        (B=Bonnie, J=Jim; actions are paired and labelled on the right of each transcript line in brackets, with the degree of embedding.)

```
 1   B: F_b→  I was wondering if you'd let me borrow your gun.        (Request:0)
 2           (1)
 3   J:      My gun?                                    (Q/Repair initiator:1)
 4   B:      Yeah.                                          (A/Repair: 1)
 5           (1)
 6   J:      What gun.              (Repair initiator on own repair initiator:2)
 7           (0.7)
 8   B:      Donchuh have a beebee gun?                       (Question:3)
 9   J:      Yeah,                                             (Answer:3)
10           (0.8)
11   B:      (I'm a-) It'[s-]
12   J:              [Oh]: I have a lotta guns.hehh          (Answer:3)
13   B:      Yuh do:?                               (Q/Repair initiator:4)
14   J:      Yeah.                                          (A/Repair:4)
15   J:      aWhat- I meant was which gun. (Redo question:2 (3rd position (repair)))
16           (0.5)
17   B:      Tch!.hhh Oh (0.4) uh::m (0.4) t!.hhh (0.5)
18           well d'j'have a really lo:ng one,              (Question: 3)
19           (0.8)
20   J:      A really l:ong one.hh[h                (Q/repair initiator:4)
21   B:                          [Yeah.                     (A/repair: 4)
22           (0.2)
23   B:      't doesn't matter what ki:nd.
24           (1)
25   J:      Why:: would you like a >>really long one.<<       (Question:4)
26           (0.8)
27   B:      Y'don' have a really long one.                   (Question:5)
28           (1)
29   J:      What?                                  (Q/Repair initiator:6)
30   B:      Y- Donchu have a l- really long ne?             (Question:6)
31   J:      ea::hhh.                                         (Answer:5)
32   J:      A- all I wan' to know why you want
33           a [gun,]                                         (Redo Q:5)
34   B:        [oh ] oh: OH::              (Sequence-closing third)
35           (0.5)
36   B:      Well↑ (0.7) becu:z, I'm do[ing       ]          (Answer:5)
37   J:                              [You're gon ]na shoot
38           your mo:m.=                                      (Redo Q:5)
39           =[Go ahead.]
40   B:       [Heheh    ]
```

```
41            (0.2)
42   B:       .hh eheheh.hh Because I'm I'm doi- heheh (0.8).hhh
43            I am doing- a pl- a thi:ng.(0.3).hhh in drama.          (Answer:5)
              (41 transcript lines omitted)
86   B:       No- I'n- it's jis' thet- everybody in the class        (Answer:5)
87            has to do a different- (.) pantomime,
88   B:       you know?                                               (Question:5)
89   J:       Uhuh,                                                   (Answer:5)
90            (0.4)
91   B:       An[:]
92   J:Sb→    [Y]eah:, you can use 't,                                (Granting:0)
```

Jim's 'Yeah, you can use 't' (l. 92) might initially seem to appear from nowhere; certainly its relevance to the immediately prior turns appears hard to fathom. The business covered in the preceding turns includes identifying the type of gun requested and what it might be for (for a fuller account of the entire sequence, see Schegloff, 1990). However, it is of course a response not to the immediately prior turns, but to the one for which its relevance is provided: that, way back, in line 1: 'I was wondering if you'd let me borrow your gun.' The entire sequence is thus scaffolded by the request–response adjacency pair, which is what gives the whole its coherence.

The notion of how units fit relevantly together, showing coherence, has been a preoccupation across a number of subdomains within linguistics (see, e.g., Halliday and Hasan, 1976, 1991; Givon, 1995; Kamp, 1995; Costermans and Fayol, 1997; Wilson and Matsui, 1998). The objects of of such inquiry have been overwhelmingly propositional, and the concern, topical coherence. The intuitive notion that the exchange above is about borrowing a gun may be adequate as a topical gloss, but as Schegloff points out:

> Focusing on 'the topic' of some unit of talk risks the danger of not addressing analysis to what participants in real worldly interaction are doing to or with one another with their talk, with their talk-about-something, or with particular parts of it; that is, all talk is then treated as talk-about, not as talk-that-does ...   (1990:52)

Examined propositionally, Jim's 'Yeah, you can use 't' (l. 92) makes little sense if considered in the light of topical coherence with what went before. However, the turn-initial 'Yeah', indicating that what is to come is responsive to something prior, shows that, rather than being *about* something, it is *doing* something: in this case, granting the request launched some minutes earlier.

In this respect, the sequence is a robust empirical demonstration of speakers' abilities to embed units hierarchically. As we saw in Chapter 1, there has been vehement debate about the claim by Hauser et al. (2002) that syntactic recursion such as 'the rat the cat the dog chased killed ate the malt' (Chomsky and Miller, 1963:286–7) is the only domain-specific feature of language, making it unique to our species. However, as Levinson observes, 'there is one central sense of the term recursion – namely embedding . . . that clearly is not exclusive to syntax, and that is exhibited in a much more fulsome way outside of sentential syntax' (2013b:149). The embeddings to which Levinson refers are of course not those within sentences, but within sequences, distributed across speakers: just the kind displayed in the sequence above.

While it is a matter of some dispute as to how many degrees of syntactic embedding are possible in the languages of the world,[14] what (39) categorically shows is what Levinson calls 'pragmatic embedding' (2013b:157) – here, up to six levels – is apparently straightforwardly done in talk; a paradigmatic display of distributed cognition. In terms of processing load, two brains can do more than one. As Levinson observes:

> our action-planning system in general needs to be able to hold a stack of subgoals, and check them off one by one – to make the coffee may require calling the water-getting subroutine, which may require the jug-finding subroutine, and so forth. Many aspects of language use are best explained in terms of joint-action planning (Clark 1996, Levinson 2013a), so that language usage is able to draw directly on the cognition of our action systems in a way that syntax cannot.   (2013b:158)

The possibility of pragmatic embedding – and joint collaborative action – is thus found to lie in the sequence. Work across a range of interactional phenomena, both linguistic and extralinguistic, has underwritten participants' orientation to sequences of action as the basis for coherence in interaction. In Chapter 5, we see how the selection of one referring term over another (e.g. 'Alice' as opposed to 'she') is done by reference to sequences. With respect to prosody, we also noted in Chapter 1 that relatively high pitch onsets relative to a speaker's baseline marks the 'reason for the call' (Couper-Kuhlen, 2001): a unit that goes beyond the turn-at-talk. Alongside the linguistic, Rossano (2005, 2012), using a videoed corpus of Italian interaction, argues that gaze behaviour is mainly organised in relation to the development of courses of action, so that most of the variation in gaze direction should be observed at the beginning or at possible completion of courses of action accomplished through one or more sequences of talk. Li (2014) describes cases in Mandarin Chinese interaction in which the questioner leans towards the addressee[15] while asking a question and maintains that position until the response – an embodiment that is clearly related to work on so-called 'holds' in other-intiations of repair (Floyd et al., 2015), discussed further in section 7.3. Similarly, in work on Norwegian, Sikveland and Ogden (2012) show a relationship between the maintenance of 'co-speech' gestures across turns until sequence closure, and a display of shared understanding. Such work

[14] Levinson maintains that degree 2 centre embedding 'occurs vanishingly rarely in spoken language syntax' (2013b:155) – one claim among a number that are hotly disputed in, e.g., Legate et al. (2014).

[15] Enfield et al. (2013:374) discuss leaning forward as a common accompaniment to other-initiated repair, noting that its prevalence across languages is rooted in the assumption that this makes it more likely that one will perceive what is being said.

shows the extent to which participants deploy multimodal resources in the collaborative construction of actions across sequences – an issue to which we return in Chapter 4.

3.5   Conclusion: 'sequence' as infrastructure and context

What adjacency pairs reveal in such a compelling way – that position in sequence matters – is, in fact, generally the case for utterances in talk; as Heritage and Atkinson remark: 'utterances are *in the first place* contextually understood by reference to their placement and participation within sequences of actions' (1984:5; emphasis added). Form alone cannot deliver what an utterance is understood to be doing. It is in the intersection of compositional form – subject to local structural variation – with the universal, language-independent constraint of sequential position that actions are constructed.[16] Sacks and Schegloff had, from the earliest days of conversation-analytic research, observed that apprehension of sequential position is first and foremost a concern *for speakers* in trying to establish what is being done by any given utterance: 'a pervasively relevant issue (for participants) about utterances in conversation is "why that now", a question whose analysis may . . . also be relevant to finding what "that" is. That is to say, some utterances may derive their character as actions entirely from placement considerations' (1973:299). In other words, participants are themselves analysts. 'Why' is, of course, the participant's question; 'that' is a compositional element of the utterance (a word, an element of stress, some aspect of articulation, word order and so on), and 'now' relates to its position: this question, in the first place for participants, is also ultimately one for the analyst.

The sequence can thus be seen to be one element of the universal infrastructure of interaction and the primary resource for the specification of context. Attempts within linguistics to characterise the context of an utterance appeal to cognitive principles such as mutual manifestness in Relevance Theory or the 'bucket theory' in sociolinguistics. Such notions of context made it difficult to specify on any given occasion what elements of context are operational for any utterance. In contrast, the recognition of context as, in the first instance, sequential makes it possible to specify precisely how utterances implement actions; for context here is both the participants' *and* the analyst's resource.

[16] After all, spatial locations are done by reference to both latitude and longitude.

4   Interaction in time: the centrality of turn-taking

This chapter examines the foundational work on turn-taking in conversation (Sacks et al., 1974) and provides an overview of its main components. The central insight of the turn-taking model – that it standardly produces 'one speaker at a time', with 'no gap, no overlap' between turns – combines social and linguistic organisation in the face of real-time constraints. We explore how the grammatical resources of a language – syntactic, phonetic and pragmatic – are mobilised alongside other resources, such as gaze and embodiments, to achieve this outcome. The construction of a turn and the allocation of a turn to a next speaker is the central focus here. The model also provides us with a resource for understanding exceptions, such as silence, choral talk and overlap, and we investigate how these are managed in the accomplishment of particular actions. The turn-taking model accommodates local linguistic variation – languages of different structures – while retaining an abstractness which accounts for the universality of its application. The chapter concludes with an overview of how some of this variation is accommodated.

The central observation to be made about interaction is that we take it in turns to talk. This is the deceptively simple fact elaborated in Sacks et al.'s (1974) paper 'A Simplest Systematics for the Organization of Turn-taking for Conversation' (henceforth 'the turn-taking paper'): a paper foundational in the development of CA and one which marks a turning-point in the empirical investigation of language. Its approach to investigating language use was revolutionary: in the first place, it is grounded in an observation that is not, on the face of it, linguistic, but concerns social organisation; and, for the first time, it provides a model of language use that places us, the users of language, at its centre, showing how we *ourselves* coordinate and regulate our participation in talk.

The observation that we take it in turns to talk is one with universal validity: one which is independent of any particular language, and independent of the number of people engaged in any given interaction. Although the turn-taking model was developed by reference to conversation in English,[1] Stivers et al.'s ten-language study of questions and their responses (2010), discussed in Chapter 3, provides evidence that suggests, across languages, the central

---

[1] Detailed qualitative research on the turn-taking model in other languages unfortunately remains sparse: Tanaka (1999) on Japanese, Sidnell (2001) on a Caribbean English Creole, Guyanese, and Gardner and Mushin (2015) on the Australian language Garrwa are exceptions. All provide empirical evidence that support Sacks et al.'s findings for English. These accounts should be set against impressionistic assertions regarding turn-taking in particular communities, e.g. Reisman's claims that Antiguan turntaking conventions 'appear . . . almost anarchic' (1974:113).

claim of the paper is robust: that, in general, overlapping talk is avoided and the gap between one speaking turn and another is minimal.[2]

Examining how this is brought off by participants is like examining the intricate mechanism under the bonnet of a car: when we see how the mechanism works, we also see what it supports and what it enables us to do. So exactly how this feat of coordination is achieved is the business of the turn-taking paper. Here we provide an overview and a sketch of the model, before exploring what it makes possible.

4.1   Turn-taking: an overview

Imagining what would happen – or fail to happen – if some form of turn-taking organisation did not exist may give us the keenest appreciation for what it actually makes possible. Things simply do not get done if we do not take turns – things which may be relatively trivial (e.g. our thanks to our host gets overlapped and obscured) but also possibly highly consequential (the dispatch of an ambulance is threatened because the speaker is hysterical, obscuring other talk; on which possibility, see Whalen and Zimmerman, 1998). If *Don't all speak at once!* is a familiar admonishment to children, instructing them to speak in turn, the turn-taking model makes explicit the methods by which, in general, speakers establish who speaks next, and when. The result is that, overwhelmingly in ordinary conversation, speakers organise themselves such that 'one speaker at a time' is achieved: effectively, the self-regulation of interactional traffic. Moreover, what that speaker does – or is able to do, before the next speaker comes in – is the fundamental concern of the turn-taking paper. What is at issue here is the production and understanding of utterances, and the actions done through utterances, *in time*. For a current speaker, the prospect of a next speaker's imminent turn acts as a constraint on what gets said, and thereby done. For the other participants, waiting their turn to speak, turn-taking provides an inherent incentive to listen: to judge when, exactly, to come in: 'the system translates a willingness or potential desire to speak into a corollary obligation to listen' (Sacks et al., 1974:728). Such are the implications of the turn-taking paper that this chapter can only give the merest overview of its significance for the study of language in interaction. However, perhaps a footnote – an aside, almost in passing – gives some indication of what it might implicate, in the observation that: 'while an addressed question requires an answer from the addressed party, *it is the turntaking system, rather than syntactic or semantic features of "the question"*, that requires the answer to come "next"' (p. 725, fn.38; italics added). So social organisation, rather than

---

[2] Since there was no difference found between response times after questions and non-questions in a corpus of Dutch conversation, Stivers et al. suggest that the question–response sequences are representative for turntaking in general (2009:10588).

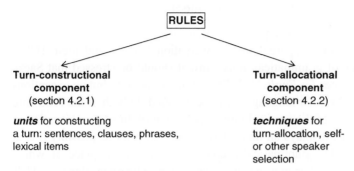

Figure 4.1 *Basic model of the turn-taking system (after Sacks et al., 1974)*

any inherent linguistic properties of an utterance, is here revealed as the mechanism by which questions elicit their answers. So judging, as a speaker, how to keep a turn, and judging, as a possible next speaker, when to come in, is where grammar and interaction meet.

4.2   A sketch of 'a simplest systematics'

In their introduction to the turn-taking paper, Sacks et al. propose that a model for the organisation of turn-taking should be able to account, in the first place, for a number of observable facts about conversation. These range from the immediately apparent (e.g. 'speaker change recurs, or at least recurs') to those requiring more scrutiny ('Occurrences of more than one speaker at a time are common, but brief'). Others concern the variability inherent in conversation; so the number of parties involved, what is said and for how long, is not specified in advance; and the order and size of turns varies. Sacks et al. note that 'Turns are valued, sought, or avoided' (1974:701) and so a turn-taking model, directed to the administration of such resources, operates effectively as an economy. The basic model consists of two components and a set of rules, summarised in Figure 4.1. If, to use our earlier analogy, interactional traffic is what gets regulated by the turn-taking model, then the turn-constructional component specifies what that traffic consists in: the units out of which turns are constructed – literally, **turn-constructional units** (TCUs). The other component specifies how turns are allocated: who goes next at any given point. Moreover, the traffic gets regulated by the participants, TCU by TCU. We examine each component, and the rules, in turn, before investigating what they reveal about interaction.

In order to participate in a conversation, participants have to monitor a turn-in-progress to establish *when* to come in (with the turn-constructional component) and *who* is being selected to speak next (the turn-allocational component). We also examine these in turn.

4.2.1   The turn-constructional component

As soon as we examine what participants actually do in conversation, it immediately becomes apparent that conversational turns, and their TCUs, comprise the range of grammatical units. Now it should be stressed that Sacks et al. refer to 'unit types *for English*' (1974:702; italics added), but no exceptions to these unit types for other languages have been found. In both of the following extracts, the recipient of the arrowed turn launches a turn directly on completion of a prior TCU. This displays an understanding of that prior as possibly (i.e. at that point, potentially) grammatically complete, and thus a place at which transition to a next speaker may occur: a **transition-relevance place**, or TRP. So TCUs may include, for example, sentences (see extracts (1) and (2)):

(1) (Sacks et al., 1974:721)
```
1   Ken→  I saw 'em last night  [at uhm school.
2   Jim                         [They're a riot
```

(2) (Sacks et al., 1974)
```
1   Lou→  I think it's really funny  [to watch.
2   Rog                              [Ohhh God!
```

In (1), Jim starts his next turn (l. 2) at the point at which Ken's turn constitutes a possibly complete sentence, at the end of 'I saw 'em last night'; as it happens, Ken has not completed his turn, and so Jim's turn overlaps with Ken's completion. Similarly in (2), Roger comes in at the point at which Louise's prior turn is possibly grammatically complete, and so potentially the end of that turn – with a similar outcome.

Of course, we do not always speak in entire sentences; and this is where the distinctiveness of the turn-taking paper's contribution becomes very marked. So, as Sacks et al. note, turns may also consist of elements below the level of the sentence, such as clauses, as in the arrowed turns in (3) and (4) below:

(3) (Sacks et al., 1974:703)
```
1   A    Uh you been down here before  [havenche.
2   B                                  [Yeh.
3   A→   Where the sidewalk is?
4   B    Yeah,
5   A→   Whur it ends,
6   B    Goes [all a' way up there?
7   A         [They c'm up tuh the:re,
8   A    Yeah.
```

(4) (Schegloff, 1996a:74)
```
1   Ton   Y'd of probly heard fr'm im already.
2         (0.9)
3   Mar   i-Ya:h.
4         (0.4)
5   Ton→  If 'e hadn' gotten a li:ft
```

Equally, turns may consists of grammatical units smaller than the clause, such as phrases (5) and (6) and lexical items (7):

(5) (Sacks et al., 1974:702)

```
1   A    Oh I have the- I have one class in the e:vening.
2   B→   On Mondays?
3   A    Y-uh::: Wednesdays.=
4   B    =Uh-Wednesday,=
5   A    =En it's like a Mickey Mouse course.
```

(6) (Schegloff, 1996a:76)

```
1   Rog    They make miserable coffee.
2   Ken    hhhh hhh
3   Ther→  Across the street?
4   Rog    Yeh
5   Ken    Miserable food hhhh
```

(7) (Clift, 2005:1644; from Parker, 2001; fragment from extract (4), Chapter 1)
     (D=David, adolescent client; T=Therapist)

```
1D   I always behave in all of them but (0.3) in=English and Maths and
2    Science and French (.) I can't.
3    (1.3)
4T→  Don't.
5    (0.8)
6D   Mm.
7    (0.5)
8T   Say to yourself (0.8) [it's not that I can't, it's that I don't.
9D                         [Mm
```

Extracts (5) to (7) show particularly clearly how radical, from a linguistic perspective, the turn-taking paper is: that phrases and lexical items are not shown to be parts of any greater whole, or as fragments of sentences, but as turns in their own right – because participants treat them as such.

In producing a next turn with no gap between the prior turn and their own, such as in (5) and (6), speakers show, in Sacks et al.'s words, that 'projectability is the case' (p. 702, fn. 12); in other words, that participants to an interaction can project the point at which an utterance is going to be possibly complete. Given that utterance planning, as we have seen, takes on average 600 ms, it is imperative that participants can identify the possible completion of these turns – and therefore an appropriate opportunity for turn transition – earlier than they actually occur, so planning can occur while the current turn is in progress.[3] Torreira et al.'s study of pre-turn inbreaths on a corpus of Dutch suggests that utterance planning involves 'early prediction of content plus late triggering of articulation based on

---

[3] Indeed, often from the beginning, so, for example, as Sacks et al. note (1974:719, fn. 32), turns beginning with *wh-* questions may have a range of interactional implications, such as possibly selecting a next speaker, possibly selecting last speaker as next speaker and – given the availability of the one-word question – possibly effect rapid turn transfer.

information present close to turn ends' (2015:8). The 'early prediction of content' would make use of the 'front-loading' of information mentioned in Chapter 3. The information 'close to turn ends' involves all the linguistic resources that are involved in turn design. The key element here, as it constitutes the units out of which turns are constructed, is thus the grammar.

Sacks et al. note that the speaker is initially entitled, in having a turn, to one TCU, whereupon turn transition becomes relevant, and therefore a possibility. As we shall see, work since the turn-taking paper shows that a number of features are implicated in projecting TCU completion, and thus possible transition. Once a turn is launched, there is an observed preference for progressivity in interaction (see Schegloff, 1979; Stivers and Robinson, 2006), which is to say that there is an observed bias in interaction towards a speaker continuing a turn to completion, rather than halting it in mid-production (we discuss preference more generally in Chapter 5, and see how the preference for progressivity is mobilised in undertaking repair in sign language, in Chapter 7).

Syntactic completion

There is ample evidence that speakers orient to syntactic completion to project a possible place for transition. See, firstly, (8) below, showing a next speaker withholding talk until Lottie comes to a syntactic completion:

```
(8)  (NB:1:6:2:R)
1  Lottie:  We leave after uh
2           (1.0)
3  Lottie:  .t u. - Yihkno:w, u. -it prob'ly leaves about
4           midni:gh[t.
5  Emma:           [Mm:hm,
```

See also in (9) below, where the end of A's turn is potentially syntactically complete, and B launches a turn at line 4:

```
(9)  (Heritage, 1:6)
1  A:  →  Uh,hh (0.2) (k) Well no:w. (0.3) Uh:: hi:s(d)- his(d)
2      →  uhm (0.2) hh He-he's there on- on Mondee ahftihhnoon I
3         know tha:t,
4  B:     He's not there until Monday no:w.
5  A:     No: he's not theh until Mondee
```

Similarly, in (10) below, the preference for progressivity and – this time – syntactic completion is again at issue as M withholds from launching his turn until C's turn is possibly complete:

```
(10)  (Goodwin, AD:11)
1  C     Keegan used to race uhruh- uhr it was uh:m (0.4)
2        used to run uh::m (3.4) oh::: sh::it. (0.3) uh::m,
3        (0.4) Fisher's ca:r.
4  M→    Three e[n a [quarter?
```

It is evident from exemplars such as the following that speakers prepare to start up at the hearable end of a prior turn; in (11) below, Ann prepares to speak as Jessie comes to a possible completion point:

```
(11)  (Jefferson, 1984b:24; Rahman:B: (13):2:R)
1  Jessie  ..cuz she's nevuh been cah[mpin[g.]
2  Ann                              [.hhh[I ]t's smashing...
```

In the following, moreover, Lottie's syntactically and prosodically complete turn (ll. 1–2) provide for Emma to respond in line 3; upon Emma's response, Lottie's turn, latched as it is to Emma's, starts up at exactly the point at which Emma's is possibly complete:

```
(12)  (Jefferson, 1984b:16; NB:IV:4:R:19:R)
1  Lottie  Ah wouldn'ev'n le-e- tell Bud I:'d jis go ahead'n
2          have the party.
3  Emma    .t Yah,=
4  Lottie  =Tuh hell with im.
```

Comparison across languages reveals how different syntactic resources are thus mobilised in the service of turn-taking. In the following fragment, we see two speakers of Japanese, a predicate-final language, finely tuning mutual entry into each other's turn spaces so that the overlaps occur precisely as the utterance final elements start to be produced, or shortly thereafter:

```
(13)  (Tanaka, 2000:20)
1  W:  'N: soo[ne
       yeah so[FP
       'Yeah isn't it?'
2  G         [Sore wa aru  deshoo[: ne
             [that TOP exist COP   [ FP
             ['That's quite plausible, isn't it'
3  W                             [Soo na n de[shoo ne
                                 [so COP N C[OP  FP
                                 ['That's probably right, isn't it?'
4  G                                         [ 'N...
                                             [yeah...
                                             ['Yeah...'
```

As Tanaka notes:

> Here, the recognition of utterance-final elements results in an exquisite chaining of consecutive turns, overlapping the next turn only at utterance-final elements. These fragments demonstrate the potential utility of utterance-final elements for turn-taking by unequivocally signaling possible TRPs.   (2000:20)

Prosodic and phonetic features of completion

The turn-taking paper itself claims syntax to be the primary determinant of possible completion (1974:721) with prosody as 'also very important' but not as central (no systematic attention is, however, given to prosody); Schegloff further-more proposes that, with respect to completion and – to paraphrase – 'grammar nominates and prosody seconds' (1998b:237). The study by Ford and Thompson (1996) of interactional units in conversational English – the first to examine closely the turn-taking paper's claims from a grammatical perspective – does not point to such a hierarchy, however, observing that, alongside the preference for progressivity, projectability involves a convergence of the grammatical constraints of syntax, the prosody and – with the action being performed by the turn – the pragmatics of the turn-in-progress. Work on conversational German by Selting (2000) suggests that transition relevance is both produced and oriented to holistically: she suggests that there is no single factor projecting completion, and although the projectability of syntactic and prosodic completion are associated, these two elements are occasion-ally decoupled. Tanaka's (2004) study of prosody in Japanese, focusing on turns unmarked by the final particles and copulas usually indicating transition relevance, suggests that a wide range of phonetic resources are mobilised to compensate for the limited capacity for syntactic projection. Furthermore, experimental data from a corpus of Dutch by Bögels and Torreira (2015) appear to underwrite the importance of intonational phrase boundaries as a means by which speakers project turn ends.

With respect to English, it is clear that turn-final intonation patterns are varied and not limited to the standardly portrayed formats of fall-to-low and rise-to-high (Szczepek Reed, 2004).[4] However, a TCU that does not come to terminal intonation either up or down may be designed to project more to come. Ford and Thompson (1996) examine the following turn:

(14) (Ford and Thompson, 1996:148; transcription as in original, with syntactic comple-
      tion points marked by a slash)
1 V   She didn't know/ what was going on/ about why they didn't
2   change the knee/.

The slash after the words 'going on' marks a point of syntactic but not prosodic completion. The fundamental frequency on these two words is relatively level, varying between only 203 and 194 Hertz. However, on the words 'the knee' at the end of the intonation unit, a point of prosodic completion, the fundamental frequency goes from 195 to 218, then down to 178. Ford and Thompson state that: 'these data are indicative of the type of difference that is conveyed by syntactic completion in cases where it is or is not accompanied by intonational completion' (1996:148).

Here is a similar instance from the turn by a doctor (D) who has been phoned by a woman caller (C) on behalf of her daughter, who has been sick several times in the night:[5]

---

[4] A number of studies examine prosodic features in signalling TRPs in particular varieties of British English. These include Wells and Peppé (1996) who examine, amongst other features, pitch, tempo, loudness and duration in Ulster English, comparing these with findings from Local et al. (1985) for London Jamaican English and Local et al. (1986) for Tyneside English.

[5] An extended extract is presented in Chapter 6, extract (8).

```
(15)  (DEC, 1:1:1)
6    D     ... I mean: it- it sounds a little bit (jis')
7    →     like'a touch a'gastroenteritis posh word really for
8    →     diarrhea and v(h)omiting i(h)sn't i(h)t? [.hh You don't really=
9    C →                                           [Yes,
10   D     =need me tuh- .hh ta tell ya that but u::m I mean what we
11         normally do: is if you can just (.) encourage >jus'< (.) fluids.
12         (.) And not bother abou:t [(.) uh:m solids,
```

The doctor's first turn is potentially syntactically complete at 'gastroenteritis'
(l. 7); however, he does not come to a prosodic completion but holds the
intonation level as he delivers, by means of an elliptical clause, an assessment
('posh word for diarrhea and v(h)omiting i(h)sn't i(h)t?'), and then comes to a
completion on the production of the tag question on rising intonation. It is only at
that point that the caller responds at line 9.

See also, for example, Bee's response in line 3 following Ava's question:

```
(16)  (Schegloff, 1996a:61)
1    B   =[Mnuh,)]
2    A   =[Oh my  ] mother wannduh know how's yer grandmother.
3    B   .hhh Uh::, (0.3) I don'know I guess she's aw- she's awright she
4        went to thee uh:: hhospital again tihda:y,
5        A Mm-hm?
```

Bee's turn in line 3, prefaced by 'Uh' and a pause, starts 'I don'know': while
this unit is syntactically possibly complete, the prosody is held level into the
next TCU; that, alongside the stress on 'I', suggests that the whole is what
Schegloff calls 'a kind of prefatory epistemic disclaimer' (1996a:62) to what is
projected next, rather than a disavowal of an answer (which, produced as an
independent unit, it might have been). And again at the next TCU after that
('she's awright'), while syntactically the turn is possibly complete ('she went to
thee uh:: hhospital today'), the prosody is nevertheless kept non-terminal and
continuative, indicating yet more to come. In the above exemplar, Bee's turn
does not in fact end with terminal, but continuative prosody; Ava produces
her continuer at the end of 'tihda:y'. What appears in this context to signal
upcoming transition relevance is the prosodic pitch peak – a phonetically
prominent major accent – in 'da:y'. Schegloff notes such pitch peaks as possible
harbingers of speaker transition, at a point in the turn he calls 'pre-possible
completion' (1996a:86). This is supported by Wells and MacFarlane (1998)
who suggest that this may be enough for participants to monitor a stretch of talk
for upcoming potential turn transition. Szczepek Reed goes further in suggesting that 'the precise pitch movement at the end of a turn may not be responsible
for whether participants treat a turn as complete or incomplete (2004:114)
(although see Fox, 2001, for a more equivocal view). So in (17) below,
Shirley can be heard preparing to speak as Geri produces a pitch peak and
sound stretch on the final word of her turn:

(17) (Frankel:TC:I:1:13)
```
1  Geri  Wul maybe we'av six. But we don't have[fi: [ve.
2  Shir                                      [.hh[Whenju get
3        out.
```

It is clear, then, that research focusing on prosody to the neglect of other phonetic parameters such as articulation, phonation and duration misses the extent to which 'the multiplicity of phonetic events . . . either jointly or in assorted bundles' (Local et al., 1986) may be involved in turn projection. So, for example, features implicated in end-of-turn marking may include diminuendo (Nolan, 2006; Local and Walker, 2010) and a slowing of speech rate (Local et al., 1986).

We have already seen how one feature, the production of audible outbreaths (see Chapter 2), may figure in projecting transition relevance. However, there is also striking evidence that articulatory features of the lexico-syntax of the talk are designed with reference to turn and TCU position. Local et al. (1986), for example, examining Tyneside English, argue that centralisation of vowels, combined with particular duration characteristics over the last metrical foot of turns, is implicated in unproblematic turn transition. In another articulatory study, Local and Walker examine the interactional realisations of the word-final English voiceless plosives /t/, /k/ and /p/ at points of possible syntactic completion; when projecting further talk they are found to display quite distinct characteristics from when they signal the possible end of the turn, showing that transition to another speaker is relevant (2012:269). So in the exchange below, Lesley comes to a point of possible syntactic completion in her turn at 'went' (l. 9, marked in bold for ease of identification) but continues the turn:

(18) (Local and Walker, 2012:262)
```
9   Les:  ↑Oh w'l I ↑am glad you ↓went cuz ↑very few ↓people'n this
10        ↓part'v the world ↑go to Ken[:t:, .h[h
11  Hal:                              [No.    [Eh-
```

Of the articulatory characteristics of *went*, Local and Walker note that it 'does not have canonical voiceless apical closure at its end but voiced velar nasality. This velar articulation is held as voicing drops off for the voiceless velar plosive which begins the following word ("cause")' (2012:261); see Figure 4.2 (note the F2/F3 velar 'pinch' in the spectrogram towards the end of the vowel (around 0.14 s onwards)).

Moreover, the end of the word 'flat' in extract (19) below is, once again, a point at which the turn is possibly syntactically complete, although Lesley has not, in fact, completed her turn:

(19) (Local and Walker, 2012:265)
```
9   Les:  An' [everybody tells us the trees are all flat still.
10  Hal:      [No.
```

Local and Walker observe that 'the apical closure for the voiceless plosive at the end of "flat" is unaspirated and released directly into apical friction for the beginning of "still"' (p. 264) (see Figure 4.3).

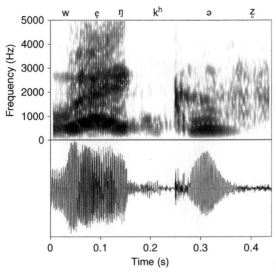

Figure 4.2 *Turn-medial anticipating token: 'went cuz', extract (18), l. 9 (Local and Walker, 2012:262)*

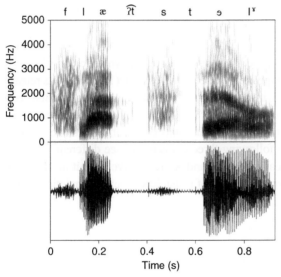

Figure 4.3 *Turn-medial token showing close proximity: 'flat still', extract (19), l. 9 (Local and Walker, 2012:265)*

Additionally, in the following extract, the final consonant of 'back' is produced as a short, lax voiceless velar fricative which is immediately followed by voicing for the first, somewhat close and front, vowel of 'again':

(20)   (Local and Walker, 2012:266)
1   Hal: so I <u>think</u> one d<u>a</u>y we should g<u>o</u> **back** again.

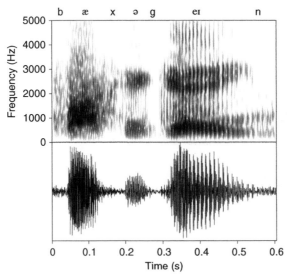

Figure 4.4 *Turn-medial reduction of word-final consonant: 'back again', extract (20) (Local and Walker, 2012:268)*

It is clear, then, that the articulatory anticipation at the end of the point of possible syntactic completion is used by the speaker as a resource to project more talk (see Figure 4.4).

So when a final voiceless plosive at a point of possible syntactic completion is followed by talk from the same speaker, we see its deletion in (18) 'went', its release without aspiration into a following sound in (19) 'flat', and its production as a fricative in (20) 'back'. By contrast, Local and Walker find that turn transition follows all final voiceless plosives released, at points of possible syntactic completion, with aspiration. So in the following three extracts, we see different voiceless plosives produced by each speaker (/t/, /k/ and /p/ respectively), but all three are released with aspiration and occur at points of possible syntactic completion which engender turn transition:

```
(21)  (Local and Walker, 2012:270)
19  Les:  Alright.
20  Hal:  ((away)) It's n<u>o</u>t dancing this Saturdee <u>is</u> it.

(22)  (Local and Walker, 2012:270)
14  Hal:  The (.) ↑wh<u>o</u>le point is Lesl' you bring your (.) <u>ow:n</u>
15        (0.3) c<u>o</u>ffee or your <u>own</u> dri:nk,
16  Les:  Yes <u>an</u>' and all ↓sh<u>a</u>re it:.

(23)  (Local and Walker, 2012:270)
1  Hal:  An' the <u>v</u>illage hall which is extremely nice is a-at th'
2        top. With[extra p<u>a</u>r:]k<u>i</u>ng?
3  Les:           [<u>O</u>h r<u>i</u>ght.  ]
```

Furthermore, Local and Kelly (1986) and Local and Walker (2005) show that different kinds of articulatory and laryngeal characteristics (e.g. glottal closure and hold versus its absence) in combination with particular lexical items in English mark that a speaker has finished talking or projects that there is more to come.

Work on Finnish by Ogden (2004) focuses on a particular form of phonation in turn transition: non-modal voice quality (NMVQ),[6] and in particular, creak, breathiness, whisper and voicelessness. Ogden finds that transition relevance in Finnish is signalled in most turns at talk (70% in his data) at least in part by a change of voice quality from modal to non-modal, and participants display an orientation to this change, as in the following extract:

(24) (Odgen, 2004:41–2)
(C=Caller; P=Radio Phone-in Presenter; P2=Presenter 2. C has requested some music sung by a Bulgarian group with a French name, '*Mystère des voix bulgares*'. The pronunciation of French and Bulgarian names has been an issue throughout the call, and neither C nor P is confident about how to pronounce them. Phonation is marked in curly brackets at appropriate points above the turn thus: {creak (C), breathiness (B), whisper (W), voicelessness (H)}.)

```
1   C                                        {B-} {H-----}
        [ja minkä  niminen]  kappale nyt  tul{ee} {sitten}hh
        and what-GEN name-ADJ piece   now come-3SG then
        and what's the name of the piece that's coming now then
2       (1.4)
3   P   hh pitääkö  mun       todellakin yr[ittää [(*  *) [tama]
        must-QCLI   1SG-GEN  really-CLI  try-1INF          this
        do I really have to try (and say) this
4   P2                                   [he    [he he [he ] hehe]
5   C                                           [no j- [j- ] .hh ]
6       £↑o↓le ↑hy↓vä£
        please
        go ahead
7   P                             {C}
    →   starobulgarski hronik{i}
        Name Name   Name
        (Bulgarian name of the track)
8   C          {C}{H------}
        kiit{o}{ks[ia ] }
        thank you
9   P                       {C---}
                    {ora]t{orio}
                    Name
        (name continued)
```

---

[6] Modal phonation is frequently considered the 'normal' mode of phonation, whereby 'the vocal folds vibrate periodically along their full length due to pressure below the glottis which is higher than the pressure above the glottis... [it] involves only moderate tension across the vocal folds ... Non-modal voice qualities ... have different degrees of vibration, involving different degrees of tension across the vocal folds, and differences in which part of the vocal folds vibrate' (Ogden, 2004:30).

```
10        (0.3)
11   C    .hjoo
          PRT
          right
```

C's information request at line 1 comes to a syntactic and pragmatic completion with a stretch of breathy voice (in the second syllable of 'tulee') followed by voicelessness and exhalation-n. The subsequent delay in responding by P, followed by P's self-deprecating display of reluctance to pronounce the name, indicate that the request cannot be granted. P's turn at line 3 is in overlap with laughter from P2 and the attempted incoming turn from C, which obscure the voice quality. At line 6, C's response to P uses stylised intonation, which, Ogden notes, may be used to handle matters intended to be treated as routine; the implication, then, is that P's implicit request to be let off the hook with respect to having to pronounce the name is rejected. In line 7, P produces the name, which is Bulgarian. Since there are no Finnish words in the turn, there is no syntactic or lexical information from which transition relevance is projectable. As Ogden notes:

> the only way in which C can orient to a TRP here is phonetically. The turn is as close as naturally-occurring talk can get to the kinds of nonsense words commonly used in experimental settings to eliminate unwanted effects of syntax or lexis. P uses creak in the last syllable of his turn at l. 7; and C displays his understanding that this signals a TRP by coming in at l. 8 and thanking P for having granted the request.   (2004:42)

The TRP in the turn at line 8 is marked by creak, and then voicelessness, in the course of which P – orienting to the indicators of transition relevance – makes an addition to his prior turn. P's production of 'oratorio' contains both a modally voiced portion and a creaky-voiced portion. Ogden notes that in other cases where a speaker continues a turn which had earlier been marked as transition-relevant, they do so with NMVQ throughout, such turn increments being designed to extend the transition space. This turn, in contrast, displays in its phonetic design that it is an addition to a prior turn rather than an extension of the transition space.

All in all, the complex of factors in the projection of turn completion is suggested in Szczepek-Reed's comment on prosody in her corpus of American English speech: 'In the case of telephone openings and closings it seems safe to conclude that the activity in which the participants are involved is so clearly structured that intonation does not need to indicate potential turn transition, but can be used for other purposes. However, in less routinized sequences... such a regulating structure is less obvious' (2004:113).

Pragmatic markers of completion

Converging with syntactic and prosodic markers of possible comple-tion, pragmatic completion relates to the completion of the action being con-ducted through the turn. So in the excerpt below, it is only on the pragmatic completion of an answer to a question in line 28 that a recipient gives her receipt:

(25) (Sidnell, 2013:97)
```
22   Deb            [s]o don't you have all your
23                  family coming today?
24   Dick    Well: they're coming around two and I .hhh left
25                  messages with Brian an:d mydad to(uh) see if
26                  they wanted to come but=uh
27                  (0.2)
28        →   .hh that's all I could do was leave messages.
29   Deb     owh
```

In response to Deb's question in lines 22–3, Dick projects an extended turn beyond one TCU. The initial 'Well' projects an unstraightforward answer (Lerner and Schegloff, 2009) of more than one TCU (Heritage, 2014), and, while the end of 'coming around two' (l. 24) might indicate a possible grammatical completion, the prosody does not indicate completion and the turn continues. The inbreath ('.hhh', l. 24) and the dysfluent 'uh' and pause (ll. 26–7) are then produced at junctures where the turn is hearably grammatically incomplete and, as such, what Schegloff calls points of 'maximum grammatical control' (1996a: 93) interdicting a possible incoming turn. At the end of 'leave messages' (l. 28), the turn is hearably syntactically and prosodically complete – and, in completing the response to the first pair part, it also constitutes a pragmatic completion, and Deb's response is duly forthcoming at that point (l. 29).

The exemplar above is a relatively straightforward exemplar of pragmatic completion. In their operationalisation of the notion of pragmatic completion, Ford and Thompson suggest that there are both 'local' and 'global' forms of completion. Local completion points are points at which the speaker is projecting more talk, but where the recipient might reasonably take a minimal turn (a so-called 'quasi-turn': Schegloff, 1997b:33), which is not turn-competitive. The following shows two exemplars of such local completion. At the end of lines 1 and 3, K has clearly not yet come to the point of his telling, but his preliminary points of completion are places where C is prosodically offered the opportunity to indicate that she is following by means of so-called try-marked, upward intoned, prosody (Sacks and Schegloff, 1979):

(26) (Ford and Thompson, 1996:151)
       (Points of syntactic completion marked by a slash; intonational completion marked
       either with period or question mark, and pragmatic completion points marked thus (>).)
```
1   K   It was like the other day/ uh.
2       (0.2)
3   K   Vera (.) was talking/on the phone/to her mom/?>
4   C   Mhm/.>
5   K   And uh she got off the pho:ne/ and she was
6       incredibly upset/?>
7   C   Mm hm/.>
```

In the following, however, at none of the points of pragmatic completion is more talk projected by the current speaker:

(27) (Ford and Thompson, 1996:151)

```
1  V   And he said we'll probably have to put an artificial knee in/
2      in five years/.>
3      (0.2)
4  V   For my Dad/.>
```

Ford and Thompson note that pragmatic completion is, then, a combination of intonation and conversational action sequencing, and emerges from the on-going monitoring of talk for possibly complete conversational actions.

Further to this, Selting (2000), focusing on an ambiguity in the turn-taking paper, has shown that TCUs may not necessarily end in TRPs. In the following German exemplar, Selting shows that an extended project beyond an initial TCU is being launched by the speaker's reference to a decision she has to make, and subsequently by the use of an 'entweder/oder' (either/or) construction. Ida is discussing her commute to work:

(28) (Selting, 2000:506)

(Global pitch higher than in surrounding units is denoted by F(\ \ ) with F=falling, R=rising, M=Mid. Unaccented local pitch movements: \=falling to mid; _=falling to low, /= rising to mid; /=rising to high; – = level . Prosodic parameters: <all>=allegro, fast; <f>=forte, loud.)

```
820   Ida   das kAm auch- (.) ich  mUßte mich entSCHEIDEN.
                (\)-              F(\            \_   )
            that was because   I   had to make a decision
821         entweder (0.7) zuHAUse wohn und fürn AUto arbeiten, (.)
                          M(/                    /          )
            either     live at home and work for a car
822         oder HIER wohn und für ne WOHnung arbeit[n.
                F(\              \_              )
            or   live here and work for a flat
823   Nat                                      [mhm,
                                                \/
            (1)
824   Ida   un da hab ich mich LIEber für das AUto entscheiden;
                              M(/              \         )
                <all                                    all>
            and then I decided in favour of the car
```

Here, Ida introduces the fact that she had to make a decision (l. 820) which projects the characterisation of the nature of the decision, and then elaborates on this by formulating the alternatives; by providing an *entweder* (either) component, she projects an *oder* (or) one. Projection is thus achieved by using particular lexical expressions. Selting concludes that

> Single-clause syntax only has scope for single TCUs, but prosody reaches beyond the current TCU and can be used to project a TCU to follow. Compound-clause syntactic, lexico-semantic, pragmatic, and activity-type-specific schemata can be used to project larger turns. After a TRP at the

possible completion of a turn, the turn may end; or it may still be continued
by adding new material in a prosodically and syntactically integrated or
exposed way.   (2000: 512)

4.2.2   The turn-allocational component

If the turn-constructional component relates to *when* a next speaker
should speak, the turn-allocational component relates to *who* should speak next.
There are two options for determining how a next turn will be allocated: current
speaker selects next speaker; and next speaker self-selects. We now examine
these in turn.

Current speaker selects next speaker

This may be done by a variety of devices; so, for example, by the first
part of an adjacency pair (see Chapter 3) in conjunction with address by means of
gaze (noted originally by Kendon, 1967) or address term; in the following, as a
family are settling down to an evening meal, Mom launches a request that is
initially formatted as a general address, but which is then repaired just before its
possible completion to be directed at a particular recipient – her son, Wesley, who
responds as she comes to complete her request:

```
(29)  (Virginia: 1)
1   Mom   (C'n) we have the blessi-ih-buh-Wesley would you ask the
2         blessi[ng¿ please¿
3   Wes        [Ahright
```

Similarly, a next-turn repair initiator (see Chapter 7) selects the prior speaker as
next (see also l. 2, extract (5)):

```
(30)  (Sacks et al., 1974:702)
1   Anna   Was last night the first time you met Missiz Kelly?
2          (1)
3   Bea→   Met whom?
4   Anna   Missiz Kelly.
5   Bea    Yes.
```

One possibility is that the speaker is explicitly chosen by name, as in extract (18). [7]
Similarly, in the following, Mary selects by name the guest, David, among a number
of family members standing in the kitchen:

---

[7] Both adjacency pair operation and selection by name converge in the action of summonsing by use
of a term of address in the following example (Lerner, 2003:188):

```
1   Nancy     Michael
2             (0.4)
3   Nancy     I thought you were going to church tomorrow?
4             (1.3)
5   Michael   I'll go Wednesday night
```

(31) (Clift, T22:47)
```
1  M→  if ↑you're very hungry David there's: s- fru:it around to e:at
2       (0.4) there are peaches and apples: (0.2) oranges and grapes-
3       whe- ↑where are these: (.) cherries around somewhere
4  D    °>oh< cherries- it's (.) (over here aren't they)°
```

While 'if you're very hungry' does not select from a number of possible recipients, the post-positioned address term does – and the selected recipient here responds at line 4.[8] Yet another possibility rests in the design of the turn. In the following, lexical choices contribute to speaker selection, with 'never' and 'ever' selecting different recipients:

(32) (Sacks et al., 1974:703, fn. 13, (b))
```
1  Sy:     See Death 'v a Salesman las' night?
2  Jim:    No.
3          ((pause))
4  Sy: →   Never see(h)n it?
5  Jim:→   No.
6  Sy: →   Ever seen it?
7  Jay:→   Yes.
```

As we saw in Chapter 3, eye gaze is a significant resource in speaker selection when participants are co-present. In his pioneering study of the interactive construction of a sentence in conversation, Goodwin (1979, 1981) charts how the gaze of the speaker, John, is directed to three different recipients over three sections of his utterance in the course of its production, so as to be gazing at a recipient for whom that part of the utterance is news. In the following, the line above the utterance indicates John's simultaneous gaze at a particular other, with the left bracket marking where the gaze meets that recipient. Dots mark gaze towards and commas mark gaze away from a recipient. It is clear from this that the recipient of John's gaze for the last portion of his utterance (the 'actually' that turns his report into an informing (see Clift, 2001)) is Ann – and it is she who speaks on the possible completion of John's utterance:

See also Clayman (2010, 2012, 2013) on other uses of address terms; we return to address terms in Chapter 6.

[8] Note, however, that some post-positioned address terms do more than strictly select next speaker. Here in line 1 is an instance:

(RC:22)
(Mary has handed David, her guest, a drink which he is trying for the first time)
```
1  M→   Don't drink it if you don't like it ↓David=
2  D→   =↑No: I do, it's lovely actually
3        (0.2)
4  D    [(-)
5  M    [You really need a zest but we haven't >got any lemons.<
```

Here, the recipient's name is appended to the injunction, acting to reassure him that he is not obliged to finish a drink with which he is not familiar; Lerner notes that this usage can be used 'as a way to underscore personal concern for a problem' (2003:185). Note that, even without the term of address, the injunction on its own would have selected David as the recipient.

(33)   (Goodwin, 1979)
       (John and his wife Beth are hosting Don and his wife Ann)

```
1   John    . . , , . . . . .  [Don,,          [Don_____
            I gave, I gave u[p smoking ci [garettes::.=
2   Don     Yea:h,
3   John    . . . [Beth               . . . [Ann_____
            1-uh: [one-one week ago t'da:[y. acshilly
4   Ann→    Rilly? En y'quit fer good?
```

In work explicitly developing the turn-taking paper's proposals regarding turn allocation, Lerner (2003) examines the role of both gaze and terms of address in speaker selection. He finds that gaze can be an explicit form of address (p. 179), as above, providing that both addressed and non-addressed participants perceive the speaker's gaze.[9] Indeed, in Stivers et al.'s (2010) cross-linguistic study of questioning and answering across ten languages, gaze appears to be the most robust resource for next-speaker selection in Japanese, with 87 per cent (N=275) of questions accompanied by speaker gaze: the highest proportion across all the languages studied (Hayashi, 2010).

The following extract shows both how gaze can be used to select a next speaker, and also how the speakers may be treated as collectivities, as co-incumbents of a particular category (in this case, that of parents) – hence, the turn-taking paper's reference to 'parties' rather than individuals as such.[10] So in (34) below, Jane is rebuking her nineteen-year-old daughter Emily, sitting on her lap, for her dissolute behaviour. At lines 22–6 she launches a strong complaining assessment, upon which Simon, Emily's father, produces an agreeing 'Yeah' (l. 26). At line 28 Jane produces a hearably terminal assessment (Goodwin and Goodwin, 1987:21) that, despite its hearably concessive beginning, reiterates her position, and, with no indication of uptake from Emily, she thereafter appends the response-mobilising 'Alright?'. In response to this pursuit, Emily, seated on her mother's lap, does not address Jane, but instead gazes at her father as she produces 'Why' (l. 35):

(34)   (Clift, Family I)
       (J=Jane (mother); S=Simon (father); E=Emily)

```
16   Jan:   [and I don't know why:: love you think you can just go out all
17   Jan:   thuh ti:me pay
18          ((E wipes eyes with left hand))
19          [get taxis all thuh time and not pay (.) fer your living.
20   Em:    [((sniff))
21          ((S looks over to J then begins to stand up))
22   Jan:   I am getting a little bit fed up with having to get up n' go
```

---

[9] However, 'one can discern at least a partial ordering among these practices when they are used concurrently, since gaze direction, if inconsistent with other forms of addressing, will ordinarily give way to them. (In other words, it is possible to gaze at one participant while addressing another participant through other means.)' (Lerner, 2003:196).

[10] That being said, Stivers (2015) proposes that the turn-taking system reveals an overwhelming bias towards dyadic over multiparty interaction, and that it is essentially a system built for two, adapted to accommodate more, rather than the other way around.

```
23          t' work, clean the house, do all the washing, while Emily goes
24          out all thuh time or sleeps
25          (0.2)
26   Si:    Yeah.
27          ((E slight shake of head - J is looking straight ahead))
28   Jan:   I love you (.) but I am getting fed up with it.
29          ((J is gazing downwards but raises gaze towards E after 'it'
30          with eyebrow flash))
31          (0.2)
32   Si:    hhh.
33   Jan:   Alright?
34          (0.4)
35   Em:→   Why. ((gazing at Simon))
36   Si:    Be[cause you're supposed to contribute you're nineteen=
37   Jan:     [hehhh. ((J produces a burst of laughter, looks towards S on
38          'supposed'. S is standing up))
39   Si:    =years old you're a young woman you've got a jo:b, .hhh n' it is
40          a [bit like uh hotel that you never pay thuh bill on isn't it¿
```

In addressing Simon with her gaze, Emily is treating Simon and Jane as a collectivity – and indeed it is Simon who responds with an account directed to underwriting Jane's previously expressed stance.

In addition to gaze behaviour, there are also tacit forms of addressing – practices used on singular occasions according to the local context. So, for example, as Lerner (2003) notes, known-in-common circumstances can restrict who is eligible to respond to a single participant. In the following, Curt solicits a first-hand account of 'the races' (l. 1) which works tacitly to select, from three possible recipients, the only person who was present – Mike – to speak next:

```
(35)  (Lerner, 2003:191; Goodwin, AD)
1    Curt    Wul how wz the races las'night.
2     →      (0.8) (Mike nods head twice)
3    Curt    Who w'n [th'feature.]
4    Mike→           [A l w o n, ]
5            (0.3)
6    Curt    [(Who)]=
7    Mike    [ A l.]=
8    Curt    =Al did?
```

We shall see further, in Chapter 6, how the issue of who knows what may figure, as it does here, in speaker selection.

Japanese provides another speaker-selection resource in the form of alternate registers, indicating social proximity or distance towards the recipient: the plain register (jootai) to address family and friends, and the polite register (keetai or desu/masu-style), reserved for social superiors or non-intimates (Hayashi, 2010). In the following extract, the host wife, Y, consistently uses the plain register when addressing her husband, K, and equally consistently uses the polite register when addressing S and M, her guests. At line 5 in the following extract, Y's question is in the polite register as indicated by the polite form of the copula *desu*:

(36) (Hayashi, 2010:2698)
       (Y and K are host wife and husband; S and M guest wife and husband.)

```
1  M:   kaeri wa tsuitsui::  (0.8) [aruichau na::.
        return TP unthinkingly        walk:AUX FP
        ((I)) walk ((home from the train station)) without thinking
        much about it
2  K:                              [so kka::.
                                    so Q
                                    I see::.
3  S:   narechau            to ne.
        get.used.to:AUX     if FP
        ((You do it)) once ((you)) get used to ((it)).
4  M:   tte yuu ka an moo nareru       to, (.)
        QT say Q um EMP get.used.to    if
        I mean, um, once ((you)) get used to it, (.)
5  Y:→  kajiritsuite ii   desu ka: hhh .hh hhh
        have.a.bite okay CP   Q
        Is it okay if (I)) have a big bite ((of this cake))? hhh .hh hhh
6  S:   haa=
        Yes.
7  M:   =doozo (doozo).
        Please go ahead.
```

As Hayashi (p. 2698) notes, Y's question in line 5 is not accompanied by an address term or gaze – she is looking down at a piece of cake in front of her that she is eating when producing the question. Nor does the question deal with a matter that falls within any particular recipient's domain of expertise or territory of knowledge. The question is also initiated interruptively and so not prompted by anything that was said previously, so it cannot be the case here that the questioner selects as next speaker the speaker of a prior turn by virtue of the fact that the question is a response to that prior turn. The major resource for next-speaker selection in this case thus appears to be the use of the polite register, which selects the guest couple (both M and S) as the next speaking party rather than her husband (K). Indeed, both S and M respond in the subsequent turns.

Next speaker self-selects

This is the case in all the three turns in the following:

(37) (Sacks et al., 1974:703, fn. 13, (c))

```
Jim:→  Any a' you guys read that story about Walter Mitty?
Ken:→  I did,
Rog:→  Mm hmm
```

Here, Jim's question does not select any particular party to speak next, but Ken self-selects, as subsequently does Roger.

With respect to self-selection, the turn-taking rules, as we shall see, state that the first speaker gains rights to the next turn, making promptness in the launch of an incoming turn a priority. The two basic requirements here are that a prospective next speaker should be able to recognise when a current speaker is coming to the end of a turn (so-called pre-possible completion), and that a prospective next speaker is able to lay claim to speaking rights to a next (at the pre-beginning of a next turn). We now examine these in turn.

(a) Pre-possible completion

In work exploring turn construction, Schegloff (1996a) identifies 'pre-possible completion' in a current TCU as a strategic place in the organisation of the turn, and visibly implicated in the understanding of self-selection in next-speaker allocation. We have already examined, in section 4.2.1 on turn construction, some linguistic means by which a next speaker can recognise that a current speaker may be projecting the end of a turn. Here we focus both on what current speakers may do in the course of their turn, such that a next speaker may recognise a place to come in, with an examination of collaboration in word searches, and anticipatory completions, and onwhat potential next speakers do in laying claim to a turn.

There are occasions, first noted in Sacks (1992a), on which a speaker displays some trouble in retrieving a word (such as a name) or phrase, so interrupting the onward progression of the turn-in-progress towards its completion. Both Lerner (1992, 1993, 1996) and Goodwin and Goodwin (1986) have identified occasions on which the word search, as such activities are generically called, may not be a solitary undertaking,[11] but, in the words of Goodwin, 'becomes formulated as a social activity, one that parties other than the speaker can actively participate in' (1987:118) (see Chapter 6 for discussion of an exchange where a search becomes an opportunity to display the partitioning of two speakers as a couple).[12] So, for

---

[11] On some occasions charted by Goodwin (1987), the speaker may display that they will undertake a search themselves for the elusive item. In the following, note the withdrawal of eye gaze and the assumption of a particular facial expression as the speaker embarks upon a search for a name:

(Goodwin, 1987:118; G.50:8:30)

```
1        C B't a-another one theh wentuh school
         Gaze withdrawn from recipient
2        with me [wa:s a girl na:med uh, (0.7)
                 [_____
         Thinking face
```

```
3        W't th'hell wz'er name]. = Karen. Right.
4        Karen. er name wz Karen something or other.
```
[12] I exclude from the main discussion here exemplars such as the extract below, discussed in detail by Goodwin and Goodwin, in which A explicitly invites collaboration in line 1, achieving it in line 6:

example, in the following, the sound stretch on the last word in line 1 indicates the first speaker displaying some trouble in retrieving a phrase, upon which the second speaker supplies a candidate completion:

```
(38)  (Lerner, 1996:262; Adato:II)
1  Jay  Well, I- I pretty much had in mi:nd the:::,
2  G→   the human race.
```

Goodwin and Goodwin (1986) identify a number of ways in which eye gaze and facial expression are mobilised to enlist, or alternatively, resist, coparticipants' collaboration in word searches (we shall see more instances of this in Chapter 7, on repair, and specifically, self-initiated other-repair). So, even when not explicitly inviting collaboration, as in (39) below, the original speaker may endorse another's intervention, here try-marked at line 2:[13]

```
(39)  (Goodwin and Goodwin, 1986:61; G.99:S:20)
                          withdraws  lowers  purses   slackens
                          eyes       lids    lips     lips
1  A  Because apparently heroin was um, (--------+) uh, (-------+--)
2  B→ Used for opiate?
3  A  Yeah.
```

```
(Goodwin and Goodwin, 1986; G.50:4:00)
1      A       °What was th'name'v the [place tch!
2      B                               [Ho: yeaum.
3      A       I can't thi[nk.
4      B                  [Sir: uh no.
5      A       I know it w[as-
6      B                  [Steak'n A:le.
7              (0.2)
8      A→      Yeah r:right.
9      B       In Mount Pleasant.
10     A       r:Right. (0.2) I knew it wz someplace out on Fifty One.=But
11             anyway thet he had a rilly good article on that.
```

[13] An example from French suggests the extent to which an incoming speaker can phonologically fit a completing unit to a preliminary one; in line 1 below, upon a first speaker hearably launching a word search for 'the:::', the second provides the candidate solution ('matches'). In the French, while the first speaker pronounces 'le:::s' in its generic articulation as a definite article ([le]), the second speaker, taking up the turn, prefaces 'allumettes' (matches) with what would be the grammatically correct sound at the end of that plural article, in a clear case of phonological juncture ([lezalu:mɛt]). (My thanks to Jacques Durand for this example.) An English example would be a completion such as 'May I have a:::' – 'Napple?'

```
(JD:FN)
1      A       Est-ce que je peux avoir le:::s
               May I have the:::
2      B→      zallumettes?
               matches?
```

```
4  B     Y[eah.
5  A      [(for opium.)
```

... or indeed resist acknowledging the intervention:

```
(40)  (Goodwin and Goodwin, 1986:61)
1  A    Her dress was white,
2       (0.7)
3  B→   Eye[let.
4  A→       [Uh Eyelet. (0.8) Embroidered eyelet.
```

Word searches show how one speaker may initiate a turn and then mandate another to supply an item that completes it. However, there are occasions on which a speaker initiating a turn does not explicitly elicit a completion, but this is in fact what happens, due to the projectability of a particular element of grammatical structure. So in the following, Ed launches an idiomatic expression, 'Out in the back'v ...' which Lesley completes – as it happens, simultaneously with Ed himself:

```
(41)  (H:10:88-1-9)
Ed:     And eh::: (0.3) also teaching a chap over at uh:m (0.3)
        .p Lovin::gton. Whi[ch is (.) o]ut in the back'v
Les:                       [ O  h  :  .  ]
Les:→   .hhh [beyond.
Ed: →        [beyo:nd.
```

Idioms such as these provide highly projectable structures facilitating collaboration. Lerner (1991, 1996, 2002, 2004) has documented a number of other cases involving TCUs with two-part structures,[14] the first part initiated by one speaker and the second completed by another. The clear projectability of the preliminary component makes it possible for another speaker to complete the turn. So, for example, *if–then* and *when–then* constructions consist of a preliminary component – the *if* or *when* clause – after the production of which, there is a clearly a projectable place for the final component to be produced:

```
(42)  (Lerner, 1991:445)
1  R    if you bring it intuh them
2  C→   ih don't cost yuh nothing
```

```
(43)  (Lerner, 2004: 240)
1  Marty   Now most machines don't record that slow. So I'd
2          wanna- when I make a tape,
3  Josh→   be able tuh speed it up.
4  Marty   Yeah.
```

Other contexts where such 'anticipatory completions' are facilitated include quotations, where the launch of the reported speech is a juncture at which another

---

[14] See also the discussion of projects beyond a single TCU in section 4.2.1 under 'Pragmatic markers of completion'.

can supply a candidate reporting;[15] in both exemplars below the prior context projects the form of the completing element. In (44), the completion of the TCU in line 4 is an extension of the preliminary component; in (45), projected by 'insteada', it constitutes a contrastive offer.

(44) (Lerner, 1991: 446)
```
1A   I just wish I were gonna eat a turkey dinner someplace ahh, he,
2    I wish that he'd say, he said, I have to be back around four,
3    because our family is having something and I wish he'd say
4B→  why don't you come over honey?
5A   yeah
```

(45) (Lerner, 1991: 450; GTS)
```
1   Ken    insteada my grandmother offering him a drink, of beer
2          she'll say
3   Lou→   wanna glass of milk?
```

These two practices – word searches and anticipatory completions – together demonstrate clearly the projectability of grammatical structures and, in the turn-taking paper's words, 'what it will take to complete them' (1974:719) (for the ways in which such projectability has been mobilised to pedagogic ends, see Koshik, 2002, and on 'designedly incomplete utterances', the former in American English, the latter in Italian, see Margutti, 2010). In order to bring off the completion of a turn launched by another, a speaker has to listen and analyse the turn-so-far, monitoring it for an appropriate place to start speaking; they launch their completions at the pre-possible completion point of a turn.

One other 'next-speaker' device illuminates the process of speaker self-selection. We have already seen next speakers' orientation to the minimisation of gap and overlap in the promptness with which they may start up a turn. This orientation can sometimes result in overlaps of a particular kind, involving what Schegloff (1987a) terms 'recycled turn beginnings'. It is sometimes the case that a speaker, oriented to the possibility of a prior turn's completion, lauches a turn, only to find that the prior speaker has not, in fact, completed their turn. The speaker, having launched a turn, thus finds the beginning of this turn to be in

---

[15] A striking instance of anticipatory completion on a literary quotation, in a case where the projected element is specific, is detailed in Patrick Leigh-Fermor's account of abducting the Nazi commandant of Crete, General Heinrich Kreipe, on 26 April 1944. Leigh-Fermor, who led the team of Special Operations Executive agents, tells of the moment where his relationship with the captured General moved to a different footing – after his completion of the Latin ode that the General starts to recite:

> We were all three lying smoking in silence, when the General, half to himself, slowly said: 'Vides ut alta stet nive candidum/Socrate . . .' It is the opening line of one of the few Horace odes I know by heart. I went on reciting where he had broken off . . . The General's blue eyes swivelled away from the mountain-top to mine – and when I'd finished, after a long silence, he said, 'Ach so Herr Major!' It was very strange. 'Ja, Herr General.' As though, for a moment, the war had ceased to exist. We had both drunk at the same fountains long before, and things were different between us for the rest of our time together.   (Leigh-Fermor, 2014)

overlap with the prior turn. This is what happens in the following sequence. It is an exchange between two couples, D and K (the hosts), and R and F (the guests), who have just come from visiting a friend in hospital who is found to have had a 'giant fullicular lympho-blastoma' (see extract (60) for the prior greetings sequence); the talk has concerned his current condition:

(46) (Schegloff, 1987a:75)
```
1   R    Well the uhm in fact they must have grown a culture, you know,
2        they must've- I mean how long- he's been in the hospital for a
3        few days, right? Takes a [bout a week to grow a culture
4   K→                           [I don' think they grow a I don' think
5        they grow a culture to do a biopsy.
```

At line 4 here, K launches his turn just after R has come to the possible completion of his turn at 'right?'. However, it turns out that R has not finished, and continues. K then finds himself in overlap; his turn, with the left bracket marking the point at which he re-launches the beginning of his turn in response to this contingency, is: 'I don' think they grow a [I don' think they grow a culture to do a biopsy'. As Schegloff notes of this instance: 'The recycle begins at precisely the point at which the "new" turn emerges "into the clear"; that is, as the overlap ends by the "old" turn coming *to* its "natural" or projected completion or by being stopped/withdrawn *before* its projected completion' (1987a:74). The analytic point is this: that, having failed to get the first start of a turn to be achieved with no gap and no overlap, the speaker here attempts to bring off the restart of the turn with no gap and no overlap – and, indeed, here succeeds. Schegloff notes that this is done, in the main, successfully (p. 75). These 'recycled turn beginnings' are, he notes, a precise repair mechanism for managing overlap in conversation; by redoing the beginning of the turn *as* a recycle, the speaker is insisting that 'what I am saying now is what I was starting to say then'. As such, it constitutes one other resource for potential 'next speakers' in the course of a current turn, once more at the pre-possible completion point in that turn.[16]

(b) Pre-beginnings

'Pre-beginnings', as Schegloff calls them, are 'just outside the beginning' of a turn (1996a:92) and constitute resources for displays of incipient speakership. These include the redirection of gaze towards a potential recipient, lip parting, coughs or throat-clearing, as well as the hearable inbreath exemplified in Chapter 2, extract (8). Such resources make pre-beginnings both visible and audible.[17] Clearly, work on multimodal corpora has been able to illuminate the

[16] Schegloff (1996a) discusses pre-possible completions, post-possible completions and pre-beginnings as places of systematic orientation in the TCU. We examine post-possible completions in Chapter 7 on repair.

[17] The salience of 'pre-beginning' elements is plain in this following anecdote from Brian Cox, a physicist and presenter of science programmes on British TV, talking about how he was given his own series to present. He is asked to appear on *Newsnight*, a BBC evening news programme, then presented by Jeremy Paxman:

process of speaker self-selection in this respect; Streeck and Hartge (1992), examining Ilokano data, show how a particular facial expression may occur in the transition space to project incipient speakership, and how gestures at TRPs may project the type of turn to come. Butler and Wilkinson (2013) examine in detail the pursuit of recipiency by a five-year-old child among adults. Mondada (2007), on a corpus of French interaction, investigates how pointing as a visible public action may be used by participants in laying claim to speakership, either in the course of a current turn, thereby projecting its end, or at the beginning of the speaker's incipient turn. In most of the cases in her corpus, pointing projects self-selection well before the end of the prior speaker's turn. The following is a case in point. The participants, who are agronomists and computer scientists, are examining land survey maps to establish a new cartographic language for modelling agricultural land. Note that Laura starts to point well before she starts to speak, in the course of Pierre-Alain's turn. His turn reaches possible completion after ' qu'elles ne l'étaient avant' ('than what they were before', l. 4), but he continues; as his voice goes into decrescendo, Laura initiates her pointing gesture, thus projecting imminent turn completion (l. 5):

(47) (Mondada, 2007:202–3)
      (L=Laura; PAL=Pierre-Alain. * * = delimits Laura's gesture; lau=participant identified when she is not the speaker; . . . . =gesture's preparation; ppp=pointing; ppp--- ->>>=gesture held till after the end of the excerpt)

```
1   PAL   et donc on voit la logique, avec cet cet aménagement du: de
          and so one sees the logic, with this this settlement of of
2         l'espace, .hh qui revient à obtenir, (.) euh: des des de- des
          space,    .hh which would make       (.) ehm
3         pâturages, (.) RElativement plus productives, qu'elles ne
```

It was 2008, and the Large Hadron Collider had just been switched on. There was a lot of news coverage around the event and Cox, justly proud of the project, was invited on to the current affairs show to talk about it. *Newsnight* being *Newsnight*, a cantankerous opponent, the president of the British Association for the Advancement of Science, had also been arranged, to slag the LHC off. 'I was ready for him,' Cox remembers. 'I'd been taught an underhand trick.' The comedian Chris Morris, an old friend . . . had spent years studying news presenters, better to pastiche them in his comedies, such as *The Day Today*. Before Cox went on *Newsnight*, Morris told his friend that when he was ready to interrupt the other guy, all he had to do was open his mouth, contort his features, and start thrashing and flailing his arms – the camera would find him. 'Chris told me: "Paxman does it all the time!" So when you want to deliver that killer blow . . .' Cox used the trick and won the debate. He says footage of it finally convinced BBC bosses to give him his own series. 'They thought, he has some attitude.'   ('The Side of Me that People Don't Tend to See Is the Side that Argues', *The Observer*, 5/10/14)

The opening of the mouth, facial contortion and gestural features mentioned here are all 'pre-beginning' elements, publicly available – and clearly deployed, here, to strategic effect.

```
          pasturelands, (.) RElatively more productive, than what they
4         l'étaient avant, grâce notamment à la: (.) <la
          were before, thanks among other things to the (.) <the
5         re*distribution des biens communs. ((decrescendo))>*
          redistribution of common goods.      ((decrescendo))>*
    lau   *..........................................................*
6   LAU   *et donc le: ce qui est en (.) orange ici là, terre assolée
          and so the: what is coloured in(.) orange there, farmland
          *ppp--- ->>
7   PAL   hum
8   LAU   c'est, (.) des prairies,
          that's, (.) grassland,
```

Laura's movement here anticipates the upcoming TRP, projecting her as possible next speaker; her point begins properly as she starts to speak, that is, as she establishes herself as self-selected current speaker. As Mondada observes:

> pointing displays a participation shift, the pointer initiating, often before even saying a word, her transition from the category of 'non-current speaker' to the category of 'incipient speaker', through the category of 'possible next speaker': in this sense, pointing gestures manifest the temporal, situated, embodied emergent process of the establishment of speakership. Moreover, this process shows publicly and visibly the way in which a 'recipient' scrutinizes, for all practical purposes, an ongoing turn and produces an online parsing of this turn in TCUs.   (2007:219–20)

We have now examined a number of means by which a next speaker may arrive at self-selection in the allocation of turns-at-talk. Having investigated aspects of turn construction and turn allocation, we now examine how speakers may extend a turn beyond the first TCU.

4.2.3   Beyond the first TCU

The fact that the turn-taking system initially allocates only one TCU to a speaker in conversation means that speakers have to design their turns so as to claim more than one unit; keeping a foot in the closing door, so to speak, of turn transition. Projecting multi-unit turns may be done by means of prefaces such as 'I have three things to say.' One practice for projecting actions, identified by Schegloff (1980), is the 'pre-pre', whereby a speaker projects an upcoming action, here a question, which effectively proposes that the other take up a recipient stance:

(48) (Schegloff, 1980:107–8)
```
1   B   I've listen' to all the things
2       that chu've said, an' I agree
3       with you so much.
4   B   Now,
```

```
5    B→    I wanna ask you something,
6    B     I wrote a letter.
7          (pause)
8    A     Mh hm,
9    B     T' the governer.
10   A     Mh hm::,
11   B     - telling 'im what I thought about
12         i(hh)m!
13   (A)   (Sh:::!)
14   B     Will I get an answer d'you think,
15   A     Ye:s/
```

Here, B's 'I wanna ask you something' (l. 5) is not followed by that 'something' but is preliminary to a further preliminary in the form of lines 6–12 before the question itself is asked at line 14. Note how the sentence 'I wrote a letter t'the governor telling 'im what I thought about i(hh)m' is here interactionally constructed, emerging incrementally, unit by unit, with the production of each unit after the projected question conditional upon the evidence of recipiency (see in particular ll. 7–8). The response at line 15 – showing how the recipient has parsed the turn for its possible completion – is produced directly thereafter.[18]

If 'pre-pre's such as in (48) are one practice for projecting upcoming actions and minimising the contribution of recipients until they are produced, a possibly more familiar conversational practice is storytelling. Storytelling prefaces (e.g. 'I'm broiling about something') indicate an extended spate of telling to come. In the extract below, Mike is telling a story, and so, despite coming to both syntactic and prosodic completion in line 1, ''n he waited' is clearly part of an on-going story; it is only at the end of line 8 that, with a hearable syntactic, prosodic and pragmatic completion, his turn gets a response:

(49)   (Goodwin: AD)
       (M=Mike; C=Curt. M. is describing a stock car race.)
```
1    M    [This, De Wa::ld spun ou:t. 'n he waited.
2         (0.5)
3    M    Al come around'n passed im Al wz leadin the feature,
4         (0.5)
5    M    en then the sekint- place guy,
6         (0.8)
7    M    en nen Keegan. En boy when Keeg'n come around he come
8         right up into im tried tuh put im intuh th'wa:ll.
9    C    Yeh¿
```

---

[18] The collaborative construction of a sentence is a topic to which we return in Chapters 6 and 7.

Storytelling is thus one more domain in which speakers can claim more than one TCU (see Sacks, 1974, 1986; Jefferson, 1978, and Schegloff, 1992c, for more on the organisation of storytelling in conversation); but these exceptions throw into relief the normative allocation of a single TCU.

4.3   The turn-taking rules

In establishing who speaks next and when, participants deploy the rules for turn-taking; that is, they put the turn-allocational possibilities into practice by reference to transition-relevance. The rules as set out below are a slightly simplified version of those formulated in Sacks et al. (1974), where S=current speaker and N=next speaker:

> 1. At the first TRP of a turn:
>   (a) If S selects N, then N, having been selected, is obliged to speak at the first TRP
>   (b) Otherwise, any other party may self-select, first speaker gaining rights to the next turn
>   (c) In the absence of a) and b) occurring, then S may, but need not, continue.
> 2. Applies at all subsequent TRPs:
> If (1c) has operated, and S has continued to a further TRP, then rules (1a–c) apply at each subsequent TRP, until transition to a next speaker.

As is evident, these rules are contingent, party administered and locally managed – that is, by the participants themselves on a turn-by-turn basis.

It is in showing how these abstract rules operate on the moment-by-moment production of actions in turns that the implications of the model become apparent. So it is clear that the rules operate such that 'one speaker at a time' is overwhelmingly the outcome:

```
(50)  (Jefferson, 1984b:18; Rahman)
1     Jessie   Hello Redcuh five oh six one?
2     Thomas   Mum?
3              (0.2)
4     Jessie   Ye:s?
5     Thomas   Me Thomas,
6     Jessie   Oh hello there what'r yih ↑doing.
7     Thomas   Ohn jis ringin tih say ah'm still alive en ah'm
8              still'eah.
9     Jessie   Yih still ali:ve'n yih still theah. Well thaht's
10             very nice, en yih don'want any tea.
11    Thomas   No I got some I'ad curry.
```

Jefferson remarks that what she calls 'unmarked next position onset', produced 'with neither haste nor delay', and embodied from lines 4–11 here, is 'the most

common, the usual, the standard relationship of one utterance to another'
(1986:162). On occasion we can discern participants monitoring a turn-in-progress in the process of 'gearing up' for the start of a next turn; in (51) below
Heatherton's pre-turn inbreath at line 3 precedes the start of his turn, which comes
at the last sound of the last word in the prior turn:

```
(51)  (Jefferson, 1984b:24; Her: OII:2:4:1)
1  Heath:    This's Heather↓ton:.
2  Steph:    Yes Heathi[ht'n.
3  Heath:→            [.h Steven look ah:: I'm phonin:g uh
4            on behah:lf'v Doreen'n myse:lf we just hehrd abah:t
5            poor um (0.4) Sondra.
```

As the turn-taking paper notes, overlaps are 'common, but brief', such as the
following, where a speaker starts up at the final sound(s) of the last word of what
constitutes a possibly complete utterance:

```
(52)  (Jefferson, 1984b:13)
1A    th'fuhrst bit'v (.) income isn'tax[ed.
2B→                                     [No: that's right, mm:
```

It is evident that speaker B here is parsing a turn in progress and projecting a point at
which it is possibly complete – given the production of 'tax' it would be semanti-
cally incoherent for the turn to continue with 'taxis' or even 'taxidermy' – and as
such constitutes what Jefferson calls a 'reasonable turn incursion' (1984b), in which
the occurrence of more than one speaker at a time is minimal and fleeting.

Another common instance of fleeting overlap is the deployment of tokens in
the course of another's extended turn by speakers passing up the opportunity to
take a complete turn; in the following at (53), E's receipt token 'Oh' at line 2 is
produced in such a way, softly and in overlap, as to be non-competitive, and the
continuers (Schegloff, 1982:87; Gardner, 1997) 'Mm' and 'hm' in line 5, constitute the quasi-turns mentioned earlier. In (54), Vera's 'yes' at line 2 is similarly
produced so as not to claim a more extensive turn:

```
(53)  (Jefferson, 1988:167; NB:II:2:R:8:SO)
1  N    You know for all of this:u[h: inten]sive thou:ght
2  E                             [°Oh::°  ]
3       (.)
4  N    bus[iness,h[.hhhh
5  E→      [Mm:    [hm,
6  N    A::nd uhm (1.8) 'tch I can't remember one: (.) one of
7       the f: ↓kids had said in his thin:g u-something abou:t...
```

```
(54)  (Jefferson, 1984b:19; Rahman:B:1(13):8)
1  J    it's only venee:r thou:gh, .hh[hhe but it's a beautiful.
2  V→                                 [Ye:s.
```

However, these brief incursions aside, there are clearly exceptions to the
general 'one-party-at-a-time' rule – indeed, insofar as their occurrence throws

into relief the normative orientation of participants,[19] these exceptions prove the rule.[20] The broad categories of exception are when two or more are speaking simultaneously for a more extended stretch of talk, and when no-one is speaking. In both cases, the rules allow us to make important distinctions within these two categories.

4.4   More than one at a time: 'interruption', overlap and choral production

The turn-taking rules, operative from 'the first TRP of a turn', suggest that a turn launched at any place other than a TRP constitutes a violation of the rules, as shown in (55) below:

(55) (Lerner, 1989: 172)

```
1   Ken   My opinion of the school system, the Los Angeles school
2         district, district, is the most fucked over,
3   Rog   Yeah well we [all got that opinion.
4   Ken→            [school syst'm WAIT is the most fucked over
5         school system in the world.
```

Roger launches his turn at a point where Ken has, in line 2, hearably not come to a possible completion – and Ken in turn, in line 4, completes his turn, making clear, with 'WAIT', that he himself has a warrant for initiating overlap; in Lerner's words, to 'violate the violater' (1989:172). This violative positioning of the incoming turn suggests that it might be characterisable by the term 'interruption' – and indeed Ken's response would appear to endorse this. However, as Schegloff (2005:452) has noted, the very term 'interruption' embodies a complaint, with 'you interrupted me!' lodging a grievance.[21] It is analytically more productive to examine such cases, independent of such evaluative overtones, as forms of overlap, characterised, following Jefferson

---

[19] For example, 'laughing is the most widely occurrent sort of thing which one can do without regard to "one party at a time." If somebody is laughing after a joke, you can laugh also. You can laugh if somebody starts up talking. And of course, not just after a joke, but after any utterance for which laughter might be appropriate. Laughing is one prototypical thing that people can be doing together at the same time, making sounds without violating the "one party at a time" rule' (Sacks, 1992a:745).

[20] 'simultaneous talk within a single conversation can, under some circumstances (e.g. when there are four or more participants in the conversation), engender the schisming of that conversation into multiple conversations' (Schegloff, 2000:5) (see, e.g., Sacks et al., 1974:713–14; Egbert, 1993, 1997).

[21] Schegloff, discussing other possible units potentially subject to interruption, observes that 'Children who have successfully learned to avoid "interrupting" by not talking while someone else *is* may find themselves bewildered to be hushed up upon starting to talk when the room is quiet and to be told nonetheless "not to interrupt". Yet they encounter this contingency if they have not yet learned to analyse the organization of storytelling in conversation and to recognize when a storytelling was "over"' (2002:290).

(1986) according to placement with respect to the prior turn. Jefferson terms the overlap embodied in (55) above 'interjacent onset' – beginning at a point where the prior turn is nowhere near possible completion and transition-ready (p. 158; see also Drew, 2009).

On other occasions overlaps can result where a next speaker launches a turn at a TRP at the same time as the current speaker opts to continue (e.g. (56) to (58)), or another speaker starts speaking (59); Jefferson calls these 'transition-space onsets' (1986:153):

```
(56)  (B:1:JMA:13)
1  J:    Anyway ah'll see you on Sunday[Ahnn.
2  A:→                                [Yes.
3  A:    O*kheh* if I don't see you befohre[ah'll see you then[Jenny.
4  J:→                                     [.hh              [Yes
```

```
(57)  (Jefferson, 1984b:17)
1  Bette     Oh theh must be some: trains.[(Intuh City)
2  Andrea→                                [Theh must be b't
3            th'point is...
```

```
(58)  (Jefferson, 1984b:17; Heritage OII:2:7:5:R)
1  Vicki     How are ↓you all. [Yer a l]ittle ti:red] °nah°
2  Doreen→                     [Oh wir ]all fi:ne,  ]Yes I'm jus:
3            sohrta clearing up a bi[t nah, ]
4  Vicki                            [°Ohhhh] deah, °
```

```
(59)  (Sacks et al., 1974:707; Frankel, 67)
1  Mike      I know who d'guy is.=
2  Vic   →   [He's ba::d.
3  James→    [You know the gu:y?
```

Since in line 1 Mike does not choose a specific other to speak next, both Vic and James legitimately self-select; and, as Sacks et al., note (p. 707), the simultaneous start shows both recipients of line 1 are able independently to project its possible completion point. However, overlaps such as the one above may also occur when a speaker does select another to speak – but when that other is a party (such as a couple), rather than a specified other, both members are mandated to speak next. In the following (which in fact precedes the extract presented earlier as (46)), A and B are a couple, and C and D a couple; in line 1 A adumbrates an announcement to C and D, whereupon both respond with sharply distinct stances towards it (ll. 2 and 3), to be met by both A's and B's simultaneous responses (ll. 5 and 6) to D's claim of familiarity with the news:

```
(60)  (Terasaki, 2004: 189; Heritage, 2013:372)
1   A    Hey we got good news.
2   C→   [What's the good ne]ws,
3   D→   [I kno:w.]
4        (.)
```

```
5    A→    [Oh ya do::?
6    B→    [Ya heard it?
7    A     Oh good.
8    C     Oh yeah, mm hm
9    D     Except I don't know what a giant follicular
10         lymphoblastoma is.
11   A     Who the hell does except a doctor.
```

It is for the very reason that the turn-taking system is designed to realise the outcome of 'one-party-at-a-time' that departures from that practice are used to achieve specific interactional objectives. There are clear occasions on which simultaneous action is licensed or mandated.[22] So, for example, we see instances such as the following:

```
(61)  (Jefferson, 1973:57)
1    Caller  Downton, though, she worked fer::I dunno
2            if you know Russ Ogle [thorpe,
3    Desk→                          [Yeah, I know'm. Mm hm,
4    Caller  She works fer him,
```

Jefferson notes of the placement of line 3: 'the timing with which the acknowledger is produced may relate to its clarity and convincingness' (1973:57), its positioning early in the prior turn underlining the claim to recognition. In such cases, the placement of a turn in overlap is clearly related to the action it is doing. In the

---

[22] In the domain of non-conversational, institutional talk, obvious instances of choral behaviour include the following, a teacher's eliciting of a choral answer from a class:

(Lerner, 1993:219)

```
1    Teacher    Where was this book published?
2               ...
3    Teacher    McMillan publishing company in?
4               (.)
5    Class →    New York ((mostly in unison))
6    Teacher    Okay,
```

As Schegloff notes, 'such outcomes are co-constructed by reference to one-party-at-a-time even though they are realised through designedly simultaneous talk' (2000:48). In addition, audiences provide clear cases of choral behaviour, such as booing (on which, see Clayman, 1993) and applause (see Atkinson, 1984). Atkinson discusses a technique called 'surfing applause' (used by particularly effective speech-makers such as Martin Luther King and Barack Obama) whereby a speaker continues to speak as applause starts:

> Unlike most speakers, surfers don't just stop whenever the audience applauds and wait until they've finished. What surfers do is to carry on speaking after the applause has started, which creates a number of positive impressions. It makes it look as though you hadn't been seeking applause at all, and are really quite surprised that the audience has interrupted you with an unexpected display of approval.
>
> Then, if you keep trying to go on while the audience is still clapping, it's as if you're telling them that, unlike less passionate politicians, you're the kind of person who regards getting your message across as much more important than waiting around to savour the applause.   (Atkinson, 2009)

following, it intercepts a turn that is clearly launching an inapt question just at the point at which it becomes recognisable where it is heading:

(62) (From Drew, 2009; Heritage:1:6:9)
```
1   Dor     If by any chance, (0.8) theh isn't anybody heuh I've got
2           tih go out jus' fer awhi:le, [.hh What is your- new-
3   Hel                                  [Ye:s
4   Dor     What is your telee[phone numbuh?
5   Helen→                    [Well we're not on the phone yet
```

It would seem that a number of actions designed to be affiliative are constructed by reference to overlap. An everyday instance might be greetings (see Lerner, 2002) and leave-takings such as the following, another case of Jefferson's interjacent onset:

(63) (Lerner, 2002; GL:FN:closing)
```
1   A:  Good luck. Nice to [↑   s e e::    y o u : : ]
2   B:                     [>Nice to< ↑   see:: you::]
```

We might also think of our own concerted attempts with others to achieve a *Happy Birthday* in greeting a friend as they open the door, toasts over drinks or how (albeit less strictly simultaneously) compliments to the cook over dinner are produced with several parties 'chiming in'.[23] This kind of 'celebratory' uptake registering 'eager supportiveness' (Schegloff, 2002:300) is evident in interjacent onsets in the following two cases, in (64) at line 5 and in (65) at line 4:

(64) (NB:II:3:R)
```
1   Lot:  Ye:ah a:n: uh:: u::: Ken Kno:x f'm Knoxberry Farm wul:
2         he's gunnuh (.) bring all the chicken for me.
3         (.)
4   Lot:  S[uh I'm j's gunnuh ha]:ve that (.) chicken.
5   Emm:→ [W o : n d e r° f'l°.]
```

(65) (Drew, 2009; NB:II:4:16)
      (Nancy has reported having met a nice eligible man.)
```
1   Nan:  He's jist a ri:l sweet GU:y. .h .t[.hhhh
2   Emm:                                    [WONderful.
3   Nan:  So: we w'r [sitting in
4   Emm:→            [YER LIFE is CHANG[ing
5   Nan:                              [EEYE::A:H
```

Moreover, while not itself talk, but produced by reference to it, on some occasions laughter may be hearable as having been elicited by a prior turn[24] (see Jefferson, 1979):

---

[23] Indeed, this is an occasion where non-participation indicates a studied withholding.

[24] 'Laughing is the sort of thing that, when it's done, it will be heard as tied to the last thing said' (Sacks, 1992a:745); but see also Holt (2014) for an exception.

(66)   (Jefferson, 1979:80)

```
1   Joyce:     Cuz she wz off in the bushes with somebuddy, tch!
2              (0.7)
3   Joyce:     ehh[hhhhhh!
4   Sidney:→       [Oh(hh)h hah huh!
```

Apart from such instances of collaboratively simultaneous action,[25] overlap is a phenomenon that may otherwise be hearably problematic for participants (see French and Local, 1983, on turn competition, and specifically the prosodic features of high pitch and loudness that characterise it) and that requires management and resolution (see Schegloff, 2000; Kurtić et al., 2013). However, in Chapter 7, we examine how other-initiated repair may freely start up in overlap, displaying none of the features described by Schegloff (2000) for overlap competition – thus suggesting that such other-initiated repair trumps the turn-taking rules (Kendrick, 2015).

4.5   No-one speaking: forms of silence

Just as the turn-taking model provides for a distinction between forms of simultaneous talk, so it also allows speakers to make distinctions within the category of no talk; that is, silence (Sacks et al., 1974:715, fn. 26; see also Levinson, 2013a:108). As we saw in Chapter 3, placement is criterial in establishing what a turn is doing. However, placement equally shapes the absence of talk. We saw, for example, how consequential was the lack of an immediate response

---

[25] One practice, described by Schegloff (2002), is not so collaborative – indeed, quite the opposite. This is when a speaker comes to the possible completion of a turn. At that point, the recipient legitimately launches a turn, but some way into that, the original speaker subsequently launches a turn that is hearably designed to 'recomplete' her prior turn that had apparently been completed earlier. Schegloff cites one exemplar; here is another such example:

(NB IV:5:R)
(Gladys is offering her neighbour, Emma, the paper (l. 1) while her husband ('he', l. 8) is out.)

```
1   Gla:   'n ah have the paypuh here I
2          thought chu might li:ke tih ↑have it. ↑.hhhh[h
3   Emm:                                          [Th[a:nk yo]u.
4   Gla:                                             [En then]you:
5          could retuhrn it ub (.) Oh along about noo:n,
6          (0.2)
7   Emm:   Yer goin up'n ge[tcher hair]: fixed t]ihda]↑:y. ]
8   Gla:                   [befo:  re ]he gets ] ho ]↑:me.]
```

So in the above, Gladys's lines 4–5 'En then you could return it ub (.) oh along about noon' is syntactically possibly complete and the prosodic pitch peak on 'noon', alongside the pause, suggest that Gladys's turn is complete. Emma launches a turn and a hearably new topic, but some way into the turn, Gladys produces what is hearably designed as a continuation and completion of her prior turn. By launching a turn that 'recompletes' her prior turn so far into Emma's own turn, Gladys effectively makes out that *she* was interrupted, rather than the one interrupting.

to the first pair part of an adjacency pair. We can now see that this is attributable to rule 1(a) of the turn-taking model, which allocates a turn to a specific next speaker. Given that the second is then immediately due, the silence that develops in its place is attributable to the recipient and, as the pursuits in lines 3 and 5 attest, continue to be so until a response is forthcoming:

```
(67)  (Atkinson and Drew, 1979:52)
1   A    Is there something bothering you or not?
2        (1.0)
3   A→   Yes or no
4        (1.5)
5   A→   Eh?
6   B    No
```

However, not all silences are so attributable; if a next speaker is not selected, as in (68) below at line 2, then either rule 1(b) (other-speaker self-selects) or 1(c) (same speaker may continue) are possibilities, but neither of these occurs immediately. The ensuing silence at line 4 is, then, a non-attributable *gap* before rule 1 (b) comes into operation. This is followed at line 6 by a *lapse* whereby none of the rules 1(a), (b) and (c) are operational (see Levinson, 1983:299, and for a detailed investigation of lapses, see Hoey, 2015):

```
(68)  (Sacks et al., 1974:714)
1   J    Oh I could drive if you want me to.
2   C    Well no I'll drive (I don' m // in')
3   J    hhh
4   →    (1.0)
5   J    I meant to offah.
6   →    (16.0)
7   J    Those shoes look nice when you keep on putting stuff on
8        'em
```

This differentiation between attributable silences, gaps and lapses is thus an important consequence of the turn-taking rules; as such, it can shed light on how parties to conversation treat silence. It is clear from extract (49), for example, when Mike is telling a story, that pauses in the incremental delivery of the story are not accountable and do not require management. Moreover, compare, for example, the treatment of a silence within a turn – an *intra-turn* silence – before the arrival of a TRP, as in Mike's first turn in (49) where the recipient withholds talk until Mike has completed his turn, with the *inter-turn* silences in (67) above. Speaker A, receiving no immediate response, twice prompts speaker B before a response is forthcoming.[26] Such inter-turn silences are thus shown to be

---

[26] Jefferson suggests the possibility of a metric for English conversation 'which has as one of its artefacts a "standard maximum" of approximately one second' (1988:188) in conversation. Ethnographic research in different speech communities has revealed variation in this respect. For example, Mushin and Gardner, in a study of the Garrwa speakers in two Aboriginal

problematic – so much so that speakers may work to minimise them, using grammatical resources to do so.

4.6   Transforming silence: the role of grammar

So, for example, a speaker may bring a turn to a possible syntactic and prosodic completion but find that the recipient is not forthcoming with a next turn. In such a context, a speaker may choose to build the next turn not as a hearably new beginning but as a resumption of the prior. See, for example, at line 13 below:

(69)   (Holt, May 88:1:5:10)
(Robbie and Lesley are supply teachers at the same school, and are comparing notes on the pupils they both teach.)

```
1    Les:    I feel very sorry f'that little boy becuz uh- I thin:k
2            e-life must be diff↑icult for im at home,
3            (0.4)
4    Rob:    D'you know I think he copes with it though,
5            (0.2)
6    Les:    [Yes.
7    Rob:    [( )-
8    Les:    [Yes.
9    Rob:    [He- when he when I fi:rst met him when he wz ↓very
10           little.↓ (0.4) uh::m (0.3) ee↓Yes. An' he used to hold
11           my ha:nd.
12           (0.2)
13   Rob:→   Which wz (.) always sort'v (w(h)arm) in a
14           chi[:ld (t'me)
15   Les:       [.hhhhh Yes that's ri:ght. 'N he'll cuddle up to you,
16           h[uh! even no:w Ye:[s
17   Rob:     [(Ye:s it's)    [Ye:s it's lovely.
```

Robbie comes to a syntactic and prosodic completion (with the pitch peak and sound stretch in the last word) after the main clause, 'An' he used to hold my hand' (ll. 10–11) indicating the possible completion of the turn. However, her turn receives no immediate response; after two-tenths of a second's pause, she

Australian communities in Northern Australia, testify to the 'relatively high frequency of silences of more than a second that do not correlate either with trouble in the interaction, nor with a coordinated activity which precludes or interrupts the flow of talk' (2009:2049). Gardner and Mushin provide some ethnographic background which may account for this: 'Long silences between turns – gaps that do not transform into lapses – are not only tolerated, but are common. In addition, these women have little to do. They sit around for hours at a time, passing the time of day in conversation. Conversations involving intimates in familiar surroundings, with a lack of pressure to talk may in fact be at least as pertinent as cultural difference in accounting for expanded transition spaces' (2015:12). However, in the light of Stivers et al.'s (2009) ten-language study, such cases appear to be exceptions where local variation inflects universal practice in particular ways.

opts to syntactically continue the turn with something that effectively 'recompletes' it (l. 13): what Schegloff (1996a, 2000, 2001) has called an *increment*, or grammatical extension to a turn, which may be lexical, clausal or sentential (for a cross-linguistic study, see Couper-Kuhlen and Ono, 2007). The clausal increment here, 'which wz always sort'v (w(h)arm) in a chi[:ld (t'me)', appends an assessment to the report at lines 10–11, and its production shows evidence of Robbie's pursuit of concurrence from Lesley: a laugh token on the assessment item 'w(h)arm' (Jefferson, 1979), the sound stretch on 'chi:ld' and the further extension of the turn with the modulation of the strength of the assessment. Lesley's subsequent agreement and confirmation at line 15, plus her own further instantiation of Robbie's assessment, ''N he'll cuddle up to you' constitutes the enthusiastic embrace of the common stance that Robbie was pursuing. Crucial in this pursuit is Robbie's increment at lines 13–14, which in effect converts an inter-turn silence into an intra-turn pause – that is, a pause within her own speaking turn. With such a practice the speaker can claim that her prior turn had not in fact been brought to completion – despite it having indeed been so, both syntactically and prosodically.[27] In so doing, the potentially interactionally damaging implications of the silence at line 12, in its lack of prompt agreement (a topic to which we shall return in Chapter 5), are headed off.

That such a practice – converting an inter-turn silence into an intra-turn pause – is neither idiosyncratic to that episode of interaction (see Clift, 2014) nor limited to relative clauses is evident in the following extract. Here, Vanessa's lack of any prompt response, firstly to Mary's topic proffer in lines 1–2, and then her resistance to Mary's proposal in line 4 result in the inter-turn silences at lines 3, 5 and 8. However, finding herself subject to the same contingency at line 11 – Mary's refusal to embrace her own proposal – Vanessa deploys the same practice as observed in (69) above. Having come to a recognisable syntactic, prosodic and pragmatic completion at line 10, and in the face of resistance from her recipient, she resumes talk with a turn that is clearly designed as a continuation ('or my purple dress', l. 12); moreover, meeting with on-going resistance, she produces a further continuation at line 14, which, as in (69) above, pursues a response, which it gets, by means of an acknowledgement:

(70) (Clift, T8:5)
      (Talk turns to the wedding anniversary party of a family friend. Vanessa is Mary's
      twenty-something-year-old daughter; she is wearing a summer dress.)
1   Mary: Listen, I don't know how dressy this is going to be
2   tomorrow.
3   (0.4)
4   Mary: I don't think you want to wear that dress do you?
5   (1.1)

---

[27] See Chapter 5, extract (43), for another such instance.

```
6    Van:    This dress¿
7    Mary:   Mm.
8            (1.2)
9    Van:    I could, I mean if its bla:zingly hot, I might wear this
10           dress.
11           (0.2)
12   Van:    Or my purple dress.
13           (0.8)
14   Van: →  Which is pre[tty.
15   Mary:               [Mmm.
```

So we can see in these cases how grammatical resources may be used to interactional ends – in such cases, deployed to head off the problematic implications of inter-turn silence.

4.7   Local variation, universal system?

In examining the claims made by the turn-taking paper, we have seen how the various linguistic resources of particular languages may be implemented in the social organisation of the turn-taking system. So, for example, it is quite clear that turn-taking imposes constraints on the information structure of utterances (Roberts and Levinson, 2014) and that the word order of a language will have implications for interaction. Schegloff (1996a) suggests that the beginning of a turn is a key locus for projectability, and this is underlined, for English, by Thompson and Couper-Kuhlen who observe that 'the recurrently regular syntactic resources deployed by speakers of English tend to permit early projection of turn trajectories' (2005:487). In this respect the recipient is at a relative advantage in being in receipt earlier, rather than later, of the main informational load of the turn: question words (*Who/What/How ...*), imperatives (*Stop ...*), conjunctions or quote attributions in English occur clause-initially, just as subject-auxiliary inversion in yes/no questions (*Have you ever ...?*) allows for early recognisability of the action being launched (Mazeland, 2013:476). By the same token, it is clear that a verb-final language such as Japanese benefits the speaker in terms of utterance planning. As Tanaka notes:

> Partly as a result of the predicate-final orientation of postpostional grammar, turns in Japanese are massively structured so that the substance of what is being talked about is articulated before the social action bearing upon that substance is made known. Put another way, turns in Japanese *do not necessarily project from their beginnings* what their ultimate shape and type will be.   (1999:141; italics in original)

As we saw from extract (13), turn-final particles in Japanese are thus an important guide to transition relevance. Tanaka shows how the linguistic structure of Japanese facilitates particular interactional possibilities not available to speakers of English, with its SVO word order; and indeed Fox et al. propose that the profusion of final particles in Japanese evolved at least in part to serve turn-taking considerations in this respect (1996:213). By contrast, many of the Mesoamerican languages standardly have a VOS word order, and this clearly has implications for the organisation of interactional sequences;[28] Brown et al. (2010), examining Tzeltal, Yucatec and Zapotec conversation, note the striking prevalence of cross-speaker repetition, where (allowing for deictic, evidential and attitudinal changes) the proposition expressed remains the same as that in a prior turn. Indeed, Brown and Levinson (2005) observe that in polite Tzeltal social interactions – in particular when a topic is winding down – adults may engage in up to eight turns of repetition of one another's utterances. The following extract shows how repetition is a general resource in Tzeltal for responding affirmatively or agreeing with a claim in the preceding utterance (Brown, 2010:2642):

(71)   (Brown, 2010:2642)
       (A is demurring from accepting the offer of a corn gruel drink.)
1 A   *ja' nax ma*   *s-k'an x-y-uch'-o*   i   *k-a'al-tik i.*
       !   PT NEG 3-E-want ASP-3E-drink-3A this 1E-water-1PLE DEIC
       It's just that   she doesn't drink our water
2 N   *aj pero* *pay-bil* *me* *ye'l*   *ek tz'i ja'* *ya k-uch'-tik.*
       ah but boil-RES if apparently too P T!   ICP 1E-drink-1PLE
       Ah but it's the case that we too drink it boiled (i.e. it's safe
       to drink)
3 A→   *aj* *pay-bil* *ya*   *'w-uch'-0*   *ek*
       ah boil-RES   ICP 2E-drink-3A   too
       Ah you drink it boiled too
4 N→   *pay[bil-*
       boil-RES
       Boiled
5 A→   *[pay-bil?*
          Boiled?
6   (0.2)
7 N→   *pay-bil.*   *melel (0.6) chikn-aj-em*   *me*   *s-k'olal.*
       boil-RES   truly   perceptible-1CH-PERF   DEIC 3-E-reason
       Boiled. Truly, (we've) heard about the reasons (for boiling
       drinking water)

Here, A in line 3 does a confirmation check, which N affirms in line 4, in the course of which A produces a second confirmation check (l. 5), which N then again confirms and then elaborates on (l. 7). The interaction thus provides a compensatory 'workaround' for the grammar (Levinson, 2014).

---

[28] Eye-tracking experiments comparing Dutch (SVO) and Tzeltal (primarily VOS) show a tight parallelism between grammatical structure and the order of encoding operations carried out during sentence formulation (Norcliffe et al., 2015).

Some languages are more equivocal than English, Japanese and Tzeltal with respect to word order, however; and it is instructive to examine how, in the same language, different word order has interactional consequences. Mandarin has both SVO and SOV structures. The following extract demonstrates an instance of the former.

(72) (Li, 2014:56)
```
164  Lei:  deguo    dao     le siyue    CHU       hai  leng    ne shuo shi.
           Germany  till  CRS April  beginning    still cold  PRT say be
           It's said that it's still cold at the beginning of April
           in Germany
165        shuo hai  yao    chuan   daYI ne.
           say  still have  to wear coat PRT
           (and) people still have to wear coats
166  Ran:  keshi (-) yinggai bu  hui xiang xianzai zheyang.
           but       should NEG will like now    this
           But (it) shouldn't be (as cold) as now.
167  →     wo juede nei ge  zuileng   de   tianqui yijing
           I think  that CL coldest   ASSC weather already
           GUOqu [le.
           over   PFV
           I think the coldest weather is already over.
168  Lei:       [bu.
                [NEG
                [No.
169        chunhanliaoqiao   yiding   ting leng  de.
           spring cold chilly  must be pretty cold PRT
           There is still chill in the air in early spring. It must be
           pretty cold.
```

Lei and Ran are talking about spring in Germany. Ran's turn at line 167 is a complex sentence with SVO structure, with the object a clause. The trajectory and action implication of the turn is recognisable as an upcoming assessment from early on 'wo juede nei ge zuileng de tianqui' (I think the coldest weather), such that there is maximal projectability at 'yijing guoqu' (already over). Lei's incoming disagreeing turn 'bu' (No) overlaps with the last syllable of this turn, showing that the recipient has already recognised the possible completion point. The SVO structure here thus allows for projection of possible turn completion (Li, 2014:57). In contrast, in the following exchange, the units in SOV structures do not allow for such early projection of turn completion:

(73) (Li, 2014:57–8)
```
1201 Fan  yihuir na   zhe shexiangji qu louxia      pai yi duanr.
          later  take ASP video camera go downstairs  film one CL
          Let's take the  video camera downstairs (to your place) and
          film there for a little while
```

```
1202   Rui    keyi a mei wenti,
              OK  PRT NEG problem
              OK, no problem
1203          ni  keyi   qu wo jia pai a;=
              you can     go my home film PRT
              You can go to my place to film
1204   Fan    =ai ya
              INT
              Heck
1205   Rui→   ba women san ge ren    jia   li dou pai   yi xia.
              BA we   three CL person home  in all film   one CL
              (You can) film in all of our places.
1206   Fan    ei nimen jia    hai  SAN    ge ren;
              INT you   home   also three  CL person
              Ei, there are already three people at your home?
1207   Rui    bu shi.
              NEG be.
              No.
       Hand   pointing to Fan, Tin and himself
1208    →     ba women SAN     ge ren     de jia   dou pai   yi xia.
              BA   we  three   CL person POSS   home all film   one CL
              (You can) film in all of our places
1209   Fan    hehehe
1210          wo shuo zheme kuai ya.
              I  say so     fast PRT
              I thought, (you're) so fast!
1211          dou    you   sa  ren  le.
              already have three person PRT
              There're already three people at your place.
```

Li and Thompson note that the BA construction, usually referring to 'something about which the speaker believes the hearer knows' (1981:465), here used by Rui at lines 1205 and 1208, in Mandarin is an SOV construction, thus:

```
Subject        ba       direct object      verb
S                        O                  V
```

In line 1205, the unexpressed subject is 'you' – the same as that in Rui's prior TCU at line 1203. The verb here, expressing the action 'pai' (film), is in this turn delayed until late in the turn, and so projectability is retarded, relative to the exemplar in (72). Li presents the online production of the unit as a whole as follows (2014:59). It is clear from the schema below that, on the production of 'ba' at (1), the direct object becomes relevant; but on the production of the object at (2), the recipient may still not be able to predict the verb (and thus the action being proposed):

```
1. ba ...
   BA ...
   ('You can')
```

```
2. ba women san     ge ren     jia li
   BA we    three  CL person home in
   ('You can')... the home of all three of us
3. ba women san     ge ren     jia li dou pai yi xia.
   BA we    three CL person home in all  film one CL
   ('You can') film the home of all three of us
```

It is only at (3) that the verb, and therefore action, is made recognisable, and the BA construction is complete. This comparison from Mandarin thus shows in a very clear way how the SVO ordering allows an early projection and prediction of the possible turn completion, whereas the SOV structure defers its recognition.

With respect to variation, not in structure but in interactional norms, work by Hoymann (2010) on the Namibian language ǂĀkhoe Haiǁom is illuminating for what it reveals about the intersection of the local and the universal. Hoymann's research was part of the Stivers et al. (2010) ten-language comparative study of questions and answers, introduced in Chapter 3. Hoymann proceeds to consider how the hunter-gatherer culture of ǂĀkhoe Haiǁom shapes interactional preferences by reference to work conducted on interaction in other hunter-gatherer cultures, such as that by Kimura (2001) on the Baka of central Africa, and Australian Aboriginal communities (see, e.g., Liberman, 1985; Eades, 1991, 1994; Walsh, 1991), as well as work on the North American Warm Springs Indian community (Philips, 1976, 2005). This ethnographic research has suggested that such societies have relatively greater tolerance for silence and a lack of next-speaker selection that shows less coerciveness on the part of the speaker (Hoymann, 2010:2737). However, the quantitative results across the ten-language study appear to suggest that while there is a certain degree of local variation, the universality of the basic turn-taking system is robust. So, for example, ǂĀkhoe silences were found to be relatively long compared to those of the other languages (but, as we saw in Chapter 3, not the longest, which was Danish), and ǂĀkhoe speakers select a next speaker less often than speakers of other languages do. ǂĀkhoe also showed a relatively high proportion of non-responses to questions (23%, but below Lao, which had the highest, at 25%), which might be down to the relative lack of explicit next-speaker selection. Hoymann suggests that the distribution of question types – a high proportion of content or open questions, and virtually no polar requests for confirmation – makes it more likely for questions to go unanswered. Some commentators (e.g. Kitamura, 1990; Sugawara, 1996,1998) propose a link here between forms of questioning and the high value attached to speakers' independence. All in all, however, as Hoymann concludes, 'there is no evidence to support an ǂĀkhoe Haiǁom mode of communication that is radically unlike other cultural groups' (2010:2738). So, as we saw in Chapter 3, across the study as a whole, answers in ǂĀkhoe are preferred over non-answers; preferred answers are faster than dispreferred ones and, contrary to some prior work, no evidence to support significantly more overlap than other languages. ǂĀkhoe Haiǁom was the only

African language represented in the ten-language comparative study, and so further research is clearly required to establish the extent of variation across languages within what appear to be the translinguistic organisations of sequences and turn-taking.

4.8 Conclusion: grammar and social organisation in context

The turn-taking system[29] is the meeting point of grammar and social organisation; it is the means by which speakers regulate their own participation in, and through, time with each other, unit by unit. It has the apparently paradoxical quality of being at the same time context free and context sensitive (Sacks et al., 1974:699): in other words, it is abstract enough to account for observable properties of talk-in-interaction, yet at the same time capable of accommodating whatever variation participants bring to each occasion, whether linguistic, as we have seen, or social. So there are, of course, particular contexts (courtrooms, interviews, debates, for example) in which who speaks when is specified or overtly regulated. In these contexts, when business in domains such as medicine, the law, politics and the broadcast media gets transacted, it does so through the distinct social institutions grounded in talk. Furthermore, these organisations are themselves adaptations of the turn-taking system for ordinary conversation (see, e.g., Drew and Heritage, 1992; Heritage and Clayman, 2010). As Sacks et al. state, 'It is a systematic consequence of the turn-taking organisation of conversation that it obliges its participants to display to each other, in a turn's talk, their understanding of other turns' talk' (1974:728); it is by such means that contexts are created, sustained and ultimately rendered visible in talk by means of a system that shows how time intersects with grammar to interactional ends.

---

[29] At this point it may be noted that the turn-taking paper is entitled 'A Simplest Systematics' and not, for example, '*The* Simplest Systematics', in an acknowledgement of the possible existence of other systems. That said, the model proposed by Sacks, Schegloff and Jefferson is the one which accounts for the 'grossly observable facts' about conversation and the one most comprehensively accountable to them.

5 The structure of sequences I: preference organisation

Preference organisation relates to the systematic bias observed in interaction towards the use of certain structures (and thus 'preferred') over others ('dispreferred'). It is the clearest means by which social and cultural constraints are brought to bear on language. Initially we examine how preference operates over the second pair parts of adjacency pairs, with respect to both the actions implemented by a turn and the format of the turn itself. While the first pair part of an adjacency pair may propose agendas or constraints on a next turn, these may be resisted; forms of compliance and resistance in responsive actions are here explored. The relationship between two actions – offers and requests – is given particular scrutiny for what it reveals about action construction. Cross-linguistic data show the exent to which preferred outcomes (e.g. the acceptance of an offer) are the result of negotiation, and an extended English exemplar shows how actions may be recognised and managed without actually being verbalised. We then explore how preference operates on another domain: that of person reference. Exploration of defaults and resistance to them shows an orientation, not to information exchange, but action. What in one language may be done en passant within a turn may, in another, be accomplished across a sequence. Cultural norms are seen to act as biasing operators over particular structural features, and in these processes we see the origins of grammaticalisation.

As we saw in Chapter 3 through examining the adjacency pair and its expansion, questions need answers, requests need responses and invitations need accepting or declining; together, speakers collaboratively build courses of action through talk, and these are done through sequences. In this and the following chapter, we pursue the ways in which actions are implemented through sequences by looking more closely at the relationship between the parts of an adjacency pair in examining the interactional constraints collectively known as preference organisation. Very broadly, this relates to how we pursue affiliation and solidarity, and how cultural norms may intersect with these constraints. It is in preference organisation that linguistic and social phenomena are brought together most clearly. We examine how this may shape the production of adjacency pairs and the shaping of sequences. We then proceed to another domain over which preference operates, that is, word selection in reference to people. In examining how local cultural norms select for particular lexical choices, we are afforded an insight into something of the processes of language change.

5.1   Preference organisation: an introduction

What has come to be known as **preference** organisation[1] shapes a number of interactional phenomena. Despite its connotations of favouritism and personal inclination, the term 'preference' in CA reflects the observation that selecting one course of action over another is 'routinely implemented in ways that reflect an institutionalised ranking of alternatives' (Heritage and Atkinson, 1984:53). We have already encountered preference briefly in Chapter 3, where we noted a preference for *yes* answers over *no* answers, and for answers over non-answers in the ten-language survey by Stivers et al. (2010). We also saw, in Chapter 4, an observed preference for progressivity in interaction – an observed inclination to continue a turn to possible completion rather than abandoning it in the course of its production. Preference is thus seen to operate in the selection of one among several options; as Lerner notes, '[t]he asymmetry of relevant action alternatives is realized through practices that produce systematic advantages for certain types of (thereby preferred) action over other types of (thereby dispreferred) action' (1996:304); this clearly has implications, ultimately, for language structure. In Chapter 7 we discuss how preference organises conversational repair; here, however, we investigate how it operates with reference to adjacency pairs and how it shapes larger sequences of talk.

5.1.1   Preference and adjacency pairs

With respect to adjacency pairs, the term 'preference' has been applied to distinct aspects of initiating turns on the one hand, and responsive turns on the other, and so some clarification is necessary to navigate its various uses in the literature.

Preference and initiating turns

With respect to initiating turns, a first pair part may be constructed in such a way as to prefer – in the sense of project – a specific form in response. As Schegloff notes: 'Whether a question (for instance) prefers a "yes" or "no" response is a matter of its speaker's construction of it . . . the preference is built into the sequence' (1988b:453). So a question, e.g. *Have you got the time?* is said to prefer a *yes* response; *You haven't got the time, have you?* to prefer a *no*. Some straightforward evidence that speakers register the distinction can be found, with respect to questions, in the ways in which questions structurally preferring one option but receiving the other may be appended, TCU-finally, with the particle *actually* (Clift, 2001). So a question preferring *yes* as in (1) and (2) receives a *no* answer; conversely, a question preferring a *no* answer in (3) receives a *yes*

---

[1] For an account of the origins of the concept within CA, see Schegloff (1992a:xxxii–xxxiii).

answer. In each case, TCU-final *actually* marks that the turn is performing an action running counter to that projected by the first pair part:

(1) (Clift, 2001:253; H:(2)H7&~2:2)

    (L=Lesley; G=Gwen)

```
1L    An' he's just had a fortnight with his mothe:r,
2G    Ye:s?
3.    (0.5)
4L    An' he's going off to have a- a week with his siste:r
5     an' you know there's a third grandchi:ld do you?
6     (.)
7G    Ah:::m (.) n:no I think I wz only aware of two
8→    actua[lly.
9L         [Mm:. There's a third one,
10    (.)
11G   Well with Hele:ne.
12    (0.7)
13L   °I s'poze so:,°
```

(2) (Clift, 2001:255; C:7:1)

    (M=Mary; G=Gus. M and G are talking about the possibility of G having picked up German as a child living in Germany.)

```
1M    but I don't- (d'you see-) did you have help in the
2     hou:se? You probably di:d.
3     (0.2)
4G→   ptk. uh:m (.) ↑not [very much actually, uhm::
5M                       [Germans probably-
6M    Mm.
7G    not- not around constantly anyway.=
8M    =No.
```

(3) (Clift, 2001:253; H:(2)HC8~3:2)

    (C=Carrie; L=Lesley)

```
1L    Okay um.p.h ngYou don't off hand know Bodwin's
2     number,
3     (0.6)
4C→   Yeah I've got it down here actually I bumped into her
5     this morning I wz lucky.
6     (.)
7L    Oh-:.
8C    Ahh hah So I didn' haf to ring her. (.) It's uhm (0.3)
9     five oh six one three.
10    (.)
11L   Lovely thank you very much.=_S[ee you la:]ter.=
```

In both (1) and (2), the questions strongly project a *yes* answer – in (2) to the extent that the speaker, in line 2, provides a candidate answer herself. In (3), by contrast, the question, formatted negatively ('you don't . . .') is designed to prefer *no*. In each case, however, the eventual response goes against the preference exhibited in the design of the question. So preference may be built into the structure of first pair parts, and speakers design their related seconds to take account of this preference.

Preference and responsive turns

Just as first pair parts can be said to display in their structure a preference for a particular response, second pair parts can be said to display a preference in both the *action* that they perform and in their *format*. We examine these in turn.

(a) Action preferences

As a question may receive a *yes* or *no* response, an invitation may receive an acceptance or declination; a request, likewise, may be accepted or rejected. Many[2] second pair parts are chosen from these two broad, asymmetrical, possibilities. Given that it is through sequences that activities get accomplished in conversation, an action that aligns positively with respect to the stance displayed in that first part, thus favouring the accomplishment of the activity, and advancing the sequence (Schegloff, 2007a:59), is said to be preferred; an action which aligns negatively with the prior first pair part, is said to be dispreferred. The closest linguistic correspondence to preference is to the notion of markedness, with preferred turns being the 'unmarked' option (Levinson, 1983: 307; see also Levinson, 2000). Exemplars (4) and (5) below show what have become paradigm cases in the literature (e.g. Levinson, 1983; Heritage, 1984b) of preferred and dispreferred actions respectively; an invitation that is accepted (4), followed by one that is rejected (5):

```
(4)  (SBL:1:1:10)
1   A      Why don't you come and see me some [times
2   B   →                                     [I would like to
3   A      I would like you to
```

```
(5)  (SBL:1:1:10)
1   A   Uh if you'd care to come and visit a little while this morning
2       I'll give you a cup of coffee
3   B   hehh well that's awfully sweet of you, I don't think I can make
4       it this morning..hh uhm I'm running an ad in the paper and- and
5       uh I have to stay near the phone
```

So in (4) above, the acceptance of the invitation at line 2 both aligns with the action and promotes affiliation; in contrast, in (5) we see, at line 3, a declination which impedes the forward progression of the action and so does the opposite of pursuing affiliation. In the difference between these two exemplars lies Heritage's encapsulation of preference as 'a "bias" intrinsic to many aspects of the organisation of talk which is generally favourable to the maintenance of bonds of solidarity between

---

[2] Of course, some first pair parts – like greetings and farewells – only have one possibility as a second pair part.

actors and which promotes the avoidance of conflict' (1984b:265). Sacks, in his observations on the preference for agreement and contiguity in conversation, notes that 'the blandest look would say that if you examine only answer turns, then "yes"s are a lot more frequent than "no"s are' (Sacks, 1987:57). However, 'the blandest look' also seems be proving empirically robust; Stivers et al.'s (2010) study of question–answer sequences across ten languages (see Chapter 3) finds a greater proportion of confirmations than disconfirmations (from 70% of all answers in Danish to 89% in Yélî Dnye). This still is the case, even when the affirming response is in negative form (e.g. *You're not coming? – No, I'm not); no*-confirmations are not significantly slower than *yes*-confirmations.

(b) Format preferences

It is not only the responsive actions that display a distinction between the preferred and dispreferred turns, but also the formats of the turns themselves: the means or practices by which they are produced. The acceptance in (4) comes before the end of the invitation is produced, and in overlap (we recall in Chapter 4 how the placement of a turn in overlap can serve to endorse an action designed to be affiliative). The acceptance itself is also stated in unequivocal terms. In contrast, the declination in (5) is more structurally complex and contains several components: a hearable delay before the turn is produced ('hehh'), and in a yet further delay, the counterpositional 'well' (Sacks, 1992a, 1992b; Pomerantz, 1984; Heritage, 2014) as preface,[3] before a statement of appreciation ('awfully sweet'), a mitigated declination focusing on the speaker's inability ('I don't think I can'), reference to a time constraint that imports a provisional element to the declination ('today') and then an account ruling out compliance, produced with a certain degree of dysfluency.

Extracts (4) and (5) show particularly starkly the distinctions between preferred and dispreferred turn shapes in the case of an invitation. However, it turns out that the features associated with these turn formats are observable across adjacency pair action types for preferred and dispreferred turns. Here, for example, are an offer (6) being accepted (l. 2), and a request (7) that is acceded to (l. 2); the second pair parts in both cases arrive with no delay (indeed, in (6), early as in (4)), and with stated agreement components – turns that are what Heritage (1984b:266) calls 'simple and unvarnished':

```
(6)  (Holt, X(C)2:1:2:5–6)
     (Gordon is Lesley's son.)
1  L:    .hh Okay I'll ↑get Gordon to tell you the ↓na[me.
2  J:→                                              [Yes.
3  J:    Alright the:n tha[nks a lot Lesle[y
```

---

[3] Kendrick and Torreira's statistical survey on English data found that 'when a response includes a turn-initial "well", the probability that it will be a dispreferred action is 0.78; when the response includes turn-initial "u(h)m" the probability is 0.67; and when it includes turn-initial in-breath, the probability is 0.6. In contrast, when a response lacks these practices, the probability that it will be a dispreferred action drops to 0.21' (2014:268).

(7) (Davidson, 1984:113)
```
1   A        .hhhhh Uh will you call 'im tuhnight for me,=
2   B    →   =eYea:h,
3            (.)
4   A        Plea::se,
```

By the same token, the following (8) and (9) display a number of dispreferred second pair parts in the context, once more, of an offer, and then an invitation:

(8) (Heritage, OII:2:4)
```
1   H     And we were wondering if there's anything we can do
2         to help
3   S     [Wel 'at's]
4   H     [ I  mean ] can we do any shopping for her or something like
5         tha:t?
6         (0.7)
7   S→    Well that's most ki:nd Heatherton hhh at the moment no:. because
8         we've still got two bo:ys at home.
```

(9) (Potter and Weatherell, 1987:86)
```
1   M     We were wondering if you wanted to come over Saturday, f'r
2         dinner.
3    →    (0.4)
4   J→    Well (.).hh it'd be great but we promised Carol already.
```

Moreover, even when first actions are not necessarily first pair parts – that is, where initiating actions do not insist on a response, responsive actions may display such markers of preference. One such case – introduced in Chapter 3 – is assessments, where responses may be optional (see Stivers and Rossano, 2010; we discuss this further in Chapter 6). In such cases, we see that when responses are produced, agreement responses (as in (10), (11) and (12)) show the features of preferred turns – fast, and with stated agreement tokens:

(10) (Pomerantz, 1984:65; JS:2.28)
```
1   J     T's- tsuh beautiful day out isn't it?
2   L→    Yeh it's just gorgeous ...
```

(11) (Pomerantz, 1984:65; MC:1)
```
    (A and B are talking about a dog.)
1   A     Isn't he cute
2   B→    O::h he::s a::DORable
```

(12) (Pomerantz, 1984:65; SBL:2:1:8:5)
```
1   B     She seems like a nice little [lady
2   A→                                 [Awfully nice
3         little person.
```

The exemplars above all show what Pomerantz identifies as upgraded agreements, that is, responsive turns that incorporate stronger evaluative descriptors than those offered in the prior turn; otherwise, the agreements would be vulnerable to being heard as 'just going along with' the first assessment (a matter to which we return in Chapter 6). So, in (10), 'beautiful' gets the response 'just gorgeous'; in (11), 'cute' gets 'adorable', and in (12) the epistemically weak 'seems like a nice little lady' gets the intensified 'awfully nice little person' – each of which thereby displays a certain independence from the first assessment. The recurrence of upgraded evaluations in agreement turns is such that absence of such upgrades (e.g. the response 'yes' on its own, for example, to 'Isn't he cute?') may be hearable as tacit *dis*agreement – and indeed, they often do preface stated disagreements.

In contrast with agreements, disagreements generally show dispreferred features, with delays and markers of hearable reluctance to disagree:

```
(13)  (Pomerantz, 1984:70–1; SBL:2.1.7.-14)
1    A     (              ) cause those things take working at,
2    →    (2.0)
3    B→   (hhhhh) well, they [do, but
4    A                       [They aren't accidents,
5    B→   No, they take working at, But on the other hand,
6          some people are born with uhm (1.0) well a
7          sense of humor, I think is something yer born
8          with Bea.
9    A     Yes. Or it's c- I have the- eh yes, I think a
10         lotta people are, but ehn I think it can be
11         developed, too.
12        (1.0)
13   B     Yeah, but [there's-
14   A               [Any-
15   A     Any of those attributes can be developed.
```

In the above, the pauses at lines 2 and 12 before the dispreferred turns (beginning '(hhhhh) well' and 'Yeah, but' respectively) clearly foreshadow the disagreement to come.

So while preferred turn shapes are characterised by their prompt (and in some cases, early) production relative to a first pair part, the dispreferred turns are characterised in the first place by delay. Such instances of delay, alongside the sort of dysfluency evident in (5) are, as Pomerantz and Heritage note, 'interpretable as "reluctantly" performed instances of the action' (2013:215), and, as such, designed to head off the disaffiliative implications of what is being done. Of course, different actions are potentially disaffiliative to varying degrees; so, for example, we see markers of delay (as well as TCU-final *actually*) in the dispreferred seconds in extracts (1), (2) and (3), alongside a certain degree of dysfluency, and in (3) an account. These dispreferred seconds, we recall, are answers to questions with a clear preference for the opposite. However, with actions where the disaffiliative implications are more evident, we clearly see how a constellation of features is implicated in formatting second pair parts to show the actions as being 'reluctantly performed'. So (8) above, declining an offer of help, has many of the features of (5), in which an invitation is turned down: the appreciation ('most kind') to counter any imputation of ingratitude, the time reference ('at the moment no'), and the account eliminating the need for help ('We've still got two boys at home') (see Heritage, 1984b:269–73, for a detailed discussion of accounts in dispreferred second pair parts). Indeed, as observed by Drew (1984), accounts themselves may stand as implicit declinations and obviate the need for any declination components; by reporting alternative commitments (here alongside hearable markers such as delay and appreciation), a speaker can leave it up to the recipient to determine the implications for a get-together; this is how the exchange between Emma and Nancy, reported in Chapter 3, extract (1), proceeds:

```
(14)  (Drew, 1984:135; NB:II:2:14)
 1    E    Wanna cum down'n [av a bighta l:unch with me:?=
 2    N                    [°(              )°
 3    E    =I got s'm bee:r en stu:ff,
 4    →    (0.2)
 5    N→   Wul yer ril sweet hon:, uh::m
 6    →    (.)
 7    N→   [l   e t-  I: ha(v)]
 8    E    [or  d'yuh'av sum]p'n el[se (t')
 9    N→                           [N o :, I haf to uh call
10    →    Rol's mother..h I told'er I:'d ca:ll 'er this
11    →    morning= I g[otta
12    E                [°(Ahh.)°
13    N→   letter from 'er en (.).hhhhh A:n'dum
14    →    (1.0)
15    N→   p.So sh- in the letter she sed  if you  can why
16    →    (.) yih know call me  Sa:turdih morn:ning en I
17    →    jist haven't hh.
18    E    Mm[hm
19    N      [.hh T's like takin' a beating. (.)mhh
20         -heh. [heh heh [hh.
21               [Mm::    [('N th' hav'n) heard a word huh.
```

There is nothing in the exchange above which is a declination as such; but by reporting a prior obligation (ll. 9–10, 'I haf to uh call Rol's mother'), the speaker can rely on the recipient to understand the upshot for herself.

Such displays of reluctance are so pervasive in the production of dispreferred turns that Heritage, in contemplating offers and invitations, wryly notes:

> a rejection or refusal which is unaccounted for may be held to be suspect because the rejecting party 'would not' or 'could not' explain it in the normal way. Or again, a speaker who asserts unwillingness to attend a party to an intending host may add insult to injury since, it may be held, 'he couldn't even be bothered to invent an excuse'. And it is in virtue of such considerations that speakers may end up attending social functions for the lack of an appropriate excuse. For, lacking such a desirable social asset, they may do the non-accountable thing, and go.   (1984b:273)

5.1.2   Actions and formats: interactional implications

The formats of the two sets are so strikingly different, and, indeed, publicly observable and accountable – 'institutionalized methods of talking' in Heritage's words (1984b:268) – that to produce any of the second pair parts in (5), (8), (9) or (14) fast and unmitigated would be interpretable as the opposite of reluctance, and therefore purposefully and studiedly disaffiliative (or, put bluntly, downright rude). By the same token, a certain delay in the production of a second pair part – thus breaking Sacks's observed preference for contiguity – appears to be taken to be a harbinger of trouble. So, in (14) Emma's 'or d'yuh'av sump'n else (t')' (l. 8) testifies to her hearing the delay in Nancy's response (l. 4), and her appreciation prefacing it (ll. 5ff.), as adumbrating a declination. Moreover, in (15) below, A's initial proposal (in l. 1) is met by silence, whereupon A's 'or'-prefaced line 3 (as in (14) above) formulates the stance that the silence is taken to indicate; L's line 5 testifies to the fact that the proposal had indeed been problematic:

```
(15)  (SBL:3–3)
1   A    Why wd'n it be nice tih play pa:rtners.
2   →    (0.7)
3   A    Or w'tchu li:ke tha:t.
4        (2.8)
5   L    tch We:ll, (0.2) I don't know how wud we get partners.
```

Similarly with questions; in (16) below, Lesley (at l. 7) plainly takes the half-second's pause (l. 5) to adumbrate – correctly as it turns out, a 'No':

```
(16)  (Raymond, 2003:946)
1   L    Eh: WE:LL eh WHAT I RANG
2        up about was ehm
3        Di- di did you have
4        anybody want a photogra:ph?
5   →    (0.5)
6   R    I'll be honest with you
7   L    No.=
8   R    =haven't a:sked th'm.
9   L    Oh: that's alright
```

Furthermore, in (17) below, first introduced in Chapter 1, the questioner's line 4 shows that the 2.2 seconds of silence in the wake of the question is taken to indicate – correctly, as line 5 shows – that the answer is going to be negative:

```
(17)  (Drew, 1990:28)
1   A:   This- chemotherapy (0.2) it won't have any lasting effects
2        on having kids will it?
3   →    (2.2)
4   A:   It will?
5   B:   I'm afraid so
```

Note here that the question is built in such a way as to prefer a *no* answer and that the silence is thus taken by the speaker, as shown by line 4, to adumbrate a *yes*.[4]

The cross-linguistic study conducted by Stivers et al. (2009) of questions and answers also provides quantificational cross-linguistic support for this observation, suggesting that speakers of first pair parts take a certain degree of delay to indicate dispreference. So confirmations are delivered faster than disconfirmations (between, on average, 100 and 500 ms faster), reaching significance in seven out of ten of the languages. Moreover, here the distinction between dispreferred actions – declinations, disagreements and so on – on the one hand and dispreferred turn formats – the way such actions are produced – on the other is an important one to make, as it appears to be one that participants themselves make (see Schegloff, 1988b, for an extended discussion of the distinction):

(18) (Sacks, [1973] 1987)

     (B is inviting A out, but A has had a toe operation.)

```
1  A   Can you walk?
2  →   (0.4)
3  A   W'd be too hard for yuh?
4  B   Oh darling, I don't know. Uh it's bleeding a little,
5      'e j's took the bandage off yes'day.
```

Here A's question adumbrating an invitation fails to get an immediate response, whereupon A reformulates the first pair part which does then receive its second pair part. However, note the distinction here between format and action: the question itself is formatted to prefer a *yes* response, but such an agreement would constitute a dispreferred response to the question. Schegloff observes that these are 'cross-cutting preferences', and that 'the actual response to the revised question is attenuated to the point of invisibility' (2007a:77), not saying that it would be 'too hard' but giving accounts for not going. This dispreferred action is, however, done in a characteristically preferred manner: immediately, and with no delay in its production. As Schegloff notes, it is 'the preference structure of *the action being implemented* which dominates here and shapes the construction of the second pair part's turn, not the action's vehicle, which at most is expressed in the contiguous startup of the responding turn' (pp. 77–8; italics in original).

---

[4] The following report is a particularly dramatic instance of an exchange where a silence is taken to be a *yes* response, but is not in fact 'on the record' as such. Two *New York Times* reporters, Robert Smith and Robert Phelps, have revealed that they were given the tip-off that would lead to the Watergate scandal and the resignation of US President Richard Nixon, some time before the *Washington Post* reporters Bob Woodward and Carl Bernstein, who became famous for breaking the story. The acting director of the FBI, Patrick Gray, had told Smith that the former Attorney General, running Nixon's re-election campaign, was involved in a cover-up of the break-in and bugging the offices at the Democratic National Committee in the Watergate hotel:

'Smith asked Gray how far up it went – all the way to the President? "He sat there and looked at me and he didn't answer. His answer was in the look," Smith said. Smith rushed back to the *Times*'s Washington office, and accosted Phelps, an editor at the bureau. Phelps took notes and recorded the conversation. But nothing happened.'

('Watergate under the Bridge: How the New York Times Missed the Scoop of the Century', *The Guardian*, 25 May 2009)

In a study examining the distinctions between actions and turn formats in the expression of preference, Kendrick and Torreira (2014:273) map the possibilities thus:

	Preferred format	Dispreferred format
Preferred action	preferred action in a preferred format	preferred action in a dispreferred format
Dispreferred action	dispreferred action in a preferred format	dispreferred action in a dispreferred format

Kendrick and Torreira examine the extent to which the timing of a response – a format-based metric – may serve as a reliable signal of incipient action. Their statistical review of the data suggests, in the first place, that gaps of up to 700 ms are, in fact, no more associated with dispreferred actions than with preferred ones and that it is relatively longer gaps (of over 700 ms), as in (15) above, that indicate a dispreferred action is likely to be undertaken in a dispreferred format. They conclude that 'the timing of a response is best understood as a turn-constructional feature, the first virtual component of a preferred or dispreferred turn format, one without a one-to-one relationship in the actions speakers use it to perform' (p. 287).

It is not, however, only the format of dispreferred turns that show speakers' orientation to preserving affiliation; there are other sorts of evidence, too. In the first place, it is clear that speakers recurrently pursue affiliation in the face of incipient disaffiliation. So in (14) and (15) above, the speaker whose proposal is met by silence thereupon submits an alternative (in the form of an *or*-prefaced clause) which, given the trouble-marking implications of the silence, is directed towards receiving a preferred response.

5.1.3   An exception

It is also clear that, while, as noted above, disagreements with prior assessments are *generally* seen to be dispreferred, there appears to be a significant exception, and that is the context in which a speaker proffers an assessment which is hearably self-deprecating; for a recipient to agree with this would amount to a criticism of the speaker. In such contexts, Pomerantz (1984) reports, disagreements may sometimes come with stated disagreement components (e.g. *no*), and are generally produced fast:

(19) (Pomerantz, 1984:85; SBL:2.2.3:15)
```
1   A    I mean I feel good when I'm playing with her because I feel
2        like uh her and I play alike hehh
3   B→   No. You play beautifully.
```

(20) (Pomerantz, 1984:85; SBL:2.2.3:40)
```
1   B    And I never was a grea(h) Bri(h)dge play(h)er Clai(h)re
2   A→   Well I think you've always been real good.
```

(21) (Pomerantz,1984:85; C)
```
1  C     ...'ere Momma. She talks better than I do
2  B→   Aw you talk fine
```

These instances of fast disagreements stand as more evidence of speakers generally pursuing affiliation, and in the absence of such affiliation, responses which are affiliative may be pursued. In the following, a speaker, Julia, who has produced a self-deprecating assessment (l.1), gets swift, indeed overlapped, alignment and affiliation from Mary in line 2. Julia's subsequent account of the outcome of her latest trip to the hairdresser's ends in the assessment 'I'm sure it's blobs' (l. 6), but this is met by withholding from Mary at line 7, whereupon Julia pursues the matter (l. 8):

(22) (Clift, 2001:253; C:28:1:180)
```
      (M=Mary; J=Julia, in their sixties; M and J are talking about their hair.)
1J     I just feel o::ld and do::w[dy,
2M                                [Oh I do know [the feeling, (thinking)
3J                                              [Huh heh heh!
4M     Well I had supposedly had highlights and lowlights: (0.9) a
5      fortnight ago, (1) and I daren't look at the back, cos I know she
6      just got it with a thick brush and it's- (.) I'm sure it's blobs.
7      (0.8)
8M     Can you see some lighter blobs?
9      (1.2)
10J→   °No, it's alright actually. (0.2) Mm::, yeah, 'tis alri[ght°.
11M                                                          [BUT (.) I
12     [have mi-
13J    [I know what you mea:n, (.) so- sort of like- (>incredibly ch-<)
14     like a ch(h)ee:ta(h)h or-
15     (0.3)
16J    [(something)
```

Despite its clear status as a self-deprecation, the assessment 'I'm sure it's blobs' is structurally equivocal with respect to whether it demands a response. However, the upgraded response-mobilising feature (Stivers and Rossano, 2009), which we discuss further in Chapter 6, of interrogative syntax and rising intonation in 'Can you see some lighter blobs?' show the speaker pursuing a response – and an affiliative one ('No, it's alright actually') duly arrives at line 10.

5.1.4   Between preferred and dispreferred: agendas, social norms and deontic authority in responsive turns

It is clear that, in the case of self-deprecations, the usual preference for agreement comes into conflict with an ultimately stronger constraint, namely the pursuit of social cohesion, manifested in the pursuit of affiliation. Evidently there are other actions whose responses may similarly be shaped by other factors. Here we examine three domains in which responses to a first pair part are shown in various ways to resist the terms of engagement proposed by that first: in certain forms of answers to questions, compliment responses and children's responses to directives.

Answers to questions: conformity and resistance

The fact that polar (yes/no questions) constrain their responses in various ways is thrown into relief by Hoymann's work (2010) on questioning in ‡Ākhoe Haillom. As we saw in Chapter 4, ‡Ākhoe Haillom makes frequent use of open questions rather than polar ones, which are less constraining on the kind of response open to the speaker. Speakers are also less likely to use requests for confirmation, which are highly coercive in preferring a *yes* answer. Hoymann notes that there are several languages (Swahili, Kera in Chad and Gciriku in Namibia) where posing questions is considered impolite, and that certain types, such as polar questions, are dispreferred (p. 2736). In the following, even though a polar question is asked, the response avoids *yes* or *no* but implies the answer:

(23) (Hoymann, 2010:2735)
```
1  Ms:  llari           go  sī    ra  ū-he    dara-n   ge hîna?
        one.day.from.now RECPST take.away PROG take-PAS wire-3-pn DECL TAG
        the wire was taken yesterday right?
2  KO:→ ti-b    goro mî i      ge
        thus-3sm RECPST say UNKN DECL
        he   said  so
```

A study such as this shows the extent to which polar questions propose constraints on their responses, which participants may accept or resist in the design of their responses. In a study of yes/no interrogatives,[5] Raymond (2003) observes that yes/no responses in English accept or reject a proposition about the state of affairs proposed in the first pair part; they are therefore constrained to respond within the terms set by the question. They are what he calls structurally 'type-conforming'. In (24) below, Sue produces a type-conforming *no* response to Gail's question, and then a further component that offers an account for why the call was timed as the questioner arrived home (Pomerantz, 1988); here, 'No' on its own would have been insufficient to respond to the inference Gail has clearly drawn from the timing of the call:

(24) (Pomerantz, 1988:364)
```
1  Sue   So how are you.
2  Gail  Okay:: dju j'see me pull up?
3  Sue   No:: I wz trying you all day.en the line wz busy for
4        like hours
```

---

[5] Raymond (2003) uses the term 'interrogative' to refer to utterance form, thus maintaining a distinction between the form of an utterance and the action it proposes, since not all interrogatives implement questions.

In (25) below, the Health Visitor asks a yes/no question, acknowledging that the mother's breasts have caused problems, and receives a *yes* answer in line 3, with some elaboration indicating that matters have improved:

```
(25)  (Raymond, 2003:948)
        (HV=Health Visitor; Mom=Mother)
1   HV      How about your breast(s) have they settled do:wn
2           [no:w.
3   Mom→    [Yeah they 'ave no:w yeah.=
4   HV      =(      ) they're not uncomfortable anymo:re.
```

Contrast this preferred *yes* answer with the one below in line 3. The Health Visitor's question here only asks about the current state of the mother's breasts, not, as above, registering the possibility of prior problems. Once again, she builds the question to receive a yes/no response. However, on this occasion, the response to the Health Visitor's question receives what Raymond calls a 'non-conforming response':

```
(26)  (Raymond, 2003:948)
1   HV      Mm.=Are your breasts alright.
2           (0.7)
3   Mom→    They're fine no:w I've stopped leaking (.) so:
4   HV      You didn't want to breast feed,
```

The response that Mom produces, in line 3, shows that, even if her breasts are 'fine now', they once were not; a *yes* or *no* response would not have conveyed this adequately, as it would only make reference to their current state – *yes* would imply that her breasts had never been problematic; *no* would imply that they currently are. So, as Raymond notes, 'type-conforming responses accept the terms of a [first pair part], while nonconforming ones indicate some trouble with it or resistance to it' (2003:949); such responses are thus the most overt means by which speakers manage misalignments faced with the choices presented to them by yes/no interrogatives in sequential context.[6] In the following exemplar from Russian, we again see a speaker resisting the categorial response proposed by the question; thus neither *yes* nor *no* here would suffice:

```
(27)  (Bolden, 2009:129)
1   Dus:    Vse    zdaro,vy/
                everybody healthy
                Everybody's healthy?
2   Olg:→   Nu: Alechka nemnozhka prasty,fshaja/
                PRT NAME    a-little   caught-cold
                Well Alla caught a bit of a cold
3               no tak [nichevo/
                but so nothing
                but otherwise it's fine
```

---

[6] Fox and Thompson (2010) examine responses to *wh*-questions and identify a distinction between phrasal responses which do 'simple answering' and clausal responses, which are produced in contexts where there is displayed trouble with the question or sequence.

By packaging this as a non-conforming answer, the speaker is able to evade the constraints of the question's form while engaging with its agenda (Bolden, 2009:129). Work in Finnish by Sorjonen (2001) similarly examines marked and unmarked forms of response. So two particles, *niin* and *joo*, and repeats, all implement affirmations (answers that provide new information) and confirmations (treating the information addressed as already known) of the state of affairs proposed by a question. Speakers select between these alternatives: repetitions, treating the question as a request for information, imply expansion of the sequence; *niin* among other features, also projects a continuation of an activity, whereas *joo* is implicated in its possible closure.

Even within the class of type-conforming responses, however, there may be distinctions between responses which merely affirm a proposition and those which elaborate on the answer. Lee (2015), examining affirmative responses in Korean, shows that affirmations are of two kinds. The first is standardly in response to an unmarked polar question – that is, a question addressing information conveyed explicitly or inexplicitly, by presupposition, in a prior turn (p. 29). This response is a straightforward confirmation that treats the question as requiring no new information. In the extract below, Eun had invited her cousins, Kim and his sister Minju, over; only Minju had come. Eun here phones Kim to establish whether he too will come.

```
(28)  (Lee, 2015:29)
1  Kim:    mwe hay.
           what do:IE
           What are you doing.
2  Eun:    cikum enni-lang  nol-ko    iss-e
           now  sister-COM play-CONN exist:IE
           now I'm playing with sister.
3  Kim:→   Minju       enni   ka-ss-e?
           ((name)) sister go-PAST-IE
           Sister Minju came?
4  Eun:→   ung:
           yes
           Yes:
5  Kim:    ung::
           yes
           Yes:: (('I see'))
6  Eun:    hanlapong-to        mek-ess-e.
           ((name of fruit)-ADD   eat-PAST-IE
           (We) also had Hanlabong   ((a special kind of Korean orange))
```

At line 3 Kim produces an unmarked polar question, explicitly drawing out the implication attached to line 2, with its reference to 'sister'. At line 4 Eun responds with the type-conforming 'ung' (yes), fully acquiescing to the terms of the question and affirming the questioner's inference. Contrast this standalone usage of 'ung' with the one at line 3 below. Mom had asked her daughter Yun to take dumplings to her aunt. They are now on the phone the day after that visit. At line 1 Mom displays a problem with remembering what she was going to say, and then proposes a topic – the dumplings – but then cuts off 'ettehkey' (how), repairing it with the polar interrogative 'cwe.ss-ni' (did you give?). Conceivably, the abandoned question was something like *How did they turn out?* or *How did she like them?* So in response to this question, Yun does not simply supply a confirmation but addresses the broader agenda implied by that abandoned question:

(29)   (Lee, 2015::34–5)
```
1  Mom:    mwusun yayki-lul ha-la    kulay.ss-na (1.2) onul-i
           What   talk-ACC  do-PURP do.so:PAST-INTERR today-NOM
     →    isip.chil   il-i-ci° (0.4)a cincca   ecekkey  ku mantu
           twenty.seven day-CP-COMM    DM really yesterday the dumpling
           ettehkey- cwe.ss-ni?
           how     give:PAST-INTERR
           °What was I going to say (1.2) today is the twenty seventh
           ci° (0.4) Oh right yesterday the dumplings how- did you give?
2           (.)
3  Yun:→  ung imo-ka      cohaha-te-la
           yes aunt-NOM like-RETROS-DECL
           Yes the   aunt  liked    (them)
4           (.)
5  Mom:    e: ku- coh- masiss-tay?
           yes    like delicious-HEARSAY
           Yes:uh-  like-   she   said they're delicious?
```

In her answer, Eun thus infers the underlying purpose of the question (Pomerantz, 1988) and so orients to it as seeking new, unknown information, rather than a mere confirmation of the matter at hand.

While both of these affirming responses are type-conforming, the latter clearly goes somewhat beyond the ostensible terms set by the question. Another form of response explicitly challenges the very relevance of the question at all, while simultaneously proposing an alternative set of presuppositions as the basis for response. For English, Heritage (1998) shows how *oh*-prefaced responses to questions propose that the question asked is problematic in terms of its presuppositions and is thus inapposite. The central semantics of *oh* as a 'change-of-state' token are hereby invoked to propose that the question came 'out of left field' (Heritage, 1998:294), given the prior talk. Here, the celebrated English aesthete, Sir Harold Acton, is being interviewed. The interviewer produces a polar question at line 5; Acton's response is *oh*-prefaced:

(30)   (Heritage, 1998:294)
       (Act=Sir Harold Acton; Har=Russell Harty, interviewer)
```
1   Act:    ...hhhh and some of thuh- (0.3) some of my students
2           translated Eliot into Chine::se. I think thuh very
3           first.
```

```
4              (0.2)
5    Har:      Did you learn to speak (.) Chine[:se.
6    Act:→                                     [.hh Oh yes.
7              (0.7)
8    Act:      .hhhh You ca::n't live in thuh country without
9              speaking thuh lang[uage it's impossible.hhhhh
10   Har:                        [Not no: course
```

With the *oh*-prefaced response, Acton conveys the inappositeness of the question, given that it should have been clear from what he said earlier (ll. 1–2) that he had learnt Chinese (Heritage, 2002a). His subsequent expansion (ll. 8–9) elaborates on this, proposing an alternative presupposition.

Work by Wu (2004) on final particles in Mandarin reveals that turn-final *a*, with a flat or slightly rising pitch, can similarly challenge the legitimacy of the question. Standardly in Mandarin, answers are not suffixed with *a* (p. 182), but in the following two cases they are. Both of the following extracts were recorded at a dinner in the USA among friends. In (31) below, H is one of the hosts, and X is a guest:

```
(31)  (Wu, 2004:181)
      (%= talk between % is produced in English.)
1    H:    ei¿ (.) weisheme hui  duo      yi wan fan zai nabian.
           PRT     why     ASP additional one C rice at   there
           Hey, (.) how come there is an additional bowl of rice over there?
2          (1.3)
3    X:→   ↑hai you %Victor% a.
           still have (friend) PRT
           ↑There  is still %Victor% A.
```

Wu observes that turn-final uses of *a* in answering propose that the questioner should have known the answer, and that therefore the question is inapposite. So as host, the questioner in (31) might have been expected to know who the extra bowl of rice is for; the *a*-suffixing on the answer embodies the challenge to the legitimacy of the question from that questioner. At line 6 in (32), the terminal 'a' takes a similar stance towards the prior question:

```
(32)  (Wu, 2004:181)
1    T:    wo jintian-
           I  today
           I today-
2    T:    wo- (.) jinnian de shaobang       dui wo  you zai jichang
           I   this-year PRT little-league team I have   at airport
           I- (.) saw- this year's (Taiwanese) little league team
3          kandao guo.
           see    ASP
           at the airport
4          (1.2)
```

```
5  L:     a  zai nali   da.
          PRT at where play
          So where's (it) playing?
6  T:→   zai weilian    pote a
          At  Williamsport    A.
7  L:     (ou zai weilianpote)
          PRT  at    (place)
          (Oh, at Williamsport)
```

In (32), L is a baseball fan who used to play for the Taiwanese Little League; the Little League Series is held annually at Williamsport. T's turn-terminal 'a' thus marks the unwarranted status of the question: L, by implication, should have known the answer (Wu, 2004:182). In contrast to Mandarin, both Japanese and Russian mobilise turn-initial resources for resistant responses; in Japanese, *eh*-prefacing displays a respondent's departure from the terms of a question (Hayashi, 2010), and in Russian (Bolden, 2009), repeat prefacing may be used to resist the agendas and presuppositions of the question (see Chapter 7, extract (35)).

Fundamentally, although these resources all show differing degrees of resistance to a question, they accept the terms on which it is produced. Somewhat more resistance to the terms of a question is built into what Stivers and Hayashi (2010) call 'transformative responses', which seek to alter the very terms on which the question is produced, indicating that there are problems with providing a direct answer. Here, in an example from Japanese, Hiroshi, who lives in Boston, has described a restaurant he has enjoyed eating at in New York. Noboru asks whether Boston is close to New York, to which Hiroshi responds with a transformative answer:

```
(33)  (Stivers and Hayashi, 2010:5)
      (Nob=Noboru; Hir=Hiroshi)
1  Nob:   (eh) nyu-bosuton tte nyuuyooku kara chikai wake.
                 Boston       QT New.York from close reason
           Is Boston close from New York
2  Hir:→  ee::to kuruma de y- yojikan gurai ssu kedo ne:.
           well   car   by   4.hours about CP but FP
           Let's see, (it)'s about 4 hours by car
3  Nob:   a yojikan ka.=
           oh 4.hours Q
           Oh 4 hours
4  Hir:   =a ha:i.
           =Yes.
5  Nob:   a soo: hu::n
           Oh is that so. I see.
```

Instead of providing the subjective measure of distance proposed by the question, Hiroshi offers an objective measure of distance, leaving it to Noboru to judge for himself whether '4 hours' constitutes 'close'; as Stivers and Hayashi observe, 'the answer Hiroshi provides can be heard to propose a retroactive transformation of the question from a question about relative proximity to a question about absolute distance' (2010:5). Research on transformative responses also includes that on German (Golato and Fagyal, 2008) and Korean (H.R.S. Kim, 2013; M.S Kim, 2013).

Compliment responses

Questions are the paradigm case of first position actions. However, there are other actions which set terms that a speaker may, in the design of the responding turn, resist. Pomerantz (1978), in a study of responses to compliments, illuminates the means by which social norms may come into conflict with structural ones to shape responsive actions in a distinctive way. We saw earlier how agreements with assessments are standardly produced with upgrade. However, if there is a structural preference for agreement, there is a social norm against self-praise, which emerges in a distinctive way in compliment responses. In the following, for example, the recipient of the compliment accepts the compliment, but firstly prefaces it with the counterpositional 'Well' (Pomerantz, 1984:72; Sacks, 1992a:76; Heritage, 2014) and then produces an epistemically weak agreement:

(34) (Pomerantz, 1978:97)
```
1  A:    Oh it was just beautiful.
2  B:→   Well thank you Uh I thought it was quite nice
```

And in the following, the response consists of a qualification of the prior compliment:

(35) (Pomerantz, 1978:97)
```
1  A:    Good shot
2  B:→   Not very solid though
```

While (34) above is an agreement, it lacks the distinctively upgraded form of agreement evident in such exemplars as (10), (11) and (12) above; and (35) concedes the compliment with 'though', while qualifying it with what, the concession apart, would be a disagreement. Pomerantz proposes that these mitigated forms of agreement are the result of a conflict between the interactional preference for agreement, and a social norm against self-praise.

Resistance in response

A study by Kent (2012) examining adults' directives to children at mealtimes further illuminates how responses may choose a middle course between a preferred and a dispreferred option. Noting that the interactionally preferred option is compliance, she identifies a number of cases in which children responding to directives engage in what she calls, following an initial proposal by Schegloff (1989), 'incipient compliance', which manages elements of both the preferred option of compliance and the dispreferred option of resistance. So, in the following, Mum at lines 12–13 produces an implicit directive,[7] 'What did she say about talking with y'mouth full¿' at a point when Daisy clearly has a mouth full of food:

```
(36)  (Kent, 2012:716)
1    Daisy:      =N(h)o, (0.4).hh you mi:sta:yke.
2                (0.2)
3    Daisy:      S'not a jo:ke..hh Guess [↑wha' ↑ha:ppe:ns in]=
4    Mum:                                [((clears throat))  ]
5    Daisy:      =schoo'hh.hh
6                (0.6)
7    Daisy:      ((takes a mouthful of food)) When Mrs Williamson
8                ge's it wrong, (0.5) Sh'goes=
9    Mum:        ((puts her glass down, slight lean and gaze towards
10               Daisy until l.23)
11   Daisy:      =[((lifts chin high, turns right and left))]
12   Mum:    →   =[What did she say about              ]ta:lking
13               with y'mou:th full¿
14               [(1.3)                                        ]
15   Daisy:→     [((straightens back, holds chin high, chews once))]
16   Daisy:→     I've ↓fi:n↑i:shed
17               [(1.7)                                   ]
18   Daisy:→     [((cranes her head back and swallows))   ]
19   Lucy:       [((starts smushing her food with her fork))]
20   Dad:        tuhhh! (('dismissive' laugh at Daisy))
21               [(1.6)
22   Mum:        [((shakes head at Daisy, gazes down at table))]
23   Dad:        [((turns to look at Lucy smushing her food))   ]
```

Instead of producing the preferred option – immediate compliance – Daisy does what Kent calls a 'crafted over-exaggeration' (2012:717), holding herself ram-rod-straight and chewing energetically (l. 15). She then announces 'I've finished' (l. 16) when she visibly has food in her mouth – the publicly available contradiction here serving to defy the directive in claiming, but not demonstrating, compliance. As Kent notes, '(w)hen a recipient resists a directive they refuse to cede control of their actions to the directive speaker' (p. 717). It is often the case that resisting directives can result in the directive being reissued in upgraded form (Craven and Potter, 2010), but here no such reiteration is produced. Daisy, at line 18, continues with an elaborate non-verbal display ('cranes her head back and swallows') showing compliance with the directive. Mum and Dad separately register Daisy's action – the former with a shake of the head, the latter with a dismissive laugh – and then turn their attention elsewhere. The key to avoiding a reissued directive, Kent argues, lies in Daisy's initial response – the elaborate

---

[7] We return to the distinction between the form of this utterance and the action it delivers in Chapter 6.

performance of chewing – that demonstrates a stance of compliance. This is, of course, distinct from actual compliance, which occurs at some remove (l. 18) from the directive.

That this incipient compliance is not idiosyncratic to Daisy is suggested in the following, where Jessica is directed by Mum to 'phlea:se finish your soup' (l. 10):

```
(37)  (Kent, 2012:718–19)
1    Emily:    [Egger yolmk (.) °ump°            ]
2    Emily:    [((picks egg up to display it))]
3    Mum:      hhh
4              (1.2)
5    Mum:      Tis ra::ther ni:ce ((turns to watch Jessica))
6              (6.2)
7    Jess:     ((Puts glass down with a bang and turns to stare
8              at mum))
9              (1.2)
10   Mum: →    No::w, would you phlea:se <finish your ↑soup>
11             (0.8)
12   Jess:→    °Soup°
13   Jess:→    [((pulls up sleeve))
14             (0.9)
15   Jess:→    I: am (.) si:rsty::
16             [(6.4)     ]
17   Jess:→    [((gets a spoonful and blows on it, then takes a
18             tiny sip))]
19   Mum:      °Mm°
20   Jess:     [((puts her spoon down))]
21   Jess:     [Nyat] say-            ] (.) THat sa:ys (0.4)
22             [S:err: (.) >dat sa:ys< (0.4) S:ou:p.       ]
23   Jess:     [((traces finger round the edge of the bowl))]
24   Mum:      No: that sa:ys SPArro:w.
```

Nearly a second passes before Jessica, showing no orientation to either compliance or resistance, simply and quietly repeats the object of the directive (l. 12). She then – in a move that might be regarded as preparatory to further action – pulls up a sleeve, further delaying full compliance. In then announcing 'I: am (.) si:rsty::' (l. 15), Jessica offers an account for why she had not been eating prior to Mum's directive, and formulates her earlier drinking as a standard, rather than deviant and sanctionable, part of mealtime behaviour. As such, it casts 'not-eating' as justifiable and, by implication, Mum's directive as unwarranted. Her account itself delays the actual compliance still further; and, in the following 6.4 seconds, Jessica does what Kent formulates as 'getting ready to comply' (2012:719) in blowing on the soup, before she does a display of actual compliance by sipping a small spoonful of soup (ll. 17–18). So when full-bodied compliance is finally delivered, it is after Jessica's own turn, rather than her mother's directive – and so, as Kent notes, 'appears to be self-motivated behaviour rather than responsive to the directive' (p. 720). Once again, an upgraded repeat directive is held off by demonstrating a compliant orientation, but without delivering compliance as such. When compliance is ultimately delivered, then, it is produced as if the action is done under the child's own auspices – indeed, virtually voluntarily.

Kent's study shows how the recipients of directives resolve the core dilemma that compliance means relinquishing autonomy and submitting to the speaker's will; resistance risks prompting a further, upgraded attempt at control which, in stalling progressivity and potential escalation, threatens intersubjectivity. Incipient compliance thus finds the middle ground between compliance and resistance.

Such work provides an important insight into deontic authority – into who, in Kent's words, 'prevails in decision making' (2012:713; see Lukes, 1979; Walton, 1997). Clayman (2013) sheds further light on this issue by examining the placement of address terms at turn beginnings: the prime site for signposting actions which depart from the implicational relevances of sequential organisation. In (38) below, Fred, from line 1, launches a presequence:

(38) (Clayman, 2013:298; from Schegloff, 1980:112–13)
      (F=Fred; L=Laurie)

```
1    F:    Oh by the way ((sniff)) I have a bi:g favor to ask ya.
2    L:    Sure go' head.
3    F:    'Member the blouse you made a couple weeks ago?
4    L:    Ya.
5    F:    Well I want to wear it this weekend to Vegas but my
6          mom's buttonholer is broken.
7    L:→   Fred I told ya when I made the blouse I'd do the
8          buttonholes.
9    F:    Ya ((sniff)) but I hate ta impose.
10   L:    No problem. We can do them on Monday after work.
```

Fred's request is flagged up prominently in the presequence, both by the 'pre-pre' and its formulation ('big favor') at line 1, and in its attribution of responsibility for the blouse to the recipient ('the blouse you made', l. 3). At lines 5–6 he conveys a specific, and moreover, immediate need: by the end of his turn, Laurie can be in little doubt as to the nature of the upcoming request. As Clayman notes:

> In this sequential environment, a pre-emptive offer is vulnerable to being seen as coerced by the pre-request and perhaps not a genuine 'offer' at all. The framing of the pre-emptive offer is geared to avoiding this eventuality. The prefatory address term foreshadows and underscores the independent and hence voluntary nature of the offer in progress, while the subsequent account invokes a motivational history for the offer that predates the present sequential moment. All of this casts the action in progress as a non-coerced and fully volitional offer, with the further consequence of implying that the request was unnecessary.   (2013:298)

However, alongside pre-emptively 'accepting' responses to pre-requests, address terms in initial position can also figure in the design of responsive turns. In the sequence below (which, incidentally, follows sometime after that in Chapter 3, extract (34)), Karen, having declined Vicky's invitation to watch TV, produces an enquiry at line 1, which, as Clayman notes, being intrinsically imposing, 'has some of the hallmarks of a request' (p. 298), and, after some delay, receives a response at lines 5–6:

```
(39)  (Clayman, 2013:298)
      (K=Karen; V=Vicky)
1   K    Will I be invited next week?
2        (0.4)
3   V    tch
4        (0.2)
5   V→   Karen you've been invited every week b'tchu dis
6        never:: (.) get around tih coming do:wn.
```

Vicky does not provide an explicitly affirmative response. The turn-initial address term, as in (38) above, projects an independently motivated response, while the subsequent talk indicates that she has been extending invitations (by their nature, first position actions), regularly and for some time. By implication, then, as Clayman observes, 'an invitation for next week, although not yet articulated explicitly, was already in the works and would have been offered without any prompting. All of this works to undercut the antecedent request, while also registering a complaint about Karen's persistent failure to take up the prior invitations' (p. 298).

Such work is a compelling demonstration of how interactional participants manage issues of deontic authority. Work by Stevanovic and Peräkylä (2012, 2014) has shown how deontic authority is one element in the shaping of action; we return to this issue in Chapter 6, in showing how agency, independence and authority figure in the understanding of indirect utterances.

In responses to compliments, directives and requests, we have thus seen evidence of the ways in which participants manage the conflicts between interactional preferences and other factors. In the first, the preference for agreement is tempered by a general social norm against self-praise; in the second, the preference for compliance is kept in check by considerations relating to individual autonomy; and, similarly, in the third, the preference for granting is constrained by concerns to construct services as volunteered rather than coerced.

5.1.5   Preference and action categories

All the evidence shows that it would be unwise, therefore, to make assumptions about preference inclinations across classes of action; as Pomerantz and Heritage point out, 'the participants themselves make distinctions within gross categories of action, and those distinctions matter for the preference principles that are relevant' (2013:223). So preferences for action categories should not be assumed, but rather empirically established in each case.[8] It is worth examining one such case where close attention has been brought to bear on two categories of action: offers and requests.

There has long been an argument in the conversation-analytic literature that offers are standardly preferred over requests (see, e.g., Levinson, 1983:355; Lerner, 1996; Schegloff, 2007a:83–4). Perhaps the most compelling of the arguments to support this are the assertions that requests are produced disproportionately late in conversational exchanges relative to offers, that they exhibit dispreferred formats and that they may masquerade as offers. It is evident in certain contexts, such as introductions, that offering one's name is preferred over waiting for a request to produce it (Pillet-Shore, 2011). Moreover, if you are approaching a door with a cup of coffee in each hand, evidently my offering to open it (or, indeed, simply opening it) is preferred over waiting for you to request that I do so. However, the work of Kendrick and Drew (2014), which finds a rather more complex relationship between offers and requests, guards against generalising across action categories. They note that, in particular circumstances, an offer may be as potentially awkward an enterprise as requesting might be perceived to be; and, indeed, across their corpus, Kendrick and Drew find there to be equivalence between offers and requests with respect to features of turn design, noting that

> just as requests may engender impositions and obligations on the other person, so too may offers engender obligations on the other and may put the other in one's debt for even small services . . . and imply something about their need for such assistance or services . . . The accounts that accompany offers may orient precisely to such matters of obligation and debt. (2014:94)

It is similarly clear that, although requests may masquerade as offers, by the same token, offers may be produced in a number of formats not, on the face of it, dedicated to doing offering. So, to cite one example:

```
(40)  (Rahman, II:6)
      (Jenny is detailing the anxiety of her young son ('ee', l. 3) in the wake of her father's
      death.)
1   Jen:   But it gets me down a bit you know[ah: mean I ca:n't
2   Ida:                                      [(Loo:k.)
3   Jen:   I ca:n't mo:ve? Yihknow 'ee[siz where yih goi:[n g,]=
4   Ida:                              [(What)            [Well]=
5   Jen:   =[(goin to- we:y-)]
6   Ida:   =[a h 'v to:ld    j]u:.
7          (.)
8   Jen:   Mm[:?
9   Ida:→    [Jis ^send im round here fer a couple'v: hou:r:s
```

---

[8] Schegloff suggests 'would you like the last piece of pie?' (2007a:60) as an instance of an offer preferring a rejection – but not one that is empirically attested.

The offer is done here (l. 9) by means of a directive, rather than in a canonical offer format (Curl, 2006; see Chapter 6 for more on canonical formats) – one made possible by the prior detailing of a problem (by Jenny) to which Ida's offer (in Kendrick and Drew's phrase, 'interactionally generated') is a possible remedy. So, as Kendrick and Drew note:

> These relationships, and the symbiosis between offers and requests that they point to, derive in large measure from specific circumstances of need, commonly but not invariably embodied in requests, and the possibility that one way of being solicitous is to anticipate the needs of others, by offering assistance. This symbiotic relationship is one aspect of social solidarity and social cohesion, but it is a contingent relationship, built upon particular circumstances . . .   (2014:12)

Whether Kendrick and Drew's conclusion that offers are not, in fact, generally preferred over requests is, of course, to be empirically determined. However, their study shows how a range of evidence can be used to illuminate the relationship between categories of action – and other forms of evidence may yet emerge. Furthermore, it reinforces the extent to which actions may be constructed across sequences, rather than being encapsulated in a single turn; it is the sequential context that enables us to hear Ida's 'Jis send im round here fer a couple'v: hou:r:s' in (40), or, say, *Let me open that door for you* as an offer, rather than the directive proposed by its form. It also should guard against assumptions that a preference for one action over another holds across all contexts. For example, Pomerantz (1980) shows how interactants use a particular device – the 'my side telling' where they report their perspective (e.g. *I hear you guys are having a party Friday*) to 'fish' for an invitation. In so doing, speakers orient to the social inappropriateness of direct self-invitations (e.g. *Can I come to your party?*; also cf. extract (39)). While it appears to be intuitively the case that inviting oneself is socially inappropriate, the following news report on the visit of Prince Charles to a Welsh brewery shows that this is evidently not without exception:

> **Owner reunited with Prince**
>
> OWNER of Felinfoel Brewery, Captain Beryn Lewis, said the Prince's visit was a great honour, but also a reunion.
>
> 'I used to work for him, so I'm excited to see him,' he said.
>
> 'I was a guards officer – I used to protect the palace.'
>
> 'We didn't invite him here – he invited himself, which is great'.   (*Llanelli Star*, 18 July 2012)

Furthermore, with the positive assessments, 'which is great', and 'a great honour' here, the self-invitation is not only treated as not inappropriate – rather, highly desirable; it is patently taken to be the vehicle for another action: a compliment. Such exceptions do not, of course, overturn the general preference – the empirical skewing – for being invited over self-invitation, but rather propose caution in making such generalisations, and attention to circumstantial particulars.

Work such as Kendrick and Drew's on categories of action is establishing an increasingly nuanced understanding of particular actions in showing how they are built across sequences. This is even the case for actions which might, on the face of it, appear to be unilaterally undertaken. So, for example, work on complaints suggests that they 'cannot simply be defined as particular expressions of discontent that are produced unilaterally by one of the participants' (Heinemann and Traverso, 2009:2) and that complaining is 'ultimately a joint activity, negotiated in a step-by-step fashion between the participants in inter-action' (p. 2). Moreover, in the course of examining the joint construction of complaints, Drew and Walker note of a collection assembled by Gail Jefferson of what they call 'dis-sings' (disagreements, discord, complainings, disputes, etc.):

> every case of what came to be an explicit expression of disagreement, etc. was found to be incipient in the prior talk. Even the handful of cases (about 5) which seemed to be 'initial actions', turned out, to be [sic] on closer inspection, to be adumbrated in the talk leading up to the overt disagreement, dispute or whatever.   (2009:2405, fn. 4)

Furthermore, there are other reasons why generalisations across action cate-gories may be risky. For example, while it may be assumed that invitations generally prefer acceptances, there are clearly cases where they do not. Isaacs and Clark (1990) identify a set of actions they call 'ostensible invitations':[9] they propose that such invitations are a member of a family of ostensible actions such as questions, compliments, assertions (we return to the formatting of such actions in Chapter 6). Many will also recognise how a first offer of second helpings at the dinner table is almost routinely declined (what Schegloff, 1988b:454, calls a 'pro-forma' declination), but then accepted upon subsequent urging; in some communities such initial declinations with subsequent acceptances are so salient that they form part of a culturally recognised and named phenomenon. The Persian norms or code of politeness collectively known as *ta'arof*, for example, involves initial declinations of invitations and refusals of offers so routinely that Persian speakers can be taken aback when, in Western contexts, their ostensible invitations are accepted first time round, and when their own refusals of offers are accepted without challenge (see, e.g., Taleghani-Nikazm, 1998; Asdjodi, 2001; Menasan, 2003).[10] Work on offers in Arabic is similarly establishing a preference for refusing an offer at least in the first instance (and on most occasions, several times) before a visible display of reluctant acceptance (Abu Abah, 2015).[11] In the

---

[9] Isaac and Clark (1990), as a study in speech acts, is concerned to identify a class of acts and establish the conventions regarding their use and recognition as ostensible acts.

[10] I am grateful to Saeed Menasan for this observation.

[11] In Levantine Arabic there is a term, translated as 'a fisherman's invitation', that bears comparison with *taa'rof* and ostensible invitations. It is said to have derived from the fishermen of Alexandria who, on passing each other in their respective boats, would each invite the other to share their food. Given that each is on his boat, an acceptance is out of the question and a refusal normative.

following Saudi Arabic exchange, Lama, the host, offers her son-in-law Nader tea (l. 1); it is met by an immediate and vigorous refusal (l. 2), whereupon the co-host, Ahmed, insists by means of the imperative to his wife (l. 3), and Lama reissues the offer by minimising it ('ša:hy Byalat ša:hy' – '(just a) cup of tea'):

(41) (Abu-Abah, 2015)
    (N=Nader is at his in-laws' house; L=Lama and A=Ahmed)

```
1  L:     (      ) ʔru:ḥ ʔjybešš↑ahy
           (  ) (I) go get the te↑a
           (  ) (Shall I) go get the t↑ea
2  N:→    >la la< tᵃdji:bi:nˤai tak[fe:n
          >no no< bring you (sig. fem) thing ple[ase
          >no no< (don't) bring anything ple[ase
3  A:                                [Illa dʒi:bai
                                     [Illa bring you (sing.fem)it
                                     [do bring it
4  L:                                [ša:hy
                                     [tea
5         Byalat¹² ša:hy
          Byalah of tea
          (just a) cup of tea
```

Several turns later, with no further reference to tea, Lama goes to prepare the tea. The following, involving participants in a wholly different relationship, also shows initial resistance to an offer. A younger man offers to carry a case for a much older man, but, while the visible actions from the outset project that the offer will be taken up, there is still initial verbal resistance from the offer recipient. The extract is taken from a reality TV show in Saudi Arabia. The young contestant, Sultan, offers to carry the suitcase of the older visitor, Ghali. Sultan approaches Ghali, who is closing the case, and points to the suitcase:

(42) (Abu-Abah, 2015)
    (S=Sultan; G=Ghali)

```
1  S:     ʔšy:l ʕannek?
          (I) carry for you?
          (shall I) carry (it) for you?
2  G:→    ʔstery:ḥ¿ ʔstery:ḥ¿
     →    [Relax¿ relax¿
3         [((S continues to point to the case))
4  G:     Jazzakallah xer
          Rewards you (sig.masc) god good
          God reward you
```

One source suggests that absence of such an ostensible invitation is the cause of great offence (see M. Sobhy, blogspot, 4 October 2011, at: http://maged-sobhy.blogspot.co.uk/2011/10/blog-post .html). My thanks to Faye Abu-Abah for drawing this term, and the source, to my attention, and for translating it for me.

¹² A small glass used for drinking tea.

```
5            Barakellah fy:k¿ šukran, ʔllah yeʕṭy:kelʕafyah
6    G:      yeʕṭy:kelʕafyah
             Bless god in you¿ thank, god give you wellness
             give you wellness
7            God bless you¿ thank you, god give you health
             give you health
8            ((S takes the bag and invites G to walk in front
9            of him and out of the room))
10   G:      Jazzakumullah xer
             Rewards you god (pl.masc) good
             God reward you
```

Ghali's first response to the offer is 'ʔstery:ḥ¿ ʔstery:ḥ¿' (Relax, relax) – not, as in the previous case, a direct refusal, but resistant nonetheless; but as he does so, Sultan continues to point to the case. Ghali's next turn 'Jazzakallah xer' (God reward you) implicitly accepts the offer (for a discussion of religious invocations in Arabic, see Clift and Helani, 2010); as he does so, he steps back from the case, allowing Sultan to pick it up. Recurrently in Saudi data, Abu Abah (2015) finds that initial resistance, if not vigorous refusal, is routinely preferred in the face of offers, even if – as is equally routine – acceptance ultimately follows. Empirical investigation of this kind across the range of Arabic varieties is limited, but anecdotal evidence suggests that this is widespread. Harris, discussing Egyptian Arabic, notes that refusal 'is freely acknowledged as occurring in a wide range of situations' and is just '"kala:m" (mere) words/talk that a person needs to say when he has been offered something' (1996:41).

Thus, normative preferences for English conversation may not always hold in exactly the same forms when subject to cross-linguistic examination, but in the face of such apparent variation the general norms for the promotion of affiliation appear to be universal. While, in the face of an offer in Arabic, vigorous initial refusal is preferred, this should not obscure the fact that acceptance is ultimately preferred overall. It is also the case that in particular non-conversational contexts the observed norms appear to differ from those shaping conversation. Perhaps because there is correspondingly less importance on personal affiliation, given the task-based nature of institutional talk, preferences pertaining in conversation may not hold. So in the disagreement sequence in extract (13) there are clear indications of reluctance to disagree; however, in contrast, televised panel interviews conducted by broadcast journalists are structured around polarised debate. As Pomerantz and Heritage note: 'In this environment, disagreements are, for the most part, offered straightforwardly and vigorously' (2013:225).[13]

---

[13] This kind of adversarial format, originating in political interviews, has also become conventionalised in some other forms of interview. One non-political interviewee, invited to appear on a programme (*Today*, BBC Radio 4) predominantly concerned with political debate, takes objection to this:

> The style of debate practised by the *Today* programme poisons discourse in this country. It is an arena where there are no positions possible except for diametrically

5.2   Preference and the recognition of action

It is clear, then, that interactional preferences are visible in the means by which sequences are developed – and indeed, they are the means by which sequences are developed. So, as we saw in Chapter 3, in the discussion of pre-expansion, pre-invitations are directed to minimising the possibility of a declination, and pre-announcements directed to minimising the possibility of informing the recipient of something already known. So an orientation to the possibility of a dispreferred action is the motivation for pres of various kinds. The following sequence – the epitome of a dispreferred sequence expansion – shows this in a particularly striking manner. Here, among other things, a request is not quite produced (the salient parts of the sequence are labelled here for clarity) – and not quite refused:

```
(43)  (Schegloff, 1995a:193)
      (M=Marcia; D=Donny)
1               Rings
2     M:        Hello?
3     D:        'lo Marcia,=
4     M:        Yea[:h
5     D:           [=('ts) Donny
6     M:        Hi Donny
7     D: F_pre→  Guess what.hh
8     M: S_pre→  What.
9     D: F_b→    .hh My ca:r is sta::lled.
10              (0.2)
11    D: F→      ('n) I'm up here in the Glen?
12    M: S→      Oh:：.
13              [(0.4)]
14    D:        [.hhh ]
15    D:        A:nd.hh
16              (0.2)
17    D:        I don' know if it's po:ssible, but [.hhh]/(0.2)] see
18              I haveta open up the ba:nk.hh
19              (0.3)
20    D:        a:t uh: (.) in Brentwood?hh
```

opposed ones, where nuance is not permitted and where politicians are forced into defensive positions of utter banality. None of it is any good for the national conversation.

Of course, I'm not saying that news interviews can't be adversarial. Sometimes, you have to be nasty Columbo or we'd never get to the truth. But I'm talking about that very specific, very artificial, very *Today* programme format of a presenter acting as referee between two people who have been chosen to represent the opposing sides of a manufactured argument. It is a binary view of politics, of life and, as a result, it is also a dishonest one ...

It was Michael in the red corner, me in the blue! Ding! Defend yourself! Justify yourself!   (Graham Linehan, 'My Today Programme Ambush', *The Guardian*, 8 June 2011)

```
21  M: S_b→   =Yeah:- en I know you want- (.) en I whoa- (.) en I
22            would, but- except I've gotta leave in aybout five
23            min(h)utes. [(hheh)
24  D:                    [Okay then I gotta call somebody
25            else. right away.
26            (.)
27  D:        Okay?=
28  M:        =Okay [Don    ]
29  D:              [Thanks] a lot. =By-.
30  M:        Bye:.
```

In his absorbing analysis of this exchange, Schegloff notes how, aside from
Marcia's 'Oh' at line 12, Donny's announcement – adumbrated by his pre-
announcement 'Guess what' (l. 7), given the go-ahead by Marcia (l. 8) – can be
rendered as: 'My car is stalled (and I'm up here in the Glen?), and I don't know if
it's possible, but, see, I have to open up the bank at uh, in Brentwood?' Nothing is
left out here – in a very literal sense – but the silences (some with audible breaths)
that constitute that 'nothing' are, in interactional terms, very much something;
once again, we see how sequential position enables us to see exactly what that
something is, on each occasion of its occurrence:

> Then we can see that – and how – this is not a unitary discourse produced by a
> single participant; and we can see that and how some of its components
> follow not the components of talk that preceded them, but the silence that
> followed the talk component that preceded them. Thereby we can come to
> see that it is not just a hearer's uptake and actions that can enter in the shaping
> of a speaker's talk; it can be the absence of them that does so.   (Schegloff,
> 1995a:194)

Thus, Donny's turn – 'My car is stalled' (l. 9) – coming as it does, to a prosodic,
syntactic and pragmatic completion, is possibly complete; as a hearable
announcement and also a possible complaint (embodied in 'stalled'), some
kind of appropriate uptake is thus relevant (cf. 'my mom's buttonholer is broken',
extract (38)). An information receipt, and/or some alignment with the misfortune,
is due here; but such a preferred response is withheld. Moreover, this absence of
an action – this silence – is, as Schegloff notes, *'as fully fledged an event in the
conversation as any utterance and as consequential for the ensuing talk'* (p. 198;
italics in original). For what follows is manifestly shaped by it, the *and*-prefacing
of the turn that ensues being designed as a continuation rather than a new
beginning. The upshot, of course, is that 'and I'm up here in the Glen?', as a
continuation, artfully converts a potential inter-turn pause (between two speakers) that would expose the brewing dispreference into an intra-turn pause, a pause
in a speaker's own turn – just like the *which* increments in extracts (69) and (70)
in the previous chapter. Indeed, not only line 11, but subsequently lines 15, 17 and
20 are built similarly as increments, in response to Marcia's relevantly *not*
responding at each possible turn completion to what is being constructed as a

potential request for help, and what is coming to fruition as such with the pre-request starting at line 17, 'I don't know if it's possible, but '. The construction of a turn incrementally as a series of 'turns-so-far' (Schegloff, 1995a:198)[14] thus deftly conceals the absence of a relevant offer of help from Marcia. Indeed, Marcia, at lines 21–3, produces an account, so illustrating the dispreferred nature of rejection, without ever having been explicitly asked – the account itself, and its response ('Okay then'), testament to the very real – oriented-to – status of the request itself, despite it never actually being formulated.

Schegloff's bravura account of this exchange fully brings out the contingency of actions through time. In showing how the absence of specific actions may be as consequential as their production, it charts the incremental building of actions which may never be fully explicitly realised in verbal form, but which, none-theless, are recognisable and real.

5.3   Preference in person reference

We have so far concentrated on preference with respect to actions in sequence. However, it is clear that preference operates, not just at this level of 'position' but also 'composition': in elements of turn construction. This speaks to a fundamental principle in interaction, that of recipient design (Pomerantz and Heritage, 2013:211) with respect to word selection. Sacks notes the preference 'for building such a description as will permit the other to see that you know that they know what you're talking about' (1992b:149). One area of word selection in particular has attracted substantial interest, perhaps because of its scope for comparative study across languages, and that is the domain of person reference; it is this topic to which we now turn.

5.3.1   Preference, principles and defaults in person reference

With respect to person reference (e.g. Sacks and Schegloff, 1979; Sacks, 1992a,b), there appears to be a systematic inclination by interactants to choose particular options over others when choosing how to refer to persons. These principles can be summed up for English as: 1. *minimisation:* 'if possible, use a single reference form' (e.g. *Naomi*) and 2. *recognition:* 'if possible, use a recognitional reference' – that is, one that the recipient will recognise (e.g. *my sister*). If *Naomi* alone is recognised by the recipient, then both conditions will be satisfied at once. However, if it is not, and *my sister* is, then, as Schegloff and Sacks point out, the principle of recognition trumps the principle of a single

---

[14] Compare, for example, Chapter 4, extract (48), 'I wrote a letter to the governor telling 'im what I thought about him', and Goodwin's (1979) analysis of the single sentence 'I gave up smoking cigarettes today one week ago today, actually' in conversation, produced incrementally with reference to eye gaze, Chapter 4, extract (33).

reference form.[15] So, in the following, we see Ann using three different forms
used in an attempt at reference (referents in bold for the sake of clarity):

```
(44)  (Schegloff, 2007b:127)
1   Ann:   ...well I was the only one other than
2      →   .hhh than thee uhm (0.7) mtch! Fo:rds.
3      →   Uh Mrs. Holmes Ford?
4          (0.8)
5   Ann:→  You know the- [the the cellist?
6   Bev                  [Oh yes. She's- she's (a)/(the) cellist.
7   Ann    Ye:s
8   Bev    Ye[s
9   Ann      [Well she and her husband were there, ...
```

At line 2, it is evident from the inbreath and the repetition of 'than', after which
the referent is due, that there are problems with the progressivity of the turn – the
'uhm', the pause, and the bilabial click indicating a search. After the referent is
produced – 'Fo:rds' – and got none of the immediate recognitional uptake
(Schegloff, 2007b:127–8) that regularly attends a successful search of this
kind, Ann goes on to produce another single recognitional reference form (l. 3),
'Mrs. Holmes Ford?', this time on upward-intoned, 'try-marked' prosody. This
getting no acknowledgement after a lengthy pause (l. 4), Ann launches a third
attempt, with another try-marked recognitional, 'the cellist?'. As it happens,
however, before the referent itself is produced, Bev produces an *oh*-prefaced
acknowledgement, finally claiming recognition.[16] So, while recognition is still
elusive, there are continued attempts to achieve it. Here, the principle of minimisation – 'use a single reference form' – is successively relaxed until recognition is secured. The principle of recognition is thus seen to trump that of
minimisation, and this appears to be the case across the languages on which
such research has been conducted (e.g. Brown, 2007 for Tzeltal; Enfield, 2007b
for Lao; Hacohen and Schegloff, 2006 for Hebrew; Hanks, 2007 for Yucatec
Maya; Levinson, 2007 for Yélî-Dnye; Oh, 2007a,b for Korean; Senft, 2007 for

---

[15] There are clearly contexts in which particular institutional constraints shape the use of specific
forms. So in English, the preference for minimisation implies that interactants do not standardly
address recipients with 'first name + last name'. However, one exception is the broadcast
interview, where such forms may be used in the service of informing the audience, e.g.

```
(Heritage and Clayman, 2002:78)
1   IE     ...and the Government is derelict in its duty if
2          it does not communicate to the four million with
3          security clearances that fact. That should be
4          done.
5   IR:→   Christopher Boyce, I think you've done it.
6          And done it very eloquently tonight. Thank
7          you very much for talking with me.
```

[16] We pursue these kinds of searches in Chapter 7 on repair.

Kilivila; Sidnell, 2007 for Bequian Creole). So even in a community such as that reported by Sidnell, on Bequia, where people may have multiple names, the unmarked option is to attempt to secure recognition with one name, as Emmanuel does at line 31 here:

(45) (Sidnell, 2007:305)

```
31   Emmanuel:→   Elis ma.
                  Ellis man.
32   Anya:        ah:::
33   Shana:       huu Elis.
                  Who Ellis?
34   Emmanuel:    Da iz wa ah doz kal Geeza somtaim.
                  That's what I call Gazer sometimes.
35   Shana:       oo - yu een biin konchriiz satadee nait.
                  oh - you didn't go to the countries Saturday night.
```

As it happens, the reference, although apparently recognised by Anya, is not so by Shana, and repair is initiated on it at line 33, whereupon Emmanuel offers another possibility at line 34.

Stivers et al. (2007:13) note that names (though not always bare names, so, e.g., 'Aunt Rebecca' as well as 'Rebecca') are broadly preferred as the unmarked reference form in English, Yélî Dnye, Kilivila, Bequian Creole and Lao. By contrast, possessed kin terms ('my aunt') are the unmarked reference form for Yucatec Maya, Tzotzil, Tzeltal and Korean. No languages so far examined prefer descriptions ('the woman in the hat') as the unmarked reference form.

5.3.2   Preference and grammaticalisation

There may be other preferences at work, too. Evidence from a number of languages leads Stivers et al. (2007:14) to suggest that there may be a preference for *association*, whereby speakers do work to associate themselves and their co-participants with the referent, such as, *my sister*, *your cousin*, *his brother's teacher* (associated with his brother, associated in turn with him). This appears to be the unmarked form of person reference in Tzeltal, Tzotzil and Yucatec. The following is an instance from Tzotzil:

(46) (Haviland, 2007:241)

```
ja 's-tot     y-ajnil    a-kumpare      Manvel.
!   3-E-father 3-E-wife 2-E compadre Manuel
He is the father of the wife of your compadre Manuel.
```

Haviland notes that the referent could, in fact, stand in a much closer relationship to the speaker. (This would be somewhat analagous to, in English, saying to an in-law on the phone *Would you like to speak to your son?* whereby the default name is substituted for a kin term, which we discuss later with reference to departures from default usage.) However, there is a convention whereby, if possible, the speaker begins a kin-chain with one's addressee and constructs the shortest path from addressee to referent. The second-person possessive prefix on *a-kumpare* (your compadre) makes explicit the indexical link between the referring expression and the addressee (Haviland, 2007:241). In this way, local norms are seen to inflect general preferences; and the operation of what Blythe (2013:912) calls 'biasing operators' is what allows selection of certain words to take place.

Levinson (2007) suggests there may also be a preference in many languages relating to *circumspection*, formulated by Blythe as: 'if possible, observe culturally specific and/or situationally specific constraints on reference and avoid the default reference forms' (2013:898). In English, such usage may be marked, but not culturally enshrined (e.g. *somebody's getting very sleepy*, said by one parent to another as their child yawns). Or take the following, fairly standard, instance of pronoun usage. Although not mentioned by name here, it is possible to derive the referent by inference, through familiarity with English social norms regarding husband-and-wife couples. Lesley's 'We have friends in Bristol' (l. 3) allows her to refer subsequently to 'he' (ll. 7 and 13) as one member of the invoked couple, the husband:

```
(47)  (Kitzinger, 2005a:249)
1    Les:     ..hh (.) Uhm (0.3).tch Well I don't know how that went,
2             .h uh (.) It's just thet I wondered if he hasn:'t (0.3)
3         →   uh we have friends in Bristol
4    Mar:     Ye:s?
5    Les:     who:- (.) uh: thet u- had the same experience.
6    Mar:     Oh↑::.
7    Les:→    And they uhm:.t (0.2).hh He worked f'r a printing an:'
8             paper (0.9) uh firm [u-
9    Mar:                         [Ye:s,
10   Les:     uh[:- which ih puh- uh: part'v the Paige Group.
11   Mar:       [Yeh,
12            (.)
13   Les:→    .hh And he now has: u- a:: um (1.1) I don't think you'd
14            call it a consultancy (0.2) They find positions for people:
15            in the printing'n paper industry:,
```

'He', then, is derived by pragmatic inference; and, as the sequence shows, the recipient displays no trouble in accessing the referent, and the reference is done en passant in the course of discussing something else ('the same experience', l. 5). This sort of passing reference may be contrasted with the work that may be done to achieve reference in languages showing a preference for circumspection. Evidence from Yélî Dnye, the language of Rossel Island, and from a number of Australian languages, suggests that circumspection may supersede the preference for recognition because of the very strong constraints associated with certain naming taboos referring to the deceased. Extract (48) shows a case where a speaker refuses to produce a name, in accordance with the Rossel principles of taboo, leading to an extended guessing sequence. In line 1, N produces a minimal description, 'that girl', using the demonstrative *wu* 'that.unseen/indirectly.ascertained'. After a pause, P initiates repair on this, only to receive, *sotto voce*, a gloss, but no specification – 'that girl I mentioned', now with the anaphoric demonstrative. There then follows three guesses, and a repetition, from the co-participants, all in terms of kinship specifications, but no names ('the daughter of Mbyaa', l. 7, 'Kpâputa's wife' from M at l. 9, repeated by P at l. 11, and then 'Kpâputa's widow' at l. 16):

```
(48)  (Levinson, 2007:60)
1    N:→   wu dmâdî a kêdê Thursday ngê anê lóó
            That girl told me she would go across on Thursday
2           (0.6)
3    P:    n:uu ngê?
            Who did?
4           (0.8)
5    N:→   °(yi          dmâdî)°
            That.mentioned girl
6           (1.2)
7    P:    Mby:aa tp:oo módó (ngê)
            The daughter of Mby:aa did?
8           (0.6)
9    M:    Kpâputa u kpâm?
            Kpâputa's wife?
10          (1.2)
11   P:    Kpâputa u kpâm?
            Kpâputa's wife?
            [
12   M:    ee! ee! ki tpóknî mwi lee dmyino, Stephen a kwo,=
            Hey kids go over there, Stephen is here,
                (
13   N:        ((Eyebrow flash))
14   M:    =mwi lee dmyino ó!
            go   right over there!
                (
15   N:    ((Head-point East))
16   P:    Kpâputa u kuknwe apii?
            Kpâputa's widow, right?
            [            [
17   N:→   (kî dmâdî) ((Eyebow flash)) mm
            (lapse) That girl) 'you got it'
```

It is only after the repetition of 'Kpâputa's wife', from P at line 11 (overlapping with an aside to some children, ll. 12 and 14) that N, the speaker of the trouble source, gives the first response: an eyebrow flash, which on Rossel Island can mark assent, and then a head-point towards the home base of the referent. P then rephrases the prior guess, 'Kpâputa's widow, right?' to which N responds with a more expansive eyebrow flash and a reintroduction of the referent 'that girl' (now with an unmarked deictic like English 'that') (Levinson, 2007:60). It transpires that N is referring to his own daughter-in-law, widowed because his son has died (p. 65). Reference in this case is far from en passant and has clearly become the priority business.

Similarly, in his study of Murrinh-Patha person reference, Blythe shows how various types of kin-based morphosyntax ('kintax', as defined by Evans, 2003) evolved to satisfy design constraints required by certain conversational preferences, in particular that relating to circumspection; Blythe notes that there are potentially hundreds of names to be avoided. The following extract shows this preference emerging in an expanded adjacency pair sequence. Mona has just recounted an amusing story told to herself and her sister Edna, at which Edna (l. 1) requests Mona to remind her who told them the story:

```
(49)  (Blythe, 2013:900)
1    Edna     ↑Nanggalardu, (.) ↓dannyiyerr↓ngime¿
              nanggalardu
              who
                  dam       -nyi          -yerr  -ngime
                  3SG/DU.SB.19.NFUT -1NSG.INCL.DO -inform -PAUC.C.NSIB
              Who was it that told us that story?
2             (0.15)
3    Mona→    <MaKA[:RDU]warda>;
              ma- kardu    warda
              NEG-living.human TEMP
              He isn't around any more.
4    Edna     [-----]
5             (1.6)
6    Edna     Nanggalyu;
              nanggal =yu
              who      =DM
              Who was it?
7             (1.3)
8    Mona→    °Birrarriya.°=
              Birrarri  =ya
              man's.name =DM
              Birrarri°.
9             (0.5)
10   Edna     Ah nyinika bere tjimngime=
              Ah nyini-ka  bere   tjim           -ngime
              COS ANAPH-TOP finish 1NS.INCL.SB.1sit.NFUT -PAUC.F.NSIB
              Oh that's right, we were sitting down
11            =da nan panguwathu;
              da    nan            pangu-gathu
              NC:PLT what's.its.name DIST -toward
              at what's that place over there.
```

While a principle of recognition might expect the prompt delivery of a name, there is firstly a brief pause and then a description which both indicates decease in its grammatical form ('MaKA:RDU warda', 'he isn't around any more', produced with markedly slower pace) and provides Edna with information for a category-specific search (someone, no longer alive, who might have told an amusing story). However, after nearly 2 seconds' pause, Edna reissues the request. After some delay, Mona produces the name, at line 8, but, as marked speech rate delivered the description at line 3, here the name is produced with marked speech volume, that is, here, *sotto voce*, used to mark attention to the impropriety of its production (Schegloff, 2003c; see also extract (48), l. 5, from Yélî Dnye, above). This fragment is exceptional in that it shows circumspection (along with minimisation) being relaxed in favour of recognition; indeed, it is plain here that the name is produced with sequential and articulatory features that mark it as dispreferred. Standardly in Murrinh-Patha, it is the other way around, and circumspection trumps the other principles,[17] and it is in the use of pronouns and kin terms that this displayed caution is expressed.

If English, ignoring case distinctions, makes six distinctions in its pronoun system (*I*, *we*, *you*, *he*, *she*, *they*), the Murrinh-Patha pronominal system has twenty-five distinctions for free pronouns and indirect objects, and twenty-three distinctions for direct objects and verbal subjects (Blythe, 2013:901). So to the outsider, the referencing may seem extremely oblique, drawing, as it does, on specific knowledge of the kinship system. However, as we see from the following extract, the referencing of four individuals is accomplished successfully through pronouns and cross-reference as a recipient, Mary, attempts to remember a particular occasion, many years previously, that a speaker, Edna, recalls in line 1:

```
(50)  (Blythe, 2013:906–7)
1    Edna→   Ne↑ki°ngi°me [tjin] tharrkatngime trak kayyu.
              nekingime              tjim              -dharrkat
              1PAUC.INCL.F.NSIB 1NSG.INCL.SB.1sit.NFUT -get.stuck
                   -ngime            trak     kanyi =yu
                   -PAUC.F.NSIB   vehicle      PROX =DM
              This is where we got bogged in a car.
2    Dora                 [Ah  ]
3                  (0.3)
4    Mary    .h°°(nganakaya)°°.h
              nganaka=ya
              maybe  =DM
                   (Maybe)((ingressed))
5                  (1.1)
6    Edna→   >nan'gungintha tjininginthadha.<
              nan'gungintha tjini           -ngintha  -dha
              2.DU.F.NSIB   2SG/DU.SB.1.sit.PIMP -DU.F.NSIB -PIMP
```

---

[17] Blythe also suggests there may be other preferences at work, namely *association*, mentioned earlier, as well as *generalisation* ('prefer general reference terms if possible and don't be overly specific') and *specification* ('prefer specific reference forms that maximize the potential for recognition') (2013:912).

```
                 You and one other person were here
7                (0.6)
8     Mary       Ngarrangu.
                 ngarra     -wangu
                 what/where -direction
                 Which way.
9                (0.5)
10    Edna→      kanyethu kura pandjedha°dh°arra.
                 kanyi-gathu kura    pandje                       -dha
                 PROX-hither NC:water 3PU/PAUC.SB.22bring/take.PIMP -PIMP
                     -dharra
                     -moving
                 The two siblings were bringing something of the water class
                 this way.
11               (1.5)
12    Mary       ngarran°uw°a:ngu mayern ngarran°uw°a:ngu.
                 ngarra     -nu wangu     mayern ngarra     -nu wangu
                 what/where –DAT direction track  what/where –DAT direction
                 Which way? Which track?
13               (0.2)
14    Edna       °kanyungu kangyungu dingalngu;°
                 kanyi-wangu    kanyi-wangu    dingalngu
                 PROX-direction PROX-direction place.nam
                 This way, this way Dingalngu
15               (0.5)
16    Edna       °↓ngarra thardidha°g°athungime.↓°
                 ngarra thardi     -dha     -gathu -ngime
                 REL    1NSG.INCL.4be.PIMP –PIMP –toward –PAUC.F.BSIB
                 toward where we were camping.
17               (3.6)
18    Edna→      °↓Aa bematha nukunu damatha kandjingarrudhangime.↓°
                 Aa bematha   nukunu damatha
                 Ah that's.all 3SG          INTS
                     kandj                         -ngarru -dha –ngime
                     3SG.22bring/take.PIMP -1DAUC.IO PIMP -PAUC.F.NSIB
                 Ah well he was the one bringing it for us
```

In this extended sequence, note that the repairs are initiated, not on the human referents but the locational ones, at lines 8 and 12; the references to people here are accomplished successfully and en passant. Blythe notes, of Mary's initial reference form in line 1:

> Both the free pronoun *nekingime* and the verb *tjintharrkatngime* are used for an initial reference to the persons in the car that became bogged. The reference (1PAUC.INCL.F.NSIB) is to several people, at least one of whom was female and whose number includes the addressee (probably Mary). Because both the addressee and the speaker are female, the others might have been males or females; we cannot tell . . . In line 6, Edna goes on by asserting that

Mary and one other person were there: *Nan'gungintha tjininginthadha*. This free pronoun plus verbal cross-reference (2DU.F.NSIB) is 'you two nonsiblings, at least one of whom is female' ... Because Mary is female, and formerly married, and because there were no particularly salient referents from the prior talk, the implication is that Mary was there with her late husband Ken.   (2013:907–8)

After a pause, Mary initiates repair on the locational reference in line 6. At line 10, Edna repairs with the deictic 'kanyethu' (in this direction), including another person reference that advances the sequence and so progresses the story: 'kanyethu kura pandjedhadharra' (the two siblings were bringing something of the water class in this direction) (p. 909). The ensuing 1.5 second silence (l. 11) suggests a problem, which at line 12 is revealed in Mary's repair initiation to be, once again, with a location: 'Ngarrangu' (Which way). The reference to the siblings, in contrast, is not treated as problematic, and Edna proceeds to produce another person pronoun in line 18 as she clarifies.

We can track an incremental process of inferencing across the sequence from line 1, which tells Mary that she is included in the 'car-load of people' (with the 'we' reference). Line 6 tells Mary her husband Ken was there; line 10 furthermore tells her that two people in the car were siblings – but is unmarked for gender, so does not distinguish between sisters or brothers. Blythe tracks the process of pragmatic inferencing thus:

Realizing that 'something of the water class' (expressed with the bare waterclass nominal classifier *kura*) is a veiled reference to beer, *kura thurrulk*, provides a clue as to the identity of the siblings. It can be inferred that these siblings liked to drink beer. The question 'Why that now?' makes relevant an inspection of line 10 as a possible elaboration on line 6. That is, might Mary's husband, Ken, be one of the two siblings? If so, then Mary need only identify a person in a sibling relation to her husband Ken, who is likely to drink beer with him. If there is such a person, why not just mention his name? Ken is deceased. Might the other 'sibling' also be deceased? One of Edna's own sons (Greg) passed away. He was a good friend of Ken's, and they liked to have a beer together. The two men both had a common ancestor who happened to be their respective mothers' fathers' father. By same-sex sibling merger (Scheffler 1978:115), the mothers' fathers can be equated, and the mothers can be equated, thus making them classificatory brothers. Finally, Edna makes singular reference to her son at line 18, stating that he had been bringing out the beer for them. Neither man is mentioned further. The story has run its course.   (2013: 909)

Four individuals, two of whom cannot be, and are not, named, are thus here successfully referenced in the course of altogether other business by means of pragmatic inferencing from kin-based morphosyntax in the service of name avoidance. As Dixon observes: 'the social custom of name taboo, and the associated proscription on lexical words that have similar form, is of utmost significance for understanding one of the ways in which Australian vocabularies change' (1980:28).

5.3.3   Departures from default usage

Cultural preferences are one general constraint shaping usage, expressed through default forms of referring. However, when departures from such defaults occur, they testify to more ephemeral considerations in the shaping of actions being implemented through the reference term. In this section we examine a number of departures from default usage, firstly in English, and then subsequently in Hebrew and Korean.

As as noted earlier, the default referring expression in English is a bare name or pronoun; to use other than this default is to accomplish something in addition to what Schegloff (1996b:440) calls 'referring *simpliciter*', that is, which does nothing above and beyond straightforwardly referring – as Enfield puts it, 'without trying to convey that one is doing it in a special way or for a special reason' (2013:439).[18] The following extract exemplifies such reference:

(51)   (Enfield, 2013:439; Field, 5/88:2:1:1)
        (Dwa: Dwayne; Mar: Margie)

```
1  Dwa:    u-How is everybody in general [(          )
2  Mar:                            [Oh we:ll: uh (0.2)
3     →    pretty good uh:m: (0.4) Kathrine seems to be alright
4     →    she's: still at Yo:rk
```

There are two instances in Margie's turn of reference *simpliciter*: the recognitional form 'Kathrine' in line 3, and the pronoun 'she' in line 4, neither doing anything beyond straightforwardly referring. However, alongside these default *forms* of reference, Schegloff (1996b) identifies default *positions* for reference, departures from which implement specific actions. So, in the extract above, 'Kathrine' not only is an initial form (as would be, e.g., *my daughter* or any other description) but is also in what Schegloff terms initial position.[19] By the same token, the pronoun *she* not only is a subsequent reference form, but is also in a subsequent position. These default relationships of form and position are thrown into relief by the implementation of subsequent forms in initial position, and initial forms in subsequent position.

The first possibility – a subsequent form in initial position – was captured from a linguistic perspective by Lasnik's (1976) observation that pronouns do not necessarily require antecedents. That there may be an interactional basis for this usage is exemplified in anecdotal form by Schegloff, who observes the following in respect of the day that President Kennedy was assassinated:

---

[18] However, see Haviland on Tzotzil (2007:249), for the view that speakers cannot simply refer without doing other things.

[19] Schegloff (1996b) uses the terms '*locally* initial/*locally* subsequent form/position' but in the interests of clarity, the terms 'initial' and 'subsequent' are used here.

> One could walk on the street or campus and observe others being approached –
> or be approached oneself – by apparently unacquainted persons who asked, 'Is
> he still alive?' What was striking was that virtually without fail the reference
> was understood; and with great regularity that reference had taken the form of
> a … subsequent reference in … initial position. It served at the time as a
> striking embodiment of community, for each speaker presumed, and presumed
> successfully, what was 'on the mind' of the other, or could readily be 'acti-
> vated' there. The … subsequent reference term tapped that directly … In the
> convergence of their orientations lay 'community'.   (1996b:451)

The reverse mapping – of an initial form onto a subsequent position – is similarly
done by reference to sequences of action. In talk which is otherwise apparently
referentially continuous with prior talk, a speaker may use an initial reference
form in a subsequent position to propose that what is being launched is a
departure from the line of talk hitherto. At line 17 in the following extract, the
locally initial form, 'Alice', is used in what is clearly subsequent position, as
evidenced by its initial usage at line 7 and subsequently with referential pronouns
at lines 11 and 13:

(52)   (Schegloff, 1996b:452; SN-4, 16:2–20)
       (Mar=Mark; Kar=Karen; She: Sheri)
```
02  Mar:   So('re) you da:ting Keith?
03         (1.0)
04  Kar:   'sa frie:nd.
05         (0.5)
06  Mar:   What about that girl 'e use tuh go with fer so long.
07  Kar:→  A:lice? I [don't-] they gave up.
08  Mar:            [ (mm) ]
09         (0.4)
10  Mar:   (°Oh?)
11  Kar:   I dunno where she is but I-
12         (0.9)
13  Kar:   Talks about 'er evry so o:ften, but- I dunno where she is.
14         (0.5)
15  Mar:   hmh
16         (0.2)
17  She:→  Alice was stra::nge,
18         (0.3) ((rubbing sound))
19  Mar:   Very o:dd. She usetuh call herself a pro:stitute,='n I
20         useteh- (0.4) ask 'er if she wz gitting any more money
21         than I: was.(doing).
```

At lines 14–16 the topical sequence has been allowed to lapse. By using an initial
form at line 17, rather than the subsequent form ('she') that would be licensed by
its subsequent position, Sheri treats it as a new spate of talk, and 'embodies this,
and incipiently constitutes it, by use of the locally intitial reference form'
(Schegloff, 1996b:452). Thus, selection between alternatives ('Alice' or 'she')
is done by reference to a sequential project. In section 6.2.1, 'Epistemics and

identity', we examine another case, showing how the departure from default usage may be implicated in the construction of identity.

There are other ways in which the use of a non-default term may be accomplishing distinct actions. It is clear that even within the category of initial forms, there are clear departures from referring *simpliciter* (such as *Madam needs her dinner* in response to a baby crying). Stivers examines such usage – what she calls an 'alternative recognitional' – at line 1 below:

(53) (Stivers, 2007:90–1)
    (Nicole just finished talking to boy on phone.)
```
1   Nic:→   Mom, can you go pick the birthday boy u:p.
2           He wants to go to the Plu:nge;
3           if there's anybody there th't he kno:ws
4           He can go swimmin' toda:y.
```

By using 'the birthday boy' rather than her son's name in line 1, Nicole better fits the form of reference to her request that her mother pick up her son from the swimming pool. As Stivers observes, the form of address here neatly embeds an account for the request and why it should be granted (2007:90). There are a number of things that such alternative recognitionals do above and beyond simply referring, and Stivers examines the means by which they can be used to manage aspects of the relationship between the speaker, addressee and referent.

There are also distinctions to be made within the category of subsequent forms. In languages where, standardly, reference forms do not require free-standing pronouns – pro-drop languages – the use of such pronouns can similarly be used to do something beyond referring *simpliciter*. In Hebrew, for example, although subject pronouns are included in the present tense, in the past and future tenses, the verb is inflected for person (speaker, recipient or other), for number (one or more) and for gender. So past tense usages where, in addition, there are free-standing pronoun references, are clearly a breach of the preference for minimisation, and informationally redundant; however, interactionally speaking, it is evident that they are anything but. In the following, two women are driving, and Dorit starts reflecting on her heavy day:

(54) (Hacohen and Schegloff, 2006:1307–8)
```
1   Dorit:   'avar   'alay yom kashe::. 'Ani
             passed on+me day har::d.  I
             I had    a  hard   day. I
2            'aye:: fa=' ex   'e:ex hayiti 'omeret et ze
             tir::ed =how h:how I+was   say  it
             am tired. How do I say it
3            tam↑id? Fe::
             alwa↑ys? Fe:: ((wipes her nose))
             usually?
4            (1.2)
5   Gali:    'an lo yoda'at. 'od   lo   shafaxt (.) kafe 'az
             I'no know.  yet  no   spilled+you (.) coffee so
```

```
                I don't know. You haven't spilled coffee yet so
6               'ani lo yoda'at.=
                I    no know.=
                I don't know. ((spilling coffee is one of Dorit's
                features))
7   Dorit:→     ='ani lo shati-ti kafe          hayom, 'anshati-ti [te::y.]
                =I   no I+drank  coffee today,  I'drank+I [te::a.]
                I didn't    drink    coffee    today,     I drank tea.
8   Gali:                                                   [SHAKRA]nit.
                                                            [L I A]R.
                                                            Liar.((shouts))
9       →       'at  shat-it          kafe    sha[xor 'ecli'al hashul]xan.=
                you drank+you coffee bla[ck by+me on the+tab]le.
                you drank black coffee in my place on the table.
10  Dorit:                                       [ze kafe shaxo:r]
                                                 [it black coff:ee]
                                                 It was black coffee.
```

Dorit's first turn solicits a word from Gali, but the latter announces herself unable
to help, invoking one of Dorit's characteristic features as an account: Dorit
usually spills coffee over herself. By line 6 each party has used a single reference
form to refer to self or recipient; either the present tense, in which the person is
not inflected on the verb and is expressed by a pronoun ("ani 'aye::fa' by Dorit in
1–2, "Anlo yoda'at' by Gali in 5), or the past tense without a pronoun ('hayiti' by
Dorit in 2, 'shafaxt' by Gali in 5). However, in line 7, where Dorit rejects the
account with her dispreferred response, both verbs are, as standard, inflected for
first-person singular on the verb (marked in the transcript with the final '-ti'
ending, 'shatiti', 'I drank'), but, in addition, there is a turn-initial pronoun 'ani'.
This rejection is in turn contested by Gali (l. 8) with the epithet 'Liar' and then the
account: that Dorit had had coffee at her house. The singular feminine past tense
verb is marked for second person 'shatit' (you drank), but it is also preceded by
the second-person pronoun 'at' (you). This use of an informationally redundant
pronoun is, across the cases studied by Hacohen and Schegloff, a means by which
participants underline the disaligning character of their actions.

If Hebrew is a 'moderately' pro-drop language, Korean features pronoun
deletion not only for subjects, but in practically all grammatical contexts.
Similar to the study for Hebrew above, Oh (2007b) examines those occasions
on which speakers depart from this preference by incorporating an overt form of
reference to themselves and/or their recipients, even though verbs are inflected
for person. Prior to the following exchange, C and J had agreed to meet L
somewhere before all going on to a restaurant to meet K. However, arriving ten
minutes late, they could not find L and had embarked on a search for an hour and a
half; L, it turns out, had simply gone to the restaurant without waiting for the
others. They have just met and are discussing the incident; in line 1 C addresses J
and K, who separately had been looking for L:

(55) (Oh, 2007b:470)

```
1  C    nuney-tul-i    olay kellyess-te-n              ke        kath-untey?
        you:PL-PL-NOM long take:ANT-RETROS-ATTR thing seem-CIRCUM
        It seems that it took long for you guys,
2       twul-I     ka-se?
        two-NOM    go-PRECED
        because you both went there?
3  L    kunikka-n (                      )
        therefore-TOP
        So,
4  J    twu pen        tol-ko.
        two times    go:around-CONN
        We went around twice, and
5  L    a choyak-i-ess-e choyak.=
              worst-be-ANT-IE  worst=
        Oh, it was the worst, the worst.=
6  L→   =sip pwun-ul    mos kitali-nun        palamey   nayka.=
        =ten minute-ACC NEG   wait-as:a: consequence   I-NOM=
        All because I couldn't wait for ten minutes.
7  J    hung hung
```

J responds to C in line 4 with a description of what they did; whereupon L launches an emphatic negative assessment, 'a choyak-i-ess-e choyak' (Oh it was the worst, the worst). In his subsequent account for this, he uses a contextually redundant form of self-reference 'nayka'. Oh remarks that it appears to have been motivated by the speaker's interactional goal of publicly attributing to himself responsibility for the incident that has just been assessed negatively; she notes that

> the function of the particle 'ka' is to highlight the status/role of the NP that it is attached to (i.e. the first-person pronoun in this case) as a participant in the event described by the predicate. Here, it serves to underscore that it is the speaker himself who did not wait for 10 minutes, and who should thus be held responsible for the negative consequences . . .   (Oh, 2007b:470)

The use of the speaker reference term 'nayka' thus plays a critical role in the speaker assuming culpability – to which J's laughter appears to be an aligning response, contrary to the standard preference for disagreement in such self-deprecations.

This is but one instance of a number of such departures from the default examined by Oh; she also shows the use of such forms in actions such as self-praise, responsibility-attribution and disagreement. They are also implicated in the management of turns: projecting further talk by the current speaker, or selecting next speaker, often marking that reference form with a particle relevant to the specific action being implemented (Oh, 2007b:486).

All in all, this work on Korean suggests that what has also been observed for Hebrew and English may hold across languages; that 'the preference for minimization is a formal preference; that is, it is a preference for the use of a single form and not necessarily for a minimization of referential information ... an additional form may carry no new referential information, other than the sheer fact of its addition' (Hacohen and Schegloff, 2006:1311). Thus what, on the face of it, appears to be one of the most straightforward functions of language, and a paradigmatic example of information transfer – person reference – is revealed to be a rather more nuanced, complex and collaborative matter when examined across interactional sequences; speakers make selections from the linguistic resources at their disposal with reference to operational preferences. In the words of Haviland: 'the linguistic and interactive resources for achieving reference ... are not simply designed as "recognitionals" but as intricate and highly structured instruments of interactive social action' (2007:251).

5.4   Conclusion: preference in the turn and the sequence

If collaborative action is the essence of interaction, sequences are the means by which action is accomplished. As collaborative achievements, actions are accomplished in turns, through time, and across sequences – and these turns within sequences are shaped by preference organisation. In this chapter we have shown the means by which preference – characterised by solidarity-seeking and conflict-avoidance – is embodied in both sequences and turns. We have seen how the pre-expansion of a sequence before a base adjacency pair is directed to minimising the possibility of a dispreferred action being done; in some cases, such as requests, the base action itself need not, as we have seen, even be done, but is recognisably projected and recognisably managed even so.

Sociocultural preferences clearly constrain the forms that these actions take. So an action such as referring may be done within the constraints of a single turn in one language, and offering across a couple of turns in another, but each may only be accomplished across a sequence of several turns in a third. The elements out of which turns themselves are constructed display the means by which participants manage their talk with respect to the unremitting constraints of preference organisation. This is not to claim that preference has either predictive or prescriptive qualities, but rather, that it provides a normative framework of orientations, departures from which are then hearable and inspectable as such. As Schegloff notes, 'inversion and omission of components can be ways of doing things or ways of avoiding doing things' (1992b:1317). It is only by reference to these orientational patterns that such inversions and omissions can be identified. In a broader context, we have seen how orientations to preference shape the selection of particular linguistic structures over time.

For linguistics, the implications are clear. If we are to understand the relationship between linguistic structures and actions, we need to look beyond the single utterance to investigate the means by which actions are accomplished collaboratively across sequences.

6   The structure of sequences II: knowledge and authority in the construction of identity

This chapter consolidates the examination of sequences by showing how orientations to identity are accomplished across sequences. It begins with a consideration of Sacks's work on the 'membership categorisation device' (MCD): the apparatus by which we organise knowledge of categories and generate social inferences about them. It then introduces two domains in interaction – those relating to knowledge and authority – to show how they may be used as resources to invoke categorial relevancies in interaction. Work on the epistemics of interaction has illuminated the means by which participants mobilise grammatical resources in particular sequential positions to make specific claims of relative authority or subordination in making assessments, and thence claims to identity categories. This, in turn, has shown how epistemic domains are implicated in action recognition and may neutralise elements of grammar (e.g. interrogative morphosyntax or prosody) in the interpretation of utterances: a major conundrum regarding the misfit of grammatical form and function is thus addressed through epistemics. It is clear that differentiating between *status* and *stance* captures that distinction between more enduring features of relationships and the moment-by-moment expression of them in interaction. Orientations to deontic status and stance in the form of entitlement is examined alongside the dimension of contingency with respect to variation in the grammatical formats embodying requests. The chapter concludes by using research in epistemic rights and deontic authority to illuminate the sequential motivations for indirect utterances in interaction.

The late MP Neil Marten used to tell the story of a tour he took around the Palace of Westminster with his Banbury constituents. Touring through the maze of corridors they turned a corner and met Lord Hailsham, the Lord Chancellor, wearing the full regalia of his office.

   Recognising his Parliamentary colleague in the midst of the Banbury constituents, Lord Hailsham boomed 'Neil.'

   Not needing to be told again, the tour party fell to their knees with some haste.   (Marten, n.d.)

How could one action, a summons – 'Neil!' – be understood as another, a directive – 'Kneel!'? The case above suggests that the authority visibly embodied in the Lord Chancellor, resplendent in the pomp of ceremonial dress, was one resource for interpretation. In this chapter we move beyond the adjacency pair and preference as organising principles for sequences to investigate two domains implicated in the construction of identity: knowledge and authority. We first examine the pioneering work of Harvey Sacks in investigating the systems of knowledge underlying social inference. Sacks's observation that culture is an apparatus for generating recognisable actions led him to propose that 'if the same procedures are used for generating as for detecting, that is perhaps as simple a solution to the problem of recognizability as is formulatable' (1992a:226). We then go on to investigate some mechanisms by which identities become relevant in interaction: how knowledge and authority are invoked in the doing of actions, and so how they are implicated in the building of sequences. First, however, a brief overview of Sacks's 'membership categorisation device'.

6.1   Identity in CA: the 'membership categorisation device'

Schegloff neatly encapsulates the perennial problem faced by the recipient of any utterance in relating a conundrum that arose in the midst of analysing data:

> in data Chuck Goodwin collected on an oceanographic research vessel, someone appears on deck with a complicated piece of equipment and says, "Where next?" In the discussion[1] of how to characterize the action this turn was doing – 'request for instructions' or 'offer of further help' – the issue was recurrently made to turn on who the speaker and addressee, respectively *were*, in hierarchical structure terms. If we could stipulate to the identity of the parties, we could get a solution to the characterization of the action.   (2007b:473)

As we shall see, Schegloff himself later suggests that the solution is not so simple and unidirectional. However, the notion that the interpretation of an utterance may be grounded in an understanding of the speaker's identity is an issue originally raised by Sacks. So, for example, examining some data involving some teenage boys and a therapist in a therapy session, he suggests that the grasping of the speaker in line 1 as a 'therapist' might be central to hearing that utterance as a hint that the session might be drawing to a close:

```
(1)  (Sacks, 1992a:595)
1   Ther→   Well, what's new, gentlemen?
2   Al      That's a hint we must get outta here before he gets
3           mad at us.
4   Roger   We adjourn to lunch now.
```

Sacks notes that: 'It's not that (the speaker) merely announces "Session's over", but that what he does is something seeable as a "hint" at that, where its seeability as a "hint" turns on seeing him as a "therapist" for that activity as a possibility' (1992a:595). So generating an identity category – in this case, occupation – becomes an interpretive resource. Such categories include the familiar demographic categories of occupations, ethnicity, family status, nationality and residence – the categories of survey interviews and census data – as well as any of the infinite number that may be potentially invokable (the newspapers

---

[1] During a data session at the second Center for Language, Interaction and Culture (CLIC) Conference on Interaction and Grammar, UCLA, 1993.

we read, the menu choices we make, our selected modes of transport, etc.). In the
suicide helpline calls that Sacks examined, such categories surfaced recurrently:

(2)   (Sacks, 1992a:44)
        (B is the caller.)
1   A   How old are you Mr. Bergstein?
2   B   I'm 48, I look much younger. I look about 35 and I'm
3   quite ambitious and quite idealistic and very inventive
4   and conscientious and responsible.

Categories, as Sacks notes, are 'inference rich' (1992a:41), that is,
invoking them generates a store of common-sense knowledge that any
reasonable person might be expected to know about them; here, the caller,
having mentioned his age, then works to counter what might be assumed to
be characteristic of a 48-year-old. In the following, the male caller invokes
a subset of occupational categories, 'hair stylist … fashions … things like
that' (ll. 4–5):

(3)   (Sacks, 1992a:46)
        (B is the caller.)
1   A   Is there anything else you can stay interested in?
2   B   No, not really.
3   A   What interests did you have before?
4   B   I was a hair stylist at one time, I did some fashions now
5   and then, things like that.
            (lines omitted)
6   A   Have you been having some sexual problems?
7   B   All my life.
8   A   Uh huh. Yeah.
9   B→   Naturally. You probably suspect, as far as the hair
10   →   stylist and uh, either one way or the other, they're
11   →   straight or homosexual, something like that

At lines 9–11 the caller takes it as entirely natural that the recipient should infer
homosexuality from mention of these categories; as Sacks asserts, 'there are ways
of introducing a piece of information and testing out whether it will be acceptable, which don't involve saying it' (1992a:47). Across the helpline calls, Sacks
was particularly struck by the recurring statement *I have no-one to turn to* (1972a:
53–5). He notes that this statement is the product of a particular procedure
'arrived at properly and reproducibly' (p. 67) and the outcome of a search for
help; in response, the counsellors typically invoke possible people the caller
could turn to: spouse or partner, parents, friends … in that order, beginning with
those assumed to have the strongest obligation to help. Moreover, Sacks notes
that callers often imply that they themselves have considered each of these, *in
that self-same order*, and yielded nothing; the upshot here is that both caller and
counsellor are working with a common set of categories in their search for
possible candidates for the caller to turn to: a powerful apparatus is at work.

The central paradox here, Sacks notes, is that often the trouble that prompted the call is the very mechanism by which the most obvious candidate to help is the one thereby removed from the category of first one to turn to. Take, for example, the case of an adulterer:

> The spouse is the most eligible and entitled person to turn to with trouble, but *this* trouble – were it disclosed to the spouse, would be grounds for the spouse to remove themselves from that category. Hence the bind: no one to turn to, if the person to turn to would become *not* such a person, if turned to. (Schegloff, 2007b:466)

Of course, the caller, in saying *I have no one to turn to* is, again, paradoxically, turning to someone: the counsellor. This paradox is resolved, Sacks suggests, because there is a set of categories that exist not by reference to relationships, but to knowledge: professional knowledge. So while by reference to relationships, the counsellor is a stranger (and thus not in the hierarchy of viable candidates, standardly, to turn to), by reference to categories organised according to professional knowledge, the counsellor is indeed a legitimate person to turn to. So Sacks, in studying the means by which common-sense reasoning is methodically applied to these kinds of dilemmas, was able to establish how someone could validly say *I have no one to turn to*. During his examination of another recurrent phrase used by callers – *I am nothing* – he asks: 'Is there some way in which we can go about constructing the procedure whereby "nothing" is a possible product?' (1992a:66): how would it be possible for someone to arrive at that conclusion? One such caller goes on to say: 'what man wants a neurotic childless forty year old woman . . . No man' (p. 68): the speaker's formulation of her present state is done in such a way as to uphold the legitimacy of the claim *I am nothing*, and to rule out the possibility that anyone selecting her as a mate is properly entitled to be called *a man* (p. 69). This sense of entitled encumbency of a category figures centrally in the helpline calls; noting the set of inferences attached to any category, Sacks notes of the callers that:

> Some person is a nominal member of a category, but feels that the set of inferences that are properly made about that category are not properly made about them. They can count down the list of inferences and find 'I'm not this, I'm not that', by reference of course to a rule of relevance as to what one is or is not. That is, one is . . . saying . . . 'I'm not one of the things that, given my categorical membership, I ought to be.'   (1992a:69)

The procedure, then, by which someone comes to see themselves as a 'proper' member of a category – or not – is an immensely powerful one, and one by which people themselves may police category boundaries (for a famous case-study, see Sacks, 1979) in establishing whether they are 'something' or 'nothing' – with potentially critical consequences.

In his 'A Tutorial on Membership Categorization' (2007b), Schegloff provides an invaluable exegesis of the two central papers (1972a, 1972b), known respectively as the 'search for help' paper and the 'baby cried' paper, in which Sacks outlined his work on the topic. Schegloff notes that one way of locating the work analytically is to understand it as part of the resources we use for reference to persons – itself part of two larger domains, one of descriptive practices and one of word selection: 'how speakers come to use the words they do, and how that informs the hearing that the talk gets from recipients' (2007b:463). Sacks set out to investigate the 'structural properties' of this kind of common-sense knowledge – the means by which, in his most famous example, anyone faced with the utterance, *The X cried. The Y picked it up* from a story told by a two-year-old (1992a:243–51) could immediately grasp that 'X' would be 'baby' and 'Y' would be 'mummy' (rather than, say, 'therapist' and 'hairstylist'). Moreover, the 'mummy' is understood to be the 'mummy' of the 'baby', and picking up the baby is understood to follow from the baby crying. Explicating these common-sense understandings – or building what he called an 'apparatus', a set of resources and practices – is what Sacks undertook to do in developing his work on membership categorisation. Sacks's membership categorisation device (MCD) – the apparatus – consists of collections of categories and a set of rules of application. What follows is a brief overview of each.

6.1.1   Categories and collections of categories

As well as the universal categories of age and gender, anyone can be categorised in myriad ways – 'stranger', as we saw earlier, can alternatively be characterised as 'counsellor'; 'neurotic childless forty-year-old woman' could alternatively be characterised as a 'caller' and a 'daughter', or, for example, 'doctor, 'dog owner', 'vegetarian' and so on. The selection of each (e.g. choosing to call someone 'a daughter' rather than, say, 'a doctor') clearly invokes different domains of knowledge and experience – and thus clearly reproduces the ideologies of any given culture.[2] What Sacks identified as the 'inference richness' of such categories is evident in the quite specific assumptions that can be made at some remove from what Moerman (1988) called the category label – so there exist culturally specific inferences about, for example, food preferences and political inclinations in assumptions about how vegetarians might vote, or indeed, occupation and sexuality, as in (3). In work on error correction as an interactional resource (the topic of which we develop in Chapter 7), Jefferson, registering that the pronunciation of the definite article *thee* adumbrates a next word starting with a vowel, whereas *thuh* adumbrates one starting with

---

[2] So, to take two fairly random examples, when the climber Alison Hargreaves was killed on K2, there was much debate in the British press about her fitness as a parent (see, e.g., Barnard, 2002) – debate that is noticeably absent from similar reports about male climbers; and, in similar vein, the appointment of Rhona Fairhead as Chair of the BBC's governing body, the BBC Trust, was announced in the *Daily Telegraph* headline as 'Mother of Three Poised to Lead BBC' (30 August 2014).

a consonant, notes of an utterance produced by a witness in court, 'I told that to thuh- uh- officer':

> in interactional terms, an occurrence such as ' . . . thuh- uh- officer' may be an elaborate act, serving as a resource for such interactional business as the proferring of identity of self and situation. So, for example, ' . . . thuh- uh- officer' can convey not merely that someone happened to be on the verge of saying 'cop' and replaced it with 'officer', but that this is the sort of person who habitually uses the term 'cop' and replaced it with 'officer' out of deference to the courtroom surround; someone who is to be recognized as operating in unfamiliar territory, e.g. a regular guy talking to a Judge in a courtroom . . . one can propose 'I am not like this but am talking by reference to the fact that you are' by finding ways to show that the terms one produces are not the terms which first come to mind.   (1974:192)

Sacks proposes that attached to particular categories are what he calls 'category bound activities' shaping the particular inferences we draw (e.g. the caller in (3) referring to an interest in 'fashions, things like that' as a way of invoking without mentioning his sexuality). In the following, a single category label – 'Catholic' – is proffered as an account:

(4) (Silverman, 1997)
     (A=HIV clinic counsellor; B=patient)
1A   How long have you been with him?
2B   Six months.
3A   Six months. (0.3) When were you last with anyone before that?
4B   About thr(h)ee years. hhh=
5A   About three yea[rs.
6B→   [hhh I'm a Catholic. =heh he[h.hhhhh
7A   [Right.

In line 4, the speaker produces the response with a slight infiltrating laugh particle, indicating the delicacy of the matter (Jefferson, 1984a) – perhaps attending to a possible public perception that 'about three years' is some length of time between relationships. Upon the counsellor's response – a repair initiator (see Chapter 7) which invites confirmation, rather than, for example, a straightforward acceptance – the patient produces, with following laugh particles, the declarative statement 'I'm a Catholic', the category label being proffered as an account for the lengthy interval. That this statement works as an account (accepted by the counsellor with 'Right', l. 7) turns on the commonly held assumptions invoked by the category label – what anyone might be expected to know about someone who is 'a Catholic' with respect to sexual behaviour. That this is commonly available, and thus, invokable, cultural knowledge is evident by considering how substituting other possible labels (e.g. 'Protestant', 'lorry driver', 'Sagittarius') would not do the work of accounting in the same way.

The embedded inferences that emerge in the sequential organisation of talk are the subject of work by Kitzinger (2005b), who identifies some of the inferences attached to family reference terms. So in the following, someone phones a doctor on behalf of her sick infant daughter:

```
(5)  (Kitzinger, 2005b:491)
1     C     my daughter who's uh:: just coming fuh nineteen
2           months old, um:.thh yesterday she was feelin' very
3           sick.
            ((74 lines omitted, of problem presentation, diagnostic
            questioning, and diagnosis))
78    D→    Who's your doctor,
```

The assumption embedded in the question at line 78 here is that family members share a doctor; word selection ('your doctor', rather than, say, 'her doctor') is thus seen to be done by reference to these sorts of normative assumptions (just as we saw, in Chapter 5, extract (47), that 'We have friends in Bristol' can allow the speaker subsequently refer to 'he' and assume correctly that the referent will be understood to be the husband). Kitzinger brings out the extent to which terminology constructs 'the family' as a distinct, co-residential, heterosexual marital unit. She argues that the lesbian or gay man contacting a doctor on behalf of a partner or child cannot call upon the same resources and inferences associated with them – the assumption displayed in (5) above, for example, that the caller and the patient share a doctor (2005b:495).

The ways in which orientations to particular labels shape sequences is further brought out by the work of Kitzinger and Mandelbaum (2013) on the construction of the 'expert' as distinct from the 'layperson'. Expectable sets of knowledge and competencies are part of the attribution of category membership. In the following extract, the call-taker on a Birth Crisis helpline uses the term 'doulas' (l. 4) but adumbrates it with an inbreath and produces it with try-marking (Sacks and Schegloff, 1979),[3] and then checks the caller's understanding of the term ('D'you know what doulas are', ll. 4–6), thus showing her understanding that she is not talking to someone occupying the identity category 'childbirth expert':

```
(6)  (Kitzinger and Mandelbaum, 2013:6)
     (CT=call-taker on a Birth Crisis helpline, here listing the occupations of the other
     call-takers servicing the helpline. DAW is the caller.)
1    CT:    I mean they're N-C-T teache:rs a:[nd   ] u:m=
2    DAW:                                   [yeah]
3    CT:    .hhhhh post-natal (.) people'n breastfeeding
4      →    people'n [.hhhh] doulas? D'you know what=.
5               [ Yes ]
6    CT:    =doulas are.
7    DAW:   No:.=
8    CT:    =Well they offer (.) woman-to-woman care in childbirth
9           along wi- you know just being another woman friend.
```

---

[3] Contrast this with the presumptive use of Murrinh-Patha person reference, as displayed in, e.g., Chapter 5, extract (50).

The call-taker's decision to check her recipient's familiarity with the term is clearly justified in this case, and the sequence gets further expanded as the call-taker provides an explanation (ll. 8–9). Compare this last sequence, expanded in its course with the Q-A adjacency pair, with the following use of the same term, used with no display of uncertainty as to whether the recipient will understand it – a confidence endorsed by the recipient:

```
(7)  (Kitzinger and Mandelbaum, 2013:7)
     (Pau=caller to Birth Crisis Helpline; CT=call-taker)
1    Pau:  Hi:: uhm (.) I wonder if you could help
2      →   me.=I'm working as a doula i[n (.)] in=
3    CT:                               [mm hm]
4    Pau:  =West London and (.) a baby has just die:d.
5    CT:   Oh I'm so so:rry:. Tell me about it.
```

Here, the announcement in line 4 that 'a baby has just died' gets immediate condolences in the next turn, and the term 'doula' is not treated as problematic by either party, with the call-taker receipting the term with a continuer in line 3. Word selection practices thus constitute participants as expert or layperson. The following, of which we saw a fragment in Chapter 4, extract (15), involves a doctor speaking to a woman who has phoned about her daughter having been sick several times that night. The doctor's design of the talk shows delicacy concerning the production of the diagnostic term 'gastroenteritis' (ll. 7–10):

```
(8)  (DEC, 1:1:1)
     (D=Doctor; C=Caller)
1    D    ... she's not under the doctor for anything¿
2    C    [No,
3    D    [.hhhh A::m >'n she's not on any regular tablets or
4         anything nasty,
5    C    No,=
6    D    No, fine..hh I mean: it- it sounds a little bit (jis')
7      →  like'a touch a'gastroenteritis posh word really for
8         diarrhea and v(h)omiting i(h)sn't i(h)t? [.hh You don't really=
9    C                                             [Yes,
10   D    =need me tuh-.hh ta tell ya that but u::m I mean what we
11        normally do: is if you can just (.) encourage >jus'< (.) fluids.
12        (.) And not bother abou:t [(.) uh:m solids,
13   C                              [(            )
```

The production of 'gastroenteritis' is assessed immediately on its production as 'posh word' by means of an elliptical clause (the use of the less specialist 'diarrhea and vomiting' echoing his earlier use of 'anything nasty' as glossing 'regular tablets'); the laughter particles infiltrating the last few words of the TCU attest to the delicacy with which the explanation is delivered (on laughter as a patient's resource in medical interactions, see Haakana, 2001), and the tag question proposes that in fact the term is not unfamiliar to the caller. In lines 8–10 the doctor produces a more extended mitigation: 'You don't really need me tuh-.

hh ta tell you that', before returning to the main business of diagnostic advice-giving. Here we see recipient design writ large, with a speaker displaying his judgement of the recipient's identity with respect to particular territories of expertise.

The inference-richness of category labels, irrespective of their grounding in actuality, is one of two notable characteristics. The other, Sacks proposes, is that they are protected against induction;[4] this means that exceptions to categories do not prompt revision against what is known about the category; they are simply seen as exceptions. What is generally known about, for example, lorry drivers or hairdressers stays robust, however many exceptions might be encountered. The robustness of this knowledge is what makes it possible to implement actions by the application of category labels to individuals who are clearly not members of that category; so, to say of a child 'she's very grown-up' constitutes a compliment; to say of an adult 'he's a real baby' is just the opposite. Moreover, as Sacks observes of his helpline calls, the consequences are all too real for those who consider themselves to be exceptions to any given category; as he notes: 'such categories as "imitation" and "phoney" provide us with something very central, in that they serve as boundary categories around the term "member"' (1992a:71).

It is in the term 'membership categorisation *device*' (MCD) that the structural properties of this common-sense knowledge become evident. Sacks notes that categories are organised by users (i.e. us) into collections. So the categories 'therapist' and 'hairdresser' are heard to be part of a larger collection, 'occupation'; 'vegetarian' and 'carnivore' of the larger collection 'dietary preferences'; 'Leo' and 'Scorpio' of the collection 'zodiac signs'. It is also the case that the same category may belong to different collections (1972b:335): 'baby' in the context 'The baby cried. The mummy picked it up' is heard – as is 'mummy' – as belonging to the collection 'family'. However, in the context 'he's a real baby', it is heard as belonging to the collection 'stage of life', where 'baby-child-adolescent-adult' are ordered in degrees of development; one of a subset of 'positioned' categories, 'where one member can be said to be higher or lower than another, as with baby ... adolescent ... adult' (Sacks, 1992a:595). This is why the studied misapplication of a label can bestow a compliment, or lodge a complaint.

6.1.2 The rules of application

Sacks proposed that in applying membership categories to an individual, there exists an economy rule (1992a:246): one category may be enough (e.g. 'a Catholic', extract (4)). The fact that 'The baby cried. The mummy picked

---

[4] For a classic social-psychological demonstration of the robustness of prior beliefs (in this case, of attitudes to the death penalty), see Lord et al. (1979).

it up' is a story from a two-year-old shows that children of that age have already acquired the principle of adequate reference (1972a:35) and have understood that categories may be grouped into collections. However, the fact that one category may be sufficient does not mean that more than one may not be used (e.g. 'my daughter . . . nineteen months old', extract (5)). As both Sacks (1992b:447) and Schegloff (2007b:471) point out, the analytic question is therefore why more than one is used when one is in fact sufficient.

A second rule of application is the consistency rule (1972a:33), whereby if one individual is categorised by reference to a particular collection, then a subsequent individual may be categorised by reference to the same collection. Thus 'baby' is heard to be from the MCD 'family' and 'mummy' is therefore heard to belong to the same collection. So, as Sacks observes, these kinds of norms underlie at-a-glance judgements of, for example, when to offer help in public; hence, a report in a newspaper that a man publicly beating up a woman gets no intervention because, in the account of a bystander, 'we thought you were married and it wasn't any of our business' (1992a:91). Or 'a woman walks away from a supermarket with the baby carriage that's not hers' (p. 254); as Sacks notes: 'It's not seeable' (p. 254).[5] These relationships – man–wife, mother–baby – are a particular subset of co-incumbents of an MCD: what Sacks called 'standardised relational pairs' (1972a:37): bound by particular standardised rights and obligations concerning the activity of giving help, in a way which other co-incumbents (e.g. Leos and Scorpios) are not. An initial issue, then, Sacks proposes, is: 'What is it that's being done about the current collection of people?' (1992b:296).[6] So this is how we come to understand that 'The mummy' is the mummy of *this* particular baby. Another such pairing, mentioned in Chapter 1, is host–guest. In (9) below, excerpted from the longer exchange first presented in Chapter 3, we see Emma repairing[7] out of one formulation about what she is doing ('sittin here with Bill 'n: Gladys'n haa:' – what is hearably about to be 'having a drink') to another ('fixin'm a drink'):

---

[5] Conversely, someone's attention to what *is* seeable may also have tragic consequences: 'Abigail Rae was a toddler who wandered out of her nursery, and drowned in a nearby pond. A male passerby told her inquest he had spotted her in the street, and been concerned. But he hadn't saved her life by stepping in, he said, for fear of looking like he was abducting her' (Aitkenhead, 2007).

[6] A misunderstanding in visible conduct grounded in the different partitioning of a couple is related by Lerner and Raymond (2014) in a study of what they call 'body trouble remediation'. They examine adjustments to manual action, such as accelerating an action or suspending one for the purposes of coordination either between participants or between manual action and talk. One such episode involves a cashier at a restaurant and two customers, a male and a female, who approach the cashier. The male customer pays the cashier, and, at the end of the transaction, the cashier shakes hands with him. Having shaken the male customer's hand, the cashier does not retract his hand but moves it from the male customer's hand to proffer it to the female customer (apparently the wife/partner of the bill payer). The recipient of the proffer, with a bag under her arm, has then to adjust her position to free her hand and accelerate the proffering of her hand to meet the cashier's. It is evident from the female customer's remedial action that she had figured the first handshake to 'suffice' to represent both, as a couple – while the cashier's conduct disaggregates them from a couple into individuals.

[7] Such self-repairs will be examined in more detail in Chapter 7.

(9) (NB:IV:9)
```
1    Mar:    ...lo:, °hhuh°
2    Emm:    How'r you:.=
3    Mar:    =Well wuhdiyuh doin. hh hnh
4            (0.5)
5    Emm:    .hhh (hhOh:) Margy?=
6    Mar:    =eeYeehuh. [a-
7    Emm:               [Oh: I'm jis sittin here with Bill'n Gladys'n
8        →   haa:eh fixin'm a drink they're goin out tih ↓dinner:
9            (.)
10   Emm:    H[e's-
11   Mar:     [Oh::::. Oh.
```

In repairing from one formulation to another, Emma reformulates her relation-ship with 'Bill'n Gladys': initially constructed as 'jis sittin here' implies no particular responsibility for them, whereas 'fixin'm a drink' clearly invokes her duties as a host – and thus the implications for her availability, which, as was noted earlier, is the issue identifiable in line 3. The repair, and the selection of an alternative formulation from 'having' to 'fixin'm' thus has sequential implica-tions detectable in Margy's hearably deflated 'oh's at line 11.

These two basic rules of application – the economy rule and the consistency rule – alongside the categories and collections of categories are together the basic constituents of the MCD for any culture. As Schegloff remarks, Sacks chose to treat the actions as unproblematic so as to problematise the actors, but in fact 'the analysis and characterization of the activity is also contingent: is it "crying," or "eyes watering," as may, for example, become problematic to someone with right-hemisphere brain damage, whose capacity to recognize emotion is impaired' (2007b:472). So, in dismissing the possibility, quoted earlier, that he himself raised, Schegloff suggests that it is not simply a question of stipulating to the identity of the actor to get a solution to the characterisation of the activity. In mobilizing the means by which actions get formed up into sequences, we also have the means for examining how identities get invoked in interaction. As Antaki et al. put it: '[Identities] never just appear, they are always used ... and ... they ... change as they are deployed to meet changing conversational demands' (1996:479).

6.2   Knowledge and authority as resources for action recognition

While it may be inuitively clear that certain actions make particular identity categories invokable, how they come to be so is less immediately obvious. We have already seen how form does not straightforwardly map on action. Thus, although 'We're all meeting Granny off the bus on Sunday evening' is delivered on rising prosody, it is clearly understood to be not the question its intonation proposes, but an informing: a crucial difference in the relative states of knowledge proposed by the utterance. Moreover, the fact that a summons (*Neil!*) may be understood as a directive suggests that an orientation to authority may similarly figure in action recognition. Here, we examine how orientations to these two basic dimensions in human relations – to knowledge, and to authority – may shape the understanding of the actions being done, and how such actions figure in making particular identities relevant.

6.2.1   Territories of knowledge in interaction

In a foundational paper bringing together action, sequence and grammar, Heritage and Raymond (2005) investigate one particular action in talk – the assessment – to examine how speakers position themselves with respect to what they know and their rights to know it. In doing so, they not only provide insights into the relationship between grammar and sequential position with respect to action, but also identify a basic facet of human social relations.

Epistemic authority and subordination in assessing

A fundamental concern of Heritage and Raymond (2005) is who produces an assessment first, and who second – and thus who is agreeing with whom. This ordering tacitly encodes speakers' differential rights to assess referents. Heritage and Raymond propose that a speaker offering a first assessment, as at the turns arrowed below, implicitly makes a claim to primary rights to evaluate what is being assessed:

```
(10)  (Heritage and Raymond, 2005:19; SBL:2-2-3:5)
      (Ch=Chloe; Cl= Claire)
1   Ch:  →   We:ll it was [fu:n Clai[re, ((smile voice))
2   Cl:             [hhh      [Yea::[:h,]
3   Ch:                             [°M ]m°
```

```
(11)  (Heritage and Raymond, 2005:23; SBL:2-1-8:5)
      (N=Norma; B= Bea)
1 N:→  I think everyone enjoyed jus sitting aroun'
2    → ta::lk[ing.]
3 B:        [ h h] I do too::,
```

In each case the assessments in first position ('fun', 'everyone enjoyed') are produced as simple declarative evaluations and receive agreements in second position. Heritage and Raymond propose that this represents a default ordering, with the producers of the agreements claiming secondary rights to assess through the sheer fact of going second. However, this default ordering is not one that speakers necessarily adhere to; it does not necessarily follow that a speaker proffering an assessment first (or second) will thereby claim primary (or second-ary) rights to assess. We saw earlier, with assessments, that agreements with assessments are commonly done with upgrade so as to defeat a possible implica-tion that a speaker going second is simply 'going along with' a first speaker. So epistemic independence is something to which participants clearly show an orientation. By the same token, participants display very nuanced positions with respect to who may have priority in the matter of assessment. So in some cases, speakers offering first assessments may work to defeat an implication that they are claiming primary rights to evaluate the matter at hand.

So a first position assessment may be modulated in specific ways in order to downgrade its claim to primary rights to assess. In the following extract, (12), Norma evidentially downgrades her assessment of a longtime acquaintance of Bea's with 'seems', and she in turn receives a declaratively asserted agreement from Bea, 'Awfully nice little person':

```
(12)  (Heritage and Raymond, 2005:18; SBL:2-1-8:5)
      (B=Bea; N=Norma)
1  B:    hh hhh We:ll,h I wz gla:d she c'd come too las'ni:ght=
2  N:→   =Sh[e seems such a n]ice little [l  a  dy]
3  B:       [(since you keh)]            [dAwf'l]ly nice l*i'l
4          p*ers'n. t hhhh hhh We:ll, I[:  j's]
5  N:                                   [I thin]k evryone enjoyed jus...
```

And in the following, two women, Jenny and Vera, are discussing Vera's son Bill, his wife Jean, and their children. In producing an assessment in first position (l. 1) Jenny modulates her assessment of Vera's family with a tag question ('aren't they'), which downgrades her rights to assess; in reponse, Vera confirms and then agrees:

```
(13)  (Heritage and Raymond, 2005:20; Rahman: B:2: JV(14):4)
      (J=Jenny; V=Vera)
1  J:→  They're [a lovely family now aren't [they.
2  V:→          [°Mm:.°                      [They are: ye[s.
3  J:                                                     [eeYe[s::,
4  V:                                                          [Yes,
5  J:   Mm: All they need now is a little girl tih complete i:t.
6  J:   [h  e h  h eh ]
```

In Vera's confirmation and agreement, we see how speakers in the position of responding to an assessment may work to defeat the implication that their rights to assess are secondary to the speaker who in fact provided an assessment first. So Vera here chooses confirmation as the priority matter over agreement, and a response such as 'that's right' to an assessment in effect claims priority in rights to assess (Heritage and Raymond, 2005:26). Moreover, a negative interrogative in a second position assessment (as in the following, at l. 8) can attenuate its second position status by providing a putatively 'new' question for the previous speaker to respond to:

(14) (Heritage and Raymond, 2005:33)
      (E=Emma; M=Margy)

```
1    E:    =Oh honey that was a lovely luncheon I shoulda ca:lled you
2          s:soo[:ner but I:]l:[lo:ved it.Ih wz just deli:ghtfu[: l.]=
3    M:         [((f))Oh:::]   [*(    )                        [Well]=
4    M:    =I wz gla[d   y o u   ] (came).]
5    E:             ['nd yer f:  ] friends] 'r so da:rli:ng,=
6    M:    =Oh:::[: it  wz:]
7    E:          [e-that P]a:t isn'she a do:[:ll?]
8    M:→                              [iY e]h isn't she pretty,
9          (.)
10   E:    Oh: she's a beautiful girl.=
```

Margy's assessment of her friend at line 8 is formatted as a negative interrogative which asserts her primacy in the right to assess someone who is, after all, her friend. However, it is also the case that even with the default entitlement supplied by first position, speakers can choose to upgrade their rights to assess still further. So in line 7, we see that Emma's first position assessment had, as a negative interrogative ('isn't she a doll?'), laid claim to further rights to assess – and this, of course, an assessment of Margy's friend. In this light, Margy's response at line 8 can be heard as a reassertion of her own epistemic rights. This, in turn, is met by Emma's *oh*-prefaced assessment – *oh*- prefacing being another means by which interactants may upgrade their rights to assess. Such epistemic battles in the course of what is ostensibly the benign and cooperative environment of offering and receiving thanks is the basis of Heritage and Raymond's reference to the 'deeply ambiguous process of agreement' (2005:33) in evidence here. Heritage and Raymond examine a range of such grammatical practices through which the producers of first and second assessments can index the relative primacy and subordination of their assessments relative to that of co-participants, summarised in Figure 6.1.

Subsequent research has identified a number of other devices speakers may use in upgrading claims to knowledge in second position (on English, see, e.g., Stivers, 2005, on modified repeats, and Clift, 2006, on reported speech). It is clear that epistemic positioning is an abiding concern for participants.

First position epistemic downgrading may be indexed by:
- evidential weakening (e.g. 'seems', 'sounds' – from ex. (12), l. 2)
- tag questions (e.g. 'aren't they' – from ex. (13), l. 1)

Second position epistemic upgrading may be indexed by:
- confirmation + agreement (e.g. 'they are, yes' – from ex. (13), l. 2)
- *oh*-prefaced second assessments (e.g. 'oh she's a beautiful girl' – from ex. (14), l. 10)
- tag questions (e.g. 'it is, isn't it')
- negative interrogatives (e.g. 'isn't it beautiful')

First position epistemic upgrading may be indexed by:
- negative interrogatives (e.g. 'isn't she a doll?' – from ex. (14), l. 7)

Figure 6.1 *Some practices for indexing relative primacy and subordination of assessments: a summary of Heritage and Raymond (2005)*

The following extract from ǂĀkhoe Haiǁom is taken from the Stivers et al. ten-language comparative study of questions and answers (2010) – so not, in the first instance, a study of epistemics. However, here in the response to the question, we see such epistemic positioning as a lively concern. Ga, Su's mother, asks Su whether Su's baby is vomiting. Su, who might have answered with a confirming 'yes' or even a repeat, 'he is vomiting', chooses instead to upgrade her answer, thus showing her primacy in the matter:

(15) Hoymann (2010:2735)

```
1  Ga:   |hûi    i   b-a?
          vomit STAT 3sm-A
          'is he vomiting?'
2  Su:→  |hûi  gara b-a    i    ge
          vomit big  3sm-A STAT DECL
          'he is vomiting a lot'
```

Alongside such work revealing epistemics to be a concern for participants, there has been a wealth of comparative linguistic research designed, in the first instance, to identify epistemic devices (see, e.g., the collection in Stivers et al. (2011)). Heinemann et al. (2011), for example, examine the Danish adverb *jo* and Swedish adverb *ju* in addressing epistemic incongruence. Further, in a study of verbal mood selection in Spanish, Raymond examines indicative (*realis*) versus subjunctive (*irrealis*) morphology in syntactic constructions that license the use of either mood, demonstrating the limitations of a dichotomous 'what speaker knows' vs. 'what hearer knows' (or even 'speaker' or 'hearer' 'knows better') system. He shows knowledge becoming co-constructed between participants, thus arguing for a system taking into account absolute vs. relative levels of knowledge (2014:262). Hayano (2011) examines how in Japanese speakers manipulate the intensity of their evaluations in order to ground their claims of epistemic primacy. So, while in English agreements are, as we have seen, standardly done with upgrades (Pomerantz, 1984), in Japanese, agreements with same-degree evaluations are about twice as common as those with upgrades. The particle *yone* marks same-degree assessments. In the following, a customer (CT) and a beautician (BT) are talking. The beautician's assistant has just sneezed loudly at the back of the salon, and in line 1 the customer's assessment is heard as an account for the sneeze:

(16) (Hayano, 2011:63)

```
1  CT:   kyoo    datte  sa^mui desu mon.
          today because cold  CP   FP
          (Well) (it's) ^cold today.
2         (.)
3  CT:   [(   )
4  BT:→  [samui desu YONE:,= kyoo  wa ne[:,
          cold   CP   FP:     today TP FP
          (It's) cold yone:,=today it is ne:,
```

```
5  CT:                                  [(so:-) [nn:,
                                                ITJ
                                        [(tha:-) Yeah:,
6                                               [kion:
                                                temperature
                                                The temperature
7   →    hai, [hikui desu yone,
         ITJ   low   CP   FP
         Yes, (it's) low yone,
8  CT:→        [kion          wa- hikui desu yo[ne:,
               temperature TP    low  CP    FP
               The temperature is- low yone:,
9  BT:                                     [ha:i,
                                            ITJ
                                            Yeah:,
```

Here, the *yone*-tagged agreements are formulated with evaluations of the same intensity as the first assessments (ll. 4 and 8), showing that in agreement neither speaker is attempting to claim superior rights to assess (Hayano, 2011: 63). Similarly with *ne*; the pottery instructor here comments on a teapot her student has made and receives an agreement from the student:

(17) (Hayano, 2011:64)
      (INST=pottery instructor; STU=student)
```
1  INST:  de- (0.2) a^tsui ne.
          and       thick FP
          And- (0.2) (it's) ^thick ne.
2  STUD:  Atsui desu[ne:.
          thick CP   FP
          (It's) thick ne:.
3  INST:             [Un:.
                      ITJ
                      Yeah:.
```

Both first and second assessments are marked turn-finally with 'ne', and the same evaluation (l. 2) is treated as an unproblematic agreement (Hayano, 2011:64).

In contrast, *yo* tags an assessment claiming priority in the matter of assessment. Two sisters-in-law, Yoko and Kazu, are having tea at Kazu's house and appreciating the flowers on her balcony. Yoko has asked about a particular flower, and Kazu's response concludes with the assessment in line 1:

(18) (Hayano, 2011:66)
```
1  Kazu:  °kore ga mata kawai[i:_
          this SP also pretty:
          °These are also pretty:_
2  Yoko:                    [kawaii yone. [au   mon=
                             pretty FP     suit FP
                             (They are)   pretty yone, (They) suit
```

```
                                   (other flowers).=
3   Kazu:                                       [nn,
                                                 ITJ
                                                 Yeah.
4   Yoko:     =choodo     [ne:.
               perfectly [FP
              =perfectly ne:.
5   Kazu→                [asa     ga ka      [waii no yo,
                          morning SP pretty   PRT FP
                          (they are) pretty in the Morning yo.
6   Yoko:                                  [n::
                                            ITJ
                                            Yeah::.
7             (0.5)
8   Kazu:     hontoni moo,
              really EMP
              Really,
9             (0.7)
10  Kazu:     >ano< (.) <asa  wa> moo me  ga sameru hodo   kawaii.
              well   morning TP EMP   eye SP wake  degree pretty
              >Like< (.) <in the morning> (they are) so pretty (they)
              wake (me) up
11  Yoko:     aa soo,=
              ITJ that
              Oh are they,=
12  Kazu:     =nn!
              ITJ
              =Yeah!
```

In response to Kazu's assessment in line 1, Yoko produces a *yone*-marked agreement (ll. 2 and 4). Yoko's second assessment claims independent access to the flowers, while *yone* marks a claim to equivalent knowledge. However, in line 5 Kazu's reformulation narrows the scope of the assessment, such that only she has access to it: how the flowers look in the morning. The use of *yo* in this turn contrasts with that of *yo* and *ne* by Yoko – and so claims epistemic primacy over Yoko. Note that this is followed by both a pause and a next-turn repair initiator by Kazu, implicating potential disagreement, but in response, Kazu upgrades the evaluation. As Hayano observes, 'By so doing, she implies that the flowers that she is talking about are qualitatively different from those that Yoko is now looking at, thus providing a basis for her claim of epistemic primacy' (2011:67). With Yoko's news receipt at line 11, she cedes epistemic primacy to Kazu.

It is clear that, beyond the initial work on assessments, the domain of epistemics has profound implications for interaction generally,[8] showing the

---

[8] The issue of epistemic rights in the construction of action has myriad implications. One, not pursued here, is in how it might matter for translation; see Clift (2012b) on how translations may not be able to capture the action implications of utterances. See, e.g., Bellos (2011:79–80) on how

interdependence of grammatical resources and sequential position in the construction of action. As we saw with the utterance 'What are you doing' in Chapter 3, it is evident from the table in Figure 6.1 above that the same grammatical resource may be doing different actions in different sequential positions; so a tag question in first position may be downgrading a speaker's right to assess, but in second position may be upgrading. So grammar is used to subvert the epistemic rights proposed by sequential ordering – an ordering that is the inevitable outcome of the real-time exigencies of interaction.

Epistemic domains, mobilising response and the epistemic engine

The work on epistemic rights shows us that 'who has primary rights to know what' is a basic – and oriented-to – issue for participants themselves in interaction. Furthermore, as Heritage (2012b) proposes, there is much to suggest that actions and sequences may be motivated, and so warranted, by imbalances of knowledge. Perhaps the paradigm case of a sequence motivated by an imbalance of knowledge is the question–answer adjacency pair in cases where questions are motivated by information-seeking. We saw in Chapter 1, extract (8) one case in which a speaker questions another, with *oh*, a 'change-of-state' token, marking a transition from a state of not knowing (schematically encapsulated as K−) to knowing (K+); the following is another instance. Lesley questions her mother about some tablets she has recommended:

```
(19)   (From Heritage, 2012b:34–5; Field, 1:1:89–94)
1    Les:   Uh diduh get yer garlic tablets.
2    Mum:   Yes I've got them,
3    Les:   Have yuh t- started tak[ing th'm
4    Mum:                          [I started taking th'm t'da:y
5    Les:→  Oh well do:n[e
6    Mum:               [Garlic'n parsley.
7    Les:   ↑THAT'S RI:ght. [BY hhoh-u-Whole Food?
8    Mum:                   [(      )
9           (0.3)
10   Mum:   Whole Foo:ds ye[s,
11   Les:                  [YES well done,
12          (0.3)
13   Mum:   (      )
14          (0.6)
15   Les:   's I've got Katharine on: th'm too: now,
```

After Mum responds to the initial question (l. 2), Lesley asks another (l. 3); Lesley greets Mum's answer (l. 4) with 'oh' and an assessment. So before this

and why the American film title *It's Complicated* was translated into French, not into the literal rendering 'C'est Compliqué', but into the less intuitively obvious *Pas Si Simple!* (Not So Simple!).

(a) Before (19)   (b) After (19)

Figure 6.2 *Relative epistemic access before and after extract (19)*

exchange, Lesley would have been K− and Mum K+ with respect to this issue, and the epistemic gradient between the two represented by a cline, as in Figure 6.2(a); after it, both would be K+, as in 6.2(b).

So each question–answer sequence in (19) is initiated by a speaker – Lesley – who is in a K− position, and then terminated, with the 'oh' indexing the epistemic shift to K+. Heritage (2012b) introduces the notion of **epistemic status** to refer to the relative positioning of participants vis-à-vis some domain of knowledge; participants 'recognise one another to be more or less knowledgable concerning some domain of knowledge as a more or less settled matter of fact' (2012b:32). That recognition – the epistemic status that each attributes to the other – is embodied in the exchange in (19). However, it is clearly the case that there is not necessarily a straightforward relationship between epistemic status and its recognition; for that reason, the notion of **epistemic stance** captures the moment-by-moment positioning of participants with respect to each other in and through the talk. So a teacher asking a class an information question – say, *What's the capital of Mali?* – relies on the assumption of a K− status, as does a barrister cross-examining a witness, for pedagogical and legal purposes respectively. In such cases, when speakers appear more or less knowledgeable than they actually are, epistemic stance may thus be deployed to occlude actual epistemic status. Clearly here linguistic form is trumped by epistemics, and more specifically, the notion of **epistemic domains**. This owes its origins to work by Labov and Fanshel (1977) who propose a distinction between A-events (known to A but not to B), B-events (known to B, but not to A) and A-B events known to both. Kamio (1997), in consolidating this proposal, suggests that both A and B have their own territories of information, and while there are elements of knowledge to which both may have access, these might be to varying degrees.

Of course, as we have seen, interrogative form does not necessarily implement an interrogative action. *Have you heard the news?* is a question format that implements a pre-announcement. Furthermore, tag questions (*It is, isn't it?*) and negative interrogatives (*Isn't she a lovely girl?*) in agreements are not initiating actions – asking questions – but responsive ones. By the same token, declarative syntax may well implement an interrogative. This is where epistemic domains figure centrally in action interpretation; in another's epistemic domain, a declarative assertion is taken to be a request for confirmation.

In a study of yes/no (polar) questions, Heritage and Raymond (2012) show how question design can establish the depth of the epistemic gradient between

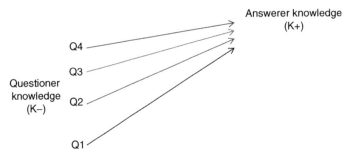

Q1. Who did you talk to?
Q2. Did you talk to John?
Q3. You talked to John, didn't you?
Q4. You talked to John?

Figure 6.3 *Epistemic gradients embodied in question design (Heritage and Raymond, 2012:181)*

questioner and answerer. So the declarative assertion, *You talked to John*, displays a shallow epistemic gradient that only seeks confirmation from the answer, whereas *Who did you talk to?* displays a much steeper gradient. While any form of question assigns ultimate authority to the respondent, Figure 6.3 shows the distinctive gradients associated with different question formats.

In the following example from Dutch, Mazeland shows how three different forms of question design display differing gradations of epistemic stance:

```
(20)  (Mazeland, 2013:485–6)
1     IR:      ohkee:h.
               okay.
2              (.)
3      →       je hee:t (.)    Johnny.
               you have-name   Johnny
               your name is    Johnny
4              (0.4)
5     JO:      Johnny ja.
               Johnny yes.
6     IR:→     .hh how oud ben je?
               how old are you?
7              (0.3)
8     JO:      >zeventien.<
               seventeen.
9              (0.4)
10    IR:→     ze:ventien..hh heb je broe:rs   en zus^(j)e?
               seventeen  have you  brothers and sister
               seventeen. do you have any brothers and sisters?
11             (.)
12    JO:      jah. één zusjeh.
               yes. one sister. DIM
               yes. one little   sister.
```

All three questions in this extract are in the recipient's epistemic domain and they presume his primary epistemic rights. However, the declarative syntax of the question 'je heet Johnny' (your name is Johnny) reveals the speaker's epistemic stance that she has good reason to assume the statement's correctness, more so than she does with the interrogative lexico-syntax of the *wh*-question in line 6 and the yes/no interrogative in line 10. The latter two questions the questioner claims to have no knowledge about. Speakers may thus index different epistemic stances in the grammatical format of their questions while leaving intact the epistemic primacy of the question recipient (Mazeland, 2013).

In Stivers et al.'s (2010) comparative study question–answer sequences in ten languages, all the languages examined were found to use epistemic asymmetries to implement questioning using forms with no formal question marking, as with 'je heet Johnny', above. For example, Lao, as a tone language, has lexically dedicated pitch contours that cannot be overridden with 'rising tone' for questioning; the following question at line 1 has no explicit marking and so exploits an epistemic imbalance:

(21) (Enfield, 2010b:2653)
```
1  A→   ñaang1 daj4  laØ
          walk   can   PRF
          (You) can  walk already
2  B    qee5  phòò2 daj4   juu1
         INTJ  enough can  FAC.WEAK
         Yeah, (I)   can  more  or less
```

It should now be evident how interrogative prosody is similarly overridden by epistemic domain. Lesley's lines 10–11 'we're all meeting Granny off the bus on Monday evening?', from extract (5) in Chapter 1, ending on rising prosody, is clearly understood to be informing, rather than questioning, being, as it is, in Lesley's own epistemic domain:

(22) (Heritage, 2012a)
```
10 Les→  .hhh Yes alri:ght..hh The -thing is (.) u-we're all
11     → meeting Granny off the bus: on Monday eve↓ni:ng?
12 Kat   ehYeah,
13 Les   .hhhh But -then Dad could come: back 'n hhhave iz ↓tea
14       'n then go on: to Glastonbur[y
15 Kat                               [Ye:s well if I'm at the
16       Kidwell's house it dzn't matter (.) I mean he c'n come:
17       pick me up whenever 'e wants to °can't h[e°
```

The apparent conundrum that the so-called high-rising terminals (see, e.g., Ching, 1982; Guy et al., 1986; Britain, 1992) on declarative assertions do not lead recipients to understand that questions are being asked is then resolved by reference to epistemic domains (see also Couper-Kuhlen, 2012). In respect of final rising prosody, Heritage proposes that

If final rise as a practice has an underlying 'semantics', it must surely be to mobilize response. In this capacity, it can contribute an urgency to whatever interactional project is 'in play', and what that project is will be grasped, at least in part, by reference to the epistemics that are also in play in the moment. The identification of final rising intonation with 'questioning' is an unnecessary burden on the signal itself: unnecessary because it involves the attribution of a misplaced concreteness to a signal that is elaborated by a multiplicity of contexts.   (2013:569)

Bolinger (1957), Horn (1978) and Quirk et al. (1985) all discuss so-called rhetorical questions, on actual instance of which was exemplified by 'For whom' (extract (10)) in Chapter 1. In what she calls 'assertive questions', Koshik (2005) examines a range of question formats that, far from seeking information, seek to challenge:

(23)   (Koshik, 2005:39)
       (Debbie and Shelley)
```
35   Deb     =I do'know,=jus don't blow off
36           your girlfriends for guy:s,
37           Shel.
38   Shel→   De:b I'm not. h[ow man-]e-
39   Deb                    [o ka:  ]
40   Shel→   when have I.=beside ya- I mean
```

These question formats convey the strong K+ stance of the questioner and so, as Koshik notes, 'the stance expressed is that of the corresponding negative statement; "when have I" implies "never have I" or "I never have"' (2005:39) (see also Heinemann (2008) and Heritage (2002b, 2012a) on polar questions that are unanswerable, such as those of the format *How could you?*). In the following, both interrogative morphosyntax and interrogative prosody at lines 23 and 26 are neutralised by context:

(24)   (From Clift, 2012:70; *The Loyalists*, first broadcast on BBC2, 1999)
       (PT=Peter Taylor, BBC journalist; PW=Paul Wilson, son of the late Senator Paddy Wilson, murdered by John White of the UFF)[9]
```
1    PT    When: you saw: your father's killer John White, walking
2          into Downing Street¿
3          (0.4)
4    PW    .HHHHaaah::::.. I jus' [(starts gently shaking head)]
5                                 [(---------3.0---------)]
```

---

[9] In one of the most brutal murders of the Northern Irish Troubles, in 1973 an Irish Catholic senator, Paddy Wilson, was murdered alongside Irene Andrews, a Protestant, by John White, a Loyalist paramilitary (an 'Ulster Freedom Fighter'), who later admits that the killing had been 'barbaric'. Twenty-five years later, John White was part of a Loyalist delegation invited to Downing Street to meet John Major, then Prime Minister, as part of the Anglo-Irish peace talks. Peter Taylor, a BBC journalist, has asked John White whether he shook hands with the Prime Minister; White responds 'I did indeed, yes, aha.' Subsequently, Taylor interviews Paul Wilson, the son of the murdered senator, and the extract that follows is taken from that interview.

```
 6   PW    = hh flabbergasted. [As- astonished. Completely=
 7   PW                         [(shaking head)
 8   PW    =astonished.
 9         (2)
10   PW    How a man can do:: [°*a- a- a-*°  ]  a double murder,↑cos=
11                            [---(1.2)----]
12   PW    =it was a double murder, there was someone with my
13         father, it just wasn't my father, Irene Andrews was
14         with him. (1.2) And then walk in and meet the Prime
15         Minister of Great [Britain w's j's- (-- [-----1-----) j's=
16                           [(----shaking head---[(licks lips)---)=
17   PW    =[unbelievable.
18   PW    =[(shaking head)
19   PT    And shake his hand.
20         (2.1)
21   PW    [°Yeah°. And shake his  [hand.
22   PW    [(nods head)            [(nodding)
23   PW→   [[Which hand  did  he [[[shake¿
24   PW    [[(shaking head-----[[[(eyebrow raise on 'shake')
25         (1.2)
26   PW→   [°Hm°. Was it the hand with the knife?
27   PW    [(shaking head)
28   PW    (1)
29   PW→   (purses lips and tilts head to left) [°Which hand did he=
30   PW                                         [(shaking head)
31   PW→   =[s(h)hake°.
32   PW    [(shaking head)
33        (1)
34   PW    (Shakes head)
```

The institutional context of the interview here of course displays a number of instances of turns treated as questions that are not formatted as such, or not completely: the interviewer's turn at lines 1–2 of the interviewer's, which is produced as prosodically complete, ending on a low-rise, but which is syntactically not; and the interviewer's line 19, where he effectively recompletes the interviewee's prior turn with the extension 'And shake his hand' – a proposal that the interviewee accepts with assent and then a repetition. In extending his responsive turn beyond the confirmation, the interviewee's subsequent 'which hand did he shake' is formatted as a question but clearly not designed to be treated as such; it is unanswerable. However, the fact that it is unanswerable is here emphatically not the point in a sequential context where we know already that the answer, informationally, would be immaterial. What the interviewee has established in his lengthy turn from lines 4–17 (and notably the assessments in ll. 6, 8 and 17) is his response to the very fact that the meeting took place at all. Upon the lengthy subsequent pause, he issues a follow-up – the polar interrogative 'was it the hand with the knife?' – once more, not designed to be answered, and not so treated. The fact that, after a second's pause, the original question is subsequently repeated on a terminal falling tone underscores the fact that that question is not designed to be answered.

The linguistic format of an utterance in sequence is therefore either under-written by relative epistemic stance, or undermined by it. However, if linguistic format can be thus either underwritten or undermined, the question thus arises as to what ends such formats are implemented in talk. One answer is to be found in the work of Stivers and Rossano (2010), who suggest that lexico-morphosyntax and interrogative prosody, gaze and recipient-tilted epistemic asymmetry are the four main resources of turn design mobilising recipient response. Consider the following extract. Bud phones his wife Emma, having walked out on her fairly recently. The exchange takes place soon after the opening of the call. Here, Emma initiates a reciprocal sequence (Schegloff, 2007a:195) with a vigorous 'Happy Anniversary!' (l. 5) and Bud responds, albeit more softly, with 'Happy Anniversary to you', marked lexically and prosodically as a reciprocal. Emma's 'I MISS you' (l. 7), launched on the heels of this, initiates what clearly could be another reciprocal sequence, but this is met instead initially by silence (l. 8) and then a next-turn repair initiator from Bud, 'Y'do?', which initiates its own sequence. Upon Emma's affirmation, Bud very softly produces what is hearably about to be some kind of assessment (conceivably, e.g., *Well that's nice*). It is upon this that Emma explicitly mobilises, by dint of the interrogative syntax and prosody ('You miss me?'), an affirmation – just – from Bud:

```
(25)  (NB:III:3:R)
1     Emm:    .p.tch Oh it's been go:rgeous tihday Bud ↑yesterday wz: a
2             mos'mizerble day thou:gh,
3     Bud:    Ya:h?
4             (0.2)
5     Emm:    .h.t Happy Anni↑VER:sery!
6     Bud:    °Happy annivers'ry tih [you:.° ]
7     Emm:                           [ .h  h ] I ↑MISSshyou.
8             (0.4)
9     Bud:    Y' [↑d o ?]
10    Emm:       [.t.hhh] .hhh -YE:↓ah.
11    Bud:    °°(Well at's [    )   °° s
12    Emm:→                [You miss me?    ((constricted))
13    Bud:→   °°Ye:-:h. °°
14            (0.2)
15    Emm:    We jus hadda vo:dka Barbr'en I: jis hadda ni:ce great
16            big double vo:dka
```

Here, where the declarative 'I miss you' gets no reciprocity, the use of inter-rogative syntax and prosody, as well as recipient-tilted epistemic asymmetry (whether he misses her) at line 12 explicitly mobilises response. In the following face-to-face interaction, where Kim and Mark are eating pasta together, Kim mobilises all of these features plus gaze in the pursuit of a response.

(26) (Stivers and Rossano, 2010:21)
```
1   Kim   [((Kim gazing down at plate))
2   Kim→  [I don't like this rainbow one.
3         [((Mark stabbing ravioli))
4         (0.5)/((Mark continues preparing bite))
5   Kim→  Do you?, ((gazing to Mark))
6         (2.4)/((Mark eats bite on fork and gazes to package))
7   Kim   I like this kinda...
```

Kim's assessment (l.1) does not strongly constrain a response and does not receive one. After the silence, Kim pursues a response, shifting to an interrogative structure that, as in the extract before, has recipient-tilted epistemic asymmetry (what he likes or does not like rather than what she likes or does not like). The pursuit also has rising intonation and is delivered while she gazes at him. In this case she still does not secure response – instead he eats the bite previously on his fork (which may or may not have been the 'rainbow one') and gazes at the packaging. She does not further pursue response but moves on to initiate another sequence about another sort of pasta. Although Mark does not, ultimately, respond, the interest here is in the resources Kim relies on to mobilise response in the face of failing in a first effort – lexico-morphosyntax, prosody, gaze and epistemic domain. It is further noticeable that this instance of 'telling my side' (l. 2) (Pomerantz, 1980) invites response but is not coercive of it, whereas the shift to a design that is highly response mobilising is more coercive of response (Stivers and Rossano, 2010:21).

It appears, then, that with certain actions, linguistic features of turn design are mobilised for purposes that are profoundly interactional because epistemic domains, or the partitioning of knowledge across parties (Heritage, 2012b), is fundamental in the interpretation of actions. As Heritage proposes:

> both interrogative morphosyntax and intonation are 'freed' to participate as 'response mobilizing' features of other classes of utterances such as assessments and noticings (Stivers and Rossano 2010). It further follows that the epistemic stance generally conveyed by interrogative morphosyntax and intonation functions as a secondary lamination on to epistemic status, fine tuning the epistemic gradient between speaker and recipient.   (2012a:24)

Figure 6.4 shows how interpretations of the action being implemented by a turn is grounded in a combination of linguistic form, both prosodic and syntactic, and the location of the utterance in the epistemic domain of either the speaker or the recipient; exemplars are taken from extracts in the book, and numbers refer to the chapters in which they appear.

Heritage invokes the hydraulic metaphor of an 'epistemic engine' driving sequences forward, with participants speaking from positions of either K+ or K−:

> when a speaker indicates that there is an imbalance of information between speaker and hearer, this indication is sufficient to motivate and warrant

	K+ epistemic status (Within speaker's epistemic domain)	K– epistemic status (Not within speaker's epistemic domain)
Turn design feature	**Action Interpretation** (Given the 'known in common' epistemic status of speaker and recipient relative to the targeted state of affairs)	
Declarative syntax	Informing *Gonna be beautiful outside (3)*	'Declarative/B-event Question' *You don't want any tea. (4)*
Declarative syntax with final rising intonation	Continuing *we're all meeting Granny off the bus on Monday evening? (1)*	Questioning *Yuh still taking shots? (3)*
Tag question	Mobilizing support for an assertion *They're a lovely family now, aren't they (6)*	Seeking confirmation *Dad couldn't pick me up from (.) even from Westbury, could he (6)*
Negative interrogative syntax	Assertion *...isn't she a doll? (6)*	Request for information *...don't you have all your family coming today? (4)*
Interrogative syntax	Pre-informing *Didju hear the terrible news? (3)* Known answer question *Is he teaching History or Divinity (1)* Rhetorical question *Which hand did he shake (6)*	Request for information *How did you get his number? (1)*

Figure 6.4 *Epistemics and action formation (adapted from Heritage, 2012a:24)*

a sequence of interaction that will be closed when the imbalance is acknowledged as equalized for all practical purposes.　　　(2012b:32)

Whereas the sequence in (19) above is initiated by a speaker in a K– position,
sequences may equally be initiated by a speaker in a K+ position. The clearest
instance of this is embodied in a news delivery sequence as in (27) below, where
the news is adumbrated first by a pre-announcement (ll. 1–2) that is then given the
go-ahead (l. 3):

(27)　(Heritage, 2012b:31)
```
1    Ron   I fergot t'tell y'the two best things that
2          happen'tuh me t'day.
3    Bea   Oh super.=What were they
4    Ron   I gotta B plus on my math test,
5    Bea   On yer final?
6    Ron   Un huh?
7    Bea→  Oh that's wonderful
8    Ron   And I got athletic award.
9    Bea   REALLY?
10   Ron   Uh huh. From Sports Club.
11   Bea→  Oh that's terrific Ronald.
```

Ron's pre-announcement in fact indicates two newsworthy events, each of which
is delivered through its own sequence, Bea's transition from K– to K+ marked in
the first instance by newsmarks (Jefferson, 1981; Heritage, 1984a) at lines 5 and

9, and subsequently by her sequence-closing receipts of 'oh'+ assessment at lines 7 and 11.

The two exemplars in (19) and (27) are relatively clear-cut instances of speakers in K− or K+ positions initiating sequences, and those sequences being terminated when the epistemic imbalance has been equalised. However, these cases aside, it is evident that topic expansion – in Heritage's metaphor, the driving forward of a topic – is generally dependent on K+ and K− contributions. By the same token, lack of any new epistemic input may lead to atrophy (2012b):

(28) (Heritage, 2012b: 45–6; Rahman:14; 25–46)
(Vera's son and family, arriving to stay with Vera but finding her absent, had been advised by a neighbour, 'Missiz Richards' (ll. 1–3) to go to Jenny's house – advice, it turns out, prompted by Vera herself, ll. 1–3.)

```
1   Ver:     eeYe- Wasn' [it lucky? Ah to:ld the w- told Missiz=
2   Jen:                 [Mm-
3   Ver:     =Richards tih te[ll (                    )
4   Jen:                     [Ye::s that wz smashing <mind he might
5            hev thoughtchu w'r up here anyw[ay
6   Ver:                                    [Ye:s he could'v done,=
7   Ver:→    =[Yes,
8   Jen:→    =[eeYe:s:: [Mm hm,
9   Ver:→              [Yes.
10  Jen:     Oh[: (          ).
11  Ver:       [I'm sorry yih hahd th'm all
12            o[n you [J e n n y] like that]
13  Jen:       [.hhh [↑Oh don't] be sill]y=
14  Jen:     =No: thaht wz luvly it wz a nice surpri:ze
```

Vera's expression of satisfaction at the outcome receives first an agreement from Jenny, followed by a somewhat deflationary observation, implying that the same outcome might have been achieved without Vera's intervention (ll. 4–5). After an agreement from Vera, the sequence of 'yes's from both parties, in Heritage's words, 'neither advance the sequence, nor wholly abandon it . . . no additional life is contributed to the topic through the see-saw of K−/K+ epistemics and the topic withers' (2012b:46). Both apparently initiate a new sequence, with Vera's apology getting taken up and subsequently topically progressed (ll. 11–14).

Brief though it may be, this extract shows clearly how information exchange – or lack of it – is criterial to the development or otherwise of a sequence, and suggests that, in Heritage's words, 'conversational sequences, and not just sentences, are the objects of complex, intersubjectively validated, management of talk as information flow' (p. 49). The 'engine' driving this progression is the public accountability of what is said; 'a person, finding some new thing to say, is warranted in saying it, and finds warrant from others in its saying, by the fact that it is a "new thing"'(Heritage, 2012c:80).

Epistemics and identity

It is evident, then, that equalising epistemic imbalances is a basic warrant for the building of sequences. Clearly, 'what each party can accountably know, how they know it, whether they have rights to articulate it, and in what terms' (Raymond and Heritage, 2006:16) are all implicated in the practices of talk. In this respect, epistemic domains may thus be seen to be conclusively allied to the identities of participants and their relative rights and responsibilities as invoked and made relevant, and so consequential, in talk.

Heritage (2012c:76) suggests epistemic domains are continuously monitored and updated by a kind of 'epistemic "ticker"' keeping track of who knows what. It is not just in the design of turns, but also in their allocation, that this mechanism becomes apparent. So Goodwin's analysis of a single utterance in conversation, discussed in Chapter 4, makes it clear that the emergent utterance, each increment of which is addressed to different primary recipients, is shaped by the basic issue of 'who knows what'. Furthermore, Goodwin's study of 'forgetfulness' as an interactional resource (1987) shows how a display of forgetfulness or uncertainty not only affords another glimpse of the mechanics of utterance production but also opens up an opportunity to make visible that two participants are a couple. In the following, Mike, who has hitherto been addressing Curt, launches a search for a name[10] at lines 2–3:

(29) (Goodwin, 1987:115)
```
1  Mike I was watching Johnny Carson one night
2    →  en there was a guy by the na- What was
3         that guy's name.=[Blake?
4  Curt                   [The Critic.
```

Just before the question is launched there is a cut-off on 'na-', and Mike turns his gaze from Curt to Phyllis, his wife. As Goodwin notes: 'signaling that a particular recipient shares with the speaker access to a specific type of information can mark those participants as a couple, and in so doing make an identity relationship such as "husband-wife" relevant to the organization of the talk of the moment' (1987:116).

It is clear that the ultimate rationale for selecting next speaker here is epistemic. In the following, speaker selection is done by reference to membership category and presumed (but, as it turns out, mistaken) category-bound activity:

(30) (Clift, 2012b:74)
      (Teacher has just used the cricketing term 'innings' in class, whereupon the following exchange occurs.)
```
1 Student 1 to Teacher:    Why is it called an 'innings'?
2 Teacher:              →  (turns eye-gaze to only middle-aged,
3                       →  English male in class, Student 2)
4 Student 2 to Teacher:    Don't look at me.
```

---

[10] We examine searches in Chapter 7.

Here is ample evidence of what Heritage calls 'an object of massive orientation' (2012b: 50). Student 2's disavowal of epistemic authority in the matter is also clearly one which simultaneously challenges the particular categorial relevancies mobilised in speaker selection.

Raymond and Heritage's use of epistemic domains to investigate what they call the 'epistemics of social relations' (2006) offers a cogent set of analytic resources for the exploration of identity. How speakers claim rights to assess certain domains is brought to bear on the data of an extended sequence in one telephone call between two women, Vera and Jenny, as they discuss Vera's grandchildren. As mediated through the resources for claiming epistemic rights, Raymond and Heritage establish how Vera's identity as a grandparent is constructed and sustained as a relevant and consequential feature of their interaction (p. 683). An early part of the phone call was presented as (28) above; the first few lines of that extract are reproduced below as (31).

(31)   (Raymond and Heritage, 2006:688)
```
1  Ver:   eeYe- Wasn' [it lucky? Ah to:ld the w- told Missiz=
2  Jen:               [Mm-
3  Ver:   =Richards tih te[ll (              )
4  Jen:                   [Ye::s that wz smashing <mind he might
5          hev thought chu w'r up here anyw[ay
```

We recall that Vera is congratulating herself on having had the foresight to tell the neighbour to suggest that her family, who have arrived for a visit, go round to Jenny's; this is formulated as a negative interrogative, 'Wasn't it lucky ...', which, as an assessment in first position, upgrades what is, by virtue of being first, already the default priority in rights to assess. As a yes/no question, it invites the recipient not only to respond but to do so in a particular format, asserting command of the terms to be used in assessing the referent; and by dint of the negative interrogative, 'the speaker invokes an established or settled position and, through that, a more extensive acquaintance with the referent state of affairs and/or rights to assess it' (Raymond and Heritage, 2006:689). Later in the exchange, talk turns to the grandchildren themselves, and, in attempting to find a precise formulation to assess one of her grandchildren, James, Vera offers a contrastive assessment of another child, Jillian:

(32)   (Raymond and Heritage, 2006:687; Rahman:14:1–2)
```
1  Ver:    Ah thi:nk it's: eh::m a nice devil. ah don't think it's
2       →  nahsty you see. hh with Jillian, she c'n be a little
3       →  nahsty little bi[tch
4  Jen:                    [Well you w'r say: ↑in thez something in
5           thaht_=It's a sha:me i[sn't i:t.]
```

Vera's assessment of Jillian, that 'she c'n be a little nahsty little bitch', delivered without equivocation or qualification, asserts her right to assess on the basis of direct access to the referent. In contrast, Jenny's subsequent assessment of Vera's family (l.1) in (33) below lacks this forthrightness, mitigated as it is by a tag

question, in an epistemic downgrade of her first position status, deferring to Vera
as the children's grandparent:

(33)   (Clift, 2006:572; Rahman: B:2: JV(14):4)
       (Jenny (J) and Vera (V) are talking about Vera's son Bill, his wife Jean, and their
       children.)

```
1    J:→  They're [a luvly family now ar'n't [they.
2    V:→          [°Mm:.                    [They are: ye[s.
3    J:                                                  [eeYe[s::,
4    V:                                                       [Yes,
5    J:   Mm: All they need now is a little girl tih complete i:t.
6    J:   [h e h  h eh ]
7    V:→  [Well I said  t]uh Jean how abou:t it so our Bill (0.2)
8         laughingly said 'ey she'll havetuh ask me fir:st no:w.
9    J:   h:ha[: ha:
10   V:       [huh huh-u huh-u [uh uh
11   J:                       ['Eez 'ad enough 'as 'ee=
12   J:   =heh [heh eh ih huh huh
13   V:        [Yea::h hih- Yea:h,
```

Vera pounces on this assessment with a confirmation – 'They are' – followed by
an agreement – 'yes'. In making confirmation the priority over agreement, Vera
proposes that she held this position prior to and independently of Jenny; she
thereby asserts her rights to assess what is, after all, her family. So in the initial
assessment sequence here, both Jenny (by downgrading her own rights to assess)
and Vera (by upgrading hers) display recognition of Vera's priority in the matter
of assessment and, in so doing, uphold her identity as grandparent. However, if
Jenny's acknowledging 'yes' and Vera's responsive 'Yes' (l. 4) provide for the
sequence to be brought to a close, what Jenny does next radically shifts from her
prior downgraded stance vis-à-vis the family. Her subsequent assessment, 'All
they need now is a little girl to complete it', in the first place, continues the
sequence. The strength of this assessment, marked in part by what Pomerantz
(1986) identifies as an extreme case formulation, 'all', is in stark contrast to the
evidential weakening that characterised her prior assessment at line 1. The only
indication of mitigation here is in the subsequent laughter (l. 6), in what Schegloff
(1996a:92) calls a 'post-completion stance marker'. However, if the laughter
constitutes an invitation to join in, as a means of affiliating (Jefferson, 1979), Vera
distinctly resists doing so. While her response starts in overlap with the laughter,
it displays no orientation to it. Instead, the launch of the turn is placed directly
after Jenny's prior turn, the 'well' at its beginning indexing what follows as both
responsive to its prior but also counterpositional to it (Davidson, 1984:110;
Pomerantz, 1984:72; Sacks, 1992a:76; Heritage, 2014). It is in this context – of
Jenny's strong assessment, and Vera's resistance to it – that Vera reports what she
said to her daughter-in-law on the matter: 'Well I said to Jean how about it.'
As Clift (2006) demonstrates, reported speech in this environment of competitive
assessment constitutes a powerful evidential display of having reached an

assessment first, and, as such, is another resource for upgrading a speaker's epistemic rights. Indeed, in response to this display of epistemic authority, and in a clear display of alignment, Jenny laughs.

In the following extract from the same conversation, we see also how forms of reference, discussed in Chapter 5, are also brought to bear on claims to epistemic priority. In the first instance, Jenny's use of the subsequent form 'he' in her assessment ('bright little boy') at line 3 reveals a discrepancy regarding the object of their agreement. While Jenny initially offers 'little James', Vera, the boys' grandmother, names 'Paul' in overlap with her. However, Jenny immediately defers to Vera by repeating 'Paul' and producing agreement tokens (ll. 5 and 7). Perhaps to display her own epistemic independence in her initial positive assessment, and counter a possible inference that she was simply 'going along with' Vera in naming Paul, she thereafter offers a negative assessment of James in line 11: 'Yeh, James's a little devil.' The initial 'yeh' proposes its turn as continuing the prior sequence; this underscores her assessment of James as contrastive with the one she offered earlier of Paul, so implying that Paul was indeed the object of her earlier positive assessment. However, in conveying that she meant to refer to Paul, Jenny, in line 11, produces a declarative, first position negative assessment of Vera's other grandson, James:

```
(34)  (Raymond and Heritage, 2006:693)
1    Ver:    ehr: they readjer comics:'n evrythink yihkn[o:w
2    Jen:                                              [Yeh: w'l
3            I think he's a bri:ght little boy: u[h:m
4    Ver:                                       [I: do=
5    Jen:    =l[ittle Ja]:[:mes,] uh [Pau:l.yes.]
6    Ver:      [ Pau:l, ]  [mm- m] mm [Pau : : l,]
7    Jen:    Mm:.[Yes.
8    Ver:        [Yes.
9            (0.3)
10   Ver:    [Yes (              )]
11   Jen:    [Yeh James's a little] divil ihhh 'heh heh
12   Ver:    [That-
13   Jen:    [.huh..hh[h He:-
14   Ver:→            [James is a little bugger [isn'e.
15   Jen:                                       [Yeh- Yeah=
16   Jen:    =[(he's into) ev'rythi]ng.
```

While agreeing with Jenny, Vera, at line 14, resists the claim to superior epistemic access proposed by the format of Jenny's turn. This resistance is embodied by two features of her own turn, 'James is a little bugger isn'e.' In the first instance, the tag question in the second position assessment marks her turn as a 'new' first pair part and thus stakes a claim to the priority of that assessment. Secondly, the use of the initial reference form 'James' in what is clearly a subsequent position from its first mention in Jenny's line 11 also serves to index the 'firstness' of her assessment – so effectively disregarding Jenny's initial mention of him. Thus, the choice of the reference form in Vera's turn is implicated in the action it implements. Indeed, this claim to first position is accepted by Jenny's type-conforming 'Yeh- Yeah' and what Raymond and Heritage call 'a potential (and decidedly pallid) specification of "little bugger": "he's into everything"' (2006:694).

While these excerpts permit only a brief foray into the extended sequence examined by Raymond and Heritage, there is surely enough in the above exchanges to show how identities are invoked and made relevant by participants themselves; as Raymond and Heritage note: 'each speaker's orientation to the relevance of Vera's status as a closely related family member is consequential (i) for the design of their turns, (ii) for the content of those turns, and (iii) for the trajectory of this series of sequences as a whole' (2006:700). Nowhere is the term 'grandparent' actually used – and yet the speakers display a sustained orientation to Vera's occupancy of this category through their positioning with respect to each other.

Work by Raymond (2014, forthcoming) on Peruvian Spanish has also shown the extent to which grammatical distinctions may be invoked in the construction of identity, further illuminating the distinction between status and interactional stance. Spanish, like many languages of the world, has a distinction in the second-person singular reference form between *tú* and *usted* – a distinction traditionally conceived of in the literature, and discussed in Chapter 1, as one between social intimacy and social distance, respectively (Brown and Gilman, 1960). As we saw in Chapter 5 with reference to pronoun use in a number of languages, either form would be grammatically correct (see, as a comparison, Lerner and Kitzinger (2007) on repairs through shifts in first-person reference forms in English) and do the job of referring, but here Raymond investigates how shifts between the two accomplish important elements of identity in the service of social action (2014:145). The following extended exchange affords a remarkable insight into how a momentary shift from one form to another can allow for a recalibration of the relationship between speaker and hearer at a particular moment in the interaction. It is taken from a Peruvian political interview in which a lawyer, Rosa María Palacios, interviews Martha Chávez, who is running for Congress. Chávez has been widely criticised for her stance on human rights and violations thereof. Chávez has, up until the extract below, been showing her dissatisfaction with how the amnesty laws are applied, in her view unjustly, such that those she views as terrorists are set free, while members of the armed forces are left in jail; she invokes and points to a legal document, the American Convention on Human Rights, in support of her position. In line 14 below we see the default reference form, *usted*, which has been used for the entirety of the interview:

(35) (Raymond, 2014:116; Prensa Libre: Rosa María interviews Martha Chávez)
      (Pal=Palacios; Cha=Chavez)
14   Cha: *Sabe usted Rosa María.* =
              know.USTED you   R   M
       →   Usted   know   Rosa Maria

```
15        =La vez pa[sada yo aquí creo      que     lo mencioné.
          The time past     I here I-think  that    it I-mentioned
          =The last time I  was here I believe     I mentioned it.
16                     [((quick point at table))
17   Pal:  [Mm,
18   Cha:  [.hhh [La convención americana    >de< derechos humanos,
                 the convention American     >of<   rights human
           .hhh  The American   Convention >on< Human Rights,
```

Palacio subsequently challenges the position of Chávez by citing an exception: those convicted of genocide, which would include those to whom Chávez referred. In response, seen at line 33 below, Chávez produces a vigorous 'multiple "no"' (Vazquez Carranza, 2013) – a multiple saying (Stivers, 2004) which itself challenges Palacio's position, asserting that 'genocide' as a category did not exist in this legal form till 2003, and that retrospective application of the law is not possible. Furthermore, at lines 36–7 Chávez self-repairs to abandon the default form of *usted* and momentarily address Palacios as *tu*:

(36) (Raymond, 2014:117; Prensa Libre: Rosa María interviews Martha Chávez)
      (Pal=Palacios; Cha=Chavez)

```
33   Cha       [No no.    No          [El genoci:dio es una (.)
               no                      the genocide is a
               No no.     No           Genoci:de is a (.)
34        tipificación que    se     da  a partir del  año=
          typification that self    gives to-leave of-the year
          classification starting in   the  year=
35        =dos mil       tres para nosotros,=
          two  thousand three for  us
          =two-thousand three  for us,=
36    →   =Y usted sabe  perfectamente Rosa María,=
          and you   know.USTED perfectly      R    M
          and   usted know perfectly       Rosa María,=
37    →   =[O tú sabes Rosa María.
           or  you know.TÚ R     M
           Or  tú know  Rosa María.
38        [((audibly/visibly out of breath by the end of l.36))
39        .hhh que
              that
          .hhh that
40        (.)
41        Los tipos penales (.) son (.) ((timeline with hands))
          The types penal       are
          Penal classes (.)  are
42        [a partir de que   se tipifican (.) ((timeline))
          to to-leave of that self typify
          from their classification (.)
43   Pal  [((raises hand))
```

44   Cha   *[en adelante para los hechos   que suceden allá. ((timeline))*
            on   forward for the deeds that   happen there
            Onward for those deeds which occur there.
45   Pal   [*.hhhhhhhhhhhhhh   hhhhhhhhhhhhhhhh*
46   Pal   *Muy bien. Entonces no va   a haber cambio en la posición.*
            Very well then   no goes to to-be change in the position
            Very well. So there is   not going to be a change in the position.

To underline the force of her position, she refers to Palacio's epistemic domain
in the preface to her assertion (ll. 36–7): 'You know perfectly Rosa María',
'*perfectamente*' and the use of the name (Clayman, 2010) underlining the
sincerity of the assertion. What the English translation cannot capture here,
however, is the decisive shift at the transition space[11] into a different form
of second-person reference: 'Y *usted sabe* perfectamente Rosa María, O *tú
sabes* Rosa María.' Raymond suggests that the shift from *usted* to *tú* – a moment
of 'alikeness through a socially-intimate reference form' (2014:119) actively
invokes common ground (Clark, 1996) with her interlocutor by embodying,
through the linguistic reference, co-membership of the category 'lawyer' and
thus equal access to the legal knowledge she is about to present (p. 119); the
lack of any challenge subsequently from Palacio does indeed suggest that it has
accomplished co-participant alignment after a sequence where confrontation
and disalignment have been very much in evidence (see Raymond, 2014:120–2,
for discussion on a switch in the other direction, from *tú* to *usted*). As Raymond
notes:

> while the underlying pragmatics of *usted* and *tú* can indeed carry with them
> the notions of social distance and intimacy, respectively, in a given dialect
> (Brown & Gilman 1960; Brown & Levinson 1987), the ground-level sig-
> nificance of invoking such distance or intimacy is no more automatic or
> predetermined than the identities of the interactants themselves. Rather, the
> interactional relevance of these pronominal options is action- and sequence-
> conditioned by way of the moment-by-moment negotiation of identities in
> and through the ongoing talk.   (2014:122)

While the 'underlying pragmatics' of *usted* and *tú* speak to notions of interactional status, the 'moment-by-moment negotiation of identities' in the talk clearly
shows here how pronouns are mobilised in the implementation of interactional
stance.

   While it may be intuitively evident that second-person reference forms, and
shifts between them, should be deployed in the service of category membership,
less so is the fact that third-person reference forms should also be so mobilised.
However, work in Korean by Oh (2010) on third-person demonstrative-based
quasi-pronouns distinguishing proximal and distal shows that selection of one or
other form is ultimately grounded in territories of knowledge – and thus category

---

[11] Transition-space repairs are a topic to which we return in Chapter 7.

membership – being invoked in the talk. So speakers may refer to a co-present party with the distal demonstrative *ce* (that)-based quasi-pronoun instead of a proximal demonstrative *i* (this)-based one to endow the referent with a different category membership from themselves, without reference to actual spatial proximity. In the following extract, M and K, former high-school class-mates, are conversing in the presence of R, who is M's daughter. M has just remarked that the granddaughter of a former classmate is already at middle school, for which K provides a possible account at line 1: 'She got married early.' M's agreement (l. 2) and possible sequence closure follow. However, at line 4, M initiates a new, topically related sequence:

```
(37)  (Oh, 2010:1227–8)
1  K:    kulehkey toy-keyss-ci[:°illccik] kyelhonhayss-nuntey.°
         like:that become-DEC:RE-COMM       early marry:ANT-CIRCUM
         It   may well be so. °She  got married  early.°
2  M:                       [ °kuchi° ]
                             be:so:COMM
                            °Right.°
3        (0.3)
4  M:→   yay-lul- (.)nuc::key nassci:.(.)↑tongchang cwungeyse nayka yay-lul
         QP-ACC       late give:birth:to:COMM schoolmate among I:NOM QP-ACC
         I gave birth to (.)  her LA::TE.   (.)I  THINK I HAD HER THE LATEST
5        ceyil nuckey nass-ul ke-ya.
         most late give:birth:to:ANT-ATTR thing-be:IE
         AMONG OUR SCHOOLMATES.
6  K:    kulay.
         be:so:IE
         Right.
7        (0.3)
8  M:    selun tases-ey nass-e.
         thirty-five-TEM give:birth:to:ANT-IE
         I had her at thirty five.
```

With her assessment, 'I gave birth to her late', M refers to her daughter, R, sitting beside her, with the proximal demonstrative-based quasi-pronoun *yay*. This is the unmarked option for referring to a person who is in physical proximity to the speaker. However, in the following extract, the very same referent in the very same position with respect to the speaker as in (37) above is referred to, not with *yay*, but with the distal demonstrative-based quasi-pronoun *cyay*. Prior to the sequence below, it has emerged that K went to 'Hanseng' middle school, and, at line 1, M offers that as an account for something she has known – that K was a year behind in the school they both attended – but for which she did not know the reason. This is confirmed by K. After a brief pause, M launches a turn at line 4 informing K that her daughter – the co-present R – graduated from Hanseng women's high school (part of the same organization as K's middle school):

(38) (Oh, 2010:1228)

```
1  M:    Han- kule- kulay- kulayse il-nyen nuc-ess-kwuya:¿
         Han- be:so- so    so     one-year late-ANT-UNASSIM
         Han- right- so- THAT'S why you were behind  by one year, huh
2  K:    e.
         yes
         Yeah.
3        (1)
4  M:→   °>ku ttay Hanseng ye-ko-              <° yay- cyay Hanseng ye-ko
         that time Hanseng woman-high:school   QP   QP  Hanseng woman-high:school
5        nawass-e. ((thump)) (.) [Payceng:- ung]
         graduate:ANT-IE          Payceng  yes
         °>At that time, Hanseng women's high-school
         -<°She (proximal)- SHE (distal) graduated from Hanseng
         women's high-school. (.) PAYCENG- Yes.
6  K:→                           [yay-ka? (    ) ((surprised tone))
                                  QP-NOM
                                  Did she? ()
7  M:    Payceng (.) miswul cenkong ha-taka¿
         Payceng   art     major   do-TRANS
         She majored in Art (.)  at PAYCENG (middle school), and
8  K:    ung
         yes
         I see.
```

In the course of her turn at lines 4–5, M self-repairs the reference to her daughter, seated beside her, from the unmarked *yay* to marked *cyay*; indeed, *cyay* is stressed, displaying its status as a correction. The use of the distal demonstrative-based quasi-pronoun *cyay* serves to distance the speaker from its referent – in this case, M from her own daughter. What is more, in contrast to M's use of *cyay*, which assigns the speaker to a different membership category from the referent, K's next turn at line 6 displays that she – who attended the same foundation (Hanseng) school – here positions herself with M's daughter R by referring to her by means of the proximal form *yay*. So despite being both physically (sitting across a table from R) and relationally more distant from R than M, K's use of *yay* indicates at once that she categorises herself with the referent, R, and away from the recipient, M (Oh, 2010:1228–9).

Grammatical resources are thus brought to bear on the configuration of social relationships made relevant by the actions being implemented in the talk. While the physical-spatial relationships between the participants – and indeed their status with respect to each other – may remain constant, the epistemic territories may shift from moment to moment, and these momentary calibrations of interactional stance are captured in the mobilisation of particular grammatical forms in the construction of action.

6.2.2   Authority in interaction

Orientations to knowledge are clearly a basic interpretive resource for participants to interaction. However, as we saw at the beginning of this chapter, orientations to authority are similarly implicated in the recognition of action. Stevanovic and Peräkylä (2012, 2014) propose that, alongside the epistemic dimension of authority, participants orient to a deontic dimension, anchored in issues of rights and obligations. The interpretation of a summons (*Neil!*) as a directive (*Kneel!*) is clearly located in an attribution of relative deontic status. The distinction, invoked with respect to epistemic rights, between attributed deontic status and the moment-by-moment adjustments to a particular deontic stance, is similarly evident in the examination of interactional sequences.

The previous chapter showed how children may find a middle way between resistance and compliance with a directive in incipient compliance; the directives they receive show a high degree of entitlement and deontic status:

(39)   (Craven and Potter, 2010:432)
```
21   Mum  Ri:gh'. Ea:' ya te:a now.
```

Furthermore, while deontic stance and deontic status (like their epistemic counterparts) are usually congruent with each other, this is not always the case; as Stevanovic and Peräkylä observe, 'highly authoritative speakers rarely need to command, while speakers with low authority sometimes can try to inflate their authority with more assertive directives' (2014:191).[12] Attributed authority may be such that it obviates the verbal altogether; Kidwell (2005) examines how this authority may be invested in eye gaze in a study of how very young children differentiate 'the look' from a mere look by their adult caregivers.

Participants' judgements about their relative deontic status are critical for their understanding whether an utterance is to be interpreted, for example, as a directive (*Kneel!*), or a request for action. Labov (1972:304) mentions that, when A requests B to do X, it is necessary for A to have the 'right to tell B to do X' for this to be heard as a valid command. So, in perhaps the most famous

---

[12] The journalist who uncovered evidence of phone hacking at the British newspaper the *News of the World* (which was closed down as a consequence), writes of the power of the press mogul, Rupert Murdoch, and his modus operandi:

> The point about real power is that it does its own work, particularly among those who deal in power. Nobody in the power elite needs to be told. They all recognise the mogul's power and, with few exceptions, they do everything they can to pacify him, to ingratiate themselves. The mogul, for the most part, does not have to make threats or issue instructions. He just has to show up. Not even that – he just has to exist, somewhere in the background. Everybody understands; the fact of power is enough. If there's a bull in the field, everybody steps carefully. The fear gives him access; the access gives him influence. Real power is passive.   (Davies, 2014:177–8)

This recalls Sun Tzu's characterisation of the most powerful person in the room: 'the one who doesn't speak in a room. He's the one who holds all the cards.'

historical instance – at least, that handed down by oral tradition,[13] is Henry II, referring to Thomas à Becket: 'Will no one rid me of this turbulent priest?' Clearly, deontic authority figures in the interpretation of this as a directive. In Lindström's study of home help visitors to senior citizens in Sweden, we see how statements are interpreted as requests:

(40) (Lindström, 2005:220)

   (The senior citizen (SC) is sitting on a board placed across the edges of the bathtub. She has a big towel across her shoulders and is drying herself while the home help provider (HH) is drying up water with a rag that she moves across the floor with her foot.)

```
1      HH      ° (U) dä:r(hh).°
                    there
2              (0.4)
3      SC→     Du får no torka
               You may PRT dry
               You should probably
               (x) (y)
4       →      me  på    ry[:ggen.
               me on the back
               dry my back
5      HH              [Ja:: a ska göra de(h).
                       Yes I will do that
(x)    HH moves toward SC
(y)    HH puts her hands on the towel on SC's shoulders and starts drying her
```

The interpretation of lines 3–4 as a directive turns on the recipient's judgement of the speaker's high deontic status – and thus high degree of entitlement relative to the recipient in this particular domain.

It is a basic observation that any action can take a number of forms (e.g. *Dry my back/Can you please dry my back?/My back needs drying* and so on), or that, to put it another way, that different forms and actions can amount to the same thing. It is tempting, when faced with alternative formats, to suppose that the motivation to choose one over the other has its origins in the external context, or considerations such as politeness (Brown and Levinson, 1987; Watts, 2003). Take requests: there is a range of ways in which these may be formatted, from simply naming what's requested (e.g. *a pint of Guinness*), to recognisable lexico-syntactic formulae (e.g. *Could you ...?*) through to intuitively less direct forms (e.g. *I wonder if you could ... ?*). Work by Curl and Drew (2008) investigating a corpus of phone calls in domestic settings and out-of-hours phone calls to doctors has uncovered a fundamental distinction between the interactional circumstances under which speakers select either *Could you ...* or *I wonder if ...* in

---

[13] Schama (2000:142) prefers the contemporary account of the biographer Edward Grim, writing in Latin, who suggests that in fact Henry said: 'What miserable drones and traitors have I nourished and brought up in my household, who let their lord be treated with such shameful contempt by a low-born cleric?' On this account, deontic status is brought explicitly to the surface. The theoretical point, of course, remains the same.

the making of requests where judgements of entitlement, and thus deontic status, play a crucial role.[14]

Modal auxiliaries such as 'could you' (in l. 7 of (41) below) in the format of requests account for two-thirds of their corpus of 'everyday' calls:

```
(41)  (Curl and Drew, 2008:137; Field SO88:2:8:1)
1    Les    Hello:?
2           (0.3)
3    Gor    It's Gordon.
4    Les    .hhhh oh Gordon. Shall I ring you back darling,
5    Gor    Uh:: no y- I don't think you can,
6           (0.3)
7    Gor→   But uh: just to (0.3) say (.) could you bring up a
8           letter.
9           (.)
10   Gor    When you come up,
```

In contrast, the *could you* format is rare in the corpus of doctors' calls, and instead the *I wonder* preface (as at l. 2 below) predominates:

```
(42)  (Curl and Drew, 2008:138; 1:1:12)
      (Doc=doctor; Clr=caller)
1    Doc    hello,
2    Clr→   mt! Hello, I wonder if you could give me some advice,
```

On the very rare occasions that the *could you* format is used, the circumstances are detailed in such a way as to make clear that a medical visit is warranted and urgent, as in the case below ('she's breathless', l. 7):

```
(43)  (Curl and Drew, 2008:139; 1:2:12)
1    Doc    Hel:lo:,
2    Clr    Hel:lo, is tha' du- doctor
3    Doc    Yes, Doctor (omitted) speaki:ng,
4    Clr→   i:i: (yeah) couldja's (call'd) an' see my wife please,
5           .h[h
6    Doc       [Yes:.
7    Clr→   She's breathless. She can't.hh get 'er breath.hh
```

Compare the *could you* format above with that used in the earlier call in (42), where 'some advice' (l. 2) is being solicited; it is clear in this latter case that the caller, in deploying *Could you* rather than *I wonder if* displays an entitlement to a visit by the doctor. Returning now to (41), Gordon's request to his mother, formatted as 'could you bring up a letter' (ll. 7–8) similarly claims an entitlement

---

[14] Curl and Drew note that their findings do not support the distinction made, in politeness theory and elsewhere in the literature, between the putatively direct and indirect forms *Would you . . .* and *Could you . . .* They also find no difference between speakers' selection of either *Would you . . .* versus *Could you . . .* Here, we therefore use *Could you . . .* as the generic form in referring to these variants. In contrast, Curl and Drew's findings do not support treating *Could you . . .* and *I wonder if you could . . .* as equivalently indirect forms (2008:133).

that *I wonder if you could bring* would not have. The following, in contrast, is taken from a call to a bookshop:

(44)   (Curl and Drew, 2008:141; 2:2:1; opening unrecorded)
```
1   Les    ... and ordered a boo:k [.hhh and you said you'd ho:ld=
2   Jon                            [yeah
3   Les    it for me
4   Les    And (.) I was supposed to be coming in around Easter
5    →     well I haven't managed to get i:n a:nd I wonder if you
6          could se:nd it to me if you've still go:t it
```

In Lesley's detailing of the circumstances leading up to her request, she is displaying awareness of the contingencies associated with being able to fulfil it; Curl and Drew note that *I wonder*-prefaced requests are a means of displaying that the request is 'contingent on knowing and following the proper procedures and practices' (2008:141). *Could you send it to me ...* would have made the assumption that the bookshop would have been able to send her the book; as it is, the format chosen avoids making such an assumption. Note that Gordon follows his 'Could you bring ... ' request in (41) with a mention of the contingency involved in meeting it ' ... when you come up'. Thus, as Curl and Drew propose:

> The actual conditions of use of modal verbs and imperatives versus *I-wonder*-prefaced requests coincide with, and are partly constitutive of, speakers' displays of entitlement; and it is the *I-wonder*-prefaced requests (as well as those questioning the possibility of an action) that display speakers' awareness of certain requests as having contingencies that they cannot anticipate.   (2008:144)

The displays of entitlement to which Curl and Drew refer are, of course, participants' orientations to their deontic status. In the following, we see a speaker changing the form of her request to display progressively diminishing entitlement, and thus diminishing deontic status. Lesley, talking to her daughter, Katherine, currently at university, raises the issue of when Katherine is to come home (l. 1). Katherine's implied proposal – that she come home the same day as her boyfriend (l. 3) – is rejected (ll. 5–6); in the wake of this rejection, and with no alternative proposal from Lesley forthcoming (l. 9), Katherine launches her request (l. 10):

(45)   (Curl and Drew, 2008:146; Field X:C:2:1:4)
```
1    Les    Anyway when d'you think you'd like to come home ↓love.
2           (.)
3    Kat    Uh:m (.) we:ll Brad's goin' down on Monday.
4           (0.7)
5    Les    Monday we:ll ah-:hh. hh w: ↑Monday  we can't manage
6           because (.) Granny's ↓coming Monday↓
7           (0.4)
8    Kat    Oh:,
9           (0.5)
10   Kat→   Could- (0.3) Dad ↑couldn't pick me up from:: (.) ee-
11          even from Westbury could he
```

```
12   Les    .hh I ↑CAN'T HEAR you very well cz of this damn machine
13          that's attached to this telephone ↑say it again,
14   Kat→   Would it be possible: for Dad to pick me up from
15          Westbury on [Monday.
16   Les                [Ye:s yes ↑THAT would be ↓alright
```

Katherine's first request is initiated at line 10 with a cut-off self-repair 'Could-'. Whether or not this is on the way to being *could* or *couldn't*, it is the latter that she initially settles on – and in both the morphosyntax ('couldn't') and the delivery of the beginning of the turn (the dysfluency) we already see an orientation that what is about to be proposed as problematic. The proposal itself (l. 11) – that her father pick her up from a nearby town on that day – is, in addition, formatted (with 'even') and the tag question ('could he') to display her awareness that he might not be able to pick her up on that day at all. Upon her mother's initiation of repair – a claim of non-hearing, rather than non-understanding – Katherine does not produce the (incidentally, very directly) requested repeat. Instead, in the wake of what had been a refusal (l. 5, 'Monday we can't manage') and a possible incipient disagreement heralded by the repair initiator at lines 12–13, Katherine reformats her request to display more diminished deontic status than she had hitherto: 'would it be possible' (l. 14). Her assessment of her entitlement to come home whenever she wishes (note the format of Lesley's initial inquiry) has thus been modified in line with her displayed attentiveness to the contingencies surrounding the granting of her request.

Selection of one or other format for making a request is therefore seen to be grounded in speakers' assessments of their entitlement to what is requested and its attendant contingencies, and thus their overall deontic status vis-à-vis their recipients. So rather than being conditioned by aspects of either speaker identity or external (institutional vs. non-institutional) context, the two dimensions of entitlement and contingency are those manifestly oriented to by speakers in the detail of the interaction. In research on requests in Italian, Rossi (2014, 2015a) examines different formats (e.g. *Passami il sale* – 'pass me the salt' vs. *Mi passi il sale* – 'will you pass me the salt') in a corpus of videoed data, establishing how the different contingencies select different formats. In the following exemplar from Cha'palaa, Floyd (2015) notes how a participant, here B, may delegate to a third party, especially when that third party is closer to a target object, or of lower social status, both of which are the case with participant C here:

```
(46)  (Floyd, 2015:9)
1   A      inu jabon
            i-nu jabon
            1SG-ACC soap
            to me, soap ((in water; points at soap on shore))
2   B  →   jabon tya'kide    apa   ñaa
            jabon tyatyu-ki-de apa    ñu-ya
            soap throw-do-IMP 'father' 2SG-FOC
            throw the soap, son, you
            ((points at soap))
3   C      ((child throws soap to A))
```

So the relative anticipatability of the request, the recognition of potential obstacles to its granting and the relation of the request to what the recipient is currently doing – whether it is consistent with, or departs from, the recipient's current course of action – are all factors in the selection of different request formats.

There is also a growing body of research on requests in particular contexts: Vinkhuysen and Szymanski (2005) on the choice between *I need* and *Can you make...?* in a photocopy shop, Heinemann (2006) on displays of entitlement through *Will you ...?* versus *Can't you ...?* in Danish requests in a home-help context. Furthermore, Antaki and Craven (2012) examine requests and imperatives between staff in a residential care home and adults with intellectual impairments, and find that directives are used far more frequently than requests, similarly showing little attention to the possible contingencies involved in compliance, but a high degree of entitlement; in the following, staff member Kath solicits the residents' preference for holidays:

(47)   (Antaki and Craven, 2012:880)
```
1   Kath    ((describing photo)) that's me and you
2       →   at missiz [Name]'s house. >now< - listen
3       →   carefully now, where do you want
4           to go on holidays.
```

Once again, high deontic status is displayed through the imperative format 'listen carefully now'. In comparison, the imperative format discussed in the previous chapter – 'Jis' send 'im round here for a couple'v hours' – adopts a high deontic stance in order to implement an offer. In a study of offers and requests, Clayman and Heritage (2015) discuss the ways in which the linguistic form of an utterance is interpreted as doing some particular action in the light of who is projected to be the agent of some particular action and who is understood to be its beneficiary. They use empirical materials to work through an observation made by Ervin-Tripp, who invites us to imagine a scenario in which you are cutting up carrots with a large kitchen knife and are approached by a small child who says 'Can I help?':

> If you consider yourself the beneficiary of the assistance of a well-trained Montessori-taught carrot-slicer, you may hear this as an offer. If you doubt the skill or even safety of the help, you may consider it a plea for permission ... The difference here is that in the case of permission requests, the speaker, as a principal beneficiary, wants the action more than the hearer ...   (1981:196–7).

There is no doubt who has deontic authority in such a situation; the issue is whether in one's dealings with the child a speaker might temporarily cede such status in adopting a deontically weaker stance. Weidner (2015), on a corpus of doctor–patient interaction in Polish, shows how the format *Proszę mi powiedzieć* (Please tell me), may be characterised by an incongruent epistemic-deontic configuration that encodes both deontic authority and epistemic subordination.

Similarly, in their investigation of Polish, Zinken and Ogiermann highlight issues of deontic stance in the course of work on requests (2011, 2013). One focus is on a particular format in Polish interaction, the impersonal *trzeba x* ('one needs to x'), commonly used in family interactions to enlist another in the accomplishment of some practical activity. They note the prevalence of this format in contrast to the much rarer person-marked declarative (2011:266). The following exchange takes place over a family dinner table. Bolek, the eleven-year-old son of the family, has been leaving the table repeatedly to see his two-year-old brother, Stás, who has left the room. At line 1 he has briefly returned to the table, complaining about the mess his brother has made in their shared bedroom, in overlap with his father's exhorting him to eat (l. 2). At line 4 Bolek runs out of the room once again, addressing Stas as he does so. After a pause, his father, Jacek, at line 8, while looking down at his plate, produces the *trzeba*-formatted turn: 'Może trzeba by go wziąć' (Maybe one would need to get him). Ilona, his wife, immediately complies, by getting up and with her verbal response in line 9, 'Zaraz go wezmę' (Right, now I'll get him):

```
(48)  (Zinken and Ogiermann, 2011:269–70)
      ( J=Jacek, father; I=Ilona, mother; B=Bolek, son)
1   B   [Kurcze, ja    (zasłałem)            nasz [pokój, (.) a
         Chick,    I (PFV-make.bed-PST-M-1SG)  our  room     and
         Oh rubbish,   I (made the beds in)    our room, and
2   J   [nie skończyłeś                            [jedz
         Not PFV-finish-PST-M-2S                    eat.IMP
         You haven't finished                       Eat
3   B   t(h)eraz¿ (1) hmhm (nie tam kurze ścieram)
         now             hmhm (no there dusts wipe-1S)
         now             hmhm (no I'm wiping dust there)
4       ((Bolek runs out of room))
5   B   °Jejciu on nie wiem (.) do   tego   wszystkiego dobierze.°
         dear   he not  know- 1S to this-GEN all-GEN.S  PFV-grab.3S
         Oh dear he I don't   know (.) gets  his   hands on this all.
6       h Stasiu¿
           Stasiu¿
7       (1.5) ((Ilona straightens her hand and taps table))
8   J→  Może  trzeba  by  go    wziąć ((looking down at plate))
         Maybe trzeba COND he.ACC take.PFV.
         Maybe one would need to get him.
9   I   ((gets up)) Zaraz  go   wezmę.
                    At.once he.ACC take.PFV-1S
         Right now (I'll) get him.
10      (1)
11  I   Sta:siu::, cho:dź słoneczko.
         Staś-VOC   come-IMP sun-DIM
         Staś, come little sun
         ((Conversation continues in another room))
```

Zinken and Ogiermann note of the *trzeba*-formatted turn:

> Jacek has built a turn in which, formally speaking, he has not asked Ilona to do anything, nor has he told Ilona to do something. Rather, he has 'pointed out' a necessary action. Doing so, he has built a turn consisting of a grammatically recognizable unit, which makes speaker transition, and a responsive action from Ilona, relevant next. Furthermore, note that Jacek builds his turn with a turn-initial może ('maybe') and conditional marking, practices that contribute to the mitigation of the 'force' of an action. (2011:270)

Zinken and Ogiermann's study of the format '*trzeba* x', proposing its action as objectively necessary, cuts across the usual classifications of request/directive. Kendrick and Drew illuminate this issue by deploying the general term 'recruitment' to refer to

> the various ways in which one person can ask for, seek, or solicit help from another, including giving indirect and perhaps embodied indications of their need for assistance; as well as another's anticipation of someone's need for help, and their offering or giving that help without being asked, without their help having been solicited.   (2016:2)

Instances of recruitment are evident in, among others, extract (38), 'My mom's buttonholer is broken', and extract (43), 'My car is stalled', in Chapter 5. A major comparative study across eight languages[15] by Floyd et al. (2014) uses multimodal data to show how such recruitments may be done non-linguistically by pointing, or holding out an object for a recipient to engage with in ways that are at once more interactionally immediate and more subtle than the verbalisation of requests or directives. They show the interactional contingencies attached to recruitments according to whether, for example, co-participants are in the same visual field; interrogative formats are used when a desired object is not visibly available. It is evident from this work that certain sets of resources recur cross-linguistically as practices for achieving similar actions. For example, in all of the languages speakers choose among imperative, declarative and interrogative sentence types, and spoken, visual or multimodal formats, and between 'bare' requests and mitigated requests including accounts or minimisers like diminutive marking: speakers select from among all these options according to interactional contingencies.

6.3   Conclusion: knowledge, authority and agency in indirection

We recall that Sacks's early work on membership categories was part of a more general enterprise investigating both description and word selection.

---

[15] Siwu (Ghana), Lao, Cha'palaa, Murrinh-Patha, Dutch, Russian, English, Mandarin Chinese and Italian.

Subsequent CA research on speakers' orientations to knowledge and authority has provided a sequential basis for this work. It has illuminated many aspects of the construction of identity by reference not only to the more enduring features of social relationships in the form of epistemic or deontic status but also to the moment-by-moment interactional shifts in epistemic or deontic stance.

Moreover, even if not labelled as such, this body of work is giving empirical foundation to, and also testing, Pinker et al.'s claim, mentioned in Chapter 1, that the function of language is to convey information and negotiate relationships. We have surely seen enough by now to acknowledge that such a proposal can be only a part of the picture. Of course, work in epistemics is showing that the conveyance of information is one element at the heart of human sociality and one motivation driving action; likewise, work on deontic authority speaks to the central role of relationships in language use. However, with respect to work in epistemics, as Hanks (2014:5) suggests, it is less 'information' that is at issue than 'knowledge', and it is speakers' relative access to and claims on that knowledge that is clearly a priority matter for participants. Reframing one linguistic function as 'knowledge' rather than 'information' as such, and investigating it as above all a social currency, methodologically also represents a significant shift away from an exclusive focus on grammar. So, to take a simple example, linguistic studies of evidentiality have focused on, and in many cases are restricted to, elements of morphosyntax.[16] However, it is clear that, interactionally, evidentiality and displays of stance (with respect to knowledge, say, or authority) emerge as much from grammar in the sequence (position + composition) as solely from the grammar.

Furthermore, it is quite clear that the reference to epistemics and deontics already provides some means of understanding how the linguistic form of an utterance relates to the action it implements in sequence. We have already seen how preference operates on the expansion or termination of sequences; we are now in a position to explore how preference and these other orders of organisation operate in the production and recognition of so-called indirect utterances. Levinson's (1983) proposal that indirect requests are collapsed presequences certainly appears to hold for one set of actions, but is not, we recall, generalisable across all. However, in identifying the origins of indirectness in the presequence Levinson captures one possible motivation for its use.

Indirect utterances indicate a preference for using minimal resources to accomplish actions. Kendrick and Drew, discussing the relationship between offers and requests, draw on the argument of Heritage and Raymond (2005) with reference to epistemics that first position carries a tacit claim of

---

[16] To cite a well-known example: 'the independent verb in Tuyuca is minimally composed of a verb root and an evidential' (Barnes, 1984:256), the morpheme indicating whether the speaker has personally seen the situation, has perceived it by hearing or some other sense, infers it, has learnt it from others or deems it reasonable to assume.

independence and primacy; in noting that first position is a locus for the expression of agency in interaction, they propose that:

> While a recipient who grants a request submits to the agency of the requester, agreeing to implement a solution devised by the requester, the recipient of a report or display of a problem finds him- or herself in a position to offer assistance voluntarily, and to determine his or her own solution to the problem, thereby exercising a greater degree of agency over the course of action.   (2014:111)

So we recall Ida's offer to Jenny in Chapter 5, extract (40) – 'Jis send im round here fer a couple'v: hou:r:s' – is produced, not as the result of a direct request, but after Jenny's detailing of her problems with her son. The recipient of a pre-request is hardly offering assistance voluntarily; yet the evidence that requests are fulfilled overwhelmingly by pre-requests rather than requests as such (and that they are conventionalised in such pres as *Can you pass the salt?* and *Have you got a light?*[17]) adds considerable weight to the argument that the speaker complying with an as-yet-unstated request is exerting a greater degree of agency over the action. Agency matters to participants: recall the resistance shown by children in the face of adult directives, and their deployment of incipient compliance to claw back autonomy and self-determination while still accomplishing compliance. In this light, we may be in a better position to understand the motivation for indirect utterances, such as Mum's directive to Daisy in Chapter 5, extract (36): 'What did she say about talking with y'mouth full¿'; while clearly a directive, its form cedes a certain degree of agency to its recipient. So the parent who issues *Is that your coat on the floor?* as a directive yields something in autonomy to the child, who, by picking it up, is effectively short-circuiting the directive it foreshadows. This is why stating 'My car is stalled' (Chapter 5, extract (43)) is preferred over soliciting help directly, and why opening the door for you because you're holding a cup in each hand is preferred over waiting for you to ask me to do so. Seen from this perspective, recruitments of various kinds (Floyd et al., 2014) are clearly anterior to requests. We can also see in contexts such as the breaking of bad news, where one might get one's recipient to guess by means of the pre (e.g. 'I had something terrible t'to tell you', Chapter 3, extract (24)) how certain actions are effectively devolved altogether. As Doris notes: 'much human agency is characterized by indirection: achieving outcomes that are not amenable to direct volitional control, but are manipulable by causal intermediaries. Securing the expression of one's values, and thereby exercising agency, frequently requires workarounds' (2015:127). In cultures where indirection is less prevalent (e.g. 'give me the string there' in Cha'palaa, Chapter 3, extract (38)), individual agency is apparently less of a priority.

---

[17] Levinson (1983:364) notes how questions of ability and the existence of goods – as in these two examples – crop up routinely in prerequests, as these are prime obstacles to the success of a request.

Thus, much CA work indicates the extent to which phenomena that, within linguistics, have been treated as exclusively grounded in logic (indirectness, see Pinker et al., 2008) and grammar (e.g. evidential or deontic markers of morpho-syntax) have an alternative basis in the sequence (Clift, 2006). Moreover, the same sequential resources are clearly mobilised by participants in their orientation to identities which, rather than being exogenously imposed by the analyst, are endogenously generated in the talk itself, in what Kitzinger and Mandelbaum call the 'micromoments of identity construction' (2013:17).

7 Halting progressivity: the organisation of repair

This final chapter on the procedural infrastructure of interaction examines repair: the means by which shared understandings are sustained and defended.
The importance of such shared understandings is such that repair can take priority over the turn-taking system. Repair can be categorised by who initiates the repair (the speaker – 'self' – or the recipient – 'other') and who completes it. In the light of this broad distinction, we provide an overview of repair practices across languages – and one form of repair initiation ('Huh?') that appears to be universal. There are explicit forms of repair initiations which are undertaken through linguistic means, and implicit forms of repair which mobilise extralinguistic resources in the form of gaze and embodiments. It is clear that repair is also a vehicle for implementing actions over and above simply repair.

If intersubjectivity – the tacit assumption of a shared world – is the bedrock on which interaction rests, then the means by which speakers maintain and defend this assumption is a necessary element of it. As Schegloff observes: 'without systematic provision for a world known and held in common by some collectivity of persons, one has not a misunderstood world, but no conjoint reality at all' (1992b:1296). This chapter is an overview of the organisation of repair – the action or actions by which speakers and recipients work to address what Schegloff et al., in their foundational work on repair in talk, call '*problems* in speaking, hearing and understanding' (1977:361; italics added).[1] These actions are unique in that they systematically supersede whatever was due next in a turn, thus disrupting the preference for progressivity (Schegloff, 1979: 277–8) that observably characterises talk. Repair is thus treated by participants as a 'priority activity' (Sacks et al., 1974:720) which, as we shall see, takes precedence over the rules for turn-taking that motivate fast transitions (Kendrick, 2015:13).

It is important here, however, to distinguish the term 'repair' from what might at first appear to be simply a matter of correcting errors or mistakes. In the first place, it is not the case that all errors in talk are corrected – they may be (and often are) overlooked by recipients who, error apart, grasp the gist of what has been said. Secondly, not all talk subject to repair is a mistake: a passing plane, say, may drown out what's been said and so necessitate its repetition. Schegloff (1997c:507) wryly notes that trouble sources need only be putative, not actual: issuing *Huh?* into the silence while sitting reading might cause others around to search for what it was they were supposed to have said. So repair is 'neither contingent upon error, nor limited to replacement' and 'nothing is, in principle,

---

[1] Repair had been introduced in Sacks et al. as a mechanism 'for dealing with turn-taking errors and violations' (1974:701).

excludable from the class "repairable"' (Schegloff et al., 1977:363). In noting the scope of repair, Schegloff draws an analogy with tailoring:

> a suit that someone tries on may be torn at the underarm; this is a trouble-source and is in need of repair. But it happens as well that there is nothing 'wrong' with the outfit, but the tailor remarks that it would be more flattering to the wearer if the lapel was a tad narrower. If agreed, the undertaking would be termed an 'alteration'; it is not that something was wrong and had to be fixed, but it could be better realized by an 'alteration'.   (2013:46–7)

This kind of adjustment is evident in the following exchange, where Bee and Ava are reminiscing on the phone. Bee asks Ava about someone they once knew:

```
(1)  (From Schegloff, 2013:47; TG, 10)
1         (0.5)
2 Bee:  °(I 'unno )/° (So anyway      ) .nn Hey do you see
3    →v-  (0.3) fat ol' Vivian anymouh?
4 Ava:  No, hardly, en if we do:, y'know, I jus' say hello
5       quick'n,
```

At line 2, Bee is heading towards producing *Hey do you see Vivian anymore* but cuts off just after the first sound of the name, pauses, and then produces 'fat ol" before repeating 'Vivian' in such a way as to frame 'fat ol" as an insertion of additional material. As Schegloff notes of Bee's repair:

> She could well be incorporating the reference form that she and Ava used to refer to Vivian in days gone by, and thereby invoking – and inviting Ava to participate in reviving – the camaraderie of the past. Not then a tear in the underarm, but a narrowing of the lapel; not fixing a trouble, but using the turn to invoke a past intimacy; not a repairing of a trouble-source, but an enhancing with an alteration.   (2013:47)

Nor are such alterations restricted to speakers; recipients may embark upon repairs of their own. In the same phone call, Bee undertakes to repair Ava's characterisation of 'playing around' (l.14) with a substitution of her own, 'fooling around' (l. 16):

```
(2)  (From Schegloff, 2007a:271)
1     Ava:  I'm so:: ti:yid. I j's played ba:ske'ball t'day
2           since the firs' time since I wz a freshm'n in
3           hi:ghsch[ool.]
4     Bee:          [Ba::] sk(h)etb(h)a(h)ll?
5           (h) [(°Whe(h)re.)
6     Ava:      [Yeah fuh like an hour enna ha:[lf.]
7     Bee:                               [.hh] Where
8     Bee:  didju play ba:sk[etbaw.  ]
9     Ava:               [(The) gy]:m.
10    Bee:  In the gy:m? [(hh)
11    Ava:             [Yea:h. Like grou(h)p therapy. Yuh know
12          [half the grou]p thet we had la:s' term wz=
```

```
13   Bee:   [ O h : : : . ] .hh
14   Ava:   =there-<'n we [jus' playing arou:nd.
15   Bee:                [.hh
16   Bee:→Uhfo[oling around.
17   Ava:        [.hhh
18   Ava:   Ehyeah so, some a' the guys who were bedder
19          y'know wen'off by themselves so it wz two girls
20          against this one guy en he's ta:ll.Y'know? [.hh
21   Bee:                                              [Mm hm?
```

What the proposed replacement of 'playing around' with its synonym 'fooling around' is grounded in is ultimately irretrievable;[2] Ava in any case tentatively accepts it with 'Eh-yeah' in line 18. However, what the proposed substitution does show is how recipients, as well as speakers, may repair something not, on the face of it, problematic.

These two instances of repair show a distinction that is highly consequential for the organisation of repair: that between *self-* and *other*-repair. While it may seem obvious that 'self' and 'other' refer to speaker and recipient, these may not be just individuals, but co-incumbents of their particular categories, just as Sacks et al.'s turn-taking model makes reference to 'parties' rather than individual speakers (see the discussion of extracts (34) and (60), Chapter 4). So, for example, Lerner (1993) notes that in the following exchange T and M are addressed by B as a couple (l. 1). T undertakes to respond to the question (l. 2) by referring to 'Hotel Six' (l. 8) – a reference that is repaired by M to 'Motel Six' (l. 11):

```
(3)  (Lerner, 1993:230)
1    B    So what've you guys bin doin?
2    T    Oh not much, we went to Santa Barbara last weekend=
3    J    =you went to what?=
4    T    Santa Barbara last [weekend.
5    J                       [Oh diju? (.) [How was it ( )
6    M                                     [(It was really
7         ni:ce)=
8    T    =It was outta si:ght. We stayed in a Hotel Six,=
9    M    =hhh=
10   J    =Was it warm up the[re?
11   M→                      [Motel Six.=
12   T    =Oh it was beautiful=Motel Six.
```

Lerner observes that 'couple' here is both a relevant and consequential unit of participation for both the topic and the emerging course of action (p. 230; see also Chapter 6, fn. 6) – one that, as we saw in the previous chapter, may itself be grounded in epistemic status. Work by Schegloff (1995b), Egbert (1997) and

---

[2] Sidnell and Barnes (2013:342) speculate that the latter removes possible sexual content from the former, or alternatively that it is a co-telling from knowledge of what the group is like.

Bolden (2013), exploring collectivities and conjoined participation – the latter with respect to epistemic entitlement – similarly support a view of 'self' and 'other' as categories of parties rather than individuals.[3]

As we shall see, within the broad distinction of 'self' and 'other' there is a further distinction to be made in the stages of repair between who *initiates* the repair and who *completes* it. The importance of this latter distinction is, of course, that with the self-initiation of repair, we see evidence in the talk itself of the work being done to construct the turn; as Drew et al. state, 'it is through self-repair that we see speakers orient to what is the appropriate form to do *this* action in *this* sequential place' (2013:93). On the other hand, with other-initiation of repair, we see a potential challenge to the 'world known and held in common': the recipient's apprehension that something has gone awry. It should be evident from these exemplars that self-initiated repair, as in (1), interrupts the progressivity of the turn, whereas other-initiated repair, as in (2), interrupts the progressivity of the sequence (Kitzinger, 2013:231). We saw in Chapter 3 how other-initiated repairs are implicated in expansions of the sequence in various ways. The early observation by Sacks, discussed in Chapter 2, that 'I can't hear you' in a call to a suicide helpline was a possible device for avoiding giving one's name is grounded in the fact that other-initiation of repair is sequence-expanding; line 2 below is an other-iniated repair of line 1, initiating the repair sequence. By the end of line 4, the conversational 'slot' where standardly one gives one's name has been occluded by the disruption to the progressivity of the sequence, such that business can be pursued thereafter without the name being accountably absent:

(4) (Sacks, 1992a:xvi)
```
1  A:   This is Mr. Smith, may I help you.
2  B:   I can't hear you.
3  A:   This is Mr. Smith.
4  B:   Smith.
```

Repair is thus very much an action in its own right, and a vehicle for other actions.

What follows is an overview of the basic operations of repair and how this extraordinary 'self-righting mechanism' (Schegloff et al., 1977:381) for language use is organised. Under the two broad categories of self- and other-repair, we examine first the initiation and then the completion of the repair in turn. In each case we investigate some of the practices by which repair is initiated and the resources used to do so. Moreover, while the two exemplars (1) and (2) above show that it is not always possible to recover the motivations for repair, in many cases we can track the interactional impact of the repair operations; they afford an illuminating glimpse into the construction of both turns and sequences – and, as such, how participants build and secure a world held in common.

---

[3] Bolden shows an example of repair initiation not addressed to the producer of a trouble-source, but to the person who arguably has greater epistemic primacy over that informational territory (2013:8).

1. Self-initiated self-repair (SISR)
  a) SISR in same TCU
  b) SISR in transition space
  c) third position repair
	3. Other-initiated self-repair

2. Self-initiated other-repair 'Word searches' and anticipatory completions	4. Other-initiated other-repair

Figure 7.1 *Forms of repair, with preference ordering*

The distinctions between the stages of repair, and who undertakes them, recognises that both a self-repair and an other-repair may issue from either self- or other-initiation. It turns out that, just as the second pair parts of adjacency pairs are subject to preference organisation, so too are forms of repair; and one – self-initiated self-repair in same turn, before a TRP – is, of all the possible types of repair, overwhelmingly preferred in talk. Furthermore, this observed skewing towards one type and one placement of repair is not happenstance, given that the turn-taking rules oblige a speaker to complete a turn-at-talk, and by the same token interdict the launch of an incoming turn until its possible completion.

Figure 7.1 shows the possibilities, outlined and exemplified, in preference order.

7.1   Self-repair

7.1.1   Self-initiated self-repair in same TCU

The first opportunity for repair is, of course, by the speaker[4] in his or her own turn, before reaching a transition relevance place in any given turn-constructional unit (TCU). This repair opportunity is displayed in (5) and (6) below:

(5) (Schegloff et al., 1977:364)
```
1   Vic    En- it nevuh happen. Now I could of wen' up there
2      →   an' told the parents myself but then the ma- the
3      →   husbin' liable tuh come t'd'doh...
```

(6) (Schegloff, 2013:46; Joyce and Stan, 4)
```
1   Sta    And fer the ha:t, I'm lookin fer somethi:ng uh a
2      →   little different. Na- uh:f: not f:: exactly funky
3          but not (.) a r-regular type'a .hhh >well yihknow I
4          I< have that other hat I wear, yihknow?
5   Joy    Yeah,
```

---

[4] Notwithstanding the earlier observations regarding the possible co-incumbency of the categories 'self' and 'other' by more than one individual, the following exemplars involve individuals occupying these categories.

In (5) Vic, in the middle of what is apparently about to be 'man', initiates repair by means of a glottal cut-off, which is an initial alert of potential problems with progressivity (see Jasperson, 2002, for the phonetic features of cut-offs as repair initiators). The forward progress of the turn is thus disrupted. Vic subsequently repeats the prior word 'the' and produces 'husbin' – a term which is hearably a substitution for 'man' – to complete the repair. The repair operation implemented here – the replacement of one item ('the ma-') for another ('the husbin') is by far the most common.[5] In (6) we see another means by which repair is initiated. In addition to the cut-off on 'Na-' (l. 2), there is subsequently what is commonly known as a 'sound stretch' (Schegloff, 1984b:268) – a prolongation of a sound (marked transcriptionally as colons), here on 'f::', before 'exactly' is produced. That the 'f' is subsequently repeated as the initial sound of 'funky' retrospectively casts 'exactly' as an insertion repair. Unlike a replacement, an insertion retains and builds on the original formulation (Wilkinson and Weatherall, 2011:87) – in this case, to render more specific the descriptor 'funky'.[6] These two exemplars of self-initiated self-repair thus show two common ways in which repair is initiated, and two repair operations – replacement and insertion. It appears to be the case that, in the words of Schegloff, 'there do not seem to be systematic relationships between the types of trouble source and the form taken by the repairs addressed to them' (1987b:216).[7] Other operations so far identified include deleting, searching (Lerner, 2013), parenthesising (Clift, 2001; Mazeland, 2007), aborting, recycling (Schegloff, 1987a), sequence-jumping, reformatting and reordering (see Schegloff, 2013, for an overview and account of each).

An increasing body of research testifies to how the universal principles of self-repair intersect with the prosodic and morphosyntactic resources of particular languages (see, e.g., Hayashi, 1994, 2003 (on Japanese); Fox et al., 1996 (Japanese and English), 2010 (German, Hebrew and English); Fincke, 1999

---

[5] One subtype of this involves extracting an individual from a collectivity, as in the following:

(Lerner and Kitzinger, 2007:541)

```
1    Din:     ... En on the way ho:me we sa:w the:
2             (0.5) most gosh u-awful WRE:ck
3    Bea:     Oh:::.
4             (0.4)
5    Din:     we have e- (.) I've ever seen.
```

It can also aggregate an individual to a collectivity and enumerate the incumbents of a collectivity; see Lerner and Kitzinger (2007).

[6] For a full account of distinctions within the category of insertion repair on a corpus of 500 exemplars, see Wilkinson and Weatherall (2011).

[7] However, there is some evidence to suggest systematicities within types of repair. So, for example, Plug (2015) examines a corpus of Dutch replacement repairs and finds correlations between those that are prosodially marked (produced with prosodic prominence) and those that are not, grounded largely in speakers' appeals to epistemic authority.

(Bikol); Uhmann, 2001 (German); Wouk, 2005 (Indonesian); Huang and Tanangkingsing, 2005 (Cebuano and Tsou); Wu, 2006 (Mandarin); Maheu-Pelletier and Golato, 2008 (French), Laakso and Sorjonen, 2010 (Finnish)). So, for example, repair initiation may be accomplished in English by the cut-off and sound stretch, neither of which are phonemic in English. However, it is reported by Daden and McLaren (1978, cited in Schegloff, 1987b) that in the Guatemalan language Quiche, the cut-off and brief sound stretches, in contrast, are phonemic – and that self-repairs are not, in Quiche, initiated by either. Nevertheless, 'over-long sound stretches' in Quiche are not phonemic, and these are, indeed, used to initiate self-repair (Schegloff, 1987b:213). Moreover, it appears that a range of typological features, such as word order, favoured anaphoric devices, morpho-logical complexity of words, degree of syntactic integration, and presence or absence of articles and adpositions influence self-repair in a variety of ways (Fox et al., 2010). Fox et al. (2009) is a cross-linguistic statistical study of the site of self-repair initiations in seven languages with very diverse morphosyntactic profiles: Bikol (spoken in the Philippines), Sochiapam Chinantec (spoken in Mexico), Finnish, Indonesian, Japanese, Mandarin and English. They propose that there are universal principles shaping the site of repair initiation, with word length and number of syllables a significant factor. So, for example, in recycling and replacement repairs, monosyllabic words tend to be repaired after recog-nisable completion in all the languages investigated; and multisyllabic words tend to be repaired prior to recognisable completion in all but Indonesian (Fox et al., 2009:999–100). Furthermore, a statistical study of repair in English and Japanese suggests that a commonly implemented practice in English – repetition of an entire clause – is extremely rare in Japanese (Hayashi, 1994; Fox et al., 1996). As we saw in Chapter 4, word order in English, in contrast to Japanese, facilitates projectability from the beginning of a TCU; Fox et al. suggest that this is because

> in English, the beginning of the clause is a coherent syntactic and inter-actional object from which a re-projection for the entire clause can be made; whereas in Japanese the beginning of the clause may not be syntactically knit to what follows in the clause, and would not be the site of re-projection. In Japanese, projection may be done much more bit-by-bit than it typically is in English, and the organization of recycling reflects this fact.   (1996:214)

If the means by which self-repair is initiated are language-specific, the uses to which it is put are not. Each same-turn repair operation modifies the emerging turn in the course of its production and so in some way adjusts what is being done, whether it be to replace the incumbent of one category with another ('man' to 'husband', 'playing around' to 'fooling around'), to alter or correct a referent ('Vivian' to 'fat ol' Vivian'; 'Hotel' to 'Motel'), or to subtly modify a description ('not funky' to 'not exactly funky').

However, the actions accomplished by same-turn repairs are diverse and do not necessarily correspond to specific repair operations. So, for example, we recall in Chapter 6 a number of exemplars in which self-repair served as the vehicle for identity-related actions – e.g. 'thuh- uh- officer' (Jefferson, 1974:192). Moreover, in extract (9) of that chapter, recall that Emma's same-turn replacement repair from what was hearably 'having a drink' to 'fixin'em a drink' is consequential as a reformulation of what she is doing, with implications for her availability – and for the sequence in which the repair is embedded. So in that exchange, Emma's description of an activity is reformulated; in the following, a reformatting self-repair results in an assertion being aborted in favour of a question:

```
(7)  (Drew et al., 2013:76)
1   Hal     Oh 'el[lo Lesl[ie?
2   Les            [.hhhh  [I RANG you up- (.) ah: think it wz
3       →   la:s' night. But you were- (.) u-were you ↑ou:t?
4           of: was it the night before per[↓haps.
5   Hal                                     [Uh:m night be↓fore
6           I expect we w'r dancing Tuesdee ni:ght.
```

At line 3, Leslie launches what is a declaratively formed assertion but cuts off to reformat this as an interrogative: 'were you out?', the repair embodying a shift from asserting something in Hal's epistemic domain (Heritage, 2012b) to enquiring as to whether he was out (Drew et al., 2013:76). The repair, then, changes the very action being implemented – a transformation that is evident from the syntactic shift from 'you were' to 'were you'.

Of the myriad actions accomplished by self-repair, there are accounts, among others, of how it reduces the accountability of an interviewer in avoiding excessively coercive forms of questioning (Heritage, 2002b) and mitigates displays of entitlement (Curl and Drew, 2008), and of how recycling secures speakership in overlap (Schegloff, 1987a). In an extended case analysis, Schegloff shows how doing something *as a repair* shows how something that was not previously taken into account is now being taken into account and how by incorporating 'a reference to an otherwise disattended utterance by another participant . . . thereby also potentially incorporates its speaker as a potentially active participant in the conversation' (1987c:111).

It is clear that self-repair can also reshape the trajectory of the emerging sequence. In the following, Charlie phones Ilene to inform her that the lift he had offered her ('th'trip teh Syracuse', l. 6) is now not a possibility, something he leaves her to infer from 'I really don't have a place tuh sta:y' (l. 26), which she then does, at line 29 ('So yih not g'nna go up this weeken'¿'). In this context, the beginning of his account at lines 10–11 is replete with the dysfluency and self-repair – hesitation being one indication that 'a possibly delicate item' (Lerner, 2013:111) is being delivered. Note, then, the self-repair from 'I spoke teh the gi:r-' to 'I spoke tih Karen' in lines 11–12:

```
(8)  (Trip to Syracuse: I)
1    Ile:   Hullo:,
2           (0.3)
3    Cha:   hHello is eh::m:: (0.2) .hh.hh Ilene there?
4    Ile:   Ya::h, this is Ile:[ne,
5    Cha:                      [.hh Oh hi this's Charlie
6           about th'trip teh Syracuse?
7    Ile:   Ye:a:h, Hi (kch)
8    Cha:   Hi howuh you doin.
9    Ile:   Goo::[d,
10   Cha:        [hhhe:h heh .hhhh I wuz uh:m: (.) .hh I wen'
11      →   ah:  (0.3) I spoke teh the gi:r I spoke tih
12          Karen.
13   (Cha): (.hhhh)/(0.4)
14   Cha:   And u:m:: (.) ih wz rea:lly ba:d because she
15          decided of a:ll weekends fuh this one tih go
16          awa:y
17          (0.6)
18   Ile:   Wha:t¿
19          (0.4)
20   Cha:   She decidih tih go away this weekend.
21   Ile:   Yea:h,
22   Cha:   .hhhh=
23   (Ile): =.kh[h
24   Cha:       [So tha:[:t
25   (Ile):            [kkhhh
26   Cha:   Yihknow I really don't have a place tuh sta:y.
27   Ile:   .hh Oh:::::.hh
28          (0.2)
29   Ile:   .hhh So yih not g'nna go up this weeken'¿
30          hhh)/(0.2)
31   Cha:   Nu::h I don't think so.
```

On the face of it, Charlie self-repairs from a non-recognitional form to the preferred recognitional (discussed in Chapter 5); this, it would seem, is evidence for the operation of preference considerations in reference to persons. However, it is also the case that, grammatically speaking, the subject requires a predicate – in other words, that 'the gir-' is shaping up to be the subject, the predicate of which would likely have been something like *I was going to stay with*. Delivered as such, this account would have put the news upfront – the repair to 'Karen' then allows the news to be delivered obliquely, such that Ilene herself is left to articulate its upshot in line 29. As Drew notes of this exchange, Charlie's self-repair makes it possible to design the turn 'so as to position the bad news in a certain way, to defer it in a way that enables him to wrap the bad news into an account that makes it Karen's fault' (2012:67). So it is evident that the formatting of the turn here has wider implications than simply a transformation from one action into another (such as the switch from an assertion to a question as in (7) above). The entire form of what Levinson calls a project ('the distribution of a job over a preparatory and delivery phase' (2013a:120; see also Pomerantz, 2014) is thus shaped by what the self-repair makes possible.

It is clear, too, that, from a methodological perspective, such self-repairs give us an invaluable glimpse of the work that goes into the building of a turn-at-talk. A number of studies (e.g. Curl, 2006 on offers; Drew, 2006 on out-of-hours requests to doctors; Clift, 2007 on reported speech; Curl and Drew, 2008 on requests) have used the evidence that self-repair provides to show how speakers select between alternative versions in the construction of action, rejecting an initial version in favour of a subsequent one. As Drew et al. put it: 'we can discern in self-repair speakers' orientations to how best to construct turns for their sequential environment, to do the interactional work they are designed to perform' (2013:92).

The foregoing exemplars should give some sense of the scope and reach of self-repair – all before a speaker reaches the transition space. Schegloff (1996a:86) notes that just before 'pre-possible completion' of a turn (on which, see section 4.2.2 under 'Next speaker self-selects') is a systematic place for self-repair to be undertaken. In the following instance, the word 'good' is inserted into its TCU just before 'pre-possible completion':

(9) (Schegloff, 1996a:86)

```
Curt   [He- he's about the only regular <he's about the only good regular out
       there'z, Keegan still go out?
```

We can see that if the repair were undertaken any later in the TCU it would be vulnerable to incipient talk by a next speaker.

7.1.2   Self-initiated transition-space repairs

The second opportunity is for self-initiated, self-repair to be undertaken at a TRP – what Schegloff calls a point of 'post-possible completion' (1996a:91):

(10) (From Schegloff et al., 1977:366)

```
1  L    An' 'en but all of the doors 'n things were taped up=
2  →    =I mean y'know they put up y'know that kinda paper
3       'r stuff, the brown paper.
```

(11) (Schegloff et al., 1977:370)

```
1  Bee   Then more people will show up. Cuz they
2  →     won't feel obligated tuh sell. Tuh buy.
```

(12) (Schegloff et al., 1977:376)

```
1  A    That sto:re, has terra cotta floors.
2       (pause)
3  A    Not terra cotta. Terrazzo.
```

On such occasions, of course, an entire TCU has been produced and, until the transition space, not been founding wanting by its producer. However, at that point, repair is initiated in order to clarify (as in (10)) or correct (as in (11) and (12)) something in the just-produced unit. This may be the case even when the just-produced TCU is apparently accepted by its recipient as unproblematic; in the following extract, Bea's receipt of Hannah's turn (with 'Mm hmmm', l. 2) provides for Bea to continue, which she does, briefly, before pulling up with a cut-off and a revision:

(13) (Schegloff et al., 1977:366)
      (Han=Hannah; Bea=Beatrice)
1   Han   And he's going to make his own paintings.
2   Bea   Mm hm,
3   Han→   And- or I mean his own frames
4   Bea   Yeah,

Here, the repair corrects 'paintings' to 'frames'. While there has been an intervening 'Mm hm' by Bea at line 2, as a continuer (as we saw in Chapter 4), this constitutes not a complete turn but what has become known as a 'quasi-turn'. This type of repair is known as third *turn* repair (for more on third turn repair, see Schegloff, 1997b) and, as such, represents a variant of transition-space repair.

As is evident from (11) above, there may be no explicit indication that a repair is underway ('Tuh buy' – the repair solution – is not in any way adumbrated). However, it also may be the case that, as with self-initiated self-repairs generally, there may be repair prefaces (Lerner and Kitzinger, 2010) beyond the alert of a cut-off, sound stretch or delay with *uh(m)*. So, as we saw in (10) and (13) above, 'I mean' can constitute one such preface. In a study of *I mean*-prefaces, Maynard (2013) shows that one such usage is to clarify a speaker's own prior talk as a complaint, as in the following:

(14) (Maynard, 2013:224)
1   E   Bud couldn't e:ven eat his breakfast. He o:rdered he
2   waited forty five minutes'n he'a:dtuh be out there
3   tuh tee off so I gave it t uh: (.) Karen's: little
4   bo:y.
5   (0.7)
6   E→   ((swallow)) I mean that's how bad the service was .hhh
7   (.) It's gone tuh pot.
8   L   °u-Oh*:::° (.) e-[Y_e_:_:_a h .]Ye<]

Emma's multi-unit turn from lines 1–4 here culminates in a report of her own benevolence, and it is in this context that Lottie withholds any response; Emma's 'I mean'-prefaced turn refocuses on the complaint and, with a figurative expression that is commonly a feature of complaints (Holt and Drew, 1988), brings it to completion. This usage of *I mean* as a preface can thus be seen to anticipate trouble with recipiency and in this respect is preemptive, as Maynard says, 'enhancing the prospects for a preferred, aligning response to the complaint'

(2013:233) – as indeed, in the above exemplar, it gets. Common repair prefaces in English include:

> *actually* (Clift, 2001) (extracts (1) and (2), Chapter 1)
> *I mean* (Maynard, 2013) (extract (14), this chapter)
> *or* (Lerner and Kitzinger, 2015) (extract (13), this chapter)
> *well* (Jackson and Jones, 2013; Heritage, 2014) (extract (6), this chapter)

There may also, in the wake of a repair, be some registering that a repair has been done. In extract (15) below, the repair is adumbrated by a sound stretch on the trouble source ('placenta'), there is delay ('uh:m'), a pre-frame ('the') before the repair solution replacement ('cord'). Here, 'sorry' extends the repair segment beyond the production of the repair solution (Kitzinger, 2013:240):

(15) (Kitzinger, 2013:240)
```
1  Ros   you let the placenta:: uh:m the cord
2        sorry (0.2) tch! detach naturally:.=
```


7.1.3   Third position repairs

If some previous self-repairs were in the third *turn* relative to the repairable, trouble-source turn, there is a category of self-repair that is not necessarily in third turn, but in third *position* relative to the trouble source. That is, when a speaker produces a turn (position 1), its recipient shows an understanding of it in responding (position 2). Where third position repairs are undertaken, the position 2 response reveals some kind of misapprehension or misunderstanding of the turn in position 1. It is, then, the speaker who produced the turn at position 1 who undertakes to clarify this misapprehension by repairing in next turn (position 3). This schema is instantiated in the following exchange:

(16) (From Schegloff, 1992b:1303)
(Ann=press officer in Civil Defence Headquarters; Zeb=Chief Engineer)
```
1  Ann    Which one::s are closed, an' which ones are open.
2  Zeb    Most of 'em. This, this, [this, this (pointing)
3  Ann→                            [I 'on't mean on the
4         shelters, I mean on the roads.
5  Zeb    Oh!
6         (8)
7  Zeb    Closed, those're the ones you wanna know about,
8  Ann    Mm[hm
9  Zeb      [Broadway...
```

Here, the speaker repairs in third position (l. 3), addressing a problem with her first position utterance (l. 1) as revealed in the understanding of it conveyed by the recipient's utterance in second position (l. 2). So third position repairs are typically produced by the speaker of the first position utterance. Overwhelmingly, third position repairs, such as the one above, are in the third turn relative to the trouble source,

but they are not invariably so. In the following case, the trouble source in the first turn
(ll. 1–2) gets repair initiated on it in line 6 ('No I mean the uh house number'):

(17)   (From Schegloff, 1992b:1318)
```
1   Dis   Now what was that house number you said=
2         =[you were=                                    [POSITION 1]
3   Cal   =[No phone. No.                                [POSITION 2]
4   Dis   Sir?
5   Cal   No phone at all.
6   Dis→  No I mean the uh house number. [Y-             [POSITION 3]
7   Cal                                  [Thirdy eight
8         oh one?
9   Dis   Thirdy eight oh one.
```

The next-turn initiated repair sequence at lines 4–5 ('Sir?' – 'No phone at all')
displaces the repair from the serially third turn. Schegloff notes that third position
repair is 'the last structurally provided defence of intersubjectivity' (1992b:1325) in
conversation because it is the last systematically provided opportunity to catch
divergent understandings. Moreover, it is because the organisation of repair is so
efficient that there are few sources of trouble to escape beyond the repair space; most
have been detected and repaired by third position.[8] The implications of not being
able to retrieve misunderstandings are, of course, profound. The very maintenance of
intersubjectivity is at stake, and 'in providing for the management of

---

[8] There have only been a few identified instances of fourth position repair, which Schegloff (1992b)
notes should thus be treated with caution. These are a form of other-initiated repair and occur when
the recipient of a first position turn (position 1), responds to it (position 2), and in turn receives
a response (position 3) which reveals that their response in position 2 was a misapprehension of the
first position turn in position 1. The speaker of the position 2 thus undertakes repair in position 4.
The following exchange embodies that schema:

   (From Schegloff, 1992b:1322)
   (Ph=Phil; J=Josh)
```
1    Ph   Hello?
2    J    Phil!                                          [POSITION 1]
3    Ph   Yeh.                                           [POSITION 2]
4    J    Josh Lehroff.
5    Ph   Yeh.
6    J    Ah:: what've you gotten so far. Any requests to
7         dispatch any trucks in any areas,              [POSITION 3]
8    Ph→  Oh you want my daddy.                          [POSITION 4]
9    J    Yeah, Phi[l,
10   Ph            [Well he's outta town at a convention.
```

   The fourth position repair here occurs in what is in fact serially the seventh turn (l. 8): 'Oh you
want my daddy.' The summons, in first position (l. 2), is answered in second position (l. 3) by
'Phil' – the truck driver's son, who understands himself to have been identified. The caller then
self-identifies (l. 4) and this is registered by the answerer (l. 5). The mutual identifications
complete (or so it seems), the caller moves to first topic at lines 6–7, and it is this move, in third
position, that reveals to the answerer that the caller is proceeding on the basis of
a misidentification – something which he makes apparent in line 8, in fourth position.

intersubjectivity in talk, provision is made as well for the management of inter-subjectivity regarding whatever can enter into the talk' (Schegloff, 1992b:1340).

7.1.4   Self-initiated other-repair

While the exemplars we have seen so far have all involved repairs initiated and completed by the same speaker, it is the case that sometimes repair is initiated by a speaker and completed by a recipient:

(18) (From Schegloff et al., 1977:364)
```
1   B→   He had dis uh Mistuh W- whatever k- I can't think of
2        his first name, Watts on, the one thet wrote [
3   A→                                               [Dan
4        Watts.
```

Speaker B here has demonstrable difficulty recovering a name, indicated initially by cut-offs and false starts and then an explicit formulation 'I can't think of his first name'; as he embarks on a description, A ventures to supply it. As we saw in the last chapter, searches may serve as a vehicle for other interactional projects. Lerner (2013), investigating hesitation in delicate formulations, examines a number of cases in which the progressivity of a turn is delayed so as to invite collaboration on a delicate matter. He suggests that the joint authorisation of a delicate item, achieved through these self-initiated other-repairs, reveals that '*the very enactment of deli-cateness is designed for collaboration – that is, for collaborative indiscretion*' (2013:111; italics in original). In the following case, a speaker pulls up short before the completion of a turn, and the recipient supplies the projected but unvoiced item:

(19) (Lerner, 2013:114)
```
1   Cur   Oh nothing she's just a(b)- (0.4)
2   Car→  bitch.
3   Cur   tch! Ye:h, .hhh
```

Moreover, in the following, other-completion is solicited by an explicit appeal in combination with hearable trouble in finding a formulation:

(20) (Lerner, 2013:115)
```
1   Mrk   an' at what point did you find out
2         that ah .hh her ah what shall we call
3         him (0.2) uhm: (.) her [um
4   Bob→                         [(her old) boyfriend?
5   Mrk   her old boyfriend (y)eah that's a good phrase
```

As Lerner puts it:

> the range of progressivity-delaying methods employed for delicate delivery affords a structurally-enabled opportunity for collaborative indiscretion – an interactional fact that puts its stamp on the habitus of social life. One might say that here we see a preference organization operating within a turn at talk.   (2013:112)

Gaze in self-initiated other-repair

In Chapter 4 we saw how Goodwin and Goodwin (1986) have shown how eye gaze may be mobilised to achieve collaborative action. It is evident that self-repair practices – notably hesitation and dysfluency – are used in conjunction with eye gaze by a speaker to secure the eye gaze of a recipient whose gaze is elsewhere. Goodwin (1980) examines restarts and pauses in such attentional repairs. In the following four exchanges, the recipient's gaze direction towards the speaker is marked by a solid line; absence of such a line indicates that the gaze is elsewhere. The point at which the recipient's gaze meets the speaker is marked by an X. In the following two exchanges, the recipients are not gazing at the speaker at the beginning of the speaker's turn; without bringing that turn to completion, the speaker in (21) produces a cut-off and in (22) a sound stretch, in both cases halting the progressivity of the turn. At the point at which the recipients' gaze turns to the speaker, the speaker resumes (in (21), by recycling the turn beginning; in (22) with a restart):

```
(21) (Goodwin, 1980:276)
Tommy     You agree wi [d- You agree wi'cher aunt
Pumpkin                [X_____
Tommy     on anything.
Pumpkin   _____
```

```
(22) (Goodwin, 1980:276)
Barbara   God that's: [:, I don't want that
Gordie                [X_____
Barbara   life.
Gordie    _____
```

Similarly, coming to a halt in the course of a TCU serves to secure the eye gaze of a non-gazing recipient. In the following two exemplars, the movement bringing the gaze to the speaker is marked by a series of dots. During a pause, each tenth of a second in the pause is marked with a dash indicating where in the pause the gaze actually arrives:

```
(23) (Goodwin, 1980:284)
Don     They've changed- (----[-] the China
John                     (. .  [X_____
Don     City.
John    _____
```

```
(24) (Goodwin, 1980:283)
Ann     Wh'n you had that big uhm:,
        (-----------[-] tropical
Jere    . . . . . .  [X_____
```

Goodwin shows that gaze is one means by which recipients indicate that they are attending to talk. For that reason, speakers' restarts and pauses, far from being evidence of defective 'performance' do, in fact, demonstrate speakers' orientations to producing turns-at-talk that are appropriately attended to; as he observes, 'the talk produced within a turn is not merely the result of the actions of the speaker, but rather is the emergent product of a process of interaction between speaker and hearer' (1980:294). Once again, repair, another part of interaction's procedural infrastructure, is here mobilised in the production of collaborative action.[9]

7.2   Other-repair

If the self-repairs we have seen temporarily suspend the onward progression of the turn, the initiation of repair by a recipient – 'other' – temporarily suspends the onward progression of the action being implemented by the sequence in which it is embedded. The other-repair thus constitutes a sequence of its own (e.g. ll. 3–5 in the third position repair exemplar at (16) above) before the main business of the sequence is resumed – constituting, as we saw in Chapter 3, a post-first insert expansion. The instance of other-initiated other-repair in (2) above is, in fact, a rarity; it is overwhelmingly the case that when repair is initiated by 'other', it is in fact completed by 'self', and it is this category of other-repair that is the focus here.

Overwhelmingly, other-repair is initiated in the turn after the trouble source turn, and of those, overwhelmingly completed by the speaker of the trouble-source turn, as in the following, seen earlier in Chapter 3:

```
(25)  (From Schegloff et al., 1977:364)
1   Ken     Is Al here today?
2   Dan     Yeah.
3           (2.0)
4   Rog→    He is? hh eh heh
5   Dan→    Well he was.
```

The other-initiation of repair (henceforth OIR) occurs here after a pause of some two seconds; as Schegloff et al. note, other-initiations are regularly withheld a little past the possible completion of a trouble-source turn, in what they call 'an organized positioning' (1977:374) (see also l. 2, extract (48), Chapter 5, for an instance in Yélî Dnye). Such a withhold of immediate other-initiation extends the transition space, affording the speaker of the trouble source further opportunity to self-initiate. Moreover, such opportunities are indeed taken, as the transition-space repair in (12) shows; such exemplars, as Schegloff et al. propose, should be

---

[9] For a detailed account of how bodily behaviour can be mobilised to repair manual action, see Lerner and Raymond (2007) and Raymond and Lerner (2014).

taken as evidence of the withholding of other-initiation, and thus the preference for self-initiation, even though no other-initiation occurs in them. This 'nearly invariable withhold' of other initiation 'provides clear evidence that self- and other-initiation are related TO EACH OTHER, that the relatedness is ORGANIZED, and that the organization is in REPAIR-SPECIFIC TERMS' (Schegloff et al., 1977:374; capitals in original). Other evidence includes exemplars such as the following, in which the initiator of the repair clearly has the means to provide the repair solution, but nonetheless leaves it to the speaker of the trouble-source turn to do so:

(26) (Schegloff et al., 1977:370)
```
1     A     Hey the first time they stopped me from sellin'
2           cigarettes was this morning.
3           (1.0)
4     B     From selling cigarettes??
5     A     From buying cigarettes.
```

In a study of the timing of OIR, Kendrick suggests that the most frequent cases occur after gaps of ~700 ms, in contrast to 300 ms for responses to polar questions (2015:6)[10] – gaps during which facial gestures, like raising or furrowing one's eyebrows, may be preliminaries to verbal other-initiations (p. 10). Kendrick further shows how these exceptions to the fast transitions motivated by the turn-taking rules suggest that other-initiations of repair supersede the turn-taking system. So in (27) below, the OIR starts up in overlap with the on-going TCU which intervenes between it and the trouble-source TCU. Although the other-initiation is not designed as competitive, here the speaker of the trouble source drops out, ceding the turn to the other who has initiated the repair:

(27) (Kendrick, 2015:14; Benjamin, 2013:188)
      (Hal=Haldeman; Nix=Nixon)
```
1     Hal:  he may be victimized on it
2           (0.6)
3     Hal:  I'm not sure he's ma[king]
4     Nix:                     [you ] mean by his lawyer
5     Nix:  [hhhhhhhhh]
6     Hal:  [yeah or  ] (.) somebody else
```

Such exemplars demonstrate, in Kendrick's words, that 'OIRs supersede not only first-starters in self-selection, but also continuations by current speakers. The window of opportunity for OIR is thus larger than for other next turns, which are subject to constraints on turn allocation and overlap that OIRs appear to outrank' (p. 14).

---

[10] Furthermore, 'OIRs that locate a source of trouble in a prior turn specifically tend to occur after shorter gaps than those that do not, and those that correct errors in a prior turn, while rare, tend to occur without delay' (Kendrick, 2015:1).

There are a range of resources for OIR, from those which show reasonable understanding and requiring only confirmation, as with the understanding checks in line 4 of (26), and line 4 of (27) above and line 3 of (28) below to, at the other end of the spectrum, those that show little grasp of the prior turn, as in line 6 of (29), which consists of the open class repair initiator (Drew, 1997) 'Huh?':

```
(28)  (Schegloff, 2007a:102; TG, 1:16–21)
1   Bee    Why whhat's a mattuh with y-Yih sou [und HA:PPY,] hh
2   Ava                                        [ Nothing  ]
3      →   u- I sound ha:p [py?]
4   Bee                   [Yee] uh.
5          (0.3)
6   Ava    No:,
```

```
(29)  (From Schegloff, 1997c:507)
1   Eddy    Oh I'm sure we c'get on at San Juan Hills.
2           That's a nice course, I only played it once.
3   Guy     Uh huh.
4           (1.0)
5   Guy     It's not too bad,
6   Eddy→   Huh?
7   Guy     'S not too bad,
8   Eddy    Oh.
9           (1.0)
10  Eddy    What time you wanna go.
```

Both 'I sound happy?' in (28) and 'Huh?' in (29) initiate repair on a prior turn, treating it as involving some kind of hearing or understanding problem; in (28) Ava's subsequent disconfirmation at line 6 shows that this kind of repair initiation, a partial repeat, is also, as we saw in Chapter 3, disagreement-implicative.

The functional and sequential properties of these resources are illuminated by a major comparative study across ten languages[11] reported by Dingemanse and Enfield (2015). So while all known languages make use of category-specific interrogatives (Ultan, 1978; Enfield et al., 2013), the forms of these words are of course language-specific. If *who* asks a question about a person in English, the same action is implemented by *phaj3* in Lao and a sign denoting 'who', eyebrows together and a head upward movement in LSA (Dingemanse and Enfield, 2015:104). Sequential properties relate to how the repair initiator ties back to a prior turn (e.g. by using repetition or a question word) and what response it makes relevant. In their comparative study, Dingemanse and Enfield found that these two dimensions – retrospective to prior turn, and prospective, to next – provide a useful distinction in grouping repair initiation formats. The retrospective dimension provides us with a distinction between the 'open' (Drew, 1997) and 'restrictive' class of repair initiator, which targets a specific form of trouble. The prospective dimension gives

---

[11] These were Argentine Sign Language (LSA), Cha'palaa, English, Icelandic, Italian, Lao, Murrinh-Patha, Russian, Siwu and Yélî Dnye.

Table 7.1 *Three basic repair initiation format types (a summary of Dingemanse and Enfield, 2015)*

Type of repair initiator	Example	Target	Makes relevant
Open request	Huh?	Whole of prior turn	Repetition and possible clarification
Restricted request	Who?	Some aspect of prior turn	Repetition, clarification and/or specification of that aspect
Restricted offer	I sound happy?	Some aspect of prior turn with candidate understanding	Confirmation or clarification

rise to three basic types of repair initiation, found across all the languages in the study (see Table 7.1).

Taking into account the sort of trouble targeted also yields an ordering with respect to both the type and the strength of repair intitiation formats. Overwhelmingly, repair in talk is initiated with explicit linguistic resources. However, as we have already noted, one resource for initiating repair is the speaker's use of eye gaze to secure a recipient's attention. Moreover, as we shall see, in a context where there is exclusive reliance on the visual channel – LSA – eye gaze may also be mobilised to initiate repair on another's talk, in an implicit form of repair called the 'freeze-look' (Manrique, 2011; Manrique and Enfield, 2015). These resources for other-initiated repair may be arranged along a spectrum from weaker (where no specific trouble is targeted) to stronger (see Figure 7.2).

We now examine these in turn.

7.2.1   Understanding checks

At the 'stronger' end of the continuum, embodied in the restricted offer-type 'I sound happy?' in (28), the trouble is not one of hearing, as evidenced by Ava's repetition, with rising prosody of the repaired portion of Bee's prior turn – for all that it is in overlap. Moreover, Bee's unelaborated confirmation displays her own understanding that her first turn requires no clarification. Clearly, then, repetitions are targeting something other than hearing. Recall extract (1), lines 5–8 in Chapter 3: 'Wuddiyuh –DOin' – 'What'm I doin¿'. Here, Emma's repair 'Cleani:ng?' displays her analysis of Nancy's 'What'm I doin¿' to be pursuing specification of the *class* of activity to be formulated (one possible response, of course, being 'talking to you'). In the following, Stan undertakes a check on a referent, 'Bullocks' (l. 2) in lines 4–6:

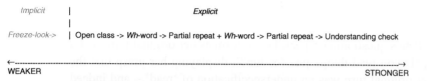

Figure 7.2 *Spectrum of other-repair initiation types (Sidnell, 2010; Manrique and Enfield, 2015)*

Note: wh-word is used here as the generic term for a question word, irrespective of language.

(30) (Kitzinger, 2013:233–4)
      (Joy=Joyce; Stn=Stan)
```
1    Joy:    Why don'tchoo: go into Westwood,
2            (0.4) and go to Bullocks.
3            (1.2)
4    Stn:→   Bullocks? ya mean that one right
5            u:m (1.1) tch! (.) right by thee:
6            u:m (.) whazit the Plaza? theatre::=
7    Joy:    Uh huh.
8            (0.4)
9    Stn:    °(memf::)°
10   Joy:    °Yeah,
```

Here Stan claims to have heard and have a grasp of the referent, subject to checking it out ('ya mean that one', l. 4) by means of a candidate understanding with the speaker of the trouble-source turn.

One particular form of understanding check is a repetition of the trouble-source turn. In a study of repeats as repair initiators on prior questions, Robinson and Kevoe-Feldman show that such full repeats on rising intonation also show understanding that a question was asked – but the repetitions suggest that the action of questioning is somehow problematic (2010:235). In the following, there has been a lapse in the conversation, whereupon Deb reinitiates talk with a question at line 1 which, after a pause (which, as we have seen, commonly adumbrates such forms of repair) has repair initiated upon it by Pete:

(31) (Robinson and Kevoe-Feldman, 2010:240)
      (Lapse in conversation)
```
1    Deb     Do you re::ad?
2            (0.4)
3    Pet→    Do I re:ad?
4            (1.4)
5    Deb     D'you read things just for fun?
6            (0.2)
7    Pet     Y:e:ah.
8            (0.5)
9    Pet     Right now I'm reading No:rma Jean thuh Termite
```

```
10          Q(h)uee(hh)n
11   Deb    £↑What's tha:t.↓£
```

In the wake of Pete's questioning repeat, Deb reformats her original turn to add a complement, 'D'you read things just for fun?', displaying her grasp that the trouble with her original turn was an underspecification of 'read' – and indeed Pete goes on to answer the reformatted question, and indeed to elaborate on it (ll. 9–10). In (32) below, from a phone call, we similarly see a questioning repeat (and similarly, a prefacing pause). The question at line 14 comes after a canonical call opening (Schegloff, 1986) and initiates the first topic:

```
(32)   (Robinson and Kevoe-Feldman, 2010:250; MTRAC:90:2:23)
14   Joe    What's been happening lately.
15          (2.1)
16   Mom→   What's been happening lately?
17   Joe    Yea:h.°
18          (1.4)
19   Mom    Li:ke- like what.
20          (0.2)
21   Joe    Like >(with your)< school (or anything).
22          (0.2)
23   Joe    (W'[=has]   an  ]ything exciting been going on?
24   Mom       [(Weh-/wha-)]
25   Mom    Y:ea:h >very< exciting. I:'m taking a le:ave.
```

The trouble-source turn at line 14 here is, like 'Do you read?' in the prior exemplar, topic-initiating; Robinson and Kevoe-Feldman note that the vast majority of their cases are in such sequential positions and as such are sequentially and/or topically incoherent with prior talk (2010:235). Both Schegloff (1979) on self-repair and Drew (1997) on OIR have shown how topic initiation is vulnerable to repair in this manner; here, once again, deriving from a combination of sequential position and composition. However, in the case above, unlike the prior exemplar, the speaker of the trouble source does not undertake to clarify further; he simply confirms what he originally said. Mom, after a pause, then reinitiates repair, but with another form – in fact, two different forms. The first, 'Li:ke-' is one of a range of grammatical resources (such as *and, because* and *which*) described by Lerner (2004) to prompt a just-prior speaker to elaborate on a turn that they have just brought to completion – thus implying that the turn is somehow insufficiently complete.[12] However, Mom cuts off and abandons this, recycling 'like' to formulate another attempt at repair initiation, 'like what'. As Robinson and Kevoe-Feldman remark, this repair initiator 'is

---

[12] The following (Lerner, 2004:162) is striking for its conciseness:

```
Jack      I just returned
Kathy     From
Jack      Finland
```

evidence that she heard and understood the words and syntactic structure of Joe's trouble-source TCU, and understood it as a possible request for information' (2010:251). Joe's first attempt at clarifying (l. 21) getting no immediate uptake, he reformats his trouble-source question at line 23, which then gets an answer at line 25.

These two instances are indicative of Robinson and Kevoe-Feldman's general finding that full repeats[13] signal the problematic nature of the questioning action – either 'the thrust of the question-as-a-whole, or what it is getting at, or what is meant by its asking' (p. 235). In a minority of cases, the repeats were shown to accept the questioning action and yet characterise it as being ridiculous (p. 235).[14]

7.2.2 Partial repeats

Such full repeats, then, are at the 'stronger' end of the other-initiated repair spectrum. Rather less strong than the repetition of the full turn is the restricted-offer-type partial repeat. So, for example, in the excerpt from extract (2), reproduced below, we see a partial repeat at line 4: 'Ba::sk(h) etb(h)a(h)ll?':

```
(33)  (Schegloff, 2007a:271)
1  Ava:     I'm so:: ti:yid. I j's played ba:ske'ball t'day
2           since the firs' time since I wz a freshm'n in
3           hi:ghsch[ool.]
4  Bee:→            [Ba::]sk(h)etb(h)a(h)ll?
5           (h)[(°Whe(h)re.)
6  Ava:        [Yeah fuh like an hour enna ha:[lf.]
```

And the following shows an exemplar from Cha'palaa, whereby A, who is washing her clothes on the shore, requests a plastic tub from B. However, before complying, B initiates repair on A's first turn in order to confirm the target object

---

[13] Benjamin and Walker examine a particular prosodic contour – the high rise-fall – on a corpus of repetitions, showing how 'matters of truth, appropriateness, and acceptability' (2013:107) are managed through such a resource. This prosodic contour sounds similar to the Italian 'hanging repeat' (Rossi, 2015b). However, the two have very different interactional import. While the English high rise-fall combines with partial repetition to prompt correction of the repeated material, this contour in Italian contrasts with two other contours, and combined with a partial repetition of material from the trouble-source turn, it prompts the co-participant to complete the turn. As Dingemanse and Enfield thus point out, the '(U)se of high-rise intonation' per se does not shed light on the cross-linguistic formats for other-initiation of repair (2015:104).

[14] The veteran British celebrity interviewer Michael Parkinson called an interview with Meg Ryan his 'most difficult TV moment' ('You Don't Have to Like Someone to Interview Them', Holly Williams, *The Independent*, 6 November 2010). The interview became notorious for Ryan's resistance to Parkinson's questions, with Ryan at one point suggesting 'Why not wrap it up?' The first indication that the interview is not destined to be a success comes with Ryan's response to the first question. Parkinson, referring to his previous fashion expert guests, asks if she finds fashion 'empowering'. Ryan, leaning forward, responds: 'Do I find it empowering?' – a repeat that foreshadows the trouble up ahead.

(note the forthrightness, in line 1 of the request, characteristic, as mentioned in Chapter 3, for Cha'palaa):

(34) (Floyd, 2015:3)
```
1     A    Daira ñaa inu tina ka' eede
           Daira ñu-ya  i-nu  tina ka-tu ere-de
           Daira 2SG-FOC 1SG-ACC tub grab-SR pass-IMP
           Daira you pass me the tub
2     B→   enstaa?      ((pointing at tub))
           ensta-a
           this-Q
           this one?
3     A    jee tsadekee
           jee tsa-de-ke-e
           yes SEM-PL-do-IMP
           yeah do that
4     B    ((throws tub to A))
```

Bolden (2009) investigates partial repeats in Russian; in the following, Tanya (Tan) asks Natasha (Nat) what she is doing the next day, the question formulating the assumption that plans have been made:

(35) (Bolden, 2009:131)
```
1   Tan:   Okej,/A::m (0.2) .hh a:: ladna chevo zavtra  delaete?/
           Okay                    okay what   tomorrow do
           Okay                    Okay what are you doing tomorrow?
2   Nat:→  Shto za, vt'a/<eta-da etava >my esch-my<eschë da sevodnja
           what tomorrow that to that    we yet we  yet   to today
           Tomorrow,/ For that- We haven't even figured
3          ne d(h)abr(h)alis' [sh(h)to m(h)y d(h)elaem/.hA zavtra
           not got            what     we   do          PRT tomorrow
           out what  what we are doing today/Tomorrow
4   Tan:                      [Nu okej/
                               PRT okay
5   Nat:   =skarej vsevo:: v: Geti   v kakojta mamet/ili pa krajnej
           most    likely  to Getty at some   point  or at least
           most       likely    we'll go  to the Getty at some point/or at
           least
6          mere [chast' nas paedet  tuda/
           least part us    will-go there
           some of us will go there
```

Natasha's partial repeat here locates the trouble source in the prior turn ('Shto za, vt'a', 'Tomorrow', the comma marking continuing intonation). She then asserts, with laughter-infiltrated talk (l. 3), that she hasn't even made plans for that day – thus explicating her problem in complying with the first pair part (Bolden, 2009:131).

7.2.3   Partial repeat + *wh*-word

A weaker format than the partial repeat is the partial repeat framed by a *wh*-question:

```
(36)  (Benjamin, 2013:122)
1     A      and she stole five hundred from Jodie
2            .hhhhhhh[hhh
3     B→            [from who?
4     A      Jodie
5            (0.3)
6     B      She did
```

```
(37)  (Benjamin, 2013:121)
1     A      ...I would definitely recommend not you know working
2            in Gunma
3            (1.0)
4     B→     Not working where?
5            (0.2)
6     A      in Gunma Prefecture [where I      ]
7     B                          [where you're] working
8     A      where I work
```

Those initiating repair in each case claim a grasp of the trouble-source turn as referring to a person (36) and a place (37), the category-specific interrogatives in each case ('who?' and 'where?') being framed by a partial repeat of the trouble-source turn. In the following German exemplar, the other-initiation in line 5 targets an adjective in the trouble-source turn:

```
(38)  (Egbert, 1997:621–2)
1     M      der mann war allerdings auch tscheche °glaub ich.°
             but the husband was     also Czech   °I believe°
2            (0.2)
3     H      oh gott [wat n düennehne (dialect)
             oh god  [what a mess
                     [
4     A               [(       )
5     I→     was war der?
             what was he?
6            (.)
7     H      tscheche
             Czech
8     M      gebürtiger tscheche
             a born Czech
```

Note that in this exemplar, the repair solution is initially provided by a speaker other than that of the trouble-source. By insisting on doing the response to the repair initiation herself, in line 8 (building on and specifying – 'a born Czech' – the first repair solution in l. 7), the speaker indicates that, having produced the trouble-source, she is the proper provider of the repair solution (Egbert, 1997:622).

As a next-turn repair initiator, this form of partial repeat may still be disagreement-implicative, as we saw in Chapter 3. The former US Secretary of State, Henry Kissinger, walked out of a radio interview with the British journalist Jeremy Paxman, soon after the exchange in (39).[15]

(39)   (*Start the Week*, BBC Radio 4, 28 June 1999)
       (I=Interviewer, Jeremy Paxman; K=Interviewee, Henry Kissinger)

```
1    P     ↑Can we turn to Indo-China for which you received the Nobel
2          Peace Prize in nineteen-seventy three. .h That deal did not
3          bring peace to Indo-China. .hh Was there any part of you felt a
4          fraud in accepting it¿
5          (0.2)
6    K→    Felt a what?
7    P     A fraud in accepting the Nobel Peace Prize.
8          (0.5)
9    K     .h I wonder what you do when you do a- a- a hostile interview=
10   P     =Heh heh. I was merely trying to explore-
11   K     Em yeah
```

The interviewer's strong assessment ('a fraud') in line 4 is the target of the interviewee's repair initiation, the framed repeat 'Felt a what?' This form of repair initiation is a form of 'ritualized disbelief' (Heritage, 1984a:339) (other tokens include 'really?' 'did you?' and the more hearably sceptical 'you're joking', which are sometimes produced as a preface to a display of surprise (Wilkinson and Kitzinger, 2006)). In response to this repair initiation, and in holding firm, the interviewer does a so-called 'Sacks substitution' (Schegloff, 1989:146–7) whereby a pro-form ('it', l. 4) is, upon the re-doing of an utterance, replaced by the full form to which it refers ('the Nobel Peace Prize', l. 7), even when that pro-form, as appears here, is plainly not the source of the trouble.[16]

---

[15] Kissinger's departure was reported in the following way: 'After two questions from his fellow guests, Dr Kissinger left the studio muttering as Mr Paxman interrupted himself to bid him a hasty "thank you and goodbye"' (Janine Gibson, 'Kissinger Walks Out of Paxman Programme', *The Guardian*, 29 June 1999).

[16] So, for instance:

```
1    Vic     My pail's there.
2    James   Hoh?
3    Vic     My pail is in yuh hallway.
```

and

```
1    Jones   What do they want with us?
2    Smith   Hm?
3    Jones   What do they want with you and me?
```

(Cited in Schegloff, 1989:147). See also extract (48).

7.2.4   *Wh*-word

A weaker version of such partial-repeat-framed category-specific interrogatives is the standalone interrogative, such as in the following, in which other-initiations target in (40) an indexical person reference ('he'), and in (41) a place reference:

(40) (Benjamin, 2013:100)
```
1   A    so i- is he poor
2        (0.4)
3   B→   who.=
4   A    =Shawn
```

(41) (Benjamin, 2013:106; transcription as in original)
```
1    A    what about h .hhhh well- (.) uh- (0.3) you know that Matt
2         Munro: is working at Sonnenshein and Nath
3         (1.1)
4    A    have [you
5    B→        [where?
6         (.)
7    A    s:- a(t) Sonnenshein and Nath?
8         (0.4)
9    B    h s@ay it again
10        (0.3)
11   B    a s[innen- sh]ein?
12   A       [um        ]
13        (.)
14   A    Sonnenshein S O N N E N .hhhhh S C H I- E I N?
15        (.)
16   B    Never heard of it where is it
```

And in the following, in which the speakers are discussing characters in a film, the genitive form 'whose' in the OIR grammatically selects the referent indicated by 'his' as trouble source, rather than the referent's 'wife':

(42) (Benjamin, 2013:105)
```
1   A   I think his old wife was way better
2       (0.4)
3   B   Whose.
4       (1.2)
5   A   the guy's old wife
```

Note that in (41) the repair initiator is on rising intonation ('where?'), whereas in (40) and (42) they are on falling intonation ('who'/'Whose') respectively. In an investigation of the prosodic patterns of these other-initiations, Benjamin (2013) establishes that these are distinct practices; that rising intonation (*who? where?*, etc.) can signal both hearing *and* recognition troubles – as indeed is evidenced in (41) above. Here, the trouble-source speaker responds to the repair initiation with a try-marked (Sacks and Schegloff, 1979) intoned repetition of the targeted referent: 'at Sonnenshein and Nath?' (l. 7), displaying a diagnosis of hearing trouble but indexing uncertainty. After the trouble-source speaker requests a repetition, and then offers a candidate hearing, and the repair-initiating speaker produces a second repetition and a spelling out of the name, B explicitly claims unfamiliarity with the place/company (Benjamin, 2013:106–7). In contrast, falling prosody (*who./whose.*) initiates repair on an indexical form or implicit reference: in (40) 'he' in 'is he poor', and in (42) 'his' in 'his old wife'. Such formats thus initiate what Benjamin calls 'specification repairs' (p. 105) in response to these underspecified forms in trouble-source turns. Prosody thus delimits both the source and the nature of the trouble (p. 229).

7.2.5   Open class repair initiator

All of the foregoing exemplars of other-initiated repair claim some grasp of the trouble-source turn in the format of their turns. The weakest format, claiming no grasp beyond the fact that something was produced in the prior talk, is the request-type format known as the open class repair initiator (Drew, 1997). These may take the form of lexical items or phrases, e.g. *Sorry?*, *Pardon?* (see Chapter 1, extract 12), *What?* (Chapter 1, extract 13) or phrases such as *Excuse me?* or (in British English) *Say again?* So, for example:

```
(43)  (Enfield et al., 2013:349)
1  Les    m-[Jem's
2  Mum      [Are the family o:ff?
3         (0.5)
4  Les→  SORRY?
5  Mum→  'Av your family gone o:ff?
6         (.)
7  Les    Ye:s,
8  Mum    Oh ↓goo:d.
```

Yoon (2010:2789) notes how the forms *e*, *um* and *ung* and their polite forms *yey* and *ney* in Korean have a basic meaning of 'yes' or the equivalent of the English affirmative answer; however, on rising intonation, they roughly correspond to *Huh?*, *pardon* or *excuse me?* (Kim, 1999a,b:145):

```
(44)  (Yoon, 2010:2789)
1  Jin:    ai    sok   kepwukha      -ntey.
           EXC stomach uncomfortable-CIRCUM
           Ah I  feel uncomfortable in my stomach.
2  Hyun:→  u:m?
           Hu:h?
3          (1)
4  Jin:    s:hh sok      kepwukha      -ntey(h).
                stomach   uncomfortable-CIRCUM
           s:hh I feel uncomfortable in my stomach.
```

In Tzeltal there is a generic other-repair initiation form, *jai*:

(45) (Brown, 2010:2630)

```
1  P    pero a'-k'inal=e tey    to   nix  ay-O
        but  2E-land=CLI there still PT EXIST-3A
        But do you still have your land there?
2  A→   jai?
        What (did you say)?
3  P    tey     to  nix ay-O  [tz'i'-k'inal.
        there still PT EXIST-3A PT 2E-land
        You still have your land there.
4                           [tey pero (.) ya j-chon-O.
                            there but     1E-sell-3A
                            (It's) there but I'm selling it.
```

The following is an instance from Danish:

(46) (Heinemann, 2010:2711)

```
1  Ester   Det ka' da ikk' gå det var så'n hver gang,
           It wouldn't be good if it was like this every time,
2          (0.5)
3  Kirst→  HVA'R,
           WHAT,
4  Ester   Nej det ku' aldrig gå det var så'n hver gang,
           No it wouldn't be good if it like this every time,
```

For German, Selting (1996) similarly shows how prosody can mark an important distinction within a category of other-initiated repair, differentiating types of trouble. She shows an action distinction between two prosodic realisations of the German open class repair initiator *Was?*:

(47) (Selting, 1996:241–2)

(Transcription as in original. Global pitch higher than in surrounding units is denoted by H(\ \ ) with H=high, F=falling, R=rising. Unaccented local pitch movements: \=falling, /= rising. Prosodic parameters: <all>=allegro, fast; <f>=forte, loud)

```
1  SOC   dann müssn se inne SEnnestadt gehn (.)
                          (\              )
         then you must go to Sennestadt
2        äh dort zum dort wo sie sich auch ANgemeldet habm
                                       (\              )
         eh there to there to where you also registered
3  KLI   ja die KINdergeld s geKOMM
               F(\              \ )
         yes the child allowance has arrived
4  SOC→  was
         (/)
         what
5  KLI   ds KINdergeld is geKOMM
```

```
          F(\                    \ )
            <all>
          the child allowance has arrived
6         (.)
7   SOC   jaa
          \
          yes
```

In (47) above, the question 'was' at line 4 initiates repair on the prior turn, realised here with what Selting terms 'a rather non-salient rising pitch' (1996:242). This repair initiation is taken to be in the service of a hearing problem, and the recipient duly repeats the problem turn. In the extract below, the same repair initiator has a very different prosodic realisation:

```
(48)  (Selting, 1996:242)
6    SOC    das KOStet allerDINGS
            it costs something though
7    SOC    sag ich Ihn ma gleich vorher
            <all                    all>
            I'll tell you beforehand
8    SOC    PRO seite drei MARK
            F(\              \ )
            per page three marks
9    KLI1→  WAS
            H(/ )
            <f >
            what
10   SOC    ich MUSS also jetz
                  (\
            I have to know
11   SOC    JEde beglaubichte SEIte nehm ich ihn drei MARK
            F(\              \                   \ )
            For every notarized page I take three marks
12          (.)
13   KLI2   WieSO kostet das den GE:LD:
             R(\                \   )
            but why does it cost money
14   KLI2   der BRAUCHT das doch für ne (.) beWERbung
               R(\                       \   )
            He needs it for an application
15          (1.5)
16   SOC    spielt KEIne ROLle
            doesn't matter
17          (.)
18   LI2    [also in GÜtersloh kostets überHAUPT nichts
            [       H(/                 \        )
            [but in Gütersloh it doesn't cost anything
19   SOC    [das EINzige was
```

```
                 [the only thing which
20   SOC     das EINziger was KOStenlos is sind ä:hm:
                 the only thing which is free is  ehm
21   SOC     äh beGLAUbigungn für RENtn (.) SACHn (.)
                 eh notarizations for old age pensions
```

In this case, 'Was?' (l. 9) has high pitch and increased loudness. Subsequent turns display no evidence that KL1 has not heard the utterance in line 8, and indeed SOC's repair does not consist of a repetition, suggesting that she does not take 'Was?' here to be a hearing problem. She launches her repair (l. 10) by referring to the regulations she must follow, but then abandons this and reformulates, in more expansive terms, the rules. However, the question from KL2 (KL1's partner) makes it clear that the issue was not one of understanding but rather a matter of expectation. Selting examines a number of these prosodically marked realisations and suggests that recipients orient to them as indicating 'astonishment' due to an expectation problem, and, like Benjamin on English, shows prosody differentiating types of problem handling within repair sequences. Dingemanse and Enfield's ten-language study (2015) similarly shows marked prosody used to signal surprise or disbelief in languages as varied as Russian, Icelandic (Gisladottir, 2015) and Siwu (Dingemanse, 2015).

There is a substantial cross-linguistic literature on other-initiated repair practices, for example, Kim (1993, 2001) on Korean; Wu (2006, 2009) on Mandarin; Svennevig (2008) on Norwegian; Sidnell (2008) on two Caribbean English Creole-speaking communities; Egbert et al. (2009) on German; Bolden (2011) and Bolden et al. (2012) on Russian; and Hayashi and Kim (2013) on Japanese and Korean. These reveal the language-specific implementations of the universal structure and organisation of repair.

The most general format for OIR, however, shows striking commonalities across languages. It is usually transcribed in English as the interjection *Huh?* but can also take the form *Hm?*[17] These offer the trouble-source speaker few resources for establishing what the trouble might be. In such cases, trouble-source speakers, lacking such resources, commonly undertake to repeat the entirety, or virtually the entirety,[18] of the trouble-source turn, as shown in (49) below, excerpted from (29) above, and (50):

(49)   (From Schegloff, 1997c:507)
```
5   Guy     It's not too bad,
6   Eddy→   Huh?
7   Guy     'S not too bad,
```

---

[17] Enfield et al. (2013:379, fn. 5) report Robinson's view that *Huh* may be more often dealing with hearing and understanding problems, whereas *What* may be more likely to extend to dealing with issues of alignment/agreement/affiliation.

[18] There are, however, contexts in which they do not: for an investigation into what gets omitted in such contexts, see Schegloff (2004a).

```
(50)  (Schegloff, 1997c:507)
1   Mom    [No, I didn' jog th[is mornin' 'cause I didn' have
2          ta:hme.
3          (1.9)
4   Wes    Wel[l uh
5   Mom         [eh-huh! _hh [I  h a d d a | s a l e t h a t  |=
6   Wes                      [I thought you|wuh getting' ready|=
7   Mom    =[startid tida-]
8   Wes    =[fuh next week.]
9          (.)
10  Mom→   Huh?
11  Wes→   I thought you were gettin' ready fuh next week.
12         (1.1)
```

Early cross-linguistic work suggested that *Huh?*, or some variant of it, was also used in other languages. So Moerman's (1977, 1988) work on Thai – the first wide-scale conversation-analytic study on a language other than English – reveals the following as one format for other-initiated repair:

```
(51)  (Moerman, 1977:878)
1   TM    pen pen xá.j   kâ.t   â
          PRN PRN   sell  market Qprt
          Do  they sell it   in  town?
2         (2.3)
3   W→    Hy.
          Huh?
4   TM    já.:      pen xá.j kâ.t ka.
          Medicine PRN sell market Qprt
          The medicine, do they sell it in town?
5   W     e.:.
          Yeah.
```

An initial survey of twenty-one languages by Enfield et al. (2013) provides further evidence of some remarkable commonalities across this format type. Where English has *Huh?* as a primary interjection strategy (Bloomfield, 1933:176), the languages surveyed[19] show a strikingly similar phonetic form: a monosyllable featuring an open non-back vowel [a,æ,ɔ,ʌ], often nasalised, sometimes with an [h] onset, and usually with rising intonation (Enfield et al., 2013:343). This has led Dingemanse et al. (2013) to propose, on a subset of ten languages, that *Huh?* is, in fact, a universal word. Examination of the OIRs *in situ* reveals much the same sequential patterning as the English exemplars, with the

---

[19] The languages surveyed (with their locations in square brackets and interjection forms in round brackets) are: ǂAkhoe Hailom [Namibia] (hɛ), Cha'palaa [Ecuador] (aː), Chintang [Nepal] (hã), Duna [Papua New Guinea] (ɛ̃ː/hm), Dutch [Netherlands] (hɜ), English [UK] (hã:/hm), French [France] (ɛ̃), Hungarian [Hungary] (hm(ha)), Icelandic [Iceland] (haː), Italian [Italy] (ɛː), Kri [Laos] (ha :), Lao [Laos] (hãː), Mandarin Chinese [Taiwan] (hãː), Murrinh-Patha [Australia] (aː), Russian [Russia] (haː), Siwu [Ghana] (hã), Spanish [Spain] (e), Tzeltal [Mexico] (hai), Yélî-Dnye [Papua New Guinea] (ɛ̃), Yurakaré [Bolivia] (æ/a) and LSA (Argentine Sign Language).

other-initiations prompting exact or near-exact repeats, in (45) above in Tzeltal, and in (52) in Yurakaré, a language of Bolivia, and in (53) in Siwu (a Kwa language of Ghana):

(52) (Enfield et al., 2013:355) Yurakaré

```
1  M    tishi   nij   da   lacha?
        tishilë nij   da   lacha
        now     NEG give.SP too
        It doesn't have enough energy now either?
2       (.)
3  A→   ë?=æ
        INTJ
        Huh?
4  M    =nij da layj tishilë
        nij  da lacha tishilë
        NEG give.SP too now
        It doesn't have enough energy right now either?
```

(53) (Enfield et al., 2013:353–4) Siwu

```
1  C    ìɖe   kàku    kere    tà-màbara   kpòkpòpò-ò?
        S.1-be funeral just PROG-3PL-do IDPH.pounding-Q
        isn't it for a funeral that the kpòkpòpò (pounding)
        is being done?
2  D    Ilè     isɛ-ɛ?
        place  S.1-sit-Q
        where is it?
3       (1.3)
4  C→   hã? [hãː]
        repair
        huh?
5       (0.3)
6  D    Ilè  isɛ-ɛ?
        place S.1-sit-Q
        where is it?
7       (3.0)
8  C    i Mempeasem ngbe!
        loc PSN    here
        in Mempeasem here!
```

In all of the cases above, the other-initiations are on rising prosody; indeed, in all but three documented cases[20] the *Huh?* word is on rising pitch. Speculating on the remarkable phonetic and prosodic similarities across unrelated languages,

---

[20] These are Icelandic, Cha'palaa and Lahu (Matisoff, 1994). In the case of Icelandic, Enfield et al. note that this is consistent with the internal organisation of pitch in questioning in Icelandic (2013:362); such exceptions illustrate how 'conventionalization and interaction with other subsystems – such as question prosody – can attenuate the forces of iconic-indexical motivation in a linguistic system' (p. 362).

Type	Example (OIR in bold)	Extract number
Understanding check	A: Why don't you. . .go to Bullocks	34
	B: Bullocks? ya mean that one. . . .	
Understanding check	A: Yih sound happy	
(full repeat)	**B: I sound happy?**	32
Partial repeat	A: I j's played basketball t'day	
	B: Basketball?	37
Partial repeat +	A: She stole five hundred from Jodie	
Wh-word	**B: From who?**	40
Wh-word	A: so i- is he poor	
	B: who.	44
Open class	A: It's not too bad,	
repair initiator	**B: Huh?**	33

Figure 7.3 *Explicit other-repair initiation types: a summary*

Enfield et al. assert that 'we can only presume that there is some kind of indexical-iconic motivation that makes the sound [ha + rising pitch] appropriate for this function' (p. 358). Furthermore, Dingemanse et al. (2013) propose that the striking similarities may be down to a mechanism of convergent cultural evolution, whereby a common conversational environment across languages pulls this specialised interjection into the same region of the possibility space in language after language.

There is, however, also a certain degree of diversity; while all but two of the languages surveyed (Tzeltal and Yélî Dnye) also have a question word used in the OIR (usually the equivalent of English *what*), these, in contrast, display wide variations in phonetic form. So ǂĀkhoe Haiǁom has *mati*, Yurakaré has *tæpʃæ*, Hungarian has *mi*; these, however, are used less frequently than the interjection (see Enfield et al., 2013, for discussion).

A summary table of explicit other-repair initiation types as discussed is given in Figure 7.3 with one exemplar for each type, from stronger to weaker.

7.3 Implicit forms of repair initiation: embodiment and gaze

In Enfield et al.'s survey of other-initiated repair across twenty-one languages, common visible behaviours associated with OIR are (1) eyebrow movements (raising and/or bringing together), (2) gaze toward the speaker of the troublesource and (3) head or body movement towards the speaker of the troublesource (2013:371).

The last of these is exemplified in a movement described by Seo and Koshik as a 'head poke' and upper body movement forward toward the recipient

(2010:2222). In the following, taken from an American family dinner conversation in the 1970s, the mother ('Mom') of fourteen-year-old Virginia invokes age in challenging the suitability of Virginia's attendance at parties with people her sister Beth's age. Virginia, in rebuttal, complains that people her age are 'gwaffs'. Mum initiates repair on the term, both verbally 'They're what?'(l. 10), and an accompanying head poke gesture (ll. 11–12). Single-headed arrows here indicate the onset of the gesture, and double-headed arrows indicate the release of the gesture (p. 2222):

```
(54)   (Seo and Koshik, 2010:2223)
1      Mom       .hhh ^Well that's something else.
2                (0.3) ^I don't think that
3                you should be going to the parties that
4                Beth goe:s to. She is eighteen years
5                old. =An' you are fou:rtee:n, da[rlin'.
6      Vir                                       [I KNOW::,
7                BUT A:LL THE REST OF MY: PEOPLE MY AGE
8                ARE GWAFFS.=I promise.=they are
9                si:[ck.
10     Mom->        [They're what?
11        ->        [((head poke and upper body movement forward))
12                (.)
13     Vir       GWAF[FS.
14        ->>          [((Mom begins to release gesture))
15     ???       (   )
16     Pru?      What's a gwaff.
17                (3.1)
18     Vir       Gwaff is jus' someb'dy who's really
19                (1.1) I just- ehh! .hh s- immature.
20                >You don't wanna
21                hang around peope like tha:t.<
22                (1.9)
```

Mum's verbal repair initiation ('They're what?'), targeting the epithet Virginia uses to describe people her age, is accompanied by a gesture, a head poke and upper body movement forward towards Virginia (see Figure 7.4).

In response to this repair initiation, Virginia simply repeats the trouble-term 'gwaffs' and Mom starts to release the gesture in the middle of the production of the word (Seo and Koshik, 2010:2223). Seo and Koshik also identify, in a specific pedagogical environment, a particular head-turn gesture that can be used without verbal accompaniment to initiate repair on its own.

With respect to gaze behaviour, work by Egbert (1996), on German, establishes that the repair initiator *bitte?* indexes the fact that 'no mutual gaze is established during the delivery of the trouble-source turn' (p. 608). The production of *bitte?* thus works to establish mutual gaze, with either the producer of the trouble-source or its recipient showing an orientation to securing

Lines 8-9   →   Lines 10-12   →   Lines 16-17

Figure 7.4 *Mum's verbal repair initiation (from Seo and Koshik, 2010:2222)*

gaze.[21] The participants in the extract below are in two different rooms, with the doors open. Timo produces a request at line 2, which is the trouble-source. At line 4, repair is initiated on this turn, and as Timo launches the repair (l. 5), he turns his head towards Rita in the other room.

```
(55)  (Egbert, 1996:606)
1              (2.0)
2     Timo     und die klammer an den blaun korb hängn bitte.
               and hang the peg on the blue hamper please.
3              (0.4)
4     Rita→    bitte?
               pardon?
5     Timo     die klammer an den wa- blaun korb da.
               and the peg on the whi- blue hamper there.
```

Shortly after the turn at line 5, Rita comes into the same room as Timo and mutual gaze is established.

Nowhere is there a more striking example of how local resources are calibrated to generic organisations than a context where interaction is exclusively in the visual channel. Work by Manrique (2011) and Manrique and Enfield (2015a,b) on LSA has identified a particular local practice in the other-initiation of repair: a particular holding configuration which they term a 'freeze-look'. Here the party initiating repair holds their bodily configuration and facial expression still in a 'frozen' posture at the completion of the trouble-source turn until the speaker of the trouble source undertakes self-repair. Clearly this resource for repair is located in the assumption of progressivity and the recipient of a trouble-source turn is, as Manrique and Enfield state, 'responding by pointedly *not* responding' (2015a:1) and clearly not engaged in other activity which might account for the delay in responding. They describe the characteristics of the 'freeze-look' (by B) as follows:

---

[21] Unlike the case of *bitte?*, there was no observable correlation between eye-gaze behaviour and *was?* or *hm?* (Egbert, 1996:606).

Sequence			Turn type	Extract (56)	
A	Question?		Trouble-source (FPP)	*Do you know SN?*	T–1
B→		Freeze-look response	Implicit repair initiation	*Freeze-look*	T–0
A		Repetition Q?	Solution	*SN?*	T+1
B		Answer	(OIR sequence closure)/ resume sequence from T1	*No, no*	T+2

Figure 7.5 *The 'freeze-look': a schema (adapted from Manrique and Enfield, 2015a:12, and Floyd et al., 2015:5)*

a. At this moment, the addressee of a question (Signer B) is normatively required to produce a relevant response (an answer to a question, or something related).
b. The addressee looks directly at the Signer of the question (Signer A).
c. The addressee temporarily holds their entire body posture in a still or 'frozen' position.
d. It is clear that the addressee has seen that they were just addressed by A; and they are not otherwise signaling any difficulty in responding.
e. Signer A then redoes the question (e.g., by repeating or rephrasing).

(Manrique and Enfield, 2015a:11)

A schematic representation of the implementation of the 'freeze-look' is in Figure 7.5, with extract (56) below mapped onto the schema. The repair initiator turn is here called 'T0', being produced in response to the trouble-source turn, T-1, and before the repair solution, T+1, usually consisting of a reformulation or clarification of the trouble source in T-1. In many sequences there is also a turn after T+1, in which the sequence is closed, either through information uptake or by continuing the sequence suspended at T-1; this turn is called T+2. In extract (56) the sequence is resumed at T+2 with B producing the answer to the question in T-1.

So in the exchange below, we see a question by A at line 4 'Do you know (sign-name)', which receives a freeze-look from B at line 5, whereupon A repeats the name (see Figure 7.6):

(56) (Manrique and Enfield, 2015a:16)

```
1   A    [HEY
         [Hey ((trying to get B's attention))
2   B    [((Stops signing movement, holding the last previous sign))
         [              Q-ET
3   A    [KNOW SN-H (1.1)                    (FIGURE 7.6.a)
4   B→   [Freeze-look response (1.1)
         [   Q-ET
5   A    [SN---H                             (FIGURE 7.6.b)
         (Sign name?)
6   B    ((Continues in freeze-look position))
7   B    NO NO
         No, no ((Drops freeze position to 'no' signing position))
```

Figure 7.6 *Extract (56) (Manrique and Enfield, 2015:15)*
    a. *Do you know SN?*, Signer A, right, asks a question to Signer B, left. Signer B suspends his signing position in a freeze-look response.
    b. *Sign-name?*, Signer A, right, end of the repetition of the question to Signer B, who answers after the end of the repeat.

The implicit form of repair initiation described by Manrique and Enfield is one instance of a general practice investigated by Floyd et al. (2015) across three structurally very different languages and termed 'holds'. These are when relatively dynamic movements are temporarily and meaningfully held static by the initiator of a repair, and only disengaged when the problem is resolved and the sequence closed. The duration of holds is timed according to the duration of sequences (Floyd et al., 2015:2). These movements may involve the head, face, eyes, hands or torso or any combination of these. Alongside the 'freeze-look' in LSA, Floyd et al. examine Northern Italian and Cha'palaa. The basic structure of these holds is captured schematically in Figure 7.5, for the 'freeze-look'. The repair sequences analysed by Floyd et al. for the most part feature some form of closure at or after T+1. This means that each sequence features a successful repair solution by A and in many cases also a sequence-closing turn by B that ratifies the solution or resumes the halted sequence. However, in some cases the trouble is not resolved at the first T+1 turn, and the sequence includes further T0 turns, thus leading to an expanded sequential structure. Since visual bodily holds orient to the continued conditional relevance of the sequence, the longer the sequence remains unresolved the longer until the hold is disengaged. For example, in extract (57), line 4 below, from the Italian data, Eva initiates repair once with the 'open class' initiator '*che*' (what?), but when the repair solution introduces a new problem of pronoun ambiguity, she pursues an additional response, this time with a more specific 'restricted class' format, *chi* (who?) (l. 9); see Figure 7.7.

(57) (Floyd et al., 2015:20–1)

```
1    Ada   ma lo sai   che il Michele si  legge  i notturni  di Chopin Eva
            but 3s.A know-2S that the NAME  3S.D read-3S the nocturnes of Chopin NAME
            do you know that Michele reads Chopin's nocturnes Eva?
```

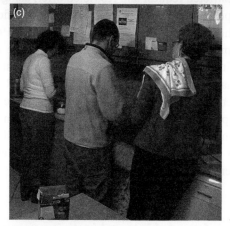

Figure 7.7 *Extract (57) (Floyd et al., 2015:21)*
    a. 'what', extract (57), l. 4
    b. 'who?', extract (57), l. 9
    c. 'no way!', extract (57), l. 11

2	Remo	*ho visto*
		have-1S see-PSTP
		I saw that
3		(0.5)
4	Eva→	*che:* ((turns to Ada))
		wha:t?
5		(0.7)
6	Ada	*si legge dei notturni di Chopin*
		3S.D read-3S some nocturnes of Chopin
		he reads Chopin nocturnes
7		(0.5)
8	Ada	*pia pian[ino con la] destra e la sinistra=*
		slowly slowly-DIM with the right and the left
		little by little with the right and the left hand

```
9   Eva→            [  chi  ] ((keeps looking at Ada))
                    who?
10  Ada    =il Michele
            the NAME
            Michele
11  Eva    ma dai ((looks away from Ada and down on the worktop))]
            but BCL
            no way!
```

This work is thus extraordinary for how it reveals the generic, universal procedural infrastructure of interaction at work through the mobilisation of available bodily resources.

Across a richly diverse range of languages, we have seen data to suggest that the operation of other-initiated repair is strikingly similar, from the three basic format types – open request, restricted request and restricted offer, using similar linguistic resources – to the preference for selecting the most specific repair initiator possible, endorsing the proposal made by Schegloff et al. (1977) for English, and one which 'minimizes the cost for addressee, and for the dyad as social unit' (Dingemanse and Enfield, 2015:110). With respect to linguistic form, there is evidence to suggest that one interjection mobilised in the OIR may be a possible universal: a conventionalised lexical item. The robust sequential patterning of other-initiated repair across languages suggests that it lends itself to strikingly similar interactional possibilities: marked prosody signalling surprise, for example, or the fact that OIR, in whichever language, is standardly taken to adumbrate disagreement.

7.4   Conclusion: the defence of intersubjectivity

In the early days of conversation analysis, Harvey Sacks entertained the possibility that 'I can't hear you' might be a methodical device. It is therefore in some sense fitting to end our examination of interaction's infrastructure with a consideration of repair, as it returns us to the origins of the enterprise, its motivations and its method. An investigation of repair puts us right in the midst of just what some linguistic approaches might have us discard: the apparently 'inherently disorderly and unresearchable mess' which is the consequence of the real-time production and understanding of utterances. However, by interrogating data across a range of languages, we have been able to identify areas of both local diversity and commonality that illuminate the interactional implementation of linguistic structures. Sacks's insistence that we could assume 'order at all points' is here underwritten. Repair, alongside turn-taking and sequence organisation, 'furnishes participants with resources for organizing social life *at the point of its production*' (Hayashi et al., 2013:2), as the means by which they maintain and defend intersubjectivity. Moreover, like those other orders of organisation, there is growing evidence to suggest that the various means, both linguistic and extralinguistic, by which participants defend shared understandings, is generic to social life. As Schegloff says, 'If the organization of talk in interaction supplies the basic infrastructure through which the institutions and social organization of quotidian life are implemented, it had better be pretty reliable, and have ways of getting righted if beset by trouble' (2006:77).

8   Conclusion: discovering order

We began this book with an assertion: that *action* and *sequence* are the two inextricable things at the core of conversation-analytic inquiry. This is because actions delivered through sequences are at the core of human social life.

We have seen that even an action as apparently straightforward as referring, done en passant in one language, may become the business of the talk itself in another, accomplished jointly over a sequence of turns. Moreover, as should now be plain, in doing something such as referring, a speaker may invoke resources that from a purely informational perspective either are wholly redundant (such as the use of subject pronouns in pro-drop languages), or appear to be synonymous ('James' and 'he'). However, clearly, selection among alternatives is a principled one, done by reference to action and sequences of action. The linguistic – and other – formats of their actions, whether they be requesting, offering, complaining, resisting and so forth, are by their nature recipient-designed and so revealing of identities and relationships between co-present participants. As we have seen, these are consituted both by the underlying pragmatics of attributed status and by the momentary assumptions of particular interactional stances in the service of social action.

Linguistic typology has long been regarded as a grammatical endeavour. However, in recognising human cognition and human language as inherently situated and indexical, subject to the unremitting constraints of spatiotemporality, CA shows how it is intricated into actions alongside other resources such as non-linguistic vocalisations, gaze and embodiments. Embodied action, both ontogenetically and phylogenetically, precedes linguistic action; and, as we have seen, in co-present interaction, it may also precede – and at times supersede – turns-at-talk. Turn-taking shows how the local resources of particular languages are calibrated to a general system. With its origins in non-verbal conduct, turn-taking is thus ultimately the fountainhead of linguistic typology. As Floyd et al. observe:

> Grammatical systems show diversity but the underlying basic interactive practices show much less variance cross-linguistically (Levinson, 2000; Enfield & Levinson, 2006; Stivers et al., 2009; Enfield et al., 2013). The reasons for this are complex and difficult to pinpoint, but we find that the best account concerns similar material, temporal and social conditions in the face-to-face speech situation. As a basic prerequisite for interaction, speakers must be able to perceive each other's turns before reacting to them, and this generates some basic constraints of temporality and bodily orientation that apply cross-linguistically. Because of their connection to the attentional dynamics of interacting in physical bodies, elements like gaze and posture are provided with natural meaning that can additionally function as semiotic displays of engagement.   (2015:25)

A focus on language to the exclusion of other semiotic resources, and the narrowing, within that, to the sentence and the utterance, methodologically only leaves us to investigate grammar – elements of composition – for anything from possible structural universals to allophones. By bringing a consideration of sequential position to the analytic table, CA has been able to identify how such elements of composition intersect with sequential position in the accomplishment of actions. Examining how participants mobilise linguistic resources from particular sequential positions has made it possible to propose a general account of indirect utterances grounded not in 'top-down' assumptions about language use but anchored in the orientations of participants themselves. While logic, maxims of conversation or concepts of face may be usefully invoked as baseline heuristics or general orientations, as resources for analysing the observable conduct of participants to interaction, they lack the empirical 'bite' that both position and composition jointly provide.

Key to the findings here is a methodological perspective that regards context as not external to the talk, but generated by it: the context is in the sequence. Like the act of referring, an offer in Arabic or a question in ǂĀkhoe Haiǀǀom displays how, in Evans's words, 'cultural preoccupations find their way into linguistic structures' (2003:14). Examining these structures without reference to the contexts that shape them risks removing just that which might illuminate them. The recognisability of actions, in their moments of linguistic stability, derives from the sequence, which makes coherence and collaborative action possible. So not-quite-a request can receive not-quite-a declination, and yet still we can recognise that something determinate has been done. As Schegloff observes, naturally occurring materials

> appear to introduce elements of contingency, of variability, of idiosyncrasy, which are often taken to undermine the attainability of ideals of clarity, comparability, descriptive rigor, disciplined inquiry, etc. Meeting such goals is taken to require experimental control, or at least investigators' shaping of the materials to the needs of inquiry – standardization (of stimuli, conditions, topics, etc.), conceptually imposed measurement instruments, etc. But in the name of science the underlying natural phenomena may be being lost, for what is being excised or suppressed in order to achieve control may lie at the very heart of the phenomena we are trying to understand. One is reminded of Garfinkel's (1967:22) ironic comment about the complaint that, were it not for the walls, we could better see what is holding the roof up.[1]   (1996b:468)

---

[1] There is a resonance here beyond language and interaction. In a discussion about genetic modification, Druker makes the following observation:

> although the bioengineering venture is based on the premise that a discrete sequence of DNA has but one meaning – and that the meaning is conserved when the sequence is randomly transplanted within the DNA of another species – in reality, the meaning can be radically revised through such an operation. That sequence may have had *multiple* meanings within its native context, and those meanings can be skewed within a foreign context because they to a large extent depend on how the information inside the sequence interacts with information arrayed outside its confines. Moreover, the

It is, then, in examining the contingency, the variability and the idiosyncrasy that has made it possible to discover order: the order that Goffman insisted was an autonomous domain of organisation. This domain is the procedural infrastructure of interaction, part of a more general language-independent human 'interaction engine' (Levinson, 2006).[2] Musing on the centrality of collaborative action to interaction, Levinson throws a gestalt switch on many assumptions regarding language evolution in proposing that

> 'Language didn't make interactional intelligence possible, it is interactional intelligence that made language possible as a means of communication' (Levinson 1995:232). So language is the explicandum, not the explicans – humans didn't evolve language, then get involved in a special kind of social life, it was just the reverse.   (2006:43)

It is only by investigating language *in* social life that an insight such as this – embedded in principled, empirical accounts of language use – is possible. A world of discovery awaits.

> inserted sequence can disrupt information networks *within* the target organism and jumble the meanings of several of its native DNA sequences as well.   (2015:346)

I thank Graeme Willis for bringing this passage to my attention.

[2] As Levinson suggests:

> Evolution is bricolage (to use Lévi-Strauss's term), seizing what is at hand in the organism's phenotype to construct an often ramshackle but adaptive system. So an 'interaction engine' could be constructed of scraps of motivational tendencies, temporal sensitivities (reaction contingencies), semi-cooperative instincts, ancient ethological facial displays, the capacity to analyze other's actions through mental simulation, and so forth. The model is a Jean Tinguely kinetic sculpture built of bric-a-brac, not a Fodorean mental module, let alone a Chomskyan point mutation.   (2006:44)

References

Abu Abah, F. 2015. Offers in Saudi Arabic. *Essex Graduate Student Papers in Language and Linguistics*. University of Essex.

Aitkenhead, D. 2007. Why We Need to Set Our Kids Free. *The Guardian*, 3 November.

Albert, S. 2015. CHAT-CA-Lite. Downloaded on 7 August 2015 from https://github.com/saulalbert/CABNC/wiki/CHAT-CA-lite.

Antaki, C. 2012. What Actions Mean, To Whom, and When. *Discourse Studies* 14 (4):493–8.

Antaki, C. and Craven, A. 2012. Telling People What to Do (and Sometimes, Why): Contingency, Entitlement and Explanation in Staff Requests to Adults with Intellectual Impairments. *Journal of Pragmatics* 44:876–89.

Antaki, C. and Wilkinson, R. 2013. Conversation Analysis and the Study of Atypical Populations. In J. Sidnell and T. Stivers (eds.), *The Handbook of Conversation Analysis*. Chichester: Wiley-Blackwell, pp. 533–50.

Antaki, C., Condor, S. and Levine, M. 1996. Social Identities in Talk: Speakers' Own Orientations. *British Journal of Social Psychology* 35 (4):473–92.

Antaki, C., Billig, M. G., Edwards, D. and Potter, J. A. 2003. Discourse Analysis Means Doing Analysis: A Critique of Six Analytic Shortcomings. *Discourse Analysis Online*, 1.

Asdjodi, M. 2001. A Comparison Between Ta'arof in Persian and Limao in Chinese. *International Journal of the Sociology of Language* 148 (1):71–92.

Atkinson, J. M. 1984. *Our Master's Voices: The Language and Body Language of Politics*. London: Methuen.

2009. Cameron's Conference Speech High Spot: Standing Ovation for 'Surfing Applause'. Downloaded on 31 May 2015 from http://maxatkinson.blogspot.co.uk/2009/10/camerons-conference-speech-high-spot.html.

Atkinson, J. M. and Drew, P. 1979. *Order in Court: The Organization of Verbal Interaction in Judicial Settings*. London: Macmillan.

Atkinson, J. M. and Heritage, J. 1984. Preference organization. In J. M. Atkinson and J. Heritage (eds.), *Structures of Social Action: Studies in Conversation Analysis*. Cambridge University Press, pp. 53–6.

Auer, P. 1984. Referential Problems in Conversation. *Journal of Pragmatics* 8 (5–6):627–48.

Auer, P., Couper-Kuhlen, E. and Müller, F. 1999. *Language in Time: The Rhythm and Tempo of Spoken Interaction*. Oxford University Press.

Austin, J. L. 1962. *How to Do Things with Words*. Oxford: Clarendon Press.

Bar-Hillel, Y. 1954. Indexical Expressions. *Mind* 63:359–79. (Reprinted in Bar-Hillel 1970:69–89.)

1970. *Aspects of Language: Essays and Lectures on Philosophy of Language, Linguistic Philosophy and Methodology of Linguistics*. Amsterdam: North-Holland.

Barnard, J. 2002. I Loved Her Because She Wanted to Climb the Highest Peak. That's Who She Was. *The Guardian*, 28 August.

Barnes, J. 1984. Evidentials in the Tuyuca verb. *International Journal of American Linguistics* 50:255–71.

Barth-Weingarten, D., Reber, E. and Selting, M. (eds.) 2010. *Prosody in Interaction*. Amsterdam: John Benjamins.

Bauman, R. and Sherzer, J. (eds.) 1974. *Explorations in the Ethnography of Speaking*. Cambridge University Press.

Beach, W. 1993. Transitional Regularities for Casual 'Okay' Usages. *Journal of Pragmatics* 19 (4):325–52.

Bellos, D. 2011. *Is That a Fish in Your Ear?: Translation and the Meaning of Everything*. London: Penguin.

Benjamin, T. 2013. Signaling Trouble: On the Linguistic Design of Other-initiation of Repair in English Conversation. PhD thesis, University of Gronigen.

Benjamin, T. and Walker, T. 2013. Managing Problems of Acceptability with High Rise Fall Repetitions. *Discourse Processes* 50 (1412):107–38.

Bloomfield, L. 1933. *Language*. New York: Holt.

Blythe, J. 2013. Preference Organization Driving Structuration: Evidence from Australian Aboriginal Interaction for Pragmatically Motivated Grammaticalization. *Language* 89 (4):883–919.

Bögels, S. and Torreira, F. 2015. Listeners Use Intonational Phrase Boundaries to Project Turn Ends in Spoken Interaction. *Journal of Phonetics* 52:46–57.

Bolden, G. B. 2008. Reopening Russian Conversations: The Discourse Particle *to* and the Negotiation of Interpersonal Accountability in Closings. *Human Communication Research* 34 (1):99–136.

2009. Beyond Answering: Repeat-Prefaced Responses in Conversation. *Communication Monographs* 76 (2):121–43.

2011. On the Organization of Repair in Multiperson Conversation: The Case of 'Other'-Selection in Other-Initiated Repair Sequences. *Research on Language and Social Interaction* 44 (3):237–62.

2013. Unpacking 'Self': Repair and Epistemics in Conversation. *Social Psychology Quarterly* 76 (4):314–42.

Bolden, G. B., Mandelbaum, J. and Wilkinson, S. 2012. Pursuing a Response by Repairing an Indexical Reference. *Research on Language and Social Interaction* 45 (2):137–55.

Bolinger, D. 1957. *Interrogative Structures of American English: The Direct Question*. Tuscaloosa: University of Alabama Press.

Borsley, R. and Ingham, R. 2002. Grow Your Own Linguistics?: On Some Applied Linguists' Views of the Subject. *Lingua* 112:1–6.

Britain, D. 1992. Linguistic Change in Intonation: The Use of High Rising Terminals in New Zealand English. *Language Variation and Change* 4 (1):77–104.

Brown, G. and Yule, G. 1983. *Discourse Analysis*. Cambridge University Press.

Brown, P. 2007. Principles of Person Reference in Tzeltal Conversation. In N. Enfield and T. Stivers (eds.), *Person Reference in Interaction: Linguistic, Cultural, and Social Perspectives*. Cambridge University Press, pp. 172–202.

2010. Questions and Their Responses in Tzeltal. *Journal of Pragmatics* 42 (10):2627–48.

Brown, P. and Levinson, S. C. 1978. Universals in Language Usage: Politeness Phenomena. In E. N. Goody (ed.), *Questions and Politeness: Strategies in Social Interaction*. Cambridge University Press, pp. 56–311.

1987. *Politeness: Some Universals in Language Usage*. Cambridge University Press.

2005. Comparative Response Systems. Paper given at the American Anthropological Association meeting, Washington, DC.

Brown, R. and Gilman, A. 1960. The Pronouns of Power and Solidarity. In T. A. Sebeok (ed.), *Style in Language*. Cambridge, MA: MIT Press, pp. 253–76.

Brown, P., LeGuen, O. and Sicoli, M. 2010. Cross-Speaker Repetition in Tzeltal, Yucatec, and Zapotec Conversation. Paper given at the International Conference on Conversation Analysis 10, Mannheim, Germany.

Butler, C. and Wilkinson, R. 2013. Mobilizing Recipiency: Child Participation and 'Rights to Speak' in Multi-Party Family Interaction. *Journal of Pragmatics* 50:37–51.

Bybee, J. 2001. *Phonology and Language Use*. Cambridge University Press.

2006. From Usage to Grammar: The Mind's Response to Repetition. *Language* 82 (4):711–33.

2010. *Language, Usage and Cognition*. Cambridge University Press.

2015. *Language Change*. Cambridge University Press.

Chafe, W. (ed.) 1980. *The Pear Stories: Cognitive, Cultural, and Linguistic Aspects of Narrative Production*. Norwood, NJ: Ablex.

Ching, M. K. L. 1982. The Question Intonation in Assertions. *American Speech* 57 (2):95–107.

Chomsky, N. 1957. *Syntactic Structures*. The Hague: Mouton.

1965. *Aspects of the Theory of Syntax*. Cambridge, MA: MIT Press.

Chomsky, N. and Miller, G. A. 1963. Introduction to the Formal Analysis of Natural Languages. In R. D. Luce, R. R. Bush and E. Galanter (eds.), *Handbook of Mathematical Psychology*, Vol. II. New York: Wiley, pp. 269–321.

Clark, H. H. 1996. *Using Language*. Cambridge University Press.

Clayman, S. E. 1993. Booing: The Anatomy of a Disaffiliative Response. *American Sociological Review* 58 (1):110–30.

2010. Address Terms in the Service of Other Actions: The Case of News Interview Talk. *Discourse and Communication* 42 (2):161–83.

2012. Address Terms in the Organization of Turns at Talk: The Case of Pivotal Turn Extensions. *Journal of Pragmatics* 44:1853–67.

2013. Agency in Response: The Role of Prefatory Address Terms. *Journal of Pragmatics* 57:290–302.

Clayman, S. E. and Heritage, J. 2015. Benefactors and Beneficiaries: Benefactive Status and Stance in the Management of Offers and Requests. In P. Drew and E. Couper-Kuhlen (eds.), *Requesting in Social Interaction*. Amsterdam: John Benjamins, pp. 55–86.

Clift, R. 2001. Meaning in Interaction: The Case of *Actually*. *Language* 77 (2):245–91.

2005. Discovering Order. *Lingua* 115:1641–65.

2006. Indexing Stance: Reported Speech as an Interactional Evidential. *Journal of Sociolinguistics* 10 (5):569–95.

2012a. Identifying Action: Laughter in Non-humorous Reported Speech. *Journal of Pragmatics* 44:1303–12.

2012b. Who Knew?: A View from Linguistics. *Research on Language and Social Interaction* 45 (1):69–75.

2014. Visible Deflation: Embodiment and Emotion in Interaction. *Research on Language and Social Interaction.* 47 (4):380–403.

Clift, R. and Helani, F. 2010. Inshallah: Religious Invocations in Arabic Topic Transition. *Language in Society,* 39 (3):357–82.

Clift, R., Drew, P. and Local, J. 2013. 'Why That, Now?': Position and Composition in Interaction (Or, Don't Forget the Position in Composition). In R. Kempson, C. Howes and M. Orwin (eds.), *Language, Music and Interaction.* College Publications, pp. 211–32.

Costermans, J. and Fayol, M. (eds.) 1997. *Processing Interclausal Relationships: Studies in the Production and Comprehension of Text.* Mahwah, NJ: Lawrence Erlbaum.

Couper-Kuhlen, E. 1992. Contextualising Discourse: The Prosody of Interactive Repair. In P. Auer and A. Di Luzio (eds.), *The Contextualization of Language.* Amsterdam: John Benjamins, pp. 337–64.

2001. Interactional Prosody: High Onsets in Reason-for-the-Call Turns. *Language in Society* 30 (1):29–53.

2009. A Sequential Approach to Affect: The Case of 'Disappointment'. In M. Haakana, M. Laakso and J. Lindström (eds.), *Talk in Interaction: Comparative Dimentions.* Helsinki: SKS Finnish Literature Society, pp. 94–123.

2012. Some Truths and Untruths about Prosody in English Question and Answer Sequences. In J. P. de Ruiter (ed.), *Questions: Formal, Functional and Interactional Perspectives.* Cambridge University Press, pp. 123–45.

2014. What Does Grammar Tell Us About Action? *Pragmatics* 24 (3):623–47.

Couper-Kuhlen, E. and Ford, C. E. (eds.) 2004. *Sound Patterns in Interaction.* Amsterdam: John Benjamins.

Couper-Kuhlen, E. and Ono, T. 2007. Turn-Continuation in Cross-Linguistic Perspective. *Pragmatics* 17 (4):505–646.

Couper-Kuhlen, E. and Selting, M. (eds.) 1996. *Prosody in Conversation: Interactional Studies.* Cambridge University Press.

2001. Introducing Interactional Linguistics. In M. Selting and E. Couper-Kuhlen (eds.), *Studies in Interactional Linguistics.* Amsterdam: John Benjamins, pp. 1–22.

Coussé, E. and Mengden, F. von. (eds.) 2014. *Usage-Based Approaches to Language Change.* Amsterdam: John Benjamins.

Craven, A. and Potter, J. 2010. Directives: Entitlement and Contingency in Action. *Discourse Studies* 12 (4):419–42.

Croft, W. 2000. *Explaining Language Change: An Evolutionary Approach.* London: Longman.

Cuff, E. C. and Payne, G. C. (eds.) 1979. *Perspectives in Sociology.* London: Allen and Unwin.

Curl, T. S. 2006. Offers of Assistance: Constraints on Syntactic Design. *Journal of Pragmatics* 38 (8):1257–80.

Curl, T. S. and Drew, P. 2008. Contingency and Action: A Comparison of Two Forms of Requesting. *Research on Language and Social Interaction* 41 (2):129–53.

Curl, T. S., Local, J. and Walker, G. 2006. Repetition and the Prosody-Pragmatics Interface. *Journal of Pragmatics* 38:1721–51.

Daden, I. and McLaren, M. 1978. Same Turn Repair in Quiche (Maya) Conversation: An Initial Report. Unpublished paper, University of California, Los Angeles.

Davidson, J. 1984. Subsequent Versions of Invitations, Offers, Requests and Proposals Dealing with Potential or Actual Rejection. In J. M. Atkinson and J. Heritage (eds.),

Structures of Social Action: Studies in Conversation Analysis. Cambridge University Press, pp. 102–28.

Davies, N. 2014. *Hack Attack: How the Truth Caught Up with Rupert Murdoch*. London: Chatto and Windus.

Dediu, D. and Levinson, S. C. 2013. On the Antiquity of Language: The Reinterpretation of Neandertal Linguistic Capacities and Its Consequences. *Frontiers in Psychology* 4:397.

De Ruiter, J. P., Mitterer, H. and Enfield, N. J. 2006. Projecting the End of a Speaker's Turn: A Cognitive Cornerstone of Conversation. *Language* 82 (3):515–35.

Dingemanse, M. 2015. Other-Initiated Repair in Siwu. *Open Linguistics* 1 (1):232–55.

Dingemanse, M. and Enfield, N. J. 2015. Other-Initiated Repair Across Languages: Towards a Typology of Conversational Structures. *Open Linguistics* 1:96–118.

Dingemanse, M., Torreira, F. and Enfield, N. J. 2013. Is "Huh?" a Universal Word? Conversational Infrastructure and the Convergent Evolution of Linguistic Items. *PLoS ONE* 8 (11):e78273.

Dixon, R. M. W. 1980. *The Languages of Australia*. Cambridge University Press.

Doris, J. M. 2015. *Talking to Our Selves: Reflection, Ignorance, and Agency*. Oxford University Press.

Drew, P. 1984. Speakers' Reportings in Invitation Sequences. In J. M. Atkinson and J. Heritage (eds.), *Structures of Social Action: Studies in Conversation Analysis*. Cambridge University Press, pp. 129–51.

1990. Conversation Analysis: Who Needs It? *Text* 10 (1–2):27–36.

1997. 'Open' Class repair Initiators in Response to Sequential Sources of Troubles in Conversation. *Journal of Pragmatics* 28:69–101.

2006. Misalignments in 'After-Hours' Calls to a British GP's Practice: A Study in Telephone Medicine. In J. Heritage and D. W. Maynard (eds.), *Communication in Medical Care: Interactions Between Primary Care Physicians and Patients*. Cambridge University Press, pp. 416–44.

2009. Quit Talking While I'm Interrupting: A Comparison Between Positions of Overlap Onset in Conversation. In M. Haakana, M. Laakso and J. Lindström (eds.), *Talk in Interaction: Comparative Dimensions*. Helsinki: Finnish Literature Society, pp. 70–93.

2012. What Drives Sequences? *Research on Language and Social Interaction* 45 (1):61–8.

Drew, P. and Heritage, J. (eds.) 1992. *Talk at Work: Talk in Institutional Settings*. Cambridge University Press.

(eds.) 2006. *Conversation Analysis*. London: Sage.

(eds.) 2013. *Contemporary Studies in Conversation Analysis*. London: Sage.

Drew, P. and Holt, E. 1998. Figures of Speech: Idiomatic Expressions and the Management of Topic Transition in Conversation. *Language in Society* 27:495–522.

Drew, P. and Walker, T. 2009. Going Too Far: Complaining, Escalating and Disaffiliation. *Journal of Pragmatics* 41 (12):2400–14.

Drew, P., Walker, T. and Ogden, R. 2013. Self-Repair and Action Construction. In M. Hayashi, G. Raymond and J. Sidnell (eds.), *Conversational Repair and Human Understanding*. Cambridge University Press, pp. 71–94.

Druker, S. M. 2015. *Altered Genes, Twisted Truth*. Salt Lake City: Clear River Press.

Dryer, M. S. 2008. Polar Questions. In M. Haspelmath, M. S. Dryer, D. Gil and B. Comrie (eds.), *The World Atlas of Language Structures Online*. Leipzig: Max Planck Institute for Evolutionary Anthropology. (Available online at http://wals.info/chapter/116, Accessed on 2015-05-18.)

Du Bois, J. W. 1980. Beyond Definiteness: The Trace of Identity in Discourse. In W. L. Chafe (ed.), *The Pear Stories: Cognitive, Cultural, and Linguistic Aspects of Narrative Production*. Norwood, NJ: Ablex, pp. 203–74.

Duranti, A., Ochs, E. and Schieffelin, B. (eds.) 2011. *The Handbook of Language Socialization*. Malden, MA: Wiley-Blackwell.

Eades, Diana, 1991. Communicative Strategies in Aboriginal English. In S. Romaine (ed.), *Language in Australia*. Cambridge University Press, pp. 85–93.

1994. A Case of Communicative Clash: Aboriginal English and the Legal System. In J. Gibbons (ed.), *Language and the Law*. London: Longman, pp. 234–64.

Edelman, G. 1992. *Bright Air, Brilliant Fire: On the Matter of the Mind*. Basic Books.

Edwards, D. 1995. Two to Tango: Script Formulations, Dispositions, and Rhetorical Symmetry in Relationship Troubles Talk. *Research on Language and Social Interaction* 28:319–50.

Edwards, D. and Potter, J. 1992. *Discursive Psychology*. London: Sage.

Edwards, D. and Stokoe, E. 2004. Discursive Psychology, Focus Group Interviews, and Participants' Categories. *British Journal of Developmental Psychology* 22:499–507.

Egbert, M. 1993. Schisming: The Transformation from a Single Conversation to Multiple Conversations. Unpublished PhD dissertation, University of California, Los Angeles.

1996. Context-Sensitivity in Conversation: Eye Gaze and the German Repair Initiator 'Bitte?'. *Language in Society* 25 (4):587–612.

1997. Schisming: The Collaborative Transformation from a Single Conversation to Multiple Conversations. *Research on Language and Social Interaction* 30 (1):1–51.

Egbert, M., Golato, A. and Robinson, J. D. 2009. Repairing Reference. In J. Sidnell (ed.), *Comparative Perspectives in Conversation Analysis*. Cambridge University Press, pp. 104–32.

Enfield, N. J. 2007a. *A Grammar of Lao*. Berlin: Mouton de Gruyter.

2007b. Meanings of the Unmarked: How 'Default' Person Reference Does More Than Just Refer. In N. Enfield and T. Stivers (eds.), *Person Reference in Interaction: Linguistic, Cultural, and Social Perspectives*. Cambridge University Press, pp. 97–120.

Enfield, N. J. 2010a. Without Social Context? *Science* 329:1600–1.

2010b. Questions and Responses in Lao. *Journal of Pragmatics* 42 (10):2649–65.

2013. *Relationship Thinking: Agency, Enchrony, and Human Sociality*. New York: Oxford University Press.

Enfield, N. J., Dingemanse, M., Baranova, J., Blythe, J., Brown, P., Dirksmeyer, T., Drew, P., Floyd, S., Gipper, S., Gisladottir, R. S., Hoymann, G., Kendrick, K. H., Levinson, S. C., Magyari, L., Manrique, E., Rossi, G., San Roque, L. and Torreira, F. 2013. *Huh? What?* A First Survey in 21 Languages. In M. Hayashi, G. Raymond and J. Sidnell (eds.), *Conversational Repair and Human Understanding*. Cambridge University Press, pp. 343–80.

Ervin-Tripp, S. M. 1972. Alternation and Co-occurrence. In J. J. Gumperz and D. Hymes (eds.), *Directions in Sociolinguistics: The Ethnography of Communication*. New York: Holt, Rinehart and Winston, pp. 218–50.

1981. How to Make and Understand a Request. In H. Parret, M. Sbisa and J. Verschueren (eds.), *Possibilities and Limitations of Pragmatics*. Amsterdam: John Benjamins, pp. 195–209.

Evans, N. 2003. Context, Culture and Structuration in the Languages of Australia. *Annual Review of Anthropology* 32:13–40.

Evans, N. and Levinson, S. C. 2009. The Myth of Language Universals: Language Diversity and Its Importance for Cognitive Science. *Behavioral and Brain Sciences* 32 (5):429–92.

Evans-Pritchard, E. E. 1937. *Witchcraft, Oracles and Magic Among the Azande*. Oxford University Press.

Everett, D. 2005. Cultural Constraints on Grammar and Cognition in Pirahã: Another Look at the Design Features of Human Language. *Current Anthropology* 46:621–46.

2009. Pirahã Culture and Grammar: A Response to Some Criticisms. *Language* 85 (3):405–42.

Fincke, S. 1999. The Syntactic Organization of Repair in Bikol. In B. A. Fox, D. Jurafsky and L. Michaelis (eds.), *Cognition and Function in Language*. Stanford: CSLI, pp. 252–67.

Floyd, S. 2015 (in prep). Recruitments in Cha'palaa. In S. Floyd, G. Rossi and N. Enfield (eds.), *Recruitments: A Typological Comparison of Pragmatic Agency*. Berlin: Language Sciences Press.

Floyd, S., Manrique, E., Rossi, G. and Torreira, F. 2015. The Timing of Visual Bodily Behavior in Repair Sequences: Evidence from Three Languages. MS.

Floyd, S., Rossi, G., Enfield, N. J., Baranova, J., Blythe, J., Dingemanse, M., Kendrick, K. H. and Zinken, J. 2014. Recruitments Across Languages: A Systematic Comparison. Talk presented at the Fourth International Conference on Conversation Analysis. University of California at Los Angeles.

Foer, J. 2011. *Moonwalking with Einstein: The Art and Science of Remembering Everything*. London: Penguin.

Ford, C. E. 1993. *Grammar in Interaction: Adverbial Clauses in American English Conversations*. Cambridge University Press.

Ford, C. E. and Thompson, S. A. 1996. Interactional Units in Conversation: Syntactic, Intonational, and Pragmatic Resources for the Management of Turns. In E. Ochs, E. A. Schegloff and S. A. Thompson (eds.), *Interaction and Grammar*. Cambridge University Press, pp. 134–84.

Ford, C. E., Fox, B. A. and Thompson, S. A. (eds.) 2002. *The Language of Turn and Sequence*. Cambridge University Press.

2013. Units and/or Action Trajectories? The Language of Grammatical Categories and the Language of Social Action. In B. Szczepek Reed and G. Raymond (eds.), *Units of Talk: Units of Action*. Amsterdam: John Benjamins, pp. 13–56.

Fowler, R. 1986. *Linguistic Criticism*. Oxford University Press.

Fox, B. A. (ed.) 1996. *Studies in Anaphora*. Amsterdam: John Benjamins.

2001. An Exploration of Prosody and Turn-Projection in English Conversation. In M. Selting and E. Couper-Kuhlen (eds.), *Studies in Interactional Linguistics*. Amsterdam: John Benjamins, pp. 79–100.

2007. Principles Shaping Grammatical Practices: An Exploration. *Discourse Studies* 9 (3): 299–318.

Fox, B. A. and Thompson, S. A. 2010. Responses to WH-Questions in English Conversation. *Research on Language and Social Interaction* 43 (2):133–56.

Fox, B. A., Hayashi, M. and Jasperson, R. 1996. Resources and Repair: A Cross-Linguistic Study of Syntax and Repair. In E. Ochs, E. A. Schegloff and S. A. Thompson (eds.), *Interaction and Grammar.* Cambridge University Press, pp. 185–237.

Fox, B. A., Maschler, Y. and Uhmann, S. 2010. A Cross-Linguistic Study of Self-Repair: Evidence from English, German and Hebrew. *Journal of Pragmatics* 42 (9):2487–505.

Fox, B. A., Wouk, F., Hayashi, M., Fincke, S., Tao, L., Sorjonen, M.-L., Laakso, M. and Flores Hernandez, W. 2009. A Cross-Linguistic Investigation of the Site of Initiation in Same-Turn Self-Repair. In J. Sidnell (ed.), *Conversation Analysis: Comparative Perspectives.* Cambridge University Press, pp. 60–103.

French, P. and Local, J. K. 1983. Turn-Competitive Incomings. *Journal of Pragmatics* 7: 17–38.

Futrell, R., Hickey, T., Lee, A., Lim, E., Luchkina, E. and Gibson, E. 2015. Cross-Linguistic Gestures Reflect Typological Universals: A Subject-Initial, Verb-Final Bias in Speakers of Diverse Languages. *Cognition* 136:215–21.

Gardner, R. 1997. The Conversation Object *Mm*: A Weak and Variable Acknowledging Token. *Research on Language and Social Interaction* 30 (2):131–56.

Gardner, R. and Mushin, I. 2015. Expanded Transition Spaces: The Case of Garrwa. *Frontiers in Psychology* 6 (251):1–14.

Garfinkel, H. 1967. *Studies in Ethnomethodology.* Englewood Cliffs, NJ: Prentice-Hall.

Geluykens, R. 1988. On the Myth of Rising Intonation in Polar Questions. *Journal of Pragmatics* 12:483–94.

Ginzburg, J. 2012. *The Interactive Stance.* Cambridge University Press.

Ginzburg, J. and Poesio, M. 2015. Grammar Is a System that Characterizes Talk-in-Interaction. MS.

Gisladottir, R. S. 2015. Other-Initiated Repair in Icelandic. *Open Linguistics* 1 (1): 309–28.

Gisladottir, R. S., Chwilla, D. and Levinson, S. C. 2015. Conversation Electrified: ERP Correlates of Speech Act Recognition in Underspecified Utterances. *Public Library of Science One* 10 (3):1–24.

Givón, T. 1979. *On Understanding Grammar.* New York: Academic Press.

    1995. *Functionalism and Grammar.* Amsterdam: John Benjamins.

    2008. *The Genesis of Syntactic Complexity: Diachrony, Ontogeny, Neuro-cognition, Evolution.* Amsterdam: John Benjamins.

Gladwell, M. 2005. *Blink: The Power of Thinking Without Thinking.* London: Penguin.

Glenn, P. 2003. *Laughter in Interaction.* Cambridge University Press.

    2010. Interviewer Laughs: Shared Laughter and Asymmetries in Employment Interviews. *Journal of Pragmatics* 42 (6):1485–98.

Glenn, P. and Holt, E. 2013. *On Laughing: Studies of Laughter in Interaction.* London: Bloomsbury.

Goffman, E. 1959. *The Presentation of Self in Everyday Life.* Garden City, NY: Doubleday.

    (ed.) 1961. *Encounters: Two Studies in the Sociology of Interaction.* Indianapolis: Bobbs-Merrill.

    1963. *Behavior in Public Places: Notes on the Social Organization of Gatherings.* New York: Free Press.

    1964. The Neglected Situation. *American Anthropologist* 66 (6, Pt. 2):133–6.

[1967] 2005. *Interaction Ritual: Essays in Face-to-Face Behavior*. Chicago: Aldine Transaction.

1983. The Interaction Order: American Sociological Association, 1982 Presidential Addess. *American Sociological Review* 48 (1): 1–17.

Golato, A. and Faygal, Z. 2008. Comparing Single and Double Sayings of the German Response Token Ja and the Role of Prosody: A Conversation Analytic Perspective. *Research on Language and Social Interaction* 41 (3):241–70.

Goodwin, C. 1979. The Interactive Construction of a Sentence in Natural Conversation. In G. Psathas (ed.), *Everyday Language: Studies in Ethnomethodology*. New York: Irvington Publishers, pp. 97–121.

1980. Restarts, Pauses, and the Achievement of a State of Mutual Gaze at Turn-beginning. *Sociological Inquiry* 50:272–302.

1981. *Conversational Organization: Interaction Between Speakers and Hearers*. New York: Academic Press.

1987. Forgetfulness as an Interactive Resource. *Social Psychology Quarterly* 50 (2):115–31.

1995. Co-Constructing Meaning in Conversation with an Aphasic Man. *Research on Language in Social Interaction* 28 (3):233–60.

(ed.) 2003a. *Conversation and Brain Damage*. Oxford University Press.

Goodwin, C. and Goodwin, M. H. 1986. Gesture and Coparticipation in the Activity of Searching for a Word. *Semiotica* 62 (1–2):51–75.

1987. Concurrent Operations on Talk: Notes on the Interactive Organization of Assessments. *IPrA Papers in Pragmatics* 1 (1):1–55.

1990. *He-Said-She-Said: Talk As Social Organization Among Black Children*. Bloomington: Indiana University Press.

2006. *The Hidden Life of Girls: Games of Stance, Status, and Exclusion*. Oxford: Blackwell.

Goodwin, M. H. and Cekaite, A. 2012. Calibration in Directive/Response Sequences in Family Interaction. *Journal of Pragmatics* 46:122–38.

Greenberg, J. H. 1963. Some Universals of Grammar with Special Reference to the Order of Meaningful Elements. In J. H. Greenberg (ed.), *Universals of Language*. Cambridge, MA: MIT Press, pp. 58–90.

1966. *Language Universals, With Special Reference to Feature Hierarchies*. The Hague: Mouton.

Greenberg, S. 1999. Speaking in Shorthand: A Syllable-Centric Perspective for Understanding Pronunciation Variation. *Speech Communication* 29:159–76.

Grice, H. P. 1975. Logic and Conversation. In P. Cole and J. Morgan (eds.), *Syntax and Semantics,* Vol. III: *Speech Acts*. New York: Academic Press, pp. 41–58.

1978. Further Notes on Logic and Conversation. In P. Cole (ed.), *Syntax and Semantics,* Vol. IX: *Pragmatics*. New York: Academic Press, pp. 113–28.

Gumperz, J. J. and Hymes, D. (eds.) 1972. *Directions in Sociolinguistics: The Ethnography of Communication*. New York: Holt, Rinehart, and Winston.

Guy, G., Horvath, B., Vonwiller, J., Daisley, E. and Rogers, I. 1986. An Intonation Change in Progress in Australian English. *Language in Society* 15: 23–52.

Haakana, M. 2001. Laughter as a Patient's Resource: Dealing with Delicate Aspects of Medical Interaction. *Text and Talk* 21 (1–2): 187–219.

2010. Laughter and Smiling: Notes on Co-occurrences. *Journal of Pragmatics* 42: 1499–512.

2012. Laughter in Conversation: The Case of 'Fake' Laughter. In A. Peräkylä and M.-L. Sorjonen (eds.), *Emotion in Interaction*. Oxford University Press, pp. 174–94.

Hacohen, G. and Schegloff, E. A. 2006. On the Preference for Minimization in Referring to Persons: Evidence from Hebrew Conversation. *Journal of Pragmatics* 38: 1305–12.

Hakulinen, A. and Selting, M. (eds.) 2005. *Syntax and Lexis in Conversation: Studies on the Use of Linguistic Resources in Talk-In-Interaction*. Amsterdam: John Benjamins.

Halliday, M. A. K. and Hasan, R. 1976. *Cohesion in English*. London: Longman.

1991. *Language, Context, and Text: Aspects of Language in a Social-semiotic Perspective*. Oxford University Press.

Hanks, W. F. 1990. *Referential Practice, Language and Lived Space Among the Maya*. University of Chicago Press.

2007. Person Reference in Yucatec Maya Conversation. In N. J. Enfield and T. Stivers (eds.), *Person Reference in Interaction: Linguistic, Cultural and Social Perspectives*. Cambridge University Press, pp. 149–71.

2014. Evidentiality in Social Interaction. In J. Nuckolls and L. Michael (eds.), *Evidentiality in Interaction*. Amsterdam: John Benjamins, pp. 2–12.

Harris, R. 1988. *Language, Saussure and Wittgenstein*. London: Routledge.

Harris, R. M. 1996. Truthfulness, Conversational Maxims and Interaction in an Egyptian Village. *Transactions of the Philological Society* 94 (1):31–55.

Hauser, M., Chomsky, N. and Fitch, T. 2002. The Faculty of Language: What Is It, Who Has It, and How Did It Evolve? *Science* 298:1569–79.

Haviland, J. B. 1998. Mu'nuk jbankil to, mu'nuk kajvaltik: 'He is Not My Older Brother, He is Not Our Lord'. Thirty Years of Gossip in a Chiapas Village. *Etnofoor* 11 (2/2):57–82.

2007. Person Reference in Tzotzil Gossip: Referring Dupliciter. In N. Enfield and T. Stivers (eds.), *Person Reference in Interaction: Linguistic, Cultural, and Social Perspectives*. Cambridge University Press, pp. 226–52.

Hayano, K. 2011. Claiming Epistemic Primacy: Yo-marked Assessments in Japanese. In T. Stivers, L. Mondada and J. Steensig (eds.), *The Morality of Knowledge in Conversation*. Cambridge University Press, pp. 58–81.

Hayashi, M. 1994. A Comparative Study of Self-Repair in English and Japanese Conversation. In N. Akatsuka (ed.), *Japanese/Korean Linguistics IV*. Stanford: CSLI, pp. 77–93.

2003. Language and the Body as Resources for Collaborative Action: A Study of Word Searches in Japanese Conversation. *Research on Language and Social Interaction* 36 (2):109–41.

2010. An Overview of the Question-Response System in Japanese. *Journal of Pragmatics* 42 (10):2685–702.

Hayashi, M. and Kim, H. R. S. 2013. Turn Formats For Other-Initiated Repair and Their Relation to Trouble Sources: Some Observations from Japanese and Korean. *Journal of Pragmatics* 57:303–17.

Hayashi, M., Raymond, G. and Sidnell, J. 2013. Conversational Repair and Human Understanding: An Introduction. In M. Hayashi, G. Raymond and J. Sidnell (eds.), *Conversational Repair and Human Understanding*. Cambridge University Press, pp. 1–40.

Heath, C. 1986. *Body Movement and Speech in Medical Interaction*. Cambridge University Press.

2013. *The Dynamics of Auction: Social Interaction and the Sale of Fine Art and Antiques.* Cambridge University Press.

Heinemann, T. 2006. 'Will You or Can't You?': Displaying Entitlement in Interrogative Requests. *Journal of Pragmatics* 38:1081–104.

2008. Questions of Accountability: Yes–No Interrogatives That Are Unanswerable. *Discourse Studies* 10:55–71.

2010. The Question–Response System of Danish. *Journal of Pragmatics* 42:2703–25.

Heinemann, T. and Traverso, V. 2009. Complaining in Interaction: Introduction. *Journal of Pragmatics* 41 (12):2381–4.

Heinemann, T., Lindström, A. and Steensig, J. 2011. Addressing Epistemic Incongruence in Question–Answer Sequences Through the Use of Epistemic Adverbs. In T. Stivers, L. Mondada and J. Steensig (eds.), *The Morality of Knowledge in Conversation.* Cambridge University Press, pp. 107–30.

Hepburn, A. 2004. Crying: Notes on Description, Transcription and Interaction. *Research on Language and Social Interaction* 37: 251–90.

Hepburn, A. and Bolden, G. 2013. The Conversation Analytic Approach to Transcription. In J. Sidnell and T. Stivers (eds.), *The Handbook of Conversation Analysis.* Chichester: Wiley-Blackwell, pp. 57–76.

Heritage, J. 1984a. A Change-of-State Token and Aspects of Its Sequential Placement. In J. M. Atkinson and J. Heritage (eds.), *Structures of Social Action: Studies in Conversation Analysis.* Cambridge University Press, pp. 299–345.

1984b. *Garfinkel and Ethnomethodology.* Cambridge: Polity Press.

1998. Oh-prefaced Responses to Inquiry. *Language in Society* 27:291–334.

2002a. Oh-prefaced Responses to Assessments: A Method of Modifying Agreement/Disagreement. In C. E. Ford, B. A. Fox and S. A. Thompson (eds.), *The Language of Turn and Sequence.* New York: Oxford University Press, pp. 196–224.

2002b. The Limits of Questioning: Negative Interrogatives and Hostile Question Content. *Journal of Pragmatics* 34:1427–46.

2008. Conversation Analysis as Social Theory. In B. Turner (ed.), *The New Blackwell Companion to Social Theory.* Oxford: Blackwell, pp. 300–20.

2011. A Galilean Moment in Social Theory?: Language, Culture and Their Emergent Properties. *Qualitative Sociology* 34:263–70.

2012a. Epistemics in Action: Action Formation and Territories of Knowledge. *Research on Language and Social Interaction* 45:1–29.

2012b. The Epistemic Engine: Sequence Organization and Territories of Knowledge. *Research on Language and Social Interaction* 45:30–52.

2012c. Beyond and Behind the Words: Some Reactions to My Commentators. *Research on Language and Social Interaction* 45 (1):76–81.

2013. Action Formation and Its Epistemic (and Other) Backgrounds. *Discourse Studies* 15 (5):551–78.

2014. Turn-Initial Position and One of Its Occupants: The Case of 'Well'. Plenary lecture at the Fourth International Conference on Conversation Analysis, University of California, Los Angeles.

Heritage, J. and Atkinson, J. M. 1984. Introduction. In J. M. Atkinson and J. Heritage. (ed.), *Structures of Social Action: Studies in Conversation Analysis.* Cambridge University Press, pp. 1–15.

Heritage, J. and Clayman, S. 2002. *The News Interview: Journalists and Public Figures on the Air*. Cambridge University Press.

2010. *Talk in Action: Interactions, Identities, and Institutions*. Chichester: Wiley-Blackwell.

Heritage, J. and Raymond, G. 2005. The Terms of Agreement: Indexing Epistemic Authority and Subordination in Assessment Sequences. *Social Psychology Quarterly* 68 (1):15–38.

2012. Navigating Epistemic Landscapes: Acquiescence, Agency and Resistance in Responses to Polar Questions. In J. P. de Ruiter (ed.), *Questions: Formal, Functional and Interactional Perspectives*. Cambridge University Press, pp. 179–92.

Heritage, J. and Sorjonen, M.-L. 1994. Constituting and Maintaining Activities Across Sequences: And-Prefacing as a Feature of Question Design. *Language in Society* 23:1–29.

Heritage, J. and Stivers, T. 2013. Conversation Analysis and Sociology. In J. Sidnell and T. Stivers (eds.), *The Handbook of Conversation Analysis*. Wiley: Blackwell, pp. 659–73.

Hoey, E. M. 2014. Sighing in Interaction: Somatic, Semiotic, and Social. *Research on Language and Social Interaction* 47 (2):175–200.

2015. Lapses: How People Arrive at, and Deal with, Discontinuities in Talk. *Research on Language and Social Interaction* 48 (4):430–53.

Holt, E. 2010. The Last Laugh: Shared Laughter and Topic Termination. *Journal of Pragmatics* 42 (6):1513–25.

2011. On the Nature of 'Laughables': Laughter as a Response to Overdone Figurative Phrases. *Pragmatics* 21 (3):393–410.

2012. Using Laugh Responses to Defuse Complaints. *Research on Language and Social Interaction* 45 (4):430–48.

2014. Laughter at Last: Laughter in Third Position. Paper given at the Fourth International Conference on Conversation Analysis, University of California, Los Angeles.

Holt, E. and Drew, P. 1988. Complainable Matters: The Use of Idiomatic Expressions in Making Complaints. *Social Problems* 35 (4):398–417.

Hopper, P. J. 1987. Emergent Grammar. *Berkeley Linguistics Society* 13:139–57.

Hopper, P. J. and Thompson, S. A. 1980. Transivity in Grammar and Discourse. *Language* 56 (2):251–99.

1984. The Discourse Basis for Lexical Categories in Universal Grammar. *Language* 60 (4):703–52.

Horn, L. R. 1978. Some Aspects of Negation. In J. H. Greenberg, C. A. Ferguson and E. A. Moravscik (eds.), *Universals of Human Language*. Stanford University Press, pp. 127–210.

Houtkoop-Steenstra, H. and Mazeland, H. 1985. Turns and Discourse Units in Everyday Conversation. *Journal of Pragmatics* 9:595–619.

Hoymann, G. 2010. Questions and Responses in ‡Ākhoe Hai‖om. *Journal of Pragmatics* 42 (10):2726–40.

Huang, H. and Tanangkingsing, M. 2005. Repair in Verb-initial Languages. *Language and Linguistics* 6 (4):575–97.

Hurford, J. R. 2007. *The Origins of Meaning: Language in the Light of Evolution*. Oxford University Press.

Huron, D. B. 2006. *Sweet Anticipation: Music and the Psychology of Expectation.* Cambridge, MA: MIT Press.

Hutchins, E. 1995. *Cognition in the Wild.* Cambridge, MA: MIT Press.

Hymes, D. H. 1966. Two Types of Linguistic Relativity. In W. Bright (ed.), *Sociolinguistics.* The Hague: Mouton. pp. 114–58.

Isaacs, E. A. and Clark, H. H. 1990. Ostensible Invitations. *Language in Society* 19 (4):493–509.

Jackendoff, R. and Pinker, S. 2005. The Nature of the Language Faculty and Its Implications for the Evolution of Language (Reply to Chomsky, Hauser and Fitch). *Cognition* 97 (2):211–25.

Jasperson, R. 2002. Some Linguistic Aspects of Closure Cut-off. In C. E. Ford, B. A. Fox and S. A. Thompson (eds.), *The Language of Turn and Sequence.* Oxford University Press, pp. 257–86.

Jefferson, G. 1972. Side Sequences. In D. Sudnow (ed.), *Studies in Social Interaction.* New York: The Free Press, pp. 448–9.

1973. A Case of Precision Timing in Ordinary Conversation: Overlapped Tag-Positioned Address Terms in Closing Sequences. *Semiotica* 9 (1):47–96.

1974. Error Correction as an Interactional Resource. *Language in Society* 3 (2):181–99.

1978. Sequential Aspects of Storytelling in Conversation. In J. Schenkein (ed.), *Studies in the Organization of Conversational Interaction.* New York: Academic Press, pp. 219–48.

1979. A Technique for Inviting Laughter and Its Subsequent Acceptance/Declination. In G. Psathas (ed.), *Everyday Language: Studies in Ethnomethodology.* New York: Irvington Publishers, pp. 79–96.

1981. Caveat Speaker: A Preliminary Exploration of Shift Implicative Recipiency in the Articulation of Topic. *Final Report to the Social Science Research Council.* Downloaded on 29 May 2015 from www.liso.ucsb.edu/liso_archives/Jefferson/topic_report.pdf.

1983. Issues in the Transcription of Naturally-Occurring Talk: Caricature Versus Capturing Pronunicational Particulars. *Tilburg Papers in Language and Literature* 34. Tilburg University, pp. 1–14.

1984a. On the Organization of Laughter in Talk About Troubles. In J. M. Atkinson and J. Heritage (eds.), *Structures of Social Action: Studies in Conversation Analysis.* Cambridge University Press, pp. 346–69.

1984b. Notes on some Orderlinesses of Overlap Onset. In V. D'Urso and P. Leonardi (eds.), *Discourse Analysis and Natural Rhetoric.* Padua: Cleup Editore, pp. 11–38.

1985. An Exercise in the Transcription and Analysis of Laughter. In T. Van Dijk (ed.), *Handbook of Discourse Analysis,* Vol. III: *Discourse and Dialogue.* New York: Academic Press, pp. 25–34.

1986. Notes on 'Latency' in Overlap Onset. *Human Studies* 9 (2–3):153–83.

1988. Notes on a Possible Metric Which Provides for a 'Standard Maximum' Silence of Approximately One Second in Conversation. In D. Roger and P. Bull (eds.), *Conversation: An Interdisciplinary Perspective.* Clevedon: Multilingual Matters, pp. 166–96.

1993. Caveat Speaker: Preliminary Notes on Recipient Topic-Shift Implicature. *Research on Language and Social Interaction,* 26, 1: 1–30.

2003. A Note on Resolving Ambiguity. In P. J. Glenn, C. D. LeBaron and J. Mandelbaum (eds.), *Studies in Language and Social Interaction: In Honor of Robert Hopper*. Mahwah, NJ: Lawrence Erlbaum, pp. 221–40.

2004a. 'At First I Thought': A Normalizing Device for Extraordinary Events. In G. H. Lerner (ed.), *Conversation Analysis: Studies from the First Generation*. Amsterdam: John Benjamins, pp. 131–67.

2004b. Glossary of Transcript Symbols with an Introduction. In G. H. Lerner (ed.), *Conversation Analysis: Studies from the First Generation*. Amsterdam: John Benjamins, pp. 13–23.

Jefferson, G. 2004c. A Note on Laughter in 'Male-Female' Interaction. *Discourse Studies* 6 (1):117–33.

2010. Sometimes a Frog in Your Throat Is Just a Frog in Your Throat: Gutturals as (Sometimes) Laughter-implicative. *Journal of Pragmatics* 42:1476–84.

Jefferson, G., Sacks, H. and Schegloff, E. A. 1987. Notes on Laughter in the Pursuit of Intimacy. In G. Button and J. R. E. Lee (eds.), *Talk and Social Organization*. Clevedon: Multilingual Matters, pp. 152–205.

Johnson-Laird, P. N. 1987. The Mental Representation of the Meaning of Words. *Cognition* 25:189–211.

Jones, J. 1962. *On Aristotle and Greek Tragedy*. Oxford University Press.

Joseph, B. D. 2003. Editor's Department: Reviewing Our Contents. *Language* 79 (3):461–3.

Kamio, A. 1997. *Territory of Information*. Amsterdam: John Benjamins.

Kamp, H. 1995. Discourse Representation Theory. In J. Verschueren, J.-O. Östman and J. Blommaert (eds.), *Handbook of Pragmatics*. Amsterdam: John Benjamins, pp. 253–7.

Kendall, T. 2013. *Speech Rate, Pause and Sociolinguistic Variation: Studies in Corpus Sociophonetics*. Basingstoke: Palgrave Macmillan.

Kendon, A. 1967. Some Functions of Gaze Direction in Social Interaction. *Acta Psychologica* 26:22–63.

Kendrick, K. H. 2015. The Intersection of Turn-taking and Repair: The Timing of Other-initiations of Repair in Conversation. *Frontiers in Psychology* 6:250.

Kendrick, K. H. and Drew, P. 2014. The Putative Preference for Offers over Requests. In P. Drew and E. Couper-Kuhlen (eds.), *Requesting in Social Interaction*. Amsterdam: John Benjamins, pp. 87–113.

2016. Recruitment: Offers, Requests and the Organization of Assistance in Interaction. *Research on Language and Social Interaction* 49 (1):1–19.

Kendrick, K. H. and Torreira, F. 2014. The Timing and Construction of Preference: A Quantitative Study. *Discourse Processes* 52 (4):255–89.

Kendrick, K. H., Brown, P., Dingemanse, M., Floyd, S., Gipper, S., Hayano, K., Hoey, E., Hoymann, G., Manrique, E., Rossi, G. and Levinson, S. C. 2014. Sequence Organization: A Universal Infrastructure for Action. Talk presented at the Fourth International Conference on Conversation Analysis. University of California, Los Angeles.

Kent, A. 2012. Compliance, Resistance and Incipient Compliance When Responding to Directives. *Discourse Studies* 14(6):711–30.

Kidwell, M. 2005. Gaze as Social Control: How Very Young Children Differentiate 'The Look' From a 'Mere Look' by Their Adult Caregivers. *Research on Language and Social Interaction* 38 (4):417–49.

Kim, H. R. S. 2013. Reshaping the Response Space with *Kulenikka* in Beginning to Respond to Questions in Korean Conversation. *Journal of Pragmatics* 57: 303–17.

Kim, K.-H. 1993. Other-Initiated Repair Sequences in Korean Conversation as Interactional Resources. In S. Choi (ed.), *Japanese/Korean Linguistics, III*. Stanford: CSLI, pp. 3–18.

1999a. Other-Initiated Repair Sequences in Korean Conversation: Types and Functions. *Discourse and Cognition* 6:141–68.

1999b. Phrasal Unit Boundaries and Organization of Turns and Sequences in Korean Conversation. *Human Studies* 22 (2–4):425–46.

2001. Confirming Intersubjectivity Through Retroactive Elaboration: Organization of Phrasal Units in Other-Initiated Repair Sequences in Korean Conversation. In M. Selting and E. Couper-Kuhlen (eds.), *Studies in Interactional Linguistics*. Amsterdam: John Benjamins, pp. 345–72.

Kim, M. S. 2013. Answering Questions about the Unquestionable in Korean Conversation. *Journal of Pragmatics* 57:138–57.

Kimura, Daiji, 2001. Utterance Overlap and Long Silence among the Baka Pygmies: Comparison with Bantu Farmers and Japanese University Students. *African Study Monographs* 26, Supplement: 103–21.

Kita, S. (ed.) 2003. *Pointing: Where Language, Culture and Cognition Meet*. Hillsdale, NJ: Lawrence Erlbaum.

Kitamura, Koji, 1990. Interactional Synchrony: A Fundamental Condition for Communication. In M. Moerman and M. Nomura (eds.), *Culture Embodied*. Osaka: National Museum of Ethnology, pp. 123–40.

Kitzinger, C. 2005a. Speaking as a Heterosexual: (How) Does Sexuality Matter for Talk-in-interaction. *Research on Language and Social Interaction* 38 (3):221–65.

2005b. Heteronormativity in Action: Reproducing the Heterosexual Nuclear Family in After-Hours Medical Calls. *Social Problems* 52 (4):477–98.

2013. Repair. In J. Sidnell and T. Stivers (eds.), *The Handbook of Conversation Analysis*. Chichester: Wiley-Blackwell, pp. 229–56.

Kitzinger, C. and Mandelbaum, J. 2013. Word Selection and Social Identities in Talk-in-Interaction. *Communication Monographs* 80 (2):176–98.

Koshik, I. 2002. Designedly Incomplete Utterances: A Pedagogical Practice for Eliciting Knowledge Displays in Error Correction Sequences. *Research on Language and Social Interaction* 35:277–309.

2005. *Beyond Rhetorical Questions: Assertive Questions in Everyday Interaction*. Amsterdam: John Benjamins.

Kurtić, E., Brown, G. and Wells, B. 2013. Resources for Turn-Competition in Overlapping Talk. *Speech Communication* 55 (5):721–43.

Kutler, S. 1997. *Abuse of Power: The New Nixon Tapes*. New York: Touchstone.

Laakso, M. and Sorjonen, M.-L. 2010. Cut-Off or Particle-Devices for Initiating Self-Repair in Conversation. *Journal of Pragmatics* 42 (4): 1151–72.

Labov, W. 1972. The Social Stratification of (r) in New York City Department Stores. In W. Labov, *Sociolinguistic Patterns*. Philadelphia: University of Pennsylvania Press, pp. 43–54.

Labov, W. and Fanshel, D. 1977. *Therapeutic Discourse: Psychotherapy as Conversation*. New York: Academic Press.

Ladd, R. 1980. *The Structure of Intonational Meaning: Evidence from English.* Bloomington: Indiana University Press.

Lasnik, H. 1976. Remarks on Coreference. *Linguistic Analysis* 2:1–22.

Lee, S. H. 2006. Second Summonings in Korean Telephone Conversation Openings. *Language in Society* 35 (2):261–83.

　　2013. Response Design in Conversation. In J. Sidnell and T. Stivers (eds.), *The Handbook of Conversation Analysis.* Chichester: Wiley-Blackwell, pp. 415–32.

　　2015. Two Forms of Affirmative Responses to Polar Questions. *Discourse Processes* 52 (1):21–46.

Legate, J. A., Pesetsky, D. and Yang, C. 2014. Recursive Misrepresentations: A Reply to Levinson (2013). *Language* 90 (2):515–28.

Lehmann, C. [1982] 1995. *Thoughts on Grammaticalization.* Munich: Lincom Europa.

Leigh-Fermor, P. 2014. *Abducting a General: the Kreipe Operation and the SOE in Crete.* London: John Murray.

Lerner, G. H. 1989. Notes on Overlap Management in Conversation: The Case of Delayed Completion. *Western Journal of Speech Communication* 53:167–77.

　　1991. On the Syntax of Sentences in Progress. *Language in Society* 20:441–58.

　　1992. Assisted Storytelling: Deploying Shared Knowledge as a Practical Matter. *Qualitative Sociology* 15 (3):247–71.

　　1993. Collectivities in Action: Establishing the Relevance of Conjoined Participation in Conversation. *Text* 13 (2):213–45.

　　1996. On the Place of Linguistic Resources in the Organization of Talk-in-interaction: 'Second Person' Reference in Multi-Party Conversation. *Pragmatics* 6 (3):281–94.

　　2002. Turn-Sharing: The Choral Co-production of Talk-in-Interaction. In C. E. Ford, B. A. Fox and S. A. Thompson (eds.), *The Language of Turn and Sequence.* Oxford University Press, pp. 225–56.

　　2003. Selecting Next Speaker: The Context-Sensitive Operation of a Context-free Organization. *Language in Society* 32 (2):177–201.

　　2004. On the Place of Linguistic Resources in the Organization of Talk-in-Interaction: Grammar as Action in Prompting a Speaker to Elaborate. *Research on Language and Social Interaction* 37 (2):151–84.

　　2013. On the Place of Hesitating in Delicate Formulations: A Turn-Constructional Infrastructure for Collaborative Indiscretion. In M. Hayashi, G. Raymond and J. Sidnell (eds.), *Conversational Repair and Human Understanding.* Cambridge University Press, pp. 95–134.

Lerner, G. H. and Kitzinger, C. 2007. Extraction and Aggregation in the Repair of Individual and Collective Self-Reference. *Discourse Studies* 9 (4):526–57.

　　2010. Repair Prefacing in the Organization of Same-Turn Self-Repair. Paper presented at the International Conference on Conversation Analysis, Mannheim.

　　2015. Or-Prefacing in the Organization of Self-Initiated Repair. *Research on Language and Social Interaction* 48 (1):58–78.

Lerner, G. H. and Raymond, G. 2007. Body Trouble: Some Sources of Interactional Trouble and Their Embodied Solution. Paper presented to the National Communication Association, Chicago.

Lerner, G. H. and Schegloff, E. A. 2009. Beginning to Respond: Well-Prefaced Responses to Wh-Questions. *Research on Language and Social Interaction* 42 (2):91–115.

Levelt, W. 1989. *Speaking: From Intention to Articulation.* Cambridge, MA: MIT Press.

Levinson, S. C. 1983. *Pragmatics*. Cambridge University Press.

2000. *Presumptive Meanings: The Theory of Generalized Conversational Implicature.* Cambridge, MA: MIT Press.

2006. On the Human 'Interaction Engine'. In N. J. Enfield and S. C. Levinson (eds.), *Roots of Human Sociality: Culture, Cognition and Interaction.* Oxford: Berg, pp. 39–69.

2007. Optimizing Person Reference: Perspectives from Usage on Rossel Island. In N. Enfield and T. Stivers (eds.), *Person Reference in Interaction: Linguistic, Cultural, and Social Perspectives.* Cambridge University Press, pp. 29–72.

2010. Questions and Responses in Yélî Dnye, the Papuan Language of Rossel Island. *Journal of Pragmatics* 42:2741–55.

2013a. Action Formation and Ascription. In T. Stivers and J. Sidnell (eds.), *The Handbook of Conversation Analysis.* Malden, MA: Wiley-Blackwell, pp. 103–30.

2013b. Recursion in Pragmatics. *Language* 89 (1):149–62.

2014. The social life of milliseconds: New perspectives on timing and projection in turn-taking. Plenary talk presented at the Fourth International Conference on Conversation Analysis (ICCA14). Los Angeles, CA.

Levinson, S. C. and Evans, N. 2010. Time for a Sea-Change in Linguistics: Response to Comments on the Myth of Language Universals. *Lingua* 120 (12):2733–58.

Li, C. N. and Thompson, S. A. 1981. *Mandarin Chinese: A Functional Reference Grammar.* Berkeley: University of California Press.

Li, X. 2014. *Multimodality, Interaction and Turn-Taking in Mandarin Conversation.* Amsterdam: John Benjamins.

Liberman, Kenneth, 1985. *Understanding Interaction in Australia: An Ethnomethodological Study of Australian Aboriginal People.* Boston: Routledge & Kegan Paul.

Lindström, A. 2005. Language as Social Action: A Study of How Senior Citizens Request Assistance with Practical Tasks in the Swedish Home Help Service. In A. Hakulinen and M. Selting (eds.), *Syntax and Lexis in Conversation: Studies on the Use of Linguistic Resources in Talk-in-Interaction.* Amsterdam: John Benjamins, pp. 209–30.

Livingston, E. 2008. *Ethnographies of Reason.* Aldershot: Ashgate Publishing.

Local, J. K. 1996. Conversational Phonetics: Some Aspects of News Receipts in Everyday Talk. In E. Couper-Kuhlen and M. Selting (eds.), *Prosody in Conversation.* Cambridge University Press, pp. 177–230.

Local, J. K. and Kelly, J. 1986. Projection and 'Silences': Notes on Phonetic and Conversational Structure. *Human Studies* 9:185–204.

Local, J. K. and Walker, G. 2004. Abrupt-Joins as a Resource for the Production of Multi-unit, Multi-Action Turns. *Journal of Pragmatics* 36 (8):1375–403.

2005. Methodological Imperatives for Investigating the Phonetic Organization and Phonological Structures of Spontaneous Speech. *Phonetica* 62 (2–4):120–30.

2010. Speaking in Time and Sequence: Phonetics and the Management of Talk-in-Interaction. Paper presented at the Colloquium of the British Association of Academic Phoneticians, London. Downloaded on 30 May 2015 from http://gareth-walker.staff.shef.ac.uk/pubs/local-walker-baap2010.png.

2012. How Phonetic Features Project More Talk. *Journal of the International Phonetic Association* 42 (3):255–80.

Local, J. K., Kelly, J. and Wells, W. H. G. 1986. Towards a Phonology of Conversation: Turn-Taking in Tyneside English. *Journal of Linguistics* 22 (2):411–37.

Local, J. K., Wells, W. H. G. and Sebba, M. 1985. Phonology for Conversation: Phonetic Aspects of Turn Delimitation in London Jamaican. *Journal of Pragmatics* 9 (2–3):309–30.

Lord, C. G., Ross, L. and Lepper, M. R. 1979. Biased Assimilation and Attitude Polarisation: The Effects of Prior Theories on Subsequently Considered Evidence. *Journal of Personality and Social Psychology* 37:2098–109.

Lukes, S. 1979. Power and Authority. In T. Bottesmore and R. Nisbet (eds.), *A History of Sociological Analysis*. London: Heinemann, pp. 633–77.

Maheu-Pelletier, G. and Golato, A. 2008. Repair in Membership Categorization in French. *Language in Society* 37 (5):689–712.

Manrique, E. 2011. Other-Repair Initiators in Argentine Sign Language: Handling Seeing and Understanding Difficulties in Face-to-Face Interaction. MA thesis, Radboud University, Nijmegen.

Manrique, E. and Enfield, N. 2015a. *Suspending the Next Turn as a Form of Repair Initiation: Evidence from Argentine Sign Language*. Ms.

2015b. Suspending the Next Turn as a Form of Repair Initiation: Evidence from Argentine Sign Language. *Frontiers in Psychology* 6:1326.

Margutti, P. 2010. On Designedly Incomplete Utterances: What Counts as Learning for Teachers and Students in Primary Classroom Interaction. *Research on Language and Social Interaction* 43 (4):315–45.

Matisoff, J. A. 1994. Tone, Intonation and Sound Symbolism in Lahu: Loading the Syllable Canon. In L. Hinton, J. Nichols and J. J. Ohala (eds.), *Sound Symbolism*. Cambridge University Press, pp. 115–29.

McNeill, W. H. 1997. *Keeping Together in Time: Dance and Drill in Human History*. Cambridge, MA: Harvard University Press.

Malinowski, B. 1923. The Problem of Meaning in Primitive Languages. In C. K. Ogden and I. A. Richards (eds.), *The Meaning of Meaning*. London: Routledge, pp. 296–336.

Marten, N. n.d. Neil Marten MP. Dowloaded on 13 July 2015 from https://en.wikipedia .org/wiki/Neil_Marten.

Maynard, D. W. 1989. Perspective-Display Sequences in Conversation. *Western Journal of Speech Communication* 53:91–113.

1992. On Clinicians Co-implicating Recipients' Perspective in Delivery of Diagnostic News. In P. Drew and J. Heritage (eds.), *Talk at Work: Talk in Institutional Settings*. Cambridge University Press, pp. 331–58.

2013. Defensive Mechanisms: I-Mean-Prefaced Utterances in Complaint and Other Sequences. In M. Hayashi, G. Raymond and J. Sidnell (eds.), *Conversational Repair and Human Understanding*. Cambridge University Press, pp. 198–233.

Mayr, A. 2008. *Language and Power: An Introduction to Institutional Discourse*. London: A. & C. Black.

Mazeland, H. 2007. Parenthetical Sequences. *Journal of Pragmatics* 39 (10):1816–69.

2013. Grammar in Conversation. In J. Sidnell and T. Stivers (eds.), *The Handbook of Conversation Analysis*. Chichester: Wiley-Blackwell, pp. 475–91.

Menasan, S. 2003. A Study of Polite Requests in Persian, Azari and English. Unpublished PhD dissertation, University of Essex.

Merritt, M. 1976. On Questions Following Questions in Service Encounters. *Language in Society* 5 (3):315–57.

Moerman, M. 1977. The Preference for Self-correction in a Tai Conversational Corpus. *Language* 53 (4):872–82.

1988. *Talking Culture: Ethnography and Conversation Analysis*. Philadelphia: University of Pennsylvania Press.

Mondada, L. 2007. Multimodal Resources for Turn-Taking: Pointing and the Emergence of Possible Next Speakers. *Discourse Studies* 9 (2):194–225.

Morris-Jones, B. 1999. *The Welsh Answering System*. Berlin: Mouton de Gruyter.

Murray, L. and Trevarthen, C. 1986. The Infant's Role in Mother-Infant Communications. *Journal of Child Language* 13 (1):15–29.

Mushin, I. and Gardner, R. 2009. Silence Is Talk: Conversational Silence in Australian Aboriginal Talk-in-interaction. *Journal of Pragmatics* 41 (10):2033–52.

Nevins, A., Pesetsky, D. and Rodrigues, C. 2009. Evidence and Argumentation: A Reply to Everett (2009). *Language* 85 (3):671–81.

Nolan, F. 2006. Intonation. In B. Aarts and A. M. S. MacMahon (eds.), *The Handbook of English Linguistics*. Oxford: Blackwell, pp. 433–57.

Norcliffe, E., Konopka, A. E., Brown, P. and Levinson, S. C. 2015. Word Order Affects the Time Course of Sentence Formulation in Tzeltal. *Language, Cognition and Neuroscience* 30 (9):1187–208.

Ochs, E., Schegloff, E. A. and Thompson, S. A. (eds.) 1996. *Interaction and Grammar*. Cambridge University Press.

Ogden, R. 2004. Non-Modal Voice Quality and Turn-Taking in Finnish. In E. Couper-Kuhlen and C. E. Ford (eds.), *Sound Patterns in Interaction: Cross-Linguistic Studies from Conversation*. Amsterdam: John Benjamins, pp. 29–62.

2009. *An Introduction to English Phonetics*. Edinburgh University Press.

2012. Prosodies in Conversation. In O. Niebuhr (ed.), *Understanding Prosody: The Role of Context, Function and Communication*. Berlin: Walter de Gruyter & Co., pp. 201–18.

2013. Clicks and Percussives in English Conversation. *Journal of the International Phonetic Association* 43 (3):299–320.

Oh, S.-Y. 2007a. The Interactional Meanings of Quasi-Pronouns in Korean Conversation. In N. Enfield and T. Stivers (eds.), *Person Reference in Interaction: Linguistic, Cultural, and Social Perspectives*. Cambridge University Press, pp. 203–25.

2007b. Overt Reference to Speaker and Recipient in Korean. *Discourse Studies* 9 (4):462–92.

2010. Invoking Categories through Co-present Person Reference: The Case of Korean Conversation. *Journal of Pragmatics* 42 (5):1219–42.

Orwell, G. [1944] 1998. Propaganda and Demotic Speech. In P. Davison (ed.), *The Complete Works of George Orwell*, Vol. 16: *I Have Tried to Tell the Truth: 1943–1944*. Secker and Warburg, pp. 310–16.

The Oxford English Dictionary. 1933. Onions, C. T. and Craigie, W. (eds.). Oxford University Press.

Parker, N. 2001. Capability and Culpability: A Study of How Inability Accounts Can Be Used in Therapy to Mitigate Culpability for Socially Undesirable Behaviour. Paper given at the conference on 'Language and Therapeutic Interaction'. Brunel University, 30–31 August.

Parsons, T. 1937. *The Structure of Social Action*. New York: McGraw-Hill.

Patel, A. 2008. The Music of Language and the Language of Music. Lecture 4 in the series 'Music and the Brain', Library of Congress. Downloaded on 21 February 2016 from www.youtube.com/watch?v=2oMvtw4aeEY.

Philips, Susan Urmston, 1976. Some Sources of Cultural Variability in the Regulation of Talk. *Language in Society* 5:81–95.

2005. A Comparison of Indian and Anglo Communicative Behavior in Classroom Interaction. In S. F. Kiesling and C. Bratt Paulston (eds.), *Intercultural Discourse and Communication*. Oxford: Blackwell, pp. 291–303.

Piatelli-Palmarini, M. 2010. What Is Language, that It May Have Evolved, and What Is Evolution, that It May Apply to Language? In R. K. Larson, V. Déprez and H. Yamakido (eds.), *The Evolution of Human Language: Biolinguistic Perspectives*. Cambridge University Press, pp. 148–62.

Pierrehumbert, J. B. 1980. The Phonology and Phonetics of English Intonation. PhD thesis, Massachussetts Institute of Technology.

Pillet-Shore, D. 2011. Doing Introductions: The Work Involved in Meeting Someone New. *Communication Monographs* 78 (1):73–95.

Pinker, S. 1994. *The Language Instinct*. New York: Morrow and Co.

Pinker, S., Nowak, M. A. and Lee, J. J. 2008. The Logic of Indirect Speech. *Proceedings of the National Academy of Sciences* 105 (3):833–8.

Plug, L. 2015. On (Or Not On) the 'Upgrading–Downgrading Continuum': The Case of 'Prosodic Marking' in Self-Repair. In D. Barth-Weingarten and B. Szczepek Reed (eds.), *Prosody and Phonetics in Interaction*. Mannheim: Verlag für Gesprächsforschung, pp. 70–86.

Pomerantz, A. 1978. Compliment Responses: Notes on the Co-operation of Multiple Constraints. In J. Schenkein (ed.), *Studies in the Organization of Conversational Interaction*. New York: Academic Press, pp. 79–112.

1980. Telling My Side: 'Limited Access' as a 'Fishing Device'. *Sociological Inquiry* 50:186–98.

1984. Agreeing and Disagreeing with Assessments: Some Features of Preferred/ Dispreferred Turn Shapes. In J. M. Atkinson and J. Heritage (eds.), *Structures of Social Action: Studies in Conversation Analysis*. Cambridge University Press, pp. 57–101.

1986. Extreme Case Formulations: A Way of Legitimizing Claims. *Human Studies* 9 (2–3):219–29.

1988. Offering a Candidate Answer: An Information Seeking Strategy. *Communication Monographs* 55 (4):360–73.

2014. Plenary lecture at the Fourth International Conference on Conversation Analysis, University of California, Los Angeles.

Pomerantz, A. and Heritage, J. 2013. Preference. In J. Sidnell and T. Stivers (eds.), *The Handbook of Conversation Analysis*. Chichester: Wiley-Blackwell, pp. 210–28.

Potter, J. 2012. Re-Reading Discourse and Social Psychology: Transforming Social Psychology. *British Journal of Social Psychology* 51 (3):436–55.

Potter, J. and Hepburn, A. 2010. Putting Aspiration into Words: 'Laugh Particles', Managing Descriptive Trouble and Modulating Action. *Journal of Pragmatics* 42 (6):1543–55.

Potter, J. and te Molder, H. 2005. Talking Cognition: Mapping and Making the Terrain. In H. te Molder and J. Potter (eds.), *Conversation and Cognition*. Cambridge University Press, pp. 1–54.

Potter, J. and Wetherell, M. 1987. *Discourse and Social Psychology: Beyond Attitudes and Behaviour*. London Sage.

Quirk, R., Greenbaum, S., Leech, G. and Svartvik, J. 1985. *A Comprehensive Grammar of the English Language*. London: Longman.

Rae, J. 2008. Lexical Substitution as a Therapeutic Resource. In A. Peräkylä, C. Antaki, S. Vehviläinen and I. Leudar (eds.), *Conversation Analysis and Psychotherapy*. Cambridge University Press, pp. 62–79.

Raymond, C. W. 2014. On the Sequential Negotiation of Identity in Spanish-Language Discourse: Mobilizing Linguistic Resources in the Service of Social Action. Unpublished PhD dissertation, University of California, Los Angeles.

  Forthcoming. Linguistic Reference in the Negotiation of Identity and Action: Revisiting the T/V distinction. *Language*.

Raymond, G. 2003. Grammar and Social Organization: Yes/No Interrogatives and the Structure of Responding. *American Sociological Review* 68:939–67.

Raymond, G. and Heritage, J. 2006. The Epistemics of Social Relations: Owning Grandchildren. *Language in Society* 35:677–705.

Raymond, G. and Lerner, G. H. 2014. A Body and Its Involvements: Adjusting Action for Dual Involvements. In P. Haddington, T. Keisanen, L. Mondada and M. Nevile (eds.), *Multiactivity in Social Interaction: Beyond Multitasking*. Amsterdam: John Benjamins, pp. 227–46.

Reber, E. 2012. *Affectivity in Interaction: Sound Objects in English*. Amsterdam: John Benjamins.

Reddy, M. J. 1979. The Conduit Metaphor: A Case of Frame Conflict in Our Language about Language. In A. Ortony (ed.), *Metaphor and Thought*. Cambridge University Press, pp. 284–310.

Reisman, K. 1974. Contrapuntal Conversations in an Antiguan Village. In R. Bauman and J. Sherzer (eds.), *Explorations in the Ethnography of Speaking*. Cambridge University Press, pp. 110–24.

Roberts, S. G. and Levinson, S. C. 2014. Interaction Constrains Variation in Linguistic Structure. Talk presented at the Fourth International Conference on Conversation Analysis (ICCA14). Los Angeles, CA.

Robinson, J. D. and Kevoe-Feldman, H. 2010. Using Full Repeats to Initiate Repair on Others' Questions. *Research on Language and Social Interaction* 43 (3):232–59.

Roitsch, P. A., Babcock, G. L. and Edmunds, W. W. 1977. *Human Factors Report on the Tenerife Accident*. Aircraft Accident Report, Pan American World Airways Boeing 747, N737 PA: KLM Royal Dutch Airlines, Boeing 747 PH-BUF, Tenerife, Canary Islands, 27 March 1977. Airline Pilots Association, Engineering and Air Safety, Washington, DC.

Rossano, F. 2005. When It's Over Is It Really Over? On the Effects of Sustained Gaze vs. Gaze Withdrawal at Sequence Possible Completion. Paper presented at the International Pragmatics Association Conference, Riva del Garda, Italy.

  2012. Gaze Behavior in Face-to-Face Interaction. Unpublished PhD Dissertation, Max Planck Institute for Psycholinguistics, Nijmegen, The Netherlands.

  2013. Gaze in Conversation. In J. Sidnell and T. Stivers (eds.), *The Handbook of Conversation Analysis*. Chichester: Wiley-Blackwell, pp. 308–29.

Rossi, G. 2014. The Request System in Italian Interaction. Talk presented at the Fourth International Conference on Conversation Analysis. University of California, Los Angeles.

2015a. The Request System in Italian Interaction. PhD dissertation, Radboud University and Max Planck Institute for Psycholinguistics, Nijmegen. MPI Series 99.

2015b. Other-Initiated Repair in Italian. *Open Linguistics* 1 (1):256–82.

Sacks, H. 1972a. An Initial Investigation of the Usability of Conversational Materials for Doing Sociology. In D. N. Sudnow (ed.), *Studies in Social Interaction*. New York: Free Press, pp. 31–74.

1972b. On the Analyzability of Stories by Children. In J. J. Gumperz and D. Hymes (eds.), *Directions in Sociolinguistics: The Ethnography of Communication*. New York: Holt, Rinehart, and Winston, pp. 325–45. (Reprinted in R. Turner (ed.), *Ethnomethodology*. London: Penguin, 1974.)

1974. An Analysis of the Course of a Joke's Telling in Conversation. In R. Bauman and J. Sherzer (eds.), *Explorations in the Ethnography of Speaking*. Cambridge University Press, pp. 337–53.

1975. Everyone Has to Lie. In M. Sanches and B. G. Blount (eds.), *Sociocultural Dimensions of Language Use*. New York: Academic Pres, pp. 57–80.

1979. Hotrodder: A Revolutionary Category. In G. Psathas (ed.), *Everyday Language: Studies in Ethnomethodology*. New York: Irvington, pp. 7–14.

1984a. On Doing 'Being Ordinary'. In J. M. Atkinson and J. Heritage (eds.), *Structures of Social Action: Studies in Conversation Analysis*. Cambridge University Press, pp. 413–29.

1984b. Notes on Methodology. In J. M. Atkinson and J. Heritage (eds.), *Structures of Social Action: Studies in Conversation Analysis*. Cambridge: Cambridge University Press, pp. 21–7.

1986. Some Considerations of a Story Told in Ordinary Conversations. *Poetics* 15 (1–2):127–38.

[1973] 1987. On the Preferences for Agreement and Contiguity in Sequences in Conversation. In G. Button and J. R. E. Lee (eds.), *Talk and Social Organization*. Clevedon: Multilingual Matters, pp. 54–69.

1992a. *Lectures on Conversation*, Vol. I, ed. Gail Jefferson. Oxford: Blackwell.

1992b. *Lectures on Conversation*, Vol. II, ed. Gail Jefferson. Oxford: Blackwell.

Sacks, H. and Schegloff, E. A. 1973. Opening Up Closings. *Semiotica* 8 (4):289–327.

1979. Two Preferences in the Organization of Reference to Persons and Their Interaction. In G. Psathas (ed.), *Everyday Language: Studies in Ethnomethodology*. New York: Irvington Publishers, pp. 15–21.

Sacks, H., Schegloff, E. A. and Jefferson, G. 1974. A Simplest Systematics for the Organization of Turn-Taking for Conversation. *Language* 50 (4):696–735.

Sadock, J. and Zwicky, A. 1985. Speech Act Distinctions in Syntax. In T. Shopen (ed.), *Language Typology and Syntactic Description,* Vol. I: *Clause Structure*. Cambridge University Press, pp. 155–96.

Schama, S. 2000. *A History of Britain: At the Edge of the World? 3000 BC-AD 1603*. BBC Worldwide.

Schegloff, E. A. 1968. Sequencing in Conversational Openings. *American Anthropologist* 70:1075–95.

1972. Notes on a Conversational Practice: Formulating Place. In D. N. Sudnow (ed.), *Studies in Social Interaction*. New York: Free Press, pp. 75–119.

1979. The Relevance of Repair to Syntax-for-Conversation. In T. Givon (ed.), *Syntax and Semantics,* Vol. 12: *Discourse and Syntax.* New York: Academic Press, pp. 261–86.

1980. Preliminaries to Preliminaries: 'Can I Ask You a Question?' *Sociological Inquiry* 50:104–52.

1982. Discourse as an Interactional Achievement: Some Uses of 'Uh Huh' and Other Things That Come Between Sentences. In D. Tannen (ed.), *Georgetown University Roundtable on Languages and Linguistics 1981: Analyzing Discourse: Text and Talk.* Washington, DC: Georgetown University Press, pp. 71–93.

1984a. On Some Questions and Ambiguities in Conversation. In J. M. Atkinson and J. Heritage (eds.), *Structures of Social Action.* Cambridge University Press, pp. 266–98.

1984b. On Some Gestures' Relation to Talk. In J. M. Atkinson and J. Heritage (eds.), *Structures of Social Action.* Cambridge University Press, pp. 266–98.

1986. The Routine as Achievement. *Human Studies* 9:111–51.

1987a. Recycled Turn Beginnings. In G. Button and J. R. E. Lee (eds.), *Talk and Social Organization.* Clevedon: Multilingual Matters. pp. 70–85.

1987b. Between Macro and Micro: Contexts and Other Connections. In J. Alexander, B. Giesen, R. Munch and N. Smelser (eds.), *The Micro-Macro Link.* Berkeley: University of California Press, pp. 207–34.

1987c. Analyzing Single Episodes of Interaction: An Exercise in Conversation Analysis. *Social Psychology Quarterly,* 50 (2):101–14.

1988a. Goffman and the Analysis of Conversation. In P. Drew and A. Wootton (eds.), *Erving Goffman: Exploring the Interaction Order.* Cambridge: Polity Press, pp. 89–135.

1988b. On an Actual Virtual Servo-Mechanism for Guessing Bad News: A Single Case Conjecture. *Social Problems* 35 (4):442–57.

1989. Reflections on Language, Development, and the Interactional Character of Talk-in-Interaction. In M. H. Bornstein and J. S. Bruner (eds.), *Interaction in Human Development.* New York: Lawrence Erlbaum, pp. 139–53.

1990. On the Organization of Sequences as a Source of 'Coherence' in Talk-in-Interaction. In B. Dorval (ed.), *Conversational Organization and Its Development.* Norwood, NJ: Ablex Publishing Co., pp. 51–77.

1992a. Introduction. In G. Jefferson (ed.), *Harvey Sacks: Lectures on Conversation,* Vol. I. Oxford: Basil Blackwell, pp. ix–lxii.

1992b. Repair After Next Turn: The Last Structurally Provided Defense of Intersubjectivity in Conversation. *American Journal of Sociology* 97 (5):1295–345.

1992c. In Another Context. In A. Duranti and C. Goodwin (eds.), *Rethinking Context: Language as an Interactive Phenomenon.* Cambridge University Press, pp. 191–228.

1993. Reflections on Quantification in the Study of Conversation. *Research on Language and Social Interaction* 26 (1):99–128.

1995a. Discourse as an Interactional Achievement III: The Omnirelevance of Action. *Research on Language and Social Interaction* 28 (3):185–211.

1995b. Parties and Talking Together: Two Ways in Which Numbers Are Significant for Talk-in-Interaction. In P. ten Have and G. Psathas (eds.), *Situated Order: Studies in Social Organization and Embodied Activities.* Washington, DC: University Press of America, pp. 31–42.

1996a. Turn Organization: One Intersection of Grammar and Interaction. In E. Ochs, E. A. Schegloff and S. A. Thompson (eds.), *Interaction and Grammar.* Cambridge University Press, pp. 52–133.

1996b. Some Practices for Referring to Persons in Talk-in-Interaction: A Partial Sketch of a Systematics. In B. A. Fox (ed.), *Studies in Anaphora*. Amsterdam: John Benjamins, pp. 437–85.

1997a. Whose Text? Whose Context? *Discourse and Society* 8 (2):165–87.

1997b. Third Turn Repair. In G. R. Guy, C. Feagin, D. Schiffrin and J. Baugh (eds.), *Towards a Social Science of Language: Papers in Honor of William Labov*, Vol. II: *Social Interaction and Discourse Structures*. Amsterdam: John Benjamins, pp. 31–40.

1997c. Practices and Actions: Boundary Cases of Other-Initiated Repair. *Discourse Processes* 23:499–545.

1998a. Reply to Wetherell. *Discourse and Society* 9 (3):413–16.

1998b. Reflections on Studying Prosody in Talk-in-Interaction. *Language and Speech* 41 (3–4):235–63.

1999. 'Schegloff's Texts' as 'Billig's Data': A Critical Reply. *Discourse and Society* 10 (4):558–72.

2000. Overlapping Talk and the Organization of Turn-Taking for Conversation. *Language in Society* 29 (1):1–63.

2001. Conversation Analysis: A Project in Progress – Increments. Forum Lecture, Linguistic Society of America Linguistics Institute, University of California, Santa Barbara.

2002. Accounts of Conduct in Interaction: Interruption, Overlap and Turn-Taking. In J. H. Turner (ed.), *Handbook of Sociological Theory*. New York: Plenum, pp. 287–321.

2003a. On Conversation Analysis: An Interview with Emanuel A. Schegloff by Světla Čmejrková and Carlo L. Prevignano. In C. L. Prevignano and P. J. Thibault (eds.), *Discussing Conversation Analysis: The Work of Emanuel A. Schegloff*. Amsterdam: John Benjamins, pp. 11–55.

2003b. Conversation Analysis and Communication Disorders. In C. Goodwin (ed.), *Conversation and Brain Damage*. Oxford University Press, pp. 21–55.

2003c. The Surfacing of the Suppressed. In P. Glenn, C. LeBaron and J. Mandelbaum (eds.), *Studies in Language and Social Interaction: A Festschrift in Honor of Robert Hopper*. Mahwah, NJ: Lawrence Erlbaum, pp. 531–40.

2004a. On Dispensability. *Research on Language and Social Interaction* 37(2):95–149.

2004b. Whistling in the Dark: Notes from the Other Side of Liminality. Proceedings of the Twelfth Annual Symposium about Language and Society, Austin. *Texas Linguistic Forum* 48:17–30.

2005. On Complainability. *Social Problems* 52 (3):449–76.

2006. Interaction: The Infrastructure for Social Institutions, the Natural Ecological Niche for Language and the Arena in which Culture is Enacted. In N. J. Enfield and S. C. Levinson (eds.), *Roots of Human Sociality: Culture, Cognition and Interaction*. Oxford: Berg, pp. 70–96.

2007a. *Sequence Organization in Interaction: A Primer in Conversation Analysis*. Cambridge University Press.

2007b. A Tutorial on Membership Categorization. *Journal of Pragmatics* 39:462–82.

2009. One Perspective on Conversation Analysis: Comparative Perspectives. In J. Sidnell (ed.), *Conversation Analysis: Comparative Perspectives*. Cambridge University Press, pp. 357–406.

2013. Ten Operations in Self-initiated, Same Turn Repair. In M. Hayashi, G. Raymond and J. Sidnell (eds.), *Conversational Repair and Human Understanding*. Cambridge University Press, pp. 41–70.

Schegloff, E. A. and Sacks, H. 1973. Opening Up Closings. *Semiotica* 8:289–327.

Schegloff, E. A., Jefferson, G. and Sacks, H. 1977. The Preference for Self-Correction in the Organization of Repair in Conversation. *Language* 53 (2):361–82.

Schenkein, J. (ed.) 1978. *Studies in the Organization of Conversational Interaction*. New York: Academic Press.

Searle, J. R. 1965. What Is a Speech Act? In M. Black (ed.), *Philosophy in America*. London: Allen and Unwin.

1969. *Speech Acts: An Essay in the Philosophy of Language*. Cambridge University Press.

1975. Indirect Speech Acts. In P. Cole and J. L. Morgan (eds.), *Syntax and Semantics*, Vol. III: *Speech Acts*. New York: Academic Press, pp. 59–82.

Selting, M. 1996. Prosody as an Activity-Type Distinctive Cue in Conversation: The Case of So-Called 'Astonished' Questions in Repair Initiation. In E. Couper-Kuhlen and M. Selting (eds.), *Prosody in Conversation: Interactional Studies*. Cambridge University Press.

2000. The Construction of Units in Conversational Talk. *Language in Society* 29 (4):477–517.

Selting, M. and Couper-Kuhlen, E. (eds.) 2001. *Studies in Interactional Linguistics*. Amsterdam: John Benjamins.

Selting, M., Auer, P., Barth-Weingarten, D., Bergmann, J., Bergmann, P., Birkner, K., Couper-Kuhlen, E., Deppermann, A., Gilles, P., Günthner, S., Hartung, M., Kern, F., Mertzlufft, C., Meyer, C., Morek, M., Oberzaucher, F., Peters, J., Quasthoff, U., Schütte, W., Stukenbrock, A. and Uhmann, S. 2011. A System for Transcribing Talk-in-Interaction: GAT2. Gesprächsanalytisches Transkriptionssystem 2 (GAT 2). Gesprächsforschung. *Zeitschrift zur verbalen Interaktion* 12:1–51. Translated and adapted for English by Elizabeth Couper-Kuhlen and Dagmar Barth-Weingarten. Downloaded on 26 May 2015 from www.gespraechsforschung-ozs.de/heft2011/px-gat2-englisch.pdf.

Senft, G. 2007. Reference and 'Référence Dangereuse' to Persons in Kilivila: An Overview and a Case Study. In N. Enfield and T. Stivers (eds.), *Person Reference in Interaction: Linguistic, Cultural, and Social Perspectives*. Cambridge University Press, pp. 309–37.

2010. *The Trobriand Islanders' Ways of Speaking*. Berlin: De Gruyter.

Seo, M.-S. and Koshik, I. 2010. A Conversation Analytic Study of Gestures that Engender Repair in ESL Conversational Tutoring. *Journal of Pragmatics* 42 (8):2219–39.

Sicoli, M. A., Stivers, T., Enfield, N. J. and Levinson, S. C. 2014. Marked Initial Pitch in Questions Signals Marked Communicative Function. *Language & Speech* 58 (1).

Sidnell, J. 2001. Conversational Turn-Taking in a Caribbean English Creole. *Journal of Pragmatics* 33 (8):1263–90.

(ed.) 2007. Repairing Person Reference in a Small Caribbean Community. In N. Enfield and T. Stivers (eds.), *Person Reference in Interaction: Linguistic, Cultural, and Social Perspectives*. Cambridge University Press, pp. 281–308.

2008. Alternate and Complementary Perspectives on Language and Social Life: The Organization of Repair in Two Caribbean Communities. *Journal of Sociolinguistics* 12 (4):477–503.

(ed.) 2009. *Conversation Analysis: Comparative Perspectives*. Cambridge University Press.

2010. *Conversation Analysis: An Introduction*. Oxford: Wiley-Blackwell.

2013. Basic Conversation Analytic Methods. In J. Sidnell and T. Stivers (eds.), *The Handbook of Conversation Analysis*. Chichester: Wiley-Blackwell, pp. 77–99.

Sidnell, J. and Barnes, R. 2013. Alternative, Subsequent Descriptions. In M. Hayashi, G. Raymond and J. Sidnell (eds.), *Conversational Repair and Human Understanding*. Cambridge University Press, pp. 322–42.

Sidnell, J. and Stivers, T. (eds.) 2013. *The Handbook of Conversation Analysis*. Chichester: Wiley-Blackwell.

Sikveland, R. O. and Ogden, R. A. 2012. Holding Gestures Across Turns: Moments to Generate Shared Understanding. *Gesture* 12 (2):166–99.

Silverman, D. 1997. *Discourses of Counselling: HIV Counselling as Social Interaction*. London: Sage.

1998. *Harvey Sacks: Social Science and Conversation Analysis*. Cambridge: Polity Press.

Simmel, G. 1959. *Georg Simmel 1858–1918: A Collection of Essays, with Translations and a Bibliography*, ed. K. H. Wolff. Columbus: Ohio State University Press.

Sleeth, C. R. 1982. The OED. *Times Literary Supplement*, 24 September, 1036.

Sorjonen, M.-L. 2001. Simple Answers to Polar Questions: The Case of Finnish. In M. Selting and E. Couper-Kuhlen (eds.), *Studies in Interactional Linguistics*. Amsterdam: John Benjamins, pp. 405–31.

Sperber, D. and Wilson, D. 1982. Mutual Knowledge and Relevance in Theories of Comprehension. In N. Smith (ed.), *Mutual Knowledge*. New York: Academic Press, pp. 61–131.

1995. *Relevance: Communication and Cognition*. Oxford: Blackwell.

Stenström, A.-B. 1984. *Questions and Responses in English Conversation*. Malmö: CWK Gleerup.

Stevanovic, M. and Peräkylä, A. 2012. Deontic Authority in Interaction: The Right to Announce, Propose, and Decide. *Research on Language and Social Interaction* 45 (3):297–321.

2014. Three Orders in the Organization of Human Action: On the Interface Between Knowledge, Power, and Emotion in Interaction and Social Relations. *Language in Society* 43 (2):185–207.

Stivers, T. 2004. 'No No No' and Other Types of Multiple Sayings in Social Interaction. *Human Communication Research* 30 (2):260–93.

2005. Modified Repeats: One Method for Asserting Primary Rights from Second Position. *Research on Language and Social Interaction* 38(2):131–58.

2007. Alternative Recognitionals in Person Reference. In N. Enfield and T. Stivers (eds.), *Person Reference in Interaction: Linguistic, Cultural, and Social Perspectives*. Cambridge University Press, pp. 73–96.

2010. An Overview of the Question-Response System in American English Conversation. *Journal of Pragmatics* 42:2772–81.

2015. Is Conversation Built for Two? Plenary Address at the 14th International Pragmatics Association Conference, Antwerp.

Stivers, T. and Hayashi, M. 2010. Transformative Answers: One Way to Resist a Question's Constraints. *Language in Society* 39 (1):1–25.

Stivers, T. and Robinson, J. D. 2006. A Preference for Progressivity in Interaction. *Language in Society* 35 (3):367–92.

Stivers, T. and Rossano, F. 2010. Mobilizing Response. *Research on Language and Social Interaction* 43 (1):3–31.

Stivers, T., Enfield, N. J., Brown, P., Englert, C., Hayashi, M., Heinemann, T., Hoymann, G., Rossano, F., de Ruiter, J.P., Yoon, K. and Levinson, S. C. 2009. Universals and Cultural Variation in Turn-taking in Conversation. *Proceedings of the National Academy of Sciences* 106 (26):10587–92.

Stivers, T., Enfield, N. J. and Levinson, S. C. 2007. Person Reference in Interaction. In N. J. Enfield and T. Stivers (eds.), *Person Reference in Interaction: Linguistic, Cultural, and Social Perspectives*. Cambridge University Press, pp. 1–20.

2010. Question–Response Sequences in Conversation Across Ten Languages. *Journal of Pragmatics* [Special Issue] 42 (10):2615–860.

Stivers, T., Mondada, L. and Steensig, J. 2011. *The Morality of Knowledge in Conversation*. Cambridge University Press.

Streeck, J. 1993. Gesture as Communication I: Its Coordination with Gaze and Speech. *Communication Monographs* 60:275–99.

Streeck, J. and Hartge, U. 1992. Previews: Gestures at the Transition Place. In P. Auer and A. Di Luzio (eds.), *The Contextualization of Language*. Amsterdam: John Benjamins, pp. 135–58.

Striano, T., Henning, A. and Stahl, D. 2006. Sensitivity to Interpersonal Timing at 3 and 6 Months of Age. *Interaction Studies* 7:251–71.

Sugawara, Kazuyoshi, 1996. Some Methodological Issues for the Analysis of Everyday Conversations among the IGui. *African Study Monographs* 22:145–64.

1998. The 'Egalitarian' Attitude in Everyday Conversations among the IGui. In A. Bank (ed.), *The Proceedings of the Khoisan Identities and Cultural Heritage Conference*. Cape Town: Infosource.

Svennevig, J. 2008. Trying the Easiest Solution First in Other-initiation of Repair. *Journal of Pragmatics* 40 (2):333–48.

Sweetser, E. E. 1990. *From Etymology to Pragmatics: Metaphorical and Cultural Aspects of Semantic Structure*. Cambridge University Press.

2006. Looking at Space to Study Mental Spaces: Co-speech Gesture as a Crucial Data Source in Cognitive Linguistics. In M. Gonzalez-Marquez, I. Mittleberg, S. Coulson and M. Spivey (eds.), *Methods in Cognitive Linguistics*. Amsterdam: John Benjamins, pp. 203–26.

Szczepek Reed, B. 2004. Turn-Final Intonation Revisited. In E. Couper-Kuhlen and C. Ford (eds.), *Sound Patterns in Interaction: Cross-Linguistic Studies from Conversation*. Amsterdam: John Benjamins, pp. 97–117.

Szczepek Reed, B. and Raymond, G. (eds.) 2013. *Units of Talk:Units of Action*. Amsterdam: John Benjamins.

Taleghani-Nikazm, C. 1998. Politeness in Persian Interaction: The Preference Format of Offers in Persian. *Cross-Roads of Language, Interaction and Culture* 1:3–11.

Tanaka, H. 1999. *Turn-Taking in Japanese Conversation: A Study in Grammar and Interaction*. Amsterdam: John Benjamins.

2000. Turn Projection in Japanese Talk-in-Interaction. *Research on Language and Social Interaction* 33 (1):1–38.

2004. Prosody for Marking Transition Relevance Places in Japanese Conversation: The Case of Turns Unmarked by Utterance-Final Objects. In E. Couper-Kuhlen and C. E. Ford (eds.), *Sound Patterns in Interaction: Cross-Linguistic Studies from Conversation*. Amsterdam: John Benjamins, pp. 63–96.

Tarplee, C. 1991. Working on Talk: Interactions Between Adults and Young Children During Picture Book Labelling Sequences. Paper Presented at a Conference on Current Work in Ethnomethodology and Conversation Analysis, Amsterdam.

Terasaki, A. 1976. Pre-announcement Sequences in Conversation, *Social Science Working Papers* no. 99, School of Social Science. University of California, Irvine.

2004. Pre-announcement Sequences in Conversation. In G. H. Lerner (ed.), *Conversation Analysis: Studies from the First Generation*. Amsterdam: John Benjamins, pp. 171–224.

Thompson, S. A. and Couper-Kuhlen, E. 2005. The Clause as a Locus of Grammar and Interaction, *Discourse Studies* 7 (4–5): 481–505. (Reprinted in *Language and Linguistics* 6 (4):807–37.)

Thompson, S. A., Fox, B. A. and Couper-Kuhlen, E. 2015. *Grammar in Everyday Talk: Building Responsive Actions*. Cambridge University Press.

Torreira, F., Bögels, S. and Levinson, S. C. 2015. Breathing for Answering: The Time Course of Response Planning in Conversation. *Frontiers in Psychology* 6:1–11.

Traugott, E. C. 2010. Dialogic Contexts as Motivations for Syntactic Change. In R. A. Cloutier, A. M. Hamilton-Brehm and W. Kretzschmar (eds.), *Variation and Change in English Grammar and Lexicon*. Berlin: Mouton de Gruyter, pp. 11–27.

Traum, D. 1994. *A Computational Theory of Grounding in Natural Language Conversation*. Technical Report 545 and PhD Thesis, University of Rochester, Rochester, New York.

Uhmann, S. 2001. Some Arguments for the Relevance of Syntax to Same-Sentence Self-Repair in Everyday German Conversation. In M. Selting and E. Couper-Kuhlen (eds.), *Studies in Interactional Linguistics*. Amsterdam: John Benjamins, pp. 373–404.

Ultan, R. 1978. Some General Characteristics of Interrogative Systems. In G. Greenberg (ed.), *Universals of Human Language*, Vol. IV: *Syntax*. Palo Alto, CA: Stanford University Press, pp. 211–48.

Van Dijk, T. A. 2007. The Study of Discourse: An Introduction. In T. A. van Dijk (ed.), *Discourse Studies*, 5 Vols. Sage Benchmarks in Discourse Studies. London: Sage, pp. xix–xlii.

Vazquez-Carranza, A. 2013. Sequential Markers in Mexican Spanish Talk: A Conversation-Analytic Study. Unpublished PhD dissertation, University of Essex.

Verhoeven, J. C. 1993. An Interview with Erving Goffman, 1980. *Research on Language and Social Interaction* 26 (3):317–48.

Vinkhuysen, E. and Szymanski, M. H. 2005. Would You Like to Do it Yourself? Service Requests and Their Non-Granting Responses. In K. Richards and P. Seedhouse (eds.), *Applying Conversation Analysis*. Basingstoke: Palgrave Macmillan, pp. 91–106.

Walker, G. 2004. On Some Interactional and Phonetic Properties of Increments to Turns in Talk-in-Interaction. In E. Couper-Kuhlen and C. E. Ford (eds.), *Sound Patterns in Interaction: Cross-Linguistic Studies from Conversation*. Amsterdam: John Benjamins, pp. 147–69.

2010. The Phonetic Constitution of a Turn-Holding Practice: Rush-throughs in English Talk-in-Interaction. In D. Barth-Weingarten, E. Reber and M. Selting (eds.), *Prosody in Interaction*. Amsterdam: John Benjamins, pp. 51–72.

2013. Phonetics and Prosody in Conversation. In J. Sidnell and T. Stivers (eds.), *The Handbook of Conversation Analysis*. Chichester: Wiley-Blackwell, pp. 455–74.

Walsh, Michael, 1991. Conversational Styles and Intercultural Communication: An Example from Northern Australia. *Australian Journal of Communication* 18 (1): 1–12.

Walton, D. 1997. *Appeal to Expert Opinion: Arguments from Authority*. University Park: Pennsylvania State University Press.

Watts, R. J. 2003. *Politeness*. Cambridge University Press.

Weber, E. 1993. *Varieties of Questions in English Conversation*. Amsterdam: John Benjamins.

Weidner, M. 2015. Telling Somebody What to Tell: 'Proszę mi powiedzieć' in Polish Doctor–Patient Interaction. *Journal of Pragmatics* 78:70–83.

Wells, W. H. G. and Macfarlane, S. 1998. Prosody as an Interactional Resource: Turn-Projection and Overlap. *Language and Speech* 41 (3–4):265–94.

Wells, W. H. G. and Peppé, S. 1996. Ending Up in Ulster: Prosody and Turn-taking in English Dialects. In E. Couper-Kuhlen and M. Selting (eds.), *Prosody in Conversation: Interactional Studies*. Cambridge University Press, pp. 101–30.

Whalen, J. and Zimmerman, D. H. 1998. Observations on the Display and Management of Emotion in Naturally Occurring Activities: The Case of 'Hysteria' in Calls to 9-1-1. *Social Psychology Quarterly* 61 (2):141–59.

Wilkinson, S. and Kitzinger, C. 2006. Surprise as an Interactional Achievement: Reaction Tokens in Conversation. *Social Psychology Quarterly* 69 (2):150–82.

Wilkinson, S. and Weatherall, A. 2011. Insertion Repair. *Research on Language and Social Interaction* 44 (1):65–91.

Wilson, D. and Matsui, T. 1998. Recent Approaches to Bridging: Truth, Coherence, Relevance. *UCL Working Papers in Linguistics* 10:1–28.

Wilson, T. and Zimmerman, D. H. 1986. The Structure of Silence Between Turns in Two-Party Conversation. *Discourse Processes* 9 (4):375–90.

Wittgenstein, L. 1953. *Philosophical Investigations*, trans. G. E. M. Anscombe. Oxford: Blackwell.

Wodak, R. (ed.) 2013. *Critical Discourse Analysis*, 4 Vols. London: Sage.

Wouk, F. 2005. The Syntax of Repair in Indonesian. *Discourse Studies* 7 (2):237–58.

Wright, M. 2011. On Clicks in English Talk-in-Interaction. *Journal of the International Phonetic Association* 41 (2):207–29.

Wu, R.-J. R. 2004. *Stance in Talk: A Conversation Analysis of Mandarin Final Particles*. Amsterdam: John Benjamins.

2006. Initiating Repair and Beyond: The Use of Two Repeat-Formatted Repair Initiations in Mandarin Conversation. *Discourse Processes* 41 (1):67–109.

2009. Repetition in the Initiation of Repair. In J. Sidnell (ed.), *Conversation Analysis: Comparative Perspectives*. Cambridge University Press, pp. 31–59.

Yoon, K. E. 2010. Questions and Responses in Korean Conversation. *Journal of Pragmatics* 42 (10):2782–98.

Žegarac, V. and Clark, B. 1999. Phatic Interpretations and Phatic Communication. *Journal of Linguistics* 35 (2):321–46.

Zimmerman, D. H. 1984. Talk and Its Occasion: The Case of Calling the Police. In D. Schiffrin (ed.), *Meaning, Form and Use in Context: Linguistic Applications.* Washington, DC: Georgetown University Press, pp. 210–28.

Zinken, J. and Ogiermann, E. 2011. How to Propose an Action as Objectively Necessary: The Case of Polish *Trzeba x* ('One Needs to x'). *Research on Language and Social Interaction* 44(3):263–87.

2013. Responsibility and Action: Invariants and Diversity of Requests for Objects in British English and Polish Interaction. *Research on Language and Social Interaction* 46(3):256–76.

Author index

General index

RAW MILK
Balance Between Hazards
and Benefits

Edited by

LUÍS AUGUSTO NERO

ANTONIO FERNANDES DE CARVALHO

ACADEMIC PRESS

An imprint of Elsevier

Academic Press is an imprint of Elsevier
125 London Wall, London EC2Y 5AS, United Kingdom
525 B Street, Suite 1650, San Diego, CA 92101, United States
50 Hampshire Street, 5th Floor, Cambridge, MA 02139, United States
The Boulevard, Langford Lane, Kidlington, Oxford OX5 1GB, United Kingdom

Notices
Knowledge and best practice in this field are constantly changing. As new research and experience
broaden our understanding, changes in research methods, professional practices, or medical treatment
may become necessary.

Practitioners and researchers must always rely on their own experience and knowledge in evaluating
and using any information, methods, compounds, or experiments described herein. In using such
information or methods they should be mindful of their own safety and the safety of others, including
parties for whom they have a professional responsibility.

To the fullest extent of the law, neither the Publisher nor the authors, contributors, or editors, assume
any liability for any injury and/or damage to persons or property as a matter of products liability,
negligence or otherwise, or from any use or operation of any methods, products, instructions, or ideas
contained in the material herein.

British Library Cataloguing-in-Publication Data
A catalogue record for this book is available from the British Library

Library of Congress Cataloging-in-Publication Data
A catalog record for this book is available from the Library of Congress

ISBN: 978-0-12-810530-6

For Information on all Academic Press publications
visit our website at https://www.elsevier.com/books-and-journals

Working together
to grow libraries in
developing countries

www.elsevier.com • www.bookaid.org

Publisher: Andre Gerhard Wolff
Acquisition Editor: Megan Ball
Editorial Project Manager: Jaclyn Truesdell
Production Project Manager: Nilesh Kumar Shah
Cover Designer: Christian Bilbow

Typeset by MPS Limited, Chennai, India

CONTENTS

LIST OF CONTRIBUTORS

Maura Pinheiro Alves
Departamento de Tecnologia de Alimentos, Universidade Federal de Viçosa, Viçosa, Brazil

Caroline Andrade Tomaszewski
National Agricultural Laboratory (LANAGRO/RS), Ministry of Agriculture, Livestock and Food Supply (MAPA), São José, Brazil

Ton Baars
Research Institute of Organic Agriculture (FiBL), Frick, Switzerland

Fabiano Barreto
National Agricultural Laboratory (LANAGRO/RS), Ministry of Agriculture, Livestock and Food Supply (MAPA), São José, Brazil

Luciano S. Bersot
Universidade Federal do Paraná, Setor Palotina, Palotina, Brazil

Margherita Caccamo
CoRFiLaC, Ragusa, Italy

Tamara Castilhos
National Agricultural Laboratory (LANAGRO/RS), Ministry of Agriculture, Livestock and Food Supply (MAPA), São José, Brazil

Sanely L. da Costa
Departamento de Veterinária, Universidade Federal de Viçosa, Viçosa, Brazil

Paulo H.F. da Silva
ICB—Departamento de Nutrição, Universidade Federal de Juiz de Fora, Juiz de Fora, Brazil

Antonio F. de Carvalho
Departamento de Tecnologia de Alimentos, Universidade Federal de Viçosa, Viçosa, Brazil

Ali Demirci
Department of Agricultural and Biological Engineering, Pennsylvania State University, University Park, PA, United States

Robert E. Graves
Department of Agricultural and Biological Engineering, Pennsylvania State University, University Park, PA, United States

Colin Hill
School of Microbiology, University College Cork, Cork, Ireland; Department of Microbiology, University College Cork, Cork, Ireland; APC Microbiome Institute, University College Cork, Cork, Ireland; APC Microbiome Ireland, Cork, Ireland

Daniel R. Hillesheim
National Agricultural Laboratory (LANAGRO/RS), Ministry of Agriculture, Livestock and Food Supply (MAPA), São José, Brazil

Louíse Jank
National Agricultural Laboratory (LANAGRO/RS), Ministry of Agriculture, Livestock and Food Supply (MAPA), São José, Brazil

Abelardo Silva Júnior
Departamento de Veterinária, Universidade Federal de Viçosa, Viçosa, Brazil

Christopher H. Knight
Department of Veterinary and Animal Sciences, University of Copenhagen, Copenhagen, Denmark

Giuseppe Licitra
Department of Agriculture, Nutrition and Environment, University of Catania, Catania, Italy

Magna C. Lima
Departamento de Veterinária, Universidade Federal de Viçosa, Viçosa, Brazil

Sylvie Lortal
INRA, Agrocampus Ouest, UMR1253 Science et Technologie du lait et de l'œuf, Rennes, France

Lisbeth Meunier-Goddik
Department of Food Science and Technology, Oregon State University, Corvallis, OR, United States

Maria A.S. Moreira
Departamento de Veterinária, Universidade Federal de Viçosa, Viçosa, Brazil

Luís A. Nero
Departamento de Veterinária, Universidade Federal de Viçosa, Viçosa, Brazil

Vanísia C.D. Oliveira
ICB—Departamento de Nutrição, Universidade Federal de Juiz de Fora, Juiz de Fora, Brazil

Tom F. O'Callaghan
Teagasc Food Research Centre, Moorepark, Fermoy, Ireland; Department of Microbiology, University College Cork, Cork, Ireland

Juliano G. Pereira
Universidade Federal do Pampa, Uruguaiana, Rio Grande do Sul, Brazil

Luana M. Perin
Departamento de Veterinária, Universidade Federal de Viçosa, Viçosa, Brazil

Ítalo Tuler Perrone
Departamento de Tecnologia de Alimentos, Universidade Federal de Viçosa, Viçosa, Brazil; Faculdade de Farmácia, Universidade Federal de Juiz de Fora, Juiz de Fora, Brazil

Virendra M. Puri
Department of Agricultural and Biological Engineering, Pennsylvania State University, University Park, PA, United States

Renata B. Rau
National Agricultural Laboratory (LANAGRO/RS), Ministry of Agriculture, Livestock and Food Supply (MAPA), São José, Brazil

Isis Rodrigues Toledo Renhe
Instituto de Laticínios Cândido Tostes, EPAMIG, Juiz de Fora, Brazil

Cristina Ribeiro
National Agricultural Laboratory (LANAGRO/RS), Ministry of Agriculture, Livestock and Food Supply (MAPA), São José, Brazil

R. Paul Ross
School of Microbiology, University College Cork, Cork, Ireland; APC Microbiome Ireland, Cork, Ireland; Department of Microbiology, University College Cork, Cork, Ireland; APC Microbiome Institute, University College Cork, Cork, Ireland; College of Science Engineering and Food Science, University College Cork, Cork, Ireland

Pierre Schuck
STLO, Agrocampus Ouest, UMR1253, INRA, Rennes, France

Catherine Stanton
Teagasc Food Research Centre, Moorepark, Fermoy, Ireland; APC Microbiome Institute, University College Cork, Cork, Ireland; APC Microbiome Ireland, Cork, Ireland

Rodrigo Stephani
Departamento de Química, Universidade Federal de Juiz de Fora, Juiz de Fora, Brazil

Ivan Sugrue
School of Microbiology, University College Cork, Cork, Ireland; Teagasc Food Research Centre, Moorepark, Fermoy, Ireland; APC Microbiome Ireland, Cork, Ireland; Department of Microbiology, University College Cork, Cork, Ireland

Guilherme M. Tavares
Faculdade de Engenharia de Alimentos, Universidade de Campinas, Campinas, Brazil

Tânia Tavares
LEPABE, Faculdade de Engenharia da Universidade do Porto, Porto, Portugal; LAQV/REQUIMTE, Departamento de Ciências Químicas, Laboratório de Bromatologia e Hidrologia, Faculdade de Farmácia da Universidade do Porto, Porto, Portugal

Conor Tobin
School of Microbiology, University College Cork, Cork, Ireland; Teagasc Food Research Centre, Moorepark, Fermoy, Ireland; APC Microbiome Ireland, Cork, Ireland

Svetoslav D. Todorov
Departamento de Veterinária, Universidade Federal de Viçosa, Viçosa, Brazil;
Food Research Center (FoRC), Department of Food and Experimental
Nutrition, Faculty of Pharmaceutical Sciences, University of São Paulo, São
Paulo, Brazil

Joy Waite-Cusic
Department of Food Science and Technology, Oregon State University,
Corvallis, OR, United States

Xinmiao Wang
Department of Food Science and Biotechnology, Zhejiang Gongshang
University, Hangzhou, China

Francisco Xavier Malcata
LEPABE, Faculdade de Engenharia da Universidade do Porto, Porto, Portugal;
Departamento de Engenharia Química, Faculdade de Engenharia da
Universidade do Porto, Porto, Portugal

CHAPTER 1

Raw Milk Physiology

Christopher H. Knight
Department of Veterinary and Animal Sciences, University of Copenhagen, Copenhagen, Denmark

1.1 INTRODUCTION

Consumption of raw milk is contentious and often ill-informed. Is raw milk "better" than other milk? Is it more hazardous? Raw milk is generally taken to be milk that has not been pasteurized, but the comparison that consumers will draw is usually with a processed milk that is not only pasteurized but also standardized, homogenized, and semi-skimmed. Although raw milk is not processed in a technological sense, it is subject to biological processing. The aqueous exocrine secretion of the mammary epithelial cell (milk) is subject to enzymatic and other modification during storage in the udder, during the milking process, once it reaches the farm's bulk tank, when mixed with milk from other farms, and during packaging and distribution to consumers. My brief in this short chapter is to describe the physiology of "raw milk" (of course, lactation physiology remains the same whatever product is being consumed) and I shall start by considering the origins and purpose of lactation, then turn to consider the mammary gland itself. The development of the mammary gland during juvenile life and, especially, during gestation is followed by lactogenesis (the initiation of secretion), secretion itself, storage of the product prior to removal, and then milk ejection. During the lactation secretory cells are subject to developmental remodeling (especially just after parturition), repeated mechanical disruption during alveolar filling and emptying, potential attack by pathogenic bacteria, and finally, at the end of the lactation, regression and involution. All of these processes have been extensively research and reviewed before, and rather than simply repeating that exercise I shall try to identify those elements of lactation physiology that are most relevant to safe consumption of raw milk and also to be prospective rather than retrospective wherever possible.

Raw Milk
DOI: https://doi.org/10.1016/B978-0-12-810530-6.00001-8

1

1.2 HISTORICAL CONTEXT AND THE EVOLUTION OF LACTATION AS A MULTIPURPOSE PHYSIOLOGICAL SURVIVAL MECHANISM

The teaching of lactation physiology is generally rudimentary, restricted to a short text at the end of a reproductive biology chapter, but the mammary gland is used as a model system by many scientific disciplines. As a consequence, literature searches that include the term "lactation physiology" return an incredibly large amount of recent literature focused on molecular investigations of mammary biology and breast cancer, but relatively little mechanistic explanation of lactation as a biological process. Fortunately the older literature, most of which is still valid, was excellently reviewed relatively recently in a series of papers published in the *Journal of Mammary Gland Biology and Neoplasia* (hereafter JMGBN; Neville, 2009). A good grasp of the topic can also be gained from the suitably short but informative textbook *Physiology of Lactation* (Mepham, 1977a) or the more recent and comprehensive "Lactation and the Mammary Gland" (Akers, 2002). For the purposes of this chapter, the different physiological processes that together constitute lactation are shown in Fig. 1.1.

There is debate regarding the evolutionary origins of lactation, some holding that the porous nature of synapsid's eggs drove the need for an aqueous skin secretion (Oftedal, 2012), while others believe that the mammary gland has evolved as a specialized component of the immune system (Mclellan et al., 2008). The reason for mentioning this is to highlight the multitasking nature of lactation, for it is quite evident that milk provides a triad of nutrition, protection, and hydration. The relative importance of these functions will vary to some extent from species to species, a simple example being the transfer of passive immunity in colostrum, which is much less essential in humans than in cows because of transplacental transfer to the human fetus *prepartum*. This reveals another important aspect, namely, the interaction and interdependency of gestation and lactation. From an evolutionary point of view, some species have attached similar importance to each of these two reproductive phases whereas other have not; marsupials give birth to incredibly immature young and have an almost total reliance on lactation (the pouch has famously been described as "a womb with a view"; Renfree, 2006), while at the other end of the spectrum young guinea pigs are born so mature that lactation is almost an optional accessory. In most species the

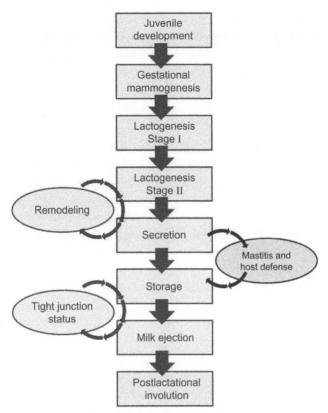

Figure 1.1 An overview of the different physiological processes that together constitute lactation.

mammary gland develops during pregnancy in order to meet the requirements of the neonate (not the mother!) so endocrine mechanisms have evolved to ensure that the fetus(es) can influence mammary growth and hence their own destiny (Knight, 1982). The secretion of the mammary gland contains species-appropriate amounts of energy in the form of fat and carbohydrate, and once again the importance attached to each will vary (Oftedal, 1984). Breastmilk supplies the majority of energy for the slow-growing human neonate as carbohydrate (lactose), while the milk of pinnipeds (seals) is incredibly rich in fat to provide for rapid growth and thermoregulatory insulation. Cow's milk is intermediate. Milk protein (caseins and whey proteins) also varies across species, the most notable feature being the low amounts present in breastmilk and equid milks. That is not to say that the importance of milk protein is less in these species: A major feature of proteins and especially peptides present in different milks is their regulatory role or bioactivity, which may require only trace quantities. "May" is an important word. On the one hand, minor components in any food can sometimes elicit major allergic or other reactions, but on the other hand, the digestive system is designed to digest, in this case to individual amino acids. Interest in health-promoting bioactivities in milk has been intense for several decades (see, e.g., Weaver, 1997), but suffice to say that the European Food Safety Authority has not yet licensed any milk product as having health-promoting effects. A recent review of breastmilk composition and bioactivity emphasizes the potential impact of oligosaccharides as probiotics (Andreas et al., 2015) and the potential biological role of specific individual fatty acids, in particular conjugated linoleic acid (CLA) (reviewed by Kim et al., 2016) demonstrates that milk is a diverse food with a broad spectrum of *potential* bioactive effects, and that is without even considering all of its minerals and trace elements. A detailed description is certainly beyond the scope of this chapter, but we shall consider how the appearance of bioactive factors might be affected by different physiological mechanisms. Another important property of milk is the way in which the nutrient is delivered, calcium being a case in point; nanoclusters of calcium phosphate are present as substructures in casein micelles at concentrations well above their solubility (Lenton et al., 2015). Occasionally a particular milk might have a specific or even unique characteristic. For instance, there is growing evidence that camel milk can deliver significant quantities of biologically available insulin (Meena et al., 2016).

Having decided to secrete milk and agreed on what to put into it, for how long should lactation continue? The consensus appears to be around 10 months in cattle and at least 6 months in women, but the physiological reality is that this is another "flexible feast" (Knight, 2001). For species that have no alternative way of feeding their young, the answer has to be "for as long as the neonate needs milk," and where ungulates are concerned this could vary enormously as a result of food availability (seasonally breeding deer will "skip" breeding for a full year if conditions are bad, since the fawn requires to be nursed for longer; Loudon et al 1983). This introduces another concept that is important for any discussion of raw milk. The biologically intended consumer of milk is the neonate, but in this book we are mainly considering older consumers. The nutritional requirements of the human neonate are normally well met by breastmilk, although there is sometimes debate about the detail (Knight, 2010) and increasing recognition that human lactation can fail (Marasco, 2014). The optimal requirements of older consumers will be very different and dependent on many lifestyle-related factors, especially other diet and exercise. There has long been an epidemiologically based belief that consumption of milk, and especially milk fat, is detrimental to health, in particular cardiovascular health. More recent reexamination of the evidence has shown this to be untrue (Thorning et al., 2016); milk is good for you!

1.3 THE PHYSIOLOGY OF MAMMARY GLAND DEVELOPMENT

1.3.1 Juvenile Development

The process of mammary growth and development is known as mammogenesis and mainly occurs during gestation under the stimulatory influence of ovarian steroids and placental lactogen. Nevertheless, there are "critical windows" of mammary development occurring earlier in life (Knight and Sorensen, 2001), which are related to the complex multicellular nature of the gland. At birth and well into juvenile life, the gland consists of relatively isolated ductular epithelial tissue lying in a fat pad. The mammary epithelium will not grow outside of that fat pad, and starting in early life there is clear evidence of regulatory interaction between the mesenchymal elements of the fat pad (and the extracellular matrix that is formed from it) and the epithelial cells of the ducts (Kratochwil, 1986; Faulkin and Deome, 1960). Later, however, an excess of adipose tissue has local inhibitory effects on the growth of the duct system. This has been demonstrated in the prepubertal heifer where it is proposed to be due to disturbance of the growth hormone (GH): insulin-like growth factor axis (Sejrsen et al., 2000). Whether this growth inhibition fully explains the subsequent reduction in milk yield observed in overfed heifers is open to debate; the udder develops progressively but slowly over a long period of time and it is not always possible to discount age-related differences in animals that grow at different rates (Daniels et al., 2009). Nevertheless, there is clear evidence in obese mice of an inhibitory effect of excess adipose deposition in the mammary fat pad on both the development and subsequent function of the secretory tissue (Flint et al., 2005). Given the growing concern surrounding lactation inadequacy in obese women (reviewed by Nommsen-Rivers, 2016) this is an area deserving of further investigation.

1.3.2 Gestational Mammogenesis

In all species studied there is exponential proliferation of mammary epithelial cells during gestation, and in most species this constitutes by far the major growth phase (significant exceptions are marsupials in which most development happens *postpartum* stimulated by local mechanisms triggered by suckling). This pattern of growth was first quantified for ruminant dairy species in goats (Fowler et al., 1990) and later in cows (reviewed in Capuco and Ellis, 2013). Classical postwar studies of the endocrine control of mammogenesis were included in the 2009 special issue of JMGBN (Forsyth and Neville, 2009). The "mammogenic complex" was established to be estrogen, GH, and adrenocortical hormones for promoting ductal outgrowth with the addition of progesterone and prolactin to stimulate lobuloalveolar (secretory tissue) proliferation. Later it became apparent that placental lactogen, a prolactin-like hormone produced by the fetoplacental unit of many species, could substitute for prolactin (Hayden et al., 1979). Berryhill et al. (2016) have recently reviewed the actions of estrogen, considered to be the major mammogen, and also shown that dietary factors (in particular CLA) can also have a major effect. Ultimately, for mammary growth to occur there must be proliferation of epithelial cells. Curiously, estrogen is a mammogen, but not apparently a mitogen; in vitro studies have failed to establish any direct stimulation of mammary cell proliferation by estrogen, and instead it is believed that the action is indirect via locally produced IGF1, which appears to be the major mammary mitogen in cattle. Numerous other factors such as photoperiod (Andrade et al., 2008) and inflammation (Gouon-Evans et al., 2002) have been shown to positively influence mammary development. Photoperiod may well act through prolactin and inflammation through other local growth factors such as colony-stimulating factor (CSF) from macrophages (the action of CLA appears to be linked to an inflammatory response). However, showing that a particular factor can affect mammary cells is not necessarily evidence of an overt action in the pregnant animal, and it is interesting to note that the photoperiod effect referred to here was observed in sheep stimulated into lactation with exogenous steroids, whereas the CSF research was done in mice and targeted toward better understanding of breast cancer. For dairy species, research interest in gestational mammogenesis has waned in the last decade (the same is certainly not true of rodents and other breast cancer model species). This probably results from the almost universal success of mammogenesis in dairy species; there is little reason for thinking that it can be improved. The mitogenic activity of IGF1 has already been mentioned. IGF1 secretion is stimulated by GH (also known as bovine somatotrophin, BST) and we shall see later that GH has a marked effect on milk secretion in ruminants. However, attempts to stimulate mammogenesis in sheep using GH have been unsuccessful (Stelwagen et al., 1993).

1.4 CONTINUED DEVELOPMENT POSTPARTUM AND DURING LACTATION

The reproductive strategy of marsupials is to give birth to altricial young after a short gestation. In this case the mammary glands are small and underdeveloped at parturition. The joey then attaches permanently to one teat, and this gland (and no other) starts to secrete milk but also begins a phase of major proliferation (Lincoln and Renfree, 1981). This concurrent proliferation and secretion represents an extreme situation, and its unilateral nature emphasizes the importance of local regulatory mechanisms. We shall return to this when considering regulation of secretion and bioactive factors in milk. In the majority of species there may be a small amount of further mammary proliferation during early lactation, but this will be small in comparison to gestation. The primary developmental characteristic of the lactating udder of dairy animals is gradual cell loss through apoptosis beginning at around peak lactation and accounting for the characteristic decline in milk yield as lactation advances. This has relevance to the duration of the lactation, which will be discussed later.

It will be evident that the development of the gland prior to the start of lactation is essential and will have major impact on the amount of milk produced. Whether there is any significant effect on milk composition is doubtful, unless there are major deficiencies in the structural integrity of the developing epithelium. This will become evident as we start to consider the secretory process.

1.5 LACTOGENESIS

1.5.1 Lactogenesis Stage I

Before secretion can begin, the secretory mechanisms must develop. Secretory cells have proliferated during pregnancy, so now we need to consider these cells and their secretory activity in more detail. Fleet et al. (1975)

defined lactogenesis stage I as "the onset of secretory activity, ie the appearance of pre-colostrum in the gland" and lactogenesis stage II as "the onset of copious milk secretion at about the time of parturition." They also reiterated the definition of the term "galactopoiesis" as "an increase of milk yield during established lactation." With the proviso that galactopoiesis has come to include "maintenance of" in addition to "increase of," these definitions have been widely accepted, although it would appear that in some breast-feeding literature galactopoiesis is incorrectly referred to as lactogenesis stage III (Suárez-Trujillo and Casey, 2016). The processes and their control are completely different, but interrelated. The term "colostrogenesis" has also been used in the animal science literature (Baumrucker et al., 2010), but this perhaps adds an unnecessary complication. The problem is one of definition; colostrum is the first milk appearing after parturition, but there is good evidence to show that its secretion starts well before that, and it is then stored within the gland for days or weeks. As we shall see, it is most unlikely that the colostrum that appears in the neonate's mouth is exactly the same as the pre-colostrum that was secreted across the apical membrane of the epithelial cell some time previously.

The Babraham group (Fleet et al., 1975) noted increased secretion of pre-colostrum during the last trimester of pregnancy in the goat and observed a changing ionic composition (from more extracellular to more intracellular), increased lactose concentration, and increased IgG concentration. This coincided with increased prolactin and placental lactogen secretion, and they hypothesized a causal relationship. The presence of milk-like concentrations of protein and fat several weeks prepartum clearly indicated that the enzymatic machinery for synthesizing milk was present, which was also supported by histological study. At the time, the reason why secretion was possible but did not happen to any appreciable extent was unknown. Also, one must add a caveat. The pre-colostrum sampling removed small but not negligible amounts, and it later transpired that this could stimulate early onset of full secretion, probably through a mechanism involving removal of locally produced prostaglandins (Maule Walker and Peaker, 1980).

The immediate requirements of any neonate are for energy, thermoregulation, and protection. Colostrum provides for these to different extents. Newborns of most species are born with some energy reserves, sufficient for survival for hours or even, in the case of human babies, a few days, so colostrum does not need to be a total energy source. Thermoregulation is assisted by the mother's behavior (licking dry, body heat) so the warmth provided directly by colostrum is not essential to survival. Some species (notably the human) are born with passive immune protection, acquired via the placenta. Farm species are not, and for them the most important contribution of colostrum (by far) is protection, and in particular immunoglobulin G1. Colostrum quality equates with IgG content. In mature milk immunoglobulin content is quite low, and IgA predominates. In colostrum it is high, and IgG exceeds IgA. How does this come about? The secretion of IgG into colostrum has been reviewed by Baumrucker and Bruckmaier (2014). Much of the detail has not been confirmed reliably, but it seems likely that secretion is by a transcytosis mechanism, whereby IgG is first internalized from plasma into secretory cell via a specific receptor, probably the neonatal Fc receptor, which is known to fulfill this same role in human placenta and neonatal intestine. The complex then translocates across the cell to the apical membrane, from where it is released into the lumen of the alveolus (the terminology will be explained more thoroughly in the secretion section). Once again, a major caveat needs to be mentioned: the "open gut" phenomenon. Absorption of immunoglobulin from the neonatal intestine occurs only during the first day or two of life, when the tight junctions (TJs) between neighboring epithelial cells are "open" and the epithelium is consequently "leaky." The implication is obvious; some or even most of the immunoglobulin transfer is via this paracellular route, not by transcytosis. Exactly the same leakiness pertains in the mammary gland during pregnancy and immediately postpartum. It is a phenomenon that has extreme relevance to the quality of mature milk, which will be discussed later. Whether it is also important in colostrum secretion is not known.

1.5.2 Lactogenesis Stage II

Endocrine changes at parturition are similar (not identical) across species and include an increase in prolactin and a fall in progesterone. Elegant experiments demonstrated clearly that prolactin in itself was not capable of initiating copious secretion in the presence of progesterone, whereas the removal of progesterone was followed by secretion. This was Nick Kuhn's "progesterone trigger" concept, first published in 1969 and reprinted 40 years later in the JMGBN special issue (Kuhn, 2009). It is still valid. Since a fall in progesterone is also implicated in the control of parturition, the mechanism ensures synchrony between birth and the availability of milk. The exception is human lactation: Progesterone does not fall until 2 or 3 days postpartum, which is when copious secretion first happens (the milk "comes in").

1.6 SECRETION

1.6.1 Synthetic Processes

Detailed accounts of the synthesis of milk components are beyond the scope of this article, and the reader is referred to reviews published in the Proceedings of the 41st Symposium of the Zoological Society (fat, Dils et al., 1977; proteins, Mepham, 1977b; lactose and other milk sugars, Jones, 1977). Some important points are deserving of emphasis. There is nothing unusual about mammary protein synthesis: Amino acids are taken up by specific transporters, protein is synthesized in the ribosomes of the rough endoplasmic reticulum, and protein granules then accumulate in the Golgi apparatus prior to secretion. The major synthesized proteins are the caseins, α-lactalbumin (all species), and β-lactoglobulin (absent from some species, including humans). Other proteins in milk are mainly derived from plasma, although there is evidence that some (acute phase proteins, for instance; Eckersall et al., 2006) may be synthesized locally within the mammary gland by endothelial or other cell types. A cross-lactational study of the bovine milk proteome (Zhang et al., 2015) revealed less than 10% variation in the number of proteins expressed at different stages of lactation, these changes being mainly in immune-related proteins; lower in mid-lactation than either early lactation (important for protection in the neonate) or late lactation (important for protection in the mammary gland). Uniquely among animal cells, α-lactalbumin orchestrates the utilization of glucose by the Golgi apparatus for the synthesis of lactose. The precursors for lactose synthesis are glucose and galactose, irrespective of species, but fat synthesis is very much species-dependent. In non-ruminants the major precursor is once again glucose, whereas in ruminants (which have relatively low glucose availability) the principal precursor is acetate. It is apparent, therefore, that glucose supply to and uptake by the mammary secretory cell is a major determinant of milk synthesis. The mammary gland is insulin-independent, possessing glucose transporters (GLUTs) 1 and 8 primarily (Zhao, 2014). The expression of these GLUTs increases dramatically during lactogenesis II, although this appears to be a consequence of local hypoxia rather than endocrine stimulation. Exactly how intracellular glucose is specifically trafficked to the Golgi for lactose synthesis is unknown.

1.6.2 Secretory Processes

The mammary gland is first and foremost an exocrine secretory gland, although it does also possess endocrine capability (Peaker, 1996). Mammary secretory cells are polarized, taking up substrates across their basolateral wall and secreting the principal components of milk (fat, proteins, and lactose) across the apical wall through two among several secretory mechanisms (Fig. 1.2 and reviewed in Shennan and Peaker, 2000). Lactose and mammary-synthesized proteins are secreted by exocytosis, whereby the Golgi and apical membranes fuse and the contents of the Golgi apparatus are released into the lumen of the alveolus (cell 2 in Fig. 1.2), whereas fat is secreted by an apocrine process whereby fat droplets become encased in apical membrane as they are extruded into the lumen, this membrane becoming the fat globule membrane (cell 3). It should be evident straight away that secretion is not straightforward, and there is considerable dynamic restructuring of membrane on a constant basis. A closer examination of the ways in which different components arrive in milk reveals a far more complex picture: 8 separate pathways are identified in the work of Baumrucker and Bruckmaier (2014) and as many as 12 scenarios of mammary phospholipid transport are envisaged in the work of McManaman (2014). However, from a physiological

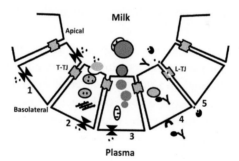

Figure 1.2 The five secretory routes present within mammary secretory cells. Cell 1 displays the membrane route: uptake of simple molecules across the basement membrane via carriers or transporters followed by trafficking across the cell and efflux across the apical membrane. Cell 2 shows exocytosis of lactose, protein, and water via fusion of Golgi and apical membranes followed by release of the Golgi content. Cell 3 shows the movement of fat into milk by apocrine secretion. Cell 4 shows transcytosis of complex molecules following binding to specific receptors on the basolateral membrane followed by internalization, trafficking via one or more cellular vesicles and extrusion across the apical membrane. These routes are all transcellular. The fifth mechanism is paracellular flux through leaky tight junctions (L-TJ), shown between cells 4 and 5.

standpoint there are five separate identifiable routes whereby major and minor components appear in milk. In addition to exocytosis and apocrine secretion, simple substances may pass first the basal membrane and then the apical membrane via carriers or transporters of some sort (the membrane route: cell 1 in Fig. 1.2). Receptor-bound complex molecules may bind, be internalized, transit through one or more intracellular vesicles, and then be extruded (this mechanism is transcytosis, shown in cell 4 with the example of immunoglobulins. Many pharmaceutical products are also secreted in this manner: Yagdiran et al., 2016). All of these four mechanisms are transcellular, that is, the route is through the secretory cell. The fifth mechanism is fundamentally different; it is paracellular (between neighboring cells) and is only possible when the junctional complexes between neighboring cells (and especially the TJs) become "leaky" (see Linzell and Peaker, 2009). It should be apparent from these multiple mechanisms that milk is likely to contain much of what is consumed or otherwise taken in by the lactating animal (see, e.g., Liston, 1998).

1.7 CONTROL OF SYNTHESIS AND SECRETION

Prolactin was named for its lactation-promoting properties when it was first discovered in rabbits in the 1930s. Its role in the stimulation of secretion and maintenance of lactation in many other species including humans is undisputed (see review by Crowley, 2015), but much less clear in ruminants. Several studies have reported that depletion of endogenous prolactin in cattle, sheep, and goats has little or even no effect on milk yield, whereas the stimulatory role of GH has been extremely well established (Bauman, 1999) to the point where recombinantly derived bovine GH (rBST) is commercially available to American dairy farmers for use as a lactation stimulant. Unfortunately, the biological mechanism is not fully understood. Homeorhesis is the repartitioning of energy and nutrients toward a specific aspect of metabolism while maintaining overall energetic balance. The mammary homeorhetic action of GH/rBST can be easily demonstrated, but it is far from clear that GH has any direct action on mammary secretory cells. Does the mammary gland "pull" nutrients, or is it "pushed"? This debate has never been properly answered, but there is a consensus that milk yield does not simply respond to greater nutrient availability. At a mammary level, the way in which GH/rBST stimulates yield remains a mystery! Recent evidence (Lacasse et al., 2016) suggests that prolactin might have more of a role in ruminant lactation than has been previously thought, and in this case it does seem to be directly on mammary secretory cells. The galactopoietic activities of prolactin are partly on synthesis of milk components and partly on secretion. This topic has recently been reviewed (Truchet et al., 2014) with emphasis on the importance of the membrane recycling events that take place on a constant basis. This requires cooperation between numerous membrane proteins, principle among these being the SNARE proteins (Soluble *N*-ethylmaleimide-sensitive factor Attachment protein Receptor) which bind arachidonic acid, believed to be the mediator of prolactin's secretagogue role.

In addition to systemic control of milk synthesis and secretion, there is also local control. The simplest example of this is milking frequency; the increased yield associated with a move from twice- to thrice-daily milking of cows is localized to the individual gland or glands that are milked more often (Hillerton et al., 1990). This local control process will be considered in more detail later.

1.8 THE IMPORTANCE OF LACTOSE (AND WATER) SECRETION

As mentioned, lactose is synthesized in the Golgi vesicle from glucose and galactose, small molecules that can easily pass the Golgi membrane. Lactose is a large molecule that cannot permeate the membrane, hence it accumulates within the Golgi and creates an osmotic potential that draws water into the vesicle. This is the principle route by which water enters into milk (Linzell and Peaker, 2009). Contrary to natural intuition, water cannot simply pass through cell membranes, because they are composed of a bilipid layer that has strongly hydrophobic characteristics. Clearly, water does enter into milk (and pass through many other cellular membranes), and the class of transporter molecules that are principally responsible for this movement are the aquaporins (AQPs) of which 13 members have been identified. We and others (Nazemi et al., 2014b) have recently demonstrated the presence and developmental regulation of AQPs 1, 3, and 5 in mammary tissue. AQP1 was mainly expressed in capillary endothelial cells. Secretory cells expressed AQP3 basolaterally and AQP5 apically, suggesting involvement of the latter in secretion. Paradoxically, expression of AQP5 decreased from pregnancy into lactation (the others increased), but these membrane proteins are extremely stable and so expression may not equate chronologically with function. We have yet to establish whether there is expression of AQP on the Golgi membrane, but we would anticipate so. There is much talk of variation in lactose concentration in milk across the course of lactation (it tends to fall in later lactation), but there is good reason to believe that, at the time of secretion, lactose concentration is constant, or very nearly so. This constancy of secreted product accompanied by variation of final ("raw") product introduces another important concept; alteration of milk composition during storage within the gland. It also begs the question, is there any significance to the fact that AQPs are developmentally regulated, if water flux is simply passive, driven by lactose synthesis. There is a major exception to this rule. The composition of marsupial milk changes quite dramatically during the course of lactation. Early lactation (Phases 1, 2a, and 2b in the terminology of Nicholas, 1988) is characterized by relatively sparse secretion of milk that is high in lactose, whereas later lactation (Phase 3) comprises copious secretion of low-lactose milk. It seems inevitable that, under these circumstances, something other than lactose secretion must be regulating water flux. The prospect of being able to manipulate water flux and hence milk volume is an exciting one.

1.9 REMODELING

The transition through lactogenesis stage II and into full secretion typically occurs smoothly, but there should be no doubting the enormity of the changes that are occurring over a short period of time. Blood flow to the mammary gland and oxygen and nutrient uptake all increase many fold, the bovine udder will suddenly flux around six times as much water as the kidneys of the nonlactating animal and at a cellular level the previously statically cuboidal-shaped secretory cells will change shape to become columnar as the alveoli fill with milk, then change back to cuboidal after milk ejection, and then continue this cyclical plasticity several or many times a day. Some years ago it was observed that a significant proportion of secretory cells fail this transition: Mammary apoptosis (physiological cell death) is high in early lactation, at least in dairy species (Sorensen et al., 2006). This remodeling of mammary tissue may be a mechanism for removing aberrant or excess cells, but there is another possible explanation. The "local hypoxia trigger" hypothesis for switching-on glucose transport into secretory cells at lactogenesis (Zhao, 2014) implies that cellular metabolism runs ahead of cardiovascular supply at this time, and we have recently obtained evidence that angiogenesis (final development of the capillary system) is a very late event in mammogenesis (we have proposed the term "lactogenesis stage III"; Agenäs et al., 2017). This is an extreme example of the remodeling that goes on in the mammary gland, but one should not underestimate the overall plasticity required of the lactation process. The lactation curve of ruminant dairy species is well known, and the decline in milk yield happening after peak is recognized to be a consequence of further apoptosis; expressed simply, the secretory cells of the late lactation animal are just as efficient as those of the peak lactation animal, there are simply fewer of them (Fowler et al., 1990). In cattle, this loss of secretory cells can be partially prevented by simply milking more often (Sorensen et al., 2008; Herve et al., 2016) raising the interesting prospect of being able to extend bovine lactation far beyond its usual 10-month duration, which would be expected to have economic (De Vries, 2006) and welfare benefits (Knight, 2008). Extended lactation is now being practiced by some dairy farmers in parts of Europe (Maciel et al., 2016), but has yet to become a popular strategy.

1.10 STORAGE OF MILK WITHIN THE GLAND AND ITS CONSEQUENCES FOR SECRETORY FUNCTION AND MILK QUALITY

Most exocrine glands operate in "secrete it and forget it" mode; the product is quickly carried away from its site of production and/or metabolized. The mammary gland is different. In dairy species there is a capacious storage area, the gland cistern, but even then a significant proportion of milk is stored within the secretory alveoli, where it is in direct contact with the cells that produced it (Knight et al., 1994). Dairy farmers typically milk at regular intervals twice or thrice daily, meaning storage times of between 8 and 16 h. For many species the storage time is much more variable than that, since it is dependent on a flexible relationship between mother and young. There are two sets of consequences: The nature of the milk is likely to change during storage, due to the presence of proteolytic enzymes, and there is an opportunity for local control of the secretory process through bioactive factors in stored milk.

1.10.1 Local Control of Mammary Function

The classic example of intramammary local control is the stimulatory effect of milking frequency. Using unilateral milking followed by reinfusion of an equal volume of biologically inert isosmotic sucrose, Henderson and Peaker (1984) were the first to show definitively that this was due to the removal of a bioactive factor in stored milk, rather than to relief of pressure. The biological rationale is quite obvious; a mechanism that matches supply of milk to demand. The practical outcome for farmers is the option of milking three times daily rather than two to obtain around 12%−15% more milk, and if this is done in an automated milking system (AMS) the benefit is achieved with no additional labor costs. Cows that choose to attend an AMS more frequently throughout lactation also have a more persistent lactation, yielding around 20% more milk overall (Pettersson et al., 2011). Furthermore, altered milking frequency changes yield, without affecting gross composition (Knight et al., 2000). Considerable effort was expended by several groups in searching for the specific lactation-regulating factor in milk, but as reviewed recently by Weaver and Hernandez (2016) no definitive answer has been forthcoming. The discovery of a small autocrine peptide or peptides (feedback inhibitor of lactation) that inhibited protein trafficking through Golgi membranes with a consequential decrease in synthesis of lactose and reduced milk yield (Wilde et al., 1995) could not be confirmed by definitive identification, and casein-derived phosphopeptides that disrupted mammary TJs could completely inhibit lactation (Shamay et al., 2002) but were not shown to have the fine control necessary for mediating milking frequency effects. More recently serotonin, 5-hydroxytryptamine (5-HT), has also been shown to have local regulatory roles in the mammary gland. Inhibition of 5-HT reuptake increases cellular exposure to serotonin and this was shown to disrupt TJs and accelerate the decline in milk yield at drying off (Hernandez et al., 2011). Serotonin also acts locally in the gland to induce the secretion of parathyroid hormone-related peptide which is important in calcium balance during lactation. Once again, definitive evidence that serotonin mediates the effect of milking frequency is lacking, nevertheless, it is evident that a number of local control mechanisms operate within the mammary gland involving bioactive factors in stored milk.

1.10.2 Proteolysis of Milk Within the Gland

Milk processors are very well aware of the problems that proteolysis can create, and there have been numerous reviews of this topic written from a dairy products standpoint (see, e.g., Ismail and Nielsen, 2010). The physiology underlying milk proteolysis has also been reviewed recently (Dallas et al., 2015), but has been much less well researched. While plasmin is by far the major proteolytic system in milk, there are actually many other systems present (nine are listed in the review), most of them are characterized by the presence of protease inhibitors and activators in addition to the active proteases themselves. There are a number of possible biological functions that can be attributed to such systems. Neonates typically have less developed digestive enzyme systems than older animals, so may benefit from consumption of a partially digested diet. Proteolysis also creates many of the bioactive peptides in milk, which can have beneficial effects on gut microbiota, immune function, appetite regulation, and many more. Within the mammary gland, proteolysis might contribute to optimal casein size distribution and generation of bioactive factors with antimicrobial activity could help to protect against mastitis. Given these potential biological benefits, one might anticipate considerable proteolysis of bovine milk stored at body temperature for, say, half a day. This is not the case; in milk from healthy, early lactation cows that are well fed the extent of proteolysis of caseins is rather modest and some proteins (lactoferrin and immunoglobulins) seem to escape proteolysis entirely. These proteins have a compact globular structure in contrast to the micellar structure of caseins, and the plasmin system (certainly) and possibly others are micelle-associated, so the differential degradation is explicable. It should also be recognized that most exocrine glands include proteases as part of their secretion; many of the glands associated with the gastrointestinal tract are obvious examples, for good reason, but there are other examples such as the extensive kallikrein system in sweat (Lundwall, 2013). In other words, the presence of these systems may represent nothing more than an evolutionary hangover from the mammary gland's origins as a skin gland. Alternatively, perhaps selection pressure has favored the appearance of protease inhibitors rather than proteases.

Modest proteolysis may be the norm in healthy early lactation, but this is often far from the case in the diseased state and in late lactation. Poor processing properties of late lactation milk produced in low-input grass-based systems are well known (Lucey, 1996) and relate primarily to breakdown of β-caseins to γ-caseins as a result of plasmin action (Brown et al., 1995). Plasmin and its inactive precursor, plasminogen, are serum proteins which are present in milk at increasing concentrations during late lactation (Politis et al., 1989). What is the origin of the proteases found in milk? There is no direct evidence of production by mammary

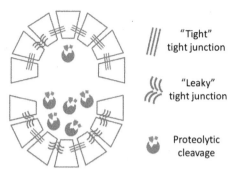

Figure 1.3 TJ status and consequences for proteolysis of secreted milk. In the top panel the majority of the TJs between neighboring secretory cells are completely tight, the paracellular passage of proteolytic enzymes into the alveolar lumen is restricted and there is little proteolysis of milk. This is the situation in the healthy mammary gland in early and mid-lactation. In the lower panel most of the TJs have become leaky, allowing paracellular flux of proteolytic enzymes with a consequent increase in proteolysis of milk within the alveolar lumen. This occurs in late lactation, during mastitis and the secretion of colostrum.

secretory cells of plasmin or indeed any of the various protease system components found in milk. Transcriptomic analysis of somatic cells derived from milk has shown the presence of mRNA for cathepsins and various plasmin elements (Wickramasinghe et al., 2012), but these cells are primarily immune cells. It is perfectly possible that some proteases are synthesized within the mammary gland, by either the secretory cells or other cell types. However, the lactation-stage relationship suggests a simpler explanation; the majority of protease activity is plasma-derived and enters into milk by the paracellular route as the mammary epithelium become "leaky" in later lactation. This is illustrated diagrammatically in Fig. 1.3.

1.10.3 Storage Anatomy

Bioactive factors in stored milk will only influence secretion if they are in contact with secretory cells, hence, the extent to which local control operates will vary according to the anatomy of the gland, and specifically the ratio of cisternal storage space to storage within secretory alveoli. This can be measured (or at least approximated) using ultrasound scanning. Dewhurst and Knight (1994) demonstrated that large-cisterned cows were less responsive to increased milking frequency because they were less restricted by local control; the same cows are also more tolerant of infrequent milking. Similar relationships have subsequently been shown for small ruminants.

1.11 TJ STATUS

1.11.1 Mammary Epithelial Integrity

The mammary epithelium comprises secretory alveolar cells joined by junctional complexes comprising (in structural order from apical to basal) *zonulae occludentes* (TJs), *zonula adherentes* (intermediate junctions), and *maculae adherentes* (desmosomes;). The physical and functional natures of mammary TJ were first described by Dorothy Pitelka and Malcolm Peaker, respectively, in the early 1970s and have recently been reviewed by Stelwagen and Singh (2014). The term "junction" carries connotations of rigidity and inflexibility, but actually these structures are dynamic and plastic, composed of two classes of membrane-spanning proteins (claudins and occludins) that are in a constant state of flux and recycling (Chalmers and Whitley, 2012). As a consequence, the integrity of the TJ can, and does, vary. Mature milk is characterized by low sodium and high potassium concentrations (intracellular fluid-like), maintained by a sealed epithelium (TJ: upper panel in Fig. 1.3). During pregnancy and very early lactation TJs are "leaky" (lower panel in Fig. 1.3) allowing an equilibration of ions and other small molecules (including lactose, for instance) between milk and plasma. In all probability, some immunoglobulin transfer also occurs by this paracellular route and it is fairly certain that proteases (especially elements of the plasmin system) and immune cells can also pass the leaky TJ. As lactation advances, the proportion of "leaky" TJ gradually increases, thus explaining the increased proteolysis evident in late-lactation milk.

1.12 CONSEQUENCES FOR MILK QUALITY

Temporary opening of TJ can be achieved by either of two mechanisms: A normal extracellular calcium concentration is essential for TJ maintenance, so infusion of calcium chelators such as EGTA (ethylene glycol-bis (β-aminoethyl ether)) will open TJ, with a consequential and immediate decrease in milk yield (Neville and Peaker, 1981). Supraphysiological doses of the milk ejection hormone, oxytocin, will also create leakiness, presumably through simple physical disruption caused by extreme contraction of myoepithelial cells (Jonsson et al., 2013 and see Milk Ejection section). The main effect in this case was a temporary increase in somatic cell count (SCC) and total protein content in milk, and the authors proposed that this treatment might serve as an improved single-visit mastitis diagnosis (for use in beef suckler cows, for instance). The same approach has also been used to temporarily increase the immunoglobulin content of porcine milk (Farmer et al., 2017). The temporary nature of these changes (around 48 h for EGTA and 24 h for oxytocin) needs to be emphasized, further evidence of the "living" and dynamic nature of TJ. This contrasts with longer term changes occurring across the length of lactation. The gradual decline in secretory cell number as a consequence of apoptosis has already been mentioned, and this is accompanied by a concomitant decrease in epithelial integrity. Whether this is due to an overall gradual loss of TJ functionality or to a complete leakiness of a proportion of TJ is unknown. From a processors point of view, the consequences are poor protein quality of the milk, as already described. From a veterinary point of view, the use of SCC as an indicator of mammary health and especially subclinical mastitis should really take into account lactation stage, but frequently does not. These longer term changes in TJ status are part of the overall developmental strategy of the mammary gland and can be reversed by the simple procedure of milking more frequently (Sorensen et al., 2001). At 52 weeks of lactation, udder-halves milked thrice daily had significantly higher α- and β-casein contents but lower plasmin, plasminogen, and γ-casein contents than the opposite half-udders milked twice daily, differences that could be partially reversed by a short period (48 h) of reversed frequency milking. These within-cow differences are another example of local control, and a clear demonstration of the importance of TJ. Finally, TJ status may be part of the mechanism that reduces milk yield when cows are milked once daily, since there is evidence of leakiness after around 18 h of milk accumulation (Stelwagen et al., 1997).

1.13 MASTITIS AND HOST DEFENSE

Pathogenic inflammation of the mammary gland, mastitis, will be the subject of a later chapter and will not be considered in detail here. However, it is important to be aware that the mammary gland does mount a local host defense mechanism, including raising an acute phase protein response (Eckersall et al., 2006) and recruiting components of the immune system via the same mechanism that has just been described, i.e., decreased TJ integrity. The mechanism is not known but may involve elevated oxytocin levels; we have observed increased endogenous oxytocin release in goats suffering from subclinical mastitis (C. H. Knight, unpublished). Mastitis in breastfeeding mothers is a common and painful problem (Scott et al., 2008), which has received surprisingly little research effort, especially when one considers that subclinical mastitis is thought to be a major vector for vertical transmission of the HIV, once again as a consequence of leaky TJ (Willumsen et al., 2000). The mammary gland may also be subject to nonpathogenic inflammation as a result of excessive milk accumulation. The cytokine repertoire present in milk differs between this "physiological inflammation" and mastitis, at least in *Staphylococcus aureus* infected mice (Nazemi et al., 2014a).

1.14 MILK EJECTION

Bovine milk ejection has been reviewed by Bruckmaier and Wellnitz (2008). Release of oxytocin form the posterior pituitary triggered by tactile stimulation of the teats at milking causes contraction of myoepithelial smooth muscle cells that surround the alveoli and run the length of smaller ducts. The alveoli are constricted, the bore of the ducts increases, intramammary pressure rises, and milk is forced into the cistern from where it can be removed by suckling or milking. In the majority of cases this reflex operates perfectly normally at milking, but it can be inhibited by stress, leading to incomplete milking. The immediate consequence for milk composition is a decreased content of fat, which as a consequence of gravity and surface tension effects is partially retained within alveolar milk. Residual milk (that left behind after a normal, complete, milking) can be removed using exogenous oxytocin and has been known to contain more than 10% fat. Experimental half-udder incomplete milking of cows additionally lead to increased SCC and decreased lactose, both changes explicable on the basis of leaky TJ (Penry et al., 2016).

Milk removal is also a function of the machine characteristics and teat anatomy. A considerable amount of research has focused on the effect of different vacuum levels, flow rate, and milking time on teat morphology, because of established links between poor morphology and mastitis risk. However, with the exception of SCC, changes in milk composition have not been reported. Similarly, there have been no detailed investigations of changes in the milk proteome as a consequence of disturbed or inadequate milk ejection.

1.15 POSTLACTATIONAL INVOLUTION

By definition, changes occurring after drying-off will not affect the raw milk arriving at the dairy, so will not be considered in detail. The process of mammary involution in dairy species was reviewed by Capuco and Akers (1999). Briefly, the changes are an extension and acceleration of what has already been described for advancing lactation. Cell death by apoptosis increases, the epithelium becomes extremely leaky due to the physical effects of milk accumulation, and milk secretion ceases. The protein composition of the final secretions is different to mature milk as production of caseins decreases and of lactoferrin and other proteins related to mammary defense increases (Wang and Hurley, 1998). The pattern of involution is very much affected by the fact that most cows are concurrently pregnant at drying off, such that the epithelial cell population is actually at least two populations, one of older cells undergoing apoptosis and one of younger cells that are proliferating.

1.16 CONCLUSIONS

The mammary gland is a dynamic, metabolically active organ that has a relatively complex physiology and is controlled by a combination of endocrine and local factors. Many of these factors can affect the detailed composition of the milk that is produced, during synthesis, secretion, and storage within the gland. An understanding of the processes involved is necessary if the objective is to optimize the quality of the product, raw milk.

REFERENCES

Agenäs, S., Safayi, S., Nielsen, M.O., Knight, C.H., 2018. Angiogenesis is a late event in bovine mammary development: evidence for lactogenesis stage 3? J Dairy Res. In press.

Akers, R.M., 2002. Lactation and the Mammary Gland. Wiley-Blackwell, Hoboken, NJ.

Andrade, B.R., Salama, A.A., Caja, G., Castillo, V., Albanell, E., Such, X., 2008. Response to lactation induction differs by season of year and breed of dairy ewes. J. Dairy Sci. 91, 2299−2306.

Andreas, N.J., Kampmann, B., Mehring Le-Doare, K., 2015. Human breast milk: a review on its composition and bioactivity. Early Hum. Dev. 91, 629−635.

Bauman, D.E., 1999. Bovine somatotropin and lactation: from basic science to commercial application. Domest. Anim. Endocrinol. 17, 101−116.

Baumrucker, C.R., Burkett, A.M., Magliaro-Macrina, A.L., Dechow, C.D., 2010. Colostrogenesis: mass transfer of immunoglobulin G1 into colostrum. J. Dairy Sci. 93, 3031−3038.

Baumrucker, C.R., Bruckmaier, R.M., 2014. Colostrogenesis. IgG1 transcytosis mechanisms. J. Mammary Gland Biol. Neoplasia 19, 103–117.

Berryhill, G.E., Trott, J.F., Hovey, R.C., 2016. Mammary gland development—it's not just about estrogen. J. Dairy Sci. 99, 875–883.

Brown, J.R., Law, A.J., Knight, C.H., 1995. Changes in casein composition of goats' milk during the course of lactation: physiological inferences and technological implications. J. Dairy Res. 62, 431–439.

Bruckmaier, R.M., Wellnitz, O., 2008. Induction of milk ejection and milk removal in different production systems. J. Anim. Sci. 86 (13 Suppl), 15–20.

Capuco, A.V., Akers, R.M., 1999. Mammary involution in dairy animals. J. Mammary Gland Biol. Neoplasia 4, 137–144.

Capuco, A.V., Ellis, S.E., 2013. Comparative aspects of mammary gland development and homeostasis. Annu. Rev. Anim. Biosci. 1, 179–202.

Chalmers, A.D., Whitley, P., 2012. Continuous endocytic recycling of tight junction proteins: how and why? Essays Biochem. 53, 41–54.

Crowley, W.R., 2015. Neuroendocrine regulation of lactation and milk production. Compr. Physiol. 5, 255–291.

Dallas, D.C., Murray, N.M., Gan, J., 2015. Proteolytic systems in milk: perspectives on the evolutionary function within the mammary gland and the infant. J. Mammary Gland Biol. Neoplasia 20, 133–147.

Daniels, K.M., Mcgilliard, M.L., Meyer, M.J., Van Amburgh, M.E., Capuco, A.V., Akers, R.M., 2009. Effects of body weight and nutrition on histological mammary development in Holstein heifers. J. Dairy Sci. 92, 499–505.

De Vries, A., 2006. Economic value of pregnancy in dairy cattle. J. Dairy Sci. 89, 3876–3885.

Dewhurst, R.D., Knight, C.H., 1994. Relationship between milk storage characteristics and the short-term response of dairy cows to thrice-daily milking. Anim. Prod. 58, 181–187.

Dils, R., Clark, S., Knudsen, J., 1977. Comparative aspects of milk fat synthesis. Symp. Zool. Soc Lond 41, 43–55.

Eckersall, P.D., Young, F.J., Nolan, A.M., Knight, C.H., McComb, C., Waterston, M.M., et al., 2006. Acute phase proteins in bovine milk in an experimental model of *Staphylococcus aureus* subclinical mastitis. J. Dairy Sci. 89, 1488–1501.

Farmer, C., Lessard, M., Knight, C.H., Quesnel, H., 2017. Oxytocin injections in the postpartal period affect mammary tight junctions in sows. J Anim. Sci 95, 3532–3539.

Faulkin, L.J., Deome, K.B., 1960. Regulation of growth and spacing of gland elements in the mammary fat pad of the C3H mouse. J. Natl Cancer Inst. 24, 953.

Fleet, I.R., Goode, J.A., Hamon, M.H., Laurie, M.S., Linzell, J.L., Peaker, M., 1975. Secretory activity of goat mammary glands during pregnancy and the onset of lactation. J Physiol 251, 763–773.

Flint, D.J., Travers, M.T., Barber, M.C., Binart, N., Kelly, P.A., 2005. Diet-induced obesity impairs mammary development and lactogenesis in murine mammary gland. Am. J. Physiol. Endocrinol. Metab. 288, E1179–E1187.

Forsyth, I.A., Neville, M.C., 2009. Introduction: hormonal regulation of mammary development and milk protein gene expression at the whole animal and molecular levels. J. Mammary Gland Biol. Neoplasia 14, 317–319.

Fowler, P.A., Knight, C.H., Cameron, G.G., Foster, M.A., 1990. In-vivo studies of mammary development in the goat using magnetic resonance imaging (MRI). J. Reprod. Fertil. 89, 367–375.

Gouon-Evans, V., Lin, E.Y., Pollard, J.W., 2002. Requirement of macrophages and eosinophils and their cytokines/chemokines for mammary gland development. Breast Cancer Res 4, 155–164.

Hayden, T.J., Thomas, C.R., Forsyth, I.A., 1979. Effect of number of young born (litter size) on milk yield of goats: role for placental lactogen. J. Dairy Sci. 62, 53–57.

Henderson, A.J., Peaker, M., 1984. Feed-back control of milk secretion in the goat by a chemical in milk. J. Physiol. 351, 39–45.

Hernandez, L.L., Collier, J.L., Vomachka, A.J., Collier, R.J., Horseman, N.D., 2011. Suppression of lactation and acceleration of involution in the bovine mammary gland by a selective serotonin reuptake inhibitor. J. Endocrinol. 209, 45–54.

Herve, L., Quesnel, H., Lollivier, V., Boutinaud, M., 2016. Regulation of cell number in the mammary gland by controlling the exfoliation process in milk in ruminants. J. Dairy Sci. 99, 854–863.

Hillerton, J.E., Knight, C.H., Turvey, A., Wheatley, S.D., Wilde, C.J., 1990. Milk yield and mammary function in dairy cows milked four times daily. J. Dairy Res. 57, 285–294.

Ismail, B., Nielsen, S.S., 2010. Invited review: plasmin protease in milk: current knowledge and relevance to dairy industry. J. Dairy Sci. 93, 4999–5009.

Jones, E.A., 1977. Synthesis and secretion of milk sugars. Symp. Zool. Soc Lond 41, 77–94.

Jonsson L., Svennerten-Sjaunja K. & Knight, C.H., 2013. Potential for use of high-dose oxytocin to improve mastitis diagnosis in dairy cows and beef suckler cows. *Proceedings of the British Society of Animal Science*. 2013, 188

Kim, J.H., Kim, Y., Kim, Y.J., Park, Y., 2016. Conjugated linoleic acid: potential health benefits as a functional food ingredient. Annu. Rev. Food Sci. Technol. 7, 221–244.

Knight, C.H., 1982. Mammary development in mice: effects of hemihysterectomy in pregnancy and of litter size post partum. J. Physiol. 3227, 17–727.

Knight, C.H., 2001. Lactation and gestation in dairy cows: flexibility avoids nutritional extremes. Proc. Nutr. Soc. 60, 527–537.

Knight, C.H., 2008. Extended lactation in dairy cows: could it work for European dairy farmers? In: Royal, M.D., Friggens, N.C., Smith, R.F. (Eds.), Fertility in Dairy Cows: Bridging the Gaps. Cambridge University Press, Cambridge, UK, pp. 138–145.

Knight, C.H., 2010. Changes in infant nutrition requirements with age after birth. In: Symonds, M.E., Ramsay, M.M. (Eds.), Maternal-Fetal Nutrition During Pregnancy and Lactation. Cambridge University Press, Cambridge, UK, pp. 72–81.

Knight, C.H., Sorensen, A., 2001. Windows in early mammary development; critical or not? Reproduction 122, 337–345.

Knight, C.H., Hirst, D., Dewhurst, R.J., 1994. Milk accumulation and distribution in the bovine udder during the interval between milkings. J. Dairy Res. 61, 167–177.

Knight, C.H., Muir, D.D., Sorensen, A., 2000. Non-nutritional (novel) techniques for manipulation of milk composition. Br. Soc. Anim. Sci. Occas. Pub. 25, 223–239.

Kratochwil, K., 1986. Hormone action and epithelial-stromal interaction: mutual interdependence. Horm. Cell. Regn. 139, 9.

Kuhn, N.J., 2009. Progesterone withdrawal as the lactogenic trigger in the rat. 1969. J. Mammary Gland Biol. Neoplasia 14, 327–342.

Lacasse, P., Ollier, S., Lollivier, V., Boutinaud, M., 2016. New insights into the importance of prolactin in dairy ruminants. J. Dairy Sci. 99, 864–874.

Lenton, S., Nylander, T., Teixeira, S.C., Holt, C., 2015. A review of the biology of calcium phosphate sequestration with special reference to milk. Dairy Sci. Technol. 95, 3–14.

Lincoln, D.W., Renfree, M.B., 1981. Mammary gland growth and milk ejection in the Agile wallaby, *Macropus agilis*, displaying concurrent asynchronous lactation. J. Reprod. Fertil. 63, 193–203.

Linzell, J.L., Peaker, M., 2009. Changes in colostrum composition and in the permeability of the mammary epithelium at about the time of parturition in the goat. 1974. J. Mammary Gland Biol. Neoplasia. 14, p271−p293.

Liston, J., 1998. Breastfeeding and the use of recreational drugs—alcohol, caffeine, nicotine and marijuana. Breastfeed. Rev. 6, 27−30.

Loudon, A.S., McNeilly, A.S., Milne, J.A., 1983. Nutrition and lactational control of fertility in red deer. Nature 302, 145−147.

Lucey, J., 1996. Cheesemaking from grass based seasonal milk and problems associated with late-lactation milk. J. Soc. Dairy Technol. 49, 59−64.

Lundwall, A., 2013. Old genes and new genes: the evolution of the kallikrein locus. Thromb. Haemost. 110, 469−475.

Maciel, G.M., Poulsen, N.A., Larsen, M.K., Kidmose, U., Gaillard, C., Sehested, J., et al., 2016. Good sensory quality and cheesemaking properties in milk from Holstein cows managed for an 18-month calving interval. J. Dairy Sci. 99, 8524−8536.

Marasco, L.A., 2014. Unsolved mysteries of the human mammary gland: defining and redefining the critical questions from the lactation consultant's standpoint. J. Mammary Gland Biol. Neoplasia 19, 271−288.

Maule Walker, F.M., Peaker, M., 1980. Local production of prostaglandins in relation to mammary function at the onset of lactation in the goat. J. Physiol. 309, 65−79.

Mclellan, H.L., Miller, S.J., Hartmann, P.E., 2008. Evolution of lactation: nutrition v. protection with special reference to five mammalian species. Nutr. Res. Rev. 21, 97−116.

McManaman, J.L., 2014. Lipid transport in the lactating mammary gland. J. Mammary Gland Biol. Neoplasia 19, 35−42.

Meena, S., Rajput, Y.S., Pandey, A.K., Sharma, R., Singh, R., 2016. Camel milk ameliorates hyperglycaemia and oxidative damage in type-1 diabetic experimental rats. J. Dairy Res. 83, 412−419.

Mepham, T.B., 1977a. Physiology of Lactation. Open University Press, Milton Keynes.

Mepham, T.B., 1977b. Synthesis and secretion of milk proteins. Symp. Zool. Soc Lond 41, 57−75.

Nazemi, S., Aalbæk, B., Kjelgaad-Hansen, M., Safayi, S., Klærke, D., Knight, C.H., 2014a. Expression of acute phase proteins and inflammatory cytokines in mouse mammary gland following Staphylococcus aureus challenge and in response to milk accumulation. J. Dairy Res. 81, 445−454.

Nazemi, S., Rahbek, M., Parhamifar, L., Moghimi, S.M., Babamoradi, H., Mehrdana, F., et al., 2014b. Reciprocity in the developmental regulation of aquaporins 1, 3 and 5 during pregnancy and lactation in the rat. PLoS One 9, e106809.

Neville, M.C., 2009. Classic studies of mammary development and milk secretion: 1945−1980. J. Mammary Gland Biol. Neoplasia 14, 193−197.

Neville, M.C., Peaker, M., 1981. Ionized calcium in milk and the integrity of the mammary epithelium in the goat. J. Physiol 313, 561−570.

Nicholas, K.R., 1988. Asynchronous dual lactation in a marsupial, the tammar wallaby (Macropus eugenii). Biochem. Biophys. Res. Commun. 154, 529−536.

Nommsen-Rivers, L.A., 2016. Does insulin explain the relation between maternal obesity and poor lactation outcomes? An overview of the literature. Adv. Nutr. 7, 407−414.

Oftedal, O.T., 1984. Milk composition, milk yield and energy output at peak lactation: a comparative review. In: Peaker, M., Vernon, R.G., Knight, C.H. (Eds.), Physiological Strategies in Lactation. Academic Press, London, pp. 33−85.

Oftedal, O.T., 2012. The evolution of milk secretion and its ancient origins. Animal 6, 355−368.

Peaker, M., 1996. Intercellular signaling in and by the mammary gland: an overview. In: Wilde, C.J., Peaker, M., Taylor, E. (Eds.), Biological Signaling and the Mammary Gland. Hannah Research Institute, pp. 3–13.

Penry, J.F., Endres, E.L., de Bruijn, B., Kleinhans, A., Crump, P.M., Reinemann, D.J., et al., 2016. Effect of incomplete milking on milk production rate and composition with 2 daily milkings. J. Dairy Sci. Available from: https://doi.org/10.3168/jds.2016-11935.

Pettersson, G., Svennersten-Sjaunja, K., Knight, C.H., 2011. Relationships between milking frequency, lactation persistency and milk yield in Swedish Red heifers and cows milked in a voluntary attendance automatic milking system. J. Dairy Res. 78, 379–384.

Politis, I., Lachance, E., Block, E., Turner, J.D., 1989. Plasmin and plasminogen in bovine milk: a relationship with involution? J. Dairy Sci. 72, 900–906.

Renfree, M.B., 2006. Society for Reproductive Biology Founders' Lecture 2006—life in the pouch: womb with a view. Reprod. Fertil. Dev. 18, 721–734.

Scott, J.A., Robertson, M., Fitzpatrick, J.A., Knight, C.H., Mulholland, S., 2008. Occurrence of lactational mastitis and medical management: a prospective cohort study in Glasgow. Int. Breastfeed. J. 3, 21–26.

Sejrsen, K., Purup, S., Vestergaard, M., Foldager, J., 2000. High body weight gain and reduced bovine mammary growth: physiological basis and implications for milk yield potential. Domest. Anim. Endocrinol. 19, p93–p104.

Shamay, A., Shapiro, F., Mabjeesh, S.J., Silanikove, N., 2002. Casein-derived phosphopeptides disrupt tight junction integrity, and precipitously dry up milk secretion in goats. Life Sci. 70, 2707–2719.

Shennan, D.B., Peaker, M., 2000. Transport of milk constituents by the mammary gland. Physiol. Rev. 80, 925–951.

Sorensen, A., Muir, D.D., Knight, C.H., 2001. Thrice-daily milking throughout lactation maintains epithelial integrity and thereby improves milk protein quality. J. Dairy Res. 68, 15–25.

Sorensen, A., Muir, D.D., Knight, C.H., 2008. Extended lactation in dairy cows: effects of milking frequency, calving season and nutrition on lactation persistency and milk quality. J. Dairy Res. 75, 90–97.

Sorensen, M.T., Nørgaard, J.V., Theil, P.K., Vestergaard, M., Sejrsen, K., 2006. Cell turnover and activity in mammary tissue during lactation and the dry period in dairy cows. J. Dairy Sci. 89, 4632–4639.

Stelwagen, K., Singh, K., 2014. The role of tight junctions in mammary gland function. J. Mammary Gland Biol. Neoplasia 19, 131–138.

Stelwagen, K., Grieve, D.G., Walton, J.S., Ball, J.L., Mcbride, B.W., 1993. Effect of prepartum bovine somatotropin in primigravid ewes on mammogenesis, milk production, and hormone concentrations. J. Dairy Sci. 76, 992–1001.

Stelwagen, K., Farr, V.C., Mcfadden, H.A., Prosser, C.G., Davis, S.R., 1997. Time course of milk accumulation-induced opening of mammary tight junctions, and blood clearance of milk components. Am. J. Physiol. 273, R379–R386.

Suárez-Trujillo, A., Casey, T.M., 2016. Serotonergic and circadian systems: driving mammary gland development and function. Front. Physiol. 7, 301.

Thorning, T.K., Raben, A., Tholstrup, T., Soedamah-Muthu, S.S., Givens, I., Astrup, A., 2016. Milk and dairy products: good or bad for human health? An assessment of the totality of scientific evidence. Food Nutr. Res. 60, 32527.

Truchet, S., Chat, S., Ollivier-Bousquet, M., 2014. Milk secretion: the role of SNARE proteins. J. Mammary Gland Biol. Neoplasia 19, 119–130.

Wang, H., Hurley, W.L., 1998. Identification of lactoferrin complexes in bovine mammary secretions during mammary gland involution. J. Dairy Sci. 81, 1896–1903.

Weaver, L.T., 1997. Significance of bioactive substances in milk to the human neonate. In: Tucker, H.A., Petitclerc, D., Knight, C., Sejrsen, K. (Eds.), Third International Workshop on the Biology of Lactation in Farm Animals. Elsevier, Amsterdam, pp. 139–146.

Weaver, S.R., Hernandez, L.L., 2016. Autocrine-paracrine regulation of the mammary gland. J. Dairy Sci. 99, 842–853.

Wickramasinghe, S., Rincon, G., Islas-Trejo, A., Medrano, J.F., 2012. Transcriptional profiling of bovine milk using RNA sequencing. BMC Genomics 13, 45.

Wilde, C.J., Addey, C.V., Boddy, L.M., Peaker, M., 1995. Autocrine regulation of milk secretion by a protein in milk. Biochem. J. 305, 51–58.

Willumsen, J.F., Filteau, S.M., Coutsoudis, A., Uebel, K.E., Newell, M.L., Tomkins, A. M., 2000. Subclinical mastitis as a risk factor for mother-infant HIV transmission. Adv. Exp. Med. Biol. 478, 211–223.

Yagdiran, Y., Oskarsson, A., Knight, C.H., Tallkvist, J., 2016. ABC- and SLC-transporters in murine and bovine mammary epithelium—effects of prochloraz. PLoS One 11, e0151904.

Zhang, L., Boeren, S., Hageman, J.A., Van Hooijdonk, T., Vervoort, J., Hettinga, K., 2015. Perspective on calf and mammary gland development through changes in the bovine milk proteome over a complete lactation. J. Dairy Sci. 98, 5362–5373.

Zhao, F.Q., 2014. Biology of glucose transport in the mammary gland. J. Mammary Gland Biol. Neoplasia 19, 3–17.

CHAPTER 2

Physicochemical Characteristics of Raw Milk

**Isis Rodrigues Toledo Renhe[1], Ítalo Tuler Perrone[2],
Guilherme M. Tavares[3], Pierre Schuck[4] and Antonio F. de Carvalho[5]**
[1]Instituto de Laticínios Cândido Tostes, EPAMIG, Juiz de Fora, Brazil
[2]Faculdade de Farmácia, Universidade Federal de Juiz de Fora, Juiz de Fora, Brazil
[3]Faculdade de Engenharia de Alimentos, Universidade de Campinas, Campinas, Brazil
[4]STLO, Agrocampus Ouest, UMR1253, INRA, Rennes, France
[5]Departamento de Tecnologia de Alimentos Universidade Federal de Viçosa, Viçosa, Brazil

2.1 STRUCTURAL AND PHYSICOCHEMICAL COMPOSITION OF MILK

The three main components in milk are water, lactose, and fat. Proteins are the fourth main constituent in cow's milk with an average content of approximately 3.3% w/w (Walstra et al., 2006). Milk's composition varies according to genetic factors (species and breed), seasons, lactation phases, illnesses, and feedings. Structure can be defined as the physical arrangement of chemical components in a system and in milk itself. Like any other system, milk's structure becomes variable once it is in thermodynamic equilibrium. Fat in milk is emulsified forming the fat globules, which are supramolecular structures of diameter ranging from 0.1 to 20 μm, and a mean diameter of about 3—5 μm (Lopez, 2011). There are around 10 trillion fat globules per liter of milk, whose develop a surface up to hundreds of square meter. The fat globules can be easily separated from the milk by centrifugation obtaining the milk plasma, which corresponds to the continuous phase in which the milk fat is emulsified (Walstra and Jenness, 1984). Casein micelles are other supramolecular structures of milk, which are in colloidal dispersion in the milk plasma. These casein micelles are highly hydrated aggregates formed by proteins and minerals (mainly calcium and phosphate), presenting a polydispersity with diameter ranging from 150 to 300 nm (Müller-Buschbaum et al., 2007). Although they represent a lower proportion of the milk dry matter, because of their smaller sizes, they are 10,000 times more numerous in milk than fat globules (Walstra and Jenness, 1984). By separating casein

Raw Milk
DOI: https://doi.org/10.1016/B978-0-12-810530-6.00002-X

29

Table 2.1 Comparative composition of cow's milk, buffalo's milk, and goat's milk

Composition (g.100 g^{-1})	Cow	Buffalo	Goat
Total dry matter	12.7	17.6	12.5
Lipids	3.7	7.0	3.8
Casein	2.6	3.5	4.7
Whey proteins	0.6	0.8	0.4
Lactose	4.8	5.2	4.1
Ash	0.7	0.8	0.8

Sources: Adapted from Jandal, J.M., 1996. Comparative aspects of goat and sheep milk. Small Rumin. Res. 22 (2), 177–185; Ahmad, S., Gaucher, I., Rousseau, F., Beaucher, E., Piot, M., Grongnet, J.F., Gaucheron, F., 2008. Effects of acidification on physico-chemical characteristics of buffalo milk: a comparison with cow's milk. Food Chem. 106 (1), 11–17.

micelles from milk plasma by ultracentrifugation or microfiltration the whey is obtained. Whey is then the fluid in which the casein micelles are dispersed. In the whey the whey proteins are dispersed, which are globular proteins presenting a diameter of few nanometers (around 5 nm). They can be fractionated from the whey by ultrafiltration.

Table 2.1 shows the average composition of the constituents that appear in highest concentrations for the three primary commercial species: cow's milk, buffalo's milk, and goat's milk, and highlights the variability among the three species. Higher concentrations do not directly correspond to a degree of importance. Minor constituents such as vitamins, enzymes, and trace elements play an important nutritional role and they also catalyze reactions and impact milk flavor. It is worth noting that contamination factors such as antibiotics and pesticides can modify milk composition and certain milk properties.

2.2 BIOSYNTHESIS OF MAJOR COMPONENTS

Milk's composition and physicochemical characteristics depend directly on its biosynthesis process, which occurs during the animal's lactation period. In essence, the process comprises three actions: secretion (intracellular synthesis), release/expulsion of secretory cells, and secretory cell storage in the alveoli, ducts, and cisterns. Lactation control depends on endocrine gland hormonal activity and is directly influenced by the animal's physiological state.

Milk constituents originate in the animal's blood. They can be passed from the blood directly into the milk or they can be synthesized from blood precursors in the secretory cells. The animal initially undergoes mammogenesis, a nonproducing stage. Then breast tissue preparation occurs accompanied by increased concentrations of progesterone and estrogen. In lactogenesis, milk secretion begins with an increase in prolactin concentration and a decrease in progesterone and estrogen. Production is maintained during galactopoiesis. As lactation progresses, prolactin levels decrease while progesterone and estrogen levels increase. Blood constituents, the modifications they undergo in secretory cells, and how they ultimately occur in milk are shown in Fig. 2.1. Fig. 2.1 also shows how milk composition depends on feeding, blood composition, animal physiology, and secretory cell processes.

Milk's fatty acid composition depends on feeding (long-chain fatty acids, acetate, and β-hydroxybutyrate availability) as well as on biohydrogenation by microorganisms in the rumen. Lactose synthesis from glucose and galactose depends on the lactose synthetase enzyme (galactosyl transferase + α-lactoalbumin). Its release into the lumen occurs in equilibrium with the passage of salts, primarily chlorides. Milk must be synthesized in isotonicity with the animal's blood. This imposes

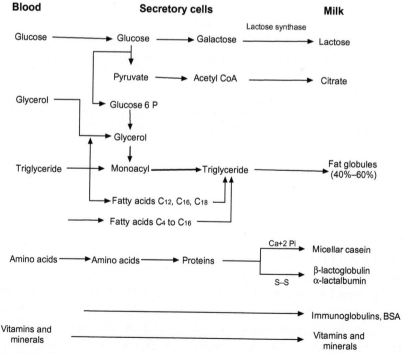

Figure 2.1 Diagram of milk constituent biosynthesis.

physiological limitations on milk composition. At the end of lactation and in cases of infection (mammary), there is an increase in the transfer of blood constituents to the milk, via a paracellular route, which results in a change in composition (lower concentration of lactose, higher concentration of chlorides and serum proteins: immunoglobulins and bovine serum albumin (BSA)) and in changes in physicochemical properties (decrease in thermal stability, change in curd characteristics during cheese production). Protein composition and properties depend on the amino acid sequence established by ribosomes and on the translational modifications that occur in the Golgi vesicles. The translational modifications worth noting are phosphorylation, glycosylation, calcium and citrate bonds, and sulfur—sulfur bonds. The fat globule trilayer membrane originates from polar lipids and proteins from the endoplasmic reticulum and from the bilayer apical membrane of the secretory cells (Heid and Keenan, 2005). This, to a large extent, determines milk's composition and properties.

2.3 INTRODUCTION TO MAIN CONSTITUENTS

The main constituents of milk are water, proteins, lactose, lipids, and salts. The physicochemical properties of milk are similar to those of water. The properties are modified, however, by the presence of substances/solutes in the aqueous phase and by the colloidal and emulsified components. The content of soluble molecules in milk (especially lactose and salts) influences its osmotic pressure (around 700 kPa), water activity (around 0.993), boiling point (around 100.15°C), and freezing point (around −0.552°C to −0.540°C) (Walstra et al., 2006). The content of salts determines the ionic strength of the milk (around 0.08 M) and, together with the protein content, are the main responsible for its titratable acidity (around 0.14%−0.18% expressed as lactic acid), pH (around 6.6−6.8 at 25°C), and buffering capacity. The color of milk is dictated, among other factors, by the scattering of visible light in fat globules and casein micelles. The content of fat and protein in milk also impacts on its viscosity (around 2.1 mPa s, at 20°C), refractive index (around 1.3440−1.3485, at 20°C), and surface tension (around 52 N m^{-1}) (Walstra et al., 2006). The fat content has also great impact on the density (between 1028 and 1034 kg m^{-3}), thermal conductivity (around 0.559 W m^{-1} K^{-1}), and specific heat (around 3.93 kJ kg^{-1} K^{-1}) of milk (Walstra et al., 2006). The redox potential of milk (around +0.25 to +0.35 V, at 25°C and pH of 6.7) is dictated by its concentration of dissolved oxygen.

2.3.1 Water

The water present in milk performs different chemical interactions with different magnitudes. Hydrophilic constituents interact strongly via ion—dipole or dipole—dipole interactions with water. Some of the water present in milk has low molecular motility; it will not freeze at temperatures of − 40°C and it is very close to the surface of the solutes and nonaqueous constituents. Water can be classified as constitutional (conducts chemical interactions of large magnitude and forms an integral part of other molecules), vicinal or monolayer (present in the first binding site of hydrophilic compound), and multilayer (occupies other binding sites around the monolayer). One of the most important aspects of water in milk and in dairy is its effect on chemical, physical, and microbiological stability. For example:

- Chemical stability: the Maillard reaction, lipid oxidation, vitamin loss, pigment stability, and protein denaturation are examples of reactions influenced by food water activity.
- Physical stability: saline balance and lactose physical state (amorphous or crystalline) are influenced by the availability of water.
- Microbiological stability: the water activity of the medium has the capacity to affect microbial growth by allowing or inhibiting the development of microorganisms.

2.3.2 Proteins and Other Nitrogen Compounds

Nitrogen compounds are important milk constituents and can be analyzed by the Kjeldahl method. The nitrogen compounds found in milk include protein nature compounds (approximately 95%, known as protein nitrogen (PN)) and nonprotein nature compounds (approximately 5%, known as nonprotein nitrogen (NPN)). NPN consists of urea, uric acid, creatine, and amino acids. The proteins can be grouped into caseins, whey proteins, proteins associated with the milk-fat-globule-membrane and enzymes, as shown in Fig. 2.2.

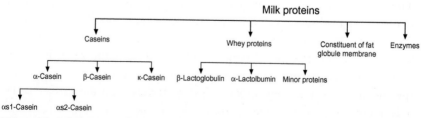

Figure 2.2 Subdivisions of nitrogenous protein fraction for cow's milk.

Caseins are the primary milk proteins and make up 78.3% of the total proteins in milk. Caseins precipitate near their isoelectric point, at pH 4.6 (Walstra et al., 2006). This distinguishes them from native whey proteins, which do not precipitate at this pH. Caseins do not present themselves as single molecules but as large, complex supramolecular structures rich in calcium phosphate presenting a diameter ranging from 150 to 300 nm, known as casein micelles (Swaisgood, 2003; Müller-Buschbaum et al., 2007). These casein micelles correspond to the self-assemble of different casein molecules (fractions): α_{s1}-, α_{s2}-, β-, and κ-caseins. The main characteristics of these caseins fractions are presented in Table 2.2. Casein micelles present a molecular mass of around 10^5 kDa and the caseins fractions obey the ratio of: α_{s1}:α_{s2}:β:κ = 4:1:4:1.3 on its structure. Caseins are calcium sensitive in this order: α_s > β > κ-casein. The formation of dairy matrices such as cheese and yogurt are based on the creation of a casein micelle protein network. Micelle structure is made up of 94% proteins and 6% salts (by mass) in the dry base. On average, milk has 10^{15} casein micelles per milliliter distanced from each other around 240 nm, they are very hydrated structures entrapping up to 3.3 g of water per gram of protein (Huppertz et al., 2017). There is still debate over of the casein micelle structure and its classification as nanocluster, dual-binding, or the submicellar. Because of the heterogeneity in microscopy image, casein micelles have been interpreted as either subunits or clusters of calcium phosphate (Dalgleish, 2011; Dalgleish and Corredig, 2012; de Kruif and Holt, 2003). This submicellar model describes the different substructures with different individual casein compositions linked by calcium phosphate. The term "nanocluster model" is derived from the thesis that the specific assembly of the casein micelles comes from the salt bridging of calcium phosphate nanoclusters to specific binding sites of calcium-sensitive caseins (de Kruif and Holt, 2003). Finally, the dual-binding model describes protein assembly from a polymerization point of view without reference to the casein micelle interior (Dalgleish, 2011). The dual-binding and nanocluster models are similar and suggest calcium phosphate nanoclusters are the structure by which calcium is present on the protein. Phosphoamino acids concentrated along the protein sequence turn into phosphate centers, with a stable link to calcium phosphate. The only general agreement on casein structure between the two casein structure seems to be that most of the κ-casein is found on the surface of the casein micelles. This protein plays a role in the protection of calcium-sensitive caseins. The protein also protects the steric stability of casein

Table 2.2 Properties and characteristics of casein fractions and whey proteins

Properties/characteristics	Casein fractions				Whey proteins	
	α_{s1}	α_{s2}	β	κ	β-lactoglobulin	α-lactoalbumin
Molecular mass (kDa)	23.6	25.2	24	19	18.3	14.2
Amino acid residues	199	207	209	169	162	123
Phosphoserine residues	8	11	5	1	0	0
Free cysteine residues	0	0	0	0 or 2	1	0
Cystine residues (S—S bonds)	0	1	0	0 or 1	2	4
Isoelectric point (pI)	4.9	5.2	5.4	5.6	5.1—5.2	4.3—4.7
Glycosylation	–	–	–	+	–	–
Ca^{2+} bond	+ + +	+ + +	+ +	+	–	+

micelles through the presence of a hairy layer. The layer is the result of an extension of κ-casein from the casein micelles' surface (Dalgleish and Corredig, 2012; de Kruif and Holt, 2003; Swaisgood, 2003).

Whey proteins represent about 20% w/w of the total protein content of milk. They are globular proteins and possess different behavior during milk processing compared to caseins, for example, different from casein the whey protein are heat sensitive (Anema, 2009; Walstra et al., 2006). β-lactoglobulin is the major whey protein and accounts for about 50% of whey proteins in milk. It is present in milk mostly as a dimer and possesses one free thiol group, which becomes highly reactive after heating (Anema, 2009; Donato and Guyomarc'h, 2009). This in turn leads to the formation of aggregates with itself as well as with other milk proteins. β-lactoglobulin tends to dominate whey properties during processing (O'Mahony and Fox, 2013) because of its higher concentration and easier denaturation. α-lactalbumin represents the second highest protein content in the whey, accounting for approximately 20% of whey proteins. It is a metalloprotein that binds to Ca^{2+}. α-lactalbumin does not usually associate, except in special conditions, and is very sensitive to heat treatment, especially when no other protein is present (O'Mahony and Fox, 2013; Walstra et al., 2006). Because α-lactalbumin takes part in lactose synthesis, these two constituents' concentrations are related and α-lactalbumin plays a major role in milk composition and production volume (O'Mahony and Fox, 2013). Other minor proteins present in the whey include BSA, immunoglobulins, proteose–peptone, and lactoferrin.

2.3.3 Lactose

Lactose is the main carbohydrate component of milk and the primary source of energy for the infant. Lactose is a disaccharide formed by the β1-4 glycosidic bond between galactose and glucose molecules. The lactose content in the milk of different species is variable, cow and human milks present an average of 4.8% and 7.0%, respectively. Lactose is considered to be a prebiotic molecule, as it favors the development of the bifid bacteria and enhances calcium and vitamin D absorption. Lactose is composed of D-galactose and D-glucose wherein the aldehyde group of galactose is attached to the C-4 group of glucose by a β-1-4-glycosidic bond. This linkage can be disrupted by the enzymatic action of β-galactosidase, which hydrolyzes lactose into its constituent monosaccharides: galactose and glucose. This conversion is of considerable interest to the dairy industry because the combined products that are the result of hydrolysis are sweeter and more soluble. They are also directly fermented and immediately absorbed by the infant's intestines. The average solubility of lactose at 20°C is 18.2 g 100 g^{-1} of water, whereas the solubility of glucose is 107 g 100 g^{-1} of water and galactose is 50 g 100 g^{-1} of water. Lactose is not as sweet as other sugars such as sucrose, glucose, and fructose. Lactose is reported to be five times less sweet than sucrose. Lactose molecule properties influence the production and characteristics of various dairy products. Production of fermented dairy products is based on the fermentation of lactose. The main by-product of this fermentation process is lactic acid. Secondary by-products include carbon dioxide, acetic acid, diacetyl, and acetaldehyde. Lactose fermentation makes it possible to transform milk into fermented milks and cheeses, and it is one of the methods used to preserve milk. The low solubility of lactose has a direct impact on milk, condensed milk, whey, and milk powder production, where saturation and supersaturation levels of lactose are reached in the solution. The appearance of crystals perceptible to the palate characterizes one of the main issues in the concentrated dairy products conservation. In condensed milk manufacturing technology, microcrystallization or forced/induced crystallization is used to obtain lactose crystals smaller than 16 μm, which makes it a fundamental step in controlling the texture of the final product. For dulce de leche, crystal size is controlled by increasing the viscosity, which can be accomplished by adding thickening agents. This technique does not prevent crystallization; it only hinders the formation of crystals that are perceptible to the palate. The use of lactase (enzyme) prevents crystallization, but it entails changes in production technology. Control or prevention of crystallization in various food products requires an understanding of the kinetics of the process and knowledge of the interactions between mass transfer, energy, and momentum properties during crystal formation and storage. For example, a solution's ultimate lactose content and product temperature are determining factors for condensed milk and dried concentrated whey crystallization. The final lactose content in the solution will depend on initial lactose content and the amount of water in the final product. A decrease in product temperature will result in a decrease in lactose solubility, favoring crystallization. In condensed milk production, a forced or induced crystallization, also known as secondary nucleation, is performed. The process consists of three steps: controlled cooling of the product, the addition of crystallization nuclei (lactose powder), and continuous stirring. The controlled and rapid cooling intensifies the driving force of the crystallization step and favors the nuclei formation. The addition of lactose powder (nuclei) helps obtain a large number of small crystals. Smaller crystals are more desirable because they hinder the consumer's sensorial perception of the crystals present.

Lactose molecules are also subject to the Maillard reaction, a nonenzymatic browning reaction that impacts several characteristics of milk and its derivatives. Productionwise some of these changes are desirable, while others have a negative impact on characteristics. Maillard reaction results include: decrease in protein nutritional value due to blocked lysine residues, which are indigestible; production of compounds that generate flavor and aroma; formation of antioxidant compounds during the reaction's more advanced stages; formation of antibacterial compounds; and development of brownish coloration due to melanoidines. The main factors that interfere in the nonenzymatic browning reaction are temperature, pH, water activity, the nature of the carbohydrate, the nature of the amino acid and catalyst effects. The Maillard reaction is slower at low temperatures and the velocity practically doubles with each increase of 10°C within the range of 40−70°C. Reaction rate is maximal at a pH close to neutral. When water activity is higher than 0.9, that is, when the reactants are very diluted and a lot of nonbound water molecules are availability, there is a decrease in the browning velocity and this velocity tends to zero when water activity reaches values below 0.2. For carbohydrates, the reaction rate is higher in monosaccharides than in disaccharides. For amino acids, the availability of nonprotonated amino groups increases the velocity of the first steps of the Maillard reaction. Finally, the Maillard reaction is accelerated in presence of phosphate and citrate anions and copper ions. Understanding the factors that influence the Maillard reaction is paramount for the production of dulce de leche and condensed milk, since the desired color intensity depends on the preferences found in each marketplace.

2.3.4 Lipids

Lipids are a class of organic compounds that are insoluble in water, but soluble in organic solvents, have hydrocarbon chains in their molecules, and occur in a wide variety of foods. The lipid class includes fatty acids, triacylglycerols, and phospholipids. Cow's milk contains lipids at concentrations of approximately $2.8 \text{ g } 100 \text{ mL}^{-1}$ to $6.0 \text{ g } 100 \text{ mL}^{-1}$, with mean values ranging from 3.5 g 100 mL^{-1} to 4.0 g 100 mL^{-1}. Milk lipids present themselves as microscopic globules with a lipoprotein membrane that contributes to the stability of the oil/water emulsion. The predominant lipid fractions in milk are triacylglycerols, but milk also contains glycolipids, fat-soluble vitamins, and flavor and aroma determinants such as lactones, aldehydes, and ketones. Fatty acid residues primarily linked to triacylglycerols and phospholipids constitute 90% (by mass) of milk lipids. However, free fatty acids are also present in milk. More than 400 types of fatty acids have been identified in milk but only a small fraction of these are present in concentrations above 1% (by mass). Milk is characterized by relatively high concentrations of short-chain fatty acid residues (C4:0 to C10:0). Butyric acid residues (C4:0) are specific to ruminant milks. Palmitic, stearic, and myristic acids are among the predominant saturated fatty acid residues present. Of the monoenoids, oleic acid residues are the most abundant. Monoenoic fatty acids also comprise transisomers, representing 3.7% (by mass) of milk lipids on average. Polyenes, especially linoleic and α-linolenic, occur at levels close to 3.0% (by mass). Milk lipids contain isomers of conjugated linoleic acid (CLA) in the range of 0.2%–2.0% (by mass), dominated by C18:2 cis-9, trans-11 (rumenic acid). Milk lipid composition is highly variable and its variations are influenced by feeding, breed, and lactation period, as well as the health and age of the animal. Feeding is the most predominant factor. In order to produce dairy products that promote human health and help reduce the risk of cardiovascular disease, there is a growing interest in changes in the qualitative composition of milk lipids. To this end, levels of oleic acid (C18:1 cis-9) and vaccinic acid (C18:1 trans-11), which is the endogenous precursor of CLA, can be increased. The increase requires reduced concentrations of saturated medium-chain fatty acids, such as lauric (C12:0), myristic (C14:0), and palmitic (C16:0) acids. Milk fat's microstructure presents itself as globules with a size of 0.1–20 μm (predominant size of 3–5 μm). The globules are surrounded by a trilayer membrane, which corresponds to 2%–6% (by mass) of the milk lipids. Fat globule membranes are asymmetric and their inner and outer layer compositions are different. Phosphatidylcholine, sphingomyelin, and glycolipids predominate on the outside surface of the globule. Neutral lipids phosphatidylethanolamine and phosphatidylserine are concentrated on the inner layer. The industrial processes used to produce dairy products influence the composition and structure of fat globules. Heating may cause the membrane constituents to interact with denatured whey proteins, especially β-lactoglobulin. Stirring may lead to fat globule coalescence and loss of membrane material. During homogenization, rupturing the globules and shrinking them to a micrometer increases their surface area so that there is no longer adequate membrane material to dispose around the newly formed globules. New membrane begins to coat the globules, a process that depends on the deposit of proteins, like caseins. In the case of butter cream, fat globule disruption leads to the loss of membrane material which migrates to buttermilk. Milk lipids are susceptible to lipolysis. Natural milk lipase is the primary responsible agent for this degradation reaction. Hydrolytic rancidification in dairy products may be caused by the thermostable lipase activity produced by psychrotrophic bacteria or by residual natural lipase activity. Fat globule membranes provide protection against lipolysis. However, some milk may exhibit spontaneous lipolysis or lipolysis which occurs without membrane rupture. Conversely, induced lipolysis, which is the result of membrane damage, is the main mechanism used for milk lipid hydrolysis. Both natural lipases and most bacterial lipases target fatty acid residues at the terminal positions of triacylglycerols. Since milk fat contains a relatively high proportion of short-chain esterified fatty acids at sn-3 position, lipolysis increases the concentration of these compounds in free form. Short-chain fatty acids, in undissociated form, can cause unpleasant taste and aroma in milk and dairy products. Autoxidation may affect milk lipids by generating hydroperoxides. These may decompose into carbonyl compounds with undesirable taste and odor. Milk fat is relatively resistant to oxidation due to the predominance of saturated fatty acids and the presence of natural antioxidants, such as α-tocopherol and β-carotene. Milk lipid oxidation may be induced by the presence of metal, especially copper, or exposure to light. Spontaneous autoxidation can occur depending on food factors and the balance of antioxidant and prooxidant compounds in milk. The oxidative process occurs mainly during milk and dairy product storage. The autoxidation rate depends on the dissolved oxygen concentration, the storage temperature, and the presence of antioxidants and prooxidants.

2.3.5 Salts

Macronutrients (protein, fat, and carbohydrates) are the main focus of milk's nutritional role, especially for infant growth, but salts also have unique nutritional value. Both the minerals present in considerable concentrations and trace minerals play important roles in bone growth and development, in cell function, and in osmolarity maintenance (Lucey and Horne, 2009). Minerals also play key roles in the formation and stabilization of casein micelles due to their buffer capacity, biological functions, and colligative properties (Lucey and Horne, 2009). In dairy production, minerals have a direct impact on protein stability during processing: they affect protein gel texture and cheese functionality and texture, not to mention emulsion stabilization (Lucey and Horne, 2009).

Milk salts are substances which are present in milk as low molar mass ions. The term "salts" does not include "ash" since the milk incineration causes organic salt loss and ash formation from nonsaline compounds. The primary cations in milk are calcium, magnesium, sodium, and potassium. Phosphates, citrates, and chlorides comprise the main anions (Gaucheron, 2005). Milk is saturated with calcium and phosphate. Mineral content in milk is not constant, but varies due to lactation stage, animal nutrition, and environmental and genetic factors.

Minerals, particularly calcium and phosphate, play an important role in the casein micelles' structure and stability. Minerals also impact protein functionality and milk properties during processing. This milk fraction is in a complex, dynamic, and strong interaction with proteins (Gaucheron, 2005). Calcium, inorganic phosphate, and other minerals are distributed between the soluble phase and the colloidal phase (casein micelles) and their distribution noticeably depends on pH, temperature, and concentration, among other factors (Lucey and Horne, 2009). On the soluble phase, they can be further divided as free, on the form of ions associations, or linked to proteins as α-lactalbumin. About two-thirds of calcium and half of the inorganic phosphate are in the colloidal phase, linked to the caseins through phosphoserine residues binding sites (Gaucheron, 2005). Micellar calcium is partially directly bound to the casein by the intermediate of these residues (calcium caseinate), and partially associated to the colloidal inorganic phosphate (calcium phosphate). Calcium can also be bind to casein micelle as calcium citrate.

Salt composition variability may come from the animal itself, while distribution changes are more likely to be induced by process technology. Acidification leads to the protonation of acid–base groups in milk with a consequent release of calcium phosphate from the caseins into the serum phase (Gaucheron, 2005). Heat treatment decreases the solubility of calcium phosphate and induces the formation of colloidal calcium phosphate (CCP) and lower concentrations of these salts can be observed in the soluble phase. This change can be reversible until 90°C for a few minutes.

Severe heating causes irreversible changes in both salt distribution and casein micelles (Gaucheron, 2005; Lucey and Horne, 2009). Cooling has an inverse effect on solubility and results in the solubilization of CCP, which can also credit to β-casein dissociation from casein micelles. Membrane concentration alters fraction proportions and increases CCP as some soluble calcium phosphate is removed. If diafiltration is applied, soluble calcium removal is more extensive and can affect micelle integrity (Li and Corredig, 2014). Chelating agents are important tecnological agent on modulation of salts fractionation. Chelating agents have affinity for cations and are capable of specially displace calcium, then increasing heat stability (de Kort et al., 2012). Increased concentration of chelating agents leads to casein micelle dissociation right up to micellar structure disintegration (Lucey and Horne, 2009).

Soluble salts present themselves in different ionic forms and in nonionized complex forms. Sodium and potassium are entirely present as cations. Chlorides and sulfates (strong acid salts) occur as anions in milk normal pH. Phosphates, citrates, and carbonates (weak acid salts) are distributed in milk as various ionic forms. The ionic calcium present in milk influences the denaturation temperature of β-lactoglobulin and promotes its aggregation, increasing the deposit and formation of bridges between adsorbed proteins on the surface of the heat exchangers. This aggregation is relevant because fouling in heat exchangers is a serious problem as it reduces heat transfer efficiency and causes an increased pressure drop in the system, which ultimately affects the profitability of a processing plant. As a result of fouling, there are increased risks of product quality deterioration because the fluid may not be heated to the required temperature for the heat treatment. Also, deposits washed away by product flow can cause significant contamination. Once calcium phosphate precipitation occurs, the concentration effect on the salt partition is a given because milk is saturated with calcium and phosphate.

Salts represent a small fraction of milk content when compared to lipids or proteins, but they play an important role in the structure and stability of casein micelles. Minor changes in the physicochemical processing conditions may induce composition variations or salt partitioning and, consequently, affect casein micelle stability. The thermal stability of milk may be reduced due to high calcium activity, low phosphate and citrate activity, and successive heat treatments. Salt imbalance may also cause a false positive alcohol or alizarol test.

REFERENCES

Ahmad, S., Gaucher, I., Rousseau, F., Beaucher, E., Piot, M., Grongnet, J.F., Gaucheron, F., 2008. Effects of acidification on physico-chemical characteristics of buffalo milk: A comparison with cow's milk. Food Chem. 106 (1), 11−17.

Anema, S.G., 2009. The whey proteins in milk: thermal denaturation, physical interactions and effects on the functional properties of milk. In: Thompson, A., Boland, M., Singh, H. (Eds.), Milk Proteins: From Expression to Food, first ed Academic Press, Amsterdam, pp. 239−282.

Dalgleish, D.G., 2011. On the structural models of bovine casein micelles—review and possible improvements. Soft Matter 7 (6), 2265.

Dalgleish, D.G., Corredig, M., 2012. The structure of the casein micelle of milk and its changes during processing. Annu. Rev. Food Sci. Technol. 3, 449−467.

Donato, L., Guyomarc'h, F., 2009. Formation and properties of the whey protein-κ-casein complexes in heated skim milk —A review. Dairy Sci. Technol. 89, 3−29.

Gaucheron, F., 2005. The minerals of milk. Reprod. Nutr. Dev. 45, 473−483.

Heid, H.W., Keenan, T.W., 2005. Intracellular origin and secretion of milk fat globules. Eur. J. Cell Biol. 84, 245−258.

Huppertz, T., Gazi, I., Luyten, H., Nieuwenhuijse, H., Alting, A., Schokker, E., 2017. Hydration of casein micelles and caseinates: implications for casein micelle structure. Int. Dairy J. 74, 1−11.

Jandal, J.M., 1996. Comparative aspects of goat and sheep milk. Small Rumin. Res. 22 (2), 177−185.

de Kort, E., Minor, M., Snoeren, T., Van Hooijdonk, T., Van der Linden, E., 2012. Effect of calcium chelators on heat coagulation and heat-induced changes of concentrated micellar casein solutions: the role of calcium-ion activity and micellar integrity. Int. Dairy J. 26 (2), 112−119.

de Kruif, C.G., Holt, C., 2003. Casein micelle structure, functions and interactions. In: Fox, P.F., Mcsweeney, P.L.H. (Eds.), Advanced Dairy Chemistry—Volume 1 Proteins Part A, third ed Kluwer Academic/Plenum Publishers, New York, pp. 233−276.

Li, Y., Corredig, M., 2014. Calcium release from milk concentrated by ultrafiltration and diafiltration. J. Dairy Sci. 97, 5294−5302.

Lopez, C., 2011. Milk fat globules enveloped by their biological membrane: unique colloidal assemblies with a specific composition and structure. Curr. Opin. Colloid Interf. Sci. 16 (5), 391−404.

Lucey, J.A., Horne, D.S., 2009. Milk Salts: Technological Significance. In: Fox, P.F., Mcsweeney, P.L.H. (Eds.), Advanced Dairy Chemistry—Volume 3—Lactose, Water, Salts and Minor Constitutents, third ed Springer, New York, pp. 351−389.

Müller-Buschbaum, P., Gebhardt, R., Roth, S.V., Metwalli, E., Doster, W., 2007. Effect of calcium concentration on the structure of casein micelles in thin films. Biophys. J. 93 (3), 960−968.

O'Mahony, J.A., Fox, P.F., 2013. Milk proteins: introduction and historical aspects. In: Mcsweeney, P.L.H., Fox, P.F. (Eds.), Advanced Dairy Chemistry—Volume 1A Proteins: Basics Aspects, fourth ed. Springer, New York, pp. 43−85.

Swaisgood, H.E., 2003. Chemistry of the caseins. In: Mcsweeney, P.L.H., Fox, P.F. (Eds.), Advanced Dairy Chemistry—Volume 1 Proteins Part A, third ed. Kluwer Academic/Plenum Publishers, New York, pp. 139−201.

Walstra, P., Jenness, R., 1984. Química y física lactológica. Editorial Acribia, Zaragoza, 423.

Walstra, P., Wouters, J.T.M., Geurts, T.J., 2006. Dairy Science and Technology, second ed. CRC Press, Boca Raton, FL, 808 pp.

CHAPTER 3

The Microbiology of Raw Milk

Luana M. Perin[1], Juliano G. Pereira[2],
Luciano S. Bersot[3] and Luís A. Nero[1]
[1]Departamento de Veterinária, Universidade Federal de Viçosa, Viçosa, Brazil
[2]Universidade Federal do Pampa, Uruguaiana, Rio Grande do Sul, Brazil
[3]Universidade Federal do Paraná, Setor Palotina, Palotina, Brazil

3.1 INTRODUCTION

Since the domestication of cattle, humans started to obtain milk for own consumption, leading to the development of a complex chain. As consequence, various dairy products were developed for human consumption, due to the versatility of milk itself and its compounds, such as fat and proteins. Also, different equipment and processes were designed for the dairy chain, since the initial steps of production in farms (milking, storage), transport to dairy industries, and processing. This complex dairy chain increases the chances of microbial contamination in milk, what can be considered as common due to nature of milk production at farms.

The control of microbial contamination in milk can be considered as a key point in the quality and safety control of dairy products. Many microorganisms that contaminate milk are pathogenic, posing as hazards for humans. Other microbial groups are relevant to indicate the hygienic conditions of milk production and storage, allowing producers, industries, and food inspectors to assess the production conditions and predict the spoilage and usage of milk for dairy products. Finally, other microbial groups can present positive and desirable features, leading their usage as probiotics or beneficial bacteria and also as starter cultures for fermented foods. All these microbial groups can contaminate milk at different steps of production, highlighting their relevance for the dairy chain.

In this chapter we will describe the main microbial groups naturally present in raw milk, focusing of their main sources of contamination and how they can impact the milk quality, as well as their consequences for the quality and safety of milk and dairy products.

Raw Milk
DOI: https://doi.org/10.1016/B978-0-12-810530-6.00003-1

3.2 MICROBIAL GROUPS PRESENT IN RAW MILK AND DAIRY PRODUCTS

Among the animal origin foods, milk is considered one of the best conditions for the development of microorganisms. It is due to factors such as pH, high water activity, and significant amount of nutrients. In this way, microorganisms find in milk favorable conditions for their multiplication.

The raw milk microbiota is very diverse and may be composed of spoilage, pathogenic microorganisms and even bacteria with significant technological importance (Montel et al., 2014; Perin et al., 2017). Anyway, microbial diversity is directly influenced by the sanitary conditions of the dairy herd, environmental hygiene, milking equipment used, and factors related to the raw milk handling, storage, cooling, and processing (Murphy et al., 2016).

Milk remains sterile inside the udder, but during milking the contamination is unavoidable once the product is exposed to air and remain in contact with equipment surfaces. Since environmental (e.g., water quality, hygiene of milking area) and operational conditions (poorly sanitized equipment, poor handling, storage temperature above recommended) are not controlled, milk is contaminated and the bacterial population find optimal conditions for development and multiplication, changing its physical—chemical characteristics and can become a source of contamination by microorganisms of importance in public health (Raza and Kim, 2018). The main routes and sources of contamination of milk during production will be described in this chapter.

3.2.1 Hygiene Indicator Microorganisms

Hygiene indicators are defined as groups or species of microorganisms which, when present in high concentrations in milk, demonstrate inadequate hygienic practices of obtaining, preserving, or processing. The groups of microorganisms most commonly used as indicators of hygiene in milk are aerobic mesophilic, psychrotrophic, and coliforms.

3.2.1.1 Mesophilic and Psychrotrophic Bacteria

Mesophilic microorganisms grow better in moderate temperatures with optimal growth temperatures ranging from 25°C to 40°C; that are optimal conditions also either spoilage and pathogenic bacteria. The main genera of mesophilic bacteria that may be present in milk are *Micrococcus*, *Staphylococcus*, *Enterococcus*, *Escherichia*, *Serratia*, *Acinetobacter*, *Flavobacterium*,

Pseudomonas, Mycobacterium, Bacillus, Lactococcus, Lactobacillus, among others (Jay, 2012). Mesophilic bacteria are considered the universal hygiene indicators and their presence in milk is unavoidable since most of these genera are present in the animal's udder, milkers' hands, equipment surfaces, water, and air. Thus, mesophilic counts are directly influenced by the conditions that milk is submitted after milking (Jay, 2012). As common sense, milk with counts of mesophilic bacteria higher than 5.0 log CFU/mL indicates poor hygienic quality during milking and production, while counts lower than 3.0 log CFU/mL indicate good production practices. In general, good manufacturing practices, adequate cooling, and refrigeration are effective measures to control mesophilic bacteria in milk.

Milk cooling must be performed immediately after milking and the temperature must rapidly reach 4°C to control the multiplication of the microbiota present until thermic treatment. The raw milk refrigeration immediately after milking constitutes the main tool of conservation of the product. However, this practice should not be applied alone, because many microorganisms that contaminate raw milk in the initial stages of production have the capacity to multiply even when submitted to refrigeration temperatures, especially in the marginal temperatures, above ideal and below 10°C (Perin et al., 2012). The microorganisms that have this capacity are named psychrotrophics and are currently considered as one of the main problems related to the microbial contamination of raw milk. The presence of psychrotrophics in milk is of relevance due to their spoilage activity and consequently one of the main limitations of the shelf-life of milk (Cousin, 1982). The main sources of psychrotrophic contamination are poorly sanitized milking equipment and water. Under suitable conditions of milking and preservation, this group generally represents 10% of the microbiota of raw milk, but when milk is obtained under poor hygiene conditions, it can represent about 75% of the total microbiota of raw milk.

The psychrotrophic group comprises several genera and *Pseudomonas* and *Bacillus* are considered the main ones. *Pseudomonas* is considered a classic psychrotrophic, due to its intense metabolic activity in the range of temperature 4–7°C (Jay, 2012). However, *Bacillus* predominates in marginal cooling temperatures, from 8°C to 10°C. Even if the ideal temperature for the multiplication of psychrotrophics is between 4°C and 10°C, in raw milks with initial mesophilic counts of 5.0 log CFU/mL (which would be considered the maximum limit for this group) and stored at temperatures of 4°C or less, psychrotrophic counts increase significantly after 24 h (Scatamburlo et al., 2015; Yamazi et al., 2013). Therefore, hygienic conditions of milking and cooling at 4°C or less are ways to prevent undesirable changes resulting from the presence of this group in raw milk.

3.2.1.2 Coliforms and Enterobacteriaceae

Coliforms are Gram-negative, mesophilic microorganisms that have the ability to ferment lactose producing gas. Coliforms when present in counts above 2.0 log CFU/mL evidence inadequate hygiene practices in the milk processing, besides indicating the possible presence of enteropathogens. Coliforms are present in soil, untreated water, equipment surfaces, and feces. *Escherichia*, *Klebsiella*, *Enterobacter*, and *Citrobacter* belong to the coliform group, however, only *Escherichia coli* has the intestinal tract of human and animals as the primary habitat (Jay, 2012). Thus, the contamination of milk by coliforms does not necessarily indicate that the product had contact with feces, it is necessary to evidence the presence of *E. coli*.

As coliforms are capable of fermenting lactose, the enumeration of Enterobacteriacea has been used as an indicator of milk contamination during milking. Enterobacteriacea is a large family composed of several genera that are capable of fermenting glucose. Since this family includes both coliforms and other genera that do not ferment lactose, the enumeration of Enterobacteriacea can be used as a broader indicator of the contamination that occurred during the various steps of the milk chain, especially milking (Martin et al., 2016).

3.2.2 Pathogenic Microorganisms

Besides the contamination by indicator microorganisms, milk can carry several pathogens, thus affecting the health of consumers, especially when they ingest raw milk or dairy products manufactured with raw milk. Detailed information regarding pathogenic bacteria presented in raw milk and dairy products is addressed in Chapter 12, Foodborne Pathogens and Zoonotic Diseases.

The pathogenic microorganisms can contaminate the milk in two different ways: (1) from diseases that affect the dairy herd, being the etiologic agents excreted by milk, such as *Mycobacterium bovis* and *Brucella abortus*; (2) resulting from nonhygienic milking and handling, allowing contamination by microorganisms through equipment, floor, soil, water, and feces, such as *Staphylococcus aureus*, *Campylobacter* spp., *Salmonella*,

Listeria monocytogenes, Shiga toxin-producing *E. coli* (STEC) (Boor et al., 2017; Gonzales-Barron et al., 2017; Zeinhom and Abdel-Latef, 2014).

Tuberculosis and brucellosis, caused by *M. bovis* and *B. abortus*, respectively, are important diseases concerning public health and economics. These diseases can affect humans either by direct contact with affected animals or by the ingestion of raw milk or dairy products that have not undergone adequate heat treatment (Jay, 2012).

Staphylococcus aureus has been a causative agent of food poisoning related to the ingestion of milk and dairy products. It occurs because *S. aureus* is a major agent of mastitis in dairy cows and also can contaminate the product during the handling of raw milk or dairy products involving food handlers who carry the pathogen in the skin, nasal cavities, and oropharynx. Since sanitary conditions of the animals are not adequate or manipulation allows the contamination by *S. aureus*, production of enterotoxin requires high amounts of the bacteria that can induce a clinical problem in humans characterized by vomiting and dehydration (Cavicchioli et al., 2015; Gonzales-Barron et al., 2017; Viçosa et al., 2010).

Campylobacter spp. is regarded as one of the main agents of foodborne diseases involving the ingestion of milk and raw products. It is estimated that in the United States, this agent represents about 70% of all outbreaks involving the intake of this type of product. However, in some countries, such as Brazil, outbreaks involving the intake of food containing this agent are not reported due, among other issues, to failures in surveillance and sub notification of foodborne diseases. This genus comprises several species, the most important is *Campylobacter jejuni*. Raw milk submitted to inadequate pasteurization is the most frequent cause of campylobacteriosis outbreaks. Contamination by this pathogen occurs during milking, because it may be present in the intestinal tract of cattle and fecal contamination occurs due to inadequate practices during milking. The use of contaminated water has also been reported as a source of contamination in the milking area (Del Collo et al., 2017; Silva et al., 2011).

Campylobacter, *Salmonella*, and STEC are enteropathogens that can be transmitted by raw milk, but less frequently. *Salmonella* and STEC are the main agents of foodborne diseases in the world; however, few outbreaks are due to the ingestion of raw milk or milk products. Since fecal contamination is their main source in food, hygienic practices should be taken to prevent fecal contact with milk, either directly or through fomites and water (Gonzales-Barron et al., 2017).

Listeria monocytogenes is widely distributed in nature and, in addition to psychrotrophic characteristic, has the ability to form biofilms, which are structures organized adhered to the surfaces of equipment and milking utensils (Kocot and Olszewska, 2017; Latorre et al., 2010). For the initial adhesion of the bacteria, it is necessary the presence of humidity and organic matter, which provides conditions for multiplication and production of extracellular polymeric substances keeping the cells strongly adhered to the surfaces (Kocot and Olszewska, 2017). Thus, the main measure to be applied during the milk production to prevent the presence of *L. monocytogenes* in raw milk is the application of hygienic practices, involving the use of detergents and sanitizers, reducing the presence of factors associated with the initial stages of adhesion for the biofilm formation and consolidation (Kumar et al., 2017).

3.2.3 Spoilage Microorganisms

Spoilage microorganisms are of great importance for the dairy industry, because for the maintenance of metabolic activities, and consequent survival in milk, they use the milk components and lead to significant changes in dairy products. Contamination by spoilage microorganisms in raw milk is unavoidable as they are distributed in the milking area, equipment, and processing environment. The milkers are the main responsible for applying measures in order to avoid contamination and consequently reducing economic losses arising from changes in products. Several bacterial species have the capacity to deteriorate milk. The main alterations involve acidification caused by saccharolytic microorganisms and proteolysis and lipolysis, due to the action of bacterial enzymes (protease and lipase) (Júnior et al., 2018).

Thus, they produce as primary metabolite lactic acid, which reduces the milk pH. The pH reduction affects the milk stability, because casein presents negative charges around the colloidal micelle when the milk pH is within the normal range (around 6.6—6.8). As the concentration of H^+ ions increases in the solution, the repulsion forces between the micelles are reduced, which leads to the destabilization of the micellar structure by reaching the isoelectric point of casein, which is at pH 4.6. In addition, the high concentration of H^+ ions also results in denaturation of the colloidal phosphate bonds, an important factor to maintain the bond between the submicelles. Thus, acidic milk presents changes in the casein stability which can lead to the coagulation during the thermal processes applied to the milk, limiting the use in the industry (Steinkraus, 1992). The main acidifying microorganisms are the mesophilic, mainly *Lactobacillus*, *Streptococcus*, *Lactococcus*, and some enterobacteria (Jay, 2012).

Psychrotrophics are dispersed in the environment and once contaminating the milk, can multiply intensely in the cooling temperature. This group includes species belonging to the genera *Pseudomonas*, *Bacillus*, *Lactobacillus*, *Listeria*, among others. Most of the psychrotrophics are thermolabile, being destroyed by the thermal treatments applied in the dairy industry, however, some genera, such as *Bacillus*, *Clostridium*, *Streptococcus*, have thermoduric characteristics, resisting the heat treatment (Júnior et al., 2018). The most important characteristic of psychrotrophics is its ability to produce heat-resistant proteolytic and lipolytic enzymes, maintaining its enzymatic activity even after heat treatment. These enzymes have sites of action in specific components of the milk and can act during the entire shelf-life (Capodifoglio et al., 2016; Scatamburlo et al., 2015).

The proteolytic action of the enzymes occurs mainly by the action on k-casein, causing protein hydrolysis and consequent micelle destabilization. This destabilization leads to milk coagulation that can be observed in milks treated by the ultra-high temperature (UHT) technology. In UHT milk, the enzymes action promotes a gel formation that deposits on the bottom of the milk package. Other change in the protein is the appearance of the bitter taste due to the presence of peptides originated from the casein breakdown. In addition, the action of proteases reduces the yield for the production of dairy products (Fairbairn and Law, 1986).

Lipases hydrolyze the phospholipids of the fat globule membrane by increasing the lipolytic potential on the triglycerides. The action of lipolytic enzymes on triglycerides results in the release of free fatty acids resulting in the release of high concentrations of butyric and caproic acid. The presence of free fatty acids causes rancid flavor in milk and dairy products (Capodifoglio et al., 2016).

3.2.4 Beneficial Microorganisms

Some microorganisms present in milk may play an important technological role once isolated from industrial environment and identified and characterized for the production of desirable metabolites. These microorganisms are used in the dairy industry as starter cultures, promoting desirable changes in milk and generating differentiated products such as fermented milks and cheeses. The beneficial microbiota of raw milk and its products is presented in Chapter 8, What Bacteriocinogenic Lactic Acid Bacteria Do in the Milk?.

The main groups of microorganisms that play a beneficial role in the milk industrialization are *Lactococcus*, *Lactobacillus*, *Streptococcus*, *Propionibacterium*, and *Leuconostoc* (Dal Bello et al., 2012; Morandi et al., 2011; Perin et al., 2016; Ribeiro et al., 2014). The main activity of these microorganisms is the fermentation, process of energy production by the microbial cell that produces various substances as primary metabolites that alter the taste, appearance, and structure of milk (Montel et al., 2014). In addition, many of these groups possess the lipolytic and proteolytic capacity and, from this metabolization, produce aromatic compounds by the conversion of amino acids and triglycerides.

Some lactic acid bacteria (LAB) have the ability to produce bacteriocins. Bacteriocins are antimicrobial peptides synthesized in the ribosomes, and a great diversity of bacteriocins has been described, which differ in amino acid composition, biosynthesis, transport, and mode of action (Cotter et al., 2005; Molloy et al., 2011). In food, bacteriocins can naturally be found as products of the normal microbiota or introduced from starter cultures.

Due to the bacteriocin activity against pathogenic and spoilage microorganisms, several studies have been published, being the use of these peptides an alternative to traditional chemical preservatives in foods. Several microorganisms produce bacteriocins, such as *Enterococcus faecium*, *Enterococcus faecalis*, *Enterococcus mundtii*, *Lactobacillus* sp., *Lactococcus* sp., *Pediococcus* sp., *Carnobacterium piscicola*, among others, producing the bacteriocins nisin, pediocin, lacticin, lactococin, leuconocin, plantaricin, enterocin, carnobacteriocin, among others (Javed et al., 2011; Kruger et al., 2013; McAuliffe et al., 1998; Perin et al., 2015; Perin and Nero, 2014). Inhibitory effects result from the action of these antimicrobial peptides on membrane permeabilization, inhibition of cell wall synthesis or inhibition of target cell RNA polymerase and RNA polymerase activity (Cotter et al., 2005; Deegan et al., 2006).

3.3 DAIRY CHAIN AS SOURCE OF MICROBIAL CONTAMINATION

Milk and milk products, like all other food types, have the potential to cause foodborne illness. Different factors can influence its quality, such as veterinary drugs, pesticides and other chemical additives, environmental pollution, nutrient degradation, but microbiological hazards are the major food safety concern regarding milk and dairy products. Milk is a complete source of nutrients, proteins, lipids, carbohydrates, minerals, and vitamins, being one of the most type of food vulnerable to physical—chemical changes and growth of microorganism, including bacteria, molds, and yeasts.

Concerning bacterial contamination, milk can carry some species of beneficial bacteria, such as LAB that can cause technological transformations in fermented dairy products and are also capable to produce antimicrobial substances (acids, diacetyl, bacteriocins, etc.) acting as biopreservatives; but it can also carry some human pathogens, such as *Salmonella*, *E. coli* O157:H7, *L. monocytogenes*, *S. aureus*, *Yersinia enterocolitica*, *Bacillus cereus*, *Clostridium botulinum*, *M. bovis*, *B. abortus*, and *Brucella melitensis*; and spoilage microorganism, mainly psychrotrophics.

The initial microbiological quality of milk can vary enormously. The microorganisms can be introduced into milk from dairy animals and farm environment, during milking procedure and subsequent storage and transport, or from dairy industry. The contact with man and equipment used during the process constitutes a cross-contamination source. This way, it is essential to follow the proper hygienic practices to control the contamination of milk throughout the dairy chain to ensure its safety and suitability for their intended use.

3.3.1 Animals and Farms

The cattle are important sources of microbial contamination in milk. The animals should be controlled by a qualified veterinary officer to ensure the absence of diseases such as brucellosis, tuberculosis, rift valley fever, and mastitis and other infectious diseases transferable to humans through milk. Also the animals should be well fed, healthy, and not on treatment (FAO/WHO, 2004). The holding area for milking animals should be clean and diseased animals should be isolated.

Milk contamination begins the moment it leaves the udder and in the case of sick animals the presence of pathogens in milk could be caused due to the secretion from the mammary gland. Intramammary infection is a common disease in the dairy industry internationally, with considerable economic costs (Cullor, 1997). Mastitis infection involves a pathogen carrier source, means of transfer, the opportunity to invade, and a susceptible host. Microorganisms enter the udder through the duct at the teat tip, and teat end damage due to injury is known to defeat the protective barrier the teat duct provides. This way they penetrate the teat end usually during milking and then attached to the tissue of the teat cistern (Chambers, 2005). Additional information of mastitis can be verified in Chapter 11, Infectious Diseases in Dairy Cattle.

The pathogens infect udders and spread the contamination in raw milk, this way the milking clusters, milker's hands, udder cloths, and other points become contaminated and represent a vehicle for transferring the disease among the herd (Chambers, 2005). *Staphylococcus aureus* and coliforms are mainly responsible for causing clinical and subclinical mastitis in ruminants (Antonios et al., 2015; Keane, 2016). Other species can also cause mastitis and be transferred to milk, such as *L. monocytogenes*, *Mycoplasma bovis*, *Streptococcus agalactiae*, and *Streptococcus uberis* (Chambers, 2005; Cullor, 1997; Nicholas et al., 2016).

Escherichia coli is a predominant isolate from many of these clinical cases particularly around parturition and early lactation when the host is immunosuppressed (Cullor, 1997). Bedding and feces serve as primary source of *E. coli* contamination. Keane (2016) investigating cases of clinical mastitis found that three *E. coli* isolates were multidrug-resistant, with one resistant to seven antibiotics. It could represent a concern related to cross-resistance for humans. Jørgensen et al. (2005) described that *S. aureus* seems to be highly prevalent in Norwegian bulk milk and isolates frequently produce enterotoxins and contain enterotoxin genes. Enterotoxigenic *S. aureus* were also found in raw milk products.

Many countries have employed control systems to reduce mastitis, including the disinfection of teat dip after milking, treatment with antibiotics, and proper sanitary preparation of the cow before and after milking. It is important to not use the milk from animals treated with antibiotics or other veterinary drugs which can be transferred to the milk (Chambers, 2005). Another interesting study demonstrated that feeding animals with farm-made total mixed ration and wet brewers' grains and the presence of dust in the milking parlor were risk factors for *Clostridium* spp. spore counts in milk (Arias et al., 2013).

The water and hygiene of farm environment are other factors influencing milk contamination and should be correctly managed. Contaminated water may contaminate feed, equipment, or milking animals leading to the introduction of hazards into milk. In farms that potable water is not available, it should be treated by purifying methods. Coliforms are an ubiquitous group in the environment, however their presence is useful to verify the quality of water used for dairy production (Chambers, 2005). Also the waste (manure, fodder residues, effluent, etc.) should be adequately managed to avoid fly population and the eventual bacterial contamination (FAO/WHO, 2004).

3.3.2 Milking

The milking process can directly affect the quality and security of raw milk and milk products (Chambers, 2005). The main sources of microbial contamination are considered the mammary gland, the exterior of the udder and teats, and milking equipment (Donnelly, 1990; Slaghuis, 1996). This way previous cleaning of udder and teats, milkers' hands, and milking area are the key to reducing contamination by spoilage and pathogenic microorganisms in milk and improve the end hygienic conditions. Steps of milking process are as follows (FAO/WHO, 2004):

1. Before milking the animals should be evaluated and the milk from each teat should be tested for visible defects. Regarding diseased animals (like animals with clinical mastitis) they should be segregated or milked last or milked by using a different milking equipment or by hand and should not be used for human consumption.
2. The udder and teats should be cleaned always using potable water and use one disposable towel per cow.
3. The initial quantity of milk from each teat should be discarded into specific receptacles and not used for human consumption.
4. After milking the udder should be washed again preferably disinfected with teat dip to avoid infection of the teats. Also during the entire procedure some precautions should be taken to avoid infections.

Milking equipment, utensils, and storage containers must be contaminated heavily to markedly increase the bacteria populations per milliliter of the milk passing through it. But clearly it should be thoroughly cleaned and disinfected before and after use (Chambers, 2005). Bacteria and milk residues accumulate as biofilms in difficult-to-clean areas and in badly designed components. Prevention of the establishment of biofilms in milking equipment is a crucial step in fulfilling the requirement of safe, high-quality milk, it represents a potential source of bulk tank milk contamination with *L. monocytogenes* (Latorre et al., 2010).

Milking can also be done by hand, but some recommendations should be followed, such as, the milkers should be healthy and their hands should be washed and dry; milkers should not wipe hands on the animals or on their own; and the milk should be drawn directly into the milking container as fast as possible. After milking the milk should be immediately cooled to avoid microbial growth.

3.3.3 Storage and Transport

The main method to control microbial growth in milk is refrigerating raw milk from the early stages of production (Bonfoh et al., 2003; Pinto et al., 2006). The ideal temperature for storage of raw milk is 4°C that properly controls the development of its microbiota (Chambers, 2005; Jay, 2012). Different countries and regions establish distinct storage methods of raw milk. Several countries establish specific microbiological criteria that must be followed independently of the adopted storage method (Table 3.1). The adopted criteria depend mainly on the characteristics of dairy farms and significance of dairy products in their economy (Perin et al., 2012). In Brazil, if farms are not adequately equipped with coolers, the raw milk can be delivered to dairy industries at ambient temperature maximum until 2 h after milking.

The storage conditions can cause changes in the milk microbiota. If milk is maintained at high temperatures for long periods, it allows the development of a specific group of microorganisms called psychrotrophics (Perin et al., 2012; Pinto et al., 2006). These microorganisms grow well at or below 7°C, and their optimal growth temperatures are between 20°C and 30°C (Jay, 2012). Many of these microorganisms are sensitive to the pasteurization temperature, but some species are able to produce heat-stable lipolytic and proteolytic enzymes which are considered to be the main spoilage factors of milk and dairy products associated with this group (Leitner et al., 2008; Marchand et al., 2008). The presence of these bacteria in milk is most commonly associated with post-pasteurization contamination.

Perin et al. (2012) compared the influence of different storage conditions of raw milk on different populations of hygiene indicator microorganisms and observed that among the psychrotrophic bacteria, *Pseudomonas* and *Serratia* were the main species of contamination. Also, they found that refrigeration at 4°C is ideal to properly control the development of mesophilic aerobes and total coliforms. However, milk samples that after milking presented poor microbiological quality, the distinct storage conditions were not sufficient to maintain the microbiological quality, especially of psychrotrophics. Highlighting the importance to

Table 3.1 Requirements and microbiological counts adopted for raw milk storage in different countries and regions according to their official rules

Country/region	Storage conditions	Microbiological criteria	Reference
Argentina	5°C or lower	200,000 CFU/mL of MA	Argentina, 1969
Brazil	4−7°C—bulk tank	300,000 CFU/mL of MA (until 2016−17)	Brazil, 2002
	7°C—milk cans immersed on cooled water	100,000 CFU/mL of MA (after 2016−17)	
	Ambient temperature (2 h after milking)		Canada, 1997
Canada	1−4°C	50,000 CFU/mL of MA	Colombia, 2006
Colombia	4 ± 2°C	700,000 CFU/mL of MA	
Equador	No specifications	No specifications	Equador, 2003
Europe	8°C—daily collection	100,000 CFU/mL of MA	European Commission, 2004
	6°C—not daily collection		
	Ambient temperature (2 h after milking)		
Mexico	5°C or lower	Minimum of 120 min in the methylene blue reduction test	Mexico, 2007
New Zealand	7°C		
	Ambient temperature (3 h after milking)	100,000 CFU/mL of MA	New Zealand, 2006
USA	4.4°C until 3 h after milking	100,000 CFU/mL of MA	USDA, 2010
	10°C until collecting		
	Ambient temperature (2 h after milking)		

MA, mesophilic aerobes; CFU/mL, colony forming units/milliliter.
Source: Adapted from Perin, L.M., Moraes, P.M., Almeida, M.V., Nero, L.A., 2012. Interference of storage temperatures in the development of mesophilic, psychrotrophic, lipolytic and proteolytic microbiota of raw milk. Semina: Ciências Agrárias, 33, 333−342.

ensure good production practices since the very first steps of milking process. It is very clear that initial microbiological quality of raw milk had a direct influence on the development of spoilage and pathogen microorganism groups in raw milk independently of storage temperature.

According to the Code of Hygienic Practice for Milk and Milk Products produced by the Food and Agriculture Organization of the United States (FAO) (FAO/WHO, 2004), the tanks and cans used to store milk should be designed, constructed, maintained, and used in a manner that will avoid the introduction of contaminants into milk and minimize the growth of microorganisms in milk. Also, sufficient potable water should be used for milking and cleaning of equipment, utensils, and instruments. After cooling at collection centers, milk shall be transported in a manner that maintains the milk temperature below 8°C. The milk transportation should be under refrigeration and without undue delay; if it is transported in cans it must be sealed properly and protected from direct sunlight. All equipment in contact with milk must be easy to clean and disinfect avoiding any possibility of cross-contamination of the next milk. Also, the contamination of milk from milk handlers should be avoided, they should wear clean clothes and not have infectious or contagious diseases that would present a risk of contaminating milk; they should adopt good practices of hygiene during transport and when discharging the tanker.

An important observation to take into consideration is that the storage of raw milk under refrigeration can mask the effects of unsanitary practices as the inadequately cleaned and sanitized milking equipment may produce off-flavors, yield poor product, and present a risk of foodborne infections in the consumer (Chambers, 2005). This use of adequate refrigeration on the farm should be associated to adoption of food sanitary and hygienic practices to ensure the final quality of milk.

3.3.4 Dairy Industries

When milk arrives at the dairy industry it should be controlled by a competent person to carry out the necessary tests for quality to determine the suitability of raw milk for processing. According to FAO/WHO (2004) the following tests are used to verify the milk quality: titratable acidity test, 10 min resazurin test, clot-on boiling test, sediment tests, half-hour methylene blue reduction test, determination of pH, determination of preservatives and antibiotics. Count of mesophilic aerobes is also a routine analysis, being useful for monitoring in quality control programs and for food inspectors, but not for ready decision or destiny of milk in a facility, once it demands 24–48 h for the end results.

In some countries sale of raw milk is allowed, but the potential risk to public health should be taken into consideration. In dairy industry raw milk can be used to produce some artisanal dairy foods, as raw milk cheeses. This type of product is very appreciated by consumers due to its sensory and organoleptic characteristics and nutritional quality. However, the milk treatment before being sold for consumption or to produce dairy products reduces spoilage and eliminates pathogens (Angelidis, 2015).

The microbial quality of raw milk that is controlled since first steps of milking is essential to prevent production losses and to achieve an optimal shelf-life of dairy products. Conventionally milk is submitted to two main thermal treatment: pasteurization and sterilization at UHT. The minimum pasteurization conditions are those having bactericidal effects equivalent to heating every particle of the milk to 72°C for 15 s (continuous flow pasteurization) or 63°C for 30 min (batch pasteurization) (Codex Alimentarius Commission, 2004). Pasteurization conditions are designed to effectively destroy the organisms *Mycobacterium tuberculosis* and *Coxiella burnetii* a rickettsia responsible to cause Q-fever (Raspor et al., 2015). Thermoduric microbiota that can survive pasteurization process include the genera *Microbacterium*, *Micrococcus*, *Bacillus* spores, *Clostridium* spores, and *Alcaligenes*; however, these microorganisms do not multiply appreciably in raw milk even at ambient temperatures, this way its high counts indicate contamination from milking equipment (Chambers, 2005). For this reason, this type of milk should be maintained, refrigerated, and its shelf-life is more limited than UHT milk. Immediately after thermal treatment the temperature of milk should be decreased very fast to avoid microbial development.

The storage conditions that allow variations in temperature of raw milk could influence the thermal resistance of *E. coli*. However, most incidences of coliforms and *E. coli* found in milk are commonly associated to post-pasteurization process in the storage and/or filling steps (Chambers, 2005). The food industry generally uses some tools to guarantee the quality of foods, such as Good Manufacturing Practice, Good Hygiene Practice, and Hazard Analysis and Critical Control Points, that include the adoption of some standard practices and reduce the risks of contamination.

3.4 CHALLENGES FOR MICROBIAL CONTROL IN DAIRY PRODUCTS

The control of microbial contamination in milk is a constant challenge faced by milk producers and farms, dairy industry, consumers, and food inspectors. The potential risks that some microorganisms naturally present in raw milk represent to consumers are evident, leading to a rigorous control and monitoring to avoid the presence of hazardous bacteria and possible consumption by humans. However, milk and dairy products are natural sources of beneficial bacteria, which must be properly isolated, characterized, and employed adequately as probiotic and/or starter cultures. Finally, specific microbial groups must be monitored as part of quality control programs and to allow the identification of production failure and poor hygienic conditions, supporting official activities of food inspectors to avoid the production of low-quality dairy products to consumers. So, controlling and monitoring the microbiota of raw milk has a direct impact on the quality of dairy products, consumers acceptance, and official guidelines requirements.

Conventional procedures for enumeration of microbial groups and detection of pathogenic bacteria, however, are extensively time consuming, and the obtained results are usually known after the processing, or even the consumption, of raw milk and its products. Despite this limitation, quality control programs demand the constant monitoring of such groups, allowing the detection of fluctuations in the counts and prevalence allowing the prediction of possible problems and proper actions to solve them. As alternatives, various rapid and automatized methods were developed in the 1970—80, with direct usage in the dairy industry to assess the quality and safety of raw milk and dairy products (Sohier et al., 2014). Many of these methods are based on conventional procedures, and molecular-based methods are being increasingly used as tools for microbial monitoring in dairy industries (Beletsiotis et al., 2011). Independently of the adopted or chosen method, it is important to highlight that the microbial contamination monitoring must be addressed in raw milk and dairy products.

The natural presence of microorganisms in raw milk and its products, and the potential risks of these products carrying pathogens, lead to an even more rigorous control of contamination in the different steps of production. These risks highlight the relevance of extreme care and hygiene during raw milk production, since the control of diseases in producing animals to rigorous hygienic procedures during milking, storage, transportation, and processing of this product. All these challenges can only be addressed if all these procedures are associated with proper and wide monitoring of different microbial groups and species. Finally, proper and reliable official monitoring by food inspectors must occur, to assure the production of products adequate for consumption.

ACKNOWLEDGMENTS

CAPES, CNPq, and FAPEMIG.

REFERENCES

Angelidis, A.S., 2015. The microbiology of raw milk. In: Papademas, P. (Ed.), Dairy Microbiology: A Practical Approach. CRC Press/Taylor & Francis Group, Boca Raton, pp. 22–69.

Antonios, Z., Theofilos, P., Ioannis, M., Georgios, S., Georgios, V., Evridiki, B., et al., 2015. Prevalence, genetic diversity, and antimicrobial susceptibility profiles of *Staphylococcus aureus* isolated from bulk tank milk from Greek traditional ovine farms. Small Ruminant Res. 125, 120–126.

Arias, C., Oliete, B., Seseña, S., Jimenez, L., Pérez-Guzmán, M.D., Arias, R., 2013. Importance of on-farm management practices on lactate-fermenting *Clostridium* spp. spore contamination of Manchega ewe milk: determination of risk factors and characterization of *Clostridium* population. Small Ruminant Res. 111, 120–128.

Beletsiotis, E., Ghikas, D., Kalantzi, K., 2011. Incorporation of microbiological and molecular methods in HACCP monitoring scheme of molds and yeasts in a Greek dairy plant: a case study. Proc. Food Sci. 1, 1051–1059.

Bonfoh, B., Wasem, A., Traore, A., Fane, A., Spillmann, H., Simbé, C., et al., 2003. Microbiological quality of cows' milk taken at different intervals from the udder to the selling point in Bamako (Mali). Food Control 14, 495–500.

Boor, K.J., Wiedmann, M., Murphy, S., Alcaine, S., 2017. A 100-year review: microbiology and safety of milk handling. J. Dairy Sci. 100, 9933–9951.

Capodifoglio, E., Vidal, A.M.C., Lima, J.A.S., Bortoletto, F., D'Abreu, L.F., Gonçalves, A.C.S., et al., 2016. Lipolytic and proteolytic activity of *Pseudomonas* spp. isolated during milking and storage of refrigerated raw milk. J. Dairy Sci. 99, 5214–5223.

Cavicchioli, V., Scatamburlo, T., Yamazi, A., Pieri, F., Nero, L., 2015. Occurrence of *Salmonella*, *Listeria monocytogenes*, and enterotoxigenic *Staphylococcus* in goat milk from small and medium-sized farms located in Minas Gerais State, Brazil. J. Dairy Sci. 98, 8386–8390.

Chambers, J.V., 2005. The microbiology of raw milk. Dairy Microbiology Handbook: The Microbiology of Milk and Milk Products. John Wiley & Sons, Hoboken, NJ, pp. 39–90.

Cotter, P.D., Hill, C., Ross, R.P., 2005. Bacteriocins: developing innate immunity for food. Nat. Rev. Microbiol. 3, 777–788.

Cousin, M., 1982. Presence and activity of psychrotrophic microorganisms in milk and dairy products: a review. J. Food Protect. 45, 172–207.

Cullor, J.S., 1997. Risks and prevention of contamination of dairy products. Rev. Sci. Tech. 16, 472–481.

Dal Bello, B., Cocolin, L., Zeppa, G., Field, D., Cotter, P.D., Hill, C., 2012. Technological characterization of bacteriocin producing *Lactococcus lactis* strains employed to control *Listeria monocytogenes* in Cottage cheese. Int. J. Food Microbiol. 153, 58–65.

Deegan, L.H., Cotter, P.D., Hill, C., Ross, P., 2006. Bacteriocins: biological tools for bio-preservation and shelf-life extension. Int. Dairy J. 16, 1058–1071.

Del Collo, L.P., Karns, J.S., Biswas, D., Lombard, J.E., Haley, B.J., Kristensen, R.C., et al., 2017. Prevalence, antimicrobial resistance, and molecular characterization of *Campylobacter* spp. in bulk tank milk and milk filters from US dairies. J. Dairy Sci. 100, 3470–3479.

Donnelly, C.W., 1990. Concerns of microbial pathogens in association with dairy foods. J. Dairy Sci. 73, 1656–1661.

Fairbairn, D.J., Law, B.A., 1986. Proteinases of psychrotrophic bacteria: their production, properties, effects and control. J. Dairy Res. 53, 139–177.

FAO/WHO, 2004. Code of Hygienic Practice for Milk and Milk Products CAC/RCP 57-2004.

Gonzales-Barron, U., Gonçalves-Tenório, A., Rodrigues, V., Cadavez, V., 2017. Foodborne pathogens in raw milk and cheese of sheep and goat origin: a meta-analysis approach. Curr. Opin. Food Sci. 18, 7–13.

Javed, A., Masud, T., ul Ain, Q., Imran, M., Maqsood, S., 2011. Enterocins of *Enterococcus faecium*, emerging natural food preservatives. Ann. Microbiol. 61, 699–708.

Jay, J.M., 2012. Modern Food Microbiology. Springer Science & Business Media, New York.

Jørgensen, H.J., Mørk, T., Høgåsen, H.R., Rørvik, L.M., 2005. Enterotoxigenic *Staphylococcus aureus* in bulk milk in Norway. J. Appl. Microbiol. 99, 158–166.

Júnior, J.R., de Oliveira, A., Silva, F. de G., Tamanini, R., de Oliveira, A., Beloti, V., 2018. The main spoilage-related psychrotrophic bacteria in refrigerated raw milk. J. Dairy Sci. 101, 75–83.

Keane, O.M., 2016. Genetic diversity, the virulence gene profile and antimicrobial resistance of clinical mastitis-associated *Escherichia coli*. Res. Microbiol. 167, 678–684.

Kocot, A.M., Olszewska, M.A., 2017. Biofilm formation and microscopic analysis of biofilms formed by *Listeria monocytogenes* in a food processing context. LWT-Food Sci. Technol. 84, 47–57.

Kruger, M.F., Barbosa, M. de S., Miranda, A., Landgraf, M., Destro, M.T., Todorov, S.D., et al., 2013. Isolation of bacteriocinogenic strain of *Lactococcus lactis* subsp. *lactis* from rocket salad (*Eruca sativa* Mill.) and evidences of production of a variant of nisin with modification in the leader-peptide. Food Control 33, 467–476.

Kumar, A., Alam, A., Rani, M., Ehtesham, N.Z., Hasnain, S.E., 2017. Biofilms: survival and defense strategy for pathogens. Int. J. Med. Microbiol. 307, 481–489.

Latorre, A.A., Van Kessel, J.S., Karns, J.S., Zurakowski, M.J., Pradhan, A.K., Boor, K.J., et al., 2010. Biofilm in milking equipment on a dairy farm as a potential source of bulk tank milk contamination with *Listeria monocytogenes*. J. Dairy Sci. 93, 2792–2802.

Leitner, G., Silanikove, N., Jacobi, S., Weisblit, L., Bernstein, S., Merin, U., 2008. The influence of storage on the farm and in dairy silos on milk quality for cheese production. Int. Dairy J. 18, 109–113.

Marchand, S., Coudijzer, K., Heyndrickx, M., Dewettinck, K., De Block, J., 2008. Selective determination of the heat-resistant proteolytic activity of bacterial origin in raw milk. Int. Dairy J. 18, 514–519.

Martin, N.H., Trmčić, A., Hsieh, T.-H., Boor, K.J., Wiedmann, M., 2016. The evolving role of coliforms as indicators of unhygienic processing conditions in dairy foods. Front. Microbiol. 7.

McAuliffe, O., Ryan, M.P., Ross, R.P., Hill, C., Breeuwer, P., Abee, T., 1998. Lacticin 3147, a broad-spectrum bacteriocin which selectively dissipates the membrane potential. Appl. Environ. Microbiol. 64, 439—445.

Molloy, E., Hill, C., Cotter, P., Ross, R., 2011. Bacteriocins, Encyclopedia of Dairy Sciences, second ed. Academic Press, San Diego, pp. 420—429.

Montel, M.-C., Buchin, S., Mallet, A., Delbes-Paus, C., Vuitton, D.A., Desmasures, N., et al., 2014. Traditional cheeses: rich and diverse microbiota with associated benefits. Int. J. Food Microbiol. 177, 136—154.

Morandi, S., Brasca, M., Lodi, R., 2011. Technological, phenotypic and genotypic characterisation of wild lactic acid bacteria involved in the production of Bitto PDO Italian cheese. Dairy Sci. Technol. 91, 341—359.

Murphy, S.C., Martin, N.H., Barbano, D.M., Wiedmann, M., 2016. Influence of raw milk quality on processed dairy products: how do raw milk quality test results relate to product quality and yield? J. Dairy Sci. 99, 10128—10149.

Nicholas, R.A.J., Fox, L.K., Lysnyansky, I., 2016. Mycoplasma mastitis in cattle: to cull or not to cull. Vet. J. 216, 142—147.

Perin, L.M., Nero, L.A., 2014. Antagonistic lactic acid bacteria isolated from goat milk and identification of a novel nisin variant Lactococcus lactis. BMC Microbiol. 14, 36.

Perin, L.M., Moraes, P.M., Almeida, M.V., Nero, L.A., 2012. Interference of storage temperatures in the development of mesophilic, psychrotrophic, lipolytic and proteolytic microbiota of raw milk. Semina: Ciências Agrárias 33, 333—342.

Perin, L.M., Dal Bello, B., Belviso, S., Zeppa, G., de Carvalho, A.F., Cocolin, L., et al., 2015. Microbiota of Minas cheese as influenced by the nisin producer Lactococcus lactis subsp. lactis GLc05. Int. J. Food Microbiol. 214, 159—167.

Perin, L.M., Belviso, S., Bello, B.D., Nero, L.A., Cocolin, L., 2016. Technological properties and biogenic amines production by bacteriocinogenic lactococci and enterococci strains isolated from raw goat's milk. J. Food Prot. 80, 151—157.

Perin, L.M., Sardaro, M.L.S., Nero, L.A., Neviani, E., Gatti, M., 2017. Bacterial ecology of artisanal Minas cheeses assessed by culture-dependent and-independent methods. Food Microbiol. 65, 160—169.

Pinto, C.L.O., Martins, M.L., Vanetti, M.C.D., 2006. Qualidade microbiológica de leite cru refrigerado e isolamento de bactérias psicrotróficas proteolíticas. Ciênc. Tecnol. Aliment. 26, 645—651.

Raspor, P., Smožina, S.S., Ambrožič, M., 2015. Basic concepts of food microbiology. In: Papademas, P. (Ed.), Dairy Microbiology: A Practical Approach. CRC Press/Taylor & Francis Group, Boca Raton, pp. 1—22.

Raza, N., Kim, K.-H., 2018. Quantification techniques for important environmental contaminants in milk and dairy products. Trends Anal. Chem. 98, 79—94.

Ribeiro, S., Coelho, M., Todorov, S., Franco, B., Dapkevicius, M., Silva, C., 2014. Technological properties of bacteriocin-producing lactic acid bacteria isolated from Pico cheese an artisanal cow's milk cheese. J. Appl. Microbiol. 116, 573—585.

Scatamburlo, T., Yamazi, A., Cavicchioli, V., Pieri, F., Nero, L., 2015. Spoilage potential of Pseudomonas species isolated from goat milk. J. Dairy Sci. 98, 759—764.

Silva, J., Leite, D., Fernandes, M., Mena, C., Gibbs, P.A., Teixeira, P., 2011. Campylobacter spp. as a foodborne pathogen: a review. Front. Microbiol. 2.

Slaghuis, B., 1996. Source and significance of contaminants on different levels of raw milk production. Symposium on Bacteriological Quality of Raw Milk. International Dairy Federation, Wolfpassing, Austria.

Sohier, D., Pavan, S., Riou, A., Combrisson, J., Postollec, F., 2014. Evolution of microbiological analytical methods for dairy industry needs. Front. Microbiol. 5, 16.

Steinkraus, K., 1992. Lactic acid fermentations. Applications of Biotechnology to Traditional Fermented Foods. A Report of an Ad Hoc Panel of the Board on Science and Technology for International Development. National Academy Press, Washington, DC.

Viçosa, G.N., Moraes, P.M., Yamazi, A.K., Nero, L.A., 2010. Enumeration of coagulase and thermonuclease-positive *Staphylococcus* spp. in raw milk and fresh soft cheese: an evaluation of Baird-Parker agar, Rabbit Plasma Fibrinogen agar and the Petrifilm™ Staph Express count system. Food Microbiol. 27, 447–452.

Yamazi, A.K., Moreira, T.S., Cavicchioli, V.Q., Burin, R.C.K., Nero, L.A., 2013. Long cold storage influences the microbiological quality of raw goat milk. Small Ruminant Res. 113, 205–210.

Zeinhom, M.M., Abdel-Latef, G.K., 2014. Public health risk of some milk borne pathogens. Beni-Suef Univ. J. Basic Appl. Sci. 3, 209–215.

CHAPTER 4

Regulations and Production of Raw Milk

Ton Baars
Research Institute of Organic Agriculture (FiBL), Frick, Switzerland

4.1 DEFINING FRESH, UNPROCESSED MILK

It is necessary to delimitate the definition of fresh, unprocessed milk, a term which will be used rather than raw milk, being any raw material taken from the milk glands of mammals, (mostly herbivores) and gathered in bulk tanks for further processing. In the German language (Fink-Keßler, 2013) raw milk (Rohmilch) is distinguished from consumption milk being processed shop milk (Trink Milch; Trinken = to drink), as if only after processing (heating, homogenization) milk will be ready for consumption. Wightman et al. (2015) discuss how the term raw milk has been used commonly and has settled in the mind of consumers, farmers, and lawmakers. They say: "Raw milk is used to describe and in some laws is defined, as any milk that has not been pasteurized. However milk that is produced for pasteurization is different from milk that is intended to be consumed by people without processing. To clarify the distinction we prefer to identify the milk intended to be pasteurized as pre-pasteurized milk, whereas whole milk, which is produced specifically for direct human consumption, is called fresh, unprocessed milk. So, milk is not milk, and intentionally farmers produce milk from different perspectives or with different security measures in mind. If you know your milk will be pasteurized afterwards, safety should come from the heating process and the killing of all food-borne pathogens. In contrast, if you consciously produce milk, which will be consumed without these technical tools, you need insight and protocols, knowledge and interest on how to produce safe raw milk. The discussion on cons and pros of raw milk consumption is pretty much stuck in meanings and often one-liners, but serious questions and answers on raw milk are present (Gumpert, 2015) and scientific discussions are present (Baars, 2013; Claeys et al., 2013; Ijaz, 2014).

Raw Milk
DOI: https://doi.org/10.1016/B978-0-12-810530-6.00004-3

65

Words to describe progression and changes strongly depend on the era and country of living. In Zürich (Switzerland) in 1925 (Brand, 1925) people distinguished between Vorzugsmilk, raw milk, and milk specialties, which was the upcoming pasteurized milk. Medical doctors preferred Vorzugsmilk as child-milk, milk to cure or health-care milk before World War II and nowadays people who give raw milk to children are mentioned as raw-milk criminals. It shows that our attitude and judgement on fresh, unprocessed milk have changed dramatically in the last century and we do not distinguish between different unprocessed milk qualities in terms of risk and safety: every milk is suspect. In this chapter, the history and development of fresh milk, meant for direct human consumption will be in focus. The status quo of several examples to sell safe, fresh, unprocessed milk will be discussed.

4.2 HISTORY OF FRESH, UNPROCESSED MILK

In the 19th century, sweet cow's milk started to be a commodity in several parts of the Western world (Atkins, 2010). Before that time, milk was mainly processed on farms into cheese and butter. Everyone living on the land had their own cow or goat and most people lived outside cities. Every profession was still connected with being a farmer, part-time or full-time. The main production areas in Europe for milk were connected with the rainy, mild climate of the coast as well as with mountainous areas. On paintings of the 17th century in The Netherlands gouda cheeses are already found. Gouda is a regional wheel-shaped cheese named after the city of Gouda in the west of The Netherlands, where enormous peat areas were grazed by cattle. The surplus of milk was processed twice a day on the farm. Local cheese markets were present all over the west of The Netherlands, whereas butter was processed mainly in the grassland areas of the Friesland province (De Vries, 1974). Nowadays the Gouda-trademark is a certification for a certain processing of cheese, independent of the region of production.

The living of people and the nutrition of their infants dramatically changed in the 19th century (Obladen, 2012, 2014). During the Industrial Revolution, the population of Europe doubled and people became city dwellers in the upcoming towns. To consume the fresh unprocessed milk, it was necessary to transport the milk into the towns, but distances became longer and at the start there was no insight in hygiene, cooling, and animal health. One way to overcome the distance of the transport was to keep cows in the towns itself, which in several areas transformed into the production of swill milk (Schmid, 2009; Obladen, 2014). Swill milk was produced from cows fed large amounts of spent grains from the waste of distilleries or other wastes from town, unsuitable for ruminants instead of grass and hay. Those cows were often ill due to the lack of roughage in their diet, and the housing in towns of animals was not very hygienic. When the sale of swill milk was prohibited in the United States in 1861 due to food-borne zoonotic problems, it became necessary to organize the transport of milk from the countryside into the towns (Obladen, 2014). Fink-Keßler (2013) mentioned the increased urbanization as an important reason that cows and farmers were repressed from the cities. However, in Germany until the late 1990s dairy farms could be settled within the boundaries of the cities. In the city-state of Bremen over 15 Vorzugsmilk farmers were delivering certified raw milk for citizens in town. During summer, cows grazed outside the towns (oral communication Gerhard Windler, retired president Vorzugsmilk-Association in Germany).

A side effect of the industrialization in the 19th century was that people were no longer living in the countryside in the direct surrounding of farms and animals. Women were necessary for industrial labor. Women could not breastfeed their babies any longer and artificial milk feeding was needed. However, in 1899 the death rate among artificial fed children in f.i. Paris was 46% compared to 5% under breast-fed children (Obladen, 2012). Nursing practices based on cows' milk existed, before any insight in bacteriology and hygiene. Poor decisions were made to give young children sterilized/pasteurized milk rather than the insight that clean and sterilized equipment, immediate cooling of milk and milk from healthy and clean cows could reduce the mortality of these young babies. Obladen, (2014) additionally described the technical development of the hand-feeding equipment and called it a bacteriological paradise. It took a while before proper rubber teats were developed, which could be cleaned and sterilized.

It was often quite a poor overall situation among the cows housed in towns (Schmid, 2009): sick cows, cows with ulcers, dirty, dark stables, no hygiene present, and no clean water. Milk sold in cities could be diluted with water, flour, chalk, and other substances were added to receive higher profits from milk sale. It was important to protect people from selling unreal milk (adulteration) and to protect children to get diseased milk (safety). At the end of the 1880s in different European countries, laws on milk and butter were formulated to protect the butter made from cream to artificial spreads or surrogate butter made by the industry. The English word "butterine" for surrogate butter was too close to the word butter and therefore margarine was accepted (www.techniekinnederland.nl). The first and main goal was to prevent food adulteration. Milk should be milk and butter should be butter. Adoptions of the laws were in the direction of food safety, the prevention of food pathogens, like *Mycobacterium*, to enter the food chain.

Due to the poor cooling systems, the mixing of bulk milk in different parts of the transport chain (trains, depots, shop), it was preferred to bottle milk already at the farm. Control of the farms, the milk, milk contents, and bacteria slowly developed. Due to the enormous problems with a safe milk supply, the wish for milk pasteurization and sterilization arose. In cities all over the Western world pasteurization plants were built.

The discussion about criminalization of raw milk applied to young children, was already present at the end of the 19th century. One of the American philanthropists Nathan Straus started up large pasteurization plants and cooled transport of bottles of cows' milk in New York City. In his review article Obladen, (2014) cited Straus, who wrote in 1895 to the mayors of every city in the United States: "I have held that the day is not far distant when it will be regarded as a piece of criminal neglect to feed young children on milk that has not been sterilized". Brand, (1925) refers to the rapid increase of pasteurized milk sales in New York City. In 1903 only 3% of the milk consumed was pasteurized, 40% in 1912, 88% in 1914, and 98% in 1918. Similar data can be found for all other large cities in the United States (Atkins, 2010). It depended often on the number of citizens how quickly pasteurization was adopted. The smaller the town, the longer the milk was delivered unpasteurized (Brand, 1925). The process of in-bottle pasteurization, also mentioned pasteurization after Koch or Holder pasteurization (60−65°C; 20−30 minutes) is one of the methods that changed apparently less on the milk quality. Temperatures above 65°C were avoided, because in those days knowledge was already present that the albumin protein became coagulated (Brand, 1925). It was preferred to pasteurize the milk into the single bottles closed by waterproof caps to avoid reinfection.

Also in Germany, there was a discussion on the need of milk pasteurization. Although 22.5% of the slaughtered cows showed signs of Tuberculosis (TB), the first point of discussion was if human and cow TB were the same, and if cows could infect humans. The main form of Tuberculosis was the lung TB, which could be transmitted from cow to cow or man to man or man to milk through coughing by infected milk-ers. All kinds of contacts (via hands, air) were possible, when people were still hand-milking in open buckets. Even up till 48% of the slaughtered swine in Berlin in 1905 were infected with TB due to the feeding of infected skim milk and mud from milk centrifuges (Fink-Keßler, 2013). A positive reaction to tuberculin test only meant that an animal had picked up the bacillus, not that it had active, shedding TB. It was esti-mated that only 0.2% of the cows were producing TB-infected milk. In contrast with the United States, the problem in Europe, however, was the high number of small producers and therefore the mixing of milk before sale. So, one infected animal could contaminate a large amount of milk (Barnett, 2000). In England and Wales two-third of those who died from TB in 1928 were under 15 years of age, with the under-fives hit hard-est—not surprising, given the amount of milk in infants' diets (Barnett, 2000). Therefore it was discussed, if raw milk for sale should be compul-sorily pasteurized. There was a pragmatic acceptance of pasteurization to control the epidemic of TB, but only till the unhygienic circumstances at the farms involved, were solved. Pasteurization was seen as a compromise and temporary solution, a stopgap measure rather than a permanent solu-tion. This argumentation was also found in other countries. One of the antipasteurization speakers was Lady Eve Balfour, founder of the Organic Movement and Soil Association in the United Kingdom. For her, "pasteuri-zation was a confession of failure. The aim should be to abandon the prac-tice just as soon as the need for it—unhealthy cows and dirty methods—can be eliminated". (Atkins, 2000). Whereas the US cities were early adopters of pasteurization, in the United Kingdom Atkins, (2000) wrote: "Gradually, pasteurization spread in the 1950s from the large cities to smaller towns and rural areas. Tuberculosis was becoming less of a threat and the tuberculin-tested grade of milk was finally abolished in 1964 as no longer necessary." Due to the culling of cows, Tuberculosis as well as Brucellosis became largely eradicated in industrialized Western countries. Nevertheless after the Second World War, pasteurization became the new standard of milk deliv-ery. A new argument against compulsory pasteurization, like in Scotland, Canada, and a number of US states, arose as "the freedom of food choice" (Atkins, 2000). This argument was used in several discussions on raw milk consumption in the last few decades.

Early initiatives to produce safe, raw milk from dairy farms in the countryside rather than from swill milk within the city boundaries already started in the early 19th century (Atkins, 2010). In the 19th century new transportation systems, mainly from railways made it possible to get milk quickly from the countryside into towns. Also industrial cooling techniques were necessary as a prerequisite before raw milk could be transported over longer distances and kept fresh during several days. Early initiatives for the production of safe raw milk were found in combination with enterprises of philanthropists. F.i. in Denmark, the Copenhagen Milk Supply Company was established in 1879: "the milk came from 40 selected farms and was brought by train in special sealed vans. It was cooled at 5°C by ice and filtered. The company was opposed to pasteurization." (Atkins, 2010). All of their milk was delivered in bottles, much earlier than in Britain. Interesting is the focus of people, who were against pasteurization. As a matter of principle they wanted a healthy environment, healthy cows, and a healthy countryside: "there is no need of pasteurization if milk production conditions were properly controlled". (Atkins, 2010). No end-of-pipe solutions through pasteurization of a poor milk quality, but safe, unprocessed fresh milk based on knowledge about cow's health and feeding, based on educated farmers, their attention and interest at work, clean and adequate housing of animals and safety procedures during milking and cleaning of all equipment.

Attention was paid to hygiene of animals, stables and people, the construction of the buildings, water supply, sanitary conditions of production, bottling and labeling of the milk, cooling of the milk after milking, and during transportation. In the United States the development took place under the flag of a local medical commission, as part of the American Association of Medical Milk Commissions and the Certified Milk Producers' Association of America (Atkins, 2010). These commissions were looking after farm hygiene and hygienic handling of milk, not at pasteurization. Also in Germany, medical doctors and hygiene workers introduced in 1875 the first sale of safe milk for young children from selected farms and controlled cows nearby cities. A start-up of raw milk sales was accepted only under conditions of sufficient and continuous check of the health status of the milking cows (Fink-Keßler, 2013). Vorzugsmilk was advised by MDs. Brand (1925) described the Swiss Vorzugsmilk, which was mentioned as Vorzugsmilch, Kindermilch, Krankenmilch, or Sanitätsmilch (respectively preferred milk, child milk, milk for suffering people, milk for medical service), in which special attention was paid on the strict hygienic conditions and health status of the farms, farmers, and cows. The immediate cooling down of the milk was part of the standard. Fink-Keßler (2013) mentioned that it was only allowed to feed cows hay plus home-grown concentrates rather than distillery products (draff, molasses) used in the swill milk production. In parallel, education of the farmers delivering raw milk as well as demonstration farms, agricultural shows, competitions, and yearly meetings took place. Education was necessary, because farmers needed to change their daily practices of milking. At the same time grading of milk in different quality standards was used to stimulate farmers as well as to get a premium price for the milk delivered.

Atkins (2010) described that in 1920, Reading researchers (United Kingdom) summarized the experiences of raw milk production in a five-point scheme to maintain a safe milk quality:

- milk should be cooled within 3 hours of milking
- the prevention of dust, hairs, etc. to fall into the open milk buckets
- sterilization of milking equipment (dairy utensils)
- looking for the cleanness of the cows, the udder, eventually washing the udder before starting milking
- training, motivation, and educating the staff involved into the milking process.

Their impulse was not very different from the standards for safe raw milk production today, described by the Association of Vorzugsmilk-producers (Germany) (www.milch-und-mehr.de) and the Raw Milk Institute (California) (www.rawmilkinsitute.net). The main focus was clean and guaranteed milk, people wanted to get rid of impure milk, and looking for pathogen-free milk, at first for their infants. It was all about risk reduction. Certified raw milk does not seek to be milk with an extended shelf life, like in the normal large-scale dairy industry, transporting milk over very long distances (ARMM, 2015). Certified raw milk looks for freshness and safety of milk, which is consumed within a period of maximum 7—10 days. Like the rhythm of milk production, fresh, unprocessed milk should be delivered in local households at least two times per week, if possible more often.

An important new tool to reflect on milk quality was the possibility to detect germs in milk (total germ counts) as well as the identification of specific germs. In the last decade of the 19th century, testing of microbes came up, milk became suspect in the transmission of several infectious diseases (Typhus, Tuberculosis). In the United States the first bacteria in milk were counted in 1892 (Atkins, 2010). Bacteriological thresholds were defined for certified milk. Tuberculin-tested certified milk was one of the triggers in the certification of raw milk. Farmers could receive a

50% premium price for such milk, and like today the animals in their herd had to be tested individually. In the United States regular counting of bacteria in milk as a control measure of hygiene was already implemented before World War I. The availability of testing offered the possibility for an objective guarantee of the promised quality as Grade A milk. In between the World Wars, regional centers for dairy microbiology were developed in the United Kingdom to control the bacteriological milk quality.

Certification systems for Grade A milk were present in both raw and heat-treated milk. Due to the gradation of milk (Grade A raw, Grade A past, Grade B past, and Grade C past) creameries in cities of the United States were pushed to improve their standards of delivery. Within a short period of time the lower graded milk disappeared (Brand, 1925). For Grade A standards the total number of germs was used as one of the selection criteria. Grade A raw milk should not exceed 30.000, and Grade A past milk not 200.000 germs per mL (before pasteurization). In the United States there was a strict system of controlling and penalty. Samples were taken for bacteriological and chemical control and transgressions were followed by warning (first), penalties (second), or withdrawal of the license to produce (third) (Brand, 1925). For the delivery of safe Vorzugsmilk in Germany nowadays the system of control and withdrawal is still quite similar, although the checklist has changed: if certain threshold levels are exceeded, farmers get warned and immediate resampling, and testing of the milk takes place or delivery can be refused, until the farmer can proof that the milk is safe again (https://www.gesetze-im-internet.de/tier-lmhv/BJNR182800007.html).

One big problem for the sale of certified raw milk was the extra cost for the farmers (certification, testing, bottling, extra hygiene). Also, the license for production was expensive, which made it attractive mainly to owners of larger herds, whereas most UK cows lived in small herds in the 1930s. By 1930 only 480 of Britain's 200,000 producers owned certified or Grade A (tuberculin tested) certificates (Barnett, 2000). Due to the high costs of certification the choice was made to reduce infections in the populations by pasteurization of milk rather than eradication of the disease.

4.3 EQUIPMENT, MILK-COOLING, AND CLEANING

There was a time that people only drank daily fresh milk from their own cows or goats, or from the neighbor farm. The time and distance between place of milking and place of consumption was short and in this period (within 12 hours) the milk did not change much due to the existing enzymes in raw milk, which could protect the first growth of bacteria. As mentioned earlier in the traditional areas of cheese processing, milk was transformed twice a day into cheese, a stabilized product that was kept for month or even years. The warm, fresh milk was processed within several hours after being milked.

Already in the early 20th century it was clear that raw milk was a risk for disease transmission and step-by-step the management around milking changed. Although the impact of single measures is hard to describe, it is clear that the buzz-words are attention for increased hygiene (cows, man and equipment), care for disease, and attention on the cooling chain. There is a huge impact of the technical development of milking, cooling, and transport on milk quality. Equipment for milking and processing went from wood till INOX and copper; systems developed from hand-milking till automatic milking; systems went from open to closed milking systems; closed pipelines rather than open buckets and cans; milk delivery in uncooled cans (30−40 L) was replaced by cooled bulk milk tanks.

To reach a high level of bacteriological milk quality (read: a low level of bacteria) traditional elements were used to change the farming practice: education and training, penalty and rewards, on-farm control and competition. Farmers received rewards, if they delivered a hygienic quality of milk over a long period of time. The reward could only be a yearly new shield on the wall in the milking room or at the barn that made farmers competitive.

The possibility to determine germs opened up the insight in spoilage and pathogenic bacteria, effect of temperatures, the way of cleaning. The impact of different choices during milking and processing led to the awareness for critical control points in the milk from single cow toward the consumer's refrigerator. It also opened up the possibility for a price policy that positively or negatively affected the income from delivered milk. Penalties were paid for milk with repeated high levels of germs, somatic cell counts (SCCs), or if antibiotics were found in the milk delivered. In the delivery of fresh, unprocessed milk meant for direct consumption threshold levels of all kind of bacteria were low, much lower than in milk meant for pasteurization and additionally potential food-borne pathogens were measured. Also here, there is a stepwise change of content depending on the techniques into the laboratory.

An important change is the change in culturing of bacteria. In the traditional plate method, not every bacteria can be shown, due to the lack of growth in specific media. DNA techniques (via PCR) are novel, strong tools to detect every germ present in milk. In Italian raw–milk–vending machines the positive samples based on real-time PCR was 2.7–9.4 times higher than the culture-based method (Giacometti et al., (2013). Especially as detection, in which farm area risks are present, this PCR technique is a helpful tool. In times, when people are germaphobic, and when quantitative risk assessment does not take place, the finding of any bacteria can, however, lead to an over-reaction of officials and health caretakers.

4.4 FRESH, UNPROCESSED MILK DISTRIBUTION NOWADAYS

The sale of fresh, unprocessed milk in the Western world is very different. In the United States several states have legalized the sale, in others it is still forbidden or limited. As the discussion on raw milk and food freedom is an important part of the United States, the contradictive interpretations and legislation between the 50 states are hard to explain. Across the United States the following legalization is found (ARMM, 2015):

- legal retail sales: 10 states
- legal on-farm sales: 15 states
- legal herd- or cow-shares: 4 states
- no law on herd-shares: 6 states
- raw milk as 'pet food': 4 states.

Canada, Scotland, and Australia completely forbid the sale of any raw milk (Ijaz, 2014), whereas in New Zealand, England, and Wales changes in the legislation make the sale of certified raw milk easier. In contrast to Australia the market for raw milk has been liberalized recently in New Zealand as it is in England and Wales, where selling of raw milk must be certified by the Food Standard Agency. Further in Europe there are still very different interpretations of the EU food safety laws. In Germany, certified raw milk (Vorzugsmilk) was allowed since the beginning of the 20th century. Also other countries had such legislation. In most EU-countries, however, raw milk is not sold in retail stores, but only directly from farms. This completely contradictive interpretation of risks within the Western world shows that there is a huge political, rather than a scientific evaluation of the pros and cons of certified, fresh unprocessed milk, milk carefully produced by farmers with the final goal not to be heated for safety reasons. For the advocates of raw milk consumption the ban of raw milk sales is a denial of an informed personal choice, the freedom to choose for their own food and feeding pattern.

Five country cases will be presented in this chapter. One of the oldest systems still present, is the German Vorzugsmilk (1). This way of delivery and the control of the milk quality are very similar toward the upcoming voluntary self-certification via the Raw Milk Institute, an independent quality assurance body (Ijaz, 2014) (2) (United States, California). There is an upcoming interest to deliver fresh, unprocessed milk via milk taps (3) in towns rather than on the producing farm itself (Italy, Slovenia). Fresh milk can also be sent by post (4) (Canada, United Kingdom). Finally there are new legal bonds between farmers and consumers (5) to overcome the legal restrictions for delivery of raw milk, known as the system of cow- or herd-sharing (United States). Generally, in all places where farmers deliver fresh, unprocessed milk meant for direct consumption, attention is paid to hygiene at the farms, control of cooling chains, and presence of food-borne pathogens. The attention for specific germs is very similar between the systems, although threshold levels can be a bit different and the control of zoonotic pathogens depends partly on the specific circumstances and history within countries or regions.

4.4.1 German Vorzugsmilk

Vorzugsmilk is processed directly after each milking or if two milking times are collected, the morning after. This fresh, unprocessed milk can be delivered in shops, but is often delivered by the farmers themselves in daily milk tours in coolers or refrigerated cars, or distributed the milk to so-called drop-off sites. The character of Vorzugsmilk was the local delivery within a region. Farmers acted like the milkman in English towns, delivering fresh milk on a regular basis. Therefore the farmers needed to be in the immediate distance of cities or to be connected to distributors, who can guarantee a within 12 hours delivery. For safety reasons the legal best-before date of Vorzugsmilk is only 4 days, although consumers experienced that if such milk is handled properly, such milk can be kept for a period longer than 1 week (www.milch-und-mehr.de).

4.4.1.1 Prerequisites for Delivery of Vorzugsmilk

According to Regulation (EC) No. 853/2004 of the European Parliament it is necessary to label any raw milk for direct human consumption with the words raw milk. Each member states can maintain or adopt national rules based on local circumstances. Criteria are based on a total plate count (TPC < 100,000/mL), somatic cell count (SCC < 400,000/mL) and absence of Tuberculosis and Brucellosis (EU, 2004). In the practice of European countries the absolute values of plate count and SCC are maintained at much lower levels, whereas the list of germs to control for, is much longer than mentioned in these basic rules.

Since the 1930s Vorzugsmilk delivery already legally existed in several European countries (Austria, Switzerland, and Germany). Only in Germany the legal status of Vorzugsmilk is still present. After the first EHEC-crisis, lawmakers have forbidden the selling of any raw milk in kindergarten, elderly homes, and hospitals nursery school. A large part of the market therefore was broken away and several farmers saved their market through the installation of a pasteurization unit on their farm. Those farmers who continued the production of Vorzugsmilk changed their market toward private households and local stores (www.milch-und-mehr.de).

To maintain their legal status to sell Vorzugsmilk, farmers need to send one bottle of milk every month to the Veterinary State Control body. There are several markers, for which the milk is tested: markers for hygiene, udder infection, and zoonosis (Table 4.1). Two threshold levels are maintained: small m and large M. If the threshold "M" for one of the deliverables is exceeded, the delivery of milk can be stopped immediately. Based on a mandatory track-and-trace system of all milk charges the

Table 4.1 Threshold levels for Vorzugsmilk

	m	M	n	c
Bacterial count/mL	20,000	50,000	5	2
Enterobacteriaceae/mL	10	100	5	2
Coagulase-positive bacteria/mL	10	100	5	2
Somatic cell count/mL	200,000	300,000	5	2
Salmonella/25 mL	Negative	Negative	5	0
Concentration pathogenic bacteria or their toxins	Negative	Negative	5	0
Sensory abnormalities	Negative	Negative	5	0
Enzyme phosphatase positive	Positive	Positive	5	0

delivered milk will be recalled. Milk is still accepted for delivery, if only one item is above "m". If failures are found (values between "m" and "M", farmers have to re-test their milk. They sent in another five bottles of milk (Column n) and only two out of these five samples can be in between "m" and "M", the other ones need to be below "m". For all zoonotic diseases, samples always need to be negative and otherwise delivery will be stopped immediately (https://www.gesetze-im-internet.de/tier-lmhv/BJNR182800007.html). In Box 4.1 an example is presented of a biodynamic farm delivering all its produced milk as Vorzugsmilk. This farm shows the potential safety of this Vorzugsmilk trading.

In contrast with farming in the past, nowadays the routine of milking has been adapted on the knowledge on the ecology of zoonotic bacteria, spoiling bacteria, environmental- and cow-depending mastitis bacteria. At milking there is an inspection of the teats and the udder; stable dirt, manure and soil is taken off the teats; the first milk is visually controlled on mastitis; teats can be predipped, washed and dried; there is a policy of one cloth per cow, if it is paper, cotton or even based on wood shavings; after milking teats can be dipped again with an antiseptical (often iodine based) to prevent penetration of germs in the open teat canal. If necessary, farmers use a sequence of milking, in which cows with a known subclinical mastitis are milked at last. Sometimes automatic systems are present that the teat cups are flushed with water in between two cows to avoid cross contamination.

The standard pathogen testing is to control for *Salmonella*, *Listeria*, *Campylobacter*, and toxins of EHEC. Depending on the local circumstances milk can be tested for additional zoonotic or mastitis germs. Additional requirements include the testing for udder infections of the cows that enter the herd as heifer or re-enter after the dry period (Box 4.2). The veterinarian monthly controls the health status of the herd during a farm visit.

Coenen (2000) described the results from Vorzugsmilk-farms in comparison to "normal" farm milk (Table 4.2). Also the German Institute for Risk Assessment (Hartung, 2008) tested yearly both Vorzugsmilk and general farm milk. Both studies concluded about the high hygienic standard of this type of Grade A raw milk, nevertheless zero-risk is absent.

BOX 4.1 Case Rengoldshausen, biodynamic farm, Überlingen, Lake Konstanz (Germany)

On this biodynamic farm 50 dairy cows produce Vorzugsmilk. The farm runs a system of nursing the calves with their own mothers, and raising all his male bull calves for meat production. The breed of cows is traditional brown cows (Orginal Braunvieh), and cows only receive grass (grazing) and hay as fodder. Ninety-five percent of the fresh, unprocessed milk is filled in bottles, sold directly from the farm, or via the neighbor organic trader (Bodan), who delivers the milk three times per week to larger cities in Baden–Wurttemberg and Bavaria.

In the below table, the data of milk samples (one bottle per month) regenerated by the state veterinarian are summarized. Data were taken into account from 2010 to 2014, presented per year and as average values. Below is the percentage of samples that exceed the accepted threshold levels ("m" and "M").

Year	Total germs ($\times$ 1.000/ mL)	Enterococci ($\times$ 1.000/ mL)	Coag. positive Staphylococci ($\times$ 1.000/mL)	Somatic cell counts ($\times$ 1.000/mL)
2010	1.4	2.7	2.7	36.7
2011	0.7	1.7	2.0	28.1
2012	1.0	8.0	1.5	23.9
2013	3.5	4.3	2.2	49.6
2014	3.2	2.4	2.0	22.6
Overall				
Mean	1.6	3.2	2.0	30.5
Median	1.7	1.7	1.5	35.0
Low	5.0	1.5	1.5	7.0
High	90.0	142.0	811.0	172.0
SD	0.0	3.2	2.9	0.0
Threshold level exceedance´				
M (capital)	1.8%	1.8%	1.8%	0.0%
m (lowercase)	3.5%	12.5%	7.0%	0.0%

Additionally seven food-borne pathogens or udder bacteria have been tested monthly: Verotoxins of *Escherichia coli*, *Campylobacter*, *Salmonella*, *Listeria*, *Yersina*, *S. agalactiae* plus multiple resistant *Staphylococcus aureus*. All milk samples always tested negative.

Source: *Own data.*

BOX 4.2 Regulatory somatic cell count (SCC) levels in cow's milk

The threshold levels of somatic cells in bulk-tank milk have been lowered over the last decades. Nevertheless, the standards were set for prepasteurized milk, not milk meant for direct human consumption. In the United States, bulk tank SCC (BTSCC) were accepted till levels of 750,000 cells/mL since 1993, whereas in Europe the levels were already reduced to 400,000 in 1992 (Schukken et al., 1993). In several Nordic European countries this level of acceptance dropped to 150,000. The signal of the high SCCs is the presence of clinical and subclinical mastitis and the presence of mastitis bacteria in the milk. A linear relationship between the BTSCC and the percentage of infected udders was described (Eberhart et al., 1982). However, for all pasteurized milk produced, the safety of the consumption milk was taken over by the dairy plant. In contrast, raw milk produced for direct human consumption cannot accept such a high SCC level. If milk is not pasteurized, hazard bacteria, like *S. aureus* or *Streptococcus agalactiae*, have to be controlled through prevention strategies, the threshold levels of milk should be much lower.

The only method to accept a threshold level for a healthy udder is from the animal itself. In the first lactation of a healthy cow the monthly SCC of the complete milking are in between 40,000 and 60,000 cells/mL. Based on the total milk delivered of a single cow, a cell count above 100,000 cells/mL, was correlated with an infection in one of the four quarters of the udder (Hamann, 2002). His conclusions were based on a set of six changed milk components. If a cow gets older, her somatic cells always will get slightly higher, but a maximum of 150,000 in older cows is the limit. From an animal welfare point of view, the upper limit of the bulk tank should not exceed 100,000 ($-$150,000) cells/mL. Exceedance indicates the risk for unwanted bacteria in milk meant for direct consumption, however not for prepasteurized raw milk.

4.4.2 Raw Milk Institute (RAWMI)

Selling of raw milk in the State of California (United States) is legally allowed and the success of the farm Organic Pastures was the basis for the start-up of the RAWMI (www.rawmilkinstitute.net). The knowledge about raw milk safety and the experiences of Organic Pastures will be used to support other farmers in their search for the production of safe raw milk. In its mission statement RAWMI mentions that, "it will improve the safety and quality of raw milk and raw milk products through training and mentoring farmers, establishing raw milk guidelines, improving raw milk accessibility and production transparency, and education, outreach and research". RAWMI will act as an independent, objective

Table 4.2 Prevalence of four food-borne pathogens in general raw milk and in Vorzugsmilk (Coenen, 2000)

	General raw milk	Vorzugsmilk
Farms (N)	115	35
Milk samples (N)	149	74
Total germs	49,000	8,700
Listeria	10.1	*16.2
VTEC	0.7	0.0
Salmonella	0.0	0.0
Campylobacter	0.0	0.0

*All positive samples came from repeated milk samples of one single farm. Due to the control system this milk cannot be delivered for consumption.

third party, when it comes to certification standards of safe raw milk; it will list up certified farmers on its website and brings in transparency by the publication of data on milk quality and hygiene/safety of raw milk produced. RAWMI offers a mentoring and training program for farmers who wanted to become certified. RAWMI undertakes teaching activities and webinars to get farmers involved about all kind of issues relevant for selling of safe raw milk. Transparency of the farm is an important goal of becoming listed and a central document of each listed farm is its self-written Risk Analysis and Management Plan (RAMP) or Food Safety Plan: "Your listing portal will contain a biography about your farm operation and a link to your website. Consumers will be able to access your Food Safety Plan and accompanying checklists along with supporting documentation that your milk has been pathogen-free and low in bacteria counts. They can use this information to make purchasing decisions based on facts they can understand." In this RAMP farmers describe how they will tackle, control, and solve important safety issues with regard to raw milk production. Through this procedure the farm crew is aware how to handle all kinds of potential risks in their farm. Organic Pastures writes about its own RAMP: "Our RAMP is a "Grass to Glass" comprehensive conditions and risk-based management system that assures consistent test outcomes through audited daily checklist-verification of all noncritical, GMP, SSOP and CCP raw milk safety elements. This management tool allows for regular team meetings and discussions to make any necessary changes to the plan as we learn more about safety issues and assess data" (ARMM, 2015).

Box 4.3 is a recent example, how Organic Pastures tackled and immediately solved the detection of a single EHEC positive milk sample.

BOX 4.3 Organic Pastures

Organic Pastures (http://www.organicpastures.com) in California produces 3800 tonnes of milk per year, which is around 12 million servings of mainly fresh, unprocessed milk, and also raw milk products. In its internal controlling system in spring 2016, the farm tested positive for *E. coli* O157:H7. It was the first *E. coli* O157:H7 case since the farm started a test and hold system for 15 years. There was an immediate recall of all milk sold and within 72 hours the internal biosafety control system detected one single cow shedding the bacteria. This action was possible due to the quick BAX PCR test present on the farm. Through a process of stepwise elimination, the problem could be traced back toward one single cow that was slaughtered. Before the State Control System on Food Risks could alarm for the situation, the farm already had detected and solved the problem.

Areas of risk, which need to be controlled, are: the introduction of new animals in the farm, handling of raw milk, environmental risks, feed sources, human, and nutritional factors. Like the German Vorzugsmilk farms, the farmer will regularly test their milk for indicator bacteria for hygiene as well as potential zoonotic bacteria. Also here there is a zero-tolerance, when it comes to the detection of zoonotic bacteria. The accepted levels of coliform bacteria are $<10/mL$, the total bacteria plate count should not exceed $5,000/mL$.

4.4.3 Milk Sent by Courier

Father and son Phil and Steve Hook farm Longleys Farm organically. During three weeks a day Hook and Son (United Kingdom) distribute milk through a nationwide service in insulated cardboard boxes ("direct from our farm, direct to your door"): cooled transport overnight, delivered within 24 hours. For this purpose only the fresh milk of the morning milking is chilled to $2°C$ and packed in polybottles (1 L). The organic, grass-fed herd lives in East-Sussex, south of the Capital of London, but Hook and Son deliver milk in Wales and Scotland. The testing procedure from the Food Standards Agency is only every 3 months (total germs and coliform bacteria). Additionally the company takes samples of raw milk, raw cream, and raw butter, which are tested every week at a commercial laboratory (total germs, coliforms, presence of pathogens). Yearly the cows are tested for TB, because of the presence of infected baggers in different areas of the United Kingdom. Further the company follows a HACCP plan (Hazard Analysis Critical Control Point), which is a personalized, systematic preventative approach to food safety that has been drawn up with feedback from the local Environmental Health officers. All personal is trained for food safety issues (www.hookandson.co.uk).

4.4.4 Raw Milk Dispensing Machines

In most European countries tapping raw, chilled milk directly from the bulk milk tank, is allowed. The raw-milk-vending machine is a technological improvement, in which milk from a single farm is delivered into cities rather than people coming and visiting the farm on their own. This system is coming up in several European countries, like Poland, Slovenia, Estonia (Kalmus et al., 2015), and Italy. Remote locations of dispensers and therefore a disconnection between the farm and the milk, are not always allowed, which was shown after a test case in the United Kingdom. The farm Hook & Son placed a self-service machine in Selfridges Food Hall. After 3 months the Food Standards Agency intervened and the sale was postponed waiting for the judgment of the FSA. A similar situation exists in Germany and The Netherlands. In case of direct sale of milk from the bulk tank there must be a clear sign in the milking room, that raw milk should be kept chilled during transport and cooked at home before consumption. Since legalization in 2004, in Italy there are almost 1200 raw-milk-vending machines (www.milkmaps.com, accessed 01.07.2016). Italian milk intended for raw consumption via vending machines must fulfill specific criteria (Bianchia et al., 2013): "biosafety measures and own-check for producers, microbiological and chemical criteria for milk, and vending machine installation and management specifications." Each dispenser is connected with milk from only one single farm. Since 2008 it must be a signposted that this milk should be boiled before consumption. So, the Italian regulation for milk from vending machines is made equal to milk sold directly from the farm bulk-tank milk. In seven Italian regions the zoonotic milk quality of these machines has been monitored (Giacometti et al., 2013). In total 61,000 samples were analyzed over a 4-year period. 178 positive samples (prevalence = 0.29%) were found for four food-borne pathogens tested (*C. jejuni* (0.09%), *Salmonella* (0.03%), *Listeria monocytogenes* (0.14%), and *E. coli* O157:H7 (0.04%)). There was an upward trend over this period of time for both *Campylobacter* and *Listeria*. The paper mentions, that in "previous Italian studies performed at the regional levels confirmed the low prevalence of raw-milk contamination in comparison to international findings. This lower prevalence is probably due to the fact that farmers intending to sell raw milk must implement specific practices such as self-monitoring for meeting microbiological and chemical criteria for milk and management systems for meeting higher standards of good dairy-farming practices than other types of dairy farms." Bianchia et al. (2013) tested Italian milk from vending machines in the Piedmont region. They found a significant correlation between a previous finding of pathogens and recurrence of contamination, which shows that the finding of pathogens is not always random, but can depend on the contaminations in a single farm. Bianchia et al. (2013) concluded that the number of positive samples in this type of milk is low. Further reduction can only be reached if the farmer is willing to adapt his herd management and follows further biosafety procedures. The existence of positive findings of food-borne pathogens at one single farm, although biosafety measures are already at a high level can be confirmed in other countries, where raw milk is sold for direct consumption. If we compare these results with the raw milk market in Estonia, the list of positive samples was much higher, although this milk was also certified for direct sale. Here, the frequency of control for zoonotic germs should be higher and threshold levels could be lower to protect the consumer of raw milk. Although several pathogens were not detected (*Salmonella* and *Campylobacter*), other germs were found (*S. agalactiae, S. aureus, Listeria*, and *E. coli*), plus the very high SCCs in general, there is a need for a better education of farmer and consumer (Kalmus et al., 2015). If such data were found under German Vorzugsmilk-regulation much of this milk was not allowed to sell.

German veterinarians and health-care professionals do not control raw milk dispensers in the same way as the Vorzugsmilk. From a legal point of view milk tapped from an on-farm vending machine is similar to milk from the bulk tank. Such milk should be boiled and this is signposted by the farmer. The sale of raw milk from vending machines therefore should not be compared to the sale of fresh, unprocessed milk meant for direct human consumption (like RAWMI and German Vorzugsmilk-Association are promoting), unless the farms are certified as fresh milk producers. Without additional control of the milk and education of the farmers, the risk of milk sold through vending machines might be at the same level as general raw milk tapped from the bulk-milk tank.

4.4.5 Cow- or Herd-Sharing

In the United States the Farmer-to-Consumer Legal Defence Fund (FCLDF) supports farmers in the legal aspects of a cow-share program. On its website FCLDF writes: "in some US states sales of raw milk are illegal. The farmer can lose his or her Grade A-license and even go to jail for selling consumers unprocessed milk directly. In these states, consumers have been able to obtain raw milk directly from farmers by purchasing a share in a cow, goat, or in the whole herd. Even in states where sales of raw milk are legal, the permits (or inspection fees) are often very expensive. Cow or goat-share programs allow farmers to provide raw milk to consumers without cumbersome and expensive paperwork mandated by the state."

About the US cow-share agreements Wightman et al. (2015) wrote: "herdshare, cow share, or agister agreements (the term agister is used in fresh milk herdshare agreements to refer to the person hired to provide boarding and other services for owners of the herd animals) are legal arrangements for obtaining fresh milk. Such contracts are legal and valid, as guaranteed by the Constitution of the United States of America. The consumer does not buy milk from the farmer. Rather, the farmer is paid for the service of keeping the dairy animal and his/her labor for milking and storing the milk. The amount of milk available to a shareholder depends on the number of shares being held, and the seasonal variation in milk production." From the point of view of pathogen transfer, there is no difference between cow-share systems and a system in which farmers sell bottled raw milk or sent raw milk by chilled post. In all cases the safety of the milk has to be in the front of discussion, and for the daily management practice related to hygiene, mastitis, and cleaning, should confirm the highest standards.

To overcome the discussion on raw milk consumption, the FCLDF writes:

- The herd is tested free of TB and brucellosis.
- Teats of cows are cleaned with approved solution before milking.
- Cows are milked in a clean barn or milking parlor.
- Milk is kept chilled.
- Milk is tested regularly to ensure absence of pathogens.

4.5 ORGANIC AND BIODYNAMIC MILK PRODUCTION SYSTEMS WORLDWIDE

As mentioned earlier Lady Eve Balfour, founder of the Soil Association, saw "pasteurization as a confession of failure" and like the practice nowadays in German Vorzugsmilk as well as RAWMI in California, she principally wanted a safe, raw milk production based on intensive knowledge. Although there is not a direct necessary relationship between raw milk sales and organic agriculture, organic farmers often feel another interest, when it comes to raw milk and raw milk products. Based on their philosophy of farming, biodynamic farmers do not homogenize their milk, if pasteurized. Biodynamic and organic farmers are staying close to nature (Verhoog et al., 2007) and respect the integrity of life. Pasteurization therefore can already be one step too far, because it destroys the integrity, the origin of the product. Raw milk is not made for pasteurization, and organic farmers want to produce a whole product, whole in terms of undisturbed, nature-like. Another level in the discussion on the use of nature is, that organic farmers want to mimic nature, and use natural rather than artificial processes to develop a healthy farming system. For that reason organic cows should have access to pasture, eat hay or silage rather than maize and concentrates. The cow is a ruminating creature, which is present to digest roughage, not grains. Cows have a complex digestion stomach system present to digest roughage based on rumination. This choice of mimicking processes in nature results in organic milk with a different fatty acid pattern, based on higher polyunsaturated fatty acid levels, especially when cows have plenty access to pasture (Kusche et al., 2014). Another aspect of the systemic approach in organic farming is that farmers look for preventive solutions rather than end-of-pipe solutions. If organic farmers choose for raw milk (products), it is because raw milk is connected with the support of health based on the whole product. Although scientists now are trying to unravel, which element(s) in raw milk is responsible for the suppression of asthma and atopic diseases, organic farmers are staying with raw milk and raw milk products, which should be safe. In their focus safety does not erase from an isolated part, but from milk as a whole. The German market for fresh, unprocessed milk (Vorzugsmilk) for direct consumption has been declined dramatically, since the EHEC-crisis in the 1990s. Vorzugsmilk was for almost 100% in the hands of conventional farmers. Most of them gave up the sale of unprocessed milk. Nevertheless still organic and biodynamic farmers converted to the sale of legalized raw milk. They experience this as a challenge of complex management to produce a safe, unprocessed food, like raw milk. From the point of view of a consumer, it makes sense that farmers combine several potential health aspects present in milk: milk should be (1) raw, unprocessed from (2) grass-based, extensive farm holdings, and (3) the production without any use of antibiotics. In practice those farmers use (4) local, dual-purpose breeds, adapted to their environment.

4.6 CONCLUSION: ACTIVE CONTROL OF FRESH, UNPROCESSED MILK FOR DIRECT CONSUMPTION

Most papers on the food safety and the hazard situation of raw milk mention the potential hazard of any raw milk (Oliver et al., 2009; Claeys et al., 2013; Bianchia et al., 2013). Bianchia et al. (2013) for instance concluded that "unpasteurized milk can be vehicle of a variety of microorganisms and can be an important source of food-borne illness outbreaks, especially if consumers are young, elderly, or ill." Others compare it with Russian roulette and you never know, when the guns fires (Gumpert, 2015). The conclusion that pasteurization is the most safest way to reduce the harmful microorganisms might be the right conclusion in general, however not in the case of farmers, who consciously produce fresh, unprocessed milk meant for direct consumption. In the case of the German Vorzugsmilch farmers and in the methodology applied by RAWMI-Institute, farmers get tools to reduce the chance of transmission of food-borne pathogens. Therefore the conclusion of Bianchia et al. (2013) is, that it is important that farmers get "trained properly on food safety measures and the application of good practices for farmers selling raw milk." An important element is a positive farmer's attitude toward the production of raw food, and the meaning of this for good conditions management with daily checklists for controls and measurements. Since several food-borne pathogens are connected with the feces of the animal, proper milking practice, and proper cleaning of cows and equipment are the most important step to reduce the risk of contamination (Ricci et al., 2013). Another important theme is the maintenance of a low mastitis-level in the herd. Good praxis could be implemented according to HACCP procedures and the exchange of experiences between raw milk producers. In the case of Organic Pastures, who is one of the biggest raw milk sellers worldwide and a pioneer in this topic, there is an internal laboratory present to test all kinds of charges of milk in different rhythms. To protect the raw milk sellers from failures, a test and hold protocol with a low cost, on-farm lab monitoring every bottling for hygienic indicator bacteria (coliform and APC/SPC) will protect the consumer far more than a once-a-month postconsumptive pathogen test. An increase of raw milk sales needs to be assisted by the latest rapid on-farm milk testing technology, which is available nowadays. Therewith certified, raw milk can be as safe as pasteurized milk.

Through law, farmers selling raw milk are responsible for the maintenance of the health of their customers. If raw milk is distributed in single packages by the farmer an active controlling system, often by the authorities, is present to prevent that people get sick and if there are problems, it must be clear, how a recall of the milk is organized or how problems can be tracked and traced, and finally solved.

4.6.1 Testing Records, Record Keeping, and Identification Systems

The control of the production of safe, fresh unprocessed milk is based on:
- chilling and cold chain control: Quickly chilling, maintenance of chilling during processing and handling, not breaking the cold chain during processing, storage and transport
- control of mastitis, mainly *S. aureus*, also *S. agalactiae*
- control of SCC per cow
- control of hygiene at milking, cleaning and in contact with milk equipment, mainly through total bacteria plate count, *E. coli* or *Enterococci*
- absence of zoonotic bacteria (zero tolerance), like EHEC, *Listeria*, *Campylobacter*, *Salmonella*, also *Brucella* or Tubercle bacteria.

4.6.2 Track and Trace Systems On-Farm

For the safe production of raw milk it is necessary to build-up such a system that a recall is possible. It depends on the intensity of the internal control system on the farm, how quickly a farmer can reply, if bacteriological mistakes are found. Two levels of control are possible, one from every batch of raw milk produced and bottled, secondly based on a systematic regular control at the farm and the maintenance of thresholds.

4.6.3 Teaching, Training, and Exchange

Maybe the most important of all, is to find motivated and skilled farmers. Farmers who are willing to produce safe, unprocessed milk, because of conviction not mainly for market purposes. In the environment of institutes, like RAWMI (United States) and the Vorzugsmilk-foundation (Germany), farmers can get information and training about raw milk handling.

REFERENCES

Australian Raw Milk Movement (ARMM) (2015) Freedom of Choice: The Case for Certified Raw Milk.

Atkins, P., 2000. The pasteurization of England: the science, culture and health implications of food processing, 1900–1950. In: Smith, D.F., Phillips, J. (Eds.), Food, Science, Policy, and Regulation in the Twentieth Century: International and Comparative Perspectives. Routledge: Psychology Press.

Atkins, P., 2010. Dirty milk and the ontology of clean. In: Atkins, P. (Ed.), Liquid Materialities, a History of Milk, Science and the Law. Routledge: Ashgate Publishing Limited, 2010.

Baars, T., 2013. Milk consumption, raw and general, in the discussion on health or hazard. J. Nutr. Ecol. Food Res. 1 (2), 91–107.

Bianchia, D.M., Barbaroa, A., Gallina, S., Vitalea, N., Chiavaccia, L., Caramellia, M., et al., 2013. Monitoring of foodborne pathogenic bacteria in vending machine raw milk in Piedmont, Italy. Food Control 32 (2), 435–439. Aug.

Brand, H., 1925. Kritische und experimentelle Studien der Pasteurisierung der Milch – Kuhmilch und Frauenmilch. Dissertation Zürich: Eidgenössischen Technischen Hochschule.

Barnett, L.M., 2000. The people's League of Health and the campaign against bovine tuberculosis in the 1930s. In: Smith, D.F., Phillips, J. (Eds.), Food, Science, Policy and Regulation in the Twentieth Century: International and Comparative Perspectives. Routledge: Psychology Press.

Claeys, W.L., Cardoen, S., Daube, G., De Block, J., Dewettinck, K., Dierick, K., et al., 2013. Raw or heated cow milk consumption: review of risks and benefits. Food Control 31 (1), 251–262.

Coenen, C., 2000. Untersuchungen zum Vorkommen und zur Risikoeinschätzung pathogener Keime in Rohmilch und Rohmilchprodukten aus der Direktvermarktung. Fakultät Veterinärmedizin an der Freien Universität Berlin, Dissertation Berlin.

De Vries, J., 1974. The Dutch Rural Economy in the Golden Age, 1500-1700. Yale University Press, New Haven and London.

Eberhart, R.J., Hutchinson, L.J., Spencer, S.B., 1982. Relationship of bulk tank somatic cell counts to prevalence of intramammary infection and to indices of herd production. J. Food Prot. 45, 1125–1128.

EU 2004. Regulation (EC) No 853/2004 of the European parliament and of the council of 29 April 2004 laying down specific hygiene rules for food of animal origin.

Fink-Keßler, A. 2013. Milch. Vom Mythos zur Massenware. Reihe Stoffgeschichten, Band 8, München: Oekom-Verlag.

Giacometti, F., Bonilauri, P., Serraino, A., Peli, A., Amatiste, S., Arrigoni, N., et al., 2013. Four-year monitoring of foodborne pathogens in raw milk sold by vending machines in Italy. J. Food Prot. 76 (11), 1902–1907. Nov.

Gumpert, D.E., 2015. The Raw Milk Answer Book: What You REALLY Need to Know About Our Most Controversial Food. Lauson Publishing, Incorporated.

Hamann, J. 2002. Relationships between somatic cell count and milk composition. Proceedings of the IDF World Summit, Auckland/New Zealand, nr. 372, pp. 56–59.

Hartung, M. (Ed.), 2008. Erreger von Zoonosen in Deutschland im Jahr 2006. BfR Wissenschaft, Berlin.

Ijaz, N., 2014. Canada's Other Illegal White Substance: Evidence, Economics and Raw Milk Policy. Health Law Rev. 22 (1), 26–39.

Kalmus, P., Kramarenko, T., Roasto, M., Merem, K., Viltrop, A., 2015. Quality of raw milk intended for direct consumption in Estonia. Food Control 51, 135–139.

Kusche, D., Kuhnt, K., Ruebesam, K., Rohrer, C., Nierop, A.F., Jahreis, G., et al., 2014. Fatty acid profiles and antioxidants of organic and conventional milk from low- and high-input systems during outdoor period. J. Sci. Food Agric. 95 (3), 529–539. Feb.

Obladen, M., 2012. Bad milk, part 1: antique doctrines that impeded breastfeeding. Acta Paediatr. Nov 101 (11), 1102–1104.

Obladen, M., 2014. From swill milk to certified milk: progress in cow's milk quality in the 19th century. Ann. Nutr. Metab. 64 (1), 80–87.

Oliver, S.P., Boor, K.J., Murphy, S.C., Murinda, S.E., 2009. Food safety hazards associated with consumption of raw milk. Foodborne Pathog. Dis. 6, 793–806.

Ricci, A., Capello, K., Cibin, V., Pozza, G., Ferrè, N., Barrucci, F., et al., 2013. Raw milk-associated foodborne infections: a scoring system for the risk-based categorisation of raw dairy farms. Res. Vet. Sci. Aug 95 (1), 69–75.

Schmid, R., 2009. The Untold Story of Milk. New Trends Publishing Inc, Washington.

Schukken, Y.H., Weersink, A., Leslie, K.E., Martin, S.W., 1993. Dynamics and regulation of bulk milk somatic cell counts. Can. J. Vet. Res. Apr 57 (2), 131–135.

Verhoog, H., Lammerts van Bueren, E.T., Matze, E., Baars, T., 2007. The value of 'naturalness' in organic farming. NJAS 54 (4), 333–345.

Wightman, T., Wilson, S., Beals, T., Beals, P., Brown, R. (Eds.), 2015. Producing Fresh Milk — Cow Edition. Farm-to-Consumer Foundation, Cincinnati, Ohio.

FURTHER READING

www.techniekinnederland.nl/nl/index.php?title = Boterwetten_in_internationaal_perspectief (accessed 22.09.16).

www.milkmaps.com (accessed 01.07.16).

www.hookandson.co.uk (accessed 01.08.16).

www.organicpastures.com (accessed 01.08.16).

www.rawmilkinstitute.net (accessed 01.09.16).

www.milch-und-mehr.de (accessed 01.08.16).

https://www.gesetze-im-internet.de/tier-lmhv/BJNR182800007.html.

CHAPTER 5

Conventional and Emerging Clean-in-Place Methods for the Milking Systems

Xinmiao Wang[1], Ali Demirci[2], Robert E. Graves[2] and Virendra M. Puri[2]

[1]Department of Food Science and Biotechnology, Zhejiang Gongshang University, Hangzhou, China
[2]Department of Agricultural and Biological Engineering, Pennsylvania State University, University Park, PA, United States

5.1 INTRODUCTION

Based on the Food and Agriculture Organization report in 2013, the global production of milk in total was 768.6 million tons; a substantial increase of 21.7% compared to the milk production a decade ago of 631.8 million tons (FAOSTAT, 2013). The consumption of dairy products keeps increasing worldwide, given the demonstrated nutritional values and health benefits. Since more than 80% of milk worldwide comes from cow (with Americas and Europe >97% and Oceania 100%), this chapter will use the milking system for cow milk as an example, and similar approaches could be adapted and applied to the milking system for other milk-producing mammals.

On a conventional dairy farm, milk is usually collected from the cow either by hand or through a milking unit under vacuum. The milk from a healthy cow should be sterile. However, during the collection phase (when using hand milking or with the milking unit) and/or the transportation phase (when milk is held in the milk pail or transported in the milk line), potential contamination of the raw milk might occur due to the undesirable cleanliness of the milk contact surfaces. Therefore, a proper cleaning and sanitizing of the milk contact surfaces is important to prevent the contamination.

The definition of clean can be interpreted in various ways; a milk contact surface could be physically cleaned to remove gross debris, or chemically cleaned using cleaning chemicals and some mechanical forces, or microbiologically cleaned through reducing the microorganisms to an

Raw Milk
DOI: https://doi.org/10.1016/B978-0-12-810530-6.00005-5

91

acceptable level (Walton, 2008). Different end-products require different processing techniques with respective "clean" standard. For the milking system, the "dirt" particles are easily removed by the installation of the milk filters at the end of the milk line; provided no chemical contamination is posed (i.e., chemical solution overuse or leak), the risk of pathogenic microorganisms contaminating raw milk is therefore the major focus of today's milk processing. *Listeria monocytogenes*, *Salmonella typhimurium*, *Bacillus cereus*, *Campylobacter jejuni*, *Yersinia enterocolitica*, *Staphylococcus aureus*, *Escherichia coli* O157:H7 are some of the commonly seen contaminating microorganisms on a dairy farm and in the raw milk. These microorganisms pose potential hazard to the quality and safety of the milk, which need to be eliminated. In this chapter, the traditional and up-to-date milking system, along with their cleaning and sanitizing approaches are introduced, the assessment and prediction of the "cleanliness" of the milking system are presented.

5.2 CONVENTIONAL CLEANING AND SANITIZING APPROACHES FOR MILKING SYSTEMS

The milking system on a typical dairy farm nowadays could be categorized as the vacuum system (Fig. 5.1) and the sanitary piping system

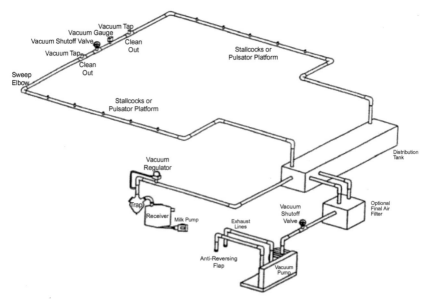

Figure 5.1 Typical milking system vacuum system layout (DPC, 2000).

(Figs. 5.2 and 5.3). The vacuum provides the power during milking and cleaning; the sizing, level testing, exhaust line design, and control of the vacuum pump are all essential to conduct an appropriate milking and cleaning. The sanitary pipes and components include milk and wash lines and accessories needed from milking units (1) to the receiver such as air inlets, milk inlets, milk meter, milking pipelines, and lowlines, (2) from the receiver to the storage cooling tank such as receiver jar with probes,

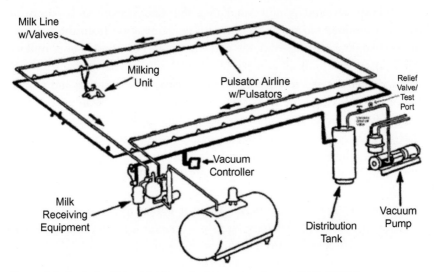

Figure 5.2 Typical milking highline pipeline system layout (DPC, 2006b).

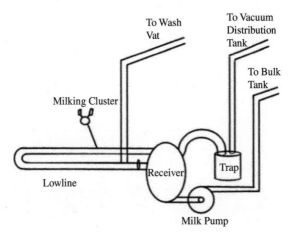

Figure 5.3 Typical milking lowline pipeline system layout (DPC, 2000).

milk pump, milk filters, heat exchangers, and discharge lines, and (3) the washing components such as diverter valve, wash lines, wash sink or vats, inlets, jetter assemblies if needed, air injectors, drainage, booster heaters if needed (Fig. 5.4). All milk contact surfaces need to be cleaned and sanitized at the completion of the milking event (Walton, 2008). These milk contact parts can be further divided into the milk delivery line, cooling tank, and milk "holder" including milking units, milk meters, and the receiver (Efficient Cleaning, 2001).

Milking by hand is now used in a few dairy farms; it is laborious, time consuming, and prone to potential contamination from the inappropriate handling during milking and cleaning. For those hand milking dairy farms, raw milk is squeezed from the teats of the cow into a milk pail and then carried to a storage cooling tank. The cleaning and sanitizing of the "milking system" is then, simplified into the cleaning and sanitizing of the milk pail, the storage cooling tank, and other associate fittings such as valves, caps, tees, gaskets, etc. This can be achieved through a diluted wash detergents, clear water, and brushes to conduct the manual wash (DPC, 2006b). The advantage of such a simple system is that it is easy to set up and no additional equipment is needed; however, the labor cost is extremely high. When it comes to the cleaning of the system, the worker might have already worked a long time during milking, leading to potential insufficient practices and higher risk of contamination. The direct contact between the worker and hazardous detergent solution and hot water during cleaning is potentially dangerous, and

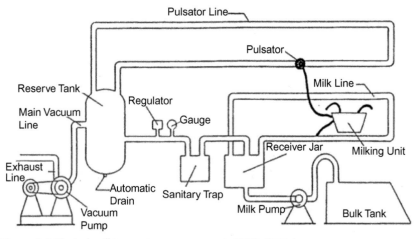

Figure 5.4 Typical milking system components (DPC, 2006a).

precautions must be taken into consideration with appropriate protections. Additionally, from a physiological point of view, workers might conduct the cleaning and sanitizing procedure inappropriately or insufficiently, and the human error is a problem particularly for missing the corners, bends, dead ends, and other unreachable places.

For most middle-to-large size dairy farms today, the milking process and the following cleaning and sanitizing process include a certain level of automation. Manual milking is replaced with bucket machine milking or vacuum-powered milking and correspondingly, the cleaning and sanitizing is upgraded into certain degree of automation with the controlling system.

Compared to the manual milking, cleaning, and sanitizing, one advanced approach is referred to as "cleaning out of place (COP)," in which the milk contact components are disassembled after the milking event and put in a circulation tank for cleaning and sanitizing. The tank is usually equipped with high-volume circulation pump and motor-driven brushes to enhance the cleaning and sanitizing performance. Due to the large surface area of the wash tank and the high possibility of temperature drop in the tank during washing, a temperature recording chart and an automatic temperature controlling steam valve are required for every COP system (DPC, 2001). The wash solution temperature can be elevated when needed to ensure the cleaning and sanitizing performance. The energy usage for COP system is typically high and the disassembly and reassembly of the milk contact surface parts takes extra labor; therefore, usage of COP is decreasing on dairy farms. Therefore, to reduce labor cost (compared to the manual cleaning and sanitizing) and energy consumption (compared to COP), and at the same time to ensure a cleaned and sanitized milk contact surface that prevents potential biofouling and biofilm formation, clean-in-place (CIP) is nowadays widely adopted on dairy farms.

CIP is a procedure during which the cleaning and sanitizing is conducted within the processing equipment in its assembled condition and the equipment/system is not dismantled during the circulation/recirculation of rinse water, wash, and sanitizing solution. CIP is typically highly automated and labor need is minimal (Tamime, 2009). Several recommendations are drafted from different organizations for the milking system CIP. Despite the minute differences in each cleaning and sanitizing cycle requirements, the basic structure for the milking system CIP includes three main functions: to remove the organic milk residues including carbohydrate, lipid, and protein (potential to form biofilm for harboring and protecting microorganisms); to remove the inorganic milk residues of various minerals (layers of scales tend to form "milkstone"); and to inactivate microorganisms and retard their growth during the idle time between milking events.

Alkaline solution is needed to remove the organic residues, while acidic solution is needed for the removal of minerals. In the United States, apart from the Food and Drug Administration recommendations, the Dairy Practices Council (DPC) had been working on the guidelines regarding milk quality, sanitation, and regulatory uniformity since 1970, and several revisions and improvements had been made to keep it updated with the technology development (DPC, 2010). They recommended that, a complete set of dairy farm milking system CIP, regardless of the system size, should include a prerinse cycle, an alkaline wash cycle, an acid wash cycle, and a sanitizing cycle prior to the next milking event (Table 5.1). The prerinse cycle utilizes clear tepid water to rinse out the loose residues (including the carbohydrates) and the one-pass rinse without recirculation eliminates redeposition of residues back onto the milking system. For prerinse step, tepid water instead of cold water is recommended, because warmer temperature removes the solid residues more effectively. However, the temperature of the tepid water should not exceed 50°C, to prevent milk proteins from denaturation.

Table 5.1 Recommended milking system CIP steps (DPC, 2010)

CIP steps	Temperature (°C)	pH	Cycle time (min)	Additional recommendations
Tepid water rinse	43.3–48.9	NA	NA	Cycle time depends on system pipeline length
Alkaline wash	Start: 71.1–76.7 End: ≥ 48.9	11.5–12	8–10	Slug number ≥ 20; chlorine concentration ≥ 120 ppm; alkalinity ≥ 1100 ppm
Clear rinse	Tepid	NA	One-pass	NA
Acid wash	NA	3.0–4.0	≥ 2–3	NA
Sanitizing	NA	NA	NA	EPA-registered product

NA, Not Applicable.

The following alkaline wash cycle uses high alkalinity solution (usually chlorinated) to remove the organic soils including milk fat and protein and the remaining carbohydrates. The alkaline wash cycle requires a high solution temperature to start with and long recirculation time duration, depending on the configuration and installation of the specific milking system. To avoid the neutralization of the following acid wash with the alkaline solution, a one-pass intermediate clear rinse is recommended (not mandatory) with tepid water.

The acid wash cycle uses acidic solution to remove the minerals. This cycle is not specified with fixed recommendations, mainly because that the application of this cycle is largely dependent on the completion of the alkaline wash cycle and the particular milking system. However, the acid solution usually has a pH around 3 with relatively shorter wash time (than the alkaline wash cycle).

The wash cycle detergents function more than just saponification of the fat and penetration into the milk residues, they also act as emulsifiers to break down the milk fat and to form more uniform residue suspensions in the wash solution (alkaline wash), chelating agent to hold minerals in especially hard water condition and prevent mineral redeposition (acid wash), lower the surface tension of wash solution and contact with the milk residue better (both alkaline and acid washes), etc. (Watkinson, 2008).

Lastly, each time before the milking event, an US Environmental Protection Agency (US EPA) registered sanitizing circulation is recommended to ensure the microbiological status of the milking system (DPC, 2010). The types of EPA-approved sanitizers include chlorine-bearing sanitizers, iodophors, acid sanitizers, and hydrogen peroxide solutions. DPC specifically emphasizes that when the sanitizing cycle is completed, the milking system and equipment must not be rinsed with water again to guarantee the performance of the sanitizing cycle (Table 5.1). However, for some potentially corrosive sanitizers (such as hypochlorites), the contact time of the sanitizers with the milking system and equipment should not exceed half an hour before the milking event (DPC, 2005).

To enhance the cleaning performance and reduce water usage, air is sometimes used in the milking system CIP to create "slugs"; pushing solutions forward and increasing the shear force exerted on the milk deposits. Air could be sucked into the milking system with similar to equal portion as the water continuously (referred to as "spontaneous slug flow formation") or whenever the water level drops below the suction pipe intake (referred to as "spontaneous flushing pulsation"), or more often practiced, a controlled periodic air and water alternating pattern into the milk line (referred to as "controlled flushing pulsation"), in which the slug speed is controlled by the air admission rate and slug size (Efficient Cleaning, 2001). DPC recommended a minimum number of 20 slugs per cycle running for typical 8–10 min for the controlled flushing pulsation CIP (DPC, 2010), and similar recommendations could also be found for Canada, Australia, New Zealand, and other countries (Canadian Quality Milk Program, 2015; Dairy Australia, 2016; Cleaning Systems, 2016).

As mentioned previously, the factors affecting the CIP performance include the mechanical forces (flow rate and slug velocity), detergents and sanitizers selection, CIP time duration, and temperature of the CIP solutions. It is necessary to especially emphasize the importance of the heat factor (i.e., solution temperature). The tepid water rinse temperature (43–49°C) (DPC, 2010) ensures that milk fat do not crystallize and redeposit on the milk contact surface while not too high to denature the milk protein and "cook on" milk solids, which can be very difficult to remove. On the other hand, the alkaline wash solution temperature should start high (71–77°C) (DPC, 2010) with adequately wash solution volume to dissolve and emulsify the milk residues, more importantly, the final return solution temperature should still be above 49°C (DPC, 2005, 2007), and also the potential redeposition of milk soils onto the milk contact surfaces should be prevented at the completion of the alkaline wash. For the acid wash cycle, however, DPC does not recommend a specific solution temperature. Room-temperature acid wash is sufficient but for a minimum contact time of 2–3 min (DPC, 2010), normally from 7 to 10 min (DPC, 2005). But if a "shock cleaning" is conducted, the acid wash temperature should be as high as the alkaline wash. Cautions must be taken when the ambient temperature changes from season to season and the detergent concentration should be adjusted based on the water hardness and other physical and chemical properties.

DPC is widely acknowledged in the United States for dairy guidelines and recommendations. Some other guidelines are available with similar recommendations in other regions around the world. For example, the guidelines in Canada are proposed by Dairy Farmers of Canada, with a developed Canadian Quality Milk (CQM) Program (2015). In the CQM Program, it specified that the starting temperature of the prerinse cycle should be between 35°C and 60°C with an ending temperature of 35°C or higher. The alkaline wash is recommended to start at 71°C or higher with an ending temperature higher than 43°C, which is a wider temperature range as compared to the DPC recommendation, but shorter in cycle time duration, only 5—10 min. They also specified the pH (11—12), alkalinity (total alkalinity of 400—800 ppm and active alkalinity of 225—350 ppm), and chlorine concentration (80—120 ppm) of the alkaline wash solution to ensure the performance. Slug is also recommended, with a minimum of 20 slugs during the alkaline wash. The acid wash cycle seems to be similar to the DPC recommendation, with a solution pH below 3.5 and no specific requirement on the acid wash solution temperature and time duration; 5-min circulation should be sufficient. Similarly, the regional recommendations for different provinces vary; for example, in Ontario, the starting temperature of the prerinse cycle is recommended to be between 43°C and 60°C with a minimum ending temperature of 38°C (Milk Quality Infosheet, 2013). Since Hazard Analysis Critical Control Points is used in drafting the CQM Program, there are also actions for each critical control point in the program and a record book along with a workbook for the farmers to work with. Of course, there are some other organizations and institutions, taking responsibility of formulating and publishing guidelines for hygienic equipment design, construction and installation, facility and plant arrangement, testing methods regulation, and so on, including the International Dairy Federation, the International Standardization Organization, the European Hygienic Engineering and Design Group, etc.

5.3 CONVENTIONAL CIP FOR THE MILK STORAGE COOLING TANK

For the milk storage cooling tank, the CIP usually follows similar cycles as of the milking system pipeline CIP, including a tepid prerinse cycle, a heated alkaline detergent wash cycle, and a cold rinse cycle (Efficient Cleaning, 2001). Static spray balls, rotary spray heads, and rotary jet heads are commonly used in the storage cooling tank CIP due to its large inner surface area. The size of the spray ball, volume of the solution, and pressure are calculated based on the size of the storage cooling tank (Packman et al., 2008). Heat in this case is an even more important factor in the CIP performance because of the large surface area and the low temperature of the inner surface. Therefore, it is recommended that the starting temperature of the CIP wash should be as high as possible to compensate the heat loss during the wash solution travel and heat exchange between the wash solution and the cold inner surface of the storage cooling tank (Efficient Cleaning, 2001). For instance, the starting temperature of the prerinse cycle in some cases could be as high as 60°C to ensure the CIP performance.

There are other less commonly used CIP approaches, such as the acidified boiling water cleaning, during which a one-pass heated acid solution is pumped into the system for 2 min followed by 4 min of water rinse. During the 2-min acid wash with the milk contact surface, a minimal temperature of 77°C is needed (Efficient Cleaning, 2001). Another type of wash is just the opposite, using highly concentrated cold caustic soda solution to clean the system and reuse the wash solutions to save energy and chemical expenditure. This solution reusing method was popular in 1970s due to limited energy supply, but rarely used today (Lloyd, 2008). In some large parlors in New Zealand and Australia, reverse flow cleaning used to be popular (Cleaning Systems, 2016; Dairy Australia, 2016). Contrary to the typical cluster-to-sink flow direction, in this method, the wash solution is pumped into the receiver, travels through the milk line, and then drains from the clusters. There is no need to detach the cluster from the jetter (and reattach them once again for milking) and, therefore, saves some time and jetter cost. However, the usage of water is usually higher than other CIP approaches and therefore apart from the purpose to rinse the plant with cold water (Cleaning Systems, 2016), nowadays the reverse flow cleaning is not recommended by industries in New Zealand or Australia (Cleaning Systems, 2016; Dairy Australia, 2016).

Since cross-contamination is a commonly occurring problem on dairy farms, an attempt was made to prevent mastitis using CoPulsation (CoPulsation, 2013), a patented technology with two codependent solenoids, one for vacuum supply and the other for fresh air supply, providing the pulsation horizontally instead of the conventionally oblique direction.

5.4 EMERGING CIP METHODS

There are attempts to replace the current CIP wash chemical detergents with alternatives. To reduce the environmental impact of using chlorinated chemical detergents, one study used chlorine-free detergents for the CIP process (Sandberg et al., 2011). The researchers developed a model milking system with removable sampling locations. Plate samples were collected from the end of the T junctions protruding different lengths from the milk pipe main loop and *B. cereus* was used as the model contaminant on the sampling plates. They were able to find that compared to using NaOH alone, using chlorine-free detergents resulted in a higher spore reduction (not significant); however, at all temperature levels (45, 55, and 65°C), when using chlorinated detergent, the spore reduction was significantly higher than the chlorine-free detergents. More interestingly, the researchers found that the cleaning performance was not significantly improved when increasing solution temperature from 55°C to 65°C, for all detergent, chlorinated or not; possible reasons might come from the limited length of the pipelines used in the milking system and the controlled environmental factors, exerting a minimal ambient temperature effect on the wash solution during recirculation.

Electrolyzed oxidizing (EO) is another environmentally friendly method that had been investigated over the past decade in our laboratory at the Pennsylvania State University. EO water is generated through the electrolysis of diluted sodium chloride solution (0.1%). From the anode of the electrified chamber, acidic EO water is generated with chlorine and hydrochloride; simultaneously from the cathode, alkaline EO water is generated with sodium hydroxide. Under certain EO water generator settings, acidic EO water has a pH of around 2.6 with a free chlorine concentration up to 80 ppm and high oxidizing reduction potential (ORP) around 1100 mV; the alkaline EO water, on the other hand, has a pH value around 11.0 and an ORP about -800 mV (Sharma and Demirci, 2003). The basic properties of alkaline and acidic EO water solutions match the traditional milking system CIP alkaline and acid wash chemical recommendations, and therefore, it was proposed in our group that alkaline and acidic EO water solutions might be applied as milking system CIP alternatives and a number of studies were conducted in the past decades.

Firstly, Walker et al. (2005a) tested the possibility of using EO water for milking system CIP. Milking system material coupons were studied as preliminary trials. The coupons were soiled with commonly seen microorganisms, then soaked with alkaline and acidic EO water solutions. The coupon surfaces were then analyzed through comparing microbial enrichment and adenosine triphosphate (ATP) bioluminescence tests. These preliminary lab coupon tests showed promising results. Subsequently, a pilot milking system with a 27-m long milk line was set up with essential parts used on a dairy milking system (Fig. 5.5). The pilot milking system was soiled with microorganism-added raw milk and then washed with

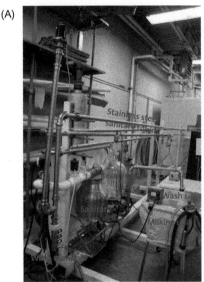

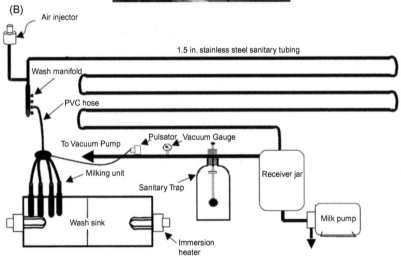

Figure 5.5 Lab-scale pilot milking system (A) to scale (Walker et al., 2005a) and (B) schematic of the pilot milking system, not to scale (Dev et al., 2014).

heated alkaline and acidic EO water solutions. It was found that EO water solutions at 60°C were able to clean the pilot system with great satisfaction and no significant differences were found in the cleanliness between the EO water cleaning for 7.5 and 10 min with the conventional cleaning approach (Walker et al., 2005b). Moreover, when conducting the EO water CIP for long-term evaluation, they found that 7.5 min wash did not reliably clean the pilot milking system, suggesting a potential need to increase the wash time duration. However, Walker et al. (2005b) did not realize that the heated acidic EO water (60°C) used during the acid wash cycle was undesirable, since the increase of solution temperature would cause the acceleration of chlorine loss, in turn decreasing a cleaning and sanitizing power and posing a potential chlorine gas release as a threat for the operator in addition to a waste of energy. Therefore, a temperature optimization study was later conducted by Dev et al. (2014) in search for the optimal temperatures of the alkaline and acidic EO water solution for the pilot-scale milking system CIP cycles. After performance analysis for different temperature combinations and mathematical modeling, the researchers showed that the logarithmic mean temperature of 58.8°C for the alkaline EO water solution and 39.3°C for the acidic EO water solution were the optimal condition of the pilot milking system CIP. Correspondingly, a starting temperature of 70°C for the alkaline EO water and 45°C for the acidic EO water to conduct the pilot milking system CIP was proposed. With this condition, a 100% ATP reduction on all sampling locations and 100% microbial reduction on all stainless steel pipe, elbow, and milk inlet sampling locations were achieved. To validate this lab optimized result in the real world, a validation study was conducted on a commercial dairy farm based on these results. Wang et al. (2013) did a 2-month EO water CIP and another 2-month conventional CIP study, with the special permission of the Pennsylvania Department of Agriculture. When comparing the performance of using EO water CIP with the conventional CIP, the researchers were able to demonstrate a comparable CIP performance, when using the EO water solutions, from both ATP bioluminescence tests and microbiological enrichment results. For some porous materials such as liners and milk hoses, the performance of EO water CIP was better than the conventional CIP, largely due to the sanitizing effect of the acidic EO water solution. Additionally, when calculating the operational cost of both CIP approaches, the researchers presented that EO water CIP per cycle was $2.15 and conventional CIP per cycle to be $2.84, which means a 25% reduction using the EO water CIP (Wang et al., 2013).

An increasing number of dairy farms are now adopting an alkaline wash and acid wash cycles combined as "one-step CIP" process to save time, energy, and operational cost from the reduction of one wash cycle. Again, in our laboratory, a lab trial was conducted on our pilot-scale milking system optimizing a blended EO water solution as an one-step

CIP alternative (Wang et al., 2016a). Through a set of optimization experiments with varying factors of acidic EO water solution percentage in the blended EO water, one-step wash cycle time duration, and the blended EO water starting temperature, an optimal condition for the blended EO water one-step CIP was found as 60% acidic EO water in the blended EO water solution, 17 min of one-step wash time, and a starting temperature of 59°C, which was then validated with replicates and the one-step CIP performance was compared with commercially available one-step wash chemicals. It was observed that the optimized blended EO water CIP had a higher ATP reduction on average than the commercial one-step CIP, and a higher microbial inactivation for the sampling locations of stainless steel pipe and elbow. Moreover, the operational cost of using the optimized blended EO water CIP on the pilot milking system is 80% lower ($0.55 per cycle for the optimized blended EO water one-step CIP and $2.82 per cycle for the commercially available one-step chemical CIP); since the solution generation only needs table salt, water, and electricity to run the EO water generator. However, to confirm the optimized blend EO water solution on a real-world scenario, commercial dairy farm study still needs to be performed for the one-step CIP.

Similarly, Yun (2014) conducted a series of studies for EO water milk tank CIPs at the Pennsylvania State University. The stainless steel milk tank had a working volume of 15 L with a 360° static spray ball installed on top center. Both refrigerated (2−4°C) and heated (74°C) milk were tested as soil, then cleaned and sanitized with EO water solutions. An additional protein test was used to test the milk contact surface protein residue level (PRO-Clean, 2015). They were able to validate the previous results from Dev et al. (2014) of alkaline and acidic EO water for the refrigerated milk tank CIP, from both ATP bioluminescence tests and residual protein tests. For the heated milk tank CIP, a response surface method was applied to achieve the optimal time and temperature conditions. They discovered, however, that only the factor of wash time for alkaline wash and acid wash cycles were significant ($P = 0.047$ for alkaline wash and $P = 0.035$ for acid wash) in achieving a satisfactory CIP; other factors such as temperature, and factor interactions, did not exhibit significant effect on the cleaning and sanitizing performance. From the ATP bioluminescence tests and residual protein tests, they showed that the 100% "cleanliness" could not be achieved, as compared to the conventional CIP washes in removing the milk deposits and fouling. Based on the optimization recommendation from the Box–Behnken response surface method, an optimal time and temperature combination of alkaline EO water at 54.6°C for 20.5 min and acidic EO water at 25°C for 10 min was proposed and validated to achieve a milk contact surface that could be considered as clean from ATP bioluminescence manufacture recommendation and the residual protein test result.

5.5 MAINTENANCE, EVALUATION, AND ASSESSMENT OF CIP PERFORMANCE

Regular maintenance and inspection of the milking system are the best ways to prevent potential problems from an inappropriately performed CIP. In addition to the dead-end fittings, corners, and elbows, the interior surface of the milk line should be inspected visually for any potential biofilm formation, especially for the upward sloping locations where wash solutions are hard to reach. Examining the wash sink and receiver jar with great care, and manual wash should be performed if needed. Rubber parts such as liners, gaskets and "O" rings, and milk hoses should be inspected and replaced on a regular basis since they are porous materials and tend to harbor microorganisms and form biofilm and biofouling. Probes in the receiver jar and wash sink should be examined for any potential clinging deposit, which might result in inaccurate indication of the solution flow, temperature, and volume (DPC, 2007). If needed, all of these should be removed and manually washed and sanitized or replaced (DPC, 2001).

The cleanliness of milk contact surfaces reveals the CIP performance and could be evaluated by several approaches. Visual evaluation is the most convenient method; however, it could be greatly misleading due to the ambient lighting condition and the physical condition, practical skills, and experience of the examiner. During the early development stages of the biofilm architecture, the attachment is not firm and the biofilm patches are not easily observed (Monroe, 2007). Therefore, visual inspection is not always an ideal approach. Microbiological tests could also be conducted, and there are several readily available methods. The milk contact surfaces can be swabbed with sterile applicators or sponges and then incubated/plated for target microorganisms. Similar to the swabbing approach, contacted agar biofilm or sticky tape could be used by simply pressing the film/tape against the milk contact surface, then incubate and count. Another method is to rinse the milk contact surface and collect the rinsed solution followed by a standard plate count; this method is more accurate compared to the swabbing method but time consuming and, therefore, not appropriate for large-scale milking systems. All of these microbiological methods are more accurate and objective compared to the visual inspection, but the downside is that the result is typically not real time and the incubation time (24 h or longer) would delay any needed immediate on-site action (Asteriadou and Fryer, 2008).

To compensate this disadvantage and achieve an on-site rapid detection, ATP bioluminescence is now widely used. ATP could be found in all viable cells from plants, animals, and microorganisms (Leon and Albrecht, 2007). The amount of ATP can be measured through the chemical reaction of luciferin and luciferase enzyme complex, resulting in an emission of light. This light is measured using a luminometer and the unit expressed as Relative Light Unit (RLU) readings (Wang et al., 2013). Now ATP bioluminescence has been widely used on dairy farms and processing facilities to estimate the existence and amount of soil as an on-site real-time detection technique (Wang et al., 2014). The increase of organisms and milk residues can be directly related to the increase of RLU readings with the increase of ATP levels. After swabbing the milk contact surfaces, the RLU reading is acquired within seconds with high sensitivity and accuracy, which makes ATP bioluminescence a desirable on-site rapid detection approach. Based on the different recommendations from the manufacturers, the criteria to access the CIP performance vary. However, one thing that needs to be pointed out is that, the RLU readings do not correlate directly with the microbial population, since the "soil ATP" contains both the environmentally residual ATP and the ATP from microbial cells (dead or alive). Cautions must be taken when analyzing and interpreting the data. In addition to the ATP swabs, there are other types of on-site rapid detection swabs available; protein swabs for instance. The color of the swabs changes after sampling and reagent released, and the extent of color changes indicates the amount range of residual protein (PRO-Clean, 2015). For certain protein swab products, heat might be needed to accelerate the chemical reaction, but still the result can be acquired within half an hour and corrective actions could be taken quickly (Clean-Trace, 2010).

For scientific research purposes, attempts were made to measure and monitor the milk deposit residue on the contact surfaces more accurately. Ellen and Tudos (2003) summarized the techniques and parameters for the online measurement and detection during milking and cleaning.

During milking, a variety of sensors could be applied to measure the temperature, density, conductivity, turbidity, viscosity, and color of the milk. In addition, pressure, flow rate, water level of milking unit and wash solution along with the potential measurement of pH, fat and protein content, lactose, flavor components, and possible contaminants could be sensed. To achieve these, a number of techniques might be useful during milking and cleaning, including Nuclear Magnetic Resonance and Magnetic Resonance Imaging, Raman spectrometry, mass spectrometry, electronic nose, tongue and other biosensors, quartz crystal microbalance, gas chromatography, Fourier Transform Middle-Infrared Spectrometry, and Fourier Transform Near-Infrared Spectrometry. Van Asselt et al. (2002) developed an online monitoring system for the dairy evaporator CIP. The major measurements were pH and conductivity changes during the CIP cycles; cycles with chemical solutions had higher conductivity compared to water, thus differentiating different CIP cycles. They were able to find comparable results of the online conductivity results with the offline conductivity measurements but not with the turbidity measurements. Lang et al. (2011) used infrared microspectroscopy to measure residual milk protein and milk fat at low concentration and succeeded in achieving repeatable data as low as $0.01 \ \mu g/cm^2$. This indicated a potential application of microspectroscopy in the online monitoring of the CIP process and the milk contact surface cleanliness assessment. Another study used ultrasound sensor to measure the milk fouling in a heat exchanger by analyzing the ultrasonic signal accompanied with temperature and mass flow rate data (Wallhäußer et al., 2013). With different decision-making classification approaches, the researchers were able to achieve more than 80% accuracy with artificial neural network method and more than 94% accuracy with support vector machine method. However, the trials are still lab-scale and not verified for commercial scale assessment.

5.6 ROBOTIC MILKING SYSTEMS

To further release the duty and reduce labor cost from the (partially) manual milking, automatic milking systems had been developed and put into practice during the past two decades. The automatic milking system is also referred to as robotic milking system since the manual teat cup attachment movement is mimicked using the robotic arm, a key component in the automatic milking system (Automatic Milking Systems, 2016). After the cows are trained (typically within 7 days), the milking robot is capable of (1) identifying the cow, (2) determining her milking status (some are even able to determine the silent heat of the cow and detect abortions and cysts), (3) dispensing the feed to the cow while she is milked, (4) evaluating the milk quality through multiple sensors installed, (5) making a record, and (6) raising alarms if needed. In an automatic milking system environment, cows can be milked 24/7 at her will and there is no need for a mandatory milk time during the day. It had been reported that with good management, the robotic milking production can be 3%–5% higher than the parlor milking (twice/day) (Robotic Milking Systems, 2011). After the teats are located, cleaned, and teat cups attached, the milking begins; based on the milk flow from each quarter, the teat cups will be removed when milking is completed. During milking, a series of data is collected including the physicals of the cows (weight, quarter yield and quarter milk time, dead milk time, etc.) and the quality of the milk (temperature, color, conductivity, fat and protein content, somatic cell count, etc.).

The cleaning of the robotic milking system varies based on different robot manufacturer's settings and models. There was a study showing that water and chemical usage for the robotic milking system is less than parlor milking system CIP (Robotic Milking Systems, 2011). For example, one robot model requires three automatic cleaning events consisting of two alkaline wash and one acid wash per day (Lely Dairy Equipment, 2014). The manufacture specifically requires that no chlorinated solution or acids other than phosphoric acid and citric acid could be used on the milking robot. To enhance the cleaning performance, they recommended their own alkaline-based detergents to remove the protein and fat which leaves no harm to the milking robot from the chlorine-free product. Another milking robot (Multi-Box Robotic Milking System) utilized short stainless steel lines and double milk filters to ensure the milk flow and debris removal (MIone, 2013). It is also programmed to conduct an automatic water rinse "backflush" in each teat cup after every milking to maintain the cleanliness of tea cups and prevent potential cross-contamination between cows. Additionally, a tepid water rinse cycle, referred as "short cleaning" is available for specific setting and programming of rinse interval and duration. The main wash cycle is a "system wash," with a tepid water rinse cycle, a heated detergent wash cycle, followed by a cold wash rinse cycle, altogether taking about 25 min to complete. Another milking robot uses a three-dimensional "time-of-light" camera to precisely locate the teats to help the teat cup attachment, and water rinse is programmed to take place between every milking for the teat cups (inside and out) and the camera glass for better precision (AMR Features, 2015). Due to the specific chemical requirements, a unique alkaline detergent was developed for the specific milking robot with a blend of sequestrates and soil suspending agents capable of removing fat and protein residues and a wide applications in both hard and soft supply water conditions (Robotic Milking, 2014).

5.7 COMPUTATIONAL CIP AND MODELING

Despite the improvements in CIP approaches and development of more effective chemicals over the years, there is always a need to better understand the CIP process for further improvements. Toward that end, mathematical models have the potential to contribute significantly. Computational fluid dynamics (CFD) simulation utilizes the available computerized numerical packages and the ever-growing computing power to conduct some computer simulation and save laboratory work. Jensen and Fris (2004) studied the flow patterns in a mix-proof valve and compared with laser sheet visualization, in an attempt to predict the CIP performance. Wall shear stress, fluid exchange, and flow patterns were considered to achieve a desirable CIP cleanliness prediction (Jensen, 2003). When treating the CIP processing as a mass exchange process, another research showed that under turbulent flow, the cleanliness of a T-junction could be predicted (Asteriadou et al., 2007). When using a finite-volume based prediction, the experimental data and predictive results compared well. This provided the possibility of mass (i.e., deposit) removal and CIP cleanliness predicting using CFD. When assuming the cleaning as a diffusion-controlled process, Föste et al. (2011) developed CFD cleaning models to predict and optimize the soil removal efficiency from pulsed flow cleaning. This expands the CFD applications to more complex system configurations with fast flow conditions.

In addition to the computational analysis and predictions, there are also some attempts experimentally to scrutinize the role of each CIP cycles in the deposit removal process and develop corresponding mathematical models. Wang et al. (2016b) constructed a stainless steel surface evaluation simulator with removable sampling pipe sections along the milk line. Milk deposit mass on the contact surface of the sampling pipes was evaluated after the milk soiling and after certain time duration of the EO water alkaline and acid wash cycles during the CIP. In this manner, the deposit mass reduction with CIP time was recorded and analyzed. A unified first-order milk deposit removal rate model dependent on nth power of remaining milk deposit mass was developed experimentally and then validated. A substantial deposit mass decrease was found within 10 s of tepid water prerinse cycle, and the deposit removal process was hypothesized to be comprised of a simultaneous fast and slow removal process. This result corroborated with the recommendation from the Ontario diary guidelines of the 90%—95% deposit removal during the tepid water rinse cycle (Milk Quality Infosheet, 2013). Based on the set of developed mathematical models, a 55% time duration reduction was achieved for the alkaline and acidic EO water CIP on the simulator and validated with the indirect ATP bioluminescence tests. The case study using the online monitoring result conducted by Van Asselt et al. (2002) also demonstrated a 50% cleaning time reduction in dairy evaporator CIP with improved cleaning efficiency. Therefore, it seems promising to apply the mathematical and computational models, equipped with online detection and monitoring technique, to the real processing facilities and to reduce energy consumption. In a similar manner as the alkaline and acidic EO water CIP modeling process, a set of two-term exponential decay kinetic models were also developed for the optimized blended EO water one-step CIP using the surface evaluation simulator, including a fast deposit removal process in the beginning of the wash cycle and a slow but steady deposit removal process throughout the entire one-step wash cycle (Wang et al., 2015). The researchers found an additional 4% deposit removal from the nondimensionalized deposit mass data during the blended EO water one-step wash cycle after the tepid water prerinse cycle. Furthermore, with the assistance of scanning electron microscopy to understand the deposit morphology on the milk contact surface, they were able to show a surface deposit coverage reduction after the tepid water rinse and after the optimized blended EO water one-step wash cycle. When evaluating the indirect ATP bioluminescence results, the average RLU readings for the sampling specimens were below 100 RLU on average, which is one order of magnitude lower than the ATP manufacture's recommendation of "clean" cutoff reading, indicating an acceptable one-step wash performance.

The deposit mass drops up to three orders of magnitude throughout the CIP process in the recent studies conducted by Wang et al. (2015, 2016b); with a sharp reduction within a really short duration (tepid water prerinse cycle), which brings the development of the multiscale modeling (mass scale and time scale) as a potential research topic, in need of the computationally feasible models for precise description and interpretation of the deposit removal process. The rapidly removed loosely bound deposits and the slower tightly bound particulate and granule deposits removal proposed by the researchers also need to be validated with more accurate visualization and inline detection technique. More work should focus on correlating the experimental results and the developed mathematical models with the CFD models for better prediction, milk deposit removal mechanism explanation, and CIP process improvement.

5.8 RECOMMENDATIONS AND FURTHER RESEARCH EXPECTATIONS

In this chapter, several milking system CIPs are summarized, from the very conventional manual milking and washing approaches to the state-of-the-art robotic milking and CIP. As stated, the very first preventative measure for contamination of raw milk is to maintain a properly cleaned and sufficiently sanitized milk contact surface along with the milking system. From this perspective, it is a continuously evolving research topic to explore new ways to conduct the milking system CIP and investigate the milk deposit removal mechanism, for different milking system configurations, with better and environmentally friendly methods equipped with accurate inline monitoring and detection techniques.

As mentioned above, attempts were made for CIP alternatives using chlorine-free detergents and EO water solutions, which can uncover the possibilities of using environmentally benign wash solutions for the milking system CIP, which also have cost and energy saving potentials. To achieve this, it is worthwhile studying the optimization of the CIP procedure and the design of milking system configuration.

High automation is always desired. During the past decades, the control of the milking system had evolved considerably; however, inline and/or real-time monitoring and detection techniques could be further studied. Based on our experiences, there is a need for user-specific CIP processes involving the particular milking system, the ambient conditions (such as temperature, elevation, air movement, and so on), the local water supply, and the configuration of the system. For instance, the water hardness affects the detergent choice and usage; the ambient temperature determines the starting temperature and circulation time duration of the wash cycles; the composition of the raw milk (milk fat and protein percentage) affects the usage of the detergent to achieve the best cleaning and sanitizing performance, the slopes of the milk line and the number of milk inlets (if existed) (which would potentially break down the slugs leading to an insufficient cleaning performance) affect the mechanical effect of the wash solution; etc., all of which might change seasonally or even more frequently. Findings have been noted of a possibly shorter time duration based on a flexible and versatile simulator milking system, pioneered by our group, and an inline monitoring system. Therefore, programs should be arranged based on the calculation of the ambient temperature, water hardness, configuration of the system (milk line length, slopes, and the degree and number of bends), etc. and real-time monitoring and detection to automatically determine and control the usage of detergent and the time duration of the CIP needed for each cycle.

There have been studies on the inline/real-time measurement and detection, but in most of these studies, only one detection method, or partially few, was studied, instead of treating the holistic system as an ensemble and evaluate the CIP process. To address this issue, the funda-mental research question lies in the deposit removal mechanism during CIP process, from the chemical reaction aspect, as well as the physical and mechanical aspect of the wash solution. As shown in the chapter, efforts were made to study the deposit removal mechanism by evaluating the deposit mass change as CIP cycle progresses. It can be better if con-tinuous measurements are applied during the CIP process to achieve a more accurate and reasonable set of deposit removal mechanism. Also, it would be more beneficial if the major components of the milk (lipids, proteins, carbohydrates, minerals) are analyzed real time with the CIP process with the mechanical actions of the wash solution (multi-physics-chemistry time-dependent modeling). In this way, the selection and usage amount of the chemicals could be designed with the configuration of the milking system and the type of milk that is being transported and processed.

EO water solutions and its efficacy are mentioned in this chapter, and the authors believe that it can be used in a wider range of cleaning-related applications. Studies should be focused on the real-world applica-tions in milking system using various types of EO water solutions, and on other dairy processing equipment as well. There is no study on the real-world practices of using blended EO water for the one-step milking sys-tem CIP yet, and certainly not on a milking robot. Some practical issues might need to be addressed when applying the EO water solutions in the real world, including the generation capacity, storage duration, possible corrosion, etc. Solving these can lead to a wider acceptance of CIP in various applications including raw milk production.

REFERENCES

AMR Features, 2015. http://www.delaval.com/en/-/Product-Information1/Milking/Systems/DeLaval-AMR/AMR-Features/ (accessed 15.06.16).

Asteriadou, K., Fryer, P., 2008. Assessment of cleaning efficiency, Cleaning-in-Place: Dairy, Food and Beverage Operations, third ed. Blackwell Publishing, Oxford, UK, Chapter 8.

Asteriadou, K., Hasting, T., Bird, M., Melrose, J., 2007. Predicting cleaning of equipment using computational fluid dynamics. J. Food Process Eng. 30, 88−105.

Automatic Milking Systems, 2016. http://www.dairynz.co.nz/media/581332/automatic_-milking_systems_booklet.pdf (accessed 15.06.16).

Canadian Quality Milk Program, 2015. Reference manual for the CQM program. https://www.dairyfarmers.ca/what-we-do/programs/canadian-quality-milk (accessed 15.06.16).

Clean-Trace, 2010. 3M Clean-Trace surface protein plus test swab pro. http://www.3m.com/3M/en_US/company-us/all-3m-products/~/3M-Clean-Trace-Surface-Protein-Plus-Test-Swab-PRO100-100-per-case?N = 5002385 + 8709314 + 8709339 + 8711017 + 8711106 + 8711414 + 8716584 + 8716596 + 3294778414&rt = rud (accessed 15.06.16).

Cleaning Systems, 2016. Milking plant cleaning. http://www.dairynz.co.nz/milking/the-milking-plant/plant-cleaning-systems/ (accessed 15.06.16).

CoPulsation, 2013. CoPulsation data. http://www.copulsation.com (accessed 15.06.16).

Dairy Australia, 2016. Check plant wash regime. http://www.dairyaustralia.com.au/Environment-and-resources/Water/Saving-water/Washing-Vat-and-Milking-Machine/Check-Plant-Wash-Regime.aspx (accessed 15.06.16).

Dev, S.R.S., Demirci, A., Graves, R., 2014. Optimization and modeling of an electrolyzed oxidizing water based clean-in-place technique for farm milking systems using a pilot-scale milking system. J. Food Eng. 135, 1−10.

DPC, 2000. Number 70, in Guidelines for the design, installation, and cleaning of small ruminant milking systems. Dairy Practices Council Publication.

DPC, 2001. Number 29, in Guidelines for cleaning and sanitizing in fluid milk processing plants. Dairy Practices Council Publication.

DPC, 2005. Number 9, in Guideline for fundamentals of cleaning and sanitizing farm milk handling equipment. Dairy Practices Council Publication.

DPC, 2006a. Number 59, in Guidelines for the production and regulation of quality dairy goat milk. Dairy Practices Council Publication.

DPC, 2006b. Number 102, in Guideline for effective installation, cleaning and sanitizing of tie barn milking systems. Dairy Practices Council Publication.

DPC, 2007. Number 2, in Guidelines for effective installation, cleaning and sanitizing of basic parlor milking systems. Dairy Practices Council Publication.

DPC, 2010. Number 4, in Guidelines for installation, cleaning, and sanitizing of large and multiple receiver parlor milking systems. Dairy Practices Council Publication.

Efficient Cleaning, 2001. www.delaval.com/Global/PDF/Efficient-cleaning.pdf (accessed 15.06.16).

Ellen, G., Tudos, A.J., 2003. On-line measurement of product quality in dairy processing. Dairy Processing: Improving Quality. Woodhead Publishing Ltd, Cambridge, UK, Chapter 13.

FAOSTAT, 2013. Production of livestock, primary: milk in total. http://faostat3.fao.org/browse/Q/QL/E (accessed 15.06.16).

Föste, H., Schöler, M., Augustin, W., Majschak, J.-P., Scholl, S., 2011. Optimization of the cleaning efficiency by pulsed flow using an experimentally validated CFD model. http://www.heatexchanger-fouling.com/papers/papers2011/45_Foeste_F.pdf (accessed 15.06.16).

Jensen, B.B.B., 2003. Hygienic Design of Closed Processing Equipment by Use of Computational Fluid Dynamics (Ph.D. thesis). Department of Biotechnology, Technical University of Denmark.

Jensen, B.B.B., Fris, A., 2004. Prediction of flow in mix-proof valve by use of CFD—validation by LDA. J. Food Process Eng. 27, 65–85.

Lang, M.P., Kocaoglu-Vurma, N.A., Harper, W.J., Rodriguez-Saona, L.E., 2011. Multicomponent cleaning verification of stainless steel surfaces for the removal of dairy residues using infrared microspectroscopy. J. Food Sci. 76, 303–308.

Lely Dairy Equipment, 2014. http://www.lely.com/uploads/original/documents/Brochures/Dairy/Dairy_equipment_brochure_2014/Lely_Dairy_equipment_2014_-_EN.pdf (accessed 15.06.16).

Leon, M.B., Albrecht, J.A., 2007. Comparison of adenosine triphosphate (ATP) bioluminescence and aerobic plate counts (APC) on plastic cutting boards. J. Foodservice 18, 145–152.

Lloyd, D., 2008. Design and control of CIP systems, Cleaning-in-Place: Dairy, Food and Beverage Operations, third ed. Blackwell Publishing, Oxford, UK, Chapter 7.

Milk Quality Infosheet, 2013. Pipeline cleaning system guidelines. http://www.omafra.gov.on.ca/english/livestock/goat/facts/info_pipecl.htm (accessed 15.06.16).

MIone, 2013. http://www.gea.com/global/en/products/automatic-milking-robot-mione.jsp (accessed 15.06.16).

Monroe, D., 2007. Looking for chinks in the armor of bacterial biofilms. PLoS Biol. 5, 2458–2461.

Packman, R., Knudsen, B., Hansen, I., 2008. Perspectives in tank cleaning: hygiene requirements, device selection, risk evaluation and management responsibility, Cleaning-in-Place: Dairy, Food and Beverage Operations, third ed. Blackwell Publishing, Oxford, UK, Chapter 6.

PRO-Clean, 2015. Rapid protein residue test. http://www.hygiena.com/pro-clean-food-and-beverage.html (accessed 15.06.16).

Robotic Milking, 2014. http://www.fullwood.com/c/automation-robotic-milking (accessed 15.06.16).

Robotic Milking Systems, 2011. https://www.extension.iastate.edu/dairyteam/sites/www.extension.iastate.edu/files/dairyteam/Robotic%20Milking%20Systems%2011%20Tranel.pdf (accessed 15.06.16).

Sandberg, M., Christiansson, A., Lindahl, C., Wahlund, L., Birgersson, C., 2011. Cleaning effectiveness of chlorine-free detergents for use on dairy farms. J. Dairy Res. 78, 105–110.

Sharma, R.R., Demirci, A., 2003. Treatment of Escherichia coli O157:H7 inoculated alfalfa seeds and sprouts with electrolyzed oxidizing water. Int. J. Food Microbiol. 86, 231–237.

Tamime, A.Y., 2009. Cleaning-in-Place: Dairy, Food and Beverage Operations, third ed. Blackwell Publishing Ltd, Oxford, UK.

Van Asselt, A.J., Van Houwelingen, G., the Eiffel, M.C., 2002. Monitoring system for improving cleaning efficiency of cleaning-in-place processes in dairy environments. Food Bioprod. Process. 80, 276–280.

Walker, S.P., Demirci, A., Graves, R.E., Spencer, S.B., Roberts, R.F., 2005a. Response surface modeling for cleaning and disinfecting materials used in milking systems with electrolyzed oxidizing water. Int. J. Dairy Technol. 58 (2), 65–73.

Walker, S.P., Demirci, A., Graves, R.E., Spencer, S.B., Roberts, R.F., 2005b. Cleaning milking systems using electrolyzed oxidizing water. Trans. ASAE 48 (5), 1827–1833.

Wallhäußer, E., Sayed, A., Nöbel, S., Hussein, M.A., Hinrichs, J., Becker, T., 2013. Determination of cleaning end of dairy protein fouling using an online system combining ultrasonic and classification methods. Food Bioprocess Technol. 7, 506–515.

Walton, M., 2008. Principles of cleaning-in-place (CIP), Cleaning-in-Place: Dairy, Food and Beverage Operations, third ed. Blackwell Publishing, Oxford, UK, Chapter 1.

Wang, X., Dev, S.R.S., Demirci, A., Graves, R.E., Puri, V.M., 2013. Electrolyzed oxidizing water for cleaning-in-place of on-farm milking systems performance evaluation and assessment. Appl. Eng. Agric. 29 (5), 717–726.

Wang, X., Demirci, A., Puri, V.M., 2014. Biofilms in dairy and dairy processing equipment and control strategies, Biofilms in the Food Environment, second ed. John Wiley & Sons, New York.

Wang X., Puri, V.M., Demirci, A., Graves, R.E., 2015. One-step cleaning-in-place for milking systems and mathematical modelling for deposit removal from stainless steel pipeline using blended electrolyzed oxidizing water. ASABE Paper No. 2189967. American Society of Agricultural and Biological Engineers. St. Joseph, MI. 10pp.

Wang, X., Demirci, A., Puri, V.M., Graves, R.E., 2016a. Evaluation of blended electrolyzed oxidizing water-based cleaning-in-place (CIP) technique using a laboratory-scale milking system. Trans. ASABE 59 (1), 359–370.

Wang, X., Puri, V.M., Demirci, A., Graves, R.E., 2016b. Mathematical modeling and cycle time reduction of deposit removal from stainless steel pipeline during cleaning-in-place of milking system with electrolyzed oxidizing water. J. Food Eng. 170, 144–159.

Watkinson, W.J., 2008. Chemistry of detergents and disinfectants, Cleaning-in-Place: Dairy, Food and Beverage Operations, third ed. Blackwell Publishing, Oxford, UK, Chapter 4.

Yun, Y., 2014. Evaluation of Electrolyzed Water for Clean-in-Place of Dairy Processing Equipment (Master of Science thesis). Department of Food Science, College of Agricultural Sciences, The Pennsylvania State University, University Park, PA.

CHAPTER 6

Alternative Processing Procedures and Technological Advantages of Raw Milk

Maura Pinheiro Alves[1], Ítalo Tuler Perrone[1], Rodrigo Stephani[2] and Antonio F. de Carvalho[1]

[1]Departamento de Tecnologia de Alimentos, Universidade Federal de Viçosa, Viçosa, Brazil
[2]Departamento de Química, Universidade Federal de Juiz de Fora, Juiz de Fora, Brazil

6.1 INTRODUCTION

Milk is a nutrient-rich food for young mammals. It allows rapid multiplication of different microbial groups which is why dairy products are processed from heat-treated milk, with the exception of certain regional cheeses produced from raw milk. The thermal treatments used for milk such as pasteurization, thermization, or ultrahigh temperature are intended to inactivate deteriorating or pathogenic microorganisms that contaminate the raw matter. However, several biological, chemical, and physicochemical changes occur in milk's components during thermal processing. Consequently, this can affect milk's nutritional and technological properties (Fox et al., 2015). One challenge to extending the shelf life of industrially produced dairy products is how to balance the inactivation of contaminating microorganisms present in raw milk, while limiting nutritional alterations and color changes in the final product (García and Rodríguez, 2014). Heat treatments used by food industries ensure the safety of milk and dairy products, although they result in irreversible changes in milk components. Among them are the changes in the physicochemical properties of calcium salts. These are insolubilized at high temperatures, which causes saline imbalance, protein modification, vitamin loss, protein denaturation, altered sensorial quality for fluid milk and dairy products, and alterations that affect the milk's cheesemaking capacity. In addition, the bacteria cells that have been inactivated by the heat treatment remain in the milk after processing. These cells retain potentially active enzymes which, along with the metabolic activity that occurs with the multiplication of thermoduric bacteria,

Raw Milk
DOI: https://doi.org/10.1016/B978-0-12-810530-6.00006-7

117

may cause modifications in the product during storage and ultimately reduce its shelf life (Correia et al., 2010).

6.2 MEMBRANE SEPARATION

In this context, there has been a growing interest in different technologies as alternatives to thermal treatments for processing milk and dairy products. Among these, membrane separation operations play a large role. Membrane separation uses membranes for the fractionation of the mixtures, solutions, and suspensions that cover substances of different molar mass and chemical nature (Kumar et al., 2013). The purpose of membrane separation is to fractionate, concentrate, or purify a liquid in order to obtain two different composition solutions. The operations are based on the selective permeability of certain components across the membrane. Molecules that are smaller than the membrane pores pass through it, while larger molecules are retained by the sieve effect or by repulsive forces on the membrane surface (Kumar et al., 2013; Saxena et al., 2009). Of all the food industries, the dairy industry has shown the greatest interest in membrane technologies, such as microfiltration (MF), ultrafiltration (UF), nanofiltration, and reverse osmosis (Carvalho and Maubois, 2010). These technologies present energy saving advantages since most membrane separation operations take place without phase change. They also feature high selectivity and simplicity of operation and scheduling. Membrane filtration can cover a wide size spectrum and separate thermolabile compounds at relatively low temperatures, which reduce the occurrence of sensorial and nutritional modifications (Saxena et al., 2009; Goulas and Grandison, 2008; Habert et al., 2006).

MF uses porous membranes with a mean pore diameter in the range of $0.1-10\,\mu m$ for the retention of suspended and emulsion materials. Depending on the pore size, milk MF allows the retention of somatic cells, bacteria, fat globules, and casein micelles. UF is used in addition to MF to retain macromolecules and colloids present in a solution, using membranes with pores in the range of $0.01-0.1\,\mu m$ (Brans et al., 2004).

MF technology improves the microbiological quality of raw milk by reducing bacteria concentration, which subsequently increases the milk's shelf life, and retains its sensorial characteristics (Zhang et al., 2016). MF membranes also allow the retention of the main bacterial spores that survive pasteurization (Sarkar, 2015; García et al., 2013).

Some countries in Africa, Asia, and South America consume raw milk and some states in the United States allow the sale of certified raw milk. France is the only country that has officially authorized the marketing of microfiltered raw milk with an extended shelf life. Microfiltered skim milk at 50°C is mixed with heated cream (95oC/20 s) for fat standardization, then the mixture is homogenized and aseptically packaged. The final product has an authorized shelf life of 3 weeks when stored at a temperature of 4–6°C (Carvalho and Maubois, 2010). In some milk processing operations around the world, rapid pasteurization high temperature for a short time (HTST—72°C/20 s) is applied to the homogenized mixture prior to packaging to extend the product shelf life by up to 5 weeks (Eino, 1997). The commercial success of microfiltered milk in these countries is due to a less apparent "cooked" flavor and better storage due to the removal of bacteria along with their thermodynamic enzymes and somatic cells (Carvalho and Maubois, 2010).

Different studies have been carried out that demonstrate the use of membrane separation technology as an alternative to the thermal processing for milk and its complementary use as a way to improve quality and minimize the sensorial and nutritional changes caused by heat (García and Rodríguez, 2014; Pinto et al., 2014a; Lorenzen et al., 2011; Elwell and Barbano, 2006). Extended shelf-life milk was produced by removing bacteria (1.4 μm) through MF. Only insignificant changes in the product composition were detected (Hoffmann et al., 2006).

The effect of heat treatment (pasteurization) and nonthermal processing (MF) on the microbiological and physicochemical qualities of milk was evaluated in the work of Silva et al. (2012). The microfiltered milk showed a greater reduction of microbial counts, lower acidity, and lower color change coordinates when compared to pasteurized milk, indicating an absence of the Maillard reaction which would have resulted from the heat treatment. Regarding sensorial acceptability, the results showed a potential market for microfiltered milk since most consumers (75%) demonstrated strong acceptance of the product.

The effectiveness of microfiltration in reducing bacterial and spore counts in milk has also been well documented (García et al., 2013; Tomasula et al. 2011; Madec et al., 1992). When Tomasula et al. (2011) carried out MF (0.8 μm) of milk prior to pasteurization heat treatment to evaluate the removal of *Bacillus anthracis* spores, they found a reduction of about 6 log cycles.

Antunes et al. (2014) produced a lactose-treated, microfiltered, pasteurized skim milk, in order to extend the shelf life of milk products available to lactose-intolerant consumers. MF of the milk in a 1.4 μm membrane reduced more than 4 log cycles of aerobic mesophiles and the product's shelf life was extended. Titratable acidity levels remained within the established regulations for pasteurized milk for more than 50 days when stored at $5 \pm 1°C$ and the number of aerobic mesophiles remained below the limit of detection during 28 days of storage.

Membrane separation technology can also be applied in raw milk cheese production to both improve the quality of the milk and preconcentrate it. Preconcentration allows increased production yield via the incorporation of whey proteins and other components of milk into the product matrix (Carvalho and Maubois, 2010; Mistry and Maubois, 2004, 2017). This process was proposed by Maubois et al. (1969) and leads to the differential concentration of the main components of milk: lipids and proteins. The technique is characterized by the direct use of the retentate obtained by the UF of the milk in cheese production. The technique does away with the desorption stage and the work (milling) of the mass in manufacturing tanks, which makes it an alternative technique in cheese production. The process was patented and became known worldwide as MMV, for the creators' surnames Maubois, Mocquot, and Vassal.

Another important application of this technology in the cheese industry is for the specific enrichment of raw milk micellar caseins to manufacture cheeses (Mercier-Bouchard et al., 2017; Maubois et al., 2001). A wide variety of cheeses with different technological variations are produced worldwide using UF and MF according to specific formulations (Mistry and Maubois, 2004).

Salvatore et al. (2014) found that during ricotta production, whey concentration by UF improved the extent of heat-induced protein aggregation during the thermal coagulation process. This led to a better recovery of the protein fractions in the product and consequently increased the yield of the product.

Membrane separation technology is also widely used in place of traditional methods for the treatment of whey. The whey concentration leads to the formation of protein products that can be used as ingredients in the food industry, improving the technofunctional properties of foods (solubility, gelation, viscosity, emulsification, foaming) (Walzem et al., 2002; Harper, 1992).

Through the application of different membranes, whey nutrients from raw milk can be concentrated, fractionated, or purified into valuable products such as whey protein, α-lactalbumin, β-lactoglobulin, lactose, and salts (Arunkumar and Etzel, 2014; Kumar et al., 2013). By applying UF and diafiltration, the protein content of whey protein concentrate can be increased from 35% to 85% of the total solids. Additionally, by removing bacteria and fat through MF, the protein content of whey protein isolates can be increased to 90% of the total solids content (Lipnizki, 2010).

Whey processing was one of the first applications for membrane technology in the dairy industry. The use of MF to treat raw milk for cheese production gave rise to the "ideal serum" (Fauquant et al., 1988), a commercially available, fat-free, and κ-GMP sterile product. This milk serum which has not been subject to heating under industrial conditions maintains the protein and salt content of the aqueous phase of raw milk (Correia et al., 2010). It is possible to concentrate and separate whey proteins in their undenatured form in the "native" serum with high functional properties when compared to the traditional sweet whey obtained from cheese manufacturing (Maubois, 2002).

6.3 COMPLEMENTARY AND ALTERNATIVE PROCEDURES

Other technologies such as pulsed electric field (Giffel and van der Horst, 2004; García et al., 2013) have been studied for milk processing and shelf-life prolongation.

Chugh et al. (2014) have studied the effect of using high hydrostatic pressure MF both separately and together on the color and composition characteristics of volatile compounds in raw skim milk. They also compared these characteristics with those of milk submitted to pasteurization. MF (1.2 and 1.4 μm) and pulsed electric field either alone or combined (barrier technology) did not cause significant changes in the color and composition of volatile compounds in skim milk. Pasteurized milk, however, underwent considerable changes in its composition, including that of ketones, free fatty acid hydrocarbons, and sulfur compounds.

According to microbiological data, previous studies have indicated that the safety of skim milk processed with a combination of pulsed electric field and MF is comparable to that achieved by heat treatment (Rodríguez-González et al., 2011; Walkling-Ribeiro et al., 2011). This shows that these nonthermal technologies present enormous potential as an alternative to pasteurization.

Bactofugation is a traditional method to reduce spores present in milk. In bactofugation, a centrifuge is used to separate microorganisms from milk based on their density, which is significantly higher than that of milk. This process reduces the concentrations of bacteria and spores in raw milk, however, bactofugation demands energy and the effect of spore reduction is quite limited (García et al., 2013).

6.4 INFLUENCE OF HEAT TREATMENT ON MILK COMPONENTS AND CHARACTERISTICS OF DAIRY PRODUCTS

During dairy processing, raw material is subject to different cumulative thermal treatments, which modify its components' properties and behavior in the final product. Among the reactions that occur under heat are the aggregation and chemical modifications of proteins through interaction with other molecules (Li et al., 2005; Liu and Zhong, 2013). Pinto et al. (2014b) evaluated the effect of the presence of glucose on β-casein and β-lactoglobulin aggregation induced by heat treatment (90°C for 24 h), and the relative digestibility of the formed aggregates. The presence of the reducing sugar strongly affected the heat-induced aggregation of proteins, retarding the kinetic aggregation of β-lactoglobulin and favoring the formation of covalently bound β-casein aggregates. In addition, the aggregates formed for both proteins in the presence of glucose were more resistant to enzymatic digestion.

Changes in the milk components due to heat treatment may also affect the composition and permeate protein yield obtained from MF. Moreover, denaturation of the whey proteins may further alter the performance of the membranes during use. In this context, Svanborg et al. (2014) evaluated the effects of heat treatment on the chemical composition of the fractions of skim milk (0.2 μm). The permeate obtained from MF of unpasteurized milk presented higher amounts of calcium, phosphorus, and native whey proteins, as well as a lower amounts of casein fragments passing through the membrane.

Due to the various changes that occur in milk components during heat treatment, when raw milk to be used as an ingredient is processed, the treatment can directly influence the technical characteristics of the final product. In the work done by Alves et al. (2014), the viscographic profile of serum protein concentrates (SPCs) produced from serum samples submitted to thermal and MF treatments was evaluated. SPCs produced from microfiltered serum in membranes of 0.8 and 1.4 µm generally had higher viscosity values when compared to the samples subject to heat treatment. According to the authors, the result can be explained by the predominance of serum proteins in the globular state that allowed a greater retention of water in its structure, resulting in a higher viscosity. In this way, they suggest that the use of SPCs as an ingredient to increase the viscosity of solutions during the processing of a given product can be optimized when the raw material used to obtain these powders is subject to a less intense heat treatment.

Stephani et al. (2015) also evaluated the behavior of the viscosity evolution of solutions of protein dairy products in different concentrations when submitted to different thermal processing conditions, with temperatures ranging from 65°C to 95°C and retention times ranged from 5 to 30 min. According to the author, the increased viscosity of the different solutions during thermal processing can be attributed to the thermal denaturation of the whey proteins and their associations with the casein micelles. This work reinforces the influence of temperature on the technological characteristics of the product during processing.

REFERENCES

Alves, M.P., Perrone, I.T., Souza, A.B., Stephani, R., Pinto, C.L.O., Carvalho, A.F., 2014. Estudo da viscosidade de soluções proteicas através do analisador rápido de viscosidade (RVA). Revista do Instituto de Laticínios Cândido Tostes 69 (2), 77–88.

Antunes, A.E., Silva E Alves, A.T., Gallina, D.A., Trento, F.K., Zacarchenco, P.B., Van Dender, A.G., et al., 2014. Development and shelf-life determination of pasteurized, microfiltered, lactose hydrolyzed skim milk. J. Dairy Sci. 97 (9), 5337–5344.

Arunkumar, A., Etzel, M.R., 2014. Fractionation of α-lactalbumin and β-lactoglobulin from bovine milk serum using staged, positively charged, tangential flow ultrafiltration membranes. J. Membr. Sci. 454, 488–495.

Brans, G., Schroën, C.G.P.H., Van Der Sman, R.G.M., Boom, R.M., 2004. Membrane fractionation of milk: state of the art and challenges. J. Membr. Sci. 243 (2), 263–272.

Carvalho, A.F., Maubois, J.L., 2010. Applications of membrane technologies in the dairy industry. In: Coimbra, J.S.R., Teixeira, J.A. (Eds.), Engineering Aspects of Milk and Dairy Products. CRC Press, Boca Raton, FL, p. 256.

Chugh, A., Khanal, D., Walkling-Ribeiro, M., Corredig, M., Duizer, L., Griffiths, M.W., 2014. Change in color and volatile composition of skim milk processed with pulsed electric field and microfiltration treatments or heat pasteurization. Foods 3, 250–268.

Correia, L.F.M., Maubois, J., Carvalho, A.F., 2010. Aplicações de tecnologias de membranas na indústria de laticínios. Indústria de laticínios 74–78.

Eino, M.F., 1997. Lessons learned in commercialization of microfiltered milk. Bull. Int. Dairy Fed. 320, 32–36.

Elwell, M.W., Barbano, D.M., 2006. Use of microfiltration to improve fluid milk quality. J. Dairy Sci. 89, E20–E30.

Fauquant, J., Maubois, J.L., Pierre, A., 1988. Microfiltration du lait sur membrane minérale. Tech Lait 1028, 21−23.

Fox, P.F., Uniacke-Lowe, T., McSweeney, P.L.H., O'Mahony, J.A., 2015. Dairy Chemistry and Biochemistry, second ed. Springer, New York.

García, L.F., Rodríguez, F.A.R., 2014. Combination of microfiltration and heat treatment for ESL milk production: impact on shelf life. J. Food Eng. 128, 1−9.

García, L.F., Blanco, S.A., Rodríguez, F.A.R., 2013. Microfiltration applied to dairy streams: removal of bacteria. J. Sci. Food Agric. 93, 187−196.

Giffel, M.C., van der Horst, H.C., 2004. Comparison between bactofugation and microfiltration regarding efficiency of somatic cell and bacteria removal. Bull. Int. Dairy Fed. 389, 49−53.

Goulas, A., Grandison, A.S., 2008. Applications of membrane separation. In: Britz, T.J., Robinson, R.K. (Eds.), Advanced Dairy Science and Technology, first ed. Blackwell Publishing, p. 300.

Habert, A.C., Borges, C.P., Nobrega, R., 2006. Processos de separação por membranas. Série Escola Piloto em Engenharia Química, COPPE/UFRJ. E-papers, Rio de Janeiro, p. 180.

Harper, W.J., 1992. New Applications of Membrane Processes. International Dairy Federation, Brussels, Belgium, pp. 77−108.

Hoffmann, W., Kiesner, C., Clawinradecker, I., Martin, D., Einhoff, K., Lorenzen, P.C., et al., 2006. Processing of extended shelf life milk using microfiltration. Int. J. Dairy Technol. 59, 229−235.

Kumar, P., Sharma, N., Ranjan, R., Kumar, S., Bhat, Z.F., Jeong, D.K., 2013. Perspective of membrane technology in dairy industry: a review. Asian Australas. J. Anim. Sci. 26 (9), 1347−1358.

Li, C.P., Enomoto, H., Ohki, S., Ohtomo, H., Aoki, T., 2005. Improvement of functional properties of whey protein isolate through glycation and phosphorylation by dry heating. J. Dairy Sci. 88, 4137−4145.

Lipnizki, F., 2010. Cross-flow membrane applications in the food industry. In: Peinemann, K.-V., Nunes, S.P., Giorno, L. (Eds.), Membrane Technology, Vol 3: Membranes for Food Applications. Wiley-VCH Verlag GmbH and Co. KGaA, Weinheim.

Liu, G., Zhong, Q., 2013. Thermal aggregation properties of whey protein glycated with various saccharides. Food Hydrocolloids 32, 87−96.

Lorenzen, P.C., Decker, I.C., Einhoff, K., Hammer, P., Hartmann, R., Hoffmann, W., et al., 2011. A survey of the quality of extended shelf life (ESL) milk in relation to HTST and UHT milk. Int. J. Dairy Technol. 64, 166−178.

Madec, M.N., Mejean, S., Maubois, J.L., 1992. Retention of *Listeria* and *Salmonella* cells contaminating skim milk by tangential membrane microfiltration (Bactocatch process). Lait 72, 327−332.

Maubois, J.L., 2002. Membrane microfiltration: a tool for a new approach in dairy technology. Aust. J. Dairy Technol. 57, 92−96.

Maubois, J.L., Mocquot, G., Vassal, L., 1969. Procédé de traitement du lait et de sous produits laitières. Patent Française, FR 2052121.

Maubois, J.L.; Fauquant, J.; Famelart, M.H.; Caussin, F. Milk microfiltrate, a convenient starting material for fractionation of whey proteins and derivatives—the importance of whey and whey components in food and nutrition. In: 3rd International Whey Conference, Munich, Germany, p. 59-72, 2001.

Mercier-Bouchard, D., Benoit, S., Doyen, A., Britten, M., Pouliot, Y., 2017. Process efficiency of casein separation from milk using polymeric spiral-wound microfiltration membranes. J. Dairy Sci. 100, 8838−8848.

Mistry, V.V., Maubois, J.L., 2004. Application of membrane separation technology to cheese production. In: Fox, P.F., McSweeney, P.L.H., Cogan, T.M., Guinee, T.P.

(Eds.), Cheese: Chemistry, Physics and Microbiology, vol. 1. third ed. Elsevier Academic Press, London, pp. 261–285.

Mistry, V.V., Maubois, J.L., 2017. Application of membrane separation technology to cheese production. In: McSweeney, P.L.H., Fox, P.F., Coter, P., Everett, D. (Eds.), Cheese: Chemistry, Physics and Microbiology, fourth ed. Elsevier Academic Press, London, pp. 677–697.

Pinto, M.S., Léonil, J., Henry, G., Cauty, C., Carvalho, A.F., Bouhallab, S., 2014a. Heating and glycation of β-lactoglobulin and β-casein: aggregation and in vitro digestion. Food Res. Int. 55, 70–76.

Pinto, M.S., Pires, A.C.S., Sant'Ana, H.M.P., Soares, N.F.F., Carvalho, A.F., 2014b. Influence of multilayer packaging and microfiltration process on milk shelf life. Food Packag. Shelf Life 1, 151–159.

Rodríguez-González, O., Walkling-Ribeiro, M., Jayaram, S., Griffiths, M.W., 2011. Factors affecting the inactivation of the natural microbiota of milk processed by pulsed electric fields and cross-flow microfiltration. J. Dairy Res. 78, 270–278.

Salvatore, E., Pes, M., Falchi, G., Pagnozzi, D., Furesi, S., Fiori, M., et al., 2014. Effect of whey concentration on protein recovery in fresh ovine ricotta cheese. J. Dairy Sci. 97, 4686–4694.

Sarkar, S., 2015. Microbiological considerations: pasteurized milk. Int. J. Dairy Sci. 10, 206–218.

Saxena, A., Tripathi, B.P., Kumar, M., Shahi, V.K., 2009. Membrane-based techniques for the separation and purification of proteins: an overview. Adv. Colloid Interface Sci. 145, 1–22.

Silva, R.C.S.N., Vasconcelos, C.M., Suda, J.Y., Minim, V.P.R., Pires, A.C.S., Carvalho, A.F., 2012. Acceptance of microfiltered milk by consumers aged from 7 to 70 years. Revista do Instituto Adolfo Lutz 71 (3), 481–487.

Stephani, R., de Almeida, M.R., de Oliveira, M.A.L., de Oliveira, L.F.C., Perrone, Í.T., da Silva, P.H.F., 2015. Study of thermal behaviour of milk protein products using a chemometric approach. Br. J. Appl. Sci. Technol. 7, 62–83.

Svanborg, S., Johansen, A., Abrahamsen, R.K., Skeie, S.B., 2014. Initial pasteurization effects on the protein fractionation of skimmed milk by microfiltration. Int. Dairy J. 37, 26–30.

Tomasula, P.M., Mukhopadhyay, S., Datta, N., Porto-Fett, A., Call, J.E., Luchansky, J.B., et al., 2011. Pilot-scale crossflow-microfiltration and pasteurization to remove spores of *Bacillus anthracis* (Sterne) from milk. J. Dairy Sci. 94 (9).

Walkling-Ribeiro, M., Rodríguez-González, O., Jayaram, S., Griffiths, M.W., 2011. Microbial inactivation and shelf life comparison of "cold" hurdle processing with pulsed electric fields and microfiltration, and conventional thermal pasteurisation in skim milk. Int. J. Food Microbiol. 144, 379–386.

Walzem, R.L., Dillard, C.J., German, J.B., 2002. Whey components: millennia of evolution create functionalities for mammalian nutrition: what we know and what we may be overlooking. Crit. Rev. Food Sci. Nutr. 42 (4), 353–375.

Zhang, S., Liu, L., Pang, X., Lu, J., Kong, F., Lv, J., 2016. Use of microfiltration to improve quality and shelf life of ultra-high temperature milk. J. Food Process. Preserv. 40, 707–714.

FURTHER READING

Pinto, M.S., Bouhallab, S., Carvalho, A.F., Henry, G., Putaux, J., Leonil, J., 2012. Glucose slows down the heat-induced aggregation of β-lactoglobulin at neutral pH. J. Agric. Food Chem. 60, 214–219.

CHAPTER 7

Nutritional Aspects of Raw Milk: A Beneficial or Hazardous Food Choice

Tom F. O'Callaghan[1,2], Ivan Sugrue[1,2], Colin Hill[2,3], R. Paul Ross[2,3,4] and Catherine Stanton[1,3]
[1]Teagasc Food Research Centre, Moorepark, Fermoy, Cork, Ireland
[2]Department of Microbiology, University College Cork, Cork, Ireland
[3]APC Microbiome Institute, University College Cork, Cork, Ireland
[4]College of Science Engineering and Food Science, University College Cork, Cork, Ireland

7.1 INTRODUCTION

Milk is a unique biological fluid which has evolved to promote development and provide optimal nourishment for young mammals from early stages of life. Milk supports nutritional, immunological, and developmental aspects of early life and is an excellent source of dietary fat and protein. Bovine milk is primarily composed of water ($\sim 87\%$), macronutrients, including protein ($\sim 3.2\%$), fat ($\sim 3.5\%$), lactose ($\sim 4.8\%$), and micronutrients consisting of salts and minerals. The composition of bovine milk is dictated by several factors which include breed, age, diet, health status, and stage of lactation. In Western societies, the consumption of liquid milk has declined in recent years, partly as a result of claimed negative health effects such as heart disease and weight gain associated with consumption of saturated fatty acids (Haug et al., 2007). In Ireland, as an example, liquid milk sales for human consumption have fallen from 530.1 million liters in the year 2000 to 507.8 million liters in 2015 (Central Statistics Office, 2016). This criticism of milk is often linked to its high content of saturated fatty acids, whose consumption has been linked to weight gain, heart disease, high cholesterol, and obesity (Insel et al., 2004). However, recent critical reviews and meta-analyses of the topic have concluded that there is at worst a neutral effect of liquid milk intake on multiple health outcomes. In fact, human ingestion of bovine milk may actually be beneficial in combating osteoporosis, cardiovascular disease, stroke, type 2 diabetes, and some cancers (Armas et al., 2016; Lamarche et al., 2016).

Raw unpasteurized milk was ingested by man for thousands of years prior to the introduction of pasteurization in the last century. The debate between the benefits and drawbacks associated with raw milk consumption over pasteurized or heated milk has been ongoing for several decades, and claims for the promotion of raw milk consumption include improved nutrition, reduced incidence of lactose intolerance, and provision of good bacteria. However, these claims have no scientific basis (Lucey, 2015). There is some evidence that heat treatment of raw milk does significantly alter its immunomodulatory effect, albeit based on in vitro studies (McCarthy et al., 2015). There is extensive epidemiological evidence suggesting health benefits associated with raw milk consumption. "GABRIELA" was a European-wide epidemiological study which reported an inverse relationship between the consumption of raw milk and incidence of asthma (Loss et al., 2011), while another European-wide study by Waser et al. (2007) also reported that the consumption of farm/raw milk may offer protection against asthma and allergy development. There is however, a very real health risk associated with consumption of raw milk contaminated with human pathogens resulting in serious illness. Pathogenic bacteria associated with raw milk include *Escherichia coli* O157, *Staphylococcus aureus*, *Mycobacterium avium* subsp. *paratuberculosis*, and *Listeria monocytogenes* (Rea et al., 1992).

Pasteurization, first implemented by Louis Pasteur in the 1860s, is centered on the realization that heating of liquids improves their keeping quality during storage. Pasteurization is now defined as the process of heating every particle of milk or milk product in properly designed and operated equipment to any of the one specified pasteurization time—temperature combinations (Food and Drug Administration, 2011), most commonly 72°C for 15 s, and is effective in destroying human pathogens or reducing their presence to a safe level. Pasteurization was made a legal requirement of dairy processors and creameries for the sale of milk in Ireland in 1958 by the Irish Department of Agriculture (Department of Agriculture, 1957) and in 1987 in an effort to reduce dairy-related foodborne illness in the United States, the Food and Drug Administration (FDA) prohibited the interstate sales of unpasteurized milk and dairy products (Food and Drug Administration, 1987). This practice has no doubt contributed to the decline in incidence of milk-borne illness in the United States, which has fallen from 25% of all food and contaminated water outbreaks in 1938 to less than 1% in 2011 (Food and Drug Administration, 2011).

In recent times, there has been an increased demand among consumers for more natural and organic foodstuffs (Palupi et al., 2012). Despite the commonly accepted food safety concerns, the consumption of raw milk has become more popular, stimulated at least in part by discussions and debates often held on the Internet where information of questionable scientific value is frequently circulated (Claeys et al., 2013). With this in mind, focusing on bovine liquid milk, this chapter presents an overview of the nutritional aspects of milk, the factors that affect its composition, and the benefits and hazards of raw milk consumption.

7.2 THE NUTRITIONAL ARGUMENT FOR MILK

The nutritional quality of any food is derived both from its composition, and potentially more importantly, the bioavailability and contribution of these nutrients to their recommended daily intakes for consumers (Claeys et al., 2013). Milk, in both raw or processed form, is a highly nutritious food product. Several arguments have been put forward in the past by advocates for raw milk consumption, a major one being that raw milk is better from a nutritional perspective than its heat-processed counterpart as a result of the denaturation of beneficial heat labile components during heat processing. The consumption of milk (either raw or processed) has also been criticized in the past, as mentioned before, because of its high content of saturated and *trans* fatty acids, and their links to dietary-related diseases. However, as mounting research has shown, generalizations about milk and milk fatty acid composition can be misleading, given the beneficial attributes of saturated and unsaturated fatty acids collectively present in milk fat (Lucey, 2015; Lock and Bauman, 2004). In fact, reviews of epidemiological studies have shown that there is no consistent relationship between high intake of dairy products and cardiovascular disease (Astrup et al., 2011). Lamarche et al. (2016) recently reported, based on meta-analysis of epidemiological data, that milk intake has a neutral effect on multiple health outcomes including coronary heart disease, stroke, and type 2 diabetes. Furthermore, Armas et al. (2016) also concluded that consumption of milk is associated with several health benefits, including reduced risk of osteoporosis, cardiovascular disease, type 2 diabetes, hypertension, some cancers, stroke, and improved weight management.

7.3 MILK FAT

Dietary guidelines in the past have recommended limited intakes of saturated fatty acids ($<7\%-10\%$ of daily energy) due to their ability to increase both total and low-density lipoprotein (LDL)-cholesterol levels in blood, which are risk factors for coronary heart disease (Parodi, 2016). However, increasing evidence and meta-analysis are now available which show an inverse association (Gillman et al., 1997; Mozaffarian et al., 2004) and no significant relationship or association of dietary saturated fatty acids with increased risk of cardiovascular disease (Chowdhury et al., 2014; Siri-Tarino et al., 2010, 2015).

Saturated fatty acids account for more than half of the milk fatty acid content, several of which have both positive and negative health effects (Haug et al., 2007). This suggests that the saturated fatty acid content of food alone is not necessarily a useful criterion on which to base food choices (Siri-Tarino et al., 2015). For example, butyric acid (C4:0) has been reported as a modulator of gene function (Smith et al., 1998) and may play a role in cancer prevention (German, 1999). Caprylic acid (C8:0) and capric acid (C10:0) may have antiviral activities and caprylic acid has been reported to delay tumor growth. Lauric acid (C12:0) has been suggested to possess antiviral and antibacterial functions and may act as an anticaries and antiplaque agent (Haug et al., 2007). In addition, stearic acid (C18:0) does not seem to increase serum cholesterol levels relative to other long-chain fatty acids and has shown no deleterious effect on cardiovascular disease risk (Grundy, 1994; Legrand and Rioux, 2015).

Milk is also a source of monounsaturated and polyunsaturated, omega-3 and omega-6 fatty acids and conjugated linoleic acid (CLA), the latter being the generic name for a group of isomers of linoleic acid ($C_{18:2\ n6}$) with a conjugated double bond. CLA has been the topic of much research because of multiple health benefiting attributes and interesting biological functions which include an impact on immune function, protective affects against cancer, obesity, diabetes, and atherosclerosis in animal studies and human cell lines; see review by Yang et al. (2015). The most prevalent form of CLA in bovine milk and ruminant derived products is the c9t11 isomer, aptly named rumenic acid, produced as an intermediate during the biohydrogenation of dietary linoleic acid to stearic acid by ruminal microorganisms including *Butyrivibrio fibrisolvens* (Kepler et al., 1966). Rumenic acid is also produced by the action of the Δ^9-desaturase enzyme on vaccenic acid (C18:1, t-11) in the mammary gland (Griinari et al., 2000). The content of CLA in bovine milk can vary considerably, but it is widely acknowledged that the dietary regimen can have a significant effect on CLA concentration (see Section 7.8). Generally, polyunsaturated and monounsaturated fatty acids are regarded as beneficial to human health. Oleic acid ($C_{18:1\ n9}$) is the most prominent monounsaturated fatty acid present in milk, while linoleic acid and α-linolenic acid ($C_{18:3\ n3}$) are the main polyunsaturated fatty acids in milk fat (Dewhurst et al., 2006). Oleic acid has been reported as favorable for health with reports that high concentrations of monounsaturated fatty acids in the diet will lower plasma cholesterol, LDL-cholesterol, and triglyceride concentrations (Kris-Etherton et al., 1999). Industrially produced *trans* fatty acids have been viewed in the past as having negative health effects, with links to increased risk of cardiovascular disease through a negative influence on ratio of LDL to high-density lipoprotein (HDL) cholesterol (Lichtenstein et al., 2003). However, the question has been raised whether ruminally derived vaccenic acid shares these negative properties. Vaccenic acid present in rumen-derived products is a known dietary precursor to CLA_{c9t11} and data suggest that consumption of this *trans* fatty acid may impart health benefits beyond those associated with CLA (Field et al., 2009). Vaccenic acid is the major *trans* C18:1 fatty acid present in milk and its concentration is heavily dependent on the cows feeding regimen, where it has been shown that fresh pasture feeding results in greater concentration of this *trans* fatty acid. Vaccenic acid is produced through the incomplete biohydrogenation of linoleic and linolenic acids by bacteria in the rumen (Lock and Bauman, 2004). Turpeinen et al. (2002) have also demonstrated that consumed vaccenic acid can be desaturated by the Δ^9-desaturase enzyme to CLA_{c9t11} in the liver of humans.

The polyunsaturated fatty acids can be further classified into two major families, the omega 3 (*n*3) and omega 6 (*n*6) fatty acids, based on the location of the final double bond relative to the terminal methyl end of the molecule (Wall et al., 2010). Linoleic acid and α-linolenic acid are termed essential fatty acids as they cannot be synthesized by the human body and these fatty acids are also precursors to the *n*6 and *n*3 series of fatty acids (Patterson et al., 2012). Both the *n*6 and *n*3 fatty acid families possess cardioprotective properties (Harris, 2015). Both are also precursors to eicosanoids, which are potent lipid mediator signaling molecules that play important roles in inflammation; in general *n*3-derived eicosanoids possess anti-inflammatory properties, while *n*6-derived eicosanoids possess pro-inflammatory properties (Patterson et al., 2012). The ideal ratio of $n3$ to $n6$ fatty acids in the diet has been reported to be 1:1–4, but changes in the Western diet in recent decades with increased consumption of fat and vegetable oils rich in $n6$ fatty acids have resulted in a ratio between 1:10 and 1:20 (Molendi-Coste et al., 2011). Coinciding with this increase in $n6$ fatty acids consumption are increases in chronic inflammatory diseases such as nonalcoholic fatty liver disease, cardiovascular disease, obesity, inflammatory bowel disease, rheumatoid arthritis, and Alzheimer's disease (Patterson et al., 2012). Many studies have concluded that reducing the ratio of $n6:n3$ fatty acids in the diet could lower risks of cardiovascular disease, metabolic syndrome, diabetes, and obesity (Benbrook et al., 2013). In milk, the ratio of $n6$ and $n3$ fatty acids is favorable compared to most other nonmarine products, particularly organic and fresh pasture derived milks (Haug et al., 2007; Benbrook et al., 2013), which could aid in ultimate goal to reduce the current $n6$ to $n3$ fatty acids ratio in the human diet to more desirable levels.

7.4 MILK FAT GLOBULE MEMBRANE

The fat globules in milk are composed of a nonpolar lipid core, surrounded by a stabilizing membrane composed of phospholipids and proteins including cholesterol, phosphatidylcholine and sphingomyelin, glycolipids, gangliosides, membrane glycoproteins, and proteins, referred to as the milk fat globule membrane (MFGM) (Ward et al., 2006). Significant quantities of MFGM are present in dairy products and are particularly concentrated in cream after the separation of milk for butter manufacturing. Buttermilk is a subsequent by-product of the butter making process and is a commercially available rich source of MFGM. Many potential benefits of MFGM have been demonstrated through both in vitro and in vivo studies, particularly involving the inhibition of pathogenic bacterial colonization. Human MFGM derived mucins have demonstrated prevention of *E. coli* adhesion to buccal epithelial cells in vitro, while bovine-derived mucin inhibited neuraminidase-sensitive rotavirus infection in MA104 cells (Kvistgaard et al., 2004; Schroten et al., 1992). Muc1 is a highly glycosylated mucin found in MFGM and bovine-derived Muc1 has been demonstrated to inhibit the binding of Gram-negative bacteria to human intestinal cells in vitro (Parker et al., 2010). Other in vitro studies have shown the ability of bovine milk oligosaccharides to prevent cellular invasion of *Campylobacter jejuni* (Lane et al., 2012).

A recent study has demonstrated the effects of defatted MFGM in inhibiting the association of *E. coli* O157:H7 with human HT-29 cells (Ross et al., 2016). Therefore, the addition of MFGM as a functional food may present an alternative approach to reduce some infections in humans.

7.5 MILK PROTEINS AND BIOACTIVE PEPTIDES

Bovine milk is regarded as an important source of protein in the human diet. Milk typically contains ~3.2% protein, which can be subdivided into two major families: the caseins (insoluble) which account for ~80% of bovine milk protein and whey proteins (soluble) which account for ~20% of total protein. Generally, milk protein composition is highly heritable and dependent on genetic factors and therefore can vary between breeds and individual cows, unlike other milk components where the dietary regimen can significantly alter their composition (i.e., milk fat). Several external factors can however affect the milk protein content, including stage of lactation, milk yield, age and health status of the cow, energy intake, and lipid supplementation. Adequate protein intake in humans is fundamental to a healthy diet with daily recommended intakes of 52−56 g/day for adult men and ~46 g/day for adult women, while these requirements can increase during pregnancy and in the elderly (Otten et al., 2006). The importance of milk proteins for health status of the elderly has received much attention in the past, particularly for preventing the loss of body and muscle mass, termed sarcopenia (Wolfe, 2015). Milk proteins have a high biological value and milk is therefore a good source of essential amino acids in the diet. In this respect, processing methods for the fractionation of milk proteins have formed the basis for the production of several high-value functional foods. Milk proteins possess a wide array of biological activities which include antimicrobial properties, improved absorption of nutrients, growth factors, enzymes, antibodies, and immune stimulants (Haug et al., 2007). The casein protein family is composed of (in descending order) α_{s1}-casein, α_{s2}-casein, β-casein, and κ-casein, while the major whey proteins include β-lactoglobulin, α-lactalbumin, serum albumin, immunoglobulins (IgG1, IgG2, IgA, and IgM), and lactoferrin (Farrell et al., 2004). Whey proteins in particular have an excellent biological value which is a measure of how well and quickly the body can utilize the consumed protein. Whey protein is a rich source of both essential amino acids and branched chain amino acids (Smithers, 2008). Branched chain amino acids (valine, leucine, and isoleucine) are thought to play an important role in tissue growth and repair, and protein metabolism in the translation—initiation pathway (Madureira et al., 2007). As a result of this, whey proteins have received much attention for the nutrition of athletes (Phillips, 2011).

Milk casein and whey proteins have been shown to be precursors of many beneficial bioactive peptides. Bioactive peptides are short amino acid chains that are inactive/dormant within the sequence of the parent protein, however during gastrointestinal digestion or through in vitro hydrolysis by proteases, the peptide sequences are released. These peptides are capable of exerting several health benefits on the host including anti-hypertensive, antioxidant, and anti-inflammatory activities (Hsieh et al., 2015). Mills et al. (2011) have comprehensively reviewed milk-derived bioactive peptides associated with human health through numerous physiological responses including antihypertensive peptides, antithrombotic peptides, opioid peptides, casein phosphopeptides, immunomodulatory peptides, and antimicrobial peptides. Angiotensin-I-converting enzyme (ACE) is a key enzyme involved in the regulation of blood pressure. As an example, it has been shown that lactic acid bacteria derived proteases can act on milk proteins particularly caseins, releasing antihypertensive peptides which inhibit ACE activity to produce angiotensin-II (Hayes et al., 2006, 2007a,b). Opioid peptides are those which have pharmacological similarities to opium. Casein and whey proteins have been highlighted as potential sources of opioid-derived peptide sequences. However, hydrolysis of β-casein in particular has been shown to produce potent opioid peptides termed β-casomorphins (Mills et al., 2011), while the hydrolysis of κ-casein has been demonstrated to produce opioid antagonist peptide sequences known as casoxins (Séverin and Wenshui, 2005). Opioid peptide sequences have also been identified within the primary sequences of the whey protein fractions β-lactoglobulin, lactoferrin, and bovine serum albumin (Mills et al., 2011). Several milk-derived peptides known as immunomodulatory peptides have also been shown to display immunostimulatory activity, of particular interest is the peptide isracidin produced by the action of chymosin on αs1-casein which has demonstrated a protective effect against mastitis when injected into the udder of sheep and cows and antibacterial activity against S. aureus and Candida albicans (Lahov and Regelson, 1996). Milk is also a rich source of potent antimicrobial proteins and peptides; an example being lactoferricin derived from the whey protein lactoferrin, which has displayed an antimicrobial effect against Gram-positive and Gram-negative bacteria, including *Listeria monocytogenes* (Clare et al., 2003). Hayes et al. (2006) demonstrated that fermentation of casein by *Lactobacillus acidophilus* DPC6026 produced antimicrobial peptides active against pathogenic strains for *E. coli* and *Cronobacter sakazakii*.

7.6 LACTOSE

Lactose is a disaccharide consisting of a galactose monomer bound to glucose. In aqueous solution, it is present in two isomeric forms: alfa (α) and beta (β). Lactose is a key source of calories in the milk of all mammals other than those of suborder Pinnipedia (seals, sea lions, and walruses), where it is present either in trace amounts or not at all (Reich and Arnould, 2007). Lactose consumption has often been discouraged in the past as a result of a majority of the global population (estimated between 70% and 75%) suffering from lactose intolerance, where the adult individual lacks the necessary enzymes to break down the carbohydrate during digestion (i.e., β-galactosidase) and several symptoms occur as a result including gas, cramps, bloating, and diarrhoea (Szilagyi, 2004). However, as a result of intense research in the area of gut microbiota and commensal microorganisms in the last 20 years, a plethora of benefits of lactose and lactose derivatives (i.e., lactulose) consumption having a prebiotic effect on the gut microbiome have come to light. Undigested lactose has also been recognized to act as a dietary fiber, which is a food component not digested in the small intestine of humans and that according to their chemical characteristics can be described as carbohydrates, carbohydrate analogs, lignin, and lignin-like compounds (Schaafsma, 2008). Intense review of the subject has resulted in calls for lactose to be redefined as a conditional prebiotic (Szilagyi, 2004). A prebiotic as originally defined by Gibson et al., (2017) is "a non-digestible food ingredient that beneficially affects the host by selectively stimulating the growth and/or activity of one or a limited number of bacteria in the colon and thus improves host health." Lactose has relatively low sweetening power, and glycemic index and promotes calcium and magnesium absorption (Schaafsma, 2008). Lactulose, a derivative of lactose (formed through the heat processing of milk) has been widely attributed to have several prebiotic properties which include stimulating the growth and/or activity of probiotic bacteria including *Bifidobacterium* and *Lactobacillus* as well as anti-inflammatory effects in inflammatory bowel disease, Crohn's disease, and ulcerative colitis and has been shown to have a laxative effect (Ebringer et al., 2008).

7.7 EFFECT OF HEAT TREATMENT ON MILK NUTRITIONAL STATUS

A number of health benefits derived from consumption of raw milk have been suggested revolving around hypothetical improved nutritional quality, from milk not subjected to heat processing. However, evidence has shown that the heat processing of milk by pasteurization temperatures for the removal of pathogenic bacteria has no significant effect on its nutritional quality (Lucey, 2015; Food Safety, 2013). While pasteurization does result in minor denaturation of whey proteins ($<7\%$) this denaturation has no impact on the nutritional quality of milk proteins. Lucey (2015) and Lacroix et al. (2006), through the use of animal studies, reported no significant difference in protein digestibility between raw milk proteins and those exposed to pasteurization heat treatment. Lacroix et al. (2008) investigated the effects of heat treatment on protein quality in human subjects, by evaluating nitrogen metabolism following a meal. The same metabolic utilization of milk protein nitrogen was observed for both raw and pasteurized milk. The commercial heat treatment of milk does not affect milk lipids and has no significant effect on the content of minerals and trace elements, including the bioavailability of calcium as reviewed by Claeys et al. (2013). Certain vitamin fractions of milk have been shown to be affected by heat treatment. MacDonald et al. (2011) conducted meta-analysis of 40 studies investigating the effects of pasteurization on vitamin levels in milks. This study reported a decrease in concentrations of vitamins B1, B2, C, and folate. For many of these aforementioned vitamins however, milk is not considered an important dietary source of these vitamins (MacDonald et al., 2011).

7.8 IMPROVING BOVINE MILK NUTRITIONAL COMPOSITION THROUGH ANIMAL DIETARY REGIMEN

As mentioned, there are several factors that can affect the composition and nutritional status of bovine milk. Dietary regimen is the single most important factor that can be targeted in an effort to manipulate the nutritional status of cow's milk for human consumption, a topic which has been reviewed by Dewhurst et al. (2006). Several factors can influence feeding systems which include land availability, climate, and dairy cow requirements. It is widely understood that the feeding system of dairy cows can have a direct impact on the composition of milk, particularly the fatty acid composition of milk fat (Chilliard et al., 2007; O'Callaghan et al., 2016a). Indeed, the level of saturated and unsaturated fatty acids in milk fat is closely dependent on the nature of the diet (Chilliard et al., 2001). Fresh grass feeding systems produce a milk fat with higher proportions of unsaturated fatty acids compared to those derived from conventional indoor housed, total mixed ration (TMR) systems (Couvreur et al., 2006). The feeding system can also have an effect on the natural color of products, where silage and TMR based diets have been shown to produce dairy products that are much whiter in color than those of pasture feeding systems which have a characteristic yellow color which has been attributed to increased concentrations of β-carotene in milks from pasture diets (Hurtaud et al., 2002; O'Callaghan et al., 2016b). Fresh grass feeding of dairy cows has been significantly correlated with increased concentrations of milk CLA_{c9t11}. Indeed Couvreur et al. (2006) demonstrated increases in CLA and vaccenic acid of cow's milk with increasing concentrations of fresh grass in the diet from 0% to 100% of total feed. The supplementation of TMR feeding systems with unsaturated fatty acids has also been shown to beneficially alter the fatty acid composition of milk (Bell et al., 2006). O'Callaghan et al. (2016a) also demonstrated that a perennial ryegrass only and perennial ryegrass with 20% white clover sward produced milks with significantly higher concentrations of fat, protein, and true protein throughout lactation than those consuming a TMR diet of maize silage, grass silage, and concentrates. O'Callaghan et al. (2017), also demonstrated the benefits of pasture feeding on the nutritional and rheological properties of Cheddar cheese, with increased CLA, vaccenic acid, and omega 3 fatty acids. Table 7.1 provides some examples of recent studies investigating the effects of different feeding systems on milk composition.

7.9 AN ALTERNATIVE TO RAW MILK: LOW-TEMPERATURE MILK PROCESSING

The consumption of raw milk poses a very real and unnecessary health risk, especially to those who may have a weak or compromised immune system such as the young, elderly, and pregnant women; thus, alternative technologies for the removal of harmful bacteria without the use of high temperatures have been developed. Moreover, post heat treatment of milk, the lysed cells remain behind with their potential active enzymes which can result in alterations to milks during storage, reducing shelf and stability, therefore the complete removal of the bacteria offers an

Table 7.1 Examples of studies investigating the effects of different feeding systems on the composition of milk

Experimental design/treatments (1–4)	Results	Reference
1: Corn silage + alfalfa hay TMR containing calcium salts and lignosulfonate-treated soybean meal 2, 3, and 4: TMR + soybeans roasted at 115, 130, or 145° C	Supplementation with roasted soybeans: ↑ Long-chain fatty acids ↑ Polyunsaturated fatty acids ↑ CLA ↓ C16:0	(Rafiee-Yarandi et al., 2016)
1. Whole flaxseed 2. Whole linola 3. Calcium salts of palm oil	Supplementation with calcium salts of palm oil: ↑ Milk yield ↑ C16:0 Supplementation with whole linola: ↑ CLA + TVA	(do Prado et al., 2016)
1. Perennial rye grass 2. Perennial rye grass + 20% white clover 3. TMR (maize silage + grass silage + concentrates)	Perennial rye, perennial rye + white clover: ↑ % Protein + % Fat ↑ % True Protein ↑ CLA ↑ Omega 3 fatty acids TMR: ↑ C16:0 ↑ Omega 6 fatty acids	(O'Callaghan et al., 2016a)
1. TMR diet (60% grass silage and 40% concentrate) no fat source 2. TMR diet + Megalac 3. TMR diet + formaldehyde-treated whole linseed 4. TMR diet + fish oil and formaldehyde-treated whole linseed	Feeding fish oil: ↓ Fat and protein content Feeding linseed oil: ↑ C18:3n3 ↓ Omega 6/omega 3	(Petit et al., 2002)
TMR + varying concentrations of whole flaxseed 1. 0 g/kg dry matter (DM) whole flaxseed (WF) 2. 50 g/kg DM WF 3. 100 g/kg DM WF 4. 150 g/kg DM WF	↑ Whole flaxseed = ↓ Yields of fat, protein, and total solids and proportions of short- and medium-chain fatty acids ↑ Whole flaxseed = ↑18:0, cis9-18:1, $trans$9-18:1, cis9, $trans$11-18:2, cis9, 12, 15-18:3 19:0, and 20:0 in milk fat ↑ Whole flaxseed = ↓cis9, 12-18:2, $trans$9, 12-18:2 and 20:4	(Petit, 2015)

(Continued)

Table 7.1 (Continued)

Experimental design/treatments (1–4)	Results	Reference
TMR diet 70:30 forage to concentrate supplemented with: 1. Corn meal plus a protein mix containing soybean meal and sunflower meal 2. Corn meal plus flaxseed meal 3. Liquid molasses plus a protein mix containing soybean meal and sunflower meal 4. Liquid molasses plus flaxseed meal	Flaxseed meal: ↓ Milk yield, milk fat, and milk lactose Liquid molasses plus flaxseed meal: ↑ Saturated fatty acids ↑ $\Delta 9$-desaturase index Corn meal plus soybean meal–sunflower meal protein mix: ↑ C4:0 and C18:0	(Brito et al., 2015)
TMR diet supplemented with: 1. Control—no sunflower oil and no monensin 2. Diet containing (dry matter basis) 42 g/kg sunflower oil 3. Control with monensin (16 mg/kg of DM) 4. Diet containing (DM basis) 42 g/kg sunflower oil and 16 mg/kg monensin	• Monensin supplementation: ↓18:0 and 22:0 ↑ cis9-17:1 Sunflower oil supplementation: ↓ Short-chain (8:0 to 13:0) and most medium-chain (14:0, 15:0, 16:0, 17:0, cis9-17:1) cis9, 12, 15-18:3, cis8, 11, 14-20:3, and cis5, 8, 11, 14-20:4. ↑ 18:0, total trans 18:1, cis9-18:1, 19:0, cis9, 12-18:2, cis9, trans11-18:2, trans10, cis12-18:2 and 22:0	(do Prado et al., 2015)
1. Control group TMR diet—9.5 kg of concentrate mainly constituted by corn, soy, barley flour, and bran, 5 kg of corn grains, and 6.5 kg of vetch and oat hay 2. Flaxseed group—control diet, 1 kg of concentrate was substituted with the same amount of whole flaxseed	Flaxseed supplementation: ↑Saturated fatty acids, monounsaturated fatty acids, and polyunsaturated fatty acids ↑ C18:3n − 3 and omega 3 fatty acids ↓ Atherogenic and thrombogenic indices	(Santillo et al., 2016)
Grass silage-based diet (forage to concentrate ratio 58:42, on a dry matter basis) supplemented with 1. 0 g of fish oil 2. 75 g of fish oil 3. 150 g of fish oil 4. 300 g of fish oil	Supplementation with fish oil: ↓Milk fat content and yield ↑ Fish oil = ↑20:5n − 3 and 22:6n − 3 fatty acids ↑ Fish oil = ↑total CLA, trans, and polyunsaturated fatty acid concentrations	(Kairenius et al., 2015)

(Continued)

Table 7.1 (Continued)

Experimental design/treatments (1–4)	Results	Reference
1. A lipid-free emulsion medium infused in the rumen (CTL) 2. Soybean oil as a source of polyunsaturated fatty acids infused in the rumen (RSO) 3. Saturated fatty acids (38% 16:0, 40% 18:0) infused in the rumen (RSF) 4. Saturated fatty acids infused in the abomasum (ASF). Fat supplements were provided continuously as emulsions at a rate of 450 g/day	The yields of energy-corrected milk, fat, and protein were greater with RSF compared with RSO The concentration of odd-chain fatty acids was decreased by RSO, whereas even-chain iso fatty acids were not affected Milk fat concentration of 17:0 + *cis*9-17:1 was higher for RSF than for RSO	(Baumann et al., 2016)

interesting alternative. Microfiltration and bactofugation have been identified as potential reduced temperature processing methods for the removal of bacteria from milk (Gésan-Guiziou, 2012). The fat content of milk however has in the past caused issues with filtration processes. Microfiltration of homogenized milk using a 0.8–1.4 μm mean pore size has been demonstrated to remove bacteria and spores (Fauquant et al., 2012). Microfiltration of milk for the removal of bacteria initially proposed by Holm et al. (1986) has led to the development of industrial plants for microfiltration of milk at 50°C using a 1.4 μm pore sized membrane known as Bactocatch by Tetra Laval Group, producing extended shelf-life milks, with averaged decimal reductions of pathogenic bacteria of 3.5–4.0 $\log_{10}$ and >4.5 $\log_{10}$ reduction in spore-forming bacteria (Saboyainsta and Maubois, 2000). It has been concluded therefore that microfiltered milk can be considered as safe as pasteurized milk (Gésan-Guiziou, 2012).

7.10 MILK COMPONENTS AS GENE REGULATORS IN HUMAN HEALTH

MicroRNAs (miRNAs) are short, single-stranded noncoding RNA molecules (~22 nucleotides in the mature form) which affect gene expression by binding to specific sequences within the 3′ UTR of mRNA. miRNAs function through direct prevention of translation or by targeting mRNA for degradation (Jing et al., 2005; Djuranovic et al., 2012). Since their discovery, they have been extensively researched, revealing a vast array of regulatory roles covering a range of biological processes (He and Hannon, 2004). Along with regulating normal gene expression, they have also been connected to a myriad of pathologies including cancer (He et al., 2016; Sianou et al., 2015; Yonemori et al., 2016), autoimmune disorders (Singh et al., 2013; Huang et al., 2016; Fenoglio et al., 2012), and diseases of the gastrointestinal tract (Pekow and Kwon, 2012; Chapman and Pekow, 2015; Actis et al., 2011).

A recently published study indicated the detection of miRNA (miR)-168a from *Oryza sativa*, the rice plant, in human and animal sera (Zhang et al., 2012). The study reported that a rice-based diet led to decreased expression of LDL receptor adaptor protein 1 in mouse liver through the activity of the exogenous miRNA (Zhang et al., 2012); however, the work remains controversial (Snow et al., 2013; Dickinson et al., 2013; Chen et al., 2013; Melnik et al., 2016). Immune-related miRNAs have been detected in breast milk (Zhou et al., 2011) and found to be present at high amounts during the first 6 months of lactation (Kosaka et al., 2010). Indeed, milk contains the highest concentration of miRNAs of all bodily fluids (Weber et al., 2010). It certainly would be a fitting narrative wherein maternal miRNAs could potentially be transferred to newborns, leading to direct regulation of gene expression beyond the known immune modulation by the transfer of immune molecules, growth factors, and nutrients (Goldman, 2007). As previously noted, miRNAs can affect health both positively and negatively. It has been demonstrated that miRNAs of bovine origin with identical sequence homology to human miRNAs in milk have impacted expression of genes in human cells (Baier et al., 2014). They have also given a probable mechanism of miRNA entry into intestinal enterocytes after milk consumption (Wolf et al., 2015). The work remains controversial (Bağcı and Allmer, 2016), but suggests potential health benefits and potential health hazards of milk consumption through complex genetic regulatory pathways. It has been demonstrated that no change occured in miRNA levels during cold storage of pasteurized whole milk, 2% milk, and skim milk, but a 63% ($\pm$ 28%) and 67% ($\pm$ 18%) decrease in concentration of miR-200c and miR-29b, respectively, following pasteurization of raw bovine milk (Howard et al., 2015). These authors speculate that disruption of milk exosomes results in degradation of the miRNAs in milk, as previously demonstrated through sonication of exosomes (Baier et al., 2014).

Examination of other milk treatments and milk fermentation on miRNA levels in bovine milk could be of interest in the future in this currently unfolding area of research.

7.11 CONCLUSIONS

Milk, raw or processed, is a highly nutritious food item and is an excellent source of proteins, minerals, and lipids, particularly important for the developing infant. Past negative reports on the fat content and composition of milk have failed to view this complex ingredient collectively rather than as individual fatty acids. As such, several benefits have been reported with the consumption of milk. Several factors can affect the nutritional composition of milk, however modification of the cows feeding system offers a simple method to achieve a more desirable nutritional profile. Raw milk consumption poses a very serious and unnecessary health risk, particularly to young, elderly, and immune-compromised individuals. Many different benefits of raw milk consumption have been put forward but these lack a scientific basis. Pasteurization processing at 72°C for 15 s does not have any significant negative effects on the nutritional quality of milk, but alleviates the potential risk of ingestion of pathogenic bacteria. Further research is required to identify particular milk components responsible for such immunomodulatory effects associated with raw milk; that may then be isolated and used in a functional food setting. Greater efforts to educate the general public are required to further alleviate food-borne illnesses associated with raw milk consumption and combat erroneous myths that are widespread on the Internet and in nonscientific material today.

ACKNOWLEDGMENTS

TFO'C and IS are in receipt of Teagasc Walsh Fellowships. The financial support of the following is gratefully acknowledged: Teagasc, JPI Food Processing for Health funded "Longlife," Science Foundation Ireland (SFI) under Grant Number SFI/12/RC/2273, and the Dairy Levy Fund administered by Dairy Research Ireland.

REFERENCES

Actis, G.C., Rosina, F., Mackay, I.R., 2011. Inflammatory bowel disease: beyond the boundaries of the bowel. Expert Rev. Gastroenterol. Hepatol. 5 (3), 401—410.
Armas, L.A.G., Frye, C.P., Heaney, R.P., 2016. Effect of cow's milk on human health. Beverage Impacts on Health and Nutrition, Cham. Springer.

Astrup, A., Dyerberg, J., Elwood, P., Hermansen, K., Hu, F.B., Jakobsen, M.U., et al., 2011. The Role of reducing intakes of saturated fat in the prevention of cardiovascular disease: where does the evidence stand in 2010? Am. J. Clin. Nutr. 93 (4), 684−688.

Baier, S.R., Nguyen, C., Xie, F., Wood, J.R., Zempleni, J., 2014. MicroRNAs are absorbed in biologically meaningful amounts from nutritionally relevant doses of cow milk and affect gene expression in peripheral blood mononuclear cells, HEK-293 kidney cell cultures, and mouse livers. J. Nutr. 144 (10), 1495−1500.

Baumann, E., Chouinard, P.Y., Lebeuf, Y., Rico, D.E., Gervais, R., 2016. Effect of lipid supplementation on milk odd-and branched-chain fatty acids in dairy cows. J. Dairy Sci. 99 (8), 6311−6323.

Bağcı, C., Allmer, J., 2016. One step forward, two steps back; xeno-microRNAs reported in breast milk are artifacts. PLoS One 11 (1), e0145065.

Bell, J.A., Griinari, J.M., Kennelly, J.J., 2006. Effect of safflower oil, flaxseed oil, monensin, and vitamin E on concentration of conjugated linoleic acid in bovine milk fat. J. Dairy Sci. 89 (2), 733−748.

Benbrook, C.M., Butler, G., Latif, M.A., Leifert, C., Davis, D.R., 2013. Organic production enhances milk nutritional quality by shifting fatty acid composition: a United States−wide, 18-month study. PLoS One 8 (12), e82429.

Brito, A.F., Petit, H.V., Pereira, A.B.D., Soder, K.J., Ross, S., 2015. Interactions of corn meal or molasses with a soybean-sunflower meal mix or flaxseed meal on production, milk fatty acid composition, and nutrient utilization in dairy cows fed grass hay-based diets. J. Dairy Sci. 98 (1), 443−457.

Central Statistics Office, 2016. Milk sales (dairy) for human consumption by type of milk and year. http://www.cso.ie/px/pxeirestat/Statire/SelectVarVal/Define.asp?maintable = AKA02&PLanguage = 0 (accessed 14.07.16).

Chapman, C.G., Pekow, J., 2015. The emerging role of miRNAs in inflammatory bowel disease: a review. Therap. Adv. Gastroenterol. 8 (1), 4−22.

Chen, X., Zen, K., Zhang, C.-Y., 2013. Reply to lack of detectable oral bioavailability of plant microRNAs after feeding in mice. Nat. Biotechnol. 31 (11), 967−969.

Chilliard, Y., Ferlay, A., Doreau, M., 2001. Effect of different types of forages, animal fat or marine oils in cow's diet on milk fat secretion and composition, especially conjugated linoleic acid (CLA) and polyunsaturated fatty acids. Livest. Prod. Sci. 70 (1), 31−48.

Chilliard, Y., Glasser, F., Ferlay, A., Bernard, L., Rouel, J., Doreau, M., 2007. Diet, rumen biohydrogenation and nutritional quality of cow and goat milk fat. Eur. J. Lipid Sci. Technol. 109 (8), 828−855.

Chowdhury, R., Warnakula, S., Kunutsor, S., Crowe, F., Ward, H.A., Johnson, L., et al., 2014. Association of dietary, circulating, and supplement fatty acids with coronary risk: a systematic review and meta-analysis. Ann. Intern. Med. 160 (6), 398−406.

Claeys, W.L., Cardoen, S., Georges, D., De Block, J., Dewettinck, K., Dierick, K., et al., 2013. Raw or heated cow milk consumption: review of risks and benefits. Food Control 31 (1), 251−262.

Clare, D.A., Catignani, G.L., Swaisgood, H.E., 2003. Biodefense properties of milk: the role of antimicrobial proteins and peptides. Curr. Pharm. Des. 9 (16), 1239−1255.

Couvreur, S., Hurtaud, C., Lopez, C., Delaby, L., Peyraud, J.-L., 2006. The linear relationship between the proportion of fresh grass in the cow diet, milk fatty acid composition, and butter properties. J. Dairy Sci. 89 (6), 1956−1969.

Department of Agriculture, 1957. Pasteurising (Separated Milk) Regulations, 1957. In S.I. No. 196/1957. Department of Agriculture, Ireland.

Dewhurst, R.J., Shingfield, K.J., Lee, M.R.F., Scollan, N.D., 2006. Increasing the concentrations of beneficial polyunsaturated fatty acids in milk produced by dairy cows in high-forage systems. Anim. Feed Sci. Technol. 131 (3), 168−206.

Dickinson, B., Zhang, Y., Petrick, J.S., Heck, G., Ivashuta, S., Marshall, W.S., 2013. Lack of detectable oral bioavailability of plant microRNAs after feeding in mice. Nat. Biotechnol. 31 (11), 965–967.

Djuranovic, S., Nahvi, A., Green, R., 2012. miRNA-mediated gene silencing by translational repression followed by mRNA deadenylation and decay. Science (New York, N.Y.) 336 (6078), 237–240.

Ebringer, L., Ferenčík, M., Krajčovič, J., 2008. Beneficial health effects of milk and fermented dairy products—review. Folia Microbiol. 53 (5), 378–394.

Farrell, H.M., Jimenez-Flores, R., Bleck, G.T., Brown, E.M., Butler, J.E., Creamer, L.K., et al., 2004. Nomenclature of the proteins of cows' milk—sixth revision. J. Dairy Sci. 87 (6), 1641–1674.

Fauquant, J., B. Robert, C. Lopez, 2012. Procede Pour Reduire La Teneur Bacterienne D'un Milieu Alimentaire Et/Ou Biologique D'interet, Contenant Des Gouttelettes Lipidiques. Google Patents.

Fenoglio, C., Ridolfi, E., Galimberti, D., Scarpini, E., 2012. MicroRNAs as active players in the pathogenesis of multiple sclerosis. Int. J. Mol. Sci. 13 (10), 13227–13239.

Field, C.J., Blewett, H.H., Proctor, S., Vine, D., 2009. Human health benefits of vaccenic acid. Appl. Physiol. Nutr. Metab. 34 (5), 979–991.

Food and Drug Administration, 1987. FDA plans to ban raw milk. FDA Consumer. US Government, Printing Office, Washington, DC.

Food and Drug Administration, 2011. Grade "A" Pasteurised Milk Ordinance. In 2011 Revision. US Department of Health and Human Services, Food and Drug Administration, USA.

Food Safety, 2013. An Assessment of the Effects of Pasteurisation on Claimed Nutrition and Health Benefits of Raw Milk. MPINZ.

Gésan-Guiziou, G. (2012). Liquid milk processing. In: Membrane Processing, A. Y. Tamime (Ed.). https://doi.org/10.1002/9781118457009.ch6.

German, J.B., 1999. Butyric acid: a role in cancer prevention. Nutr. Bull. 24 (4), 203–209.

Gillman, M.W., Cupples, L.A., Millen, B.E., Ellison, R.C., Wolf, P.A., 1997. Inverse association of dietary fat with development of ischemic stroke in men. JAMA 278 (24), 2145–2150.

Gibson, G.R., Hutkins, R., Sanders, M.E., Prescott, S.L., Reimer, R.A., Salminen, S.J., et al., 2017. Expert consensus document: The International Scientific Association for Probiotics and Prebiotics (ISAPP) consensus statement on the definition and scope of prebiotics. Nat. Rev. Gastroenterol. Hepatol 14, 491.

Goldman, A.S., 2007. The immune system in human milk and the developing infant. Breastfeed. Med. 2 (4), 195–204.

Griinari, J.M., Corl, B.A., Lacy, S.H., Chouinard, P.Y., Nurmela, K.V.V., Bauman, D.E., 2000. Conjugated linoleic acid is synthesized endogenously in lactating dairy cows by Δ9-desaturase. J. Nutr. 130 (9), 2285–2291.

Grundy, S.M., 1994. Influence of stearic acid on cholesterol metabolism relative to other long-chain fatty acids. Am. J. Clin. Nutr. 60 (6), 986S–990SS.

Harris, W.S., 2015. N-3 and N-6 fatty acids reduce risk for cardiovascular disease. Preventive Nutrition. Springer, Cham.

Haug, A., Høstmark, A.T., Harstad, O.M., 2007. Bovine milk in human nutrition—a review. Lipids Health Dis. 6 (1), 1.

Hayes, M., Ross, R.P., Fitzgerald, G.F., Hill, C., Stanton, C., 2006. Casein-derived antimicrobial peptides generated by Lactobacillus acidophilus Dpc6026. Appl. Environ. Microbiol. 72 (3), 2260–2264.

Hayes, M., Stanton, C., Slattery, H., O'Sullivan, O., Hill, C., Fitzgerald, G.F., et al., 2007a. Casein fermentate of Lactobacillus animalis Dpc6134 contains a range of novel propeptide angiotensin-converting enzyme inhibitors. Appl. Environ. Microbiol. 73 (14), 4658−4667.

Hayes, M., Stanton, C., Fitzgerald, G.F., Ross, R.P., 2007b. Putting microbes to work: dairy fermentation, cell factories and bioactive peptides. Part II: bioactive peptide functions. Biotechnol. J. 2 (4), 435−449.

He, L., Hannon, G.J., 2004. MicroRNAs: small RNAs with a big role in gene regulation. Nat. Rev. Genet. 5 (7), 522−531.

He, Y., Lin, J., Ding, Y., Liu, G., Luo, Y., Huang, M., et al., 2016. A systematic study on dysregulated microRNAs in cervical cancer development. Int. J. Cancer 138 (6), 1312−1327.

Holm, S., Malmberg, R., Svensson, K., 1986. Method and plant for producing milk with a low bacterial content. World Patent WO 86, 01687.

Howard, K.M., Kusuma, R.J., Baier, S.R., Friemel, T., Markham, L., Vanamala, J., et al., 2015. Loss of miRNAs during processing and storage of cow's (*Bos taurus*)milk. J. Agric. Food Chem. 63 (2), 588−592.

Hsieh, C.-C., Hernández-Ledesma, B., Fernández-Tomé, S., Weinborn, V., Barile, D., de Moura Bell, J.M.L.N., 2015. Milk proteins, peptides, and oligosaccharides: effects against the 21st century disorders. BioMed Res. Int. 2015, 146840.

Huang, Q., Xiao, B., Ma, X., Qu, M., Li, Y., Nagarkatti, P., et al., 2016. MicroRNAs associated with the pathogenesis of multiple sclerosis. J. Neuroimmunol. 295−296, 148−161.

Hurtaud, C., L. Delaby, J.L. Peyraud, J.L. Durand, J.C. Emile, C. Huyghe, et al., 2002. Evolution of milk composition and butter properties during the transition between winter-feeding and pasture. Paper presented at the Multi-function Grasslands: Quality Forages, Animal Products and Landscapes. Proceedings of the 19th General Meeting of the European Grassland Federation. La Rochelle, France, 27−30 May 2002.

Insel, P., R.E. Turner, D. Ross, 2004. Nutrition. Second. American Dietetic Association. Jones and Bartlett, USA.

Jing, Q., Huang, S., Guth, S., Zarubin, T., Motoyama, A., Chen, J., 2005. Involvement of MicroRNA in Au-rich element-mediated mRNA instability. Cell 120 (5), 623−634.

Kairenius, P., Ärölä, A., Leskinen, H., Toivonen, V., Ahvenjärvi, S., Vanhatalo, A., et al., 2015. Dietary fish oil supplements depress milk fat yield and alter milk fatty acid composition in lactating cows fed grass silage-based diets. J. Dairy Sci. 98 (8), 5653−5671.

Kepler, C.R., Hirons, K.P., McNeill, J.J., Tove, S.B., 1966. Intermediates and products of the biohydrogenation of linoleic acid by *Butyrivibrio fibrisolvens*. J. Biol. Chem. 241 (6), 1350−1354.

Kosaka, N., Izumi, H., Sekine, K., Ochiya, T., 2010. MicroRNA as a new immune-regulatory agent in breast milk. Silence 1 (1), 7.

Kris-Etherton, P.M., Thomas, A.P., Wan, Y., Hargrove, R.L., Moriarty, K., Fishell, V., et al., 1999. High-monounsaturated fatty acid diets lower both plasma cholesterol and triacylglycerol concentrations. Am. J. Clin. Nutr. 70 (6), 1009−1015.

Kvistgaard, A.S., Pallesen, L.T., Arias, C.F., Lopez, S., Petersen, T.E., Heegaard, C.W., et al., 2004. Inhibitory effects of human and bovine milk constituents on rotavirus infections. J. Dairy Sci. 87 (12), 4088−4096.

Lacroix, M., Léonil, J., Bos, C., Henry, G., Airinei, G., Fauquant, J., et al., 2006. Heat markers and quality indexes of industrially heat-treated [15n] milk protein measured in rats. J. Agric. Food Chem. 54 (4), 1508−1517.

Lacroix, M., Bon, C., Bos, C., Léonil, J., Benamouzig, R., Luengo, C., et al., 2008. Ultra high temperature treatment, but not pasteurization, affects the postprandial kinetics of milk proteins in humans. J. Nutr. 138 (12), 2342−2347.

Lahov, E., Regelson, W., 1996. Antibacterial and immunostimulating casein-derived substances from milk: casecidin, isracidin peptides. Food Chem. Toxicol. 34 (1), 131−145.

Lamarche, B., Givens, I., Soedamah-Muthu, S., Krauss, R.M., Jakobsen, M.U., Bischoff-Ferrari, H.A., et al., 2016. Does milk consumption contribute to cardiometabolic health and overall diet quality? Can. J. Cardiol. 32 (8), 1026−1032.

Lane, J.A., Mariño, K., Naughton, J., Kavanaugh, D., Clyne, M., Carrington, S.D., et al., 2012. Anti-infective bovine colostrum oligosaccharides: *Campylobacter jejuni* as a case study. Int. J. Food Microbiol. 157 (2), 182−188.

Legrand, P., Rioux, V., 2015. Specific roles of saturated fatty acids: beyond epidemiological data. Eur. J. Lipid Sci. Technol. 117 (10), 1489−1499.

Lichtenstein, A.H., Arja, T.E., Schwab, U.S., Jalbert, S.M., Ausman, L.M., 2003. Influence of hydrogenated fat and butter on CVD risk factors: remnant-like particles, glucose and insulin, blood pressure and C-reactive protein. Atherosclerosis 171 (1), 97−107.

Lock, A.L., Bauman, D.E., 2004. Modifying milk fat composition of dairy cows to enhance fatty acids beneficial to human health. Lipids 39 (12), 1197−1206.

Loss, G., Apprich, S., Waser, M., Kneifel, W., Genuneit, J., Büchele, G., et al., 2011. The protective effect of farm milk consumption on childhood asthma and atopy: the Gabriela study. J. Allergy Clin. Immunol. 128 (4), 766−773. e4.

Lucey, J.A., 2015. Raw milk consumption: risks and benefits. Nutr. Today 50 (4), 189−193.

MacDonald, L.E., Brett, J., Kelton, D., Majowicz, S.E., Snedeker, K., Sargeant, J.M., 2011. A systematic review and meta-analysis of the effects of pasteurization on milk vitamins, and evidence for raw milk consumption and other health-related outcomes. J. Food Prot. 74 (11), 1814−1832.

Madureira, A.R., Pereira, C.I., Gomes, A.M.P., Pintado, M.E., Malcata, F.X., 2007. Bovine whey proteins—overview on their main biological properties. Food Res. Int. 40 (10), 1197−1211.

McCarthy, R.J., Ross, R.P., Fitzgerald, G.F., Stanton, C., 2015. The immunological consequences of pasteurisation: comparison of the response of human intestinally-derived cells to raw versus pasteurised milk. Int. Dairy J. 40, 67−72.

Melnik, B.C., Kakulas, F., Geddes, D.T., Hartmann, P.E., John, S.M., Carrera-Bastos, P., et al., 2016. Milk miRNAs: simple nutrients or systemic functional regulators? Nutr. Metab. (Lond) 13, 42.

Mills, S., Ross, R.P., Hill, C., Fitzgerald, G.F., Stanton, C., 2011. Milk intelligence: mining milk for bioactive substances associated with human health. Int. Dairy J. 21 (6), 377−401.

Molendi-Coste, O., Legry, V., Leclercq, I.A., 2011. Why and how meet n-3 PUFA dietary recommendations?. Gastroenterol. Res. Pract. 2011, 364040.

Mozaffarian, D., Rimm, E.B., Herrington, D.M., 2004. Dietary fats, carbohydrate, and progression of coronary atherosclerosis in postmenopausal women. Am. J. Clin. Nutr. 80 (5), 1175−1184.

Otten, J.J., Hellwig, J.P., Meyers, L.D., 2006. *Dietary Reference Intakes: The Essential Guide to Nutrient Requirements*. National Academies Press, Washington D.C.

O'Callaghan, T.F., Hennessy, D., McAuliffe, S., Kilcawley, K.N., O'Donovan, M., Dillon, P., et al., 2016a. Effect of pasture versus indoor feeding systems on raw milk composition and quality over an entire lactation. J. Dairy Sci. 99 (12), 9424−9440.

O'Callaghan, T.F., Faulkner, H., McAuliffe, S., O'Sullivan, M.G., Hennessy, D., Dillon, P., et al., 2016b. Quality characteristics, chemical composition, and sensory properties of butter from cows on pasture versus indoor feeding systems. J. Dairy Sci. 99 (12), 9441−9460.

O'Callaghan, T.F., Mannion, D.T., Hennessy, D., McAuliffe, S., O'Sullivan, M.G., Leeuwendaal, N., et al., 2017. Effect of pasture versus indoor feeding systems on quality characteristics, nutritional composition, and sensory and volatile properties of full-fat cheddar cheese. J. Dairy Sci. 100 (8), 6053—6073.

Palupi, E., Jayanegara, A., Ploeger, A., Kahl, J., 2012. Comparison of nutritional quality between conventional and organic dairy products: a meta-analysis. J. Sci. Food Agric. 92 (14), 2774—2781.

Parker, P., Lillian, S., Pearson, R., Kongsuwan, K., Tellam, R.L., Smith, S., 2010. Bovine Muc1 inhibits binding of enteric bacteria to Caco-2 cells. Glycoconj. J. 27 (1), 89—97.

Parodi, P.W., 2016. Dietary guidelines for saturated fatty acids are not supported by the evidence. Int. Dairy J. 52, 115—123.

Patterson, E., Wall, R., Fitzgerald, G.F., Ross, R.P., Stanton, C., 2012. Health implications of high dietary omega-6 polyunsaturated fatty acids. J. Nutr. Metab. 2012, 539426.

Pekow, J.R., Kwon, J.H., 2012. MicroRNAs in inflammatory bowel disease. Inflamm. Bowel Dis. 18 (1), 187—193.

Petit, H.V., 2015. Milk production and composition, milk fatty acid profile, and blood composition of dairy cows fed different proportions of whole flaxseed in the first half of lactation. Anim. Feed Sci. Technol. 205, 23—30.

Petit, H.V., Dewhurst, R.J., Scollan, N.D., Proulx, J.G., Khalid, M., Haresign, W., et al., 2002. Milk production and composition, ovarian function, and prostaglandin secretion of dairy cows fed omega-3 fats. J. Dairy Sci. 85 (4), 889—899.

Phillips, S.M., 2011. The science of muscle hypertrophy: making dietary protein count. Proc. Nutr. Soc. 70 (01), 100—103.

do Prado, R.M., Côrtes, C., Benchaar, C., Petit, H.V., 2015. Interaction of sunflower oil with monensin on milk composition, milk fatty acid profile, digestion, and ruminal fermentation in dairy cows. Anim. Feed Sci. Technol. 207, 85—92.

do Prado, R.M., Palin, M.F., do Prado, I.N., dos Santos, G.T., Benchaar, C., Petit, H.V., 2016. Milk yield, milk composition, and hepatic lipid metabolism in transition dairy cows fed flaxseed or linola. J. Dairy Sci. 99, 8831—8846.

Rafiee-Yarandi, H., Ghorbani, G.R., Alikhani, M., Sadeghi-Sefidmazgi, A., Drackley, J. K., 2016. A comparison of the effect of soybeans roasted at different temperatures versus calcium salts of fatty acids on performance and milk fatty acid composition of mid-lactation Holstein cows. J. Dairy Sci. 99, 5422—5435.

Rea, M.C., Cogan, T.M., Tobin, S., 1992. Incidence of pathogenic bacteria in raw milk in Ireland. J. Appl. Bacteriol. 73 (4), 331—336.

Reich, C.M., Arnould, J.P.Y., 2007. Evolution of Pinnipedia lactation strategies: a potential role for alpha-lactalbumin? Biol. Lett. 3 (5), 546—549.

Ross, S.A., Jonathan, A.L., Kilcoyne, M., Joshi, L., Hickey, R.M., 2016. Defatted bovine milk fat globule membrane inhibits association of enterohaemorrhagic *Escherichia coli* O157: H7 with human HT-29 cells. Int. Dairy J. 59, 36—43.

Saboyainsta, L.V., Maubois, J.-L., 2000. Current developments of microfiltration technology in the dairy industry. Le Lait 80 (6), 541—553.

Santillo, A., Caroprese, M., Marino, R., d'Angelo, F., Sevi, A., Albenzio, M., 2016. Fatty acid profile of milk and Cacioricotta cheese from Italian Simmental cows as affected by dietary flaxseed supplementation. J. Dairy Sci. 99 (4), 2545—2551.

Schaafsma, G., 2008. Lactose and lactose derivatives as bioactive ingredients in human nutrition. Int. Dairy J. 18 (5), 458—465.

Schroten, H., Hanisch, F.G., Plogmann, R., Hacker, J., Uhlenbruck, G., Nobis-Bosch, R., et al., 1992. Inhibition of adhesion of S-fimbriated *Escherichia coli* to buccal epithelial cells by human milk fat globule membrane components: a novel aspect of the protective function of mucins in the nonimmunoglobulin fraction. Infect. Immun. 60 (7), 2893—2899.

Séverin, S., Wenshui, X., 2005. Milk biologically active components as nutraceuticals: review. Crit. Rev. Food Sci. Nutr. 45 (7-8), 645—656.

Sianou, A., Galyfos, G., Moragianni, D., Andromidas, P., Kaparos, G., Baka, S., et al., 2015. The role of microRNAs in the pathogenesis of endometrial cancer: a systematic review. Arch. Gynecol. Obstet. 292 (2), 271−282.

Singh, R.P., Massachi, I., Manickavel, S., Singh, S., Rao, N.P., Hasan, S., 2013. The role of miRNA in inflammation and autoimmunity. Autoimmun. Rev. 12 (12), 1160−1165.

Siri-Tarino, P.W., Sun, Q., Hu, F.B., Krauss, R.M., 2010. Meta-analysis of prospective cohort studies evaluating the association of saturated fat with cardiovascular disease. Am. J. Clin. Nutr. 91 (3), 535−546.

Siri-Tarino, P.W., Chiu, S., Bergeron, N., Krauss, R.M., 2015. Saturated fats versus poly-unsaturated fats versus carbohydrates for cardiovascular disease prevention and treatment. Annu. Rev. Nutr. 35, 517.

Smith, J.G., Yokoyama, W.H., German, J.B., 1998. Butyric acid from the diet: actions at the level of gene expression. Crit. Rev. Food Sci. 38 (4), 259−297.

Smithers, G.W., 2008. Whey and whey proteins—from 'gutter-to-gold'. Int. Dairy J. 18 (7), 695−704.

Snow, J.W., Andrew, E.H., Isaacs, S.K., Baggish, A.L., Chan, S.Y., 2013. Ineffective delivery of diet-derived microRNAs to recipient animal organisms. RNA Biol. 10 (7), 1107−1116.

Szilagyi, A., 2004. Redefining lactose as a conditional prebiotic. Can. J. Gastroenterol. Hepatol. 18 (3), 163−167.

Turpeinen, A.M., Mutanen, M., Aro, A., Salminen, I., Basu, S., Palmquist, D.L., et al., 2002. Bioconversion of vaccenic acid to conjugated linoleic acid in humans. Am. J. Clin. Nutr. 76 (3), 504−510.

Wall, R., Ross, R.P., Fitzgerald, G.F., Stanton, C., 2010. Fatty acids from fish: the anti-inflammatory potential of long-chain omega-3 fatty acids. Nutr. Rev. 68 (5), 280−289.

Ward, R.E., Bruce German, J., Corredig, M., 2006. Composition, applications, fractionation, technological and nutritional significance of milk fat globule membrane material. Advanced Dairy Chemistry Volume 2 Lipids. Springer.

Waser, M., Michels, K.B., Bieli, C., Flöistrup, H., Pershagen, G., Von Mutius, E., et al., 2007. Inverse association of farm milk consumption with asthma and allergy in rural and suburban populations across Europe. Clin. Exp. Allergy 37 (5), 661−670.

Weber, J.A., David, H.B., Zhang, S., Huang, D.Y., Huang, K.H., Lee, M.J., et al., 2010. The microRNA spectrum in 12 body fluids. Clin. Chem. 56 (11), 1733−1741.

Wolf, T., Scott, R.B., Zempleni, J., 2015. The intestinal transport of bovine milk exosomes is mediated by endocytosis in human colon carcinoma Caco-2 cells and rat small intestinal Iec-6 cells. J. Nutr. 145 (10), 2201−2206.

Wolfe, R.R., 2015. Update on protein intake: importance of milk proteins for health status of the elderly. Nutr. Rev. 73 (1), 41−47.

Yang, B., Chen, H., Stanton, C., Ross, R.P., Zhang, H., Chen, Y.Q., et al., 2015. Review of the roles of conjugated linoleic acid in health and disease. J. Funct. Foods 15, 314−325.

Yonemori, K., Kurahara, H., Maemura, K., Natsugoe, S., 2016. MicroRNA in pancreatic cancer. J. Hum. Genet. 62, 33.

Zhang, L., Hou, D., Chen, X., Li, D., Zhu, L., Zhang, Y., et al., 2012. Exogenous plant MIR168a specifically targets mammalian LDLRAP1: evidence of cross-kingdom regulation by microRNA. Cell Res. 22 (1), 107−126.

Zhou, Q., Mingzhou, L., Wang, X., Li, Q., Wang, T., Zhu, Q., et al., 2011. Immune-related microRNAs are abundant in breast milk exosomes. Int. J. Biol. Sci. 8 (1), 118−123.

CHAPTER 8

What Bacteriocinogenic Lactic Acid Bacteria Do in the Milk?

Svetoslav D. Todorov[1,2]

[1]Departamento de Veterinária, Universidade Federal de Viçosa, Viçosa, Brazil
[2]Food Research Center (FoRC), Department of Food and Experimental Nutrition, Faculty of Pharmaceutical Sciences, University of São Paulo, São Paulo, Brazil

8.1 INTRODUCTION

Lactic acid bacteria (LAB) produce various antimicrobial substances during fermentation, such as organic acids, hydrogen peroxide, carbon dioxide, diacetyl, low-molecular-weight antimicrobial substances, and bacteriocins (Cotter et al., 2005). These specific antimicrobial compounds act as biopreservatives in food, with records dating back to approximately 6000 BC (De Vuyst and Vandamme, 1994).

Since discover of nisin, a bacteriocin authorized in several countries as a preservative in a food industry, a scientific and industrial interest in the discovery of new bacteriocin was raised. An overview of the literature only on Science Direct research engine (www.sciencedirect.com, accessed end of September 2016) was showing more than 7000 documents containing key word "bacteriocins" for last decade. However, when key words "bacteriocins" and "milk" or "dairy" were crossed, only 600 documents were located. Even if this is a relatively low result, we need to acknowledge that application of bacteriocins and specifically nisin is one of more explored examples for biopreservation in dairy industry. Nisin is a bacteriocin worldwide applied in biopreservation (de Arauz et al., 2009). Wiedemann et al. (2001) described a model membrane study where lipid II (the principal transporter of peptidoglycan subunits from the cytoplasm to the cell wall) acts as a docking station for nisin. At high concentrations of nisin, pore formation may occur even in the absence of lipid II, resulting in the cell membrane containing at least 50% negatively charged phospholipids (Wiedemann et al., 2001).

Even, nisin was discovered in 1933, it was first marketed in England in 1953 and since then it has been approved for use in over 50 countries (Favaro et al., 2015). Nowadays, nisin is licensed as a food preservative

Raw Milk
DOI: https://doi.org/10.1016/B978-0-12-810530-6.00008-0

149

(E234) and is recognized to be safe for food by the Joint Food and Agriculture Organization/World Health Organization (FAO/WHO) Expert Committee on Food Additives in 1969. There are numerous applications of nisin as a natural food preservative, including dairy products and processed cheese. In these cases, the bacteriocin is incorporated into the product as a dried concentrated powder, though not purified, preparation made with food-grade techniques (Favaro et al., 2015).

According to the FAO/WHO Codex Committee on milk and milk products allowed nisin as a food additive for processed cheese at a concentration of 12.5 mg/kg (as pure nisin) product (Reis et al., 2012). However, there is no standardized international rules related to the use of nisin. For instance, nisin can be added to cheese without limit in the United Kingdom, while a maximum concentration of 12.5 mg/kg in that food is allowed in Spain (Sobrino-López and Martín-Belloso, 2008). In Brazil, Argentina, Italy, and Mexico, nisin is allowed for application in cheese up to 12.5 mg/kg and up to 500 IU/g (Cleveland et al., 2001). However, in the United States much higher level of 10,000 IU/g is permitted (Cleveland et al., 2001). Nisin is innocuous, sensitive to digestive proteases and it does not influence sensory properties of the food products (Pongtharangkul and Demirci, 2004). For these reasons, it has been proved to be an effective natural food biopreservative.

In this review we would like to give some examples of the isolation of bacteriocinogenic LAB (different from nisin) from milk and dairy products and application of semi-purified or pure bacteriocins produced by LAB cultures or bacteriocinogenic culture themselves. However, a summarized information about all bacteriocins and their producers in one paper is almost impossible taking in consideration of the papers published. For these reasons we have been decided to focus on some example works in order to highlight importance and perspective of application of these natural biopreservatives.

8.2 WHAT ARE LAB AND WHAT THEY DO IN THE MILK?

The role of LAB in milk is still much undefined. Even large number of LAB were being isolated from milk and different dairy products, the question why LAB are in the milk is still not well answered. The role of LAB in biopreservation and technological properties of preparation of different dairy products are well defined. A large number of scientific works were being dedicated to the specific technological role of LAB in the preparation of different dairy products. However, this is a subject on different works. In this review we give some examples of the application of bacteriocins producing LAB and its antimicrobial peptides in the bio-preservation of dairy products, including extensions of shelf life. However, most of these cases are related to dairy products, where the presence of LAB can be explained with the addition of starter cultures, addition of coagulating agents, specificity of the fermentation and matura-tion processes, etc. At several steps of the production process, these dairy products are in contact with environmental factors and specific LAB can be introduced to these products.

However, how and why LAB are present in the raw milk? Milk is sterile at secretion in the udder, but is contaminated by bacteria even before it leaves the udder. Except in the case of mastitis, the bacteria at this point are harmless and few in number. Further infection of the milk by microorganisms can take place during milking, handling, storage, and other preprocessing activities (http://www.fao.org/docrep/004/t0218e/t0218e03.htm). Different bacteria, including LAB, can get into the milk via feces of the animal; from infected udder animals, e.g., mastitis; animal diseases, e.g., bovine tuberculosis; bacteria living on the skin of the animals; environments, e.g., feces, dirt, processing environments; insects, rodents, and other animal vectors; humans, e.g., hands of the milking operators, etc. In fact, based on mentioned previous, we can describe a very apocalyptic scenario. However, if we compare use of raw and pasteurized milk, it is important to acknowledge that longest part of the human consumption history was related to use of raw milk. Only after the invention of pasteurization process by Louis Pasteur in the 19th century, this process has been recommended for increased safety of milk. Moreover, pasteurization can be a good process for eliminating patho-genic bacteria, while reducing important and beneficial LAB. During centuries, the natural selection of LAB used as part of starter cultures influenced safety of different fermented dairy products related to the production of different antimicrobial substances by applied LAB. As an example, raw-milk cheeses present almost 20% of French total cheese production and are considered far superior compared to pasteurized cheeses. Many traditional French cheeses have solely been made from raw milk for hundreds of years.

8.3 WHAT ARE BACTERIOCINS?

LAB are known for their production of antimicrobial compounds, including bacteriocins or bacteriocin-like peptides (De Vuyst and Vandamme, 1994). Bacteriocins of LAB are defined as ribosomally synthesized proteins or protein complexes usually antagonistic to genetically closely related organisms (De Vuyst and Vandamme, 1994). Bacteriocins are generally low-molecular-weight proteins that gain entry into target cells by binding to cell surface receptors. Their bactericidal mechanism varies and may include pore formation, degradation of cellular DNA, disruption through specific cleavage of 16S ribosomal DNA, and inhibition of peptidoglycan synthesis (De Vuyst and Vandamme, 1994; Heu et al., 2001). In recent papers, specific environmental conditions, including those found in food, have been studied to determine their effect on the production of bacteriocins (Leroy and De Vuyst, 2003; Motta and Brandelli, 2003). Bacteriocin production dramatically changes upon altering of environmental conditions and optimum production may require a specific combination of specific parameters (Leal-Sánchez et al., 2002). Little is known about the interactions these factors have on the production of bacteriocins, especially in a complex food environment.

Although bacteriocins display antibiotic properties, they differ from antibiotics in that they are synthesized ribosomally, exhibit a narrow spectrum of activity, and the organisms responsible for their production have immunity against them (Cleveland et al., 2001). Most bacteriocins from Gram-positive bacteria are produced by LAB (Nes and Tagg, 1996; Ennahar et al., 2000). Previous studies have reported the antimicrobial activity of bacteriocins produced by LAB against Gram-negative bacteria (Todorov and Dicks, 2004, 2006; Von Mollendorff et al., 2006).

Bacteriocins are of great importance to humans as they can play a considerable role in food preservation and human therapy. They can be used as an alternative or replacement to various antibiotics (Richard et al., 2006). This can limit the use of antibiotics and thus reduce the development of antibiotic resistance. Some of bacteriocins can be used in combination with antibiotics and can present an important synergetic effect of combined application (Minahk et al., 2004; Todorov et al., 2010). Furthermore, bacteriocins are more easily accepted by health-conscious consumers, because they are naturally produced compared to chemically synthesized preservatives. According to Deegan et al. (2006) the ongoing study of existing bacteriocins and discovery of new bacteriocins look promising for application in the food industry.

According to Heng et al. (2007), as shown in Fig. 8.1, bacteriocins are divided into four main classes: (I) Lantibiotic peptides, containing linear, globular, and multicomponent bacteriocins. Nisin was classified as linear lantibiotic peptide (Heng et al., 2007); (II) Smaller than 10 kDa bacteriocins. Pediocin PA-1 was one of most studied bacteriocins belonging to this group (Heng et al., 2007); (III) Larger than 10 kDa bacteriocins; and (IV) Cyclic bacteriocins with enterocin AS48 as a most studied example (Martínez Viedma et al., 2008). The Class I and II bacteriocins are considered the most important due to their potential commercial applications.

By definition bacteriocins are bioactive molecules affecting closely related microorganisms (Todorov, 2009). However, it is very intersecting to know if some of bacteriocins may be active against important food or human pathogens or against other LAB, included LAB from same ecological niche. A few bacteriocins are active against a number of food spoilage and pathogenic bacteria, including Gram-negative bacteria (Todorov and Dicks, 2004, 2005; Todorov et al., 2006; Von Mollendorff et al., 2006). This unusual activity includes apart from Gram-negative bacteria, some viruses, *Mycobacterium tuberculosis*, yeast, and fungi (Wachsman et al., 1999, 2003; Todorov et al., 2010, 2013).

Apart from bacteriocins, LAB produce lactic acid, hydrogen peroxide, benzoic acid, fatty acids, diacetyl, and other low-molecular-weight compounds. Bacteriocinogenic probiotic bacteria could be beneficial when used as starter cultures, as it may prolong the shelf life of the products and provide the consumer with a healthy dietary component at a considerable

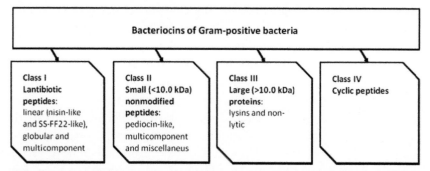

Figure 8.1 Classification of bacteriocins produced by Gram-positive bacteria. *Adapted from Heng, N.C., Wescombe, P.A., Burton, J.P., Jack, R.W., Tagg, J.R., 2007. The diversity of bacteriocins in Gram-positive bacteria. In: Bacteriocins. Springer, Berlin, Heidelberg, pp. 45–92.*

low cost. To qualify as starter cultures LAB have to be present at sufficient numbers in fermented products. Furthermore, starter cultures should not enhance acidification during storage and should not have adverse effects on the taste and aroma profiles (Heller, 2001).

8.4 LAB AND THEIR BACTERIOCINS

8.4.1 Application of *Lactobacillus plantarum* in Food Fermentations and Its Bacteriocin

Lactobacillus plantarum is a heterofermentative, micro-aerophilic, Gram-positive microorganism, with rod morphology, occurring singly or grouped in short chains. This species has well-accepted GRAS (Generally Recognised as Safe) status and numerous strains of *Lb. plantarum* have been isolated from different ecological niches including meat, fish, fruits, vegetables, milk, and cereal products. *Lactobacillus plantarum* has been used as a starter culture in various food fermentation processes contributing to the organoleptic properties, flavor, and texture. Due to production of lactic acid and other antimicrobial compounds, *L. plantarum* also contributes to the safety of the final products (Todorov and Franco, 2010).

The use of LAB in dairy products is the one of the oldest and more traditional areas of application. Strains such as *Lactobacillus acidophilus*, *Lactobacillus delbrüeckii* subsp. *bulgaricus*, *Streptococcus thermophilus*, *Lactococcus lactis* subsp. *lactis*, *Lc. lactis* subsp. *cremoris*, *Lactobacillus rhamnosus*, and *Lb. plantarum* have been used for centuries for the preparation of yoghurt, fermented milk products, and different types of cheese (Fernandes et al., 1992; Powell et al., 2007; Danova et al., 2005). In these fermentation processes, LAB are responsible for organoleptic characteristics of these products resulting from the degradation of lactose, acidification, and production of aromatic compounds.

Numerous strains of bacteriocin producing *Lb. plantarum* have been isolated in the last two decades from different ecological niches including milk and dairy products. Several of these plantaricins have been characterized and the amino-acid sequence determined. Different aspects of the mode of action, fermentation optimization, and genetic organization of the bacteriocin operon have been studied. However, numerous of bacteriocins produced by different *Lb. plantarum* strains have not been fully characterized (Todorov, 2009).

Kefir is a fermented milk product with a slightly acidic taste, yeasty flavor, and creamy consistency (Powell et al., 2007). The starter cultures, which consist mainly of LAB, propionibacteria, and yeasts, are entrapped in kefir grains held together by polysaccharides (Kwak et al., 1996; Saloff-Coste, 1996). The antimicrobial activity of Kefir has been well documented and the beverage is known to inhibit a number of spoilage microorganisms and foodborne pathogens, including *Bacillus cereus*, *Clostridium tyrobutyricum*, *Escherichia coli*, *Listeria monocytogenes*, and *Staphylococcus aureus* (Saloff-Coste, 1986; Van Wyk et al., 2002). The reason for growth inhibition is related with the presence of lactic acid, volatile acids, hydrogen peroxide, carbon dioxide, diacetaldehyde, acetaldehyde, and bacteriocins (Powell et al., 2006). The possibility of organic acids being responsible for antimicrobial activity was ruled out by growth inhibition obtained with pH-neutralized kefir (Morgan et al., 2000).

In the study of Powell et al. (2006) *Lb. plantarum* ST8KF, isolated from kefir grains, produces a 3.5 kDa bacteriocin (bacST8KF) active against *Enterococcus mundtii* ST. *Lb. plantarum* ST8KF harbors at least six plasmids (Powell et al., 2006). Growth in the presence of 80 µL/mL novobiocin resulted in the loss of a 3.9 kb plasmid from *Lb. plantarum* ST8KF and the ability to produce bacST8KF. Based on these results, the genes encoding bacST8KF production are located on the plasmid (Powell et al., 2006). This is in agreement to most other reports for bacteriocins of *Lb. plantarum*. The genes coding for plantaricin 423 and plantaricin C11 are located on bigger plasmids of approximately 9 kb (Olasupo, 1996; Van Reenen et al., 2003). Only a limited number of plantaricins are encoded by genes located on the genome, e.g., plantaricin UG1 (Enan et al., 1996) and plantaricin ST31 (Todorov et al., 1999).

Kefir produced with grains containing *Lb. plantarum* ST8KF prevented the growth of *E. mundtii* ST in situ. No inhibition of *E. mundtii* ST was recorded when kefir was produced from grains containing a plasmid-free and bacteriocin-negative variant (ST8KF⁻). Cells of *E. mundtii* ST were detected by fluorescent in situ hybridization. This is the first report on the incorporation of a bacteriocin-producing starter culture in kefir grains and in situ control of microbial growth (Powell et al., 2006).

Amasi is a traditional fermented milk product consumed in different regions of Southern African, including Zimbabwe, South Africa, and Lesotho. The product is an unsweetened curd with a consistency slightly thicker than yoghurt and with a pH between 3.6 and 4.2. Although normally consumed with thick corn-meal porridge, Amasi is also consumed between meals with ground sorghum, similar to muesli (Todorov et al., 2007). Traditionally Amasi is produced from unpasteurized bovine (cow's) milk and is allowed to ferment spontaneously in an earthenware (clay) pot or gourd ("calabash") for 2—3 days at ambient temperature. The microbiota responsible for the fermentation is derived from the air, raw milk, and walls of the containers. After coagulation, the whey is drained through a plugged hole at the bottom of the container (Todorov et al., 2007).

In previous work the characterization of a bacteriocin produced by *Lb. plantarum* AMA-K was described (Todorov et al., 2007). The cell-free supernatant containing bacteriocin AMA-K inhibited the growth of *Listeria innocua* and *Enterococcus faecalis*. Based on tricine—SDS-PAGE, bacteriocin AMA-K is 2.9 kDa in size. Activity levels of 12 800 AU/mL were recorded in MRS broth at 30°C and 37°C. Bacteriocin AMA-K remained stable after 2 h of incubation at pH 2.0—12.0 and at 100°C, respectively. The bacteriocin do not adhere to the surface of the producer cell and has a bacteriolytic mode of action. Bacteriocin production is stimulated by the presence of *L. innocua*. *Lb. plantarum* AMA-K grows in milk, but produces only 800 AU bacteriocin per mL after 24 h (Todorov et al., 2007).

In the study of Todorov (2008) some aspects of mode of action of bacteriocin produced by *Lb. plantarum* AMA-K were determined. Adsorption of the bacteriocins to the test-microorganism is essential for performing their antibacterial activity. Several factors may have an influence on this adsorption (Todorov, 2008). However, when we are planning to apply a bacteriocin in a food biopreservation we need to take into consideration that temperature, pH, presence of lipids, proteins, food additives, NaCl, and preservants may influence bioavailability of bacteriocins, their stability as well, and may affect their adsorption to the microbial contaminates. Optimal adsorption of bacteriocin AMA-K (75%) to *Listeria* strains was recorded at pH 7.0. However, temperatures of 4°C and 15°C resulted in reduction of 50% of adsorption of bacteriocin AMA-K to cells of *L. innocua* LMG13568 and *Listeria ivanovii* spp. *ivanovii* ATCC19119. Decreased adsorption of bacteriocin AMA-K to *Listeria* strains was observed in the presence of Tween 20, Tween 80, and different concentrations of NaCl. Ascorbic acid and potassium sorbate did not affect adsorption of bacteriocin AMA-K to cells of *L. innocua* LMG1568, but reduced this process to cells of *L. monocytogenes* Scott A and to *L. ivanovii* spp. *ivanovii* ATCC19119. The presence of 1% sodium nitrate increased adsorption of bacteriocin AMA-K to cells of *L. innocua* LMG13568 and *L. monocytogenes* Scott A. Bacteriocin AMA-K shares high homology to pediocin PA-1 (Todorov, 2008).

Seven isolates from donkey milk samples presenting antimicrobial activity were successfully identified as *Lb. plantarum* according to physiological, biochemical tests and 16S ribosomal DNA sequencing in the work presented by Murua et al. (2013). Bacteriocin produced by *Lb. plantarum* LP08AD was able to inhibit the growth of many food spoilage bacteria and foodborne pathogens including *Enterococcus faecium, Lactobacillus curvatus, Lactobacillus fermentum, Pediococcus acidilactici,* and *L. monocytogenes* (Murua et al., 2013). The produced bacteriocin was been characterized, including possible presence of plantaricin W in the genomic DNA from studied strain (Murua et al., 2013). In addition, authors were investigated potential probiotic properties of *Lb. plantarum* LP08AD. Based on the reported results, including bacteriocin LP08AD activity and mode of action, authors suggested that bacteriocin-producing *Lb. plantarum* LP08AD might be useful in the design of novel functional foods with potential probiotic or biopreservation properties (Murua et al., 2013).

8.4.2 Other *Lactobacillus* spp. Bacteriocin Producers

A bacteriocin-producing *Lactobacillus paracasei* subsp. *tolerans,* isolated from Tibetan kefir, was the subject of the study of Miao et al. (2014). This bacteriocin was characterized, purified, and molecular mass estimated to be 2113.842 Da. Expressed bacteriocin exhibited a wide range of antimicrobial activity, including some fungi (*Aspergillus flavus, Aspergillus niger, Rhizopus nigricans,* and *Penicillium glaucum*), but also Gram-negative bacteria (*E. coli* and *Salmonella enterica*) and Gram-positive bacteria (*S. aureus* and *Bacillus thuringiensis*) (Miao et al., 2014). Bacteriocins from LAB that have a wide antimicrobial spectrum against Gram-negative and Gram-positive bacteria and fungi are still not frequently reported.

Lactobacillus casei was isolated from fermented camel milk (Lü et al., 2014), and produced bacteriocin was purified by performing ammonium sulfate precipitation, gel filtration, anion exchange chromatography, and reversed-phase HPLC separation. According to MS spectrum, the molecular mass of expressed bacteriocin was 6352 Da, which was significantly different from previously reported bacteriocins produced by *Lb. casei* strains (Lü et al., 2014). Antibacterial activity of bacteriocin was characterized with inhibition of broad range of Gram-positive and Gram-negative foodborne pathogenic strains including some antibiotic-resistant pathogenic strains, *L. monocytogenes, E. coli,* and *S. aureus.* Some aspects of mode of action have been determined using scanning electron microscopy and transmission electron microscopy analyses, where it was demonstrated that the bacteriocin is involved in pore formation in the cytoplasmic membrane (Lü et al., 2014).

Avaiyarasi et al. (2016) evaluated bacteriocinogenic potential of *Lactobacillus sakei* GM3 isolated from goat milk. *Lb. sakei* GM3 exhibited acid and bile tolerance (that maybe can be a positive characteristic for a potential probiotic application) and produced bacteriocin showed antagonistic activity against several foodborne pathogens, including *Pseudomonas aeruginosa*, *S. aureus*, *L. monocytogenes*, *Salmonella typhi*, *S. enterica*, *Klebsiella pneumonia*, *E. coli*, *Candida albicans*, and *Candida tropicalis*. The molecular mass was determined to be 4.8 kDa after subjecting to salting out, size exclusion chromatography, reversed-phase HPLC on C18 column and MALDI-TOF-MS system. In addition, the cytotoxicity on HT29 cell line by bacteriocin GM3 showed maximum survival inhibition. Avaiyarasi et al. (2016) suggest that the *Lb. sakei* GM3 can be applied in food industry as a biopreservative.

Lactobacillus curvatus was isolated from traditional artisanal cheese *Brinza* manufactured in Azerbaijan from cow's milk (Ahmadova et al., 2013). Apart from characterization of produced bacteriocin, authors have focus on safety of producer strain in order to evaluate application not only on expressed antimicrobial peptide, but as well of producer strain as a beneficial culture in cheese manufacture. In addition to inhibitory activity of the bacteriocin against *E. faecium*, *L. innocua*, *L. ivanovii*, *L. monocytogenes*, and *B. cereus* authors explore inhibitory effect of the strain itself against some fungus. The coculture in dual slab agar of *Lb. curvatus* with several fungi displayed the same extent of inhibition of the growth of mold for *Cladosporium* spp. and *Fusarium* spp.; however, no antifungal activity was observed against *Penicillium roqueforti* (Ahmadova et al., 2013).

8.4.3 Bacteriocin Produced by *Lactococcus lactis*

Different *Lc. lactis* strains are most used LAB components of commercial starter cultures used by the dairy industry for the manufacture and ripening of cheese and fermented milk products (Limsowtin et al., 1995). Most probably bacteriocins produced by different strains of *Lactococcus* spp. were most studied antimicrobial peptides, including lanthibiotic and non-lanthibiotic bacteriocins produced by *Lc. lactis* from different sources (Venema et al., 1995). In addition, the first bacteriocin isolated from *L. lactis* was nisin (Mattick and Hirsch, 1947), 34 amino acids belonging to the group of lanthibiotic. Nisin is currently approved and exploited in over 50 countries as a food additive, with commercial code "E234" (Delves-Broughton et al., 1996).

Alegría et al. (2010) reported on collection of 60 bacterial strains, identified as Lc. lactis (Lc. lactis subsp. lactis and Lc. lactis subsp. cremoris) and differentiated by RAPD-PCR and rep-PCR, collected during the manufacturing and ripening stages of five traditional, starter-free cheeses made from raw milk. Among the 60 strains, 17 were shown to be a bacteriocin producers, including evidences for production and expression of nisin A, nisin Z, lactococcin 972, and lactococcin G-like.

Other bacteriocin, lactococcin MMFII, produced by Lc. lactis MMFII isolated from a Tunisian dairy product had been reported by Ferchichi et al. (2001). The bacteriocin was characterized, including purified to homogeneity by sulfate ammonium precipitation, cation exchange chromatography, Sep-Pack chromatography, and two steps of reverse-phase chromatography. Its amino acid sequence, obtained by Edman degradation, revealed a 37-amino acid peptide with calculated mass of 4144.6 Da and laser desorption mass spectrometry analysis molecular mass of 4142.6 Da, suggesting the presence of a disulfide bond within the purified bacteriocin. Lactococcin MMFII, a IIa class bacteriocin, presented remarkable anti-listerial activity and contains the N-terminal YGNGV consensus motif.

Lc. lactis MMFII was able to coagulate milk, indicating that this strain has potential technological properties and is a good candidate to be incorporated in dairy starters to protect fermented dairy products against listerial contamination (Ferchichi et al., 2001). Authors pointed as well, that expressed bacteriocin was not showing inhibitory activity against other Lactococcal indicator strains.

Lc. lactis subsp. lactis strain was isolated from goat milk obtained from farm located in Sao Paulo metropolitan area (Furtado et al., 2014a). Authors were evaluated expressed bacteriocin, including remarkable activity against different strains of L. monocytogenes from different serological groups. In addition to previouslly studied bacteriocins characteristics, authors were evaluated probiotic potential of bacteriocin produced strain (Furtado et al., 2014b) and evaluated potential for application of studied Lc. lactis subsp. lactis as a coculture for control of L. monocytogenes in fresh cheese model (Furtado et al., 2015). However, even expressed bacteriocin by Lc. lactis subsp. lactis was able to inhibit different strains of L. monocytogenes as effect of direct interaction between bacteriocin and pathogenic bacteria, in coculture condition in a model cheese system, efficacy was not significantly different from the used non-bacteriocinogenic control strain of *Lc. lactis* (Furtado et al., 2015). This maybe is one of several examples that environmental conditions can be responsible for the production and expression of antimicrobial peptides and can influence inhibitory effect of bacteriocinogenic strains when they were applied in model food systems. However, authors were applied nisin as a control and positive results on control of *L. monocytogenes* were recorded (Furtado et al., 2015).

8.4.4 Bacteriocin Producers From *Leuconostoc mesenteroides*

Different species from the group of LAB have been isolated from milk samples, including strains of *Le. mesenteroides* (Paula et al., 2015; Alrakawa et al., 2016). Further, some LAB strains with antimicrobial activity iso-lated from airag or koumiss have been reported (Batdorj et al., 2006; Wulijideligen and Miyamoto, 2011; Wulijideligen et al., 2012; Xie et al., 2011; Wang et al., 2012; Belguesmia et al., 2013). *Leuconostoc* sp. has a promisor future in dairy foods as bacteriocinogenic and probiotics strain and/or through enhancement of physical–chemical characteristics of dairy products, mainly in cheese.

Paula et al. (2015) investigated bacteriocinogenic potential of *Le. mesenteroides* isolated from water buffalo cheese produced in Brazil. Including the study on characterization of produced antimicrobial pep-tide, authors have to pay attention on extended spectrum of activity of expressed bacteriocin, including several *Listeria* and *Enterococcus* species with potential in bioconservation of dairy products. Expressed bacteriocin was purified using ammonium sulfate precipitation, affinity column and reversed-phase chromatography, and mass spectrometry and amino acids analyses showed that the bacteriocin produced by *Le. mesenteroides* SJRP55 was similar to mesenterocin Y105 and mesenterocin B105 (Paula et al., 2015). In addition to beneficial properties of expressed bacteriocin/s authors have to pay attention to safety of producer strain itself with determination of presence of potential virulence genes by biomolecular approach (Paula et al., 2015).

"Airag," a Mongolian fermented milk product, was served as a source for isolation of bacteriocinogenic strains in the study of Alrakawa et al. (2016). In total of 235 isolated were obtained from "airag" and authors have selected *Le. mesenteroides* subsp. *dextranicum* (strain 213M0) for deeper study and characterization of the expressed bacteriocin. According to authors, bacteriocin produced by *Le. mesenteroides* subsp. *dextranicum* 213M0 was inhibited all tested *Listeria* spp. and just seven strains of LAB among 53 tested in total and according to estimated molecular mass determined by SDS-PAGE differ to already known bacteriocins expressed by same species (Alrakawa et al., 2016).

8.4.5 Bacteriocin Produced by *Streptococcus gallolyticus* subsp. *macedonicus*

An LAB, isolated from Bulgarian-style yoghurt, produced a bacteriocin ST91KM. The strain was identified as *Streptococcus gallolyticus* subsp. *macedonicus*. The inhibitory activity of ST91KM includes a narrow spectrum of Gram-positive bacteria including mastitis pathogens, *Streptococcus agalactiae*, *Streptococcus dysgalactiae*, and *Staphylococcus epidermidis*. The macedocin ST91KM is approximately 2.0−2.5 kDa in size as estimated by tricine−SDS-PAGE. The bacteriocin remained stable after incubation for 2 h at pH 2.0 to 10.0. No decrease in activity was recorded after treatment at 100°C for 100 min, but the bacteriocin was inactivated at 121°C after 20 min. Macedocin ST91KM had a proteinaceous structure as treatment with pronase, pepsin, and trypsin inactivated the bacteriocin. Activity was not reduced after treatment with α-amylase, suggesting that the bacteriocin is not glycosylated. Macedocin ST91KM was produced at a maximum activity of 800 AU/mL in MRS (pH 6.4) after 12−15 h incubation at 30°C. The bacteriocin activity was influenced by the addition of nutrients to MRS indicating that the bacteriocin production is not only dependent on cell mass but is also influenced by nutrient factors. A recovery of 43.2% was achieved after purification with 60% ammonium sulfate and elution through a Sep-Pak C18 in 40% isopropanol (Pieterse et al., 2008).

Macedocin ST91KM produced by *S. gallolyticus* subsp. *macedonicus* appears to be a novel bacteriocin-like substance that has a very narrow spectrum of activity. In vitro studies indicated that this bacteriocin should be characterized further as it could find possible application as an antimicrobial agent against pathogenic streptococci that cause mastitis. The macedocin ST91KM activity remains stable at physiological pH and over a wide temperature range; making it a possible candidate for a medicament or topical preparation. Current treatment strategies for mastitis in dairy cattle include the use of antiseptic chemicals such as iodophors (Sears et al., 1992) and antibiotics. Dairy and beef animal products are destined for human consumption and therefore need to be strictly controlled to reduce the presence of chemical or drug residues. The presence of the macedocin ST91KM in animal products such as milk would be regarded as safe as it is inactivated by the enzymes, pepsin and trypsin, and would therefore be easily degraded by the digestive system. The current data indicates that further characterization studies of the mode of action of the macedocin ST91KM against mastitis pathogens should be done to evaluate its efficacy and possible therapeutic application as an alternative to antibiotic treatment (Pieterse et al., 2008).

The action of macedocin ST91KM resulted in efflux of cellular components in sensitive strains. The peptide adsorbed to both sensitive and nonsensitive cells, indicating that activity is not species-specific but rather dependent on specific cell-surface receptors. Binding sites for the peptide could be lipid in nature, as the addition of solvents reduced adsorption. Salts prevented the adsorption of macedocin ST91KM to target cells, possibly due to competitive ion adsorption on the cell surface. Optimal adsorption of macedocin ST91KM was recorded at physiological pH and temperature, suggesting that the peptide could be included in a teat seal. Macedocin ST91KM is also heat stable remaining active at 100°C (Pieterse et al., 2008). This may be an important consideration to ensure that macedocin ST91KM would remain active after storage at a variety of storage conditions in a final teat seal product. Macedocin ST91KM could potentially be used as an antimicrobial agent against pathogens associated with mastitis due to the rapid bacteriocidal mode of action against the mastitis pathogen *S. agalactiae* RPSAG2 (Pieterse and Todorov, 2010). It is important to keep in mind that mastitis-related microbial contaminants may be transferred to the consumers during the production of yoghurt or cheeses. Inhibitory effect of bacteriocin produced by *S. gallolyticus* subsp. *macedonicus* against selected pathogens, related to mastitis was showed *in situ* by DGGE analysis of the total DNA extracted from the mixed population containing this bacteriocin producer and mastitis pathogens and show that at least six from eight tested microbial contaminates were inhibited by coculture of *S. gallolyticus* subsp. *macedonicus* and this mastitis related pathogens in a model system.

8.4.6 Bacteriocins Produced by *Enterococcus* spp.

Enterococcus is a genus part of the LAB group. Enterococci are Gram-positive cocci that often are presented in pairs (diplococci) or short chains and based only on microscopical observation it is difficult to distinguish them from *Lactococcus* and *Streptococci* on physical characteristics alone. Two species of Enterococci are common commensal organisms in the intestines of humans: *E. faecalis* (90–95%) and *E. faecium* (5–10%). Enterococci are facultative anaerobic organisms, i.e., they are capable of cellular respiration in both oxygen-rich and oxygen-poor environments. Though they are not capable of forming spores, enterococci are highly tolerant of a wide range of environmental conditions, including extreme for other LAB temperature (10–45°C), pH (4.5–10.0), and high sodium chloride concentrations. Enterococci typically exhibit gamma-hemolysis on sheep's blood agar.

Several *Enterococcus* spp. isolated from different ecological niches, including dairy environment, were studied for their potential to produce a variety of antibacterial proteins (enterococcins) with activity against foodborne pathogens, such as *L. monocytogenes* or even pathogenic *Clostridium* spp. In addition, several enterococcins have been assessed for inhibition of *Listeria* spp., in dairy systems, where enterococci are often isolated as desirable microflora. Moreover, even if application of enterococcins in food systems is still disputable point and will require additional genetic and biochemical data in order to ensure safety of application of this LAB, enterococcin-producing organisms share a number of characteristics which may be useful for dairy use (Giraffa, 1995).

In his earlier work, Tarelli et al. (1994) (team headed by Giraffa) reported on collection of 116 different *Enterococcus* spp. isolated from dairy environment. Several of these strains, belonging to *E. faecium* and *E. faecalis*, were described as bacteriocin producers with activity against *L. monocytogenes* and *C. tyrobutyricum*. Even if several works been dedicated to bacteriocinogenic LAB and their application in milk and dairy products, still role of these antimicrobial peptides is not fully characterized. Piard et al. (1990) almost 25 years ago mentioned that milk is appropriate medium for production of bacteriocins during a fresh cheeses manufacture processes, and most probably it is related to the competition interaction with other LAB.

Based on traditional dairy fermentation processes, we can state that Enterococci have a long history of application in food production with positive influence on favorable metabolic activities (lipolysis, esterolysis, citrate utilization, etc.) contributing to the typical taste and flavor of fermented dairy products (Centeno et al., 1996; Manolopoulou et al., 2003). However, it is important to state the opposite fact of the story, some *Enterococcus* strains are human and animal pathogens. The control of enterococci in food processing has assumed a different importance in the recent years, as the conviction of the harmlessness of these bacteria has been partly changed by the increase of their incidence in nosocomial infections. Some of them were associated with important medical cases related with endocarditis, bacteremia, intraabdominal and pelvic infections, and infections in the urinary tract and central nervous system (Foulquié Moreno et al., 2006).

Some of arguments against applications of enterococci in foods, is antibiotic resistance, issue of special concern because genetic determinants of resistance in these bacteria are generally located in conjugative plasmids or transposons, prone to genetic exchange (Zanella et al., 2006). Multiresistance has been more commonly reported for *E. faecalis* due to its notorious ability to acquire and transfer antibiotic-resistance genes (McBride et al., 2007). In a worst scenario, from raw milk, bacteria may be transferred into raw milk cheeses and then to the consumers.

Bacteriocinogenic strains of *Enterococcus* spp. have been isolated from a variety of fermented food products, including cheese and milk (Ennahar et al., 2001; Sarantinopoulos et al., 2002; Leroy and De Vuyst, 2002; Cocolin et al., 2007; Ghrairi et al., 2008; Izquierdo et al., 2009; Farias et al., 1996) (Table 8.1).

Cocolin et al. (2007) described two strains of *E. faecium* (M241 and M249), isolated from goat milk, as bacteriocin producers with activity against *L. monocytogenes* and *Clostridium butyricum*, however, with not detected any activity with respect to other species of LAB. Based on genetic screening by PCR, both strains were caring genes for enterocins A and B. Authors (Cocolin et al., 2007) showed potential of application of these strains in dairy environment by coculture experiment of bacteriocin producers with *L. monocytogenes* in skimmed milk. In the presence of the *E. faecium* strains, *L. monocytogenes* showed a delay in the growth with respect to the control. An interesting point to highlight from the coculture experiments was the capability of the two enterococci strains to produce higher amounts of bacteriocins in skimmed milk than in MRS medium (Cocolin et al., 2007). Most probably these facts can be explained by admitting the presence of stimulating compounds in the milk that allow a higher production. This result is supporting again the suggestion for direct use of the enterococci strains as bioprotective starter cultures in dairy fermentation processes, alone, related to their acidification capabilities, or in mixture with other LAB (Cocolin et al., 2007).

Table 8.1 Some examples of bacteriocinogenic LAB isolated from milk and dairy products

Species of LAB	Isolated from	Reference
Enterococcus faecalis	Milk	Tarelli et al., 1994
Enterococcus faecium	Milk	Tarelli et al., 1994
Enterococcus faecium	Goat milk	Cocolin et al., 2007
Enterococcus faecium	Dairy product	Ghrairi et al., 2008
Enterococcus faecium	White brine cheese	Favaro et al., 2014
Enterococcus faecium	Coalho cheese	dos Santos et al., 2014
Enterococcus faecium	Goat milk	Schirru et al., 2012
Enterococcus faecium	Yellow cheese	Furtado et al., 2009
Enterococcus mundtii	Yellow cheese	Farias et al., 1996
Lactobacillus casei	Camel milk	Lü et al., 2014
Lactobacillus curvatus	Cheese *Brinza*	Ahmadova et al., 2013
Lactobacillus paracasei subsp. tolerans	Kefir	Miao et al., 2014
Lactobacillus plantarum	Kefir	Powell et al., 2007
Lactobacillus plantarum	Amasi	Todorov et al., 2007
Lactobacillus plantarum	Donkey milk	Murua et al., (2013
Lactobacillus sakei	Goat milk	Avaiyarasi et al., 2016
Lactococcus lactis	Dairy product	Ferchichi et al., 2001
Lactococcus lactis subsp. *cremoris*	Cheeses	Alegría et al., 2010
Lactococcus lactis subsp. *lactis*	Cheeses	Alegría et al., 2010
Lactococcus lactis subsp. *lactis*	Goat milk	Furtado et al., 2014a
Leuconostoc mesenteroides	Water buffalo cheese	Paula et al., 2015
Leuconostoc mesenteroides subsp. *dextranicum*	Airag	Alrakawa et al., 2016
Staphylococcus equorum	Cheese brine	Bockelmann et al. 2017
Streptococcus gallolyticus subsp. *macedonicus*	Yoghurt	Pieterse et al., 2008

Screening for bacteriocin production by strains of LAB from a Tunisian dairy product resulted in the detection of *E. faecium* and bacteriocin producing strain was subject of the work of Ghrairi et al. (2008). Authors characterized the expressed bacteriocin and pointed that produced bacteriocins were active against closely related LAB and also *L. monocytogenes* and *S. aureus*. However, further authors showed based on reversed-phase HPLC purification results and mass spectrometry analysis that *E. faecium* MMT21 produce two bacteriocins enterocin A (4828.67 Da) and enterocin B (5463.8 Da). This result was confirmed by amplification by PCR of enterocins A and B genes (Ghrairi et al., 2008). In addition, the bacteriocin producing strain *E. faecium* MMT21 was not hemolytic, sensitive to vancomycin and other clinically relevant antibiotics and was an anti-listerial strain. Therefore, it may be useful to improve the safety of fermented food products (Ghrairi et al., 2008). Enterocins or starter cultures containing bacteriocin producing *Enterococcus* spp. have been applied in model dairy studies to improve organoleptic traits and safety of certain traditional cheeses (Sarantinopoulos et al., 2002; Sulzer and Busse, 1991). However, different levels of success were obtained, most probably related to different levels of activity and expression of produced bacteriocins at these specific conditions. Taking into account bacteriocinogenic antagonism against *L. monocytogenes*, lack of hemolytic activity, and sensitivity to vancomycin, *E. faecium* MMT21 might be good candidate for future use to prevent growth of these pathogens in dairy food products. Further, it also has high peptidases activities and so can be employed to enhance the organoleptic properties of these foods (Ghrairi et al., 2008).

Four *E. faecium* strains, isolated from Bulgarian homemade white brine cheese, were investigated for their inhibitory activity against *L. monocytogenes* (Favaro et al., 2014). These *E. faecium* strains were described as bacteriocin producers with evidences for the presence of occurrence of several bacteriocin genes (*ent*A, *ent*B, *ent*P, *ent*L50B). In addition, authors were evaluated the safety of application of these *E. faecium* strains, based on the presence of virulence potential and safety including both PCR targeted to the genes *gel*E, *hyl*, *asa*1, *esp*, *cyl*A, *efa*A, *ace*, *van*A, *van*B, *hdc*1, *hdc*2, *tdc*, and *odc* and by phenotypical tests for antibiotic resistance, gelatinase, lipase, DNAse, and α- and β-hemolysis. Considering their strong antimicrobial activity against *L. monocytogenes* strains, the four *E. faecium* strains exhibited promising potential as biopreservatives cultures for fermented food productions. Moreover, due to their safety characteristics and technological properties, authors proposed that they could be used as adjunct NSLAB (nonstarter LAB) rather than as starter culture (Favaro et al., 2014).

Two *E. faecium* strains isolated from artisanal Coalho cheese originated from Vale do Jaguaribe and Sertões Cearenses, Ceara, Brazil, were the subject of characterization of expressed bacteriocins and determination of the beneficial properties of producer strains (Dos Santos et al., 2014, 2015). Bacteriocins were characterized, including detection of enterocin A and B genes was recorded (Dos Santos et al., 2014). In addition to production of antimicrobial peptides, authors explore the safety of both *E. faecium* strains and their potential technological and beneficial properties (Dos Santos et al., 2015) in order to apply these two strains as a possible coculture in the production of Coalho cheese.

Schirru et al. (2012) evaluated goat milk from Sardenia (Italy) as a source of bacteriocin producing LAB. Goat breeding in Sardinia constitutes an important source of income for farming and shepherding activities. In the above-mentioned study (Schirru et al., 2012), 170 LAB strains were isolated from Sardinian goat's milk and tested for bacteriocins production against several foodborne pathogenic microorganisms. Moreover, based on the selection criteria, four *E. faecium* strains (SD1, SD2, SD3, and SD4) were further selected and their bacteriocins characterized with the aim of inhibition of *L. monocytogenes*. Since the strains exhibited a strong antimicrobial activity against different 21 *L. monocytogenes* strains and 6 *Salmonella* spp. isolates, they should be considered as potential biopreservatives cultures for fermented food productions. Moreover, due to their technological features, the four strains could be taken into account for using as adjunct NSLAB rather than as starter culture (Schirru et al. 2012).

Enterococcus mundtii CRL35 was isolated from regional Argentinian yellow cheese (Farias et al., 1996) and *E. faecium* ST88Ch was isolated from yellow cheese obtained from the local market at Butanta, Sao Paulo, SP, Brazil (Furtado et al., 2009). Both strains were used in the experiment of biopreservation of fresh cheese and control of *L. monocytogenes* contaminations. It was interesting to observe that both strains showed potential in control of *L. monocytogenes* in preliminary experiments; however, when they were applied in a model system, only *E. mundtii* CRL35 was showing to be effective. Authors pointed out that inhibitory effect on *L. monocytogenes* can be a result of different antimicrobial factors related to LAB, including not only produced bacteriocins (Pingitore et al., 2012). However, comparing behavior of *L. monocytogenes* in cheeses prepared with *E. mundtii* CRL35, *E. faecium* ST88Ch, and control (non-bacteriocin producing strain of *E. faecalis* ATCC 19443), inhibitory effect can be clearly linked to the bacteriocin expressed by *E. mundtii* CRL35 (Pingitore et al., 2012).

8.4.7 Bacteriocin Produced by *Staphylococcus equorum*

Apart from the isolation and identification of bacteriocin produced by *S. equorum* isolated from cheese brine, Bockelmann et al. (2017) tested the efficacy of expressed bacteriocin in two different model cheese systems to ascertain its potential for use as a protective culture for smear cheese ripening. Cocultivation of *L. monocytogenes* and the anti-listerial *S. equorum* was performed on model cheese surface system. *Staphylococcus equorum* was able to completely inhibit the growth of *L. monocytogenes* inoculated in model system within 24 h of incubation.

8.5 WHAT ARE THE LIMITATIONS OF APPLICATION OF BACTERIOCINS IN BIOPRESERVATION?

After enthusiasms of all examples of potential application of bacteriocins or bacteriocinogenic cultures, the reality is a different story. We need to accept that the application of bacteriocinogenic cultures in control of spoilage microorganisms cannot be presented as the magical "silver bullet" ready to solve all the problems related to the preservation of fermented dairy products. It is true, that starter or nonstarter adjunct cultures can contribute to the safety of the final product, but it is necessary to consider that the antimicrobial compounds have their limitations. And most probably truth is somewhere between a combination of traditional and new approaches of biopreservation.

Subject for application of bacteriocinogenic LAB in dairy processes was reviewed by Favaro et al. (2015). Authors of this review pointed out several possible limitations/factors that can influence the effect of bacteriocins when applied in dairy systems. Some of the key points mentioned by Favaro et al. (2015) were (1) no sufficient level of bacteriocin expression, (2) antagonism of other bacteria toward the producer strain, (3) inadequacy of producer strain as a starter, (4) low capacity for bacteriocin production in food system, (5) safety of the producer strain, (6) the interaction between produced bacteriocin and food matrix; (7) the effect of the physicochemical parameters on the bacteriocin activity. The production of bacteriocins is ribosomal process and can be controlled by complex genetic machinery. In parallel with expression of the bacteriocin, immunity protein and induction factors are also expressed since they are part of the same reading frame. In this way, the bacteriocin producer guarantees its own safety from the killing action of its own bacteriocin (Cotter et al., 2005). This process can be induced by the presence of pathogenic bacteria, but can be repressed as well with the over produced bacteriocin or similar structure protein molecules. However, the biochemical machinery of LAB will need sufficient nutrients for the production of bacteriocins (Favaro et al., 2015). In addition, we have to consider dairy products that can be related to the conditions not very favorable for growth and expression of biological active molecules by LAB. Some of them, as presence of high levels of NaCl and low temperature (during ripening and storage) can be critical in production of bioactive molecules. Specifically, the low temperature, together with different physical and chemical parameters, in the cheese matrix may have inhibited the production and the following interaction of the bacteriocins with the target spoilage microbe. Favaro et al. (2015) mentioned one other relevant point—the presence of milk fat. We need to consider that fat can vary from 10% to 60% on dry basis in different cheese (Mistry, 2001) and this can be factor influencing effect of bacteriocins as well.

Yes, bacteriocins have a great potential in biopreservation of dairy products, and the fact that nisin is applied with high success is an argument that needs to encourage research in this area of applied microbiology. However, a deep study taking into consideration the complexity of dairy products, nutritional matrix, specificity of process conditions, and different technological parameters needs to be evaluated as a complex research approach.

ACKNOWLEDGMENTS

The author has been supported by grants from CNPq, FAPEMIG, USP, and FoRC.

REFERENCES

Ahmadova, A., Todorov, S.D., Hadji-Sfaxi, I., Choiset, I., Rabesona, H., Messaoudi, S., et al., 2013. Antimicrobial and antifungal activities of *Lactobacillus curvatus* strain isolated from Azerbaijani cheese. Anaerobe 20, 42–49.

Alegría, A., Delgado, S., Roces, C., López, B., Mayo, B., 2010. Bacteriocins produced by wild *Lactococcus lactis* strains isolated from traditional, starter-free cheeses made of raw milk. Int. J. Food Microbiol. 143, 61–66.

Alrakawa, K., Yoshid, S., Aikawa, H., Hano, C., Bolormaa, T., Burenjarg, S., et al., 2016. Production of a bacteriocin-like inhibitory substance by *Leuconostoc mesenteroides* subsp. *dextranicum* 213M0 isolated from Mongolian fermented mare milk, airag. Anim. Sci. J. 87, 449–456.

Avaiyarasi, N.D., Ravindran, A.D., Venkatesh, P., Arul, V., 2016. In vitro selection, characterization and cytotoxic effect of bacteriocin of *Lactobacillus sakei* GM3 isolated from goat milk. Food Control 69, 124–133.

Batdorj, B., Dalgalarrondo, M., Choiset, Y., Pedroche, J., Metro, F., Prevost, H., et al., 2006. Purification and characterization of two bacteriocins produced by lactic acid bacteria isolated from Mongolian airag. J. Appl. Microbiol. 101, 837–848.

Belguesmia, Y., Choiset, Y., Rabesona, H., Baudy-Floch, M., LeBlay, G., Haertlé, T., et al., 2013. Antifungal properties of durancins isolated from *Enterococcus durans* A5-11 and of its synthetic fragments. Lett. Appl. Microbiol. 56, 237–244.

Bockelmann, W., Koslowsky, M., Goerges, S., Scherer, S., Franz, C.M.A.P., Heller, K.J., 2017. Growth inhibition of *Listeria monocytogenes* by bacteriocin-producing *Staphylococcus equorum* SE3 in cheese models. Food Control 71, 50–56.

Centeno, J.A., Menendez, S., Rodriguez-Otero, J.L., 1996. Main microbial flora present in natural starters in Cebreiro raw cow's milk cheese, Northwest Spain. Int. J. Food Microbiol. 33, 307–313.

Cleveland, J., Montville, T.J., Nes, I.F., Chikindas, M.L., 2001. Bacteriocins: safe, natural antimicrobials for food preservation. Int. J. Food Microbiol. 71, 1–20.

Cocolin, L., Foschino, R., Comi, G., Fortina, M.G., 2007. Description of the bacteriocins produced by two strains of *Enterococcus faecium* isolated from Italian goat milk. Food Microbiol. 24, 752–758.

Cotter, P.D., Hill, C., Ross, R.P., 2005. Bacteriocins: developing innate immunity for food. Nat. Rev. Microbiol. 3, 777–788.

Danova, S., Petrov, K., Pavlov, P., Petrova, P., 2005. Isolation and characterization of *Lactobacillus* strains involved in koumiss fermentation. Int. J. Dairy Technol. 58, 100–105.

de Arauz, L.J., Jozala, A.F., Mazzola, P.G., Vessoni Penna, T.C., 2009. Nisin biotechnological production and application: a review. Trends Food Sci. Technol. 20, 146–154.

De Vuyst, L.D., Vandamme, E.J., 1994. Bacteriocins of Lactic Acid Bacteria: Microbiology, Genetics and Applications. Blackie Academic & Professional, London.

Deegan, L.H., Cotter, P.D., Hill, C., Ross, P., 2006. Bacteriocins: biological tools for biopreservation and shelf-life extension. Int. Dairy J. 16, 1058–1071.

Delves-Broughton, J., Blackburn, P., Evans, R.J., Hugenholtz, J., 1996. Applications of the bacteriocin, nisin. Antonie van Leeuwenhoek 69, 193–202.

Dos Santos, K.M.O., Vieira, A.D.S., Rocha, C.R.C., do Nascimento, J.C.F., Lopes, A.C.S., Bruno, L.M., et al., 2014. Brazilian artisanal cheeses as a source of beneficial *Enterococcus faecium* strains: characterization of the bacteriocinogenic potential. Ann. Microbiol. 64, 1463–1471.

Dos Santos, K.M.O., Vieira, A.D.S., Salles, H.O., Oliveira, J.S., Rocha, C.R.C., Borges, M.F., et al., 2015. Safety, beneficial and technological properties of *Enterococcus faecium* isolated from Brazilian cheeses. Braz. J. Microbiol. 46, 237–249.

Enan, G., El-Essawy, A.A., Uyttendaele, M., Debevere, J., 1996. Antibacterial activity of *Lactobacillus plantarum* UG1 isolated from dry sausages: characterization production and bactericidal action of plantaricin UG1. Int. J. Food Microbiol. 30, 189–215.

Ennahar, S., Deschamps, N., Richard, J., 2000. Natural variation in susceptibility of *Listeria* strains to class IIa bacteriocins. Curr. Microbiol. 41, 1–4.

Ennahar, S., Asou, Y., Zendo, T., Sanomoto, K., Ishizaki, A., 2001. Biochemical and genetic evidence for production of enterocins A and B by *Enterococcus faecium* WHE 81. Int. J. Food Microbiol. 70, 291–301.

Farias, M.E., Farias, R.N., de Ruiz Holgado, A.P., Sesma, F., 1996. Purification and N-terminal amino acid sequence of enterocin CRL35, a "pediocin-like" bacteriocin produced by *Enterococcus faecium* CRL35. Lett. Appl. Microbiol. 22, 417–419.

Favaro, L., Basaglia, M., Casella, S., Hue, I., Dousset, X., Franco, B.D.G.M., et al., 2014. Bacteriocinogenic potential and safety evaluation of non starter *Enterococcus faecium* strains isolated from home made white brine cheese. Food Microbiol. 38, 228–239.

Favaro, L., Penna, A.L.B., Todorov, S.D., 2015. Bacteriocinogenic LAB from cheeses—application in biopreservation? Trends Food Sci. Technol. 41, 37–48.

Ferchichi, M., Frere, J., Mabrouk, K., Manai, M., 2001. Lactococcin MMFII, a novel class IIa bacteriocin produced by *Lactococcus lactis* MMFII, isolated from a Tunisian dairy product. FEMS Microbiol. Lett. 205, 49–55.

Fernandes, C.F., Chandanm, R.C., Shahani, K.M., 1992. Fermented dairy products and health. In: Brian, J.B.W. (Ed.), The Lactic Acid Bacteria in Health and Disease. Elsevier Applied Science, London, pp. 297–339.

Foulquié Moreno, M.R., Sarantinopoulos, P., Tsakalidou, E., De Vuyst, L., 2006. The role and application of enterococci in food and health. Int. J. Food Microbiol. 106, 1–24.

Furtado, D.N., Todorov, S.D., Chiarini, E., Destro, M.T., Landgraf, M., Franco, B.D.G. M., 2009. Goat milk and cheeses may be a good source for antilisterial bacteriocin-producing lactic acid bacteria. Biotechnol. Biotechnol. Equip. 23, 775–778.

Furtado, D.N., Todorov, S.D., Landgraf, M., Destro, M.T., Franco, B.D.G.M., 2014a. Bacteriocinogenic *Lactococcus lactis* subsp *lactis* DF04Mi isolated from goat milk: characterization of the bacteriocin. Braz. J. Microbiol. 45, 1541–1550.

Furtado, D.N., Todorov, S.D., Landgraf, M., Destro, M.T., Franco, B.D.G.M., 2014b. Bacteriocinogenic *Lacococcus lactis* isolated from goat milk: evaluation of the probiotic potential. Braz. J. Microbiol. 45, 1047–1054.

Furtado, D.N., Todorov, S.D., Landgraf, M., Destro, M.T., Franco, B.D.G.M., 2015. Bacteriocinogenic *Lactococcus lactis* subsp *lactis* DF04Mi isolated from goat milk: application in the control of *Listeria monocytogenes* in fresh Minas-type goat cheese. Braz. J. Microbiol. 46, 201–206.

Ghrairi, T., Frere, J., Berjeaud, J.M., Manai, M., 2008. Purification and characterisation of bacteriocins produced by *Enterococcus faecium* from Tunisian rigouta cheese. Food Control 19, 162–169.

Giraffa, G., 1995. Enterococcal bacteriocins: their potential use as anti-*Listeria* factors in dairy technology. Food Microbiol. 12, 291–299.

Heller, K.J., 2001. Probiotic bacteria in fermented foods: product characteristics and starter organisms. Am. J. Clin. Nutr. 73, 374–375.

Heng, N.C., Wescombe, P.A., Burton, J.P., Jack, R.W., Tagg, J.R., 2007. The diversity of bacteriocins in Gram-positive bacteria. Bacteriocins. Springer, Berlin, Heidelberg, pp. 45–92.

Heu, S., Oh, J., Kang, Y., Ryu, S., Cho, S.K., Cho, Y., et al., 2001. gly gene cloning and expression and purification of glycinecin A, a bacteriocin produced by *Xanthomonas campestrris* pv. *glycines* 8ra. Appl. Environ. Microbiol. 67, 4105–4110.

Izquierdo, E., Marchioni, E., Aoude-Werner, D., Hasselmann, C., Ennahar, S., 2009. Smearing of soft cheese with *Enterococcus faecium* WHE 81, a multi-bacteriocin producer, against *Listeria monocytogenes*. Food Microbiol. 26, 16–20.

Kwak, H.S., Park, S.K., Kim, D.S., 1996. Biostabilization of kefir with a non lactose-fermenting yeast. J. Dairy Sci. 79, 937–942.

Leal-Sánchez, M.V., Jimenez-Diaz, R., Maldonado-Barragan, A., Garrido-Fernandez, A., Ruiz-Barba, J.L., 2002. Optimization of bacteriocin production by batch fermentation of *Lactobacillus plantarum* LPCO10. Appl. Environ. Microbiol. 68, 4465–4471.

Leroy, F., De Vuyst, L., 2002. Bacteriocin production by *Enterococcus faecium* RZS C5 is cell density limited and occurs in the very early growth phase. Int. J. Food Microbiol. 72, 155–164.

Leroy, F., De Vuyst, L., 2003. A combined model to predict the functionality of the bacteriocin-producing *Lactobacillus sakei* strain CTC 494. Appl. Environ. Microbiol. 69, 1093–1099.

Limsowtin, G.K.Y., Powell, I.B., Parente, E., 1995. In: Cogan, T.M., Accolas, J.-P. (Eds.), Dairy Starter Cultures. VCH Publishers, New York, pp. 101–130.

Lü, X., Hu, P., Dang, Y., Liu, B., 2014. Purification and partial characterization of a novel bacteriocin produced by *Lactobacillus casei* TN-2 isolated from fermented camel milk (Shubat) of Xinjiang Uygur Autonomous region, China. Food Control 43, 276–283.

Manolopoulou, E., Sarantinopoulos, P., Zoidou, E., Aktypis, A., Moschopoulou, E., Kandarakis, I.G., et al., 2003. Evolution of microbial population during traditional Feta cheese manufacture and ripening. Int. J. Food Microbiol. 82, 153–161.

Martínez Viedma, P., Sobrino López, A., Ben Omar, N., Abriouel, H., Lucas López, R., Valdivia, E., et al., 2008. Enhanced bactericidal effect of enterocin AS-48 in combination with high-intensity pulsed-electric field treatment against *Salmonella enterica* in apple juice. Int. J. Food Microbiol. 128, 244–249.

Mattick, A.T.R., Hirsch, A., 1947. Further observation of an inhibitory substance (nisin) from lactic streptococci. Lancet 2, 5–12.

McBride, S.M., Fischetti, V.A., LeBlanc, D.J., Moellering Jr., R.C., Gilmore, M.S., 2007. Genetic diversity among *Enterococcus faecalis*. PLoS One 2, e582.

Miao, J., Guo, H., Ou, Y., Liu, G., Fang, X., Liao, Z., et al., 2014. Purification and characterization of bacteriocin F1, a novel bacteriocin produced by *Lactobacillus paracasei* subsp. *tolerans* FX-6 from Tibetan kefir, a traditional fermented milk from Tibet, China. Food Control 42, 48–53.

Minahk, C.J., Dupuy, F., Morero, R.D., 2004. Enhancement of antibiotic activity by sublethal concentrations of enterocin CRL35. J. Antimicrob. Chemother. 53, 240–246.

Mistry, V.V., 2001. Low fat cheese technology. Int. Dairy J. 11 (4), 413–422.

Morgan, S.M., Hickey, R., Ross, R.P., 2000. Efficient method for the detection of microbially produced antibacterial substances from food systems. J. Appl. Microbiol. 89, 56–62.

Motta, A.S., Brandelli, A., 2003. Influence of growth conditions on bacteriocin production by *Brevibacterium lineus*. Appl. Microbiol. Biotechnol. 62, 163–167.

Murua, A., Todorov, S.D., Vieira, A.D.S., Martinez, R.C.R., Cencič, A., Franco, B.D.G. M., 2013. Isolation and identification of bacteriocinogenic strain of *Lactobacillus plantarum* with potential beneficial properties from donkey milk. J. Appl. Microbiol. 114, 1793–1809.

Nes, I.F., Tagg, J.R., 1996. Novel lantibiotics and their pre-peptides. Antonie Van Leeuwenhoek 69, 89–97.

Olasupo, N.A., 1996. Bacteriocins of *Lactobacillus plantarum* strains from fermented foods. Folia Microbiol. 41, 130–136.

Paula, A.T., Jeronymo-Ceneviva, A.B., Silva, L.F., Todorov, S.D., Franco, B.D.G.M., Penna, A.L.B., 2015. *Leuconostoc mesenteroides* SJRP55: a potential probiotic strain isolated from Brazilian water buffalo mozzarella cheese. Ann. Microbiol. 65, 899–910.

Piard, J.C., Delorme, F., Giraffa, G., Commissaire, J., Desmazeaud, M., 1990. Evidence for a bacteriocin produced by *Lactococcus lactis* CNRZ 481. Neth. Milk Dairy J. 44, 143–158.

Pieterse, R., Todorov, S.D., 2010. Bacteriocins—exploring alternatives to antibiotics in mastitis treatment. A review. Braz. J. Microbiol. 41, 542–562.

Pieterse, R., Todorov, S.D., Dicks, L.M.T., 2008. Bacteriocin ST91KM, produced by *Streptococcus gallolyticus* subsp. *macedonicus* ST91KM, is a narrow-spectrum peptide active against bacteria associated with mastitis in dairy cattle. Can. J. Microbiol. 54, 525–531.

Pingitore, E.V., Todorov, S.D., Sesma, F., Franco, B.D.G.M., 2012. Application of bacteriocinogenic *Enterococcus mundtii* CRL35 and *Enterococcus faecium* ST88Ch in the control of *Listeria monocytogenes* in fresh Minas cheese. Food Microbiol. 32, 38–47.

Pongtharangkul, T., Demirci, A., 2004. Evaluation of agar diffusion bioassay for nisin quantification. Appl. Microbiol. Biotechnol. 65, 268–272.

Powell, J.E., Todorov, S.D., van Reenen, C.A., Dicks, L.N.T., Witthuhn, R.C., 2006. Growth inhibition of *Enterococcus mundtii* in Kefir by *in situ* production of bacteriocin ST8KF. Le Lait 86, 401–405.

Powell, J.E., Witthuhn, R.C., Todorov, S.D., Dicks, L.M.T., 2007. Characterization of bacteriocin ST8KF produced by a kefir isolate *Lactobacillus plantarum* ST8KF. Int. Dairy J. 17, 190–198.

Reis, J.A., Paula, A.T., Casarotti, S.N., Penna, A.L.B., 2012. Lactic acid bacteria antimicrobial compounds: characteristics and applications. Food Eng. Rev. 4, 124–140.

Richard, C., Canon, R., Naghmouchi, K., Bertrand, D., Prevost, H., Drider, D., 2006. Evidence on correlation between number of disulfide bridge and toxicity of class IIa bacteriocins. Food Microbiol. 23, 175–183.

Saloff-Coste, C.J., 1996. Kefir. Nutritional and health benefits of yoghurt and fermented milks. Danone World Newsl. 11, 1–7.

Sarantinopoulos, P., Leroy, F., Leontopoulou, E., Georgalaki, M.D., Kalantzopoulos, G., Tsakalidou, E., et al., 2002. Bacteriocin production by *Enterococcus faecium* FAIR-E 198 in view of its application as adjunct starter in Greek Feta cheese making. Int. J. Food Microbiol. 72, 125–136.

Schirru, S., Todorov, S.D., Favaro, L., Mangia, N.P., Basaglia, M., Casella, S., et al., 2012. Sardinian goat's milk as source of bacteriocinogenic potential protective cultures. Food Control 25, 309–320.

Sears, P.M., Smith, B.S., Stewart, W.K., Gonzales, R.N., Rubio, S.D., Gusik, S.A., et al., 1992. Evaluation of a nisin-based germicidal formulation on teat skin of life cows. J. Dairy Sci. 75, 3185–3190.

Sobrino-López, A., Martín-Belloso, O., 2008. Use of nisin and other bacteriocins for preservation of dairy products. Int. Dairy J. 18, 329–343.

Sulzer, G., Busse, M., 1991. Growth inhibition of *Listeria* spp. on Camembert cheese by bacteria producing inhibitory substances. Int. J. Food Microbiol. 14, 287–296.

Tarelli, G.T., Carminati, D., Girafa, G., 1994. Production of bacteriocins active against *Listeria monocytogenes* and *Listeria innocua* from dairy enterococci. Food Microbiol. 11, 243–252.

Todorov, S., Onno, B., Sorokine, O., Chobert, J.M., Ivanova, I., Dousset, X., 1999. Detection and characterization of a novel antibacterial substance produced by *Lactobacillus plantarum* ST 31 isolated from sourdough. Int. J. Food Microbiol. 48, 167–177.

Todorov, S.D., 2008. Bacteriocin production by *Lactobacillus plantarum* AMA-K isolated from Amasi, a Zimbabwean fermented milk product and study of adsorption of bacteriocin AMA-K to *Listeria* spp. Braz. J. Microbiol. 38, 178–187.

Todorov, S.D., 2009. Bacteriocins from *Lactobacillus plantarum*—production, genetic organization and mode of action. A review. Braz. J. Microbiol. 40, 209–221.

Todorov, S.D., Dicks, L.M.T., 2004. Screening of lactic acid bacteria from South African barley beer for the production of bacteriocin-like compounds. Folia Microbiol. 49, 406–410.

Todorov, S.D., Dicks, L.M.T., 2005. *Lactobacillus plantarum* isolated from molasses produces bacteriocins active against Gram-negative bacteria. Enzyme Microb. Technol. 36, 318–326.

Todorov, S.D., Dicks, L.M.T., 2006. Screening for bacteriocin producer lactic acid bacteria from boza, a traditional cereal beverage from Bulgaria. Characterization of produced bacteriocins. Process Biochem. 41, 11–19.

Todorov, S.D., Franco, B.D.G.M., 2010. *Lactobacillus plantarum*: characterization of the species and application in food production. A review. Food Rev. Int. 26, 205–229.

Todorov, S.D., Danova, S.T., Van Reenen, C.A., Meincken, M., Dinkova, G., Ivanova, I.V., et al., 2006. Characterization of bacteriocin HV219, produced by *Lactococcus lactis* subsp. *lactis* HV219 isolated from human vaginal secretions. J. Basic Microbiol. 46, 226–238.

Todorov, S.D., Nyati, H., Meincken, M., Dicks, L.M.T., 2007. Partial characterization of bacteriocin AMA-K, produced by *Lactobacillus plantarum* AMA-K isolated from naturally fermented milk from Zimbabwe. Food Control 18, 656–664.

Todorov, S.D., Wachsman, M., Tomé, E., Dousset, X., Destro, M.T., Dicks, L.M.T., et al., 2010. Characterisation of an antiviral pediocin-like bacteriocin produced by *Enterococcus faecium*. Food Microbiol. 27, 869–879.

Todorov, S.D., Franco, B.D.G.M., Wiid, I.J., 2013. In vitro study of beneficial properties and safety of lactic acid bacteria isolated from Portuguese fermented meat products. Benef. Microbes 5, 351–366.

Van Reenen, C.A., Chikindas, M.L., Van Zyl, W.H., Dicks, L.M.T., 2003. Characterization and heterologous expression of a class IIa bacteriocin, plantaricin 423 from *Lactobacillus plantarum* 423, in *Saccharomyces cerevisiae*. Int. J. Food Microbiol. 81, 29–40.

Van Wyk, J., Britz, T.J., Myburgh, A.S., 2002. Arguments supporting kefir marketing to the low-income urban African population in South Africa. Agrekon 41, 43–62.

Venema, K., Venema, G., Kok, J., 1995. Lactococcal bacteriocins: mode of action and immunity. Trends Microbiol. 3, 299–304.

Von Mollendorff, J.W., Todorov, S.D., Dicks, L.M.T., 2006. Comparison of bacteriocins produced by lactic acid bacteria isolated from boza, a cereal-based fermented beverage from the Balkan Peninsula. Curr. Mirobiol. 53, 209–216.

Wachsman, M.B., Farías, M.E., Takeda, E., Sesma, F., De Ruiz Holdago, A., De Torres, R.A., et al., 1999. Antiviral activity of enterocin CRL35 against herpes viruses. Int. J. Antimicrob. Agents 12, 293–299.

Wachsman, M.B., Castilla, V., Holgado, A.P.D., De Torres, R.A., Sesma, F., Coto, C.E., 2003. Enterocin CRL35 inhibits late stages of HSV-1 and HSV-2 replication in vitro. Antiviral Res. 58, 17–24.

Wang, J., Zhang, W., Zhong, Z., Wei, A., Bao, Q., Zhang, Y., et al., 2012. Gene expression profile of probiotic *Lactobacillus casei* Zhang during the late stage of milk fermentation. Food Control 25, 321–327.

Wiedemann, I., Breukink, E., van Kraaij, C., Kuipers, O.P., Bierbaum, G., de Kruijff, B., et al., 2001. Specific binding of nisin to the peptidoglycan precursor lipid II combines pore formation and inhibition of cell wall biosynthesis for potent antibiotic activity. J. Biol. Chem. 276, 1772–1779.

Wulijideligen, A.T., Hara, K., Arakawa, K., Nakano, H., Miyamoto, T., 2012. Production of bacteriocin by *Leuconostoc mesenteroides* 406 isolated from Mongolian fermented mare's milk, airag. Anim. Sci. J. 83, 704–711.

Wulijideligen, S., Miyamoto, T., 2011. Screening and identification of lactic acid bacteria from airag for antifungal activity. J. Anim. Vet. Adv. 10, 2751–2757.

Xie, Y., An, H., Hao, Y., Qin, Q., Huang, Y., Luo, Y., et al., 2011. Characterization of an anti-Listeria bacteriocin produced by *Lactobacillus plantarum* LB-B1 isolated from koumiss, a traditionally fermented dairy product from China. Food Control 22, 1027–1031.

Zanella, R.C., Castro Lima, M.D.J., Tegani, L.S., Hitomi, A., de Cunto Brandileone, M.C., Pilazzo, I.C.V., et al., 2006. Emergence of VanB phenotype-vanA genotype in vancomycin-resistant enterococci in Brazilian hospital. Braz. J. Microbiol. 37, 117–118.

CHAPTER 9

Artisanal Products Made With Raw Milk

Giuseppe Licitra[1], Margherita Caccamo[2] and Sylvie Lortal[3]
[1]Department of Agriculture, Nutrition and Environment, University of Catania, Catania, Italy
[2]CoRFiLaC, Ragusa, Italy
[3]INRA, Agrocampus Ouest, UMR1253 Science et Technologie du lait et de l'œuf, Rennes, France

9.1 ACTUAL PROBLEMATIC OF RAW-MILK CHEESES PRODUCTION

In recent decades, raw-milk cheeses have been categorized as "risky" foods. In the developed countries, raw-milk cheeses are almost banned, even in Europe, despite the exceptional derogation of Directive 92/46 Article 8 of the EEC (European Commission, 1992).

In 1998, a trade group representing American industrial cheesemakers began actively lobbying the US Food and Drug Administration (FDA) (U.S. FDA, 1998) to require that all cheeses produced and marketed in the United States be pasteurized (Halweil, 2000; Kummer, 2000). Big cheesemakers companies also lobbied the EU to ban raw-milk cheese production and sale (Lichfield, 1999).

Pasteurization as well as thermization ostensibly allows the industrial producers to eliminate the external risk factors and to focus on factors under their control. In addition, pasteurized milk also affords predictability and controllability in the production process, allowing industrial cheesemakers to reduce wastage, to maximize output, and to insure price competitiveness. These fears, and related values, explain why industrial producers work with pasteurized milk, but not why they seek to make pasteurized milk mandatory for all cheesemakers (West, 2008).

Furthermore, we need to consider that very few raw-milk cheesemakers (small scale and/or family cheese factories) could afford the purchase of pasteurizer even if they wished to acquire it (Kummer, 2000; Lichfield, 1999). Offsetting such investment costs would require the expansion of volume (larger scale), effectively transforming them into industrial producers (Lichfield, 1999).

175

Mandatory pasteurization would eliminate any link with the territory. The use of raw milk imposes constraints (breaking ties) in time and places of cheesemaking. Raw-milk cheeses provide a very restricted timeline: farming, milking, and cheesemaking are allocated in neighboring places and occur within a few hours.

The use of pasteurized milk enables industrial dairies to buy milk from geographically distant farmers and or companies, even from other countries. This last condition, in particular, require heat treatments of the milk and the standardization of the quality of the milk itself, in order to reduce, as already mentioned, the external risk factors. The industry is rightly forced to simplify processes to govern and to optimize productivity, the yield.

To emphasize, the importance of worldwide traditional cheeses does not mean a lack of support for industrial products. There is need to educate consumers, the press, and opinion leaders to distinguish the difference. Industrial cheeses have reached considerably good quality, but the meaning of the term "quality" must be interpreted in a different way when we talk about traditional or industrial cheeses. The industrial ones deliver nutritious food (e.g., protein, calcium, etc.) and offer convenience at an economical price to the majority of consumers. These products are standardized, deliver consistent quality every day, and most of the time are fresh cheeses with mild flavors. The industrial cheeses are usually produced on a large scale by big companies at any place in the world, and producers are able to obtain almost the same final product. Conversely, the traditional raw-milk cheeses are niche products that are usually handmade and produced at the farm or village level and are unique expression of the symbiotic interaction between human resources, the culture of rural communities, and nature.

In summary, the traditional production companies and industrial ones are totally different production worlds and often poles apart. It would be reasonable to think that these so different systems should not be subject to the same rules, albeit with the common goal of producing healthy products for consumers.

It is also necessary to point out that in any case, regardless of the milk heat treatments, the production of milk and the farming systems must undergo regulations that guarantee the healthiness of the milk and the presence of animals free from any disease (zoonoses) that can affect health by man (e.g., the so-called hygienic package from the EU regulation No. 852/2004 and 853/2004 in Europe). We reiterate that no matter if you produce cheese with raw or pasteurized milk, for which the milk used to produce raw-milk cheeses must in itself respect the standard hygiene parameters to guarantee consumers.

There is sufficient scientific evidence that the consumption of traditional raw-milk cheeses is safe, and in any case not riskier than pasteurized milk cheeses. Just as it is scientifically proved, as we will see later in this chapter, that mandatory pasteurization would eliminate the highly distinctive aromas, textures, colors, and flavors that raw-milk cheeses afford, all made possible by the biodiversity factors (West, 2008).

Many international governmental authorities, industrial producers, traditional producers, journalists, opinion leaders, as well as the international scientific community, continue to maintain active debate on the use of raw milk vs pasteurized milk to produce safe cheeses.

It is reasonable to think that a debate over raw milk vs pasteurized milk for cheesemaking is not the issue. "Raw milk vs pasteurized milk" is a false problem or at the least it is not "the problem." The real issue to determine the "food safety" is to take into account the overall production systems and not just the use or not of raw milk, including issues related to postproduction phases, during distribution, in-store and even in-home refrigerators (postcontaminations). Several authors affirmed that outbreaks of milk-borne diseases have occurred despite pasteurization, caused either by improper pasteurization or by recontamination (Altekruse et al., 1998; Delgado daSilva et al., 1998; Hartman, 1997).

The use of pasteurization (discovered in 1865 by the French scientist Louis Pasteur), to ensure the safety of fluid milk, is perhaps the most significant public health achievement for the last centuries. Prior the advent of milk pasteurization, serious illnesses, including typhoid fever, scarlet fever, diphtheria, tuberculosis, and brucellosis, were associated with raw-milk consumption (Donnelly, 2005).

Drinking raw milk is, however, not comparable with the consumption of raw-milk cheeses, because in the traditional systems of production of raw-milk cheeses, a multiplicity of practices are used (Johnson et al., 1990) beyond pasteurization or heat treatment that significantly contribute to the microbiological safety of cheese.

Many factors are influencing microbial activity during raw-milk cheesemaking and aging process generating synergic effects for microbial pathogens inhospitality, injury of microbial cell, and generation of bacteriostatic and/or bactericidal actions. The main factors in synthesis are time and level of pH and acidity; temperature; oxygen; redox potential through the overall process; antimicrobial activity from fresh raw milk: content and activity of key enzymes including lactoperoxidase, lysozyme, lactoferrin, xantinoxidase, and the level of sulfhydryl groups and carbon dioxide (Fox et al., 2004); competition for nutrients due to the elevated number of different microorganisms in raw milk; microbial production of bacteriocin in situ or bacteriocin-like substances (Abee et al.,1995; Elotmani et al., 2002; Genigeorgis et al., 1991; Johnson et al., 1990); speed of curd acidification (fast curd acidification to reach pH 5—5.5 is unfavorable to pathogenic microorganisms); time and level of the temperature of the curd at cooking, molding and stretching stages; cheese composition throughout the overall process: a_w and osmotic pressure, moisture and ingredients' concentration (salt, sugar and spice), free fatty acid (FFA) and monoglycerides (Sun et al., 2002; Wang and Johnson, 1992), casein fragment α- and β-casein-derived peptides released in water-soluble extract (Rizzello et al., 2005).

For these reasons in Europe, under the Directive 92/46 Article 8 of the EEC (European Commission, 1992), member states may grant derogations for the manufacture of cheese with a period of aging or ripening of at least 60 days, laying down the health rules for the production and placing on the market of raw-milk, heat-treated and milk-based products. Member states should identify which requirements of this directive are likely to affect the manufacture of milk-based products with traditional characteristics, leveling off typical flavors, aromas, and smells, conferred by natural dairy microflora. The most important cases are related to traditional tools on cheesemaking and aging, and aging rooms. Finally, the FDA recently have also introduced the concept of "equivalence of pasteurization," to consider other factors that could make the cheese safe.

In any production system, raw-milk screening, good manufacturing practices, and postproduction control system, able to avoid environmental contamination of cheeses, may be the most effective strategy to improve and control products safety.

9.2 THE COMPLEXITY OF TRADITIONAL PRODUCTION SYSTEMS OF RAW-MILK CHEESES

Traditional cheeses are produced worldwide, in direct relationship with nature, and, even if unconsciously, they are an example of sustainable agriculture. The European Community has been careful toward rural reality of its member countries considering that the production, manufacture, and distribution of agricultural products and foodstuffs play an important role. It has defined a common agricultural policy for the diversification of agricultural production and encouraged to achieve a better balance between supply and demand on the markets, whereas the promotion of products having certain characteristics could be of considerable benefit to the rural economy, in particular to less-favored or remote areas, by improving the incomes of farmers and by retaining the rural population in these areas [Council Regulation (EEC), 1992].

Consumers tend to give greater importance to the quality of foodstuffs rather than to quantity. Considering the wide variety of products marketed and the abundance of information concerning them provided to consumers, they need clear and succinct information regarding the origin of the product in order to be able to make the best choice. They ask for specific products generating a growing demand for agricultural products or foodstuffs with an identifiable geographical origin [Council Regulation (EEC), 1992]. The desire to protect agricultural products or foodstuffs with an identifiable geographical origin has led certain member states to introduce "registered designations of origin." These have proved successful with producers, who have secured higher incomes in return for a genuine effort to improve quality, and with consumers, who can purchase high quality products with guarantees as to the method of production and origin [CCouncil Regulation (EEC), 1992].

Considering these successful results, Council of the European Community has decided to adopt the Council Regulation (EEC) (1992), that define, nowadays, the two most important protections of product or foodstuff characteristics linked to the existing geographical origin, named, ***protected designation of origin (PDO) and protected geographical indication (PGI)***, with the following specifications:

1. **PDO**: The name of a region, a specific place or, in exceptional cases, a country is used to describe an agricultural product or a foodstuff:
   a. originating in that region, specific place, or country, and
   b. whose quality or characteristics are essentially or exclusively due to a particular geographical environment with its inherent natural and human factors, and whose production, processing, and preparation take place in the defined geographical area;

2. **PGI**: The name of a region, a specific place or, in exceptional cases, a country is used to describe an agricultural product or a foodstuff:
   a. originating in that region, specific place, or country, and

b. which possesses a specific quality, reputation, or other characteristics attributable to that geographical origin and whose production **and/or** processing **and/or** preparation take place in the defined geographical area.

The difference between the two recognition, in few words, is due to the fact that the PDO products must take place in the defined geographical area *(production, processing, and preparation)* and give specific importance to the *"natural and human factors."* The PGI is a little bit more generic and not all the phases *"production and/or processing and/or preparation"* must take place in the defined geographical area. In total, 186 cheeses got to date in Europe the recognition of PDO distributed by country as follows: Italy 49, French 45, Spain 26, Greece 21, Portugal 11, United Kingdom 10, Austria 6, Germany 6, Slovenian 4, Netherlands 4, Poland 3, Belgium 1, Ireland 1, Romania 1, and 14 countries have no PDO cheeses. Among these, only 8% of the PDO regulations demand that the milk be pasteurized to produce PDO cheeses; 39% require to use only raw milk; and 53% allow the use of raw or pasteurized milk, among the latter, many small artisan producers continue to use raw milk.

In total, 41 cheeses got to date in Europe the recognition of **PGI** distributed by country as follows: Slovakia 8, French 7, United Kingdom 6, Netherlands 3, Czech Republic 3, Germany 3, Spain 2, Poland 2, Denmark 2, Lithuania 2, Portugal 2, Italy 1, Sweden 1, and 15 countries have no PGI cheeses. The overall cheese production in EU—28 countries in the 2015—amounts to around 9.2 million of tons. The biggest cheese producers are Germany (2.3 million tons equivalent to 25% of the total EU production), France (1.8 million tons, 20%), and Italy (1.2 million tons, 13%).

It is interesting to notice that in Italy, the production of PDO cheese accounts for approximately 42% of total cheese production (0.5 million tons), whereas in France only 14% are PDO cheeses (0.25 million tons), and in Germany less than 5% of the total country production. In Italy PDO and PGI cheeses absorb 70% of the national milk production. This shows how deeply rooted the culture of quality food in Italy and the link with the territory of origin are. In Italy in fact, the first 10 PDO cheeses, ordered by produced quantity, account for approximately 95% of the total production. Consequently, the other 39 PDO cheeses as a whole account for only 5% of the national PDO production, with an average production of about 680 t/cheese. Despite the limited quantity produced, these cheeses play a social and cultural role that goes far beyond the commercial value of the products. It follows that even in per capita cheese consumption, Italians buy and consume a highest percentage of PDO cheeses (approximately 10 kg/capita). Italy in EU-28 is the seventh country for cheese consumption with 21.8 kg/capita. The countries that most consume cheeses are France with 26.3 kg; Germany, Luxembourg, and Iceland with 24.2 kg; and Greece with 23.4 kg/capita.

Outside Europe, there are no common policies in defense of the areas of origin and of traditional products. Individual states have developed specific policies and not always of international relevance. Nevertheless, hundreds of traditional cheeses are produced worldwide, *in direct relationship with nature, and, even if unconsciously, as example of sustainable agriculture.* These products have contributed as part of the diet for billions of people for centuries. All around the world, each traditional cheese originates from complex systems related to the various "biodiversity factors" applied, such as the environment, the macro- and microclimate, the natural pasture, the breed of the animals (often autochthonous breeds), the use of raw milk and its natural microflora, the use of natural coagulants, the use of natural ingredients (e.g., saffron, pepper, herbs, sugar, flour, spice), the use of traditional equipment, the natural aging conditions including the ancestral practice of sun-drying, and the overall expertise of the cheesemakers and ripeners (Licitra, 2010a).

Manufacture using traditional systems, based on empirical experience of the producers, is much more complex than producing with standard and simplified systems applied in large industrial systems, to reduce risks on productivity. Every traditional production system is characterized by the sequence of countless biological and natural processes, each one marked by their own natural characteristics and rhythms. The cheesemakers and ripeners have to understand, support, and coordinate the delicate harmony between the characteristic of the raw materials, the sequence of the actions, and timing of the cheesemaking and of the aging process in order to produce the most exciting form of the milk, the "cheese."

Some examples may help to clarify the previous paragraph:

- To prepare a balanced diet for the animals fed on pasture (with dozens of wild forage species) is much more difficult than preparing a total mixed ration (TMR). As a consequence, the aromatic and sensory components of the grazing animals' milk are much more complex, with many positive effects on the quality of the final products (including e.g., cheeses, meat).

- Producing a cheese using raw milk with its enzymatic kit and the multiplicity of microorganisms present, compared to a pasteurized milk, inoculated with the starter cultures composed of a reduced number of microorganisms, leads to completely different products both from a sensory and aromatic point of view. Thermal elevations related to pasteurization, denature most of the enzymatic kit of raw milk, determine the volatilization of several odorous components, and nearly erase the natural microflora present in milk.
- The use of traditional wooden equipment in the production of cheeses with its biofilms composed by countless lactic microorganisms, compared to nearly sterile equipment made with steel or plastic, also determines a different quality of the final products.
- A cheese ripened in a cave (with its microflora, moisture, temperature, and natural ventilation) is much more complex than in the cold room with controlled and standardized conditions.

In summary, standardized animal feeding (no grazing), pasteurized milk, use of sterile equipment, and ripening cheeses in cold room are much easier, controllable, and programmable, resulting from laboratory recipes, without any link with the territory of origin. This results in mass-product, standardized, and often with anonymous flavor cheeses. They can be produced anywhere in the world, ignoring the historical, cultural, and human experience of local realities passed down for hundreds of generations to the present days.

Each biodiversity factor involved in the traditional production systems will synergistically influence the quality of the final products, with their intense and diversified flavors even within cheese variety, depending on the specific origin of the product (Licitra, 2010a). It is reasonable to assume that the daily empiric practices have led the historical cheesemakers and ripeners to select practices, tools, and places that most would allow the production of good products. In few words, "learning by doing" where, the need to store milk, passion and creativity have led them to establish production processes that have lasted over time for thousands of years. Therefore, the traditional systems need more attention and respect and cannot be canceled by law for a hypothetical risk on food safety, never deeply scientifically demonstrated, and to favor the interests of big industrial holdings (Licitra, 2010a). Only during last decades, scientists started to study the complexity and the real meaning of traditional cheese production and ripening systems.

9.3 MAIN BIODIVERSITY FACTORS EFFECT ON TRADITIONAL CHEESEMAKING AND RIPENING

9.3.1 The Influence of Native Pasture on the Aroma, Sensory Profile, and Health Properties of Dairy Products

Traditional cheeses are typically produced in small factories or on farms using a combination of preserved feeds and fresh pasture to feed animals. The sensory properties of the cheeses produced in this way often reflect the characteristics of the fresh pasture plants (Dumont and Adda, 1978; Mariaca et al., 1997; Viallon et al., 2000; Bugaud et al., 2001b) and the contribution of the natural microbiota from both the animal and cheese-making environment.

The impact of consumption of fresh pasture plants or different types of pasture plants on the composition of the volatile compounds in cheese (Dumont and Adda, 1978; de Frutos et al., 1991; Mariaca et al., 1997; Bugaud et al., 2001a,b,c) has been reported for several cheese varieties.

Ragusano cheeses obtained from milk produced by cows fed with native pasture plants presented more odor-active compounds compared to cheese made from milk of cows fed with TMR, confirming the strong link between product and territory (Carpino et al., 2004b). In 4-month-old pasture cheese, 27 odor-active compounds were identified, whereas only 13 from TMR. The pasture cheeses were much richer in odor-active aldehyde, ester, and terpenoid. A total of eight unique aroma-active compounds (i.e., not reported in other cheeses evaluated by gas chromatography—olfactometry) were detected in Ragusano cheese made with milk by cows fed with native Sicilian pasture plants. These compounds were two aldehydes ([E,E]-2,4-octadienal and dodecanal), two esters (geranyl acetate and [E]-methyl jasmonate), one sulfur compound (methional), and three terpenoid compounds (1-carvone, L(−) carvone, and citronellol).

In a subsequent study, Carpino et al. (2004a) on the same samples of Carpino et al. (2004b) reported that sensory analysis (performed by trained panelists) confirmed the difference between the two experimental treatments (native pasture vs TMR). The color of Ragusano cheeses produced from milk of cows consuming fresh native pasture plants (due to the transfer of β-carotene and related compounds from the diet) was much more yellow than cheeses from TMR-fed cows. The intensity of the odor attributes of floral and green/herbaceous were higher ($P <$ 0.05) for the 4-month pasture compared to TMR cheeses. This research demonstrated clearly that some unique odor-active compounds found in pasture plants can be transferred to the cheese and identified by human beings.

A study was conducted on Piacentinu Ennese, a traditional Sicilian ewes' milk cheese produced in Sicily (Horne et al., 2005). The experiment was conducted by comparing cheeses produced experimentally with raw milk with traditional methods (including animal on pasture) and pasteurized milk plus starter culture with nontraditional methods. Cheeses made from raw milk contained a higher level of terpenes. Belitz and Grosch (1986) noted that terpenes in cheeses are of plant and not of microbial origin. Reducing the influence of local pasture may in turn reduce or eliminate the ability to trace a cheese to a specific location or farm (Bugaud et al., 2001b), causing the cheese to lose some of its identity. This link to the territory of production is of particular importance because consumers may be drawn to the individuality that a cheese obtains from local pastures (Licitra et al., 2000; Bellesia et al., 2003).

It has been shown that grazing cows resulted in conjugated linoleic acid (CLA) concentrations 5.7 times higher in milk compared with milk from cows fed with diets containing preserved forage and grain at 50:50 ratio (Dhiman et al., 2000).

The α-tocopherol concentration in fresh pasture is four to five times higher than that found in a typical TMR according to National Research Council values (NRC, 7th edn. 2001). Nevertheless, pasture is unique in terms of increase of polyunsaturated fatty acids and fat-soluble antioxidants. Furthermore, cows fed with fresh pasture produce milk with increased amounts of CLA (Kay et al., 2003).

In agreement with the abovementioned research, it was found that CLA, vaccenic acid, eicosapentaenoic acid (EPA), and docosahexaenoic acid (DHA) significantly ($P < 0.05$) increased in plasma and in milk as a function of the proportion of pasture in the diet (La Terra et al., 2006). Such changes in fatty acid composition were accompanied by a concomitant increase in the concentrations of α-tocopherol and β-carotene both in plasma and milk. No change in the retinol content was found in the plasma and milk samples. The increase in EPA, DHA, and CLA, β-carotene and α-tocopherol in plasma may have a beneficial impact not only for milk and meat quality but also for animal and human health. The level of CLA also increases in the cheeses when they are obtained from raw milk produced by grazing animals.

9.3.2 Effects of Heat Treatments of Milk to Produce Cheese

9.3.2.1 Physical, Chemical, and Microbiological Properties Related to Milk Heat Treatments (Raw/Pasteurized)

Until nowadays, a lively debate persists on the use of raw milk for the production of cheese, in contrast with different international regulations and the industrial lobby, which tend to impose the pasteurization of milk, for the reasons presented previously. In the last decade, scientific research has addressed the effects of milk heat treatments on its physical, chemical, and microbiological properties.

The specific goal of pasteurization is the total destruction of pathogens. However, heat treatment of milk generates other consequences such as the elimination or the reduction of the various microorganisms [species and strains of indigenous microbiota, starter lactic acid bacteria (SLAB), and non-SLAB (NSLAB)] present in milk and some physical–chemical or enzymatic modifications which are important in cheesemaking and ripening.

Probably one of the major points that the researchers have ignored is the antimicrobial activity of fresh milk with its enzymatic kit including lactoferrin, lysozyme, and lactoperoxidase. These enzymes are inhibitory to the growth of some pathogens. They are heat labile and deactivated at various degrees by pasteurization.

Grappin et al. (1997) in a literature review with the objective of understanding the influence of pasteurization on cheese ripening and on the quality of end product report as consequences of milk pasteurization: a partial or total activation or inhibition of the plasmin/plasminogen complex (increase of plasmin activity), cathepsin D, lipoprotein lipase (LPL), alkaline phosphatase. Enzymes from psychrotrophic bacteria, acid phosphatase, and xanthine oxidase, which may be active during ripening, withstand pasteurization; a slight (7%) denaturation of serum protein and little or no modification of the cheesemaking properties (acidification by lactic acid bacteria, slight increase in clotting time, and reduction of curd firmness and syneresis); possible disruption of fat globules membrane.

Also Delores et al. (2010) affirm that milk pasteurization reduces lipolysis and proteolysis, both of which generate a diversity of odiferous compounds, including acids, alcohols, ketones, esters, and amino acids. Beuvier et al. (1997) stated that Swiss-type cheeses made with the raw-milk microbiota showed a more extensive proteolysis and a stronger propionic acid fermentation leading to more pronounced flavor. A number of NSLAB have been shown to possess lipolytic (El-Soda et al., 1986) or esterolytic (Piakietwiecz, 1987) activity. Williams and Banks (1997) found that NSLAB isolated from Cheddar cheese had esterase activity, which was the highest against triglycerides containing short-chain fatty acids and suggested that NSLAB have the potential to contribute to the release of fatty acids during the ripening of Cheddar cheese.

The importance of indigenous microbiota and the relative elimination or reduction by pasteurization was underlined by several authors: Andrews et al. (1987) reported that indigenous milk lipase is almost completely inactivated by pasteurization (72°C—15 s). McSweeney et al. (1993) in Cheddar cheese remark that NSLAB are more important and diversified in raw milk with its wide range of hydrolytic enzymes. In Swiss-type cheese, Demarigny et al. (1997) stressed the "Specificity of the flora according to the origin of the milk," and Beuvier et al. (1997) indicated that "In raw milk cheese higher populations of facultatively hetero-fermentative lactobacilli, propionibacteria and enterococci are present."

Data on the antimicrobial properties are shown by Genigeorgis et al. (1991). Some lactic acid bacteria, especially those producing bacteriocins or bacteriocin-like substances, have been shown to inhibit *L. monocyto-genes* growth in culture media and fermented milks. Messens et al. (2003) suggested that the rate of bacteriocin inactivation increased with high temperature because this is probably a result of a higher protease activity or a more pronounced cell—bacteriocin or bacteriocin—bacteriocin inter-action. Suma et al. (1998) stated that the heat-stable bacteriocins, com-bined with their ability to inhibit a wide range of bacteria comprising Gram-positive and negative food poisoning and spoilage bacteria, repre-sent a good opportunity for its use as a biopreservative in food systems.

9.3.2.2 Flavor in Raw and Pasteurized Milk Cheeses

Taste and aroma are very important features of cheese. They are consid-ered by consumers as important criteria for choosing cheese at the time of purchase. The typical cheese flavor results from lipolysis, proteolysis, and further degradation of amino acids by starter cultures and NSLAB. The concentrations of low molecular weight peptides and free amino acids have considerable influence on the cheese flavor (Lowrie, Lawrence, 1972). These products of proteolysis either contribute directly to flavor (Visser, 1993) or act as precursors of flavor compounds. In addition, the concentration of FFAs, especially the short chain ones, is responsible for the characteristic cheese flavor (Kanawjia et al., 1995).

Pasteurized milk cheeses have always lower levels of FFAs than raw-milk cheeses: lipolysis was 50% lower in Cheddar (McSweeney et al., 1993); 38% lower in Manchego (Gaya et al., 1990).

In an experiment on ripening of Cheddar cheeses made from raw milk or pasteurized milk (Pa) and from pasteurized milk added of 1% (PR1), 5% (PR5), and 10% (PR10) of raw milk, Rehman et al. (2000) showed that lipolysis was considerably higher in raw, PR10, PR5, and PR1 cheeses than in Pa cheese. The indigenous milk LPL and lipases of the indigenous NSLAB may have contributed to a higher level of FFAs in PR1, PR5, PR10, and raw cheeses than Pa cheese. It is very interesting to note, in these experiment conditions, as with the addition of only 1% of raw milk, the results are significantly different compared to only pasteurized milk.

The effect of milk pasteurization on flavor properties of seven French cheeses (Brie, Coulommier, Camembert, San Nectair, Muenster, Chevrè, Blue) has been studied by Delores et al. (2010), who highlighted relevant differences in the flavor characteristics in pasteurized-milk cheese compared to the flavor profiles of raw-milk cheese. Further proves, regardless of who are better or worse, that the raw-milk cheeses are different than pasteurized milk cheeses.

Goméz-Ruiz et al. (2002) observed that in Manchego cheese, FFAs behaved differently during the ripening period in the artisanal and industrial cheeses. At the end of ripening, FFA values were much higher in the artisanal cheese samples than in the industrial ones.

The authors observed furthermore that the odor attributes evaluated in artisanal and industrial Manchego cheeses (aged 2 months) were significantly different with higher values for "intensity, brine, rancid, pungent, and dry hay" in artisanal cheeses and for "milk and butter" in the industrial ones. Volatile compounds on Manchego cheeses aged 12 months have shown a further and even more marked difference, with the presence of a higher number for the artisanal cheeses.

Piacentinu Ennese cheeses made from raw milk, compared to cheeses made from pasteurized milk, contained a more diverse group of volatile organic compounds, especially with respect to terpenes, and had significantly stronger overall aroma intensities in most categories: green/herbaceous, floral, butyric, mushroom/earthy, roasted, hay, spicy aromas, and off-odors, except fruity (Horne et al., 2005).

The Malatya (a farmhouse Halloumi-type) cheeses made with raw milk contained higher levels of acids, esters, and lactones and lower levels of aldehydes and sulfur compounds than did the cheeses made with pasteurized milk. The authors in the experimental design included also scalding treatment (60, 70, 80, or 90°C) of the curd. Results suggest that the pasteurization of cheese milk had a greater effect on volatile composition of cheese than scalding temperature of the curd (Hayaloglu et al., 2007a).

Raw-milk cheeses usually have a more intense flavor than the corresponding pasteurized milk cheeses (Lau et al., 1991) and reach an optimum flavor faster. These results are confirmed also by Awad (2006) in the Egyptian Ras cheese produced using a mixture of cow and buffalo milks (80:20), raw or pasteurized (63°C/30 min). The author observed that the increase in water-soluble nitrogen was at a higher rate in raw-milk cheese than in pasteurized milk cheeses throughout ripening. The level of free amino groups was higher in the raw-milk cheese than in pasteurized milk cheeses at all stages of ripening. Raw-milk cheese consistently showed higher FFA levels throughout ripening. Raw-milk cheeses at 60, 120, and 180 days of ripening received higher scores for flavor intensity and flavor and texture acceptability compared to pasteurized milk cheeses, but both aged cheeses were considered acceptable. The flavor intensity increased as the ripening period progressed. The typical Ras cheese flavor was not noticed in aged cheeses made from pasteurized milk. This might be due to their relatively lower levels of free amino groups and FFAs and lower level of short chain of FFA (Kanawjia et al., 1995).

9.3.3 Traditional Equipment

Farmers and cheesemakers since prehistoric times have used tools from natural materials to collect, transform milk and to age the cheeses. Most of artisanal cheeses are produced by small family farmers leaving *in less favored areas* with limited resource, so also cheesemakers historically have had to adapt to the use of equipment and places that nature offered them. Wood has been safely used for centuries in direct contact with food. In cheese- and wine-making, wooden boards and barrels have been indispensable in traditional production.

Because of its irregular surface (crevices, cracks, etc.) and its high porosity, wood is not theoretically easy to clean, at least according to hygiene standards imposed by regulations adopted by various states in different continents. Later we will see that some scientific research shows that wood offers greater cleaning guarantees, or at least not lower than the plastic and stainless steel. Nevertheless, there are objections to the use of wood in direct contact with food, as it is usually considered less hygienic than other smooth or synthetic materials. To date, there is no evidence that any food-borne disease has been fostered by the proper use of wood, considering hygienic standards for production, storage, and applications (Lortal et al., 2014; Aviat et al., 2016).

Wooden tools are an example of a great need of scientific knowledge. The complexity of biofilms that set up on the wood surface, with hundreds of species, clones, strains, is an absolute example of biodiversity (Licitra et al., 2007; Mariani et al., 2007; Lortal et al., 2009). Wood therefore cannot be replaced by metals or plastics materials, without any demonstration of obvious risk or imposing by law, by simply stating that an appropriate use of starter cultures (with few microorganisms) on pasteurized milks solve the problems.

The traditional equipment (from wood or other natural material) cannot be considered simple containers, or insignificant tools with mechanical functions, therefore easy to replace, because they represent one of the most important source of biodiversity to produce traditional cheeses. The replacement of wooden or natural utensils by other materials, like polypropylene, high-density polyethylene, or stainless steel, will change the characteristics of cheese, affecting the traditional flavor and texture (Galinari et al., 2014).

Wood in contact with raw milk and cheeses is covered by a microbial biofilm. Wooden vat, used for milk coagulation, and wooden shelves, used for cheese ripening, have been studied mainly in the last decade. It has been demonstrated an effective interaction between wooden vat and milk (solid vs liquid), and between wooden shelves and cheeses (solid vs solid or semisolid) where the contact is extended for weeks, even months, with stabilized pH and ambient humidity.

Biofilms of wooden vats have been studied for Italian Ragusano PDO (Licitra et al., 2007; Lortal et al., 2009), Vastella della Valle dl Belice PDO (Scatassa et al., 2015), Caciocavallo Palermitano (Settanni et al., 2012; Di Grigoli et al., 2015; Scatassa et al., 2015), and for the French Cantal and Salers cheeses (Richard, 1997; Didienne et al., 2012). In all these studies, the researchers showed a very efficient and rapid inoculation (in few minutes) of desirable lactic acid and ripening bacteria from wood biofilm into milk, contributing to acidification and the final cheese characteristic, and thus safe for cheese ripening (Lortal et al., 2014). Furthermore, the results underline a large biodiversity of biofilms microorganisms not only between the different types of cheeses studied but also within the same cheese variety, among different wooden vats (*tine* or *gerle*) used in different cheese plant. The detected biodiversity confirms and demonstrates the strong characterization of the territorial origin of the products.

Cheesemakers and ripeners are very careful in choosing the wooden shelves from the sawmill. The wood for its intrinsic hygroscopic properties can lose or retain humidity depending on the temperature and ambient humidity. Wood must be correctly dried (15%–18% humidity), which might require 3–5 months when done under natural environmental conditions. No chemical treatments should have been applied to wood. A shelf which is too humid favors mold defects on the surface of cheese, and sometimes *Pseudomonas fluorescens*. If too dry, it favors the development of thick, strong rinds, and red defects (*Serratia*).

Wooden shelves have two different roles: one related to the biofilms microbial ecology of the cheese surface and the other related to hydric exchange between cheese surfaces and cellar air humidity. Both factors will influence the correct setup of the rind and its microbial ecology (Lortal et al., 2014). Wooden shelves used for ripening of Reblochon de Savoie PDO (Mariani et al., 2007), Swiss cheese (Schuler, 1994), Turkey Kulek cheese (Dervisoglu and Yazici, 2001) have been studied and the microorganisms of the biofilms characterized. Furthermore, most likely, the water flux from the cheese to the shelves also carries with it nutrients, microorganisms, and antimicrobial components (Miller et al., 1996; Schulz, 1395; Lortal et al., 2014).

The compounds most frequently studied belong to a small number of classes: phenols, lignans, tannins, stilbenes, flavonoids, and terpenoids (Pearce, 1996). Also Dumont et al. (1974) and Bosset et al. (1997) demonstrated the presence, in cheeses, of specific volatile compounds, in particular terpenic molecules, after contact with wood. Their effects are described as antimicrobial against bacteria, but it is not clear whether these are bacteriostatic or bactericidal (Mourey and Canillac, 2002), usually depending on the concentration of the antimicrobial component and the microorganism strain.

The presence of pathogens (*Listeria, Salmonella, Escherichia coli* O157, and *Staphylococcus aureus*) was analyzed in more than 15 *tina* (wooden vats) from different farms producing Ragusano PDO in Sicily. Except for very rare and very low levels of contamination with *S. aureus* (only seen after enrichment by the BAX system), none of these pathogens was detected within the biofilm (Lortal et al., 2009). Many hypotheses can explain this resistance to the establishment of pathogens on the wood. First of all, this observation is in agreement with findings for many other positive bio-films: the local pH of the wooden vat is below 5.0; the temperature cycle for Ragusano cheesemaking includes a heating step (even if never exceeding 45°C); nutritional competition with the positive microbiota can occur; and the predominant species, *S. thermophilus*, can also produce bacteriocins (Fontaine and Hols, 2007). Last, brushing and washing can also limit the potential adhesion of milk pathogens on the surface of the bio-film. All these factors are likely combined to make an efficient barrier toward pathogens.

The complete absence of pathogens was also found in 10 *gerle* examined in Cantal cheesemaking. When raw milk before contact with the wooden vats was artificially contaminated with high levels of *Listeria* organisms and *Staphylococcus* (Didienne et al., 2012), pathogens were still not able to be established within the biofilm.

Mariani et al. (2011) carried out a study to characterize the development of *Listeria monocytogenes* on wooden shelves used for cheese ripening. The authors compared inoculations on native or autoclaved wooden samples after cleaning-drying, and also on native wooden samples before cleaning-drying after two incubations. Two strains of *Listeria monocytogenes* were selected according to their behavior after inoculation on wooden shelves: the most and the least resistant. In presence of a native microbial flora on the shelves, deposited populations of *L. monocytogenes* remained stable or even decreased by up to $2 \log_{10}$ (CFU/cm^2) after 12 days of incubation at 15°C in all tested conditions. By contrast, *L. monocytogenes* populations increased by up to $4 \log_{10}$ (CFU/cm^2) when the resident bio-film was thermally inactivated (autoclaved), suggesting a microbial origin of the observed inhibitory effect. Mariani et al. (2011) concluded that the resident microbial biofilm living on wooden ripening shelves displayed a stable anti-*Listeria* effect according to the experimental ripening conditions. The overall results suggest that the biocontrol of pathogens' multiplication on wooden shelves by resident biofilms should be considered for the microbiological safety of traditional ripened cheeses.

Recently Scatassa et al. (2015), in a study on Sicilian Caciocavallo Palermitano and Vastedda della Valle del Belìce PDO, have concluded that the microbiota of wooden vat plays an active role in the achievement of the food safety objectives through the biocompetitive activity of lactic acid bacteria (LAB) and the inhibitory activity against pathogenic bacteria, particularly *L. monocytogenes.*

Since the 1990s, a number of scientific studies on wood and its microbiological status have been performed to investigate the impact of cleaning, disinfection, moisture content, and wood *properties* on the survival and transfer of microorganisms. The very interesting and update review of Aviat et al. (2016), based on 86 international references, demonstrates that the porous nature of wood, especially when compared with smooth surfaces, is not responsible for the limited hygiene of the material used in the food industry and that it may even be an advantage for its microbiological status.

The traditional worldwide procedures of cleaning wooden equipment after use involve most of the time a brushing step with hot water, or hot deproteinized whey (resulting from the production of *ricotta*) and an adequate period of drying (12−24 hours, ACTIA 2000; Lortal et al., 2009). Sicilian cheesemakers leave the wooden vat full with the deproteinized whey overnight and reuse the next morning for cheesemaking (Scatassa et al., 2015). The surface pH just after washing the *tina* was acid, between 4.5 and 5.0; the lowest values were in the bottom. This low pH at the surface is likely related to the local lactic acid production of LAB. Aviat et al. (2016) conclude that wood represents ecological ideas that are attractive to consumers (Gigon, Martin, 2006; FEDEMCO and Partner España S.A. 2002) and these have resulted in a new interest in wood for use in food packaging. It is clear for the authors that wooden packaging and wooden tool surfaces contribute beneficially to the final quality, safety, and character of many food products.

From the surveyed literature, it seems clear that wooden vats and shelves act as a reservoir of microbial biodiversity contributing to the final quality, safety, and character of dairy products. Moreover, the natural biofilms which form on wooden surfaces are safe and able to inhibit and limit pathogen implantation with mechanisms that still need to be further explored. Wood, as a tool to regulate cheese and cellar humidity, has also been proved to be difficult to replace by any other synthetic materials. Its role is important in the hydric balance and drying of cheese, which are subsequently crucial for the development of the expected microbial ecosystem on the rind; this ability has never been equaled by any other kind of shelving material.

Wood is not the only material with which the containers used in artisanal cheese production are constructed. Traditional containers made of whole sheep's skin (Motal) are used for producing of Motal Paniri in Ardabil, Iran. It is known as Khik in Khorasan, Iran and used to produce

Panire Khiki, as well as Panire Assalem and Tavalesh in the north of Iran. Tulum is the same traditional container often made of goat's skin and used to produce Tulum Peyniri in Turkey. Another traditional container is a specific earthenware similar to the pitcher, having larger mouth, named Kupa (Küpə), which is used in the manufacture of peculiar cheeses called Kupa Paniri (Küpə Pəniri), Jjikhli Panir, or Penjarli Panir, Zirali Panir, and Panire Koozei. A similar earthenware pot is used in production of Testi Peynir or Carra Peynir (Jarra Peynir) of Turkey. Different devices were also used for clots collecting like bowl and springy metal grill as the cloth folded on it.

9.3.4 Caves and Others Ripening Environment

Despite the use of *caves* in the traditional systems of cheese ripening is very widespread in the world, an equally large scientific documentation was not found, showing the specificity of the different natural environments, as well as the empirical processes that take place in them, compared to the refrigerated systems developed in industrial processes. More research is needed on this important step of traditional cheese production.

Among the few scientific works found, we report some results on the *pit* used to age the "Formaggio di Fossa di Sogliano PDO." Avellini et al. (1999) experimentally compared different systems of maturing Formaggio di Fossa (pit cheese): in factory (cells) and in the pits. The pit-aged cheese showed notable differences compared to the cheese aged in the factory. The pit cheese was less hard, but moister, saltier, sharper, and sourer, with a more pronounced aroma, than the factory-aged cheese. Chemical analyses showed significantly different values of water content, noncasein and nonprotein nitrogen, amount of free amino acids and composition of free amino acids and FFA fractions for the pit-aged cheese. Microbiological analyses showed no significant differences between the amount and distribution of lactic and nonlactic microflora in cheeses aged with different modalities. The environmental conditions of the pit, probably together with the presence of molds on the surface of the pit-aged cheese, could be responsible for the development of the unique chemical and sensorial characteristics of Fossa cheese.

The microbiology and biochemistry of Fossa cheese have been studied by Gobbetti et al. (1999), with interesting results, where several common features seemed to be shared by the Fossa cheeses: no hygienic risks; selection of NSLAB during ripening and very low survival of LAB starters; very high degree of proteolysis; very high concentration of free amino acids which increased the flavor; and moderate lipolysis which varied within samples and was also considerable in cheeses produced from bovine or mixture of bovine and ewes' milks.

The safety of Fossa cheese was considered satisfactory also by Massa et al. (1988) in a study on the hygienic quality of Fossa cheese, as well Barbieri et al. (2012), confirming the absence of hygienic risks to the consumer. The same authors characterized the genetic diversity of microbial Fossa cheese by the occurrence of *Lactobacillus plantarum*, *Lactobacillus casei*, *Lactobacillus paracasei*, *Lactobacillus rhamnosus*, and *Lactobacillus fermentum*, all NSLAB species. The fungal microflora from the traditional aged Fossa cheese mostly present were *Penicillium* and *Aspergillus* despite the high microbial diversity of the pit environment, suggesting that these strains better adapt to the particular conditions.

Skin bags have been studied by Hayaloglu et al. (2007b), for Tulum cheeses ripened in in goat's skin bags or plastic containers to understand the effect of ripening container on the chemical composition, biochemistry, microbiology, and volatile composition during 150 d of ripening. Tulum cheese ripened in goat's skin bag has unique chemical, microbiological, and sensorial properties compared to cheeses ripened in other packaging materials. It was reported that use of goat's skin bag for cheese ripening causes more decrease in moisture contents of cheeses due to its porous structure and lower microbial counts in comparison with cheeses ripened in plastic containers. The authors concluded that cheeses ripened in skin bags or plastic had similar aroma patterns, but the concentrations of some components were different. Quantitative differences in several volatile compounds were evident among the cheeses. Also, goat's skin bag is much preferred than sheep's as a packaging material of cheese because of stronger structure.

9.4 CONSUMERS PERSPECTIVE

Kupiec et al. (1998), in their research, answer to the question *"Why do consumers choose artisanal cheese?"*, by stating that overall "quality" and "flavor" of the cheeses were recognized as the most important cheese properties influencing consumers' purchase decisions, followed closely by their "superiority" and "difference from industrial cheeses." The "artisanal," "handmade," and "farmhouse" image of the cheeses are likely to increasingly influence consumer choice—especially when contrasted with the staid and unimaginative image of mass-produced industrial cheeses.

Almli et al. (2011), in their study on *"General image and attribute perceptions of traditional food in six European countries"* (Belgium, France, Italy, Norway, Poland, and Spain), found that traditional food (including cheeses) have a unanimously positive general image across Europe, with the highest scores in Spain and Poland. The authors affirm that the positive image of traditional food may be explained by the fact the traditional food products (TFP) can both offer sensorial experiences and meet ethical concerns of the production systems. The authors find that sensory properties, instead, are negatively correlated to convenience and purchase (extrinsic properties). This finding is both in accordance with Chambers et al. (2007), who found that people focusing on convenience in food choice had a more negative attitude and indicated a lower consumption of local foods, and with Pieniak et al. (2009), who concluded that convenience acted as a barrier to traditional food consumption. The results of the research point out that TFP present satisfying sensory, health, and ethical properties, but less positive purchase and convenience attributes. Common to all countries, the positive general image of TFP is significantly correlated to high quality, time consuming to prepare, and expensive. Additional attributes contribute significantly to a positive general image of TFP when the pan-European sample is studied as a whole: special taste, good appearance, consistent quality, healthy, safe, high nutritional value, difficult to prepare, and low availability. Furthermore, the results of Almli et al. (2011) give evidence that European consumers trade off some degree of inconvenience in the purchase and preparation of TFP in order to enjoy their specific taste, quality, appearance, nutritional value, healthiness, and safety. Further, results indicate that not necessarily the most typical attributes of TFP, but rather the most valued ones, contribute to shaping a positive general image of TFP. Finally, their results also suggest that festive consumptions of traditional foods, rather than daily consumptions, are the ones that most strongly shape the general image of TFP in the European consumers' minds.

Reed and Bruhn (2003) developed a study to gather information about the shopping habits and opinions of specialty cheese consumers that will help cheesemakers develop successful strategies to target that market segment. They conducted telephone surveys, focus group interviews and in-store consumer evaluations of point-of-sale materials. Focus group participants were asked to use a printed form to rank the importance of several sociopolitical factors related to food production and purchases, such as potential health benefits, sustainable and organic farming, and locally produced food, and direct from farm. The results indicate that all sociopolitical factors are influencing specialty cheeses purchases. The average response across all focus groups indicate as "very important and important": 94% for the "potential health benefits," 79% for "direct from farm," 71% for "organic farming," 68% for "locally produced food," and 65% for "sustainable production." Similar results were found in 2007 in a Sicilian consumer survey (933 interviews), suggesting that the first seven criteria on cheese purchase intention are food safety, use of natural ingredients, health properties of the products, local products, PDO denomination, artisanal production, and typical flavor (Pasta and Licitra, 2007).

Despite the participants of California focus groups (Reed and Bruhn, 2003) rated that "Buying foods that have potential health benefits," 53% as very important, and 41% said it was important (total 94%), the main concerns expressed were related to the guarantee that the cheeses were antibiotic free and hormone free; also it showed that they liked the animals were raised on pasture. The focus group responses about food safety were consistent with the telephone surveys. Most specialty cheese consumers are not concerned about the potential health issues related to consuming raw-milk cheese. Those who choose to purchase raw-milk cheeses often do so for a perceived complexity of flavor not found in pasteurized cheeses, or because they believe the process is more natural or traditional.

Furthermore, in the list of sociopolitical questions provided to participants, in the study of Reed and Bruhn (2003), the authors did not include a question about product quality or freshness. However, all the groups qualified their comments on sociopolitical issues with the statement that the actual and perceived quality and freshness of the product were more important factors than whether it is organic, sustainable, or made locally. Specialty cheese consumers may try to support organic or local production, but not at the expense of perceived quality, freshness, or flavor.

In France, the Sofres survey (http://www.fromages-de-terroirs.com/marche-fromage1.php3?id_article = 652,2005) "les Français et le fromage" on 3000 people interviews in metropolitan area indicates that adults over 36 years old (representing the 36% of the sample) base their cheese preference on the following criteria: quality, PDO certification, sustainability, and naturalness, whereas younger people look for functional products giving importance to price and accessibility.

West affirms, "the expanding market for raw-milk cheeses in recent years has been associated with consumer desires for greater traceability in the food system and produce accountability. The corollary of this is that raw-milk cheesemakers survive only on good reputation" (West, 2008).

To confirm the importance of the specific characteristics of traditional products, Guerrero et al. (2009) studied the acceptance of innovations in traditional products in terms of packaging, convenience, nutrition, and sensory properties. These authors found that consumers are open to packaging and convenience-oriented innovations, on the condition that they do not modify the fundamental intrinsic characteristics of the product. Further, changes in sensory quality such as modified flavors are not welcome in traditional foods (Guerrero et al., 2009). These results were confirmed by Vanhonacker et al. (2010), who observed that European traditional food consumers welcome innovations that highlight the authenticity and origin of traditional foods and improve their shelf-life but reject innovations that may affect the sensory properties of the product, and the authentic character of TFP (Almli et al., 2011).

Guerrero et al. (2009), in a qualitative cross-cultural study assert that TFP constitute an important element of European culture, identity, and heritage (Committee of the Regions, 1996; Ilbery and Kneafsey, 1999) contributing to the development and sustainability of rural areas, protecting them from depopulation, entailing substantial product differentiation potential for producers and processors (Avermaete et al., 2004), and providing ample variety in food choice for consumers.

9.5 SOCIAL, CULTURAL, AND ECONOMIC IMPORTANCE OF ARTISANAL RAW-MILK CHEESES

Hundreds of traditional cheeses are produced worldwide. Family Farming World Conference of 2011 remarks, "Family farming represents a sector of strategic value because of its economic, social, cultural, environmental, and territorial functions. Women and men engaged in family farming produce 70% of the world's food. Family farming is the basis of sustainable food production aimed towards food security and food sovereignty, of environmental management of land and its biodiversity, of the preservation of the important socio-cultural heritage of rural communities and nations."

Traditional products have a strong linkage to the territory of origin, are testimonial of the history, of the culture, and of the life style of those communities that produce them, handed down from generations, most of the time orally. Traditional cheeses are unique expression of the symbiotic interaction between human resources, the culture of rural communities, and the nature (Licitra, 2010a). Even in the 21st century, in Europe most of the traditional cheeses are produced in less-favored areas (including most of the PDO cheeses), in an environment that would otherwise be abandoned, where livestock and farming are often the only way to use the land. If "the overall world governance" in the era of globalization, will not be able to stop the rural exodus, beyond the need of offering them new job and lodging, the conservation of natural resources of the planet will be compromised. Farmers of disadvantaged rural areas (such as mountains, high hills, developing countries) play also a role of guardian of the environment due to protection of natural resources, reducing soil erosion, reducing deforestation and desertification, keeping animal and vegetal biodiversity.

Hundreds of artisanal products, especially in the era of globalization, nowadays not only in the developed countries, must coexist and compete with industrial products. The mass productions obtained on a large scale, to fulfill the business objectives for the holding companies that produce them, and as previously noted, provide nutrients for consumers forced to run, for the little time imposed by globalization, which rely on fast-food, both in terms of preparation (ready meals and products of IV–V gamma) and in consumption patterns, with more than 50% of the meals consumed not at home, and in stolen time to the many daily activities (fast meal).

Artisanal products are produced in small farms (family farming), in small quantities; their producers find enormous difficulty competing with the multinationals for their extraordinary distribution capacity and promotion of the products due to production volumes from which follows an incomparable financial power than traditional manufacturers. In fact, the artisanal products are for family consumption, local markets, in specialty stores, and anyway for short distribution channels. The survival of artisanal products is strongly linked to their superior quality and to the fact that they represent experiences, ancient cultures, and a strong and direct relationship with nature that leads back conscious consumers, also in the developed countries, to a quality of life that risk to lose values and primary needs for a human dimension thereof.

The artisanal production, obtained with natural systems, represents a sustainable agriculture and contributes to respecting and protecting the natural and environmental resources of the planet. Therefore, it requires the support not only of consumers but also by the media, opinion leaders, and politicians. The defense of traditional products cannot be considered just an economic "food challenge," but rather social, cultural, environmental. Just think that even today, about 50% (geographical atlas of Treccani Encyclopedia) of the world's population lives in rural areas of the planet and that the food is produced from the conjunction of local resources and creativity of man, and processes realized without special equipment and without the cold chain. These products have fed billions of people for centuries.

9.6 EXAMPLES OF FERMENTED MILKS AND TRADITIONAL CHEESES IN THE WORLD

The fermented milks and traditional cheeses that are listed below were chosen as examples of link with the territory of origin and of human creativity, but also because of the casualness of their discovery, and some not only for their economic relevance but also because they identify the countries of origin such as Parmigiano Reggiano PDO, the Beaufort PDO, the Queso de la Serena PDO.

The specificity of the production processes of the presented products, as well as for other hundreds of traditional products, makes it difficult, sometimes impossible, to reproduce at industrial level. The key factor is always the man with his experience and its empirical choices in governing the natural processes and the relationship with environmental conditions that change all the time, even during the single cheesemaking or ripening.

9.6.1 Natural Fermented Milks Products

Nowadays over 5000 fermented foods are produced worldwide, among which we find jewels of creativity and local cultures (e.g., bread, cheese, cured meats, fermented vegetables, wine, beer) (Tamang and Kailasapathy, 2010; Salque et al., 2012; Yang et al., 2014).

All raw edible material for man, animal, or plant will deteriorate under the influence of ambient microorganisms. The man has always competed with the microorganisms to preserve the harvested raw materials, from gathering and hunting, and therefore difficult to secure over time. Not only they could be damaged and lost, but they could also conceal dangerous germs. Using his five senses and his genius, the man, by observation and using simple processes, was able to select and guide the microorganisms present to stabilize the food in its evolution. The empirical knowledge of developed fermentation not only extends the shelf life of the raw material but also protects, at least partially, from unwanted germs, and also diversifies the flavors and appearance of the finished product. All this has taken place for 10,000 years without having any idea of the existence of microorganisms and the possibility to use in his favor, far before the recognition by Pasteur in 1865 of the role of microorganisms.

In the developing countries, the mean daily temperature may range from as low as 15—17°C in the highland areas to as high as 35—40°C in semiarid and arid areas. These high ambient temperatures coupled with the general lack of refrigeration facilities imply that milk, often containing high initial bacterial count, becomes sour in 12—24 hours. The standard of hygiene applied to milk production in the developing countries is poor and as a result the quality of milk is poor. Fermentation of milk to control the growth of spoilage bacteria and some pathogens is the most common aspect of technology in the preparation of traditional milk products.

The use of natural fermentation of milk was adopted as a storage system, being the most important means of achieving the necessary souring either in the preparation of fermented milk products, ready for consumption, or in an acidification or souring intermediate stage in a product's preparation. The value of lactic fermentation not only affects the shelf-life but also the quality and characteristics of the products.

Licitra (2010b) investigated 129 dairy products from Eastern Africa (26.4%), Central-Western Africa (23.3%), Middle East (19.4%), Northern Africa (14%), and Southern Asia (13.2%) and reported the main systems used to process milk. Fermented milks products represent in this investigation the most found categories with 30% of the products, followed by butter and clarified butter (20.9%), soft cheeses (20.2%), semihard and hard cheeses (20.1% of which 6.7% are sun dried), and 6.7% sweet dairy products (adding sugar mainly in India). It is interesting to mention some products stored with the oldest and natural technique which is drying under the sun, such as Lakila cheese (Marocco), Gapal cheese (Burkina Faso), Gashi cheese (Mali), Takumart cheese (Niger), Wagashi (Benin).

In general, in the developing countries acid curdling (acid-alcoholic and the acid-thermal ones) is the most spread technique (44.4%) till today and is used for 58 over 129 dairy products investigated. Soured milk, besides being liquid dairy product, is the basis for the production of unsalted butter, ghee, and curd in the household of local villages. Animal rennet is used for the production of 31 cheeses (23.3%) and only few cheeses (3) are produced by using vegetable rennet (2.3%).

Natural fermented milks are spread worldwide, and beyond the most famous, i.e., Kefir in various countries of Caucasus and Koumiss in various countries in Central Asia, that have been also imitated in some developing countries, there are many other products that daily feed family of many countries. A list of fermented milks is reported in Licitra (2010b): Akile, Nukadwarak, Ambere, Iria Imata, Mariwa, Mazia Maivu and Kamabele in Kenya; Maziwa and Mgando in Tanzania; Amacunda, Sawa, Ikuvugoto and Mabisi in Zaire; Amasi and Umlaza in Zimbawe; Dahi and Lassi in India; Kadam in Mali; Nono Koumou in Burkina Faso; Pindidaam in Cameroon; Raib and Rouaba in Chad; Roab in Sudan; Fadhi and Suusac in Somalia; Shenglish in Syria. All these fermented foods are obtained at the household level without special equipment and without the cold chain. They contribute, especially in arid areas, to preserve milk at high temperatures, transforming it in a healthy and refreshing drink, including the drinkable whey after curdling separation.

Globalization is forcing the industrialized versions of these products, and the addition of yeast selected will quickly become indispensable. However, in a large part of the world, Africa, India, and parts of Asia, artisanal practices still survive. Even within developed country highly standardized industrial fermented foods, which are exported worldwide, cohabit with a great variety of natural (traditional) fermented products, made on a small scale, and entering shorter distribution channels.

9.6.2 Traditional Cheeses

9.6.2.1 Roquefort PDO

Roquefort is the most famous among French blue cheeses and is named after the small village of Roquefort which lies on a chalky mountain, called the Combalou, between the Auvergne and Languedoc in the Aveyron region of France.

The mountain's partial collapse was caused by series of earthquakes and landslides (water erosion) and in prehistoric times. This geological accident occurred three times, the third opened a series of caves in the debris. Vertical faults and fissures in these caves provide natural ventilation and are known as "*Fleurines.*" These chimney or wind holes may be up to 100 m high and connect the caves to the outside world. They serve as an immense storage area that maintains a constant temperature of 9°C and humidity of 95% (Aussibal, 1985).

"Fleurine" ensure that the temperature and humidity remain constant throughout the year because when the temperature outside the cave is higher, the faults draw air inwards and downwards, and when the temperature rises in the caves, the air is drawn upwards and outwards (http://www.paxtonandwhitfield.co.uk/roquefort.html).

A legend tells that Roquefort was discovered when *"once a shepherd, caught sight of a beautiful girl perched in the distance at dusk. Determined to find her, he left his dog to guard the flock and hastily placed his lunch — bread and ewe's milk curds — in the nearby Combalou caves to keep cool. The shepherd was away for days, looking for his maiden, but unfortunately, he never found her. Dejected, he returned to his sheep, tired and hungry. When he took his lunch out of the caves, he found that the bread and milk curds were moldy. His hesitation was brief due to his mounting hunger. With some trepidation, the shepherd took a bite and was pleasantly surprised to find that his moldy lunch tasted quite delicious! The Penicillium roqueforti had done its work, the Roquefort was born."* This blue cheese is referred to as the "King of Cheeses" and is considered to be the most famous cheese of France.

Roquefort is made only from raw Lacaune sheep's milk, fed on grass, fodder, and cereals, except for the winter period, grazing is compulsory. The mold may either be added to the curd or introduced, after 8 days from production, by piercing the white cheeses with needles. Carbon dioxide caused by fermentation in the pate escapes, and spore laden air is introduced. Traditionally, the cheesemakers extracted the mold by leaving bread in the caves for 6—8 weeks until it was consumed by the mold. The interior of the bread was then dried to produce a powder. In modern times, the mold can be grown in a laboratory, which allows for greater consistency. Roquefort is especially famous for its pungent smell and characteristic blue veins of mold that have a sharp tang, as well as its unique production process. It is a white, crumbly, and slightly moist cheese.

Roquefort cheese benefits from a designation of origin since 1925 (the first one in France), a registered Appellation d'Origine Contrôlée (AOC) since 1979, and PDO since 1996, throughout the European Union.

9.6.2.2 *Formaggio di Fossa di Sogliano PDO*

The cheese "**Formaggio di Fossa di Sogliano**" (pit cheese) is produced in Italy in the region of Emilia Romagna and Marche, where along the ridge foothills and hills of the Apennines were obtained the pit, "Fosse." Since 2009, it received the European recognition of PDO mainly for its uniqueness of aging the cheese, in the traditional pit, *"fosse."*

The tradition of pit was introduced during the middle ages and soon became an integral part of rural culture of the territory between the Rubicon and Marecchia valleys, to the river Esino, overlapping the Romagna and Marche. The use of pit was naturally linked to the need for preservation of the product, as well as the desire to protect it from raids by the tribes and armies, which over the centuries, tried to occupy the territory.

According to legend, the special cheese processing pit would be born purely by chance. It appears that in 1486, Alfonso of Aragon, defeated by the French, had obtained the hospitality by Girolamo Riario, lord of Forli. But the resources of Forli did not allow long-sustenance of the troops, who soon began to despoil on the surrounding neighborhood. These, to defend themselves, made a habit of hiding provisions in the pits. In November, once armies left and the raids end, farmers unearthed supplies and discovered that the cheese had changed their organoleptic characteristics, improving them.

The Fosse were artificially excavated into the rock and left rough, geologically they consist of sandstone source rocks, sediments with clay, sand, or alternations of them, belonging to the deposits of the Pliocene and Quaternary current. They present a single access opening higher, having a width between 70 and 120 cm.

The Fossa cheese must be produced using a mixture of whole cow's milk (up 80%) and whole ewe's milk (minimum 20%). Traditionally it is made from raw milk. However, recently someone started to use pasteurized milk. The animals' diet is made by spontaneous forages (rich in flora species with herbaceous plants, shrubs, and trees) or cultivated forages composed of grasses and legumes collected from meadows grown in the territories of origin of the PDO cheese.

In short, it is a semihard cheese, without rind, presents an ivory color with straw yellow—orange shades. With aging, the cheese acquires a strong taste and intense aroma that recalls not only the smell of brushwood, wood, truffle, musk, and hints of herbs but also the aroma of mushroom, boiled chestnut, the smell of the pit and of the cloths where the cheeses were kept in the pits. Its flavor is distinctive and unique and goes from sweet to slightly spicy.

The aging processes are developed in two phases. In the first phase, cheese ripening takes place in appropriate locations adjacent to the dairy plant, at temperatures of 10–15°C and a relative humidity of 70%–85%, for a period of 60–70 days.

The second phase, that it is considered the true specificity of Fossa Cheese from Sogliano, is related to the use of ancient pit (flask-shaped), with a depth of about three meters, for the anaerobic maturation of the cheeses. The cheeses, collected in varying numbers in bags of cloth tightly closed and identified, are laid in the pit, by experts, called *"infossatori"* (professional profile unique in the international dairy). The bags are stacked up to the entrance of the pit, which is then filled and covered with canvas to avoid the maximum transpiration. The pits are closed by the application of a wooden lid sealed with plaster. The length of this phase varies from a minimum of 80 days to a maximum of 100 days.

The traditional opening of the pits takes place on November 25, the day of St. Catherine of Alexandria, martyred in the early 4th century.

The safety of Fossa (pit) Cheese has been studied by Massa et al. (1988), Gobbetti et al. (1999), Barbieri et al. (2012): the authors confirmed the absence of hygienic risks to the consumers.

9.6.2.3 Tuma Persa

The Tuma Persa cheese is unique for its history and for the cheesemaking technology. It is produced in Sicily (Castronovo of Sicily, a small town between Palermo and Agrigento) and has been recognized in 1998 from the Regional Government of Sicily as a historical product of Sicily.

Also, the origin of this cheese is purely accidental. Several legends are known, the most credited seems the report of a producer after producing a classic toma cheese (a pressed cheese to obtain the canestrato cheese), forgot (lost) one or few forms in a dark corner of the aging room (historically, places with thick wall, humid, sometime underground, reminding the French caves). In Italian, the word "persa" means "lost" hence the current name "Tuma Persa."

After a few weeks, the cheesemaker, going back to the aging room, noticed these forms, the tuma "lost," covered with mold. After a rough dusting of the surfaces, vowing to knock them as soon as possible.

In the following weeks, having found the opportunity to eliminate them, he finds the cheeses still full of mold. Before throwing them, he decided to open a form to see what had happened to those cheeses. The producer was surprised to find the dough inside the cheeses in excellent condition from which emerged a good smell; thus, he felt the need to taste a piece. The flavor was excellent enough to make him decide to repeat what happened accidentally.

As result of the above experience, he began using this "lucky" technology for other cheese of its production, having a great success among consumers.

A Sicilian producer in the early 1990s, having learned, from the literature, of this particular historical cheese, started experiments to reproduce it, and to get the product, known today as "Tuma Persa." The uniqueness of Tuma Persa is related to the double natural fermentations; the first in the early stages of maturation, as the legend tells, once set in shape, is not touched for about a week (with development of external molds) then washed and kept to rest for another 10 days of fermentation (second fermentation). Only after 3 weeks, it is ready to be cleaned from the mold and finally salted.

Tuma Persa is a pressed semihard cheese. Licitra (2006) made with thermized whole cow's milk. Its taste ranges from sweet to spicy, no salty or bitterness, aftertaste has a very special, long and aromatic persistency due to an excellent combination of flavors that recall the double natural fermentations, and the mold formed.

9.6.2.4 Vastedda della valle del Belice PDO

The "Vastedda della Valle del Belìce" has obtained the PDO by the European Union, October 29, 2010. The Vastedda della Valle del Belìce is a unique cheese, or at least rare in international dairy scene, because it represents one of the few stretched cheese from ewe's milk.

The older cheesemakers evoke the origin somewhat unique and especially tell that once the shepherds in a particularly hot season had problems to mature Pecorino cheese. The cheeses had defects in the crust with cracks evident that prevented a proper maturation of the cheese and in any case a large commercial depreciation of the same.

In the local dialect, when a product shows signs of wear, to say that it will ruin, it is called "si vastau," has spoiled, hence the current name "vastedda." The old shepherds tell that one of them, having seen many of his Pecorino cheeses with crust defects, sharpened the wits and began to experiment to try to recover these ruined cheeses. He took a cheese aged about 20–30 days with cracks in the crust, he open it and found that the interior of the cheese was good with no further defects. He cut it into slices and dipped it in the hot whey (85–90°C), just after the production of ricotta cheese, with the objective to remake the same type of pressed cheese. While waiting for the whey to cool, the cheesemaker dipped their hands into the container to control the cheese, and with surprise saw that the cheese mass began to stretch and various pieces of cheese began to melt.

It was a spontaneous attempt to apply the technique of stretching the curd, so he began to knead the dough to promote the fusion of the slices of the curd to form a compact block of cheese, which subsequently divided into small forms of cheeses. In the following days, he invited other shepherds to try the product of his "discovery," without telling them the background. He received appreciations from all of them, for the pleasant taste as sweet, delicate and different from the typical smell and taste of the classic Pecorino, thinking it was a product from cow's milk, goat or mixed. Technically, what happened is justifiable because the Pecorino of 20−30 days had undergone fermentation that decrease the pH from about 6.3 to a pH suitable for stretching, which in combination with the hot whey and the accidental intuition of the cheesemaker end up with the production of a new cheese.

Thus, the "vastedda" was born as a by-product created to recover the cheese with a rind defect, becoming even more prized than the Pecorino cheese. The "vastedda" found a high consensus by consumers and the value, from producer to retailer, sometimes doubles the price of the classic Pecorino. The name of the cheese "Vastedda della Valle del Belice" is derived from the birthplace of origin of the product, the Belice Valley (between the Sicilian provinces of Agrigento, Trapani and Palermo).

The cheese Vastedda della Valle del Belìce PDO is a fresh stretched cheese made with whole raw milk, with natural fermentation, and only from the autochthones Valle del Belice sheep breed, fed on natural pastures. The taste is typical of fresh sheep cheese with a slightly tangy but never too sharp (Licitra, 2006).

9.6.2.5 Wagashi

Wagashi cheese is a traditional dairy product produced in Benin, a country in sub-Saharan Africa. Wagashi, obtained using a unique technology reserved to Peulh women, aimed to nourish rural communities living in poor conditions. The uniqueness of the production process of Wagashi is related to two specific features: the use of vegetable coagulant extracted from the latex of leaves and/or stem of *Calotropis procera* (a local wild and toxic plant, but at higher doses, in addition to the fact that the high temperatures of the cheesemaking process, will denature any residual toxins); the empirical process of boiling the cheese in every 2 days for 20–30 days after production.

Women in Western Africa leaving in rural village play a crucial role in daily life of the entire communities. They are responsible of the whole household: food production, preparation and distribution; in the market days, only women are managers of small food sales, spices, etc. Usually, milk that exceeds the direct consumption is sold. In this context, a legend tells that Peulh women discovered the coagulant properties of the plant *C. procera* because, in ancient times, in order to transport the milk from the village to the market, they use a *calebasse* (pumpkin container) full of milk covered with the leaves of *C. procera* in order to prevent pollution (sand, insect, etc.). The legend tells that in dry and very hot days, some women reached the markets, observed that the milk had curdled with the separation of the curd from the whey. It was a very important discovery for women, as it allowed to depend less on the market, because they could store milk in a different form, the cheese, and also obtained a refreshing drinkable whey, particularly useful in the desert. Women then started with daily empirical practices to develop the technique of their cheese production.

Wagashi cheese is produced in Benin from women of the Peulh ethnic group using whole raw milk from Zebù. It is characterized by the use of vegetable coagulant extracted from the latex of *C. procera*. They learned the exact moment to add the latex extracted from leaves and/or stem of *C. procera* in the milk. They also discovered empirically that best activities occurred when milk reached at least 65–70°C, and then understood that to get the highest curd separation from the whey, it was necessary to rise the temperature to over 95°C for about 5 minutes.

This ancient technology makes the Wagashi cheese proteolytic activity very low (Licitra G., data unpublished), this may be due to a combination of factors such as a specific break down of the casein from the Calotropic enzymes, in a different position than any other rennet (aa 105–106), and heat protein denaturation. Further studies are needed to characterize the coagulation property of the enzymes of the *C. procera* in cheesemaking.

A further discovery by women was the possibility, may be due to the very low level of proteolysis in the cheese, to boil the cheese over and over again, in every 2 days, for about 20–30 days since it has been produced, without any apparent modification of the cheese structure.

This empirical practice guarantees the Wagashi cheese safety not only during cheesemaking but also from post contamination. Sometimes women in this phase of boiling, especially after long transportation to far away markets, color the cheese with leaves, stems and inflorescence of *Sorghum vulgare* to give red color to the cheese. This coloration helps to improve the esthetic covering of any pollution on the surface of the cheeses.

9.6.2.6 Queso de la Serena PDO

A special group of traditional cheeses are those produced with vegetable rennet. One of the most famous is the Queso de la Serena PDO, produced in La Serena district in the province of Badajoz (Extremadura), Spain. La Serena is a soft to semihard cheese made from whole raw milk from the Merino sheep breed, using natural plant rennet from the dried flowers of Cynara Cardunculus, known locally as Yerbacuajo. The pistils of these thistles are soaked in water for 12 hours in a cool, dark place. The amount of rennet to be added depends on the time of the year and the desired level of creaminess.

Cheeses are ripened on wooden shelves in a storage room called bodega or cellar under constant moisture and temperature conditions. They are turned and the bands are tightened every day until the cheese achieves the characteristic degree of creaminess and flavor. Twenty days after molding, the cheese usually reaches the stage at which the paste becomes fluid, so it has to be handled very carefully to avoid breaking the rind.

Characteristic aroma of sheep's milk has an intense, but slightly bitter flavor and not at all salty. Buttery and persistent on the palate, with a slight piquancy in very ripened cheeses. The texture varies from creamy to spreadable, edible with spoon. Similar cheeses are Queijo Serra da Estrela PDO, Queijo Azeitão from Portugal, Fromage Vacherin du Haut Doubs or Mont d'Or AOC and Cabri Ariégeois from France.

9.6.3 Pot Cheeses

Pot cheeses refer to a group of ripened cheeses which are produced from ewe's, goat's, or cow's milk. The remarkable point in their manufacture is maturation that occurs in the particular earthenware pot that is buried underground for 4—6 months. This earthenware pot, called Kupa (Küpə) or Koozeh in Iran and Carra (Jarra) or Testi in Turkey, has a larger opening compared to the conventional pot. The preparation of pot cheeses varies between regions and countries. Sometimes the earthenware pots are coated with a lacquer layer. The use of glazed pots is also preferred because they keep better cheese moisture. Their capacity ranges from 1 to 5 L (0.26−1.32 gal). The opening of pots are finally closed by grapevine leaves and a sheet of paper or clean cloth, or both of them. The prepared pots, obstructed by clay, are lowered into deep pits (about 5−6 m below the ground surface). They are disposed, upside down, in holes containing washed and wet sand, so that their bottom is flush barely. Potting usually starts in late June to early July, when milk is abundant and white cheese is cheap. The famous traditional pot cheeses are from Iran (Kupa Paniri, Jajikhli Panir, Ziraly Panir) and from Turkey (Carra or Testi Peynir).

The pot cheeses present spicy flavor due to the addition, for example, of cumin-seeds in Ziraly Panir, black cumin and thyme placed as layers in earthenware jugs for the production of Carra or Testi Peynir, herbs or vegetables in the Jajikhli Panir.

9.6.4 Sheep and Goat Skin Cheeses

Sheep and goat skin cheeses refer to a group of traditional cheeses ripened in the specific traditional whole skin bag prepared from sheep's or goat's skin. These types of cheeses are undoubtedly the oldest cheeses in the world and their history of production is tied to the history of cheese discovery for the first time, accidentally by a person carrying milk supply in the pouch made from a sheep's stomach, over 4000 years ago. Some examples for this group of cheeses are Motal Paniri, Panire Khiki or Panire Pousti, Panire Tavalesh and Assalem of Iran, Tulum Peyniri of Turkey and Bouhezza of Algeria.

After preparation of fresh cheese, it is salted and transferred to the ripening rooms for 10 to 30 days. Then ripened cheeses are broken to small pieces of 10−15 cm (3.9−5.9 in.) sizes and filled into the sheep's or goat skin bags and maintained at the cold and moist places like basement and storehouse for 2−3 months to be well ripened. Goat's skin bag is much preferred than sheep's as a packaging material of cheese because of stronger structure.

9.6.5 Skorup Dairy Product

Fresh milk is filtered, poured into the pot, and gradually heated to boiling. When milk starts to boil, it stays at the same temperature for 30 minutes to increase the total solid in milk. Higher content of total solid contributes to a better quality of Skorup. Then, milk is poured into shallow and wide wooden vessels. In vessels, milk is gradually cooled, whereby the formation of Skorup is started by separation of fatty globules and other ingredients to the surface of milk. Formation of Skorup lasts for 1−3 days. After collection, Skorup is placed in wooden tubs, layer by layer. Each layer is dry salted. At the bottom of the tubs there is a hole through which excess of milk is discharged. When the tub is filled and Skorup is drained, Skorup from tub goes into specially prepared anaerobic sheep skins. Skorup can be consumed immediately after collecting from milk (young Skorup), after a month of ripening in the tubs (mature Skorup) and after ripening it in sheep skin 6−12 months (old Skorup). There are dairies in Montenegro that produce young Skorup in an industrial way. Production of old Skorup is not possible, except on traditional way (Dozet, 1996).

9.6.6 West Country Farmhouse Cheddar PDO

The name of the cheese comes from the village of Cheddar and the Cheddar Gorge where the cheese was originally stored. West Country Farmhouse Cheddar is made using the traditional recipe to produce the real Cheddar flavor and texture. It can only be made on farm in Dorset, Somerset, Cornwall, and Devon in England, from milk produced on the farm and, where necessary, supplemented with locally farmed milk. The cheese can be made in cylindrical or block form from raw milk and recently also from pasteurized milk. The most famous part of the Cheddar making process is "Cheddaring" which entails stacking and turning slabs of curd to facilitate drainage this must be done by hand and not mechanically. The curds are milled, salted, put into molds and pressed. The cheese is put into store and graded at regular intervals being kept for a minimum of 9 months before sale. It is a hard-textured cheese with a creamy background flavor and varying degrees of complexity depending on age and the individual farm. Nowadays, large cheese factories in the English-speaking nations of the world produce this typology of cheese, obtaining different products compared to the traditional production system, sharing only the name. Cheddar is one of the most heavily consumed cheeses in the world.

9.6.7 Beaufort—PDO

Beaufort is a renowned cheese, one of the noble Alpine cheeses. Beaufort is produced year-round in three different varieties: Standard Beaufort,

Summer Beaufort, and Beaufort Chalet d'Alpage. The standard Beaufort is made from November to May when the cows are in the valleys. They are fed almost exclusively from the past summer's harvested hay, and the first consumer-ready wheels hit the stores at the start of April. Summer Beaufort and Beaufort Chalet d'Alpage are made through different processes during the same period: June to November. For summer Beaufort, the cows graze in the mountain pastures. The Beaufort Chalet d'Alpage, however, is the product of "high mountain pasture," over 1500 m, where cheesemaking takes place twice a day according to traditional methods. Both Summer Beaufort and Beaufort Chalet d'Alpage have a fruitier taste and more of a yellow color than standard Beaufort (http://frenchfoodintheus.org/534).

Beaufort was recognized at the national level in 1968 when it received its status as an AOC and again by the EU in 2009, when it obtained its PDO status. It is produced exclusively from raw cow's milk in the French Alps of the Haute-Savoie, from the milk of Tarine and Abondance cows, which according to the specification for the PDO cannot produce more than 5000 L/year/cow. The limit of the production level of the cows is a rare indication to find among all the production regulations of the European PDO, reflecting an extensive farming system in harmony with nature and the environment. It is a behemoth of a cheese, with wheels shaped (4.5−6.5 in. thick and 13.5−29.5 in. across) weighing up to 60 kg that, for its concave bottom, derived from the wooden hoops, called "Beaufort hoop" utilized for molding and pressing the curd, practical for its transportation by mules in bygone days (Baboin-Jaubert, 2002).

Beaufort is a full fat pressed cooked between semihard and hard cheese, aged on wooden shelves at least five months. It presents a unique grassy, flowery aroma to the meaty cheeses, related to grazing on sustainable mountain pastures. Furthermore, it has a firm yet buttery taste which melts easily in the mouth.

Similar French cheeses are the Comtè PDO, Salers PDO, and the Cantal PDO, at least for the large format and weight, but everyone keeping its own territorial characteristics and identity.

9.6.8 Comtè PDO

The Comtè was recognized at the France national level in 1958 when it received its status as an AOC and by the EU in 1996, when it obtained its PDO status.

Comté is an ancient cheese. It has been produced since the time of Charlemagne. Comté is still traditionally made in more than 190 cheese dairies, known as the "fruitières" in the Massif du Jura region of eastern France.

The **Comtè** cheese presents as flat wheels, up to 28 in. diameter and 3.5−5 in. high, and weighs from 32 up to 50 kg. It is a pressed cooked cheese, made from whole raw milk from the Montbéliard or Pie Rouge de l'Est breeds that graze in the pasture of the Comtè region. It is ripened on wooden spruce board (shelves), from 4 months to 2−3 years (Comtè Extra Vieux) with an average of about 8 months.

Comté has a smooth texture, an ivory-colored paste scattered of holes the size of a hazelnut. Comté has a complex flavor, ranging from nutty, creamy, and caramelized taste.

9.6.9 Salers Haute Montagne PDO

The Salers was recognized at the France national level in 1961 when it received its status as an AOC and by the EU in 2009, when it obtained its PDO status.

The Salers cheese can only be made with milk of one single breed, Salers cow (the name of the Salers breed gives the denomination to the cheese), while they are grazing in the summer pastures in the Auvergne Mountains. Salers is the *fermier* version of the Cantal. Cheesemakers can only make Salers during the summer months from April 15 to November 15, whereas Cantal can be made from milk of other seasons. Salers cheesemakers follow traditional methods, which remained fundamentally the same since the origin. The production begins immediately after milking, twice a day. The whole raw cow's milk, unheated, is coagulated in the traditional wooden vat called *gerle*.

The Salers cheese presents a cylindrical shape (12−15.5 in. high) and weighs up to 55 kg. It is a pressed uncooked cheese and is ripened from 3 months to 1 year on wooden shelves. It has a golden crust with molds in red and orange spots. Pasta is yellow, with homogeneous consistency. The Salers flavor is aromatic and slightly acidic, with herbal (grass, hay, and alliaceous), fruity (nuts, hazelnut and citrus), lactic (butter and fermented cream), and earthy scent.

9.6.10 Cantal PDO

Cantal is one of the oldest France cheese and was recognized at the France national level in 1956 when it received its status as an AOC and by the EU in 2007, when it obtained its PDO status.

The name of the cheese comes from the region of origin, the Cantal, located in south-central France. It is produced in the Auvergne Mountains, but not in the summer months, when the Saler cheese is mainly produced.

The Cantal cheese presents a cylinder—shape (17—18 in. high) and weighs up to 40—45 kg for the regular size. It can be produced smaller in size, about 20 kg and the Cantalet at about 10 kg. It is a pressed uncooked cheese, made from whole raw-milk cows (recently also from pasteurized). It is ripened on wooden shelves and present three stages of aging: Cantal Jeune aged between 30 and 60 days characterized by its white color, softness, sweet, and milk-batter taste; Cantal Entre-Deux or Doré aged 90—120 days, with its golden color, and the test is balanced of medium intensity; Cantal Vieux aged over 6 months with its yellow color and its powerful spicy test.

9.6.11 Parmigiano Reggiano PDO

The area of origin of Parmigiano Reggiano is the Po valley in the north of Italy through the provinces of Parma, Reggio Emilia, Modena, and parts of the provinces of Mantua and Bologna, on the plains, hills, and mountains enclosed between the rivers Po and Reno.

The milk produced in the area of origin undergoes an artisan process that is entrusted to the skills and passion of cheese masters. The result of a thousand years of expertise and culture, the choices made by the cheese masters are fundamental in the production of Parmigiano-Reggiano, since craftsmanship is one of its distinctive features. In fact, every cheese master must "interpret" milk every day and turn it into cheese by favoring and enhancing the distinctiveness of its indigenous microflora.

The cheesemakers are the custodians and interpreters of the secrets of the true craft of milk processing, and although in hundreds of artisan cheese dairies (about 350), they all work with their hands in the same way. The result of their work is inextricably linked to their personal experience and sensitivity giving an appreciable diversity of taste and aromas.

Raw cow's milk (evening skimmed milk is added to fresh morning milk) with the addition of fermented whey, rich in natural lactic ferments obtained from the processing of the day before, is used to produce Parmigiano Reggiano PDO. It is a hard-semi-fat cooked cheese, today still identical to how it was eight centuries ago, having the same appearance and the same extraordinary fragrance, made in the same way, in the same places, with the same expert ritual gestures. Each cheese must be inspected by experts of the Consortium of Parmigiano Reggiano to receive full approval to be sold as a PDO (fire-branded mark).

The cheese body inspection is exceptionally singular and unique, in its combination, worldwide. It is done by skilled experts using traditional instruments, such as the hammer, screw-needle, and a probe. The hammer is a small stainless steel tool and is an irreplaceable instrument for the experts that taps the cheese at various points while listening carefully to the way the crust takes the blows. Depending of the sound that comes up, the experts are able to detect formation of irregular holes in the cheese (swelling), or reveal cracks in the pasta, defects due to abnormal fermentative phenomena. All this tells him what is going on inside in much the same way as a stethoscope does.

Usually, the organoleptic characteristics of hard cheeses can be tested with the screw-needle (a long instrument similar to a screw) that allows piercing the cheese to extract a minute sample of its content. The sample let the expert judge the aroma, the degree of maturation, and taste (and consequently to verify the presence of defects linked to these characteristics). The probe will confirm texture uniformity and consistency, and sensory profile of the cheese.

Parmigiano Reggiano is ripened in wooden shelves for a minimum maturation time of 12 months, but may be aged for years. When the cheese has matured for 18 months, the mark "Extra" or "Export" can be added. A system of colored seals helps the consumer identify the level of maturation of the prepackaged products available in retailers: 18-month red; 22-month silver; 30-month gold.

Recently, the Regulation (EU) n. 1151/2012 introduced the possibility to use a further quality indication related to the products obtained in the mountain areas, for which it can also be branded as "Parmigiano Reggiano prodotto di montagna." Another important denomination is related to products obtained exclusively from the autochthone "Reggiana" breed milk (also called Red Cow). The Consortium of red cows may use the denomination "Parmigiano Reggiano delle Vacche Rosse (red cows)," when the cheeses have reached 24 months of maturation. The cheeses are subject to an additional quality control and then may receive the precious brand of Red Cows: an unmistakable fire branding embossed on the plate form.

9.7 CONCLUSIONS

The fight between raw milk vs pasteurized is a false problem or at least is not the main question to address. Traditional raw-milk cheeses are produced at an artisanal scale all over the world. They have nourished people since millenaries, and still do in the developing countries. They are reservoirs of knowledge empirically accumulated by humans over centuries of optimization and represent a sustainable, testimonial, safe, gustative outstanding form of valorization of local milk. Cheesemakers making artisanal raw-milk cheeses valorize the expression of all the biodiversity factors associated to raw-milk production, which is a very complex and territory-linked process. By chance, at least in some countries, those cheeses beneficiate from "a registration of origins" and some are known worldwide. However, despite about 180 cheeses with a protected designation of origin over the world, how many artisanal raw-milk cheeses precious receipts are not described and protected, in particular in the developing countries?

Since Pasteur, cheeses started to be made from pasteurized milk, and industrial development of standardized cheese production occurred during the 19th century with a drastic upscaling. They can be produced everywhere, deconnected from territories, in a highly regular manner. However, in terms of safety, the scientific community highlighted frequently that pasteurization is not an absolute "security" and that raw-milk cheeses, well produced, are not riskier.

Both systems should not be opposed, but the consumer must be more aware of the difference. Moreover, if the goals are common, i.e., to produce safe and healthy cheeses, it would be reasonable to consider that the systems are so different that to apply the same legal rules is not realistic. If not, the risk is to erase for sure in a middle term the raw-milk artisanal cheeses, which would be a big mistake, loosing centuries of human local creativity, and leading to social and rural major consequences, as these cheeses are often produced in less-favored areas. Only consumers can decide the future by better knowing what kind of cheeses they are eating and the consequences behind. Also, scientists have the responsibility to further characterize and describe the sense and technical pertinence of artisanal raw-milk cheeses production systems. Finally, policy makers are decisive, and hopefully, this chapter can help them to make the right evolution.

REFERENCES

Abee, T., Krockel, L., Hill, C., 1995. Bacteriocins: modes of action and potentials in food preservation and control of food poisoning. Int. J. Food Microbiol. 28, 169–185.

ACTIA, 2000. Evaluation et maîtrise du risque microbiologique dans l'utilisation du bois pour l'affinage des fromages. ACTIA, Paris, France.

Almli, V.L., Verbeke, W., Vanhonacker, F., Næs, T., Hersleth, M., 2011. General image and attribute perceptions of traditional food in six European countries. Food Qual. Prefer 22, 129–138.

Altekruse, S.F., Timbo, B.B., Mowbray, J.C., Bean, N.H., Potter, M.E., 1998. Cheese-associated outbreaks of human illness in the United States, 1973 to 1992: sanitary manufacturing practices protect consumers. J. Food Prot. 61, 1405–1407.

Andrews, A.T., Anderson, M., Goodenough, P.W., 1987. A study of the heat stabilities of a number of indigenous milk enzymes. J. Dairy Res. 54, 237–246.

Aussibal, R., 1985. Roccailleux Royaume De Rowuefort. In: Masui, K., Yamada, T. (Eds.), French Cheeses. Dorling Kindersley Limited, London, 0-7513-0346-1pp. 178–181.

Avellini, P., Clementi, F., Marinucci, M.T., Goga, B.C., Rea, S., Brancari, E., et al., 1999. Formaggio di fossa: Caratteristiche compositive, microbiologiche e sensoriali | ["Pit" cheese: compositional, microbiological and sensory characteristics]. Ital. J. Food Sci. 11 (4), 317–333.

Avermaete, T., Viaene, J., Morgan, E.J., Pitts, E., Crawford, N., Mahon, D., 2004. Determinants of product and process innovation in small food manufacturing firms. Trends Food Sci. Technol. 15, 474–483.

Aviat, F., Gerhards, C., Rodriguez-Jerez, J.J., Michel, V., Le Bayon, I., Ismail, R., et al., 2016. Microbial Safety of Wood in Contact with Food: A Review. Institute of Food Technologists. Comprehensive Reviews in Food Science and Food Safety, Vol. 00, 2016.

Awad, S., 2006. Texture and flavour development in Ras cheese made from raw and pasteurised milk. Food Chem. 97 (3), 394–400.

Baboin-Jaubert, A., 2002. Cheese. Selecting, Tasting, and Serving the World's Finest. Laurel Glen, San Diego, California1-57145-890-5.

Barbieri, E., Schiavano, G.F., De Santi, M., Valloni, L., Casadei, L., Guescini, M., et al., 2012. Bacterial diversity of traditional Fossa (pit) cheese and its ripening environment. Int. Dairy J. 23, 62–67.

Belitz, H.D., Grosch, W., 1986. Food chemistry. In: Hadziyev, D. (Ed.), Aromasubstances. Springer, New York, NY, pp. 257–303. Chapter 5.

Bellesia, F., Pinetti, A., Pagnoni, U.M., Rinaldi, R., Zucchi, C., Caglioti, L., et al., 2003. Volatile components of Grana Parmigiano-Reggiano type hard cheese. Food Chem. 83, 55–61.

Beuvier, E., Berthaud, K., Cegarra, S., Dasen, A., Pochet, S., Solange Buchin, S., et al., 1997. Ripening and quality of Swiss-type cheese made from raw, pasteurized or microfiltered milk. Int. Dairy J. 7, 311–323.

Bosset, J.O., Butikofer, U., Berger, T., Gauch, R., 1997. Etude des composes volatils du Vacherin fribourgeois et du Vacherin Mont-d'Or. Mitt Gebiete Lebensmitteluntersuch Hyg 88, 233–258.

Bugaud, C., Buchin, S., Coulon, J.B., Hauwuy, A., Dupont, D., 2001a. Influence of the nature of alpine pastures on plasmin activity, fatty acid and volatile compound composition of milk. Lait 81, 401–414.

Bugaud, C., Buchin, S., Hauwuy, A., Coulon, J.B., 2001b. Relationships between flavour and chemical composition of Abundance cheese derived from different types of pastures. Lait 81, 757–773.

Bugaud, C., Buchin, S., Noel, Y., Tessier, L., Pochet, S., Martin, B., et al., 2001c. Relationships between Abundance cheese texture, its composition and that of milk produced by cows grazing different types of pastures. Lait 81, 593−607.

Carpino, S., Horne, J., Melilli, C., Licitra, G., Barbano, D.M., Van Soest, P.J., 2004a. Contribution of native pasture to the sensory properties of Ragusano cheese. J. Dairy Sci. 87, 308−315.

Carpino, S., Mallia, S., La Terra, S., Melilli, C., Licitra, G., Acree, T.E., et al., 2004b. Composition and aroma compounds of Ragusano cheese: native pasture and total mixed rations. J. Dairy Sci. 87, 816−830.

Chambers, S., Lobb, A., Butler, L., Harvey, K., Traill, B., 2007. Local, national and imported foods: a qualitative study. Appetite 49, 208−213.

Chambers, D.H., Esteve, E., Retiveau, A., 2010. Effect of milk pasteurization on flavor properties of seven commercially available French cheese types. J. Sensory Stud 25, 494−511.

Committee of the Regions, 1996. Promoting and Protecting Local Products: A Trumpcard for the Regions. Committee of the Regions, Brussels.

Council Regulation (EEC), 1992. Council Regulation (EEC) No 2081/92 of 14 July 1992 on the protection of geographical indications and designations of origin for agricultural products and foodstuffs. WIPO Database of Intellectual Property Legislative Texts.

de Frutos, M., Sanz, J., Martinez-Castro, I., 1991. Characterization of artisanal cheeses by GC and GC/MS analysis of their medium volatility (SDE) fraction. J. Agric. Food Chem. 39, 524−530.

Delgado daSilva, M.C., Hofer, E., Tibana, A., 1998. Incidence of *Listeria monocytogenes* in cheese produced in Rio de Janeiro, Brazil. J. Food Prot. 61, 354−356.

Demarigny, Y., Beuvier, E., Buchin, S., Pochet, S., Grappin, R., 1997. Influence of raw milk Microflora on the characteristics on Swiss-type cheeses: II Biochemical and sensory characteristics. Lait 77, 151−167.

Dervisoglu, M., Yazici, F., 2001. Ripening changes of Kulek cheese in wooden and plastic containers. J. Food Eng. 48 (3), 243−249.

Didienne, R., Defargues, C., Callon, C., Meylheuc, T., Hulin, S., Montel, M.C., 2012. Characteristics of microbial biofilm on wooden vats ('gerles') in PDO Salers cheese. Int. J. Food Microbiol. 156 (2), 91−101.

Di Grigoli, A., Francesca, N., Gaglio, R., Guarrasi, V., Moschetti, M., Scatassa, M.L., et al., 2015. The influence of the wooden equipment employed for cheese manufacture on the characteristics of a traditional stretched cheese during ripening. Food Microbiol. 46, 81−91.

European Commission, 1992. Directive 92/46/EEC of the European Commission of 16 June 1992. OJEC L. 268, 14.09.1992.

Dhiman, T.R., Satter, L.D., Patriza, M.W., Galli, M.P., Albright, K., Tolosa, M.X., 2000. Conjugated linoleic acid (CLA) content of milk from cows offered diets rich in linoleic and linolenic acid. J. Dairy Sci. 83, 1016−1027.

Donnelly, C.W., 2005. The pasteurization dilemma. In: Kindstedt, P. (Ed.), American Farmstead Cheese: The Complete Guide to Making and Selling Artisan Cheeses, White River Junction, 2005. Chelsea Green Publishing Company, USA, pp. 173−195.

Dozet, N., 1996. Autohtoni mliječni proizvodi. [Autochtonous Dairy Products]. Poljoprivredni Institut, Podgorica, Montenegro, p. 1996.

Dumont, J.P., Roger, S., Cerf, P., Adda, J., 1974. Etude de composes volatils neutres presents dans le Vacherin. Lait 54, 243−251.

Dumont, J.P., Adda, J., 1978. Occurrence of sesqiterpenes in mountain cheese volatiles. J. Agric. Food Chem. 26, 364−367.

Elotmani, F., Revol-Junelles, A.M., Assobhei, O., Milliere, J.B., 2002. Characterization of anti-*Listeria monocytogenes* bacteriocins from *Enterococcus faecalis, Enterococcus faecium* and *Lactococcus lactis* strains isolated from Raib, a Moroccan traditional fermented milk. Curr. Microbiol. 44, 10–17.

El-Soda, M., Desmazeaud, M.J., Le Bars, D., Zevaco, C., 1986. Cell wall-associated proteinases of *Lactobacillus casei* and *Lactobacillus plantarum*. J. Food Prot. 49, 361–365.

FEDEMCO and Partner España S.A. 2002. Computed assisted telephone consumer interviewing omnibus on Wood Packing, La limpieza de los envases hortofrutícolas preocupa a más del 80% de los consumidores. Agroenvase 26.

Fontaine, L., Hols, P., 2007. The inhibitory spectrum of thermophilin 9 from *Streptococcus thermophilus* LMD-9 depends on the production of multiple peptides and the activity of BlpGSt, a thiol-disulfide oxidase. Appl. Environ. Microbiol. 74, 1102–1110.

Fox, P.F., Guinee, T.P., Cogan, T.M., McSweeney, P.L.H., 2004. Fundamentals of Cheese Science. Aspen Publishers, Inc, Gaithersburg, USA.

Galinari, E., Escarião da Nóbrega, J., de Andrade, N.J., de Luces Fortes Ferreira, C.L., 2014. Microbiological aspects of the biofilm on wooden utensils used to make a Brazilian artisanal cheese. Braz. J. Microbiol. 45 (2), 713–720.

Gaya, P., Medina, M., Rodriguez-Marin, M.A., Nunez, M., 1990. Accelerated ripening of ewes' milk Manchego cheese: the effect of elevated ripening temperatures. J. Dairy Sci. 73, 26–32.

Genigeorgis, C., Carniciu, M., Dutulescu, D., Farver, T.B., 1991. Growth and survival of *L. monocytogenes* in market cheeses stored at 4 to 30 °C. J. Food Prot. 54, 662–668.

Gigon, J., Martin, B., 2006. Le bois au contact alimentaire: peut-on s'en servir comme outil de communication?. Report Univ. of Polytech'Lille, France.

Gobbetti, M., Folkertsma, B., Fox, P.F., Corsetti, A., Smacchi, E., De Angelis, M., et al., 1999. Microbiology and biochemistry of Fossa (pit) cheese. Int. Dairy J. 9, 763–773.

Gomez-Ruiz, J.A., Ballesteros, C., Gonzalez Vinas, M.A., Cabezas, L., Martinez-Castro, I., 2002. Relationships between volatile compounds and odour in Manchego cheese: comparison between artisanal and industrial cheeses at different ripening times. Lait 82, 613–628.

Grappin, R., et al., 1997. Possible implications of milk pasteurization on the manufacture and sensory quality of ripened cheese. Int. Dairy J. 7, 751–761.

Guerrero, L., Guardia, M.D., Xicola, J., Verbeke, W., Vanhonacker, F., Zakowska-Biemans, S., 2009. Consumer-driven definition of traditional food products and innovation in traditional foods. A qualitative cross-cultural study. Appetite 52 (2), 345–354.

Halweil, B., 2000. Setting the cheez whiz standard. World Watch 13, 2.

Hartman, P.A., 1997. The evolution of food micro-biology. In: Doyle, M.P., Beuchat, L. R., Montville, T.J. (Eds.), Food Microbiology: Fundamentals and Frontiers. ASM Press, Washington, USA, pp. 3–13.

Hayaloglu, A.A., Brechany, E.Y., 2007a. Influence of milk pasteurization and scalding temperature (heated at 60, 70, 80, or 90 °C) on the volatile compounds of Malatya, a farmhouse Halloumi-type cheese. Lait 87 (2007), 39–57.

Hayaloglu, A.A., Cakmakci, S., Brechany, E.Y., Deegan, K.C., McSweeney, P.L.H., 2007b. Microbiology, biochemistry, and volatile composition of tulum cheese ripened in goat's skin or plastic bags. J. Dairy Sci. 90 (2007), 1102–1121.

Horne, J., Carpino, S., Tuminello, L., Rapisarda, T., Corallo, L., Licitra, G., 2005. Differences in volatiles, and chemical, microbial and sensory characteristics between artisanal and industrial Piacentinu Ennese cheeses. Int. Dairy J. 15, 605–617.

Ilbery, B., Kneafsey, M., 1999. Niche markets and regional speciality food products in Europe: towards a research agenda. Environ. Plann. A 31, 2207–2222.

Johnson, E.A., Nelson, J.H., Johnson, M., 1990. Microbiological safety of cheese made from heat treated milk. Part II. Microbiology. J. Food Prot. 53, 519—540.

Kay, J.K., Mackle, T.R., Auldist, M.J., Thomson, N.A., Bauman, D.E., 2003. Endogenous synthesis of cis-9, trans-11 conjugated linoleic acid in dairy cows fed fresh pasture. J. Dairy Sci. 87, 369—378.

Kanawjia, S.K., Rajesh, P., Latha, S., Singh, S., 1995. Flavour, chemical and texture profile changes in accelerated ripened Gouda cheese. Lebensm. Wiss. Technol. 28, 577—583.

Kummer, C., 2000. Craftsman cheese. Atl. Mon. 286, 109—112.

Kupiec, B., Revell, B., 1998. Speciality and artisanal cheeses today: the product and the consumer. Br. Food J. 100, 236—243.

La Terra, S., Carpino, S., Banni, S., Manenti, M., Caccamo, M., Licitra, G., 2006. Effect of mountain and sea level pasture on conjugated linoleic acid content in plasma and milk. J. Anim. Sci. 84 (1), 277—278.

Lau, K.Y., Barbano, D.M., Rasmussen, R.R., 1991. Influence of pasteurization of milk on protein breakdown in Cheddar cheese during aging. J. Dairy Sci. 74, 727—740.

Lichfield, J., 1999. Liberté! fraternité! fromage!: a new crisis is dividing France [Freedom! Brotherhood! Cheese!], Cheese, The Independent.

Licitra, G., Leone, G., Amata, F., Mormorio, D., 2000. In: Motta, F. (Ed.), Heritage and Landscape: The Art of Traditional Ragusano Cheese-Making. Consorzio Ricerca Filiera Lattiero-Casearia, Ragusa, Italy, pp. 163—166.

Licitra, G., 2006. Historical Sicilian Cheeses. CoRFiLaC Press, Ragusa.

Licitra, G., Ogier, J.C., Parayre, S., Pediliggieri, C., Carnemolla, T.M., Falentin, H., et al., 2007. Variability of bacterial biofilms of the "tina" wood vats used in the Ragusano cheese-making process. Appl. Environ. Microbiol. 73, 6980—6987.

Licitra, G., 2010a. World wide traditional cheeses: banned for business. Dairy Sci. Technol. 90 (4), 357—374.

Licitra, G., 2010b. Femmes et fromages traditionnels dans les pays en voie de développem, ent [Traditional women cheesemakers in developing countries: the challenge of food safety]. Les Cahiers de l'Ocha 15, 273—289. Available from: www.lemangeur-ocha.com.

Lortal, S., Di Blasi, A., Madec, M.-N., Pediliggieri, C., Tuminello, L., Tanguy, G., et al., 2009. Tina wooden vat biofilm: a safe and highly efficient lactic acid bacteria delivering system in PDO Ragusano cheese making. Int. J. Food Microbiol. 132 (1), 1—8.

Lortal, S., Licitra, G., Valence, F., 2014. Wooden tools: reservoirs of microbial biodiversity in traditional cheesemaking. Microbiol. Spectr. 2, 420.

Lowrie, R.J., Lawrence, R.C., 1972. Cheddar cheese flavour. IV. A new hypothesis to account for the development of bitterness. N. Z. J. Dairy Sci. Technol. 7, 51—53.

Mariaca, R.G., Berger, T.F.H., Gauch, R., Imhof, M.I., Jeangros, B., Bosset, J.O., 1997. Occurrence of volatile mono- and sesquiter-penoids in highland and lowland plant species as possible precur-sors for flavor compounds in milk and dairy products. J. Agric. Food Chem. 45, 4423—4434.

Mariani, C., Briandet, R., Chamba, J.-F., Notz, E., Carnet-Pantiez, A., Eyoug, R.N., et al., 2007. Biofilm ecology of wooden shelves used in ripening the French raw milk smear cheese Reblochon de Savoie. J. Dairy Sci. 90, 1653—1661.

Mariani, C., Oulahal, N., Chamba, J.-F., Dubois-Brissonnet, F., Notz, E., Briandet, R., 2011. Inhibition of *Listeria monocytogenes* by resident biofilms present on wooden shelves used for cheese ripening. Food Control 22, 1357—1362.

Massa, S., Turtura, G., Trovatelli, L.D., 1988. Qualité hygiénique du fromage de "*fosse*" de Sogliano al Rubicone (Italie). Lait 68, 323—326.

Miller, A., Brown, T., Call, J., 1996. Comparison of wooden and polyethylene cutting boards: potential for the attachment and removal of bacteria from ground beef. J. Food Prot. 59, 854—858.

Mourey, A., Canillac, N., 2002. Anti-*Listeria monocytogenes* activity of essential oils components of conifers. Food Control 13 (4), 289–292.

Mc Sweeney, P.L.H., Fox, P.F., Lucey, J.A., Jordan, K.N., Cogan, T.M., 1993. Contribuition of the indigenous microflora to the maturation of Cheddar cheese. Int. Dairy J. 5, 321–336.

Messens, W., Verluyten, J., Leroy, F., De Vuyst, L., 2003. Modelling growth and bacteriocin production by *Lactobacillus curvatus* LTH 1174 in response to temperature and pH values used for European sausage fermentation processes. Int. J. Food Microbiol. 81 (1), 41–52.

Nationa Research Council, Nutrient Requirements of Dairy Cattle, 2001. seventh ed. Revised National Academy of Science, Washington, DC.

Pasta, C., Licitra, G., 2007. Tradition or technology? Consumer criteria for choosing cheese. In: Seventh Pangborn Sensory Science Symposium. 12–16th August, Minneapolis, MN, USA.

Pieniak, Z., Verbeke, W., Vanhonacker, F., Guerrero, L., Hersleth, M., 2009. Association between traditional food consumption and motives for food choice in six European countries. Appetite 53 (1), 101–108.

Pearce, R., 1996. Antimicrobial defences in the wood of living trees. New Phytol. 132 (2), 203–233.

Piakietwiecz, A.C., 1987. Lipase and esterase formation by mutants of lactic streptococci and lactobacilli. Milchwissenschaft 42, 561–564.

Reed, B.A., Bruhn, C.M., 2003. Sampling and farm stories prompt consumers to buy specialty cheeses. Calif. Agric. 57, 76–80.

Rehman, S.U., McSweeney, P.L.H., Banks, J.M., Brechany, E.Y., Muir, D.D., Fox, P.F., 2000. Ripening of Cheddar cheese made from blends of raw and pasteurised milk. Int. Dairy J. 10, 33–44.

Richard, J., 1997. Utilisation du bois comme matériau au contact des produits laitiers. Comptes rendus de l'Académie d'agriculture de France 83 (5), 27–34.

Rizzello, C.G., Losito, I., Gobbetti, M., Carbonara, T., De Bari, M.D., Zambonin, P.G., 2005. Antibacterial activities of peptides from the water-soluble extracts of Italian cheese varieties. J. Dairy Sci. 88, 2348–2360.

Schulz H., Holz im Kontakt mit Lebensmitteln. Hat Holz antibakterielle Eigenschaften? *Holz. Zentralbl.* 84, 1395.

Settanni, L., Di Grigoli, A., Tornambè, G., Bellina, V., Francesca, N., Moschetti, G., et al., 2012. Persistence of wild Streptococcus thermophilus strains on wooden vat and during the manufacture of a traditional Caciocavallo type cheese. Int. J. Food Microbiol. 155, 73–81.

Scatassa, M.L., Cardamone, C., Miraglia, V., Lazzara, F., Fiorenza, G., Macaluso, G., et al., 2015. Characterisation of the microflora contaminating the wooden vats used for traditional Sicilian cheese production. Ital. J. Food Saf. 4 (4509), 36–39.

Schuler, S., 1994. Einfluss der Käseunterlage auf die Schmierebildung und die Qualität von Halbhartkäse. Switzerland. Milchwirtsch. Forsch. 23, 73–77.

Salque, et al., 2012. Earliest evidence for cheese making in the sixth millennium BC in Northern Europe. Nature. Available from: https://doi.org/10.1038/nature11698.

Suma, K., Misra, M.C., Varadaraj, M.C., 1998. Plantaricin LP84, a broad-spectrum heat-stable bacteriocin of *Lactobacillus plantarum* NCIM 2084 produced in a simple glucose broth medium. Int. J. Food Microbiol. 40, 17–25.

Sun, C.Q., O'Connor, C.J., Roberton, A.M., 2002. The antimicrobial properties of milk-fat after partial hydrolysis by calf pregastric lipase. Chem. Biol. Interact. 140, 185–198.

Tamang, J.P., Kailasapathy, K., 2010. Fermented food and beverages of the world. CRC Press, Boca Raton, Florida, United States.

U.S. FDA, 1998. Food Compliance Program. Domestic and Imported Cheese and Cheese Products. ⟨http://vm.cfsan.fda.gov/~comm/cp03037.htlm⟩.

Vanhonacker, F., Lengard, V., Hersleth, M., Verbeke, W., 2010. Profiling European traditional food consumers. Br. Food J. 112 (8), 871−886.

Viallon, C., Martin, B., Verdier-Metz, I., Pradel, P., Garel, J.P., Coulon, J.B., et al., 2000. Transfer of monoterpenes and sesquiterpenes from forages into milk fat. Lait 80, 635−641.

Visser, S., 1993. Proteolytic enzymes and their relation to cheese ripening and flavour: an overview. J. Dairy Sci. 76, 329−350.

Wang, L.L., Johnson, E.A., 1992. Inhibition of *Listeria monocytogenes* by fatty acids and monoglycerides. Appl. Environ. Microbiol. 58, 624−629.

Williams, A.G., Banks, J.M., 1997. Proteolytic and other hydrolytic enzyme activities in non-starter lactic acid bacteria isolated from Cheddar cheese manufactured in the United Kingdom. Int. Dairy J. 7, 763−774.

West, H.G., 2008. Food fears and raw-milk cheese. Appetite 51, 25−29.

Yang, Y., Shevchenko, A., Knaust, A., Abuduresule, I., Li, W., Hu, X., et al., 2014. Proteomics evidence for kefir dairy in Early Bronze Age China. J. Arch. Sci 45, 178−186.

FURTHER READING

Alix, B.-J., 2002. Cheese:selecting, tasting, and serving the world's finest. Lauren Glen Publiscing, San Diego, CA, ⟨www.laurenglenbooks.com⟩. 1-57145-890-5.

Chambers, D.H., Esteve, E., Retiveau, A., 2010. Effect of milk pasteurization on flavor properties of seven commercially available French cheese types. J. Sens. Stud. 25, 494−511.

European Union, 2004a. Regulation (EC) No 852/2004 of the European Parliament and of the Council of 29 April 2004 on the hygiene of foodstuffs. Off. J. Eur. Union L 139, 1−54.

European Union. 2004b. Regulation (EC) No. 853/2004 of the European Parliament and of the Council of 29 April 2004 laying down specific hygiene rules for the hygiene of foodstuffs. Off. J. Eur. Union L 139, 55−205.

Family Farming World Conference: IYFF Final Declaration: Feeding the Word, Caring for the Earth; http://www.asiadhrra.org/wordpress/2011/11/20/iyff-final-declaration-feeding...; http://www.agriculturesnetwork.org/resources/extra/news/family-farming-world-conference.

⟨http://frenchfoodintheus.org/534⟩.

⟨http://www.fromages-de-terroirs.com/marche-fromage1.php3?id_article = 652,2005⟩.

⟨http://www.clal.it/index.php⟩.

⟨http://iledefrancecheese.com/index.php/roquefort/roquefort.html⟩.

⟨http://www.Formaggio-di-Fossadi-Sogliano-DOP.Formaggio.it⟩.

⟨http://www.Agrarian.it/il-fossa/Conosrzio-di-Tutela-Formaggio-di-Fossa-di-Sogliano-DOP⟩.

⟨http://www.paxtonandwhitfield.co.uk/roquefort.html⟩.

⟨http://www.treccani.it/enciclopedia/sviluppo-urbano-e-aumento-della-popolazione_. (Atlante-Geopolitico)/⟩.

Masui, K., Yamada, T., 1996. French Cheeses. Dorling Kindersley Limited, London, 0-7513-0346-1pp. 178−181.

Schultz, T.P., Nicholas, J.J., 2000. Naturally durable heartwood: evidence for a proposed dual defensive function extractives. Phytochemistry 54, 47−52.

Yvon, M., Rijnen, L., 2001. Cheese flavor formation by amino acid catabolism. Int. Dairy J. 11, 185−201.

CHAPTER 10

Alternative Dairy Products Made With Raw Milk

Tânia Tavares[1,2] and Francisco Xavier Malcata[1,3]
[1]LEPABE, Faculdade de Engenharia da Universidade do Porto, Porto, Portugal
[2]LAQV/REQUIMTE, Departamento de Ciências Químicas, Laboratório de Bromatologia e Hidrologia, Faculdade de Farmácia da Universidade do Porto, Porto, Portugal
[3]Departamento de Engenharia Química, Faculdade de Engenharia da Universidade do Porto, Porto, Portugal

10.1 INTRODUCTION

Organic foods have been increasing in popularity worldwide, and artisanal foods—like raw dairy products and raw milk itself, are also undergoing a renaissance. More and more people realize that industrialization of food system has considerably reduced food intrinsic quality. The promotion of raw milk as "healthy food" has been on the rise, and a public debate about possible benefits regarding consumption of raw milk remains in order. The most frequently cited arguments by raw milk advocates are decreased incidence of allergies, higher nutritional quality, and better taste when compared to pasteurized milk.

The ultimate decisions about food and food safety are to be taken by the consumers, so they need to access trustworthy and reliable information. Family and friends, manufactures, scientists, and consumer associations are the usual sources of this information; however, data are sometimes contradictory, and even distorted by beliefs, values, science and public interest.

Access to food safety information has been changing all over the world. Although internet has become an increasingly important way of communication for food risk hazards and benefits (Sillence et al., 2016), consumers are warned on the validity of some information conveyed thereby. Studies focusing on online raw milk and raw milk dairy products have shown that there is a staged way of approaching the concepts; consumers more readily adhere to online information, and only when they doubt their credibility will they move to a more in-depth assessment of available information (Sillence et al., 2016). Informal channels for purchasing raw milk beyond the farm gate are also being increasingly used.

Raw Milk
DOI: https://doi.org/10.1016/B978-0-12-810530-6.00010-9
223

The demand for raw milk and associated dairy products is to be balanced against the increased risk of illness resulting from microbial contamination of milk, on the one hand, and the claims of benefits conveyed by raw milk ingestion, on the other. This chapter will accordingly present a brief overview of traditional products made with raw milk (cheeses and fermented milks), and the main focus will be the alternative raw milk dairy products.

10.2 RAW MILK

Raw milk is a living food, with claimed nutritional and biological properties. It usually comes from cows, goats, and sheep, or other domesticated ruminants that have been grass-fed, and it could vary between individual animals from the same specie (Aspri et al., 2015; Bailone et al. 2017; Claeys et al., 2014). Raw milk consists of unpasteurized and unhomogenized milk and often considered a "complete food"—since it contains natural enzymes, fatty acids, vitamins, and minerals. Raw milk is claimed to have a unique nutritional profile, being one of the most nutrient-dense foods. Common descriptors encompass "fresh," "real," "alive," "creamy," "full of flavors," "rich," "distinct," "satisfying," "tastier," and "delicious"; and it is surely a food possessing a superior flavor and texture relative to pasteurized and homogenized milk (Headrick et al., 1997; Jayarao et al., 2006). Consumer research demonstrates that flavor is one of the top reasons for consumers to choose raw milk in countries where it can be legally bought (Jayarao et al., 2006; Headrick et al., 1997). There are people who live on it exclusively (Headrick et al., 1997), and during the last century, raw milk from grass-fed cows was used as a medicine with supposed healing properties. Chronic diseases were treated and claimed to be sometimes cured upon ingestion of milk straight from the udder (Crewe, 1929).

10.3 PASTEURIZED VS UNPASTEURIZED MILK

Raw milk has the entitlement of incredibly complex whole food, supported by its digestive enzymes and its own antiviral, antibacterial, and antiparasitic compounds, as well as fat and water-soluble vitamins, a wide range of minerals, trace elements, all eight essential amino acids, and conjugated linoleic acid. However, there are significant concerns raised by some authors, as well as regulatory and public health organizations like

Food and Drug Administration (FDA) and Centers for Disease Control and Prevention, highlighting the realistic microbiological risk for the consumer (Cisak et al., 2017; Fratini et al., 2016) due to the presence of some human pathogens (Lucey, 2015). Studies have shown that a third of all raw milk contain at least one type of pathogen, even when sourced from clinically healthy animals or from milk that appeared to be of good quality (i.e., showing a low total bacterial count) (Desmasures et al., 1997; Griffiths, 2010a; Lucey, 2015; Soboleva, 2014). They can originate from animals, or from environmental contamination during milk collection and storage. Surveys from different countries have monitored the presence of various types of pathogens in raw milk (*Campylobacter, Listeria, Salmonella,* and human pathogenic verocytotoxin-producing *Escherichia coli*) that are most commonly reported as causative factors of milk-borne infections (Cisak et al., 2017; Claeys et al., 2013; Hudopisk et al., 2012; O'Mahony et al., 2009; Robinson et al., 2013; Van den Brom et al., 2015). Raw milk becomes contaminated by pathogens via direct passage from the animal blood into milk, mastitis, fecal contamination, or contact with human skin (Labropoulos et al., 1981), and their prevalence is influenced by farm size, number of animals, hygiene, farm management practices, milking facilities, and season, among others (Goff).

Pasteurization is an efficient way to ensure milk lasts longer, and all risks are eliminated upon killing pathogens. However, as a living food, raw milk is rich in beneficial bacteria that are critical for health, once human being cannot live without them. As shown above, they are responsible for stimulating and training the immune system, and working in conjunction with it to keep pathogenic bacteria away. Indeed, they can be effective in prevention and treatment of some bacterial infections. On the other hand, several strains of bacteria naturally present, or added later (*Lactobacillus, Leuconostoc,* and *Pediococcus*) and via fermentation, can transform milk into an even more digestible food. As protein and lipid nutrients, such bacterial allies are also destroyed by pasteurization—and are thus absent in pasteurized and ultrahigh temperature (UHT) processing milk.

Raw milk supporters claim that raw dairy retains health-promoting components that are lost in the pasteurization process and therefore not present in pasteurized or UHT milk; these include several of milk natural components, including beneficial bacteria, food enzymes, natural vitamins, and immunoglobulins, all of which are heat-sensitive and prevent lactose intolerance while providing improved nutrition or provision for "good" bacteria. These claims have been widely checked (Anonymous, 2014; Claeys et al., 2013; Davis et al., 2014; French et al., 2013; MacDonald et al., 2011; Ontario Agency for Health Protection and Promotion, 2013).

At the same time, consumer interest in raw milk cheeses has been continuously growing—namely based on demand for new and more intense, and more varied flavors by consumers. Raw milk cheeses exhibit a more intense and strong flavor than pasteurized or microfiltered ones (Casalta et al., 2009; Masoud et al., 2012). The diversity between cheeses and stronger sensory attributes has been associated to milk itself and its adventitious dynamic microbial community (Montel et al., 2014). The microbiological safety of raw milk cheese is a highly controversial topic. It is expected that pasteurization eradicates pathogenic bacteria from raw milk, yet it also gets rid of beneficial and unique microorganisms; however, pasteurized milk cheese may still contain pathogenic bacteria that can cause outbreaks of food-borne illness—and even to higher incidence rates than for raw milk cheese (Koch et al., 2010) because the original microbial balance was disrupted (Little et al., 2008; Ryser, 2007). Due to the potential microbiological risk posed by raw milk, it is of utmost importance that cheesemaking is followed by a sufficiently long ripening period further to hygiene enforcement in the local dairies and a representative microbiological monitoring at postmanufacturing stage (Yoon et al., 2016).

Europe began issuing general conduct regulations in the 1990s, with the aim of supporting survival of raw-milk cheese production, while guaranteeing consumer safety. Around the Mediterranean Basin, a large variety of traditional cheeses are still manufactured to significant numbers. Since 1992, manufacture of raw milk cheeses in EU Member States was allowed provided that they follow strict regulations related to raw material quality, namely, milk microbiological content, ageing period (60 days as minimum period), and hygiene in processing facilities. However, there are a few exceptions regarding processing facilities and materials when such products bear specific labels, e.g., protected designation of origin, protected geographical indication (PGI), or prodotti agroalimentari tradizionali. In fact, if the surrounding environment contributes to development of unique characteristics in said cheeses, the facilities and materials used can be different from those routinely established (Slow Food Foundation for Biodiversity, 2010).

Regulations for raw milk sales in the USA vary from state to state; however, raw milk cheese laws apply nationwide. FDA states that artisanal cheese production is to be subjected to legislation that effectively prevents manufacture, for sale in interstate commerce, of any cheese made from raw milk, unless it has undergone an ageing process of no less than 60 days.

Canada also allows sale of raw milk cheeses aged over 60 days. In 2009, the Province of Quebec modified regulations so as to allow raw milk cheeses aged for less than 60 days—provided that stringent safeguards are met (Slow Food Foundation for Biodiversity, 2010). In Australia, Standard 4.2.4A currently allows manufacture of specific raw milk cheeses, according to Swiss regulations and French Ministerial Orders. Food Standards Australia New Zealand are currently assessing the requirements in the Food Standards Code for sale of raw milk products, yet their work is restricted to regulating production and sale of very hard, aged cheeses only (no less than 6 months) (Slow Food Foundation for Biodiversity, 2010).

Akio (2010) reported a new method and apparatus for cheese manufacture able to support coagulation and suitable lactic acid fermentation, thus reducing milk decay substantially. Raw milk microbiota vary according to region and livestock breed; in general, however, it contains lactic acid bacteria (LAB) that produce pathogen-inhibiting substances, able to fight proliferation of many contaminating bacterial pathogens, and thus allowing production of cheese with minimum microbiological quality (Montel et al., 2014; Yoon et al., 2016). This has lead raw milk cheese to the status of microbiologically safe food (Masoud et al., 2012). In order to keep microbiota richness and diversity between cheeses, abiding to traditional practices is extremely important (Montel et al., 2014).

In what concerns raw milk cheese biological functions, there are some data relating to raw milk consumption; further studies are, nevertheless, needed to ascertain whether such association extends to traditional raw milk cheese (Montel et al., 2014).

Since early in the last century, industry began producing cheese with pasteurized milk—and nowadays, only species recognized as safe can be used (Bourdichon et al., 2012), with the notable exception of Europe where traditional cheeses are protected by Protected Designation of Origin (PDO) labels. However, the list of microorganisms allowed lags far behind the actual microbial diversity of traditional cheeses (Montel et al., 2014). In order to keep sensory cheese characteristics, it is crucial to preserve raw milk cheese microbial diversity, in attempts to exploit its benefits while also preserving traditional practices that have been improved from generation to generation.

10.4 ALTERNATIVE PRODUCTS

To increase pre- and probiotic properties of dairy products, and to improve the associated organoleptic indicators, new methods to obtain dairy products have been developed and patented. Chen et al. (2010) disclosed a preparation method of symbiotic goat milk powder, via combination of freeze–drying probiotic powder from raw goat milk with prebiotics. The probiotics can be protected, and their survival rate and the functionality of the goat milk powder can still be improved. Another example is the use of raw milk with addition of vegetable pumpkin powder, or beet powder, or Jerusalem artichoke powder, or even carrot powder to 2%–3% of milk weight—subjected to mild heating and homogenization, and final addition of a probiotic "Bifilact-Pro" to aid in fermentation (Anatolevich et al., 2017). Liping et al. (2016) produced a probiotic fermented milk, in which *Lactobacillus rhamnosus* and *Streptococcus thermophilus* were added to produce a product with stable quality and good mouth feel—without the need of food additives, and where LAB viable counts reach regular thresholds. The production of cultured milk beverage with the prebiotic ingredient inulin (Viktorovna et al., 2017) appeared along the same lines—where raw milk, skimmed milk (in liquid and powder forms), and inulin were mixed, homogenized, and submitted to mild thermal treatment. A starter culture, consisting of strains *S. thermophilus* and *Lactobacillus bulgaricus*, was then added to bring about fermentation. This invention apparently leads to a fermented milk beverage, with nutritional and biological added-value—able to overcome such defects as excessive liquid consistency and whey separation, to improve organoleptic features, and to stabilize the structure of the final product.

Sato and Yoshikawa (2017) patented a method to produce fermented dairy product, with addition of LAB to raw milk, followed by fermentation as first step; and a second step entailing addition of *Paenibacillus*-derived protease. These two steps assured the characteristic smoothness of the fermented dairy product, yet hardness of the fermented dairy product can be adjusted to will. Another study (Mingna and Xiaojing, 2016) focused on production of fermented dairy products promoted by *Lactococcus lactis* subsp. *cremoris*, *Leuconostoc*, *L. lactis* subsp. *Diacetyl*, and *L. lactis* subsp. *lactis*. Refreshing and unique texture products were obtained, where sodium citrate was used to control fermentation and production of carbon dioxide and special flavors. Li and De (2016) reported an invention pertaining to fermented milk flavored with cherry and raspberry jam. Coagulation effected by the cherry and raspberry jam leads to an alternative method of obtaining traditional products. Jam promotes lactic acid fermentation, leading to a new refreshing and delicate fruity flavor. Such products have a market potential. Wei et al. (2006) found a new *Lactobacillus plantarum* strain (CW006) with antihypertensive effect, due to its proteolysis activity responsible for production of angiotensin-converting enzyme inhibitor via raw milk fermentation. It can apparently be used as starting culture in the dairy industry and applied in different health care and medical products.

There are five Guangxi Baise Zhuang Niu Animal Husbandry Co. patents encompassing manufacture of new products from raw buffalo milk (Zhangzhi, 2015a,b,c,d,e). Novel and peculiar raw milk products were supposedly obtained through combination of raw buffalo milk with tomato, *Ziziphus mauritiana*, grape, pumpkin and *Passiflora edulis* flavors. All of them possess a nutritive value higher than conventional buffalo milk, and the health benefits are obvious—further to a full-bodied flavor, a sweet mouth feel and a faint-scent taste. Market competitive advantages accordingly resulted, with greater profit margins expected when compared to existing products. In addition, such raw milk products are suitable for both young and elderly.

Yali et al. (2011) developed a new dairy product based on yoghurt, where the raw material is ca. 90% raw milk, but the dry matter content (of which 1%–2% is lactalbumin and 8% sugar) was improved without resorting to additives. The yoghurt coagulation rate is high, clots are stable, and display a stiff and smooth texture and color, moderate in sweetness and acidity, but thick in mouth feeling without whey separation. A new technology to produce brown drinking yoghurt was also proposed (Yang et al., 2016); a fermented food was indeed obtained, with ca. 90% raw milk and a Danisco strain. The brown color and a unique flavor were developed via Maillard's reaction. Nutritional ingredients became concentrated due to addition of whey protein powder as gel protein; the protein content and the stability of the drinking yoghurt were both enhanced.

Jiahua et al. (2016) developed a refreshing jackfruit ice cream rich in raw milk. Another novel technology, in which raw milk is used to 80% as raw material, was developed by Sheng (2015). His invention discloses a formula for a condensed raw milk cryoconcentrated product, flavored with sweet condensed milk, whey protein powder, and specific essences. The mixture is spray-dried to generate the unique caramel flavor. This product is easy to carry and convenient to use—presenting a long storage time, and being suitable for production of many other products, such as milky tea, baking goods, cold drinks, candies, and chocolates.

Another novel product pertains to a flavor enhancer for food or drink (Washizu et al., 2008), comprising a treated product obtained by subjecting raw milk proteins to lactic acid fermentation and proteases; a balanced flavor of fresh milk was accordingly obtained.

Xi'an Zhen Yuan Yu Yang Diary Product Co. filed a patent for production of sheep milk powder with omega 3 fatty acids; this product based on raw milk supported claims in such fields as intestinal health, blood sugar balance, and cardiovascular protection (Hua and Xiaoju, 2015).

Yong et al. (2015) were able to produce a Maca nutritional health care milk; raw milk and Maca can be combined to promote body absorption and utilization of nutrients, namely, to aid in resistance to fatigue, increase energy, regulate endocrine system, enhance immunity, benefit lung and stomach, and moisten the intestines.

A new Kasha product—i.e., an instant dry grain milk, containing raw milk (20%−27%), flour (53.5%−63.5%), sucrose (9%−11%), a fruit additive (3%−14%) as source of dietary fibers and macro- and microelements, a vitamin−mineral premix as additional source of vitamins was meanwhile proposed by Dmitrievich et al. (2017).

Some innovative products relate to pastry food—and one was patented by Yanzi (2015a), with a formula for sun-shaped biscuit made with such raw materials as raw milk powder. Cake products with unusual shapes, and crisp and soft taste and milk flavor can respond to the demand by the market. Another related invention disclosed peanut butter, nut cheese, walnut milk soda, and black sesame biscuits, as well as pistachio nut small crispy cake, made with raw milk powder further to other ingredients (Pengfei, 2015a,b,c,d,e). Although many kinds of biscuit products are available in the market, the individual characteristics of all those five products were claimed to be novel in high quality, deliciousness, and delicacy. The moderate saltiness of the small crispy products produces an excellent mouthfeel; the peanut butter biscuit and walnut milk soda are moderate in sweetness and apparently conveyed a good taste. Starting with raw milk powder as ingredient, Xiaopeng, 2015a,b,c,d) and Yanzi (2015b) created different bread products. The first one claimed his products as novel in appearance, fragrant and sweet in taste, fine, smooth, mellow, and milk- and banana-flavored, or else fruity or vanilla-type taste; the second one descried his products as delicate in taste, mellow, green-tea-fragranced, and slightly milk-flavored.

A final alternative application for raw milk is as chemical fungicide against cucumber powdery mildew. Application of raw milk (40% concentration) in vegetable crops conveys a reasonable degree of disease control—being able to act as fertilizer; it apparently increases chlorophyll content, growth parameters, and yield by infected cucumber plants (Kamel et al., 2017).

10.5 CONCLUSIONS

Economic and technological development is expected to lead to improvement of quality of life, along with awareness on nutrition issues—with a tendency of food requirements to evolve from quantity to quality of food. Hence, great taste and flavor, and diversified nutrition will constitute a strategic target for the food industry in the near future. The amount of novel (safe) raw milk products available on supermarket shelves has been on the rise—thus reflecting the underlying efforts of research and development. Those products are able to keep the unique raw milk nutritional and functional characteristics intact and already include plain milk, ice cream, yoghurt, cheese, powdered milk, LAB-containing beverages, and pastry products (among others).

ACKNOWLEDGMENTS

This work received partial financial support for author T.T. via a postdoctoral fellowship (ref. SFRH/BPD/89360/2012)—supervised by author F.X.M.; under the auspices of ESF (III Quadro Comunitário de Apoio) and the Portuguese State. This work was financially supported by Project PTDC/BBB-EBB/1374/2014—POCI-01-0145-FEDER-016640— and UID/QUI/50006/2013—POCI/01/0145/FEDER/007265 funded by FEDER funds through COMPETE2020—Programa Operacional Competitividade e Internacionalização (POCI), and by national funds through FCT—Fundacão para a Ciência e a Tecnologia, I.P.

REFERENCES

Akio, O., 2010. Method for Producing Cheese, and Apparatus for the Same. 2010148473.
Anatolevich, D.R., Aleksandrovna, K.M., Viktorovna, B.T., Aleksandrovna, K.I., Mikhajlovna, M.A., Aleksandrovna, D.T., 2017. Method for Obtaining Dairy Functional Product. 0002626536.
Anonymous, 2014. An assessment of the effects of pasteurization on claimed nutrition and health benefits of raw milk. MPI Technical Paper No. 13.

Aspri, M., Bozoudi, D., Tsaltas, D., Hill, C., Papademas, P., 2015. Raw donkey milk as a source of *Enterococcus* diversity: assessment of their technological properties and safety characteristics. Food Control. 73, 81−90.

Bailone, R.L., Borra, R.C., Roça, R.O., Aguiar, L., Harris, M., 2017. Quality of refrigerated raw milk from buffalo cows (*Bubalus bubalis bubalis*) in different farms and seasons in Brazil. Ciênc. Anim. Bras. 18, 1−12.

Bourdichon, F., Casaregola, S., Farrokh, C., Frisvad, J.C., Gerds, M.L., Hammes, W.P., et al., 2012. Food fermentations: microorganisms with technological beneficial use. Int. J. Food Microbiol. 154 (3), 87−97.

Casalta, E., Sorba, J.-M., Aigle, M., Ogier, J.-C., 2009. Diversity and dynamics of the microbial community during the manufacture of Calenzana, an artisanal Corsican cheese. Int. J. Food Microbiol. 133, 243−251.

Chen, H.C., Qi, M., Tao, Q., Guowei, S., Juanna, S., Zhangfeng, W., et al., 2010. Preparation Method of Synbiotic Goat Milk Powder. 101810220.

Cisak, E., Zając, V., Sroka, J., Sawczyn, A., Kloc, A., Dutkiewicz, J., et al., 2017. Presence of pathogenic rickettsiae and protozoan in samples of raw milk from cows, goats, and sheep. Foodborne Pathog. Dis. 14 (4), 189−194.

Claeys, W.L., Cardoen, S., Daube, G., Block, J., Dewettinck, K., Dierick, K., et al., 2013. Raw or heated cow milk consumption: review of risks and benefits. Food Control. 31 (1), 251−262.

Claeys, W.L., Verraes, C., Cardoen, S., Block, J., Huyghebaert, A., Raes, K., et al., 2014. Consumption of raw or heated milk from different species: An evaluation of the nutritional and potential health benefits. Food Control. 42, 188−201.

Crewe, J., 1929. Raw milk cures many diseases. Certified Milk Magazine.

Davis, B.J., Li, C.X., Nachman, K.E., 2014. A literature review of the risks and benefits of consuming raw and pasteurized cow's milk: a response to the request from The Maryland House of Delegates' Health and Government Operations Committee 2014.

Desmasures, N.F., Bazin, F., Gueguen, M., 1997. Microbiological composition of raw milk from selected farms in the Camembert region of Normandy. J. Appl. Microbiol. 83, 53−58.

Dmitrievich, L.A., Vladimirovna, B.A., Alekseevich, E.I., 2017. Instant Dry Grain Milk Kasha. 0002626534.

Fratini, F., Turchi, B., Ferrone, M., Galiero, A., Nuvoloni, R., Torracca, B., et al., 2016. Is Leptospira able to survive in raw milk? Study on the inactivation at different storage times and temperatures. Folia Microbiol. (Praha). 61 (5), 413−416.

French, N., Benschop, J., Marshall, J., 2013. Raw milk: is it good for you? Proceedings of the food safety. Anim. Welfare Biosecur. Branch NZVA. 327, 11−20.

Griffiths, M.W., 2010a. Improving the safety and quality of milk. Volume 1: Milk production and processing. Woodhead Publishing Limited, Guelph, p. 520.

Headrick, M.L., Timbo, B., Klontz, K.C., Werner, S.B., 1997. Profile of raw milk consumers in California. Public Health Rep. 112 (5), 418−422.

Hua, W., Xiaoju, S., 2015. Sheep Milk Powder Containing Omega 3 and Preparation Method for Sheep Milk Powder. 104904858.

Hudopisk, N., Korva, M., Janet, E., Simetinger, M., Grgic-Vitek, M., Gubensek, J., et al., 2012. Tick-borne encephalitis associated with consumption of raw goat milk. Slov. Emerg. Infect. Dis. 19, 806−808.

Jayarao, B.M., Donaldson, S.C., Straley, B.A., Sawant, A.A., Hegde, N.V., Brown, J.L., 2006. A survey of foodborne pathogens in bulk tank milk and raw milk consumption among farm families in Pennsylvania. J. Dairy Sci. 89 (7), 2451−2458.

Jiahua, W., Jun, W., Xiaowei Z., 2016. Jackfruit Ice Cream and Manufacture Method Thereof. 106107009.

Kamel, S.M., Ketta, H.A., Emeran, A.A., 2017. Efficacy of raw cow milk and whey against cucumber powdery mildew disease caused by *Sphaerotheca fuliginea* (Schlecht.) Pollacci under Plastic House Conditions. Egypt. J. Biol. Pest Control. 27 (1), 135–142.

Knoll, L., 2005. Origins of the Regulation of Raw Milk Cheeses in the United States. http://nrs.harvard.edu/urn-3:HUL.InstRepos:8852188.

Koch, J., Dworak, R., Prager, R., Becker, B., Brockmann, S., Wicke, A., et al., 2010. Large listeriosis outbreak linked to cheese made from pasteurized milk, Germany, 2006–2007. Foodborne Pathog. Dis. 7, 1581–1584.

Labropoulos, A.E., Palmer, J.K., Lopez, A., 1981. Whey protein denaturation of UHT processed milk and its effect on rheology of yogurt. J. Texture Stud. 12 (3), 365–374.

Li, Z., De Z., 2016. Coagulation Type Flavored Fermented Milk Containing Cherry and Raspberry Jam and Preparation Method Thereof. 106070627.

Liping, Z., Yuanyang, N., Xinlu, W., Haiyan, L., Qiming, L., 2016. Probiotic *Lactobacillus Rhamnosus* Fermented Milk and Preparation Method Thereof. 105961588.

Little, C.L., Rhoades, J.R., Sagoo, S.K., Harris, J., Greenwood, M., Mithani, V., et al., 2008. Microbiological quality of retail cheeses made from raw, thermized or pasteurized milk in the UK. Food Microbiol. 25, 304–312.

Lucey, J., 2015. Raw milk consumption—risks and benefits. Nutr. Food Sci. 50 (4), 189–193.

MacDonald, L., Brett, J., Kelton, D., Majowicz, S.E., Snedekerr, K., Sargeant, K.M., 2011. A systematic review and meta-analysis of the effects of pasteurization on milk vitamins, and evidence for raw milk consumption and other health-related outcomes. J. Food Prot. 74 (11), 1814–1832.

Masoud, W., Vogensen, F.K., Lillevang, S., Abu Al-Soud, W., Sorensen, S.J., Jakobsen, M., 2012. The fate of indigenous microbiota, starter cultures, *Escherichia coli*, *Listeria innocua* and *Staphylococcus aureus* in Danish raw milk and cheeses determined by pyrosequencing and quantitative real time (qRT)-PCR. Int. J. Food Microbiol. 153, 192–202.

Mingna, W., Xiaojing, Y., 2016. Aerogenesis Fermentation Dairy Product and Production Method Thereof. 105613732.

Montel, M.-C., Buchin, S., Mallet, A., Delbes-Paus, C., Vuitton, D.A., Desmasures, N., et al., 2014. Review Traditional cheeses: Rich and diverse microbiota with associated benefits. Int. J. Food Microbiol. 177, 136–154.

O'Mahony, M., Fanning, S., Whyte, P., 2009. Chapter 6: the safety of raw liquid milk. In: Tamine, A.Y. (Ed.), Milk Processing and Quality Management. Blackwell Publishing Ltd./John Wiley and Sons Ltd, West Sussex, UK, pp. 139–167.

Ontario Agency for Health Protection and Promotion, 2013. PHO Technical Report: Update on Raw Milk Consumption and Public Health: A Scientific Review for Ontario Public Health Professionals. Public Health Ontario, Toronto, ON.

Pengfei, C., 2015a. Black Sesame Biscuit. 104542850.

Pengfei, C., 2015b. Nut Cheese Biscuit. 104542855.

Pengfei, C., 2015c. Peanut Butter Biscuit. 104542848.

Pengfei, C., 2015d. Pistachio Nut Small Crispy Cake. 104542847.

Pengfei, C., 2015e. Walnut Milk Soda Biscuit. 104542851.

Robinson, T.J., Scheftel, J.M., Smith, K.E., 2013. Raw milk consumption among patients with non-outbreak-related enteric infections, Minnesota, USA, 2001 e 2010. Emerg. Infect. Dis. 20, 38–44.

Ryser, E.T., 2007. Incidence and behavior of *Listeria monocytogenes* in cheese and other fermented dairy products. In: Ryser, E.T., Marth, E.H. (Eds.), Listeria, Listeriosis and Food Safety, 3rd ed CRC Press, Boca Raton, FL, pp. 405–502.

Sato, T., Yoshikawa, J., 2017. Fermented dairy product and method for manufacturing same. WO/2017/104729.

Slow Food Foundation for Biodiversity, 2010. Slow Cheeses. http://slowfood.com/slowcheese/eng/85/legislation.

Sheng, X. (2015). A Formula of a Condensed Milk Flavored Milk Powder. 104904856.

Sillence, E., Hardy, C., Medeiros, L.C., LeJeune, J.T., 2016. Examining trust factors in online food risk information: the case of unpasteurized or 'raw' milk. Appetite. 99, 200−210.

Soboleva, T., 2014. Assessment of the Microbiological Risks Associated with the Consumption of Raw Milk. MPI Technical Paper No. 2014/12.

Van den Brom, R., Santman-Berends, I., Luttikholt, S., Moll, L., Van Engelen, E., Vellema, P., 2015. Bulk tank milk surveillance as a measure to detect Coxiella burnetii shedding dairy goat herds in the Netherlands between 2009 and 2014. J. Dairy Sci. 98, 3814−3825.

Viktorovna, B.E., Vladimirovna, L.K., Yurevna, S.Y., Vladimirovna, Z.O., 2017. Method of Producing Cultured Milk Beverage with Inulin. 0002622080.

Washizu, Y., Eiji Emoto, E., Kono, M., 2008. Flavor Enhancer for Food or Drink, Production Method Thereof, and Food or Drink Comprising Flavor Enhancer. 20100112129.

Wei, C., Hao, Z., Fengwei, T., Jianxin, Z., Liangliang, S., Wenli, H., et al., 2006. *Lactobacillus Plantarum* CW006 with Antihypertensive Function. 1844363.

Xiaopeng, L., 2015a. Banana Bread. 104621209.

Xiaopeng, L., 2015b. Corn Bread. 104621206.

Xiaopeng, L., 2015c. Strawberry Bread. 104621207.

Xiaopeng, L., 2015d. Vanilla Bread. 104621208.

Yali, Z., Bangwei, O., Fuhai, Z., Hongwei, W. (2011). Preparation Method for Set Yoghurt and Prepared Set Yoghurt. 102283285.

Yang Xu, Y., Shengqu, W., Yana, Y., 2016. Brown Drinking Yoghurt and Production Method Thereof. 105901136.

Yanzi, L., 2015a. Sun-Shaped Biscuit. 104509567.

Yanzi, L., 2015b. Green Tea Bread. 104509561.

Yong, L., Ning, H., Yanke, M., Liyang, C., Abuduaini, M., 2015. Production Process of Maca Nutritional Health Care Milk. 105638903.

Yoon, Y., Lee, S., Choi, K.-H., 2016. Review: microbial benefits and risks of raw milk cheese. Food Control. 63, 201−215.

Zhangzhi, W., 2015a. Method for Preparing Grape-Flavor Buffalo Milk Product. 104782776.

Zhangzhi, W., 2015b. Tomato Buffalo Milk Product. 104782774.

Zhangzhi, W., 2015c. *Ziziphus Mauritiana* Buffalo Milk and Preparation Method Thereof. 104782771.

Zhangzhi, W., 2015d. Pumpkin Buffalo Milk Product. 104782772.

Zhangzhi, W., 2015e. *Passiflora Edulis*-Flavor Buffalo Milk Product. 104782775.

FURTHER READING

Griffiths, M.W., 2010b. The microbiological safety of raw milk. In: Griffiths, M.W. (Ed.), Improving the Safety and Quality of Milk, Volume 1: Milk Production and Processing. CRC Press, Boca Raton, FL, pp. 27−63.

CHAPTER 11

Infectious Diseases in Dairy Cattle

Maria A.S. Moreira, Abelardo Silva Júnior, Magna C. Lima and Sanely L. da Costa
Departamento de Veterinária, Universidade Federal de Viçosa, Viçosa, Brazil

11.1 INTRODUCTION

Bovine mastitis is a worldwide problem in dairy cattle that has a great effect on animal welfare and milk production (Keefe, 2012; Peton and Le Loir, 2014). Bovine mastitis is the most important disease for the dairy industry, as economic losses resulting from the disease constitute direct and indirect losses. The direct losses include treatment costs (medicament and labor), discarded milk, time, deaths, and costs associated with a recurrent mastitis. Indirect costs include decreased milk production, decreased milk quality, increased numbers of discarded animals, stopping lactation earlier than expected, animal welfare as well as a concomitant occurrence of other related health problems (Petrovski et al., 2006).

The increase in information about food safety, the role of mastitis-causing pathogens as potential zoonotic agents has been duly taken into importance. Further research are needed on the risks of *Staphylococcus aureus* enterotoxins from mastitis milk for human health, it is documented that most outbreaks of foodborne diseases come from the contamination of human food handlers. *S. aureus* deserves special attention also due to the numerous hospital infections related to methicillin resistant *S. aureus*, strains that already were identified in bovine milk (Moon et al., 2007).

Milk-borne zoonoses are important, especially in developing countries, where there is a high consumption of milk without proper heat treatment (Shaheen et al., 2015). *Mycobacterium bovis* is the causative agent of tuberculosis mastitis. The HIV/AIDS pandemic in parts of the world has raised new questions about the epidemiological impact of immunosuppression related to *M. bovis* (De La Rua-Domenech, 2006).

Raw Milk
DOI

11.2 MASTITIS

11.2.1 Concept and Classification

Intramammary bacterial infection is a common problem in dairy cows. It may cause clinical mastitis associated with an excessive inflammatory response or subclinical mastitis presenting as persistent infection (Schukken et al., 2011). The etiology of mastitis has been changing with the evidence of new microbial species. There are about 150 bacterial species isolated from cows with mastitis. Regarding the etiological agent, the disease can be classified into four types: bacterial, fungal, viral, and mastitis caused by algae. Viruses as an etiologic agent for mastitis have limited clinical significance. The major viral agents causing mastitis are *bovine herpesvirus 2*, *vaccinia*, and *pseudovariola virus*. Generally, viruses reach the dermis and epidermis of the udder, unlike the other agents that surround the secretory alveoli. Viral agents involved in mastitis have little clinical significance unless a secondary bacterial invasion occurs, which affects intramammary (IMM) tissue (Shaheen et al., 2015). There are numerous etiologic agents that are responsible for mastitis; however, majority of infections are caused by bacteria of the genera *Staphylococcus*, *Streptococcus*, and *Enterobacteriaceae* group.

There are two types of mastitis: the clinical and the subclinical. The mode of transmission can be contagious or environmental. The main contagious microorganisms are *S. aureus* and *Streptococcus agalactiae*, the main source of infection being the mammary gland of infected cows. On the other hand, the main source of pathogens causing environmental mastitis is the animal's habitat. *Streptococcus uberis*, *Escherichia coli*, and *Klebsiella* spp. are examples of microorganisms that can be transmitted from the environment (Table 11.1) (Bogni et al., 2011). The different clinical signs of the disease are often related to the species of the pathogen. Intramammary infection caused by *E. coli* usually cause acute clinical mastitis, associated with visible changes in milk, swelling, udder pain, and possibly a systemic inflammatory syndrome that severely affects cows (Burvenich et al., 2003).

Coagulase-negative staphylococci (CNS) have traditionally been considered to be minor mastitis pathogens, especially in comparison with major pathogens such 12 as *S. aureus*, streptococci, and coliforms. More than 10 different CNS species have been isolated from mastitis, and the species most commonly reported are *Staphylococcus chromogenes*, *Staphylococcus simulans*, *Staphylococcus hyicus*, and *Staphylococcus epidermidis*. The main reason for this is that mastitis caused by CNS is very mild and usually remains subclinical. It is difficult to determine whether CNS species behave as contagious or

Table 11.1 The major and minor mastitis pathogens
Mastitis

Contagious mastitis	Environmental mastitis
Staphylococcus aureus	**Coliforms**
Streptococcus agalactiae	*Escherichia coli*
Streptococcus dysgalactiae	*Klebsiella* spp.
	Klebsiella oxytoca
	Enterobacter spp.
	Citrobacter spp.
Corynebacterium bovis	**Gram-positive cocci**
	Streptococcus uberis and enterococci
	Gram-negative
	Pseudomonas spp.
Mycoplasma spp.	*Prototheca*
filamentous fungi *or yeasts*	

Coagulase-negative staphylococci (CNS): *Staphylococcus chromogenes, Staphylococcus simulans, Staphylococcus hyicus,* and *Staphylococcus epidermidis.*

environmental pathogens. Control measures against contagious mastitis pathogens, such as postmilking teat disinfection, reduce CNS infections in the herd (Pyörälä and Taponen, 2009).

In contrast, *S. aureus* is responsible by subclinical mastitis. In this situation, there are not visible signs of inflammation in the udder; however, it causes long term losses due to increased somatic cell count (SCC), reduction in milk quality and quantity, and an increased risk of spreading of the pathogen within the herd (Halasa, 2012). *S. aureus* is usually the most isolated pathogen from cow's milk because it is part of the normal microbiota of the udder skin and teat. Occasionally, *S. aureus* may enter the teat canal and colonize internal parts of the mammary gland causing clinical or subclinical mastitis. Intramammary infection by *S. aureus* predominantly causes subclinical mastitis resulting in a persistent chronic infection (Benić et al., 2012). During the early stages of infection, the damage is mild and can be reversed. However, there are cases of *S. aureus* infections, which may present hyperacute mastitis (Wall et al., 2005). Bovine mastitis may also be associated with *Mycobacterium* infection. In this case, it is usually associated with tuberculosis in other organs. However, the mammary gland disease can occur only, which represents zoonotic potential. Tuberculous mastitis is caused by *M. bovis* and *Mycobacterium tuberculosis*. *M. bovis* circulates predominantly in cattle. Although *Mycobacterium tuberculosis* predominantly infects humans, it can infect cattle (Pardo et al., 2001).

Mastitis by *Brucella abortus* is chronic and often clinically inapparent. Infected cows excrete a large number of viable bacteria in the milk for months or years. In this case, it appears that normal glands are important sources of infection not only for other calves but also for humans (Halling et al., 2005). The prevalence of fungal mastitis is low (1%–12% of all cases of mastitis) but can sometimes occur in epidemic proportions. Fungal infections of the mammary gland are predominantly caused by yeasts of the *Candida* genus. Bovine mastitis caused by fungi is usually associated with contaminated antibiotics (Krukowski and Saba, 2003). These fungi are related to situations in which bacterial mastitis control programs use indiscriminate antibiotic therapy. Important fungal agents of mastitis are *Candida albicans, Aspergillus fumigatus,* and *Aspergillus niger* (Pachauri et al., 2013). However, some other fungi such as *Cryptococcus neoformans, Trichosporon, Torulopsis,* and *Saccharomyces* are species related to bovine mastitis. Invasion of fungi in bovine mammary tissue often occurs as a mixed infection (Krukowski and Saba, 2003), Algae are others etiologic agents of mastitis. *Prototheca zopfii* causing bovine mastitis in cases of food, fodder, and water contamination. The disease is more prevalent in regions where cattle graze near public parks, lakes, and tourist places (Marques et al., 2008).

11.2.2 Defenses of the Mammary Gland and Pathophysiology of Mastitis

The innate immunity occurs at the beginning of the infection, being mediated by anatomical or physical defense mechanisms, nonspecific substances and cellular. Once the pathogen enters the mammary gland, it can be eliminated by the innate immune system, but if this does not occur, the acquired immune system is triggered (Rainard and Riollet, 2006). Since most infections of the mammary gland occur via the ascending route, the pathogen needs to enter via the teat canal which is normally closed due to the presence of a muscular ring in the hole of the teat and keratin. In the period between milking, this ring is a physical and chemical barrier. Keratin buffer consists of scaly cells of the stratified epithelium of the canal wall. Cationic proteins associated with keratin buffer may promote inactivation of bacteria by electrostatically binding to pathogens, altering the cell wall and making them more susceptible to osmotic pressure (Rainard and Riollet, 2006; Viguier et al., 2009). Resident cells and cells recruited together play a key role in immediate defense against local infection. Recruitment of extensive neutrophils from the circulation into the lumen of the mammary gland is a milestone in the immune response to early breast infection (Klimiene et al., 2011).

Several nonspecific antimicrobial factors are found in the mammary gland, such as lactoperoxidase–thiocyanate–hydrogen peroxide, lysozyme, lactoferrin, and complement system. Lactoperoxidase is the enzyme most abundant in bovine milk, which in association with hydrogen peroxide and the ion produce chemical reactions, producing the hypothiocyanic acid and the hypothiocyanite ion, these have an antimicrobial activity, being so called lactoperoxidase–thiocyanate–hydrogen peroxide system (Atasever et al., 2013; Sordillo et al., 1997). Gram-negative and catalase-positive bacteria, such as *Pseudomonas* spp., *Salmonella* spp., and *Shigella* spp., are inhibited or inactivated by this system, while Gram-positive and catalase-negative bacteria such as *Streptococcus* spp. and *Lactobacillus* spp. are only inhibited (Kussendrager and Van Hooijdonk, 2000).

Lysozyme is an enzyme produced by epithelial cells and leukocytes, has bactericidal activity that hydrolyzes the cell wall peptidoglycans of Gram-positive and Gram-negative bacteria, resulting in cell lysis. Gram-positive bacteria are more sensitive, because their cell wall has 90% peptidoglycans (Rainard and Riollet, 2006).

Lactoferrin is a glycoprotein produced by epithelial cells, macrophages, and neutrophils with bacteriostatic action, binds to iron ions making them unavailable for bacterial growth. Its concentration increases at the beginning of the dry period and during infections (Oviedo-Boyso et al., 2007).

Fig. 11.1 summarizes the main mechanisms the innate immunity of the bovine mammary gland showing the most important anatomic factors that act as defense barriers.

The complement system consists of a set of plasma proteins that act on the opsonization of microorganisms, and on the recruitment of phagocytes to the site of infection or death of the pathogen. Activation occurs through three pathways: the classical, the alternative, and the lecithin, each of which is triggered by different factors, but converging in a common pathway from the formation of C3b (Abbas et al., 2011). The classical complement activation pathway is not clearly functional in the mammary gland, and the alternative pathway is activated leading to the deposition of opsonizing components in the bacterium and the production of proinflammatory mediators C4a, C3a, and C5a (Barrio et al., 2003).

Among the immune modulators secreted by the mammary gland, cytokines play an important role in the defense of the mammary gland,

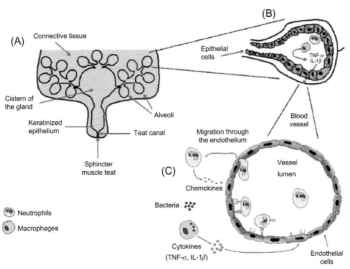

Figure 11.1 (A) Schematic diagram of the bovine mammary gland showing the most important anatomic factors that act as defense barriers. The teat sphincter muscle represents the first line of defense, whereas the keratinized epithelium of the teat cistern is considered the second line. (B) Cellular and soluble factors that participate in the innate immune response of the mammary gland. Macrophages located in the alveoli phagocytize bacteria that enter the mammary gland cistern. Activated macrophages release cytokines such as TNF-α and IL-1b. (C) Endothelial cells from blood vessels adjacent to alveoli express adhesion molecules in response to proinflammatory cytokines; this, in turn, facilitates neutrophil recruitment from the bloodstream to the site of infection in order to eliminate the invading bacteria (Oviedo-Boyso et al., 2007).

especially the interleukin-type cytokines (IL-1, IL-6, IL-8, IL-12) and tumor necrosis factor-α (TNF-α). Due to changes in the repertoire of cytokines, in the normal or mastitic udder, its use has been investigated in the diagnosis and prognosis of mastitis (Alluwaimi, 2004).

Adaptive or acquired immunity has as its main characteristic the most immediate response capacity in repeated exposures to the same microorganism. There are two types of adaptive response: humoral and cellular immunities (Abbas et al., 2011).

The acquired humoral immune response is mediated by blood molecules and mucosal secretions, called antibodies, which are produced by B lymphocytes. There are four isotypes of antibodies involved in the defense of the bovine mammary gland: IgM, IgG1, IgG2, and IgA. These antibodies have different functions, and their concentration in the milk varies with the health status of the udder and the lactation phase. IgG1 is the primary isotype found in mammary secretions of healthy animals. IgG2 increases during the inflammatory process of the mammary gland, and IgA does not aid in the opsonization of bacteria but promotes the agglutination of bacteria. Serum IgM is quite effective in neutralizing some types of toxins and opsonizing pathogens in blood and milk, being more effective in protecting against toxic shocks than in reducing signs of local inflammation (Kehrli and Harp, 2001; Mallard et al., 1998).

Cellular immunity is mediated by T lymphocytes, and it promotes the destruction of microorganisms residing in macrophages or the destruction of infected cells in order to eliminate infection reservoirs. Macrophages also play an important role in the specific immune response by the processing and presentation of antigens in association with MHC class II antigens (major class II histocompatibility complex) (Abbas et al., 2011). During postpartum, the number of macrophages increases in the mammary glands of the cows; these cells trigger mechanisms of release of prostaglandins, leukotrienes, and cytokines that can greatly increase the local inflammatory processes. However, the phagocytic capacity of the macrophages is reduced, possibly due to less opsonic activity in mammary secretions, in addition to the reduction in MHC II expression, which may contribute to a lower antigen presentation, and this possibly explains the higher occurrence of mastitis in the cows in this period (Mallard et al., 1998).

CD8 + T lymphocytes predominate in the mammary gland of healthy cows, while CD4 + T lymphocytes prevail during mastitis. These are activated in response to recognition of the antigen–MHC class II complex of the antigen presenting cells, such as B lymphocytes or macrophages. CD8 + lymphocytes can eliminate the host cell due to immune response during bacterial infection, as well as eliminating old or damaged cells from the mammary gland (Park et al., 2004).

11.2.3 Diagnosis

Detection of mastitis is usually based on indicators of inflammation in the mammary gland that originate during local or generalized microbial infection. When the infection occurs, the leukocytes gather to kill the bacteria and prevent the spread of the infection. Therefore, the number of leukocytes high in milk strongly indicates the presence of bacteria that cause mastitis. These processes include increased leukocyte infiltration, resulting in changes in chemical composition and physical properties of milk (Viguier et al., 2009).

Use of the "strip cup" test is the most simple and efficient method for the detection of clinical mastitis, being held in all cows and all milking. Besides, mug test can be done palpation of the udder in cases of suspected mastitis; udder stiffer than normal, warm, and red can be a sign of mastitis.

The test run occurs with the removal of the first three, each teat milk jets on a "strip cup." Gross changes in the milk may be observed at the time of milking such as the presence of flakes, clots, or serous milk. This is the most common means of detection of clinical mastitis. Stripping the first few squirts of milk from each quarter into a strip cup at the beginning of milking is a preferred method of detecting flakes or clots in the milk.

The affected cows may have swollen and greater touch sensitivity udder. The subclinical mastitis can be detected by direct or indirect SCC in milk. These are basically composed of two main types of cells: cell shedding from the secretory epithelium and leukocytes, and these are present in high concentrations in the cases of mastitis. The California mastitis test (CMT) is one of the most common tests for the diagnosis of subclinical mastitis, and an indirect indicator of the SCC in milk. The SCC is currently the standard used for the detection of subclinical mastitis and is an important indicator of milk quality. However, this parameter can be altered by lactation stage (beginning and end of lactation), age of the animal, nutritional imbalance, weakness, concomitant diseases, convalescence, parasitism, and lack of challenge to IMM infection (Shaheen, Tantary and Nabi, 2015).

Traditionally, methods of detection have included estimation of SCCs, an indication of inflammation, measurement of biomarkers associated with the onset of the disease (e.g., the enzymes N-acetyl-b-D-glucosaminidase and lactate dehydrogenase), and identification of the causative microorganisms, which often involves culturing methods. These methods have their limitations, and there is a need for new rapid, sensitive, and reliable assays (Viguier et al., 2009).

Continuous monitoring of mastitis, and its careful management, is essential for the well-being of a dairy herd. However, the development of novel analytical platforms incorporating enzymatic assays, immunoassays, biosensors, and nucleic acid tests are progressively replacing the more conventional methods. Also, with advances in proteomics and genomics, new biomarkers are being discovered, allowing the disease to be detected at earlier stages (Viguier et al., 2009).

Another form of diagnosis of recently used mastitis is infrared thermography that measures the surface temperature of the skin and sphincters of the teats of dairy cows and is similar to CMT findings. The efficacy of infrared thermography is not dependent on environmental conditions, and inflammation can be easily detected, being a noninvasive, high sensitivity, fast alternative, and a portable method for detecting subclinical mastitis or used in subclinical mastitis screening and subsequent detection (Pampariene et al., 2016).

11.2.4 Treatment

The most common of mastitis treatment is administration of antibiotics; however, this strategy has some disadvantages, including low cure rate, as it increases the occurrence of resistance, and the presence of antibiotic residues in milk, as well as increased cases of mastitis recurrent. Therefore, a wide variety of alternatives to antibiotics has been investigated by several groups of researchers. Bacteriophages, vaccines, nanoparticles, cytokines, and bioactive molecules are some examples of therapies alternative to antibiotics (Gomes and Henriques, 2015).

The basis for all antimicrobial therapies is the susceptibility of the pathogen to the drug used during treatment (Barlow, 2011). However, the uses of antibiogram and MIC (minimal inhibitory concentration) have limitations and cannot be considered a predictor of cure, since there are several factors that affect the efficiency of the drug, such as the distribution of antimicrobial at the site of infection, pharmacokinetics, pharmacodynamics, and data of clinical trials (Eskine et al, 2003a).

The most common route of administration for the treatment of mastitis is IMM (Ruegg, 2010). Parenteral treatment of mastitis has been suggested to be more efficient than IMM treatment because of the improved distribution of the drug along the mammary gland. This would be particularly applicable to invasive infections, such as mastitis caused by *S. aureus* (Intorre et al., 2013). The advantages of the IMM pathway relative to parenteral administration include low concentrations of the substance in milk and lower consumption of the antimicrobial because the dose of the drug directly applied to the mammary gland is small compared to the parenteral treatment. The disadvantage of IMM treatment is nonuniform distribution of the antimicrobial in the upper parts of the udder and risk of contamination when applied through the teat canal (Eskine et al., 2003b).

Cefquinome sulfate exhibits antibacterial activity against a broad spectrum of Gram-positive and Gram-negative bacterial species. Most *S. aureus* isolated from bovine mastitis are susceptible to cefquinome (Intorre et al., 2013; Kirkan et al., 2005). Evidence of the efficacy of antimicrobial treatment for mastitis caused by *E. coli* is limited. Fluoroquinolones and cephalosporins showed some scientific evidence of positive effects. In mastitis caused by *E. coli* that show mild to moderate clinical signs, antiinflammatory treatment, frequent milking, and fluid therapy should be the better option than antimicrobial treatment. In cases of severe mastitis by *E. coli*, parenteral administration of fluoroquinolones and third or fourth generation cephalosporins is recommended because of the risk of bacteremia. However, the antimicrobial treatment by IMM route for *E. coli* mastitis is not recommended (Suojala et al., 2013).

The possible reason for the persistence of most bacteria in the udder is the formation of biofilms. Biofilms are present in the form of bacteria bound to the surfaces that are incorporated in matrices composed of polysaccharides. Biofilm formation can be explained as a mechanism of protection of bacteria against the host immune system and the action of antibiotics. The correlation between biofilm production and the persistence of bovine *S. aureus* has already been described (Barkema et al., 2006; Costerton, 1999).

Research has shown that the low concentrations of some antimicrobials are capable of inducing biofilm formation by certain bacterial species. Biofilm present in bovine mammary glands contributes to antimicrobial resistance. Subinhibitory doses of enrofloxacin induce biofilm production in *E. coli*, this may be related to the recurrence of mastitis due to the same microorganism through persistence in the mammary gland (Costa et al., 2014).

The use of antimicrobials for the treatment of farm animals has the potential to affect human health. Antimicrobial residues could result in antimicrobial resistant foodborne pathogens. The risk of antimicrobial residues is well known and has been addressed with regulatory mechanisms. However, it is understood that control is not always efficiently performed (Aarestrup et al., 2008).

Drug associations of different origins are being studied in order to reduce the concentration of traditional antimicrobials and/or to return with the sensitivity profiles of the pathogens against them. In a study carried out by Ospina et al, 2014 using 27 *E. coli* isolates obtained from bovine milk with clinical mastitis, the MIC decreased when in the presence of inhibitors of multidrug efflux systems—phenylalanine-arginyl β-naphthylamide and 1-(1-naphthylmethyl)-piperazine (NMP). Other studies have demonstrated that bioactive substances extracted from plants with and without chemical modifications have demonstrated synergistic associations with the traditional antimicrobials against bacteria causing mastitis (Kinde et al., 2015; De Barros et al., 2017; Pasca et al., 2017).

11.3 OTHER DAIRY CATTLE DISEASES

11.3.1 Salmonellosis

Salmonellosis is an infectious disease characterized by the occurrence of fever, diarrhea, dehydration, and weakness and may also cause reproductive losses as abortions in late gestation and septicemia in newborn calves. It is observed a large variability in clinical signs and severity of the infection according to the health status and production level of the flock, besides the serotype of the bacterium (Cardoso and Carvalho, 2006). The disease manifests itself not only in calves between 15 and 90 days of life but also in adult animals. In adult dairy cattle, clinical signs often occur during periods of reduced immune function such as the periparturient period. The abortion can occur due to bacteremia or endotoxemia. The serotypes most commonly found in severe clinical cases are *Salmonella* Typhimurium, *Salmonella* Dublin, and *Salmonella* Newport.

The animals may be presented clinically sick patients and continue eliminating the bacteria in feces, and finally, animals latent patients who have lymph nodes bacteria, but are not eliminated in the feces. *Salmonella* contaminated foods and water and the survival time of bacteria can be long, depending on temperature and humidity (Fica et al., 2001).

The diagnosis is based on clinical examination, a thorough history of an outbreak and laboratory testing. They require prompt treatment with antibiotics and supporting therapy to save lives and slow spread of the disease. A vaccine is available that cattle protects against the most important strains of *Salmonella*. Treatment protocols should be defined according to the specific management of each dairy property (Fica et al., 2001).

All herds in which salmonellosis is an active or an endemic disease should organize a plan of action to identify, treat, and separate the suspected and confirmed cases of the disease. Cows and calves with serious cases of salmonellosis will deteriorate very quickly. Feces, colostrum, and milk animals affected are spread sources. It is suspected that a broad exposure to *Salmonella* present in the environment and in subclinical enteric infections can affect the quality of the herd milk, needing more study on the subject (Shinohara et al., 2008). *Salmonella* spp. has been recognized as a foodborne pathogen for well over 100 years; it is one of the most important causes of gastroenteritis in people. Most cases occur after consumption of contaminated food.

11.3.2 Leptospirosis

Leptospirosis is an infectious disease of worldwide distribution, caused by bacteria of the genus *Leptospira* with more than 200 serological varieties affecting among domestic animals: cattle, horses, pigs, and dogs also can occur in wildlife (Sarkar et al., 2002).

In dairy herd, leptospirosis results in large losses in productivity, in addition to zoonotic aspect. It is manifested clinically through abortions; usually occurring in half ahead of pregnancy, reproductive disorders such as retained placenta, stillbirth, congenital abnormalities, birth of weak calves. Also, leptospirosis can lead to decrease in milk production, increased calving interval, and subfertility, signals that reflect directly on the animal reproductive efficiency. It is also observed a greater or lesser severity of clinical manifestations depending on the serovar of the bacterium and the host species (Adler and de la Peña Moctezuma, 2010).

The epidemiological control of leptospirosis depends directly of the maintenance and accidental hosts. Rats are important natural reservoirs and important vectors of *Leptospira* spp. in urban and rural areas. The main reservoirs of bacteria within a bovine property are themselves contaminated/infected animals that spread the bacteria through their secretory products. In these animals, *Leptospira* spp. can remain for a long period in the kidneys, being disposed for weeks or months in urine. Transmission can occur through direct contact with skin, oral mucosa and conjunctival mucosa with urine and/or organs from animal. An important epidemiological aspect being evaluated in affected herds is to identify this serovar in the property to make vaccination with serovar causing the disease because there is no cross-protection (Arduino et al., 2009).

The diagnosis of leptospirosis is herd or is considered an epidemiological profile of the property based on vaccination records and a history of clinical symptoms compatible with the disease, to be laboratory confirmed. The laboratory test most commonly performed in routine practice is the rapid microscopic agglutination. This test is a presence of antibodies in which the suspected sera are diluted and placed in contact with samples of *Leptospira* spp. more likely to be causing the disease. Other indirect methods less frequently used in the diagnosis of leptospirosis are complement fixation, indirect immunofluorescence, and enzyme-linked immunosorbent assay (ELISA) (Blanco and Romero, 2014).

Control of the disease in the herd should start from the laboratory diagnosis of current serovar on the property, then the sick animal's treatment in order to control the elimination of bacteria in the urine and vaccination of the herd. When treated, the animals should be reviewed as they may present the clinical cure, but no bacteriological cure. Contact reduction of animal bogs, damp places, wetlands, and rodents help control bovine leptospirosis.

11.3.3 Johne's Disease

Paratuberculosis or Johne's disease is a chronic intestinal disease caused by *Mycobacterium avium* subsp. *paratuberculosis* (MAP). Clinical illness is characterized by chronic diarrhea, and the disease is smelly and resistant to treatments. The intestinal chronic inflammatory process triggers a series of changes cascading producing malabsorption syndrome that can be translated by diarrhea, dehydration, weight loss, acidosis, no fever, sudden drop in milk production, increased cases of mastitis, infertility, general cachexia, and death (Gonda et al., 2007).

Paratuberculosis is a problem that involves the dairy ruminants, especially. MAP has been implicated as a causative agent or associated with Crohn's disease, which affects humans and presents in the form of a proliferative ileocolitis similar to those observed in sick cows. There are clinical similarities, both radiographic and macroscopic, as microscopic between the two diseases. Many researchers consider paratuberculosis as a potential zoonosis (Grant, 2005). Foods such as milk and possibly the meat may become sources of infection and thus the disease has gained attention from the point of view of food safety (Faria et al., 2014).

The disease was first described in 1895 in Germany by Johne and Frothingham and has a worldwide distribution, especially in dairy herds (Stabel, 1998). It causes direct and indirect economic losses in dairy and beef cattle, the elimination of infected animals; the death of patients; the drop in milk production, estimated at 15%–16%; the increase in the incidence of mastitis; and reproductive changes that extend the calving interval (Ayele et al., 2005; Bush et al., 2006).

The diagnosis considered the gold standard is the MAP insulation in different culture media (solid and liquid) with the addition of growth factors and specific antimicrobials. The processing of tissue samples, milk, and feces is laborious and extremely time-consuming time of growth, taking about 8 or 16 weeks at 37°C. The ELISA is also used. Due to the difficulty of cultivation, the diagnosis is based on clinical history, findings pathological and/or molecular detection (Giese and Ahrens, 2000). The disposal of the positive animals, changes in management, and cutting the fecal−oral transmission from mother to her offspring are fundamental measures to control the disease in the herd (Juste and Perez, 2011).

The treatment of paratuberculosis in animals with antibacterial drugs is uneconomical and ineffective; they showed no blocking effect on fecal elimination. Vaccination is contradictory, because the vaccinated animals react to serological tests used in the detection of infection and can presenting cross-react with other mycobacteria. The vaccination is prohibited in some countries, such as Brazil (Ayele et al., 2005; Juste and Perez, 2011).

11.3.4 Tuberculosis

The tuberculosis is a chronic disease caused by bacteria of the genus *Mycobacterium* that affects ruminants, pigs, birds, wild animals, and humans. The bovine tuberculosis is caused by *M. bovis* and is responsible for significant economic losses in addition to being one of the major important zoonoses to public health, especially in the elderly, children, and immunocompromised patients (Grange and Yates, 1994).

The disease is widespread throughout the world, and eradication programs target in many countries. The main agent of transmission is air, the inhalation being the most common aerosols. Direct contact with nasal secretions and ingestion of raw milk from infected animals are also possible routes of transmission, the latter being the main route of infection for humans may result in zoonotic tuberculosis (Pollock and Neill, 2002). The test most commonly used for in vivo diagnosis of tuberculosis is the tuberculin, which can be basically three ways: flow rate, simple cervical, or cervical compared. The inspection after slaughter is critical in identifying positive animals, too (Waters et al., 2003).

Besides the economic impact, due to spending on testing, loss of milk production and the value of the animal, bovine tuberculosis is one of the most important public health zoonoses especially when considering developing countries where the disease is uncontrolled and consumption of raw milk and dairy products is common. There is no treatment with proven efficiency, testing and eliminating the positive animals of the property is the essential strategy to eradicate tuberculosis in cattle, in addition to biosecurity measures (Grange and Yates, 1994; Pollock and Neill, 2002).

11.3.5 Brucellosis

The bovine brucellosis is a zoonotic disease of global importance, caused by *B. abortus*. It is a disease that affects the sexually mature animals, a major cause of abortions, sometimes accompanied by temporary or permanent infertility, causing great economic losses. This disease exists throughout the world, but some countries have managed to eradicate it, and others are in the eradication phase. Infection rates vary from one country to another and in different regions, especially in countries with large territorial extension, such as Brazil (BRASIL, 2006). There are eight biovars of *B. abortus*, and biovar 1 is universal and dominant over the others (Le Flèche et al., 2006).

The losses to livestock because of this disease can be of great importance caused by the decrease in milk production, loss of calves and interference in the breeding program extending the average period between births, as well as a possible sequel, infertility. The disease results in domestically and internationally economic, and it is a zoonosis, being the dairy products the main vehicles for human contamination (Sardana et al., 2010).

Clinical findings depend on the herd immunity status, the main feature being the abortion after the final third of pregnancy. In subsequent pregnancies, the fetus generally comes forward, although there can occur a second or third abortion in the same cow. The retention of placenta and metritis are common abortion sequel (BRASIL, 2006). In bulls, orchitis and epididymitis occur occasionally, and the infertility is not always observed. The bacterium is intracellular, and the treatment is long and unsuccessful, so it is not recommended. In many countries, due to the control and eradication programs, treatment is prohibited (Sardana et al., 2010).

11.3.6 Infectious Bovine Rhinotracheitis

Infectious bovine rhinotracheitis (IBR) is a viral disease caused by bovine herpesvirus 1 (BoHV-1). BoHV-1 causes significant economic losses for dairy cattle. Infections and outbreaks originated by BoHV-1 cause impact on animal health in field conditions with reduced milk production, increased respiratory diseases, increased calf mortality, and reproductive problems (Jones, 2010; Rissi et al., 2008).

The rates of infection described vary widely. In Britain, the percentage of seropositive herds ranges from 40% to 50%; in Belgium, this figure is 62% (Ackermann and Engels, 2006). In Brazil, studies showed a prevalence rate of 29.2%–58.2% (Rocha et al., 2001).

Transmission occurs in the absence of visible lesions by artificial insemination (AI) with semen of infected bulls. Genital infections are the most common in cattle. The incubation period for respiratory and genital forms of BoHV-1 is from 2 to 6 days (Jones, 2010). Inoculation of BoHV-1 in the uterus by AI can cause infertility due to endometritis (Graham, 2013).

Infection by BoHV-1 exists in three stages: a preliminary infection, lasting about two weeks; a long latent infection; and an occasional viral recrudescence, reactivating viral spread to other animals. Endogenous release of glucocorticoids hormones stressful conditions or exogenous administration of high doses of glucocorticoids can reactivate the productive infection. Thus, control of the disease becomes difficult because animals that do not show clinical signs are able to release virus to the environment when the productive phase is reactivated, conveying it effectively to other susceptible animals (Field et al., 2006).

In respiratory disease cases, the animal shows excessive salivation, nasal discharge, conjunctivitis, and nasal lesions. In the absence of bacterial pneumonia, the animal recovers from 4 to 5 days after the onset of signs (Jones, 2010). In genital infections, the animal shows frequent urination, swollen vulva. In bulls, lesions on penis and prepuce are seen. Secondary bacterial infections can cause temporary infertility (Jones, 2010).

The most common complication caused by BoHV-1 in immunocompromised adult animals is abortion. If the pregnant cow is carrying the BoHV-1, is able to pass it on to the fetus, which can come in term so weak and continue as a carrier and disseminator of the virus when in stressful situations. However, there may also be abortion, mainly from the second month of pregnancy, due to degeneration of the placentomes. Abortion may coincide with respiratory signs or occur without other clinical manifestations in pregnant female. The fetus usually presents autolysate; however, neither the fetus nor the placenta typically presents macroscopic changes (Pituco, 2009).

In countries where control for sanitary sacrifice is not applied, commercially available vaccines are used. However, its effectiveness has not reached large proportion, as the clinical signs of the disease only decrease relatively, but they are not eliminated. Furthermore, it does not prevent the development of the latent stage. Serological testing and elimination of infected animals have been used to eliminate BoHV-1 in Austria, Denmark, and Switzerland (Ackermann and Engels, 2006). It is an expensive procedure (Raaperi et al., 2015), impairing its eradication. More studies are needed to better understand the dynamics of infection and the impact and losses associated with the herd when it is affected by BoHV-1 (Graham, 2013).

11.3.7 Bovine Viral Diarrhea

Bovine viral diarrhea (BVD) virus (BVDV) is an important pathogen in cattle, which causes abortion, birth of weak and infected calves. BVD has worldwide distribution with significant economic losses to bovine livestock (Dezen et al., 2013).

BVD has two genotypes, BVDV-1 and BVDV-2, and two biotypes, cytopathogenic (CP) and non-CP (NCP). BVDV-1 strain can be separated into two subgroups, 1a and 1b. Epidemiological researches suggest 1b and 1a strains predominate in respiratory cases and fetal infections in late gestation, respectively (Chaves et al., 2010).

The transmission rate of BVDV within the herds depends on the prevalence of persistently infected (PI) animals of the existence of areas with high density of animals and of virulence of viral strains (Thurmond, 2005). Studies show that the prevalence of IP cattle is between 0.5% and 2% of the general bovine population (OIE, 2008).

BVDV has been reported in several countries, including Norway, Denmark, Sweden, Germany, Austria, France, Brazil, Uruguay, and Chile. In Brazil, serological studies are being carried out in several regions to verify the prevalence in PI cattle (Del Fava, Pituco and D'Angelino, 2002). In North America, the prevalence of BVDV-1 is high. In the United States, respiratory and reproductive forms are frequent, combating the use of vaccines with attenuated or inactivated virus in the herds (Fulton et al., 2002).

Most viruses found in nature are NCP, but CP viruses are isolated from animals with mucosal diseases or postvaccinated animals. NCP crosses placenta and fetus, causing persistent infection in the fetus. NCP is responsible for various congenital, enteric, and reproductive diseases (Andrews et al., 2004).

Persistently infected animals (PI) are the primary reservoir of BVDV, and the largest source of infection. These viruses are immunotolerant to the virus. Their immune system does not respond to BVDV, so the virus continues to multiply, infects tissues, and is excreted throughout the animal's life. PI cattle are more likely to develop mucosal disease and frequently die before 2 years of age. PI calves may be born below normal size and present slower growth rate, reproductive changes, and early death (Flores et al., 2005)

Pathogenesis of immunosuppression involves the immune system. The virus has affinity for immune cells and the destruction of some of these cells is the consequence of infection. Lymphocytes and macrophages are an important target for BVDV replication. A reduction of CD 4 + and CD 8 + T lymphocytes, B-lymphocytes, and neutrophils occurs with the infection (Graham, 2013).

Methods for serological diagnosis are impaired by interference of maternal antibodies, which happens because PI animals are not identified until colostral immunity has decreased. Virus identification can also be performed by serological techniques such as virus neutralization, immunofluorescence, immunoperoxidase, and ELISA (Pilz et al., 2005).

There is no specific treatment for the animals. In cattle suspected of having acute infection, treatment is supportive and preventive against secondary bacterial infection Animals with chronic BVD should be eliminated from the herd (Chi et al., 2002).

11.4 CONCLUSION

Infectious diseases such as brucellosis, tuberculosis, Johne's disease, Leptospirosis, salmonellosis, BVD, and IBR may compromise the milk production chain, but mastitis is undoubtedly the main problem in dairy herds and has a great effect on animal welfare and milk production. The mammary gland has several mechanisms (physical, immunological, enzymatic) that protect it from infection, but if there is an imbalance between the environment, microorganism, and host factors, mastitis develops. Several etiologic agents have a significant role in the development of mastitis and among these, several pathogens with high zoonotic potential. The traditional treatment is the use of antibiotics based on the result of the antibiogram, but even so, the results are not always satisfactory, mainly due to the phenomenon of resistance. Different groups of researchers are investigating alternative treatment methods, such as the use of bacteriophages, vaccines, nanoparticles, and bioactive molecules. Despite all efforts, mastitis remains the main disease of dairy herds, so research must continue to search for methods that help reduce the incidence and prevalence of the disease that has a major impact on the milk production chain.

REFERENCES

Aarestrup, F.M., Wegener, H.C., Collignon, P., 2008. Resistance in bacteria of the food chain: epidemiology and control strategies. Expert Rev. Anti. Infect. Ther. 6, 733−750. Available from: https://doi.org/10.1586/14787210.6.5.733.

Abbas, A.K., Lichtman, A.H., Pillai, S., 2011. Imunologia Celular e Molecular. Elsevier, Rio de Janeiro.

Ackermann, M., Engels, M., 2006. Pro and contra IBR-eradication. Vet. Microbiol. 113, 293−302. Available from: https://doi.org/10.1016/j.vetmic.2005.11.043.

Adler, B., de la Peña Moctezuma, A., 2010. *Leptospira* and leptospirosis. Vet. Microbiol. 140, 287−296. Available from: https://doi.org/10.1016/j.vetmic.2009.03.012.

Alluwaimi, A.M., 2004. The cytokines of bovine mammary gland: prospects for diagnosis and therapy. Res. Vet. Sci. 77, 211−222. Available from: https://doi.org/10.1016/j.rvsc.2004.04.006.

Andrews, A.H., Blowey, R.W., Boyd, H., Eddy, R.G., 2004. Bovine Medicine: Diseases and Husbandry of Cattle, second ed. Blackwell Science Ltd., Oxford, UK, pp. 853−857.

Arduino, G.G.C., Girio, R.J.S., Magajevski, F.S., Pereira, G.T., 2009. Títulos de anticorpos aglutinantes induzidos por vacinas comerciais contra leptospirose bovina. Pesqui. Vet. Bras. 29, 575−582. Available from: https://doi.org/10.1590/S0100-736X2009000700013.

Atasever, A., Ozdemir, H., Gulcin, I., Irfan Kufrevioglu, O., 2013. One-step purification of lactoperoxidase from bovine milk by affinity chromatography. Food Chem. 136, 864−870. Available from: https://doi.org/10.1016/j.foodchem.2012.08.072.

Ayele, W.Y., Svastova, P., Roubal, P., Bartos, M., Pavlik, I., 2005. *Mycobacterium avium* subspecies *paratuberculosis* cultured from locally and commercially pasteurized cow's milk in the Czech Republic. Society 71, 1210−1214. Available from: https://doi.org/10.1128/AEM.71.3.1210.

Barkema, H.W., Schukken, Y.H., Zadoks, R.N., 2006. Invited review: the role of cow, pathogen, and treatment regimen in the therapeutic success of bovine *Staphylococcus aureus* mastitis. J. Dairy Sci. 89, 1877−1895. Available from: https://doi.org/10.3168/jds.S0022-0302(06)72256-1.

Barlow, J., 2011. Mastitis therapy and antimicrobial susceptibility: a multispecies review with a focus on antibiotic treatment of mastitis in dairy cattle. J. Mammary Gland Biol. Neoplasia 16, 383−407. Available from: https://doi.org/10.1007/s10911-011-9235-z.

Barrio, M.B., Rainard, P., Poutrel, B., 2003. Milk complement and the opsonophagocytosis and killing of *Staphylococcus aureus* mastitis isolates by bovine neutrophils. Microb. Pathog. 34, 1−9. Available from: https://doi.org/10.1016/S0882-4010(02)00186-9.

Benić, M., Habrun, B., Kompes, G., 2012. Cell content in milk from cows with *S. aureus* intramammary infection. Vet. . . . 82, 411−422.

Blanco, R.M., Romero, E.C., 2014. Evaluation of nested polymerase chain reaction for the early detection of *Leptospira* spp. DNA in serum samples from patients with leptospirosis. Diagn. Microbiol. Infect. Dis. 78, 343−346. Available from: https://doi.org/10.1016/j.diagmicrobio.2013.12.009.

Bogni, C., Odierno, L., Raspanti, C., 2011. War against mastitis: current concepts on controlling bovine mastitis pathogens. A. Méndez-Vilas (Ed.), Science Against Microbial Pathogens: Communicating Current Research and Technological Advances, pp. 483–494.

Burvenich, C.B., Erris, V.V.A.N.M., Ehrzad, J.M., Raile, A.D.I.E.Z., Uchateau, L.D., 2003. Review article severity of *E. coli* mastitis is mainly determined by cow factors. Vet. Res. 34, 521–564. Available from: https://doi.org/10.1051/vetres.

Bush, R.D., Windsor, P.A., Toribio, J.-A., 2006. 12 infected flocks over a 3-year period. Aust. Vet. J. 84.

Cardoso, T., Carvalho, V., 2006. Toxinfecção alimentar por *Salmonella* spp. Rev. Inst. Ciênc Saúde 24, 95–101.

Chaves, N.P., Bezerra, D.C., Sousa, V.E., de Santos, H.P., Pereira, Hde M., 2010. Frequência de anticorpos e fatores de risco para a infecção pelo *vírus da diarreia viral bovina* em fêmeas bovinas leiteiras não vacinadas na região Amazônica Maranhense, Brasil. Ciência Rural 40, 1448–1451. Available from: https://doi.org/10.1590/S0103-84782010005000089.

Chi, J., VanLeeuwen, J.A., Weersink, A., Keefe, G.P., 2002. Direct production losses and treatment costs from *bovine viral diarrhoea virus, bovine leukosis virus, Mycobacterium avium* subspecies *paratuberculosis*, and *Neospora caninum*. Prev. Vet. Med. 55, 137–153. Available from: https://doi.org/10.1016/S0167-5877(02)00094-6.

Costa, J.C.M., Espeschit, I.B., Pieri, F.A., Benjamin, L.A., Moreira, M.A.S., 2014. Increase in biofilm formation by *Escherichia coli* under conditions that mimic the mastitic mammary gland. Ciência Rural 44, 666–671.

Costerton, J.W., 1999. Bacterial biofilms: a common cause of persistent infections. Science 284, 1318–1322. Available from: https://doi.org/10.1126/science.284.5418.1318.

De Barros, M., Perciano, P.G., Dos Santos, M.H., De Oliveira, L.L., Costa, É.D.M., Moreira, M.A.S., 2017. Antibacterial activity of 7-epiclusianone and its novel copper metal complex on *Streptococcus* spp. isolated from bovine mastitis and their cytotoxicity in MAC-T cells. Molecules 22. Available from: https://doi.org/10.3390/molecules22050823.

De La Rua-Domenech, R., 2006. Human *Mycobacterium bovis* infection in the United Kingdom: incidence, risks, control measures and review of the zoonotic aspects of bovine tuberculosis. Tuberculosis 86, 77–109. Available from: https://doi.org/10.1016/j.tube.2005.05.002.

Del Fava, C., Pituco, E.M., D'Angelino, J.L., 2002. *Herpesvírus Bovino tipo 1* (HVB-l): revisão e situação atual no Brasil. Rev. Educ. Contin. 5, 300–312. CRMV-SP.

Dezen, S., Otonel, R.A.A., Alfier, A.F., Lunardi, M., Alfieri, A.A., 2013. Perfil da infecção pelo *vírus da diarreia viral bovina* (BVDV) em um rebanho bovino leiteiro de alta produção e com programa de vacinação contra o BVDV1. Pesqui. Vet. Bras. 33, 141–147. Available from: https://doi.org/10.1590/S0100-736X2013000200002.

Eskine, S., De Graves, F.J., Wagner, R.J., 2003a. Mastitis therapy and pharmacology. Vet. Clin. Food Anim. Pract.

Eskine, R.J., Wagner, R.J., De Graves, F.J., 2003b. Mastitis therapy and pharmacology. Vet. Clin. Food Anim. Pract. 19, 109–138.

Faria, A.C.S., Schwarz, D.G.G., Carvalho, I.A., Rocha, B.B., De Carvalho Castro, K.N., Silva, M.R., et al., 2014. Short communication: viable *Mycobacterium avium* subspecies *paratuberculosis* in retail artisanal Coalho cheese from Northeastern Brazil. J. Dairy Sci. 97, 4111–4114. Available from: https://doi.org/10.3168/jds.2013-7835.

Fica, A., Alexandre, M., Prat, S., Fernández, A., Fernández, J., Heitmann, I., 2001. Cambios epidemiológicos de las *Salmonelosis* en Chile. Rev. Chil. Infect. 18, 85–93. Available from: https://doi.org/10.4067/S0716-10182001000200002.

Field, H.J., Biswas, S., Mohammad, I.T., 2006. Herpesvirus latency and therapy—from a veterinary perspective. Antiviral Res. 71, 127–133. Available from: https://doi.org/10.1016/j.antiviral.2006.03.018.

Flores, E.F., Weiblen, R., Vogel, F.S.F., Roehe, P.M., Alfieri, A.A., 2005. A infecção pelo *Vírus da Diarréia Viral Bovina* (BVDV) no Brasil Viral—histórico, situação atual e perspectivas. Pesq. Vet. Bras. 25, 125–134.

Fulton, R.W., Ridpath, J.F., Saliki, J.T., Briggs, R.E., Confer, A.W., Burge, L.J., et al., 2002. *Bovine viral diarrhea virus* (BVDV) 1b: predominant BVDV subtype in calves with respiratory disease. Can. J. Vet. Res. 66, 181–190.

Giese, S.B., Ahrens, P., 2000. Detection of *Mycobacterium avium* subsp. *paratuberculosis* in milk from clinically affected cows by PCR and culture. Vet. Microbiol. 77, 291–297. Available from: https://doi.org/10.1016/S0378-1135(00)00314-X.

Gomes, F., Henriques, M., 2015. Control of bovine mastitis : old and recent therapeutic approaches. Curr. Microbiol. Available from: https://doi.org/10.1007/s00284-015-0958-8.

Gonda, M.G., Chang, Y.M., Shook, G.E., Collins, M.T., Kirkpatrick, B.W., 2007. Effect of *Mycobacterium paratuberculosis* infection on production, reproduction, and health traits in US Holsteins. Prev. Vet. Med. 80, 103–119. Available from: https://doi.org/10.1016/j.prevetmed.2007.01.011.

Graham, D.A., 2013. Bovine Herpes Virus-1 (BoHV-1) in Cattle—A Review with Emphasis on Reproductive Impacts and the Emergence of Infection in Ireland and the United Kingdom.

Grange, J.M., Yates, M.D., 1994. Zoonotic aspects of *Mycobacterium bovis* infection. Vet. Microbiol. 40, 137–151. Available from: https://doi.org/10.1016/0378-1135(94)90052-3.

Grant, I.R., 2005. Zoonotic potential of *Mycobacterium avium* ssp. *paratuberculosis*: the current position. J. Appl. Microbiol. 98, 1282–1293. Available from: https://doi.org/10.1111/j.1365-2672.2005.02598.x.

Halasa, T., 2012. Bioeconomic modeling of intervention against clinical mastitis caused by contagious pathogens. J. Dairy Sci. 95, 5740–5749. Available from: https://doi.org/10.3168/jds.2012-5470.

Halling, S.M., Peterson-burch, B.D., Betsy, J., Zuerner, R.L., Qing, Z., Li, L., et al., 2005. Completion of the genome sequence of *Brucella abortus* and comparison to the highly similar genomes of *Brucella melitensis* and *Brucella suis* completion of the genome sequence of *Brucella abortus* and comparison to the highly similar genomes of *Brucella melitensis*. Society 187, 2715–2726. Available from: https://doi.org/10.1128/JB.187.8.2715.

Intorre, L., Vanni, M., Meucci, V., Tognetti, R., Cerri, D., Turchi, B., et al., 2013. Antimicrobial resistance of *Staphylococcus aureus* isolated from bovine milk in Italy from 2005 to 2011. Large Anim. Rev. 19, 287–291.

Jones, C., 2010. Bovine herpesvirus type 1 (BHV-1) is an important cofactor in the bovine respiratory disease complex. Vet. Clin. North Am. Food Anim. Pract. 26, 303–321. Available from: https://doi.org/10.1016/j.cvfa.2010.04.007.

Juste, R.A., Perez, V., 2011. Control of *Paratuberculosis* in sheep and goats. Vet. Clin. North Am.—Food Anim. Pract. 27, 127–138. Available from: https://doi.org/10.1016/j.cvfa.2010.10.020.

Keefe, G., 2012. Update on control of *Staphylococcus aureus* and *Streptococcus agalactiae* for management of mastitis. Vet. Clin. North Am.—Food Anim. Pract. 28, 203–216. Available from: https://doi.org/10.1016/j.cvfa.2012.03.010.

Kehrli, M.E., Harp, J.A., 2001. Immunity in the mammary gland. Vet. Clin. North Am. Food Anim. Pract. 17, 495–516. Available from: https://doi.org/10.1016/S0749-0720(15)30003-7. vi.

Kinde, H., Regassa, F., Asaye, M., Wubie, A., 2015. The in-vitro antibacterial effect of three selected plant extracts against *Staphylococcus aureus* and *Streptococcus agalactiae* isolated from bovine mastitis. J. Vet. Sci. Technol. s13, 1−7. Available from: https://doi.org/10.4172/2157-7579.1000S13-001.

Kirkan, S., Göksoy, E.O., Kaya, O., 2005. Identification and antimicrobial susceptibility of *Staphylococcus aureus* and coagulase negative *Staphylococci* from bovine mastitis in the Ayd Region of Turkey. Turk. J. Vet. Anim. Sci. 29, 791−796.

Klimiene, I., Ruzauskas, M., Pakauskas, V., Mockeliunas, R., Pereckiene, A., Butrimaite-Ambrozeviiene, C., 2011. Prevalence of gram positive bacteria in cow mastitis and their susceptibility to beta-lactam antibiotics. Vet. Ir. Zootech. 56 (78).

Krukowski, H., Saba, L., 2003. Bovine mycotic mastitis: a review. Folia Vet. 1, 3−7. Available from: https://doi.org/10.1017/CBO9781107415324.004.

Kussendrager, K.D., Van Hooijdonk, A.C., 2000. Lactoperoxidase: physico-chemical properties, occurrence, mechanism of action and applications. Br. J. Nutr. 84 (1), S19−S25. Available from: https://doi.org/10.1017/S0007114500002208.

Le Flèche, P., Jacques, I., Grayon, M., Al Dahouk, S., Bouchon, P., Denoeud, F., et al., 2006. Evaluation and selection of tandem repeat loci for a *Brucella* MLVA typing assay. BMC Microbiol. 6, 9. Available from: https://doi.org/10.1186/1471-2180-6-9.

Mallard, B.A., Dekkers, J.C., Ireland, M.J., Leslie, K.E., Sharif, S., Lacey Vankampen, C., et al., 1998. Alteration in immune responsiveness during the peripartum period and its ramification on dairy cow and calf health. J. Dairy Sci. 81, 585−595. Available from: https://doi.org/10.3168/jds.S0022-0302(98)75612-7.

Marques, S., Silva, E., Kraft, C., Carvalheira, J., Videira, A., Huss, V.A.R., et al., 2008. Bovine mastitis associated with Prototheca blaschkeae. J. Clin. Microbiol. 46, 1941−1945. Available from: https://doi.org/10.1128/JCM.00323-08.

Moon, J.-S., Lee, A.-R., Kang, H.-M., Lee, E.-S., Kim, M.-N., Paik, Y.H., et al., 2007. Phenotypic and genetic antibiogram of methicillin-resistant *Staphylococci* isolated from bovine mastitis in Korea. J. Dairy Sci. 90, 1176−1185. Available from: https://doi.org/10.3168/jds.S0022-0302(07)71604-1.

OIE, 2008. World Organization for Animal Health. Chapter 2.4.8. − Bovine viral diarrhoea. In: Manual of Diagnostic Tests and Vaccines for Terrestrial Animals 698−711. Disponível http://www.oie.int/fileadmin/Home/eng/Health_standards/tahm/2.04.08_BVD.pdf. (accessed 07.11.16).

Ospina, M.A., Pieri, F.A., Pietralonga, P.A., Moreira, M.A.S., 2014. Sistemas de efluxo multidrogas em *Escherichia coli* isoladas de mastite bovina e uso de seus inibidores como possíveis adjuvantes. Arq. Bras. Med. Vet. Zootec 66 (2), 381−387.

Oviedo-Boyso, J., Valdez-Alarco, J.J., Ochoa-Zarzosa, A., López-Meza, J.E., Bravo-Patinõ, A., Baizabal-Aguirre, V.M., 2007. Innate immune response of bovine mammary gland to pathogenic bacteria responsible for mastitis. J. Infect. Available from: https://doi.org/10.1016/j.jinf.2006.06.010.

Pachauri, S., Varshney, P., Dash, S.K., Gupta, M.K., 2013. Involvement of fungal species in bovine mastitis in and around Mathura, India. Vet. World 6, 393−395. Available from: https://doi.org/10.5455/vetworld.2013.393-395.

Pampariene, I., Veikutis, V., Oberauskas, V., Zymantiene, J., Zelvyte, R., Stankevicius, A., et al., 2016. Thermography based inflammation monitoring of udder state in dairy cows: sensitivity and diagnostic priorities comparing with routine California mastitis test. J. Vibroeng. 18 (1), 511−521.

Pardo, R.B., Langoni, H., Mendonça, L.J.P., Chi, K.D., 2001. Isolation of *Mycobacterium* spp. in milk from cows suspected or positive to *Tuberculosis*. Braz. J. Vet. Res. Anim. Sci. 38, 284−287. Available from: https://doi.org/10.1590/S1413-95962001000600007.

Park, Y.H., Joo, Y.S., Park, J.Y., Moon, J.S., Kim, S.H., Kwon, N.H., et al., 2004. Characterization of lymphocyte subpopulations and major histocompatibility complex haplotypes of mastitis-resistant and susceptible cows. J. Vet. Sci. (Suwon-si, Korea) 5, 29−39.

Pasca, C., M rghitas, L., Dezmirean, D., Bobis, O., Bonta, V., Chiril , F., et al., 2017. Medicinal plants based products tested on pathogens isolated from mastitis milk. Molecules 22. Available from: https://doi.org/10.3390/molecules22091473.

Peton, V., Le Loir, Y., 2014. *Staphylococcus aureus* in veterinary medicine. Infect. Genet. Evol. 21, 602−615. Available from: https://doi.org/10.1016/j.meegid.2013.08.011.

Petrovski, K.R., Trajcev, M., Buneski, G., 2006. A review of the factors affecting the costs of bovine mastitis. J. S. Afr. Vet. Assoc. 77, 52−60. Available from: https://doi.org/ 0038-2809.

Pilz, D., Alfieri, A.F., Alfieri, A.A., 2005. Comparação de diferentes protocolos para a detecção do vírus da diarreia viral bovina por RT-PCR em grupos de sangue total e de soro sanguíneo, artificialmente contaminados. Ciências Agrárias 219−228. Available from: https://doi.org/10.5433/1679-0359.2005v26n2p219.

Pituco, E.M. 2009. Aspectos clínicos, prevenção e controle da IBR. São Paulo: Centro de pesquisa e desenvolvimento de sanidade animal. Instituto Biológico. Comunicado Técnico, n. 94. Disponível em http://www.infobibos.com/Artigos/2009_2/IBR/ Index.htm. Acesso em 01 de Maio de 2016.

Pollock, J.M., Neill, S.D., 2002. *Mycobacterium bovis* infection and *Tuberculosis* in cattle. Vet. J. 163, 115−127. Available from: https://doi.org/10.1053/tvjl.2001.0655.

BRASIL, 2006. Programa Nacional de Controle e Erradicação da Brucelose e da Tuberculose Animal (PNCEBT). In: Programa Nacional de Controle E Erradicação Da Brucelose E Tuberculose Animal (PNCEBT)—Manual Técnico. p. 188.

Pyörälä, S., Taponen, S., 2009. Coagulase-negative *Staphylococci*—emerging mastitis pathogens. Vet. Microbiol. 134, 3−8. Available from: https://doi.org/10.1016/j. vetmic.2008.09.015.

Raaperi, K., Orro, T., Viltrop, A., 2015. Effect of vaccination against *bovine herpesvirus 1* with inactivated gE-negative marker vaccines on the health of dairy cattle herds. Prev. Vet. Med. 118, 467−476. Available from: https://doi.org/10.1016/j.prevetmed.2015.01.014.

Rainard, P., Riollet, C., 2006. Innate immunity of the bovine mammary gland To cite this version. Vet. Res. 37, 369−400. Available from: https://doi.org/10.1051/vetres.

Rissi, D.R., Pierezan, F., Sa, M., Flores, E.F., Severo, C., De Barros, L., 2008. Neurological disease in cattle in southern Brazil associated with *Bovine herpesvirus* infection. J. Vet. Diagn. Invest. 349, 346−349.

Rocha, M.A., Gouveia, A.M.G., Lobato, Z.I.P., Leite, R.C., 2001. Pesquisa de anticorpos para IBR em amostragem de demanda no Estado de Minas Gerais, 1990−1999. Arq. Bras. Med. Vet. e Zootec. 53, 645−647.

Ruegg, P.L., 2010. The Application of Evidence Based Veterinary Medicine to Mastitis Therapy. World Buiatrics Congress, Santiago, Chile, pp. 14−18.

Sardana, D., Upadhyay, A.J., Deepika, K., Pranesh, G.T., Rao, K.A., 2010. *Brucellosis*: review on the recent trends in pathogenecity and laboratory diagnosis. J. Lab. Phys. 22, 55−60. Available from: https://doi.org/10.4103/0974.

Sarkar, U., Nascimento, S., Barbosa, R., Martins, R., Nuevo, H., Kalofonos, I., 2002. Population-based case−control invertigation of risk factors for leptospirosis during an urban epidemic. Am. J. Trop. Med. Hyg. 66, 605−610. Available from: https://doi. org/10.4269/ajtmh.2002.66.605.

Schukken, Y.H., Günther, J., Fitzpatrick, J., Fontaine, M.C., Goetze, L., Holst, O., et al., 2011. Host-response patterns of intramammary infections in dairy cows. Vet. Immunol. Immunopathol. 144, 270−289. Available from: https://doi.org/10.1016/j. vetimm.2011.08.022.

Shaheen, M., Tantary, H.A., Nabi, S.U., 2015. A treatise on bovine mastitis: disease and disease economics, etiological basis, risk factors, impact on human health, therapeutic management, prevention and control strategy. Adv. Dairy Res. 4, 1−10. Available from: https://doi.org/10.4172/2329-888X.1000150.

Shinohara, N.K.S., Barros, V.B., Jimenez, S.M.C., 2008. *Salmonella spp.*, importante agente patogênico veiculado em alimentos. Ciências e sáude coletivaáude coletiva 13, 1675—1683.

Sordillo, L.M., Shafer-Weaver, K., DeRosa, D., 1997. Immunobiology of the mammary gland. J. Dairy Sci. 80, 1851—1865. Available from: https://doi.org/10.3168/jds.S0022-0302(97)76121-6.

Stabel, J.R., 1998. Johne's disease: a hidden threat. J. Dairy Sci. 81, 283—288. Available from: https://doi.org/10.3168/jds.S0022-0302(98)75577-8.

Suojala, L., Kaartinen, L., Pyörälä, S., 2013. Treatment for bovine *Escherichia coli* mastitis—an evidence-based approach. J. Vet. Pharmacol. Ther. 36, 521—531. Available from: https://doi.org/10.1111/jvp.12057.REVIEW.

Thurmond, M.C., 2005. Virus transmission. In: Goyal, S.M., Ridpath, J.F. (Eds.), Bovine Viral Diarrhea Virus: Diagnosis, Management and Control, first ed Blackwell Publishing, Oxford, UK, pp. 91—104.

Viguier, C., Arora, S., Gilmartin, N., Welbeck, K., O'Kennedy, R., 2009. Mastitis detection: current trends and future perspectives. Trends Biotechnol. 27, 486—493. Available from: https://doi.org/10.1016/j.tibtech.2009.05.004.

Wall, R.J., Powell, A.M., Paape, M.J., Kerr, D.E., Bannerman, D.D., Pursel, V.G., et al., 2005. Genetically enhanced cows resist intramammary *Staphylococcus aureus* infection. Nat. Biotechnol. 23, 445—451. Available from: https://doi.org/10.1038/nbt1078.

Waters, W.R., Palmer, M.V., Whipple, D.L., Carlson, M.P., Nonnecke, B.J., 2003. Diagnostic implications of antigen-induced gamma interferon, nitric oxide, and tumor necrosis factor alpha production by peripheral blood mononuclear cells from *Mycobacterium bovis* infected cattle. Clin. Diagn. Lab. Immunol. 10, 960—966. Available from: https://doi.org/10.1128/CDLI.10.5.960.

CHAPTER 12

Foodborne Pathogens and Zoonotic Diseases

Ivan Sugrue[1,2,3], Conor Tobin[1,2,3], R. Paul Ross[1,3],
Catherine Stanton[2,3] and Colin Hill[1,3]
[1]School of Microbiology, University College Cork, Cork, Ireland
[2]Teagasc Food Research Centre, Moorepark, Fermoy, Ireland
[3]APC Microbiome Ireland, Cork, Ireland

12.1 INTRODUCTION

Milk and milk product consumption has long been associated with good health, but it can also pose a potential health risk when ingested in the raw state, particularly if it has been improperly processed, or when product manufacturing conditions are not of sufficiently high standard. Raw milk is defined by the European Food Safety Authority (EFSA) as "milk produced by farmed animals which has not been heat treated to more than 40°C nor had any equivalent treatment" (Hazards, 2015). Human and zoonotic animal pathogens and their toxins may be present in raw milk and raw milk products which can lead to many illnesses, the severity of which depends on the pathogen(s) present, the infectious dose, and the health of the individual consuming the product. The US Center for Disease Control and Prevention estimate a number of 48 million foodborne illnesses in the United States every year, of which 128,839 lead to hospitalizations and as many as 3037 deaths (Scallan et al., 2011). While the percentage of the US population who consume unpasteurized milk and cheese is relatively small (3.2% and 1.6%, respectively), they are >800 times more likely to become ill and 45 times more likely to require hospitalization (Costard et al., 2017). Consumption of raw milk increases the risk of foodborne illness due to the potential presence of pathogenic microbes. According to EFSA, the major risk organisms present in raw milk include *Campylobacter* spp., *Salmonella* spp., Shiga toxin-producing *Escherichia coli* (STEC), *Bacillus cereus*, *Brucella abortus*, *Brucella melitensis*, *Listeria monocytogenes*, *Mycobacterium bovis*, *Staphylococcus aureus*, *Yersinia enterocolitica*, *Yersinia pseudotuberculosis*, *Corynebacterium* spp., and *Streptococcus suis* subsp. *zooepidemicus* (EFSA, 2015). The parasites;

Raw Milk
DOI: https://doi.org/10.1016/B978-0-12-810530-6.00012-2

Toxoplasma gondii, Cryptosporidium parvum, and the virus; tick-borne encephalitis virus are also considered a microbiological hazard of raw milk, though this chapter will focus on the more common bacterial pathogens found in cow's milk. The potential of raw milk to cause illness after contamination depends largely on the storage conditions of the milk which is usually designed to prevent overgrowth of harmful organisms. Most milk collected, thermally processed, and packaged under high quality conditions poses little risk to the consumer, though problems with ineffective heat treatment, high initial microbial load, or poor packaging conditions can lead to contaminated milk. Products of raw milk also pose risk to consumers, with unpasteurized cheeses and other soft-style cheeses being a potential vector for foodborne pathogens which can survive or even grow at refrigeration temperatures. Great care must therefore be taken when choosing to ingest raw milk over its processed counterpart as there are many risk factors which could lead to illness.

12.2 *CAMPYLOBACTER* SPP.

The genus *Campylobacter* is composed of Gram-negative, nonspore forming spiral rods (Penner, 1988), which colonize the intestinal tract of many animal species, and can be shed in feces intermittently and therefore is commonly found in the farm environment. *Campylobacter jejuni* and *Campylobacter coli* are the most important species with regard to health, with *C. jejuni* as the predominant pathogen. The infectious dose of *C. jejuni* is estimated at between 500 and 800 organisms (Robinson, 1981). Symptoms of campylobacteriosis are similar to that of other lower gastrointestinal (GI) tract bacterial infections and include abdominal discomfort, cramps, fever, diarrhea, and bloody stools. Severe cases can lead to the development of Guillain Barré Syndrome, an autoimmune disorder of the peripheral nervous system (Nachamkin et al., 1998). *Campylobacter* are a leading cause of foodborne illnesses worldwide, though the number of reported infections is decreasing globally (Taylor et al., 2013). They are an environmental contaminant of milk, and their presence is generally due to contamination from feces (Humphrey and Beckett, 1987), though their direct excretion into milk has also been described (Orr et al., 1995). Pasteurization is effective at eliminating *Campylobacter* spp. from milk, though care must be taken that effective pasteurization is performed as poor processing and postprocessing environments can lead to contamination of milk or milk products (Fernandes et al., 2015).

12.3 *ESCHERICHIA COLI*

E. coli is a Gram-negative, facultative anaerobe and a normal commensal of the human gut, which is often used as an indicator of fecal contamination and poor hygiene practices. Some strains of *E. coli* have acquired virulence factors enabling pathogenesis in the human gut leading to illness. Shiga toxin–producing *E. coli* (STEC), also known as verotoxigenic *E. coli* (VTEC), are human enteric pathogens, the most well-known of which is *E. coli* serotype O157:H7, which causes diarrhea, hemorrhagic colitis, and hemolytic uremic syndrome (HUS). HUS can potentially lead to loss of kidney function, and in extreme cases can be fatal (Griffin et al., 1988). *E. coli* O157:H7 is a major hazard due to its extreme virulence, with an infectious dose as low as 5–50 cells (Farrokh et al., 2013). STEC growth has been recorded in milk at temperatures below 15°C, due to mechanisms not present in nonpathogenic *E. coli* (Vidovic et al., 2011). Ruminants are a significant reservoir for STEC and frequently shed them in feces. Defecation of the cows during milking is considered a critical event for potential transmission of STEC to raw milk; therefore, good milking and subsequently good hygiene practices must be maintained (Martin and Beutin, 2011). STEC have shown to be susceptible to heat treatment at 72°C for 15 seconds, and therefore pasteurization is sufficient to eliminate them from milk (D'Aoust et al., 1988).

12.4 *YERSINIA ENTEROCOLITICA*

Y. enterocolitica are a heterogenous group of Gram-negative facultatively anaerobic pathogens associated with raw milk, raw or undercooked pork, untreated water, and feces (Bancerz-Kisiel and Szweda, 2015). The species is classified into six biovars, five of which are pathogenic to humans (Singhal et al., 2014), represented by more than 30 serotypes (Dhar and Virdi, 2014). *Y. enterocolitica* is the most common etiological agent of yersiniosis followed by *Y. pseudotuberculosis*. Yersiniosis is an illness with a range of symptoms from acute gastroenteritis, to terminal ileitis, mesenteric lymphadenitis, and in severe cases, septicemia (Ostroff, 1995). *Y. enterocolitica* are ubiquitous in the environment, and have been shown to grow at low temperatures, propagating even at refrigeration temperatures (Hudson and Mott, 1993). Pasteurization of milk at 72°C for 15 seconds has been shown to be effective for inactivation of *Y. enterocolitica* in milk (D'Aoust et al., 1988). However, as *Y. enterocolitica* can grow at low temperatures, it remains a hazard if pasteurization is not performed effectively. Yersiniosis has previously been associated with outbreaks following consumption of pasteurized milk, due to deficiencies in the heat treatment facility (Longenberger et al., 2014).

12.5 *STAPHYLOCOCCUS AUREUS*

S. aureus is an important opportunistic pathogen which causes mastitis, inflammation of the mammary gland in the udder of dairy cows, causing major economic losses worldwide. While most strains are commensals of human and other animal skin, many of the Gram-positive facultative anaerobic cocci have been implicated as potential hazards in raw milk. Many *S. aureus* strains can produce a host of extracellular protein toxins and virulence factors which contribute to their pathogenicity, such as heat stable enterotoxins which remain stable during and after pasteurization (Balaban and Rasooly, 2000). Ingestion of food contaminated with *S. aureus* or staphylococcal enterotoxins is the cause of staphylococcal food poisoning (Le Loir et al., 2003), an illness characterized by acute gastroenteritis, with vomiting and diarrhea within 2—6 hours of consumption (Tranter, 1990). Antimicrobial resistance is a significant problem with strains of *S. aureus*, with some strains having developed high level of resistance to β-lactam antibiotics through acquisition of resistance genes which are now well established in farm populations (Smith and Pearson, 2011). Methicillin resistant *S. aureus* (MRSA), the increasingly common nosocomial acquired pathogen, have been found in milk samples since the 1970s (Devriese and Hommez, 1975) and pose a serious risk to consumers (Holmes and Zadoks, 2011). Overuse of antibiotics in the dairy and agriculture industries has contributed to the prevalence of antimicrobial and multidrug resistant (MDR) strains among herds, and in milk, with MDR strains frequently playing a role in mastitis (Holmes and Zadoks, 2011; Kreausukon et al., 2012; Haran et al., 2012). Significantly higher levels of antibiotic resistance have been found in milk from lactating Holsteins with clinical mastitis than without mastitis (Wang et al., 2014). A recent study investigating the effect of pasteurization as a means for inactivating staphylococcal enterotoxins found that heat treatment of 40 milk samples at 72, 85, and 92°C all had samples containing toxin post treatment (87.5%, 52.5%, 45% of samples, respectively) (Necidova et al., 2016).

12.6 SPOREFORMERS: *BACILLUS* AND *CLOSTRIDIUM* SPP.

Gram-positive bacteria of the phylum *Firmicutes* which can form spores when placed under environmental stress are a major problem in the food industry and the dairy sector in particular (Doyle et al., 2015). A spore can form in a bacterial cell which experiences harsh conditions for growth and survival such as high osmotic pressure, nutrient deficient environments, or large temperature differentials (Piggot and Hilbert, 2004). Spores can overcome these conditions, surviving pH changes, radiation, heat, cold, and chemical damage until conditions become favorable and allow for germination (Setlow, 2006). Spores are commonly found in soil (Barash et al., 2010), silage (Te Giffel et al., 2002), animal feces, and on udders with poor hygiene (Christiansson et al., 1999), all of which are common in the milking environment which can lead to contamination of bulk tank milk. Food pathogens of note which form spores in milk are those of the genera *Bacillus* and *Clostridium* which are aerobic and anaerobic, respectively. Many species of these genera are psychrotrophic thermophilic bacteria, which can not only survive but also grow at refrigeration temperatures. They pose a very real threat of contaminating milk and multiplying in the refrigerated bulk milk tank (Murphy et al., 1999).

B. cereus, while not on EFSA's list of harmful pathogen risk factors associated with raw milk (EFSA, 2015), is considered a major hazard due to the ability of some strains to cause illness in humans through the production of toxins. Such strains can release emetic and/or diarrhea causing toxins while growing in milk prior to heat treatment and when growing in the small intestine after consumption of contaminated milk (Kramer and Gilbert, 1989). In 2010, 3.8% of all milk samples which were tested in the EU indicated as positive for *Bacillus* toxin (European Food Safety, 2013). A recent study investigating the effects of storage temperature and duration on the microbial quality of bulk tank milk in Ireland isolated what was denoted as presumptive *B. cereus* in 8%−12% of all bulk milks samples, with no significant difference between altered storage conditions, though inadequate sample size may have been a factor (O'Connell et al., 2016). They are also a notable spoilage hazard, given their ability to produce lipolytic enzymes which can act at temperatures close to those of pasteurization and thermization (Chen et al., 2003). Indeed, the thermoduric sporeformers are a major hazard associated not only with raw milk but also with milk products, fermented products, and powders, and great care must be taken to prevent their contamination and ensure the absence of any toxins. Some investigated methods for the inactivation of *Bacillus* spores in milk include high-pressure homogenization (Amador Espejo et al., 2014; Dong et al., 2015), mild pressure and heat treatment (Van Opstal et al., 2004), the combined effects of high temperature and the food preservative and bacteriocin, nisin (Aouadhi et al., 2014).

Clostridium spp. are a major problem in the dairy industry (Doyle et al., 2015), many of the sporeformers which are found can be toxigenic, neurotoxigenic, or spoilage bacteria. Contamination of bulk tank milk can occur during and after milking from the farm environment, including feeds, feces, soil, and animal bedding (Gleeson et al., 2013). *Clostridium* sp. have been found in raw milk (McAuley et al., 2014), and pasteurization is insufficient to eradicate this bacterium due to the spores formed (Gleeson et al., 2013). Spores pose huge problems for manufacturing standards as they are difficult to eradicate. Illnesses from *Clostridium* spp. are due to ingestion of toxins produced by the genus or germination of ingested spores in the milk or milk product once inside the GI tract. *Clostridium perfringens* and *Clostridium botulinum* are the species of most concern in milk, as both are frequently isolated from the farm environment and are capable of toxin production, most notably enterotoxin and botulinum toxin, the potent neurotoxin (Doyle et al., 2015). Good farm practices must be ensured to avoid contamination with clostridia as some toxins produced in milk are heat stable and are not inactivated by heat treatment (Rasooly and Do, 2010). Similar to *Bacillus*, high pressure heat and treatment with nisin have been investigated as methods for elimination of *Clostridium* spores in milk (Gao et al., 2011).

12.7 *LISTERIA MONOCYTOGENES*

L. monocytogenes is a nonspore forming Gram-positive facultative anaerobe which causes listeriosis, a condition of particular concern for pregnant women, the immunocompromised, and the elderly (Farber and Peterkin, 1991). *Listeria* spp. are ubiquitous in the environment, and contamination of products is common from poor manufacturing conditions such as open water tanks or poor water heating systems (McIntyre et al., 2015). Risk of *Listeria*-related illness is high from consumption of raw milk and milk products such as unpasteurized cheeses held for extended periods of time at low temperatures at which the bacteria can still grow (Bemrah et al., 1998; Latorre et al., 2011). *L. monocytogenes* has a long history of pathogenesis in milk and dairy products (Boor et al., 2017) and is arguably one of the most worrying foodborne pathogens associated with the dairy industry. Several outbreaks have occurred globally in recent years connected with raw milk and raw milk products (Montero et al., 2015); however, illnesses due to *L. monocytogenes* are more often associated with consumption of unpasteurized cheeses (Costard et al., 2017).

12.8 OTHER ZOONOSES AND TOXINS

Other zoonotic bacterial species of note found in milk are *M. bovis* and *Coxiella burnetii*. *M. bovis* causes bovine tuberculosis (TB) in animals, a chronic disease which is now rare in the developed world. The pathogen can spread to humans through consumption of raw milk which is contaminated from infected cows, causing zoonotic TB which presents as identical to TB caused by the well-known human pathogen *Mycobacterium tuberculosis* (Thoen et al., 2006*)*. *M. bovis* is rarely found in milk outside the developing world except in outbreaks associated with the consumption of nonpasteurized milk (Mandal et al., 2011), and contaminated milk. Heat treatment by standard high temperature short time (HTST) pasteurization has been demonstrated to eliminate *M. bovis* (Mandal et al., 2011).

C. *burnetii* is the causative agent of Query (Q) fever, a ubiquitous zoonosis which can infect many animal species including humans, cattle, sheep, and goats. Infection by *C. burnetii* has largely been investigated in sheep and goats, where infections usually remain asymptomatic until pregnancy where the bacterium can increase incidence of abortion (Arricau-Bouvery and Rodolakis, 2005). Bacterial shedding has been described in raw milk among dairy cattle, though consumption of raw milk is considered an inefficient route of transmission (Ho et al., 1995).

Brucella spp. are similar to *Y. enterocolitica* as they not only survive but may grow at refrigeration temperature, both in raw milk (Falenski et al., 2011) and after contamination of pasteurized milk (Oliver et al., 2005). *Brucella* spp. are Gram-negative aerobes which are known to cause brucellosis, a zoonotic infection common among cattle populations. Practically, all human cases of brucellosis are due to close contact with an infected animal or through ingestion of unpasteurized dairy products contaminated with the organism (Young, 2005). It is an infection associated with poor hygiene practices particularly in developing regions of the world as major eradication programs have taken place in much of Northern Europe, North America, and Australia (Whatmore, 2009). *Brucella abortus* and *B. melitensis* are the two main species which infect cattle and pose risk associated with raw milk consumption (Meyer and Shaw, 1920). Manifestations of brucellosis in humans present as high, undulating fever, but chronic brucellosis can lead to organ damage, arthritis, hepatitis, encephalomyelitis, and endocarditis (Dean et al., 2012). Bovine brucellosis is associated with miscarriage, reduced fertility, and milk yields (Aznar et al., 2014).

Mycotoxins are organic chemicals produced in mold-contaminated foods and can be harmful to humans if ingested at high enough concentrations. Aflatoxins and ochratoxins are two such mycotoxins which can be found in raw milk. Mycotoxins are secondary metabolites from species within the *Aspergillus* and *Penicillium* genera (Cullen and Newberne, 1994). These toxins are not associated with an infection in a dairy animal but are associated with the dairy animal eating mold-contaminated foodstuff, therefore, ingesting the toxins which then enter the milk. Both aflatoxins and ochratoxins are regarded as carcinogenic and classified as class 1 known human carcinogens (IARC, 2012) and class 2b possible human carcinogens, respectively (IARC, 1993). Exposure to high levels of these mycotoxins can lead to disease and possibly death. Elevated quantities of aflatoxin can cause hepatic necrosis (Marroquín-Cardona et al., 2014), while ochratoxin is linked to nephropathy (Heussner and Bingle, 2015). Aflatoxin is a relatively heat-stable compound and pasteurization is not sufficient to completely destroy the toxin in milk, but it significantly reduces its level (Rustom, 1997).

12.9 EPIDEMIOLOGICAL CONCERNS

The outbreak-related disease burden associated with the consumption of unpasteurized cow's milk and cheese is estimated at 761 illnesses and 22 hospitalizations annually in the United States, of which 95% are salmonellosis and campylobacteriosis (Costard et al., 2017). Between 2007 and 2012, there were 27 reported epidemics associated with consuming raw milk in Europe, 24 of which were bacteria in nature, largely *Campylobacter* spp. Of 24 outbreaks, 21 were likely due to contamination by *C. jejuni*, two due to *Salmonella enterica* ser. Typhimurium and one from STEC (EFSA, 2015). Four of the 27 outbreaks were due to consumption of raw goat's milk, and the remaining 23 were due to raw cow's milk consumption. Over the same time period in the United States, there were a total of 81 reported outbreaks throughout 26 states associated with raw milk consumption, which led to 979 illnesses and 73 individuals hospitalized. This was a fourfold increase in outbreaks associated with the consumption of unpasteurized milk over a period of six years with the number of outbreaks caused by *Campylobacter* spp. nearly doubling in that time (Mungai et al., 2015). Seventy eight of the 81 outbreaks were linked with a single infectious agent, the most common of which were *Campylobacter* spp., causing 81% (62) of outbreaks. Unlike in Europe, STEC was the next most common with 17% (13) of outbreaks, followed by *S. enterica* ser. Typhimurium present in 3% (2) of outbreaks, and *C. burnetii* was the causative agent in one outbreak (Mungai et al., 2015). Between 2007 and 2009, outbreaks caused by raw milk consumption accounted for 2% of outbreaks related to food in the United States, and this increased to 5% between 2010 and 2012 (Mungai et al., 2015), most likely due to recent relaxation of laws banning the sale of unpasteurized milk in certain states (David, 2012). In 2012 alone, there was an outbreak of *Campylobacter* infections in multiple states of the USA which was traced back to a single dairy farm in Pennsylvania with a permit to sell unpasteurized milk, and which was carrying out the recommended testing for microbial contaminants of milk. The outbreak resulted in 148 individuals falling ill, 10 of whom had to be hospitalized (Longenberger et al., 2013). With the number of outbreaks associated with raw milk consumption having increased in the United States in recent years, there have been calls for the sale and distribution of unpasteurized milk to be legislated against, and continued public education with regard to the dangers of consuming unpasteurized milk (Mungai et al., 2015).

Raw milk products such as unpasteurized cheeses were responsible for 38 outbreaks between 1998 and 2011 in the United States, the pathogens responsible were *Salmonella* (34%), *Campylobacter* (26%), *Brucella* (13%), and STEC (11%) in order of most common single organism cause to least common, and soft cheeses were implicated in 26 of these outbreaks (Gould and Mungai, 2014). Soft cheeses have higher moisture content enabling bacterial growth and are commonly manufactured using raw milk. Thus, soft cheeses have been commonly linked with pathogens such as *E. coli*, *S. aureus*, *Salmonella*, and *Listeria* (Johler et al., 2015; De Valk et al., 2000; Choi et al., 2014; Quinto and Cepeda, 1997). The Food and Drug Administration in the United States requires that unpasteurized cheese be aged for 60 days to improve microbiological quality.

The aging process ensures sufficient time for acid producing starter cultures to act, thereby limiting the growth and survival of potential pathogens. Though this has been the standard for over 60 years, its effectiveness is still a matter of debate as studies have shown both its efficacy and its limitations (Brooks et al., 2012; Schlesser et al., 2006; D'Amico et al., 2008). The pathogenic potential of raw milk remains a very real risk, even in areas where raw milk may be legally sold. A recent study of 902 raw drinking milk samples for retail sale in the United Kingdom found almost half to contain indicators of poor hygiene, and 1% were deemed "unsatisfactory and potentially injurious to health" because of the presence of STEC, *Campylobacter, L. monocytogenes*, or coagulase positive staphylococci (Willis et al., 2017). Those who are immunocompromised, pregnant, elderly, and very young are discouraged from ingesting raw milk as they are high-risk subjects for complications which arise from infections from milk-associated pathogens.

12.10 CONCLUSION

Controversy remains on the potential benefits of raw milk consumption versus heat treated milk. The arguments for raw milk consumption are increased nutritional content, prevention of lactose intolerance, and consumption of "good" bacteria, but these have largely been debunked (Lucey, 2015). Raw milk poses a serious risk to consumers due to the potential presence of pathogens and their toxins. Standard HTST pasteurization is an effective means of eradicating most microbial organisms in milk, ensuring safety for consumption, though not all harmful microbes, such as sporeformers, are susceptible. Similarly, some toxins may not be heat labile and remain postprocessing if conditions allow for their production prior to heat treatment. Good farming practices are essential to reduce the risk of contamination from the environment, along with proper cold chain storage. Current legislation allows for the sale of raw milk in certain states in the United States, and Europe, under strict regulation and monitoring, and it is recommended that raw milk is not ingested by those at the extremes of life, infants and the elderly, the immunocompromised, or by pregnant women, as they are more susceptible to infections by potential contaminants. Raw milk sale and consumption will likely continue while there is demand, and should therefore be monitored thoroughly to limit any potential harm.

ACKNOWLEDGMENTS

Ivan Sugrue and Conor Tobin are in receipt of Teagasc Walsh Fellowships. The financial support of the following is gratefully acknowledged: JPI Food Processing for Health funded "Longlife" and Science Foundation Ireland (SFI) under Grant Number SFI/12/RC/2273 in APC Microbiome Ireland.

REFERENCES

Amador Espejo, G.G., et al., 2014. Inactivation of Bacillus spores inoculated in milk by ultra high pressure homogenization. Food Microbiol. 44, 204–210.

Aouadhi, C., et al., 2014. Inactivation of *Bacillus sporothermodurans* spores by nisin and temperature studied by design of experiments in water and milk. Food Microbiol. 38, 270–275.

Arricau-Bouvery, N., Rodolakis, A., 2005. Is Q fever an emerging or re-emerging zoonosis? Vet. Res. 36 (3), 327–349.

Aznar, M.N., et al., 2014. Bovine brucellosis in argentina and bordering countries: update. Transboundary Emerg. Dis. 61 (2), 121–133.

Balaban, N., Rasooly, A., 2000. Staphylococcal enterotoxins. Int J Food Microbiol. 61 (1), 1–10.

Bancerz-Kisiel, A., Szweda, W., 2015. Yersiniosis—a zoonotic foodborne disease of relevance to public health. Ann. Agric. Environ. Med. 22 (3), 397–402.

Barash, J.R., Hsia, J.K., Arnon, S.S., 2010. Presence of soil-dwelling clostridia in commercial powdered infant formulas. J. Pediatr. 156 (3), 402–408.

Bemrah, N., et al., 1998. Quantitative risk assessment of human listeriosis from consumption of soft cheese made from raw milk. Prev. Vet. Med. 37 (1), 129–145.

Boor, K.J., et al., 2017. A 100-year review: microbiology and safety of milk handling. J. Dairy Sci. 100 (12), 9933–9951.

Brooks, J.C., et al., 2012. Survey of raw milk cheeses for microbiological quality and prevalence of foodborne pathogens. Food Microbiol. 31 (2), 154–158.

Chen, L., Daniel, R.M., Coolbear, T., 2003. Detection and impact of protease and lipase activities in milk and milk powders. Int. Dairy Journal 13 (4), 255–275.

Choi, M.J., et al., 2014. Notes from the field: multistate outbreak of listeriosis linked to soft-ripened cheese—United States, 2013. MMWR Morb. Mortal. Wkly. Rep. 63 (13), 294–295.

Christiansson, A., Bertilsson, J., Svensson, B., 1999. *Bacillus cereus* spores in raw milk: factors affecting the contamination of milk during the grazing period. J. Dairy Sci. 82 (2), 305–314.

Costard, S., et al., 2017. Outbreak-related disease burden associated with consumption of unpasteurized cow's milk and cheese, United States, 2009–2014. Emerg. Infect Dis. 23 (6), 957–964.

Cullen, J.M., Newberne, P.M., 1994. 1—Acute hepatotoxicity of aflatoxins A2—Eaton, David L. In: Groopman, J.D. (Ed.), The Toxicology of Aflatoxins. Academic Press, San Diego, CA, pp. 3–26.

D'Amico, D.J., Druart, M.J., Donnelly, C.W., 2008. 60-day aging requirement does not ensure safety of surface-mold–ripened soft cheeses manufactured from raw or pasteurized milk when *Listeria monocytogenes* is introduced as a postprocessing contaminant. J. Food Prot. 71 (8), 1563–1571.

D'Aoust, J.Y., et al., 1988. Thermal inactivation of *Campylobacter* species, *Yersinia enterocolitica*, and hemorrhagic *Escherichia coli* 0157:H7 in fluid milk. J. Dairy Sci. 71 (12), 3230–3236.

David, S.D., 2012. Raw milk in court: implications for public health policy and practice. Public Health Rep. 127 (6), 598–601.

De Valk, H., et al., 2000. A community-wide outbreak of *Salmonella enterica* serotype Typhimurium infection associated with eating a raw milk soft cheese in France. Epidemiol. Infect. 124 (1), 1–7.

Dean, A.S., et al., 2012. Clinical manifestations of human brucellosis: a systematic review and meta-analysis. PLoS Negl. Trop. Dis. 6 (12), e1929.

Devriese, L., Hommez, J., 1975. Epidemiology of methicillin-resistant *Staphylococcus aureus* in dairy herds. Res. Vet. Sci. 19 (1), 23–27.

Dhar, M.S., Virdi, J.S., 2014. Strategies used by *Yersinia enterocolitica* to evade killing by the host: thinking beyond Yops. Microbes Infect. 16 (2), 87–95.

Dong, P., et al., 2015. Ultra high pressure homogenization (UHPH) inactivation of Bacillus amyloliquefaciens spores in phosphate buffered saline (PBS) and milk. Front. Microbiol. 6, 712.

Doyle, C.J., et al., 2015. Anaerobic sporeformers and their significance with respect to milk and dairy products. Int. J. Food Microbiol. 197, 77–87.

EFSA, 2015. Scientific opinion on the public health risks related to the consumption of raw drinking milk. EFSA J. 13 (1), 3940.

European Food Safety Authority, European Centre for Disease Prevention and Control, 2013. The European Union summary report on trends and sources of zoonoses, zoonotic agents and food-borne outbreaks in 2011. EFSA J. 11 (4), 3129–3133.

Falenski, A., et al., 2011. Survival of *Brucella* spp. in mineral water, milk and yogurt. Int. J. Food Microbiol. 145 (1), 326–330.

Farber, J.M., Peterkin, P.I., 1991. *Listeria monocytogenes*, a food-borne pathogen. Microbiol. Rev. 55 (3), 476–511.

Farrokh, C., et al., 2013. Review of Shiga-toxin-producing Escherichia coli (STEC) and their significance in dairy production. Int. J. Food Microbiol. 162 (2), 190–212.

Fernandes, A.M., et al., 2015. Partial failure of milk pasteurization as a risk for the transmission of *Campylobacter* from cattle to humans. Clin. Infect. Dis. 61 (6), 903–909.

Gao, Y., et al., 2011. Assessment of *Clostridium perfringens* spore response to high hydrostatic pressure and heat with nisin. Appl. Biochem. Biotechnol. 164 (7), 1083–1095.

Gleeson, D., O'Connell, A., Jordan, K., 2013. Review of potential sources and control of thermoduric bacteria in bulk-tank milk. Ir. J. Agric. Food Res. 217–227.

Gould, L.H., Mungai, E.A., 2014. Outbreaks attributed to cheese: differences between outbreaks caused by unpasteurized and pasteurized dairy products, United States, 1998–2011. Foodborne Pathog. Dis. 11 (7), 545–551.

Griffin, P.M., et al., 1988. Illnesses associated with *Escherichia coli* O157:H7 infections. A broad clinical spectrum. Ann. Intern. Med. 109 (9), 705–712.

Haran, K.P., et al., 2012. Prevalence and characterization of *Staphylococcus aureus*, including methicillin-resistant *Staphylococcus aureus*, isolated from bulk tank milk from Minnesota dairy farms. J. Clin. Microbiol. 50 (3), 688–695.

Hazards, E.P.O.B., 2015. Scientific opinion on the public health risks related to the consumption of raw drinking milk. EFSA J. 13 (1), 3940–3943.

Heussner, A.H., Bingle, L.E., 2015. Comparative ochratoxin toxicity: a review of the available data. Toxins (Basel) 7 (10), 4253–4282.

Ho, T., et al., 1995. Isolation of *Coxiella burnetii* from dairy cattle and ticks, and some characteristics of the isolates in Japan. Microbiol. Immunol. 39 (9), 663–671.

Holmes, M.A., Zadoks, R.N., 2011. Methicillin resistant *S. aureus* in human and bovine mastitis. J. Mammary Gland Biol. Neoplasia 16 (4), 373–382.

Hudson, J.A., Mott, S.J., 1993. Growth of *Listeria monocytogenes, Aeromonas hydrophila* and *Yersinia enterocolitica* on cold-smoked salmon under refrigeration and mild temperature abuse. Food Microbiol. 10 (1), 61–68.

Humphrey, T.J., Beckett, P., 1987. *Campylobacter jejuni* in dairy cows and raw milk. Epidemiol. Infect. 98 (3), 263–269.

IARCInternational Agency for Research on Cancer, 1993. Some Naturally Occurring Substances: Food Items and Constituents, Heterocyclic Aromatic Amines and Mycotoxins., Vol. 56. World Health Organization, Geneva, p. 599.

IARC, 2012. Chemical agents and related occupationsI.W.G.o.t.E.o.C.R.t.H. IARC Monogr. Eval. Carcinog. Risks Hum. 100 (PT F), 9–562.

Johler, S., et al., 2015. Outbreak of staphylococcal food poisoning among children and staff at a Swiss boarding school due to soft cheese made from raw milk. J. Dairy Sci. 98 (5), 2944–2948.

Kramer, J.M., Gilbert, R.J., 1989. *Bacillus cereus* and other Bacillus species. Foodborne Bact. Pathog. 19, 21–70.

Kreausukon, K., et al., 2012. Prevalence, antimicrobial resistance, and molecular characterization of methicillin-resistant *Staphylococcus aureus* from bulk tank milk of dairy herds. J. Dairy Sci. 95 (8), 4382–4388.

Latorre, A.A., et al., 2011. Quantitative risk assessment of listeriosis due to consumption of raw milk. J. Food Prot. 74 (8), 1268–1281.

Le Loir, Y., Baron, F., Gautier, M., 2003. *Staphylococcus aureus* and food poisoning. Genet. Mol. Res. 2 (1), 63–76.

Longenberger, A.H., et al., 2013. *Campylobacter jejuni* infections associated with unpasteurized milk-multiple States, 2012. Clin. Infect. Dis. 57 (2), 263–266.

Longenberger, A.H., et al., 2014. *Yersinia enterocolitica* infections associated with improperly pasteurized milk products: southwest Pennsylvania, March–August, 2011. Epidemiol. Infect. 142 (8), 1640–1650.

Lucey, J.A., 2015. Raw milk consumption: risks and benefits. Nutr. Today 50 (4), 189–193.

Mandal, S., et al., 2011. Investigating Transmission of *Mycobacterium bovis* in the United Kingdom in 2005 to 2008. J. Clin. Microbiol. 49 (5), 1943–1950.

Marroquín-Cardona, A.G., et al., 2014. Mycotoxins in a changing global environment—a review. Food Chem. Toxicol. 69 (Supplement C), 220–230.

Martin, A., Beutin, L., 2011. Characteristics of Shiga toxin-producing *Escherichia coli* from meat and milk products of different origins and association with food producing animals as main contamination sources. Int. J. Food Microbiol. 146 (1), 99–104.

McAuley, C.M., et al., 2014. Prevalence and characterization of foodborne pathogens from Australian dairy farm environments. J. Dairy Sci. 97 (12), 7402–7412.

McIntyre, L., Wilcott, L., Naus, M., 2015. Listeriosis outbreaks in British Columbia, Canada, caused by soft ripened cheese contaminated from environmental sources. Biomed. Res. Int. 2015, 131623.

Meyer, K., Shaw, E., 1920. A comparison of the morphologic, cultural and biochemical characteristics of *B. abortus* and *B. melitensis** studies on the genus *Brucella* Nov. Gen. I. J. Infect. Dis. 27 (3), 173–184.

Montero, D., et al., 2015. Molecular epidemiology and genetic diversity of *Listeria monocytogenes* isolates from a wide variety of ready-to-eat foods and their relationship to clinical strains from listeriosis outbreaks in Chile. Front. Microbiol. 6 (384).

Mungai, E.A., Behravesh, C.B., Gould, L.H., 2015. Increased outbreaks associated with nonpasteurized Milk, United States, 2007-2012. Emerg. Infect. Dis. 21 (1), 119–122.

Murphy, P.M., Lynch, D., Kelly, P.M., 1999. Growth of thermophilic spore forming bacilli in milk during the manufacture of low heat powders. Int. J. Dairy Technol. 52 (2), 45–50.

Nachamkin, I., Allos, B.M., Ho, T., 1998. Campylobacter species and Guillain-Barré syndrome. Clin. Microbiol. Rev. 11 (3), 555–567.

Necidova, L., et al., 2016. Short communication: pasteurization as a means of inactivating staphylococcal enterotoxins A, B, and C in milk. J. Dairy Sci. 99 (11), 8638–8643.

O'Connell, A., et al., 2016. The effect of storage temperature and duration on the microbial quality of bulk tank milk. J. Dairy Sci. 99 (5), 3367–3374.

Oliver, S.P., Jayarao, B.M., Almeida, R.A., 2005. Foodborne pathogens in milk and the dairy farm environment: food safety and public health implications. Foodbourne Pathog. Dis. 2 (2), 115–129.

Orr, K.E., et al., 1995. Direct milk excretion of *Campylobacter jejuni* in a dairy cow causing cases of human enteritis. Epidemiol. Infect. 114 (1), 15–24.

Ostroff, S., 1995. Yersinia as an emerging infection: epidemiologic aspects of Yersiniosis. Contrib. Microbiol. Immunol. 13, 5–10.

Penner, J.L., 1988. The genus Campylobacter: a decade of progress. Clin. Microbiol. Rev. 1 (2), 157–172.

Piggot, P.J., Hilbert, D.W., 2004. Sporulation of Bacillus subtilis. Curr. Opin. Microbiol. 7 (6), 579–586.

Quinto, E.J., Cepeda, A., 1997. Incidence of toxigenic *Escherichia coli* in soft cheese made with raw or pasteurized milk. Lett. Appl. Microbiol. 24 (4), 291–295.

Rasooly, R., Do, P.M., 2010. *Clostridium botulinum* neurotoxin type B is heat-stable in milk and not inactivated by pasteurization. J. Agric. Food Chem. 58 (23), 12557–12561.

Robinson, D.A., 1981. Infective dose of *Campylobacter jejuni* in milk. Br. Med. J. 282 (May), 1584.

Rustom, I.Y.S., 1997. Aflatoxin in food and feed: occurrence, legislation and inactivation by physical methods. Food Chem. 59 (1), 57–67.

Scallan, E., et al., 2011. Foodborne illness acquired in the United States—unspecified agents. Emerg. Infect. Dis. 17 (1), 16–22.

Schlesser, J.E., et al., 2006. Survival of a five-strain cocktail of *Escherichia coli* O157:H7 during the 60-day aging period of Cheddar cheese made from unpasteurized milk. J. Food Prot. 69 (5), 990–998.

Setlow, P., 2006. Spores of Bacillus subtilis: their resistance to and killing by radiation, heat and chemicals. J. Appl. Microbiol. 101 (3), 514–525.

Singhal, N., Kumar, M., Virdi, J.S., 2014. Molecular analysis of beta-lactamase genes to understand their differential expression in strains of *Yersinia enterocolitica* biotype 1A. Sci. Rep. 4, 5270.

Smith, T.C., Pearson, N., 2011. The emergence of *Staphylococcus aureus* ST398. Vector Borne Zoonotic Dis. 11 (4), 327–339.

Taylor, E.V., et al., 2013. Common source outbreaks of *Campylobacter* infection in the USA, 1997–2008. Epidemiol. Infect. 141 (5), 987–996.

Te Giffel, M.C., et al., 2002. Bacterial spores in silage and raw milk. Antonie Van Leeuwenhoek 81 (1–4), 625–630.

Thoen, C., LoBue, P., De Kantor, I., 2006. The importance of *Mycobacterium bovis* as a zoonosis. Vet. Microbiol. 112 (2), 339–345.

Tranter, H.S., 1990. Foodborne staphylococcal illness. Lancet 336 (8722), 1044–1046.

Van Opstal, I., et al., 2004. Inactivation of *Bacillus cereus* spores in milk by mild pressure and heat treatments. Int. J. Food Microbiol. 92 (2), 227–234.

Vidovic, S., Mangalappalli-Illathu, A.K., Korber, D.R., 2011. Prolonged cold stress response of *Escherichia coli* O157 and the role of rpoS. Int. J. Food Microbiol. 146 (2), 163–169.

Wang, X., et al., 2014. Antimicrobial resistance and toxin gene profiles of *Staphylococcus aureus* strains from Holstein milk. Lett. Appl. Microbiol. 58 (6), 527–534.

Whatmore, A.M., 2009. Current understanding of the genetic diversity of Brucella, an expanding genus of zoonotic pathogens. Infect. Genet. Evol. 9 (6), 1168–1184.

Willis, C., et al., 2017. An assessment of the microbiological quality and safety of raw drinking milk on retail sale in England. J. Appl. Microbiol 124 (2), 535–546.

Young, E., 2005. *Brucella* species. Princ. Pract. Infect. Dis. 6.

CHAPTER 13

Chemical Residues and Mycotoxins in Raw Milk

Fabiano Barreto, Louíse Jank, Tamara Castilhos, Renata B. Rau, Caroline Andrade Tomaszewski, Cristina Ribeiro and Daniel R. Hillesheim
National Agricultural Laboratory (LANAGRO/RS), Ministry of Agriculture, Livestock and Food Supply (MAPA), São José, Brazil

13.1 INTRODUCTION

Raw milk consumption is characteristic of many populations. Some special and traditional products are made with raw milk being a representation of popular customs. Raw milk impacts could be greater in terms of foodborne illness for susceptible groups as young children, the elderly, and individuals with weakened immune systems, such as people with cancer, an organ transplant, or HIV/AIDS. Internationally, unpasteurized dairy products are the most common cause of dairy-associated foodborne illness (Langer et al., 2012).

Dairy products have experienced an important and rapid growth in consumption in several countries in developing world, driven by economic growth. Since the early 1960s, per capita milk consumption in developing countries has increased almost twofold. However, the consumption of milk has grown more slowly than that of other livestock products; meat consumption has more than tripled and egg consumption has increased fivefold. Per capita milk consumption range, second FAO data, from 30 to 150 kg/person/year making an important vector in terms of consumers exposure to contaminants (FAO, 2008).

Based on increasing demand, production growth has been driven by technological change in the sector, which has permitted substantial improvement in productivity and appearance of large-scale commercial dairy farms. However, dairy farmers on a large scale with high technological level associated is not the most common situation around the world, such as the situation in developing countries where most of production is

Raw Milk
DOI: https://doi.org/10.1016/B978-0-12-810530-6.00013-4

associated with small producers with limited access to those technologies (Gerosa and Skoet, 2012).

Taking in account harmonization of national policies with international requirements, contaminants control has been one of the main factors aimed at trade issues. The introduction of risk analysis tools and implementation of residues and contaminants monitoring programs has become mandatory. To adequate risk evaluation and intending to introduce risk management techniques, some conditions are extremely relevant to milk and dairy products. Specifically evaluating residues, chemical contaminants, and some toxins produced by microorganisms, there is a particularly aggravating issue that is the stability of these compounds even after heat treatments (Nag, 2010).

Countries with weak control systems are subject of increased risks of chemical and microorganism's toxins contamination in food. Additionally, proximity of production with industrial areas represents an important factor of nonintentional introduction of contaminants in food chain. Moreover, new techniques of management (e.g., veterinary medicines) are available even in developing countries being mandatory introduction of Good Agricultural Practices (GAP) to ensure safe food providing. Small and local producers are susceptible to free access to pesticides and vet drugs with no adequate use information being at high risk to provide a contaminated food after off-label/misuse or failure to comply with withdrawal periods.

Different classes of compounds intended to different purposes are available and, in many countries, the tools to an accurate control are limited, lacking data about use profile which avoid a suitable control. Between the most important compounds to be monitored are pesticides, antibiotics, antiparasitic, heavy metals, mycotoxins/toxins, persistent pollutants, and compounds that have received more attention recently as the case of plant toxins.

To a suitable control is necessary an adequate support for identification and quantification of concentration in food samples. It is important to highlight the integration between environmental, food safety and health services to a consistent control of chemical hazards in food chain.

13.2 RISK ASSESSMENT

Scientific risk assessment plays an increasing role internationally for global risk governance and as a tool to support sustainable trade practices, there is the need for standardization of risk assessment procedures. The Codex Alimentarius Commission is the international forum for standardization. Compounds traces (pesticides or veterinary drugs) leave in treated products are called residues and need an evaluation to ensure safety aspects. A maximum residue level (MRL) is the highest level of a veterinary medicine or pesticide that is legally tolerated in or on food or feed when applied correctly in accordance with GAP.

Action levels need for pesticides and veterinary drugs may also be applicable to animal feeds. Evaluation goal is to recommend suitable standards for contaminants, pesticide residues, and veterinary drugs in food commodities. Residue evaluation is complex, and the available information should be used in the context of understanding residue behavior. Residue data evaluation is based on the result from pesticide and veterinary drug's use according to GAP to estimate MRLs in food and feed commodities. Under GAP, a compound is used for effective pest control but leaves a residue that is the smallest amount practicable. The use must be safe for the user and the environment, and residues in food must be safe for consumers.

13.3 RELEVANT COMPOUNDS AND LABORATORIAL SUPPORT TO RESIDUES AND CONTAMINANTS CONTROL

Adequate control of residues and contaminants in food is essential in terms of public health and consumers protection. To achieve this goal, an adequate laboratory support and rational planning of samples number to be analyzed is required.

To create control points at different stages, rapid screening methods for contaminants and residues are desired to be applied directly at food processing plants. The most widespread screening kits are intended for analysis of antibiotics and are usually used in milk before accessing the industry. These kits can detect only a few classes of antibiotics providing a qualitative result.

For monitoring compounds such as mycotoxins, pesticides, and veterinary drugs in a more accurate perspective, more modern approaches are based on analytical instrumentation applying multiresidues methods employing chromatographic techniques coupled to mass spectrometry. In this scenario emerges, techniques like liquid chromatography tandem—mass spectrometry (LC—MS/MS), liquid chromatography coupled to quadrupole time of flight mass spectrometry(LC—qTOF), and gas chromatography tandem–mass spectrometry (GC–MS/MS) methods allowing to work with concentration in order of ppb and ppt levels. An increased number of methods were introduced covering different compound classes and monitoring key compounds at same analytical run.

13.3.1 Pesticides

Pesticides could be introduced by feed contaminated, drinking water, use of household cleaning products in milking places, and directly by application of pesticides to control of insects. The main classes that are used to cattle management are pyrethroids, carbamates, and organophosphate (Oliveira-Filho et al., 2010). It has been shown levels of contamination of milk by organophosphates being one of the most important vehicles, animal feed (Fagnani et al., 2011).

Persistent pesticides like organochlorines have lower levels of notification after long-term prohibition. If compared with previous results, even in countries with a ban on its use occurring late, they are at lower levels (Gutierrez et al., 2012; Nag and Raikwar, 2008).

Different methods are available to control residues of pesticides in milk. The most actual approaches are based on LC–MS/MS and GC–MS/MS and multiresidues methods which provide a reliable option to control at same time different types of contaminants simultaneously providing helpful information to risk management (Bandeira et al., 2014; dos Anjos et al., 2016).

13.3.2 Antiparasitic

Antiparasitic drugs are used worldwide for treatment and prevention of parasitic diseases in food-producing animals and are particularly important for cattle raising in tropical regions where cattle graze on rangelands and are intensively affected by both endo and ectoparasitosis (Rübensam et al., 2011; Rübensam et al., 2013). Between the most common antiparasitic drugs administered to cattle are the avermectins ivermectin (IVR), abamectin, doramectin, eprinomectin, and the milbemycin moxidectin.

These compounds, although limited data are available about its stability, have demonstrated an important persistence after thermal treatment (Imperiale et al., 2009). Avermectins have no significant impact on dairy products production industrial process, as fermentation products (Imperiale et al., 2002). In other hand, due its lipophilic characteristics, avermectins and other antiparasitic compounds (e.g., benzimidazoles) may concentrated in fat-based products like butter and cheese and residues remain in final products (Gomez Perez et al., 2013).

Most compounds are not allowed for use in animals from which milk is produced for human consumption (Commission, 2010). But data from National Residues Control Plan demonstrated a controlled level of positive samples for IVR in milk samples. Due to its intensive use, cases of resistant parasites to avermectins are being demonstrated. This fact introduces a risk of over dosage and higher residues levels in milk and dairy products.

Multiresidues methodologies are available for determining antiparasitic being LC−MS/MS methods the most actual approach (Stubbings and Bigwood, 2009; Wei et al., 2015).

13.3.3 Heavy Metals

Unlike microorganisms that are removed after heat treatment, heavy metals are stable to treatment processes remaining on milk and dairy products (Bajwa and Sandhu, 2014). Milk and dairy products are poor sources of essential elements (iron, copper, and zinc). However, it is susceptible to contamination with nonessential or toxic elements (lead and cadmium). The presence of toxic elements above the MRL defined has deleterious consequences as metabolic disorders with extremely serious consequences. Only Pb has MRL in milk and secondary dairy products (MRL = 0.02 mg/kg w.w.) (Meshref et al., 2014).

Dairy animals ingest metals while grazing on the pasture and when fed on contaminated concentrate feeds. However, in the cow, transfer of minerals to milk is highly variable. Moreover, along the food chain, contaminants could be introduced from low-quality materials used in the transport and packaging of milk. In addition, inputs during transport, process tanks, and cleaning materials are potential sources of significant contaminants in milk samples.

In other hand, the introduction of management tools in order to increase productivity of the most widespread actions is the mineral supplementation of cattle, including milk-producing animals. Thus, this has been one of the main gateways to the introduction of contaminants such as heavy metals by low-quality materials present in supplements offered to the herd.

Different types of instrumentation are available to metal analysis resulting different limits of detection. Highly sensitive spectroscopic techniques such as flame or graphite furnace atomic absorption spectrometry, inductively coupled plasma optical emission spectrometry and inductively coupled plasma mass spectrometry (ICP−OES and ICP−MS) are the most widely used methods to determine heavy metals in food and environmental samples (Meshref et al., 2014). Although a more expensive technique, ICP−MS has emerged as a key tool for monitoring different metals in milk and dairy products simultaneously, with high sensitivity.

13.3.4 Mycotoxins

Mycotoxins are produced mainly by fungi belonging to genera *Aspergillus*, *Fusarium*, and *Penicillium* being extremely toxic when ingested to humans and other vertebrate animals presenting carcinogenic, teratogenic, and mutagenic potential (Hymery et al., 2014). This group is defined as secondary metabolites and compounds of low molecular weight. There are evidences that ruminants are less susceptible to mycotoxins intoxication than monogastrics, being more effective in the degradation, deactivation, and binding of these toxic molecules (Gallo et al., 2015).

Mycotoxins presence in feed and leading to contamination of food for human consumption is not only a matter of concern for human health but also in economic aspects, once mycotoxins are responsible for significant economic losses due to adverse effects and consequent reduction productivity (Flores-Flores et al., 2015). Most mycotoxins are very stable chemically and once formed in a feedstuff will continue to contaminate that commodity and feeds manufactured from it (Bryden, 2012). As cited by Sassahara et al., aflatoxin B1 (AFB1) presents the highest degree of toxicity for animals, followed by the aflatoxins M1 (AFM1), G1 (AFG1), B2 (AFB2), and G2 (AFG2) (Sassahara et al., 2005). AFM1 is a hydroxylated biotransformation product of AFB1, detected within 12−24 hours after the first ingestion of AFB1 and excreted into milk from 1% to 6% of dietary intake (Bryden, 2012).

Other mycotoxins (and its conjugated derivatives) such as ochratoxin A, (Tsiplakou et al., 2014) zearalenone, fumonisins, T-2 toxin, and deoxynivalenol have also been identified in milk samples and dairy products and even present at low concentrations; they have high toxicological relevance mainly to consumers of large quantities of this product, particularly children (Becker-Algeri et al., 2016; Flores-Flores et al., 2015).

Several studies have been published trying to analyze simultaneously mycotoxins of interest in milk and other matrices like feed. These approaches are of fundamental importance for generation of epidemiological data about the incidence of mycotoxins residues for those compounds that have limited scientific information on dairy products, compared with AFM1 (Tsiplakou et al., 2014; Zhang et al., 2013). New lines of research have directed efforts to analyze these compounds based on LC−MS/MS methods with other compounds of interest as veterinary drugs and pesticides (Wang et al., 2011).

13.3.5 Enterotoxins

In this field, the search for direct and more selective and sensitive methods has led researchers to lay hold of different technologies. Currently, the technology is more sensitive to these analyzes using enzyme-linked immunosorbent assay methodology type ELFA (a variation of the sandwich ELISA with fluorescent enzyme substrate).

A new approach proposed is based on typical proteomics tools, where the samples are subjected to enzymatic proteolysis with trypsin and the peptides generated are analyzed by LC−MS/MS (Andjelkovic et al., 2016; Zuberovic Muratovic et al., 2015).

Enterotoxins are a serious problem primarily related to dairy products, mainly involving milk and cheese; thus, the development of a sensitive method that allows quantification and unequivocal identification of these substances is of paramount importance to ensure the safety of the product. Analysis of enterotoxin using LC−MS/MS can be a complement to classical microbiological methods, as implemented by the network laboratories, as well as those methods employing methods based on molecular biology tools.

As mycotoxins, the enterotoxin of *Staphylococcus aureus* is the unwanted contaminants originating from microorganisms. The inclusion of methods able to detect in a direct way the presence of these compounds in foods is advancing in control tools.

13.3.6 Antimicrobials

A very important group of compounds used in veterinary medicine is antimicrobials. Antimicrobials are compounds which act against microorganisms, inhibiting their growing or causing their destruction. These substances were discovered in the beginning of twentieth century, by the discover of the penicillin, and since then, many other compounds were revealed and synthetized, always looking for better results when a compound is not effective anymore.

Antimicrobials have their use diffused in human and veterinary medicine, and many classes are used in both of them. Beyond the therapeutic application in case of infections, these substances also presented efficiency with prophylactic purposes and as improvers of feed conversion. The objective of these last two applications is to reduce the competition for nutrients by microorganisms present in the digestive tract in food-producing animals, decreasing the time needed to rise the ideal weight to slaughter, as well as the feed consumption, mortality, and improving the health of these animals. Therefore, antimicrobials are currently administrated in large scale in livestock.

The main classes used in food-producing animals are sulfonamides, quinolones, fluoroquinolones β-lactams (penicillins and cephalosporins), tetracyclines, macrolides, aminoglicosides, and amphenicols. Antimicrobials can be used as single compound presentation or in association with other antimicrobials or other compounds.

The main use of antimicrobials in dairy cattle is for the treatment of calves and adult cows. Diarrhea, pneumonia, and tick fever are some diseases which can affect calves and can be treated with antimicrobials. In cows, the main uses of antimicrobials are for treating mastitis, metritis, hoof problems, and uterine washes postpartum, as well as prophylactic at the end of lactation period (Andreotti and Nicodemo, 2004).

The control and prevention of mastitis is the main challenge in dairy cattle. This disease is responsible for significant economic losses, both for producers, as decrease of milk production and discard of milk of unhealthy animals, or even the discard of sick cows, and for dairy industry, by reducing cheese production efficiency and the shelf life of dairy products (Santos and Fonseca, 2007).

Mastitis is one of the major responsible for mortality in dairy cows and for decreasing productivity in industry (Langoni, 2013; Ruegg, 2011), as well as changing in milk properties, as calcium, lactose, sodium, chloride, and casein content. Parameters which are indirectly associated with mastitis occurrence, as somatic cells count (SCC), are linked to problems in dairy products, like cheese (Coelho et al., 2014) and yogurt (Fernandes et al., 2007), as microbiological and nutritional composition, decreasing the shelf life of these products. In pasteurized milk, the high SCC causes proteolysis and lipolysis, and, thus, sensory defects related, as rancidity and bitterness (Ma et al., 2000).

Results obtained with antimicrobials therapy are reduction of infected animals and of SCC. In terms of milk production, cows treated with antimicrobials before partum produce more milk in comparison with ones not treated and have a lower SCC, what justifies, in economic terms, the application of intramammarian infusion before partum in cattle where the occurrence of mastitis was identified (Santos and Fonseca, 2007).

The use of antimicrobials, as well as other active pharmaceutical compounds, in food-producing animals, can lead to the presence of residues of these compounds in the foods from treated animals. For the dairy industry, the main problem is the inhibition of sensible lacteous cultures used in production of cheese, yogurt, and other fermented products, difficult to obtain these products, or changing its quality. Other problems are the formation of unpleasant odors in butter and cream. Pasteurization has little or no effect on the content of residues of antibiotics milk.

Problems related to public health included the possibility of allergic or toxic reactions development in individuals who are ingesting milk containing antimicrobials residues. It is estimated, e.g., that about 4% of the population has allergies to penicillins, in greater or lesser degree, and may residues thereof, in severe cases, cause anaphylactic shock in these individuals (Jank et al., 2015b; Stolker et al., 2008b).

The main manifest allergic reactions are generally represented by the symptoms as urticaria, dermatitis, rhinitis and bronchial asthma. They are mainly related to the penicillins, but tetracyclines, streptomycin, and sulfonamides may also cause this type of reaction.

Toxic reactions are related to some antimicrobial with carcinogenic potential, i.e., they can develop tumors in laboratory animals (e.g., sulfamethazine, nitrofurans) or lead to hematological changes in susceptible individuals (chloramphenicol).

Another problem, perhaps the most worrying, is that the use of antimicrobials in large-scale livestock farming also contributes selective pressure of bacteria, favoring the incidence and developing of resistance. The constant use of these compounds and therefore the constant input of residues in the environment where there are farm animals become prone to spread of antimicrobial resistance genes. The public health concern is the potential impact of transmission of resistant bacteria to humans through the food chain, such as raw milk from subclinical mastitis animals. Concern about antimicrobial resistance was first reported in 1965, by Anderson, who described resistance in bovine *Salmonella* isolates, emphasizing that usage of these compounds with therapeutic and prophylactic purposes is the major agent in maintenance, coselection, vertical, and horizontal spread of antimicrobial resistance.

Presently, it is known that all new compounds and all new classes of antimicrobials will, sooner or later, show resistance due to originate selective pressure of their use, and these compounds may become ineffective, to a greater or lesser degree, which it becomes worrisome in view of public health. Both commensal bacteria as pathogenic bacteria present today antimicrobial resistance.

Nowadays, the approach "one-health" is a matter of discussion when it comes to resistance to antimicrobials. This means that resistance can occur in bacteria in animals and be transfer to human through the food chain. In other words, the use of antimicrobials in livestock, although appropriate and prudent, can be the way for these bacteria reach the human being, due to its wide use in veterinary medicine. When you consider that, in some cases, such use is held at higher levels than the necessary, the scenario becomes even more dramatic in relation to antimicrobial residues in raw milk, governmental agencies, and international organisms such as Codex Alimentarius, European Medicines Agency—EMA (European Union), and Food and Drug Administration—FDA (USA) defined MRLs for several veterinary drugs in food, including several classes of antimicrobials. In Table 13.1, MRLs values for some antimicrobial compounds defined by European Commission are presented (Queenan et al., 2016).

Many techniques are presented in literature for analysis regarding presence and concentration of residues in raw milk. In general, they can be divided in two different types: screening and confirmatory methods (Cháfer-Pericás et al., 2010). Screening methods can detect the presence of a compound or a class of compounds (e.g., tetracyclines), and some of them can provide semiquantitative results. Microbiological screening methods are widely used for rapid analysis, due to its application to a large amount of different antimicrobials, and its advantage is the great cost-effectiveness, as well as it does not need special training or equipment (Pikkemaat et al., 2009). Other authors also highlight the low rate of false-positive samples, high throughput, good selectivity, and low cost (Cháfer-Pericás et al., 2010).

Microbiological screening tests can be divided in tube tests and multiplate tests. Tube tests contain agar medium, a bacteria sensible to compound or class, and a pH or redox indicator. The absence or presence of the antimicrobial residue allows the bacteria to grow or not, respectively,

Table 13.1 MRLs values for some antimicrobial compounds defined by European Commission

Class	Analyte	MRL milk EMA[10]
Macrolides	Azithromycin	NA
Macrolides	Erythromycin	40.0
Macrolides	Spiramycin	200.0
Macrolides	Tilmicosin	50.0
Macrolides	Tulathromycin	NA[c]
Macrolides	Tylosin	50.0
Lincosamides	Clindamycin	NA
Lincosamides	Lincomycin	150.0
Lincosamides	Pirlimycin	100.0
Sulfonamides	Sulfachloropyridazine	100.0[a]
Sulfonamides	Sulfadiazine	100.0[a]
Sulfonamides	Sulfadimethoxine	100.0[a]
Sulfonamides	Sulfadoxine	100.0[a]
Sulfonamides	Sulfisoxazole	100.0[a]
Sulfonamides	Sulfamerazine	100.0[a]
Sulfonamides	Sulfametazine	100.0[a]
Sulfonamides	Sulfamethoxazole	100.0[a]
Sulfonamides	Sulfaquinoxaline	100.0[a]
Sulfonamides	Sulfathiazole	100.0[a]
Fluoroquinolones	Ciprofloxacin	100.0[b]
Fluoroquinolones	Danofloxacin	30.0
Fluoroquinolones	Difloxacin	NA[c]
Fluoroquinolones	Enrofloxacin	100.0[b]
Quinolones	Flumequine	50.0
Quinolones	Nalidixic acid	NA
Fluoroquinolones	Norfloxacin	NA
Quinolones	Oxolinic acid	20.0[c]
Fluoroquinolones	Sarafloxacin	NA
Dihydrofolate reductase inhibitors	Trimethoprim	50.0
Tetracyclines	Chlorotetracycline	100.0
Tetracyclines	Doxycycline	NA[c]
Tetracyclines	Oxytetracycline	100.0
Tetracyclines	Tetracycline	100.0
β–Lactams	Amoxicillin	4.0
β–Lactams	Ampicillin	4.0
β–Lactams	Cefalexin	100.0
β–Lactams	Cefapirin	60.0
β–Lactams	Cefalonium	20.0

(*Continued*)

Table 13.1 (Continued)

MRL milk

Class	Analyte	EMA[10]
β–Lactams	Ceftiofur	100.0[d]
β–Lactams	Cefoperazone	50.0
β–Lactams	Cefquinome	20.0
β–Lactams	Cloxacillin	30.0
β–Lactams	Dicloxacillin	30.0
β–Lactams	Nafcillin	30.0
β–Lactams	Oxacillin	30.0
β–Lactams	Penicillin G	4.0
β–Lactams	Penicillin V	4.0
Amynoglicosides	Apramycin	NA[c]
Amynoglicosides	Dihydrostreptomycin	200.0
Amynoglicosides	Gentamicin	100.0
Amynoglicosides	Kanamycin	150.0
Amynoglicosides	Neomycin	1500.0
Amynoglicosides	Paromomycin	NA[c]
Amynoglicosides	Spectinomycin	200.0
Amynoglicosides	Streptomycin	200.0
Cyclic polipeptide	Bacitracin	100.0
Cyclic polipeptide	Colistin	50.0

[a]The combined total residues of all substances within the sulfonamide group should not exceed 100 μg/kg.
[b]Sum of enrofloxacin and ciprofloxacin.
[c]Not for use in animals from which milk or eggs are produced for human consumption. NA, not applicable.
[d]Sum of all residues retaining the beta-lactam structure expressed as desfuroylceftiofur.

and the color of medium change due to substances released by its evolution (Pikkemaat et al., 2009). Increasing in temperature allows results in few hours. Many commercial microbiological tube tests for milk analysis are available, e.g., Charm Cowside/Charm Sciences Inc., and Delvotest/DSM.

For (multi-)plates assays, an agar layer is on the top of the plate where the samples are placed. In case of noncompliant sample, after a one night incubation, a growth inhibition zone can be observed around, for whose size is related to the concentration of residue (Pikkemaat et al., 2009).

Although presented as a practical solution having sensitivity to more than one class of antibiotics, microbiological screening tests do not provide specificity, requiring confirmatory methods such as those employing

LC—MS/MS. Mass spectrometry is a tool that has proven valuable in this research field, as it enables simultaneous analysis of compounds with different chemical characteristics (Diaz et al., 2013).

Different techniques for mass spectrometry, especially coupled with liquid chromatography, have been used for the determination of organic contaminants in food samples and may provide important information that are related to quantification with high selectivity and sensitivity by LC—MS/MS, or a comprehensive assessment of contaminants in the sample, data provided by an analysis using LC—QTOF—MS.

The techniques of mass coupled to liquid chromatography spectrometry represented an advance with regard to analysis of organic contaminants to be more sensitive (possibility of trace analysis and ultratrace—µg/L and ng/L); it does not require derivatization and allow the determination of labile, nonpolar, and volatile compounds, and detection of analytes without chromophore groups. Moreover, coupling to a mass spectrometer provides further data regarding the sample and the analyte under study due to mass spectral information.

LC—QTOF—MS has shown great potential in screening and confirmatory analysis of organic contaminants, as antimicrobials. The combination of mass accuracy with a complete data set acquisition allows the monitoring of several components at same time which could be extracted applying software tools (Pitarch et al., 2010) and is the approach of selected compounds as unselected. Still, it is possible to perform an evaluation of data already acquired at any time to search for additional compounds (initially not included) (Hernandez et al., 2011), without the need for additional analysis—from the extraction method applied, it is able to select the compound in question. Further, it is possible to obtain a similar analysis, accurate mass, and fragmentation data of compound through the information dependent acquisition mode which may be useful for the determination of an unknown sample compound (Bueno et al., 2012). These reasons justify this technique as the choice for qualitative methodologies with confirmatory purposes.

LC—MS/MS has been the most widely used analytical technique for the quantitative determination of residues in food and feed samples (Malone et al., 2009). By making use of ion monitoring mode multiple reaction monitoring, which allows obtaining data only in respect of the selected ions, significantly better responses for sensitivity and selectivity parameters are observed.

Because of this, the vast majority of the work done for the qualitative and quantitative analysis of antimicrobials in milk samples have used liquid chromatography coupled to mass spectrometry technique in recent years (Arsand et al., 2016; Bohm et al., 2009; Gaugain-Juhel et al., 2009; Jank et al., 2015a; Jank et al., 2015b; Kantiani et al., 2009; Martins et al., 2014; Riediker et al., 2001; Stolker et al., 2008a, 2008b; Turnipseed et al., 2008, 2011; Wang et al., 2006).

13.3.7 Antiinflammatory Compounds

Nonsteroidal antiinflammatory drugs (NSAIDs) are compounds that suppress inflammation by reducing prostaglandin biosynthesis (responsible for the pain and tumescence) and are classified as selective inhibitors of cyclooxygenase (COX-1 and COX-2), nonselective COX inhibitors, and selective COX-2 inhibitors. Most NSAIDs, with exceptions as metamizole, compounds are acids with pKa in the range 3−5, an essential characteristic for inhibition of COX. Structurally NSAIDs can be classified as follows: salicylic acid and derivatives, indolacetic acids (indomethacin), hetero–aryl–acetic acid (diclofenac), arylpropionic acids (carprofen), anthranilic acids or fenamates (flunixin), enolic acids (meloxicam), pyrazole derivatives (phenylbutazone), diaryl-substituted furanone (firocoxib), and sulphonamide (nimesulide) (Peterson et al., 2010).

The use of these drugs takes place in veterinary medicine since 1970 and its use has evolved similarly to the use in human medicine, being this class the second most commonly prescribed, exceeded only by antimicrobials (Lichtenberger et al., 1995). They are often considered as initial therapy for inflammatory disorders of animals of various species, prescribed for suppression or prevention of musculoskeletal disorders, pulmonary diseases, mastitis, enteritis, fever, and pain. Another approach is the use of combination with antibiotics to treatment of mammary gland inflammation (Jedziniak et al., 2013).

Although acid drugs are excreted in the milk at low levels, there is little information about the exhaustion of this same product. In veterinary practice, the use of flunixin meglumine is very widespread, being inadequate in the consumption of milk produced before 24 hours of the last dose (Jedziniak et al., 2013).

The consumption of foods with residues of NSAIDs is a risk to human health, with effects such as hepatotoxicity, aseptic meningitis, diarrhea, and depression of the central nervous system (Baert, 2003). For this reason, residues control is required, as well as the development of methods to monitor the presence of NSAIDs residues with confidence and compliance with the regulatory limits. Table 13.1 shows the MRLs established in the European Community (European Commission, 2010).

The chemical structural differences of this class transformed challenge in the development of multiresidues methods for treating principally sample (extraction and clean-up). Extraction with acetonitrile, provides an efficient extraction and suitable clean-up due protein precipitation and low fat solubility, being the most widely used organic solvent as extractor of organic compounds like vet drugs and pesticides (Dowling et al., 2008; Gentili et al., 2012; Jedziniak et al., 2012; Malone et al., 2009). However, methanol (Dubreil-Chéneau et al., 2011), as well as mixtures acetonitrile/methanol (Gallo et al., 2008) or acetonitrile/ethyl acetate (Peng et al., 2013), also showed good overall recovery when used.

Few confirmatory methods have been developed to NSAIDs analysis of milk samples. They are usually based on LC−MS/MS, although the use of gas chromatography has also been described (Dowling et al., 2008; Stolker et al., 2008a).

Whereas the LC−MS system is susceptible to matrix effects, and milk is a complex matrix, most of the methods except the proposed by some authors (Dubreil-Chéneau et al., 2011; van Pamel and Daeseleire, 2015) include a cleanup step of the extracts. Several strategies have been described, such as liquid−liquid extraction with hexane to remove fats (Malone et al., 2009; Peng et al., 2013) and the longer applied, solid phase extraction with different sorbents (amino, octadecyl, or polymeric phases) according with the set of compounds included in method (Gallo et al., 2008; Gentili et al., 2012).

LC−MS/MS is the technique of choice for confirmatory methods for determining residues of NSAIDs. The chromatographic separation is usually performed with octadecyl column and a mobile phase based on the mixture acetonitrile/water with acid pH. With regard to MS detection, most of the methods use a QqQ instrument with an ESI source, in negative or positive mode, depending on the compounds.

13.3.8 Plant Toxins

Some plant toxins like pyrrolizidine alkaloids (PAs) are present in many plants belonging to the families of *Asteraceae*, *Boraginaceae*, *and Fabaceae*. Those compounds are responsible for intoxications and severe losses in productivity terms. PAs present in ragwort species (Senecio), which are held responsible for hepatic disease in horses and cows and may lead to the death of the affected animals being transferred to edible products of animal origin and as such be a threat for the health of consumers (Hoogenboom et al., 2011).

PA intoxication is caused by consumption of plant material containing these alkaloids. The plants may be consumed as food, for medicinal purposes, or as contaminants of other agricultural crops. Cereal crops and forage crops are sometimes contaminated with pyrrolizidine-producing weeds, and the alkaloids find their way into flour and other foods, including milk from cows feeding on these plants. Many plants from the *Boraginaceae, Compositae,* and *Leguminosae* families contain well over 100 hepatotoxic PAs (Valese et al., 2016).

Unfortunately, there is no international regulation of PAs in foods, unlike those for herbs and medicines (Vacillotto et al., 2013). In relation to milk, based on limited data available, no more than about 0.1% of the ingested alkaloid base will be excreted in milk (Authority, 2001). PAs and PA N-oxides are known to be excreted in cow's milk, but due to milk bulking, it is unlikely that significant exposures would come from this source. The main technique to control these compounds is based on LC—MS/MS methods (Valese et al., 2016).

13.4 CONCLUSIONS

Regardless if used raw milk or processed, as well as dairy products, control of residues of chemical contaminants and toxins is indispensable aiming consumers safety and mitigate negative outcomes both acute and chronic.

Adequate control of materials used in the production of feed and diet supplementation for the animals, as well as water quality and environmental pollution, is essential to avoid occurrence of nonacceptable levels of contaminants in milk.

Providing sensitive analytical methods as control tools has allowed to obtain reliable results as well as the search for degradation products and metabolites. The use of multiresidues methodologies is an important example of these changes. The application of laboratory analysis based on surveillance programs aimed to monitoring simultaneously residues of veterinary drugs, pesticides, and toxins has significantly altered the information available from monitoring programs allowing a risk assessment more accurate and significant increase in food safety.

REFERENCES

Andjelkovic, M., Tsilia, V., Rajkovic, A., De Cremer, K., Van Loco, J., 2016. Application of LC−MS/MS MRM to determine staphylococcal enterotoxins (SEB and SEA) in milk. Toxins 8 (4), 118.

Andreotti, R., Nicodemo, M.L.F., 2004. Uso de Antimicrobianos na Producão de Bovinos e Desenvolvimento de Resistência Campo Grande. Embrapa, Brazil.

dos Anjos, M.R., Castro, I.M.D., Souza, M.D.L.M.D., de Lima, V.V., de Aquino-Neto, F. R., 2016. Multiresidue method for simultaneous analysis of aflatoxin M1, avermectins, organophosphate pesticides and milbemycin in milk by ultra-performance liquid chromatography coupled to tandem mass spectrometry. Food Addit. Contam.: A 33 (6), 995−1002.

Arsand, J.B., Jank, L., Martins, M.T., Hoff, R.B., Barreto, F., Pizzolato, T.M., et al., 2016. Determination of aminoglycoside residues in milk and muscle based on a simple and fast extraction procedure followed by liquid chromatography coupled to tandem mass spectrometry and time of flight mass spectrometry. Talanta 154, 38−45.

Authority, A.N.Z.F., 2001. Pyrrolizidine alkaloids in food. A Toxicological Review and Risk Assessment. *ANZFA Australia, Canberra.*

Baert, K., 2003. Pharmacokinetics and Pharmacodynamics of Non-Steroidal Anti-Inflammatory Drugs in Birds. Universiteit Gent, Gent.

Bajwa, U., Sandhu, K.S., 2014. Effect of handling and processing on pesticide residues in food—a review. J. Food Sci. Technol. 51 (2), 201−220.

Bandeira, D.D., Munaretto, J.S., Rizzetti, T.M., Ferronato, G., Prestes, O.D., Martins, M. L., et al., 2014. Determinação de resíduos de agrotóxicos em leite bovino empregando método QuEChERS modificado e GC−MS/MS. Química Nova 37, 900−907.

Becker-Algeri, T.A., Castagnaro, D., de Bortoli, K., de Souza, C., Drunkler, D.A., Badiale-Furlong, E., 2016. Mycotoxins in bovine milk and dairy products: a review. J. Food Sci. 81 (3), R544−R552.

Bohm, D., Stachel, C., Gowik, P., 2009. Multi-method for the determination of antibiotics of different substance groups in milk and validation in accordance with Commission Decision 2002/657/EC. J. Chromatogr. A 1216 (46), 8217−8223.

Bryden, W.L., 2012. Mycotoxin contamination of the feed supply chain: implications for animal productivity and feed security. Anim. Feed Sci. Technol. 173 (1−2), 134−158.

Bueno, M., Ulaszewska, M., Gomez, M., Hernando, M., Fernandez-Alba, A., 2012. Simultaneous measurement in mass and mass/mass mode for accurate qualitative and quantitative screening analysis of pharmaceuticals in river water. J. Chromatogr. A 1256, 80−88.

Cháfer-Pericás, C., Maquieira, A., Puchades, R., Miralles, J., Moreno, A., 2010. Fast screening immunoassay of sulfonamides in commercial fish samples. Anal. Bioanal. Chem. 396 (2), 911−921.

Coelho, K.O., Mesquita, A.J., Machado, P.F., Lage, M.E., Meyer, P.M., Reis, A.P., 2014. The effect of somatic cell count on yield and physico-chemical composition of Mozzarella cheese. Arq. Bras. Med. Vet. Zootec. 66 (4), 1260−1268.

Commission, E., 2010. Commission regulation no. 37/2010. Off. J. Eur. Union, L 15/ 1−L 15/72.

COMMISSION REGULATION (EU), 2010. *No 37/2010.* Chapter Brussels.

Diaz, R., Ibanez, M., Sancho, J., Hernandez, F., 2013. Qualitative validation of a liquid chromatography-quadrupole-time of flight mass spectrometry screening method for organic pollutants in waters. J. Chromatogr. A 1276, 47−57.

Dowling, G., Gallo, P., Fabbrocino, S., Serpe, L., Regan, L., 2008. Determination of ibuprofen, ketoprofen, diclofenac and phenylbutazone in bovine milk by gas chromatography-tandem mass spectrometry. Food Addit. Contam. A Chem. Anal. Control Exposure Risk Assess 25 (12), 1497−1508.

Dubreil-Chéneau, E., Pirotais, Y., Bessiral, M., Roudaut, B., Verdon, E., 2011. Development and validation of a confirmatory method for the determination of 12 non steroidal anti-inflammatory drugs in milk using liquid chromatography-tandem mass spectrometry. J. Chromatogr. A 1218 (37), 6292−6301.

FAO, 2008. Dairy Production and Products: Milk and Milk Products.

Fagnani, R., Beloti, V., Battaglini, A.P.P., Dunga, K. d S., Tamanini, R., 2011. Organophosphorus and carbamates residues in milk and feedstuff supplied to dairy cattle. Pesquisa Veterinária Brasileira 31, 598−602.

Fernandes, A.M., Oliveira, C.A.F., Lima, C.G., 2007. Effects of somatic cell counts in milk on physical and chemical characteristics of yoghurt. Int. Dairy J. 17 (2), 111−115.

Flores-Flores, M.E., Lizarraga, E., López de Cerain, A., González-Peñas, E., 2015. Presence of mycotoxins in animal milk: a review. Food Control 53, 163−176.

Gallo, A., Giuberti, G., Frisvad, J.C., Bertuzzi, T., Nielsen, K.F., 2015. Review on mycotoxin issues in ruminants: occurrence in forages, effects of mycotoxin ingestion on health status and animal performance and practical strategies to counteract their negative effects. Toxins 7 (8), 3057−3111.

Gallo, P., Fabbrocino, S., Vinci, F., Fiori, M., Danese, V., Serpe, L., 2008. Confirmatory identification of sixteen non-steroidal anti-inflammatory drug residues in raw milk by liquid chromatography coupled with ion trap mass spectrometry. Rapid Commun. Mass Spectrom. 22 (6), 841−854.

Gaugain-Juhel, M., Delepine, B., Gautier, S., Fourmond, M., Gaudin, V., Hurtaud-Pessel, D., et al., 2009. Validation of a liquid chromatography-tandem mass spectrometry screening method to monitor 58 antibiotics in milk: a qualitative approach. Food Addit. Contam. A—Chem. Anal. Control Exposure Risk Assess. 26 (11), 1459−1471.

Gentili, A., Caretti, F., Bellante, S., Mainero Rocca, L., Curini, R., Venditti, A., 2012. Development and validation of two multiresidue liquid chromatography tandem mass spectrometry methods based on a versatile extraction procedure for isolating non-steroidal anti-inflammatory drugs from bovine milk and muscle tissue. Anal. Bioanal. Chem. 404 (5), 1375−1388.

Gerosa, S., Skoet, J., 2012. Milk availability. *Trends in production and demand and medium-term outlook.*

Gomez Perez, M.L., Romero-Gonzalez, R., Martinez Vidal, J.L., Garrido Frenich, A., 2013. Analysis of veterinary drug residues in cheese by ultra-high-performance LC coupled to triple quadrupole MS/MS. J. Sep. Sci. 36 (7), 1223−1230.

Gutierrez, R., Ruiz, J.L., Ortiz, R., Vega, S., Schettino, B., Yamazaki, A., et al., 2012. Organochlorine pesticide residues in bovine milk from organic farms in Chiapas, Mexico. Bull Environ. Contam. Toxicol. 89 (4), 882−887.

Hernandez, F., Ibanez, M., Gracia-Lor, E., Sancho, J., 2011. Retrospective LC−QTOF−MS analysis searching for pharmaceutical metabolites in urban wastewater. J. Sep. Sci. 34 (24), 3517−3526.

Hoogenboom, L.A., Mulder, P.P., Zeilmaker, M.J., van den Top, H.J., Remmelink, G.J., Brandon, E.F., et al., 2011. Carry-over of pyrrolizidine alkaloids from feed to milk in dairy cows. Food Addit. Contam. A Chem. Anal. Control Exposure Risk Assess. 28 (3), 359−372.

Hymery, N., Vasseur, V., Coton, M., Mounier, J., Jany, J.-L., Barbier, G., et al., 2014. Filamentous fungi and mycotoxins in cheese: a review. Compr. Rev. Food Sci. Food Saf. 13 (4), 437−456.

Imperiale, F., Sallovitz, J., Lifschitz, A., Lanusse, C., 2002. Determination of ivermectin and moxidecin residues in bovine milk and examination of the effects of these residues on acid fermentation of milk. Food Addit. Contam. 19 (9), 810−818.

Imperiale, F.A., Farias, C., Pis, A., Sallovitz, J.M., Lifschitz, A., Lanusse, C., 2009. Thermal stability of antiparasitic macrocyclic lactones milk residues during industrial processing. Food Addit. Contam. A Chem. Anal. Control Exposure Risk Assess. 26 (1), 57–62.

Jank, L., Martins, M.T., Arsand, J.B., Campos Motta, T.M., Hoff, R.B., Barreto, F., et al., 2015a. High-throughput method for macrolides and lincosamides antibiotics residues analysis in milk and muscle using a simple liquid–liquid extraction technique and liquid chromatography–electrospray–tandem mass spectrometry analysis (LC–MS/MS). Talanta 144, 686–695.

Jank, L., Martins, M.T., Arsand, J.B., Hoff, R.B., Barreto, F., Pizzolato, T.M., 2015b. High-throughput method for the determination of residues of β-lactam antibiotics in bovine milk by LC–MS/MS. Food Addit. Contam. A Chem. Anal. Control Exposure Risk Assess. 32 (12), 1992–2001.

Jedziniak, P., Szprengier-Juszkiewicz, T., Pietruk, K., Sledzinska, E., Zmudzki, J., 2012. Determination of non-steroidal anti-inflammatory drugs and their metabolites in milk by liquid chromatography-tandem mass spectrometry. Anal. Bioanal. Chem. 403 (10), 2955–2963.

Jedziniak, P., Olejnik, M., Szprengier-Juszkiewicz, T., Smulski, S., Kaczmarowski, M., Żmudzki, J., 2013. Identification of flunixin glucuronide and depletion of flunixin and its marker residue in bovine milk. J. Vet. Pharmacol. Ther. 36 (6), 571–575.

Kantiani, L., Farre, M., Sibum, M., Postigo, C., de Alda, M., Barcelo, D., 2009. Fully automated analysis of beta-lactams in bovine milk by online solid phase extraction-liquid chromatography–electrospray–tandem mass spectrometry. Anal. Chem. 81 (11), 4285–4295.

Langer, A.J., Ayers, T., Grass, J., Lynch, M., Angulo, F.J., Mahon, B.E., 2012. Nonpasteurized dairy products, disease outbreaks, and state laws—United States, 1993–2006. Emerg. Infectious Dis. 18 (3), 385–391.

Langoni, H., 2013. Milk quality: an utopia without a rigorous monitoring program for bovine mastitis control. Pesquisa Veterinária Brasileira 33 (5), 620–626.

Lichtenberger, L.M., Wang, Z.M., Romero, J.J., Ulloa, C., Perez, J.C., Giraud, M.N., et al., 1995. Non-steroidal anti-inflammatory drugs (NSAIDs) associate with zwitterionic phospholipids: insight into the mechanism and reversal of NSAID-induced gastrointestinal injury. Nat. Med. 1 (2), 154–158.

Ma, Y., Ryan, C., Barbano, D.M., Galton, D.M., Rudan, M.A., Boor, K.J., 2000. Effects of somatic cell count on quality and shelf-life of pasteurized fluid milk. J. Dairy Sci. 83 (2), 264–274.

Malone, E.M., Dowling, G., Elliott, C.T., Kennedy, D.G., Regan, L., 2009. Development of a rapid, multi-class method for the confirmatory analysis of anti-inflammatory drugs in bovine milk using liquid chromatography tandem mass spectrometry. J. Chromatogr. A 1216 (46), 8132–8140.

Martins, M.T., Melo, J., Barreto, F., Hoff, R.B., Jank, L., Bittencourt, M.S., et al., 2014. A simple, fast and cheap non-SPE screening method for antibacterial residue analysis in milk and liver using liquid chromatography-tandem mass spectrometry. Talanta 129, 374–383.

Meshref, A.M.S., Moselhy, W.A., Hassan, N.E.-H.Y., 2014. Heavy metals and trace elements levels in milk and milk products. J. Food Meas. Charact. 8 (4), 381–388.

Nag, S.K., 2010. 5-Pesticides, veterinary residues and other contaminants in milk A2—Griffiths. In: Mansel, W. (Ed.), Improving the Safety and Quality of Milk,. Woodhead Publishing, pp. 113–145.

Nag, S.K., Raikwar, M.K., 2008. Organochlorine pesticide residues in bovine milk. Bull. Environ. Contam. Toxicol. 80 (1), 5–9.

Oliveira-Filho, J.C., Carmo, P.M.S., Pierezan, F., Tochetto, C., Lucena, R.B., Rissi, D.R., et al., 2010. Intoxicação por organofosforado em bovinos no Rio Grande do Sul. Pesquisa Veterinária Brasileira 30, 803–806.

van Pamel, E., Daeseleire, E., 2015. A multiresidue liquid chromatographic/tandem mass spectrometric method for the detection and quantitation of 15 nonsteroidal anti-inflammatory drugs (NSAIDs) in bovine meat and milk. Anal. Bioanal. Chem. 407 (15), 4485–4494.

Peng, T., Zhu, A.-L., Zhou, Y.-N., Hu, T., Yue, Z.-F., Chen, D.-D., et al., 2013. Development of a simple method for simultaneous determination of nine subclasses of non-steroidal anti-inflammatory drugs in milk and dairy products by ultra-performance liquid chromatography with tandem mass spectrometry. J. Chromatogr. B 933, 15–23.

Peterson, K., McDonagh, M., Thakurta, S., Dana, T., Roberts, C., Chou, R., et al., 2010. Drug class reviews. Drug Class Review: Nonsteroidal Antiinflammatory Drugs (NSAIDs): Final Update 4 Report. Oregon Health & Science University Oregon Health & Science University, Portland (OR).

Pikkemaat, M.G., Rapallini, M.L., Dijk, S.O., Elferink, J.W., 2009. Comparison of three microbial screening methods for antibiotics using routine monitoring samples. Anal. Chim. Acta 637 (1-2), 298–304.

Pitarch, E., Portoles, T., Marin, J., Ibanez, M., Albarran, F., Hernandez, F., 2010. Analytical strategy based on the use of liquid chromatography and gas chromatography with triple-quadrupole and time-of-flight MS analyzers for investigating organic contaminants in wastewater. Anal. Bioanal. Chem. 397 (7), 2763–2776.

Queenan, K., Häsler, B., Rushton, J., 2016. A one health approach to antimicrobial resistance surveillance: is there a business case for it? Int. J. Antimicrob. Agents 48 (4), 422–427.

Riediker, S., Diserens, J., Stadler, R., 2001. Analysis of beta-lactam antibiotics in incurred raw milk by rapid test methods and liquid chromatography coupled with electrospray ionization tandem mass spectrometry. J. Agric. Food. Chem. 49 (9), 4171–4176.

Rübensam, G., Barreto, F., Hoff, R.B., Kist, T.L., Pizzolato, T.M., 2011. A liquid–liquid extraction procedure followed by a low temperature purification step for the analysis of macrocyclic lactones in milk by liquid chromatography–tandem mass spectrometry and fluorescence detection. Anal. Chim. Acta 705 (1–2), 24–29.

Rübensam, G., Barreto, F., Hoff, R.B., Pizzolato, T.M., 2013. Determination of avermectin and milbemycin residues in bovine muscle by liquid chromatography-tandem mass spectrometry and fluorescence detection using solvent extraction and low temperature cleanup. Food Control 29 (1), 55–60.

Ruegg, P.L., 2011. Managing mastitis and producing quality milk. In: Retamal, C.A.R.A. P.M. (Ed.), Dairy Production Medicine. Blackwell Publishing Ltd, Oxford, UK.

Santos, M.V.D., Fonseca, L.F.L.D., 2007. Estratégias para o controle da mastite e melhoria da qualidade do leite. Editore Manole, São Paulo.

Sassahara, M., Pontes Netto, D., Yanaka, E.K., 2005. Aflatoxin occurrence in foodstuff supplied to dairy cattle and aflatoxin M1 in raw milk in the North of Parana state. Food Chem. Toxicol. 43 (6), 981–984.

Stolker, A., Rutgers, P., Oosterink, E., Lasaroms, J., Peters, R., van Rhijn, J., et al., 2008a. Comprehensive screening and quantification of veterinary drugs in milk using UPLC–ToF–MS. Anal. Bioanal. Chem. 391 (6), 2309–2322.

Stolker, A.A.M., Rutgers, P., Oosterink, E., Lasaroms, J.J.P., Peters, R.J.B., Van Rhijn, J. A., et al., 2008b. Comprehensive screening and quantification of veterinary drugs in milk using UPLC–ToF–MS. Anal. Bioanal. Chem. 391 (6), 2309–2322.

Stubbings, G., Bigwood, T., 2009. The development and validation of a multiclass liquid chromatography tandem mass spectrometry (LC–MS/MS) procedure for the determination of veterinary drug residues in animal tissue using a QuEChERS (QUick, Easy, CHeap, Effective, Rugged and Safe) approach. Anal. Chim. Acta 637 (1-2), 68–78.

Tsiplakou, E., Anagnostopoulos, C., Liapis, K., Haroutounian, S.A., Zervas, G., 2014. Determination of mycotoxins in feedstuffs and ruminant s milk using an easy and simple LC—MS/MS multiresidue method. Talanta 130, 8—19.

Turnipseed, S., Andersen, W., Karbiwnyk, C., Madson, M., Miller, K., 2008. Multi-class, multi-residue liquid chromatography/tandem mass spectrometry screening and confirmation methods for drug residues in milk. Rapid Commun. Mass Spectrom. 22 (10), 1467—1480.

Turnipseed, S., Storey, J., Clark, S., Miller, K., 2011. Analysis of veterinary drugs and metabolites in milk using quadrupole time-of-flight liquid chromatography—mass spectrometry. J. Agric. Food. Chem. 59 (14), 7569—7581.

Vacillotto, G., Favretto, D., Seraglia, R., Pagiotti, R., Traldi, P., Mattoli, L., 2013. A rapid and highly specific method to evaluate the presence of pyrrolizidine alkaloids in Borago officinalis seed oil. J. Mass. Spectrom. 48 (10), 1078—1082.

Valese, A.C., Molognoni, L., de Sá Ploêncio, L.A., de Lima, F.G., Gonzaga, L.V., Górniak, S.L., et al., 2016. A fast and simple LC—ESI—MS/MS method for detecting pyrrolizidine alkaloids in honey with full validation and measurement uncertainty. Food Control 67, 183—191.

Wang, H., Zhou, X.-J., Liu, Y.-Q., Yang, H.-M., Guo, Q.-L., 2011. Simultaneous determination of chloramphenicol and aflatoxin M1 residues in milk by triple quadrupole liquid chromatography — tandem mass spectrometry. J. Agric. Food. Chem. 59 (8), 3532—3538.

Wang, J., Leung, D., Lenz, S., 2006. Determination of five macrolide antibiotic residues in raw milk using liquid chromatography-electrospray ionization tandem mass spectrometry. J. Agric. Food. Chem. 54 (8), 2873—2880.

Wei, H., Tao, Y., Chen, D., Xie, S., Pan, Y., Liu, Z., et al., 2015. Development and validation of a multi-residue screening method for veterinary drugs, their metabolites and pesticides in meat using liquid chromatography-tandem mass spectrometry. Food Addit. Contam.: A 32 (5), 686—701.

Zhang, K., Wong, J.W., Hayward, D.G., Vaclavikova, M., Liao, C.-D., Trucksess, M.W., 2013. Determination of mycotoxins in milk-based products and infant formula using stable isotope dilution assay and liquid chromatography tandem mass spectrometry. J. Agric. Food. Chem. 61 (26), 6265—6273.

Zuberovic Muratovic, A., Hagström, T., Rosén, J., Granelli, K., Hellenäs, K.-E., 2015. Quantitative analysis of staphylococcal enterotoxins A and B in food matrices using ultra high-performance liquid chromatography tandem mass spectrometry (UPLC—MS/MS). Toxins 7 (9), 3637—3656.

FURTHER READING

Bueno, M.J.M., Aguera, A., Hernando, M.D., Gomez, M.J., Fernandez-Alba, A.R., 2009. Evaluation of various liquid chromatography-quadrupole-linear ion trap-mass spectrometry operation modes applied to the analysis of organic pollutants in wastewaters. J. Chromatogr. A 1216, 5995—6002.

Jank, L., Hoff, R., Tarouco, P., Barreto, F., Pizzolato, T., 2012. Beta-lactam antibiotics residues analysis in bovine milk by LC—ESI—MS/MS: a simple and fast liquid-liquid extraction method. Food Addit. Contam. A—Chem. Anal. Control Exposure Risk Assess. 29 (4), 497—507.

Le Loir, Y., Baron, F., Gautier, M., 2003. Staphylococcus aureus and food poisoning. Genet. Mol. Res. 2 (1), 63—76.

Morandi, S., Brasca, M., Lodi, R., Cremonesi, P., Castiglioni, B., 2007. Detection of classical enterotoxins and identification of enterotoxin genes in Staphylococcus aureus from milk and dairy products. Vet. Microbiol. 124 (1-2), 66—72.

CHAPTER 14

Cow's Milk Protein Allergy and Lactose Intolerance

Paulo H.F. da Silva[1], Vanísia C.D. Oliveira[1] and Luana M. Perin[2]
[1]ICB—Departamento de Nutrição, Universidade Federal de Juiz de Fora, Juiz de Fora, Brazil
[2]Departamento de Veterinária, Universidade Federal de Viçosa, Viçosa, Brazil

14.1 COW'S MILK PROTEIN ALLERGY: CONCEPT, PHYSIOPATHOLOGY, SYMPTOMS, EPIDEMIOLOGY, DIAGNOSIS, AND TREATMENT

Adverse food reaction is an abnormal reaction by the body to the ingestion, contact, or inhalation of foods or food additives. This reaction could be classified as toxic or nontoxic according to the susceptibility of the person. Toxic reactions are independent of previous state of health and occur when the patient ingests sufficient amounts of food to trigger undesirable reactions (Brasil, Associação Brasileira de Alergia e Imunopatologia, 2008). Nontoxic reactions are those that depend on the susceptibility of the person and can be classified as immune-mediated or nonimmune mediated. Immune-mediated reactions are food allergies. Nonimmune-mediated reactions are food intolerances and occur without the involvement of the immune system (Brasil, Associação Brasileira de Alergia e Imunopatologia, 2008).

Genetic predisposition; immature intestinal mucosa, inherent in children in the first 2 years of life; early introduction of cow's milk in infant feeding and premature weaning of breast milk; and the intestinal permeability barrier are the most important factors that contribute to the development of cow's milk protein allergy (CMPA) in childhood. The maturity of the intestinal mucosa is reached with age and is demonstrated by the ability to process the ingested antigens. Such ability is known as oral tolerance (OT) (Brasil, Associação Brasileira de Alergia e Imunopatologia, 2012; Brasil, Sociedade Brasileira de Pediatria, 2012).

CMPA is an adverse reaction to food, which depends on immune intervention. These reactions could be classified as: Type I hypersensitivity or IgE-mediated hypersensitivity; Type II hypersensitivity or cytotoxic

Raw Milk
DOI: https://doi.org/10.1016/B978-0-12-810530-6.00014-6

295

hypersensitivity; Type III hypersensitivity or immune complex mediated; and Type IV hypersensitivity or cell-mediated hypersensitivity. However, the most prevalent are Type I (IgE-mediated) and Type III (immune complex mediated) (Falcão and Mansilha, 2017).

The allergic reactions caused by Type I hypersensitivity are easy to diagnose due to the rapid onset of symptoms (from seconds—minutes to 8 hours after milk ingestion) and by the identification of specific IgE antibody formation (Ferreira et al., 2014). Allergic reactions caused by Type III hypersensitivity are caused by T cells (lymphocytes), immunoglobulin G, and immunoglobulin M and are characterized by delayed manifestations, which may occur days or weeks after milk ingestion (Ferreira et al., 2014; Antunes and Pacheco, 2009). Mixed allergic reactions are IgE-mediated and non-IgE-mediated (i.e., IgE-mediated with involvement of immune cells—T lymphocytes, eosinophils, proinflammatory cytokines, and complex cellular mechanisms—demonstrated by the presence of CD8 lymphocytes in the epithelium) (Ferreira et al., 2014).

The most allergenic milk proteins are casein, α-lactalbumin, β-lactoglobulin, globulin, and bovine serum albumin, which can cause both IgE-mediated and non-IgE-mediated allergic reactions. The patient and/or their family should pay attention to the presence of these proteins in foods and medical drugs (Lifschitz and Szajewska, 2015). Eight foods account for 90% of allergic food reactions: milk, egg, peanut, seafood, fish, nuts, soy, and wheat. However, CMPA is the most frequent (American Academy of Pediatrics, 2000; Delgado et al., 2010).

CMPA symptoms are variable and nonspecific and may include oral and perioral swelling (more evident in cutaneous manifestations—atopic dermatitis, urticaria, angioedema), gastrointestinal symptoms (eosinophilic esophagitis, reflux, vomiting, dyspepsia, rectal bleeding with or without malabsorption, food refusal, severe colic, constipation, and eosinophilic gastritis), and respiratory tract symptoms (persistent asthma, allergic rhinitis, wheezing, or chronic cough); and the patient may also experience chest pain, arrhythmia (cardiovascular system), drowsiness, seizure, or mental confusion (nervous system) and in more severe cases, anaphylactic shock (Koletzko et al., 2012).

A recent study conducted in the United States showed that 3.9% of people up to 18 years of age had CMPA, and it observed an increase of 18% in cases from 1997 to 2007. In Europe, it is estimated that the prevalence of CMPA is 2%—3% in the first year of life and 1% from the age of 6. The risk of allergy increases by 40% when a first-degree relative (parents or siblings) is allergic (Branum and Lukacs, 2009; Koletzko et al., 2012).

In Brazil, the incidence and prevalence of CMPA are 2.2% and 5.4%, respectively. The incidence of CMPA ranges from 2% to 3% in the first year of life. Of these, 56% of the children up to 1 year, 87% at 3 years, and 97% at 15 years present improvement of the symptomatology. Children up to 5 years old who are diagnosed as allergic to milk protein show a positive evolution in 80%–90% of cases (Delgado et al., 2010). However, even in children who developed tolerance, there is a tendency for the development of asthma, rhinitis, or dermatitis, in a process called "atopic gait" (Vandenplas et al., 2017).

The most specific and sensitive tests for the diagnosis of food allergy are skin tests, blood tests Radioallergosorbent (RAST) and (ELISA), upper and lower gastrointestinal endoscopy, intestinal biopsy, exclusion diet (elimination diet), and oral food challenge (Morais et al., 2010). Skin tests such as prick or patch test are immediate hypersensitivity tests that detect specific IgE. The formation of papule with 3 mm of diameter or more after 15 minutes of the contact with the standardized extract confirm the test. This test is widely used because it is fast, safe, and simple (can be done in the doctor's office or medical outpatient) and has low cost. However, it is necessary well-trained professionals to perform the test. The negative predictive value is 95% (Cruz et al., 2006).

The oral food challenge test can be open, single-blind, and double-blind. Open-food challenge is the one in which the doctor, the family, and the patient know which food is being offered. It is simpler and can be conducted inside the doctor's office; however, it has a greater potential for errors and must be confirmed with other tests. Single-blind food challenge test is done when only the doctor knows which food is being given. It may or may not be placebo controlled, but when it is used, it is important that the smell, texture, consistency, and taste are not similar to milk (Mendonça et al., 2011).

The double-blind, placebo-controlled food challenge test is the gold standard test for the diagnosis of CMPA and the only one with reliable results when compared to the others. This test does not have a standard protocol and varies according to the hospital where it is performed. The patient makes the total elimination diet (including medications that may influence the test result). Usually, the milk is put in contact in the perioral region with the aid of gauze. After 30 minutes, 10 mL of whole milk or infantile formula is administered orally, with a progressive increase in volume, folding the dose every 20–30 minutes for 2.5 hours. The test is discontinued and considered positive when one or more allergic reactions to milk protein are present (Mendonça et al., 2011).

Although the double-blind food challenge test is the gold standard test, it is rarely done—it is time-consuming, laborious, and expensive and is not covered by public and private health-care system. Thus, CMPA diagnosis is most often based on clinical history, physical examination, RAST, ELISA, skin tests, and improvement of symptoms when exclusion diet is used. However, the correct diagnosis of CMPA is worth it due to the importance of dairy products in human health, its sociocultural impact, and its nutritional benefits for children (Mendonça et al., 2011).

The treatment of food allergy is essentially nutritional and is based on the exclusion diet or, in the case of infants, on the use of hypoallergenic or "HA" formulas or diets (Lifschitz and Szajewska, 2015). Milk is rich in proteins of high nutritional value; lipids; lactose; vitamins especially those of B complex, such as riboflavin and cobalamin; minerals such as calcium and phosphorus; and in whole milk, vitamins A and D (Matanna, 2011). The diagnosis of CMPA and lactose intolerance (LI) should be performed with caution and responsibility, as the treatment is based on the exclusion of milk from diet. Elimination of milk without adequate replacement and supplementation may impair normal growth and nutritional quality of the diet (Lifschitz and Szajewska, 2015).

The main goals of nutritional treatment are to prevent the onset of symptoms, disease progression, and worsening of allergic manifestations and to provide the adequate growth and development of the child. In this way, it is important to enlist a multidisciplinary team to elaborate the diet aiming at the planning and choose the essential foods to the nutritional needs of the child. All efforts must be made to carry out the necessary food replacements in order to guarantee the adequate nutritional supply according to the current nutritional recommendations of the technical regulation on recommended dietary intakes of proteins, vitamins, and minerals.

Breastfeeding is the most appropriate for infants allergic to milk protein. It promotes adequate growth and nutrition, protection against diseases and infections, as well as strengthening the bond between mother and child. The number of breastfed children is still small and the early introduction of other types of milk is common. Exclusive breastfeeding is indicated up to 6 months of life, with the introduction of complementary feeding after this age (according to the World Health Organization;

Gasparin et al., 2010). In these conditions, if the allergy is identified, the mother is submitted to the exclusion diet of milk and dairy products with adequate nutritional guidance for her and for the child and maintenance of breastfeeding (Gasparin et al., 2010).

However, this must be analyzed with caution, since there are no studies confirming the success of the exclusion diet during pregnancy and lactation in the prevention of allergy for the baby. Maternal weight gain may be compromised (Cruz et al., 2016). However, if the exclusion of milk is carried out, it should be nutritionally calculated with caution and calcium and multivitamin complex supplementation should be indicated.

When breastfeeding is not possible and CMPA is diagnosed, the choice of which formula will be used should be based on the child's age and on the presence of other associated food allergies (Lifschitz and Szajewska, 2015).

The formulas indicated for children under 1 year suffering with CMPA are soy protein formulas (over 6 months old), with purified and supplemented proteins, formulas and diets based on extensively hydrolyzed protein (protein hydrolysates), and diets based on free amino acids (the only one considered completely nonallergenic) (Lifschitz and Szajewska, 2015).

The use of soy protein-based formulas in infant feeding is controversial. It is not safe to introduce soy in patients with an inflamed intestinal mucosa barrier who have been injured for at least 1 month because the allergen promotes an inflammatory reaction in the mucosa, considering the allergic potential of soybeans (Agostoni et al., 2006). Due to inflammation, there is an increase in the permeability of the mucosa with increase of macromolecules penetration, the inflammatory process perpetuates and, in most cases, the person become allergic also to soy protein (Agostoni et al., 2006).

Soy-based preparations, such as extracts, in liquid or powder formula, are not indicated for infants up to 6 months old since it does not correspond to nutritional recommendations for its age group and does not contain isolated and purified proteins. Also, goat, sheep, and other mammal's milk should not be indicated due its antigenic similarity (Agostoni et al., 2006).

Soy protein-based formulas are indicated for infants after 6 months of age that suffer CMPA IgE-mediated; LI; galactosemia; and by family option (vegetarian or vegan). Soy drinks or extracts can be used for children with allergies or intolerance, from the age of 2 years old. As soybean has low L-methionine, L-carnitine, and taurine concentrations, essential compounds for infants, soya drinks should be supplemented with these nutrients (Agostoni et al., 2006).

Due to the presence of phytates that interfere with the absorption and decrease the bioavailability of iron and zinc, the soy formulas should be supplemented with these minerals, and also with calcium and phosphorus, aiming at adequate bone mineralization. Besides the phytates, soy contains high amounts of aluminum and phytoestrogen (belonging to the isoflavones, genistein, and daidzein class) (Agostoni et al., 2006).

Studies show the relationship between high phytoestrogen content and effect on sexual and reproductive development. However, further studies on the adverse effects of long-term soybean use are needed. Soy formulas are contraindicated for preterm infants, as there is evidence of low weight gain and decrease of total serum and total protein levels (Agostoni et al., 2006).

Formulas named as HA, which are partially hydrolyzed, are indicated for the allergies prevention and are contraindicated for the treatment of milk allergy (American Academy of Pediatrics, 2000). The aim in developing HA products is to prevent the primary sensitization of infants and, at the same time, to stimulate the OT to milk antigens. Other possible advantages of the partially hydrolyzed formulas over the extensively hydrolyzed ones are their better organoleptic properties as well as their lower cost. However, further studies are needed to prove the effectiveness of using this type of allergy prevention formula (American Academy of Pediatrics, 2000).

The consumption of goat milk is unsafe for CMPA patients, since 92% of them may present reactions to goat's milk. This is because cow and goat's milk protein may have the same amino acid sequence containing the epitope domain or may have similar structures (the same three-dimensional conformation) that allow the binding of specific antibodies. Although this, the exclusion of goat's milk from diet is only indispensable when undesirable reaction is proven in more than one diagnostic test or in the occurrence of clinical symptoms. The consumption of goat's milk should not be a substitute for cow's milk in patients with CMPA (Agostoni et al., 2006).

Exposure to small amounts of formula containing cow's milk during the first days of birth may increase the chance of milk allergy. Both the hydrolyzed formula and breast milk protect against allergy, compared to the uninterrupted used of milk-based formula.

14.2 LACTOSE INTOLERANCE: CONCEPT, PHYSIOPATHOLOGY, SYMPTOMS, EPIDEMIOLOGY, DIAGNOSIS, AND TREATMENT

LI is a disease of the intestinal mucosa (small intestine) characterized by the inability to digest and absorb lactose due to the low activity (hypolactasia) or low production of the β-D-galactosidase enzyme, popularly known as lactase (Canani et al., 2016).

Under optimal conditions, lactase hydrolyzes lactose releasing the galactose and glucose monosaccharides for bloodstream absorption. These monosaccharides pass through the portal system and are transported to the liver where the galactose will be converted to glucose. This enzyme is present on the apical surface of enterocytes with higher production in the jejunum (Liberal et al., 2012).

In the intestinal lumen, the lactose that has not been digested increases the local osmolarity, attracting water and electrolytes, causing diarrhea. Intestinal dilation caused by osmotic pressure accelerates intestinal transit increasing malabsorption (Mazo, D.F. de C., 2010).

If lactose is not metabolized, it will not be absorbed in the small intestine and reaches the colon, where it is fermented by bacterial microbiota releasing CO_2 and H_2 gases and short chain fatty acids producing acetate, butyrate, and propionate. This way, the feces become more acidy and liquid, causing abdominal distension and perianal hyperemia, common symptoms in LI (Mazo, D.F. de C., 2010). The symptoms of LI manifest from 30 minutes to 2 hours after the ingestion of dairy products and are characterized by flatulence, abdominal discomfort, diarrhea, nausea, borborygmic, vomiting, and constipation (Lomer et al., 2008).

After weaning from breastmilk, the person could be capable of digesting lactose, known as "persistent lactase" or "normolactasia" or could not be capable of digesting lactose, known as "nonpersistent lactase" or "hypolactasia," which correspond to 75% of the world's population. Nonpersistent lactase can be classified as primary or acquired lactase deficiency, secondary or transient lactase deficiency, and congenital or genetic lactase deficiency (Canani et al., 2016; Mazo, D.F. de C., 2010).

The primary or acquired lactase deficiency occurs from the age of 3 years. Over the years, the decrease in the production of lactase in humans is genetically programed and irreversible, but it occurs very slowly and gradually (Bacelar Júnior et al., 2013). The secondary or transient lactase deficiency has its origin in any disease or drug that causes damage to the small intestine mucosa or that accelerates the intestine transit, and/or diminishes the absorption surface, as in intestinal resections (Lomer et al., 2008). Secondary deficiency may occur, for example, in infectious enteritis, giardiasis, celiac disease, inflammatory bowel disease (especially Crohn's disease), drug-induced or radiation-induced enteritis, and in diverticular disease of the colon. Lactase is an intestinal brush-border-associated enzyme, so if there is any morphological change in this region, it may lead to decrease the capacity to hydrolyze lactose (Liberal et al., 2012). The LI prognosis is very good and after the treatment, the symptoms disappear and the patient can eat food containing lactose (Liberal et al., 2012).

The congenital or genetic lactase deficiency is extremely rare and is an autosomal recessive inheritance (by modification of lactase gene). This deficiency was found only in 42 patients from 35 Finnish families in a study between 1966 and 2007, with an incidence of 1:60,000 (Mazo, D.F. de C., 2010; Burgain et al., 2012).

Prevalence of LI varies according to the people ethnicity. Australians and Americans have the lowest prevalence. Prevalence of LI is 5% in Northeast Europe, 4% in Denmark, 5% in Great Britain, 1%–7% in Sweden, 25% in Finnish, 15% in French, more than 50% in South America and Africa, and almost 100 in some Asian countries (Mazo, D.F. de C., 2010). In Brazil, the incidence is 44.11%, and the most affected is the age group from 0 to 10 years old (23.71% of the cases), a decrease in the incidence occur after age 40, with a lower percentage after the age of 60 years (6.71%—73 cases) (Pereira Filho and Furlan, 2004; Canini et al., 2016).

The causes of this ethnic difference are still unknown (Lomer et al., 2008; Canini et al., 2016). However, in Asian and African countries, the inappropriate climate for dairy cows and the high mortality of cattle before 1900 reduced the availability of milk for population and may culminate in a difficulty in digesting milk. The theory that slaves were normally deprived of milk, support the fact that intolerance is more common in black than in white people. The ability to digest and metabolize lactose is a recent evolutionary trait that coincided with the domestication of cattle (Mazo, D.F. de C., 2010).

The diagnosis of LI is based on the clinical exam and complete anamnesis, seeking the gestational history, family history, food history, and research of triggering factors, such as early introduction of complementary feeding (Liberal et al., 2012). The jejunal biopsy is the gold standard diagnosis. However, it is very invasive and expensive.

The OT test can be indicated, since it has 93% of specificity and 78% of sensitivity. During the test, the glycemic rates must be monitored to not influence the results. The fasting blood glucose is titrated, and the glycemic curve is calculated after ingestion of 50 g of lactose (1 L of milk). The patient should be checked at times 15, 30, 60, and 90 minutes after ingestion (Mazo, D.F. de C., 2010).

In the urine test, ethanol and lactose are ingested together. It prevents the hepatic conversion of galactose into glucose, facilitating its excretion through the urine (Mazo, D.F. de C., 2010; Canini et al., 2016). The hydrogen excretion test is observed through respiration after lactose ingestion. H_2 is formed by bacterial fermentation of undigested lactose; the gas is absorbed and eliminated by the lungs (Mazo, D.F. de C., 2010).

The genetic test is based on DNA extraction for the detection of genetic polymorphism. Genetic tests allow the analysis of the C/T-13910 and G/A-22018 polymorphism of the lactase-phlorizin hydrolase gene. There is a relation between the genetic mutation and the lactose malabsorption. This test has 100% of sensitivity and 96% of specificity and confirms the results obtained by hydrogen excretion test. It dispenses fasting, does not cause collateral effects, and the collection of blood is simple (Mazo, D.F. de C., 2010).

The raffinose and stachyose fibers, contained in beans, broccoli, potatoes, cauliflower, onions, and dietary products used as sweeteners (sucralose, mannitol, and sorbitol), are not digested by the intestine and cause similar symptoms to those of LI. An accurate and well-conducted diagnosis would avoid an unnecessary milk-exclusion diet.

LI treatment is based on the partial exclusion of dairy products from diet (for infant and adult), breastfeeding, or the use of "lactose-free" infant formulas (for infant) (Liberal et al., 2012). Each patient reacts to dairy consumption in different ways. Small portions of lactose should be offered and gradually increased in the diet. Apparently, increased or continuous exposure to increasing amounts of lactose may lead to OT. However, most patients prefer to eliminate lactose from the diet to avoid clinical manifestations (Mazo, D.F. de C., 2010).

For children and adults, some dairy foods are better tolerated than others. Milk chocolate, for example, is much more tolerated than white chocolate. Also, hard cheeses (cheddar, Swiss, Parmesan) are better tolerated due the insignificant amount of lactose and high solids content. Ripened cheeses contain a minimum amount of lactose due the removal of whey during manufacturing and the conversion of lactose into lactic acid and other acids. Lactose-free milk has an 80%−90% reduction in lactose. Cheeses (Brie, Camembert, Cheddar, Kingdom, Emmental, Gorgonzola, Parmesan, Prato, Provolone, Roquefort and Swiss), except the fresh ones, are also good options; they contain small amounts of lactose (Antunes and Pacheco, 2009).

Yogurts are also tolerated: lactose is digested by *Lactobacillus* sp. or by lactase, produced by the starter cultures after consumption. The semisolid texture of the yogurt delays gastric emptying and intestinal transit and consequently the release of lactose in the intestine. Recent studies indicate that yoghurts produced with *Lactobacillus acidophilus* and *Lactobacillus bulgaricus* strains stimulate the lactase production (Canini et al., 2016).

Variability of responses after food ingestion can be caused by osmolality, fat content of the food, gastric emptying time, sensitivity to abdominal distension due the osmotic load of unhydrolyzed lactose, intestinal transit, and the colon response to the carbohydrate load (Mazo, D.F. de C., 2010).

Usually is necessary the ingestion of 12 g of lactose (240 mL of milk) to appearing the symptoms. However, some patients are able to ingest small portions of lactose and do not show symptoms (Canini et al., 2016).

Some recommendations are important to ensure the absence of symptoms, such as ingestion of dairy products with other foods, their fractionation throughout the day, and the consumption of fermented and ripened product.

In both syndromes, it is necessary to encourage families and patients to read and interpret correctly the food and drug labels. Due its technological potential, lactose and milk protein are added to foods to modify texture, color, and water retention capacity. In drugs, lactose acts as a vehicle or excipient. Therefore, there is a wide variety of nondairy products containing milk nutrients (Antunes and Pacheco, 2009).

14.3 EXCLUSION DIET CONSEQUENCES

In order to reduce the nutritional impacts of the exclusion diet, supplementation with some nutrients is necessary, especially calcium, zinc, phosphorus, and vitamins A and D. The supplementation recommendation should consider the dietary history, biochemical tests, and symptoms caused by nutrient deficiency (Mazo, D.F. de C., 2010).

This way, CMPA and LI diets construction is a complex process and goes beyond the elimination of carbohydrate or protein from the diet. It is important to highlight that child with CMPA or LI with no satisfactory clinical and nutritional evolution even using adequate diet should be investigated, especially in cases that the diet is strictly followed, and there is no remission of symptoms. A review of dietary calculus and confirmation of the CMPA and LI diagnosis should be carried out for these patients (Morais et al., 2010).

In most cases of secondary lactase deficiency, the enzyme takes 1−8 months to restore its activity in the intestine. However, there is no reason to exclude dairy foods from the diet. This exclusion can impair the ingestion of many essential nutrients for the proper functioning of the organism (Santos et al., 2014). It is believed that some intolerant women reestablish the ability to digest lactose during gestation. This phenomenon could be an adaptation, because during gestation, the diet is increased in several nutrients, especially calcium (Ruzynyk and Still, 2001).

Lactose has an important role for the infant during the breastfeeding, also reflecting in its adult phase. Lactose ensures important source of energy for the infant and due to its intestinal acidification allow the absorption of calcium. In addition, there is a relation between strengthening of the immune system and low intestinal pH (Medeiros et al., 2004).

Medeiros et al. (2004) compared the nutritional status of children with CMPA and without CMPA and observed that energy, lipid, protein, carbohydrate, calcium, and phosphorus consumption was lower in children with restrictive diets. In addition, the group with a diet free of cow's milk and dairy products had a deficit for all indices: height/age, weight/height, but statistically significant difference was found only for the weight/age index. In another study evaluating children with CMPA was observed low weight/age, low weight/height, and low height/age. Villares et al. (2006) evaluated the growth of children with CMPA and other allergies and children with CMPA only. A significant difference for weight between groups was observed. The results showed that children with CMPA only, who received adequate replacement diets, presented at 2 years, a weight-stature development similar to that of a healthy population.

It is important to highlight that calcium, phosphorus, and vitamin D have a direct relation with bone health. Its deficiencies can cause fracture and lower weight gain (Imataka et al., 2004). Rickets disease is related to the concentration of vitamin D, calcium, and phosphorus, which may be reduced by dietary deficiency, genetic alterations, or by abnormal metabolism of these minerals. It is a bone mineralization disorder and occurs due to abnormalities in bone formation at the epiphyseal growth plate. Rickets that occur between infants and children can be attributed to low dietary calcium intake when exposed to cereal-based diets and poor access to dairy products. In these situations, the use of dietary supplements can guarantee the cure of bone disease (Imataka et al., 2004).

Many experts still confuse CMPA and LI pathologies or are unaware of correct diagnose method and treatment. This problem may delay the diagnosis and consequently the illness treatment or, in some cases, exclusion diet could be unnecessarily indicated. In addition, inadequate treatments for CMPA have been widely indicated, such as substitution of cow milk by goat or soy milk. Many studies have alarmed medical societies about this fact (Cruz et al., 2006).

In a recent study conducted by the Brazilian Society of Pediatrics (BSP), a questionnaire was developed and knowledge of pediatricians about diagnosis, symptomatology, and treatment of CMPA was evaluated. The study showed the need for a consensus on the diagnosis method and treatment of food allergy, avoiding disastrous dietary attempts to children. The BSP also realized that the lack of an ideal diagnostic method makes clinical history an important tool. However, ignorance of the symptoms, as well as their evolution, has favored the incorrect diagnosis of food allergy and, consequently, the imposition of exclusion diets inappropriately. The study also showed the improvement of food allergy to cow's milk due the ingestion of goat's milk (Sole et al., 2007).

In another study, Cortez et al. (2007) concluded that pediatricians and nutritionists demonstrated errors regarding the main therapeutic recommendations in cow's milk allergy. Evaluating the dietary intervention, it was observed that products such as goat's milk, lactose-free formula, partially hydrolyzed milk formula, soy-based drink, and other mammal's milk were considered adequate by some professionals. In addition, it was observed that the professionals did not indicate the hydrolyzate-based formulas and amino acid formulas as the safest therapeutic options. Regarding the knowledge about the daily calcium recommendation, both professionals did not know the recommended quantity in all the age groups questioned (Cortez et al., 2007).

Therefore, it is important to encourage the adoption of a standard recommendation of nutrients by professionals in order to assist in the evaluation of diet and in the prescription of supplements, mainly calcium. LI has often been confused with cow's milk proteins allergy.

REFERENCES

Agostoni, C., et al., 2006. Soy protein infant formulae and follow-on formulae: a commentary by the ESPGHAN Committee on Nutrition. J. Pediatr. Gastroenterol. Nutr. 42 (4), 352–361.

American Academy of Pediatrics, 2000. Committee on Nutrition. Hypoallergenic infant formulas. J. Am. Acad. Pediatr. 106 (2), 346–349.

Antunes, A.E.C., Pacheco, M.T.B., 2009. Leite para adultos: mitos e fatos frente à ciência, 1. ed. Varela, São Paulo.

Branum, A.M., Lukacs, S.L., 2009. Food allergy among children in the United States. J. Am. Acad. Pediatr. 124 (6), 1549–1555.

Brasil, Associação Brasileira de Alergia e Imunopatologia, 2008. Consenso brasileiro sobre alergia alimentar: 2007. Rev. Bras. Alerg. Imunol. 31 (2), 64–89 (Brasília).

Brasil, Associação Brasileira de Alergia e Imunopatologia, 2012. Guia prático de diagnóstico e tratamento da Alergia às Proteínas do Leite de Vaca mediada pela imunoglobulina E. Rev. Bras. Alerg. Imunol. 35 (6), 203–233. Brasília).

Brasil, Sociedade Brasileira de Pediatria, 2012. Manual de orientação para a alimentação do lactente, do pré-escolar, do escolar, do adolescente e na escola, 3. ed. The publisher is Associação Brasileira de Alergia e Imunopatologia, Rio de Janeiro, p. 148, p.

Burgain, J., et al., 2012. Maldigestion du lactose: formes cliniques et solutions thérapeutiques. Cahiers de nutrition et de diététique. Cahiers de nutrition et de diététique 47, 201–209 (Paris).

Canani, R.B., et al., 2016. Diagnosing and treating intolerance to carbohydrates in children. Nutrients v. 8 (n. 157), 1–16. Itália.

Cortez, A.P.B., et al., 2007. Conhecimento de pediatras e nutricionistas sobre o tratamento da alergia ao leite de vaca no lactente. Rev. Paul. Pediatr. 25 (2), 106–113 (São Paulo).

Cruz, A.G., Oliveira, C.A., Sá, P., Corassim, C.H., 2016. Química, Bioquímica, Análise Sensorial e Nutrição no Processamento de Leite e Derivados, first ed Elsevier, Rio de Janeiro.

Delgado, A.F., Cardoso, A.L., Zamberlan, P., 2010. Nutrologia básica e avançada, 1. ed. Manole, São Paulo.

Falcão, I., Mansilha, H.F., 2017. Cow's Milk Protein Allergy and Lactose Intolerance. Acta Pediátr. Portuguesa v. 48 (n. 1), 53–60. Portugal.

Ferreira, S., et al., 2014. Alergia às proteínas do leite de vaca com manifestações gastrointestinais. Nascer e crescer v. 23 (n. 2), 72–79. Revista de pediatria do centro hospitalar do Porto, Portugal.

Gasparin, F.S.R., et al., 2010. Alergia à proteína do leite de vaca versus intolerância à lactose: as diferenças e semelhanças. Rev. Saude Pesqui. 3 (1), 107–114 (Maringá).

Imataka, G., Mikami, T., Yamanouchi, H., Kano, K., Eguchi, M., 2004. Vitamin D deficiency rickets due to soybean milk. J. Paediatr. Child Health 40 (3), 154–155.

Koletzko, S., et al., 2012. Diagnostic approach and management of cow's milk protein allergy in infants and children: ESPGHAN GI Committee practical guidelines. J. Pediatr. Gastroenterol. Nutr. 55, 221—229.

Liberal, E.F., et al., 2012. Gastroenterologia Pediátrica, 1. ed. Guanabara Koogan, Rio de Janeiro.

Lifschitz, C.E., Szajewska, H., 2015. Cow's milk allergy: evidence-based diagnosis and management for the practitioner. Eur. J. Pediatr. v. 147, 141—150.

Lomer, M.C.E., et al., 2008. Review article: lactose intolerance in clinical practice—myths and realities. Aliment. Pharmacol. Ther. 27 (2), 93—103.

Matanna, P. Desenvolvimento de requeijão cremoso com baixo teor de lactose produzido por acidificação direta e coagulação enzimática. Dissertação (Mestrado em Ciência e Tecnologia dos Alimentos) — Universidade Federal de Santa Maria, Santa Maria, RS, 2011.

Mazo, D.F. de C. Intolerância à lactose: mudanças de paradigmas com o biologia molecular. 2010. Rev. Assoc. Med. Bras. 2010. 56 (2), 230—236 (São Paulo).

Medeiros, L.C. Nutrient intake and nutritional status of children following a diet free from cow's milk and cow's milk by-products. 2004. J. Pediatr. 2004. 80 (5), 363—370 (Rio de Janeiro).

Mendonça, R.B., et al., 2011. Teste de provocação oral aberto na confirmação de alergia ao leite de vaca mediada por IgE: qual seu valor na prática clínica? Rev. Paul. Pediatr. 29 (3), 415—422.

Morais, M.B., et al., 2010. Alergia à proteína do leite de vaca. Rev. Pediatr. Mod. 46 (5), 165—182.

Pereira Filho, D., Furlan, S.A., 2004. Prevalência de intolerância à lactose em função da faixa etária e do sexo: experiência do laboratório Dona Francisca, Joinville (SC). Revista Saúde e Ambiente 5 (1), 24—30 (Joinville).

Ruzynyk, A., Still, C., 2001. Lactose intolerance. J. Am. Osteopath. Assoc. 101, 10—12.

Santos, F.F.P., et al., 2014. Intolerância à lactose e as conseqüências no metabolismo do cálcio. Revista Interfaces: Saúde, Humanas e Tecnologia 2, 1—7 (especial) (Juazeiro do Norte).

Sole, D., et al., 2007. O conhecimento de pediatras sobre alergia alimentar: estudo piloto. Rev. Paul. Pediatr. 25 (4), 311—316 (São Paulo).

Vandenplas, Y., et al., 2017. Prevention and management of cow's milk allergy in non-exclusively breastfed infants. Nutrients 9 (731), 2—15.

Villares, J.M.M., et al., 2006. Cómo crecen los lactantes diagnosticados de alergia a proteínas de leche de vaca? J. An. Pediatr. 64 (3), 244—247.

FURTHER READING

Bacelar Júnior, A.J., et al., 2013. Intolerância à lactose-revisão de literatura. J. Surg. Clin. Res. 4 (4), 38—42 (Ipatinga).

Caffarelli, C., et al., 2010. Cow's milk protein allergy in children: a practical guide. Ital. J. Pediatr. 36 (5), 1—7.

Christie, L., Hine, J.R., Parker, J.G., Burks, W., 2002. Food allergies in children affect nutrient intake and growth. J. Am. Diet. Assoc. 102 (11), 1648—1651.

Correa, F.F., et al., 2010. Teste de desencadeamento aberto no diagnóstico de alergia à proteína do leite de vaca. J. Pediatr. 86 (2), 163—166. Rio de Janeiro.

Dias, J.C., 2012. As raízes leiteiras do Brasil, 1. ed. Barleus, São Paulo.

Host, A., 2002. Frequency of cow's milk allergy in childhood. Ann. Allergy Asthma Imunol. 89 (6), 33—37.

Johansson, S., et al., 2004. A revised nomenclature for allergy for global use: report of the nomenclature review Committee of the World Allergy Organization. J. Allergy Clin. Immunol. 56, 832–836.

Medeiros, L.C., Lederman, H.M., de Morais, M.B., 2012. Lactose malabsorption, calcium Intake, and bone mass in children and adolescents. J. Pediatr. Gastroenterol. Nutr. 54 (2), 204–209.

Pereira, P.B., Silva, C.P., 2008. Alergia a proteína do leite de vaca em crianças: repercussões da dieta de exclusão e da dieta substitutiva sobre o estado nutricional. Rev. Pediatr. 30 (2), 100–106 (São Paulo).

Rafael, M.N., et al., 2014. Alimentação no primeiro ano de vida e prevenção de doenças alérgicas: evidências atuais. Braz. J. Allergy Immunol. 2 (2), 50–55 (São Paulo).

Ramos, R.E.M., et al., 2013. Alergia alimentar: reações e métodos diagnóstico. J. Manage. Prim. Health Care 4 (2), 54–63.

Salvador, M., et al., 2013. Alergia a proteínas de leite de vaca em idade pediátrica—abordagem diagnóstica e terapêutica. Rev. Port. Dermatol. Venereol. 71 (1), 23–33 (Lisboa).

Savaiano, D., et al., 2013. Improving lactose digestion and symptoms of lactose intolerance with a novel galacto-oligosaccharide (RP-G28): a randomized, double-blind clinical trial. Nutr. J. 12 (1), 160–169. Estados Unidos.

Sole, D., et al., 2012. Guia prático de diagnóstico e tratamento da alergia às proteínas do leite de vaca mediada pela imunoglobulina E. Rev. Bras. Alerg. Imunopatol. 35 (6), 203–233.

Spolidoro, J.V., et al., 2005. Cow's milk protein allergy in children: a survey on features in Brazil. J. Parenter. Enteral Nutr. 29 (1), p. s.27.

Vieira, M.C., et al., 2010. A survey on clinical presentation and nutritional status of infants with suspected cow' milk allergy. J. BMC Pediatr. 10, 25.

Wortmann, A.C., et al., 2013. Análise molecular da hipolactasia primária do tipo adulto: uma nova visão do diagnóstico de um problema antigo e frequente. Rev. AMRIGS 57 (4), 335–343 (Porto Alegre).

Yonamine, G.H., et al., 2011. Uso de fórmulas à base de soja na alergia à proteína do leite de vaca. Rev. Bras. Alerg. Imunopatol. 34 (5), 187–182.

Yu, J.M., Pekeles, G., Legault, L., Mccusker, C.T., 2006. Milk allergy and vitamin D deficiency rickets: a common disorder associated with an uncommon disease. Ann. Allergy Asthma Immunol. 96 (4), 615–619.

CHAPTER 15

Consumers Acceptance of Raw Milk and its Products

Lisbeth Meunier-Goddik and Joy Waite-Cusic
Department of Food Science and Technology, Oregon State University, Corvallis, OR, United States

15.1 INTRODUCTION

Dairy products are an important part of the diet in many regions of the world. Dairy products often serve as the foundation for the first foods introduced to infants as they provide a good balance of bioavailable nutrients as well as a variety of essential vitamins and minerals. Dairy product consumption, in the form of fluid milk, cheeses, yogurts, and other products, continues during childhood and throughout adulthood. Approximately 78.5% of the adult US population consumes fluid milk at least weekly (Centers for Disease Control and Prevention, 2007). Due to these high consumption rates, it is essential to public health efforts that dairy products be produced and distributed to the consumer in a manner that retains the nutritional integrity of the product while minimizing the risk of foodborne illness.

The primary objective of this book chapter is to communicate the complexity of consumer acceptance and attitudes of raw milk and its products. The primary context of this chapter will be presented from the perspective of the United States; however, cultural and geographical differences will be discussed.

15.2 HISTORY OF DAIRY PRODUCTION IN THE UNITED STATES

To understand consumer attitudes related to raw-milk consumption, it is necessary to evaluate the historical context and evolution of milk production and consumption in the United States. This context provides perspective of the opinions of regulators, scientists, producers, and consumers at various points in US history.

Prior to mass urbanization in United States in the 1800s, most families obtained their dairy products from their personal livestock or from that of their neighbors or local farms. Purchases or bartering occurred to supply the needs of the local area with minimal oversight. As US cities grew, the dairy industry began to form into a system of mass production and distribution. However, a poor understanding of sanitation and handling practices coupled with the lack of refrigeration on farm and in distribution channels led to outbreaks of serious milk-borne diseases (e.g., tuberculosis, typhoid fever, diphtheria) (Potter et al., 1984). The US dairy industry approached reducing these illnesses using two strategies: the certified milk movement and the pasteurized-milk movement (Potter et al., 1984).

15.2.1 The Certified Milk Movement

In the late 1800s, physicians worked with veterinarians and dairymen to create sanitation standards for dairies that provided milk to medical facilities, particularly those treating infants and children. These extensive animal husbandry and dairying practices became the foundation of the *Methods and Standards for the Production and Distribution of "Certified Milk"* (American Association of Medical Milk Commissions, 1912). Dairies operating under these requirements, including inspection and documentation, produced milk that were classified as "certified" by the American Association for Medical Milk Commissions (Currier, 1981). The implementation of certified milk production standards had a positive impact on infant survival (Potter et al., 1984).

15.2.2 The Pasteurized-Milk Movement

In the early 1900s, thermal pasteurization was introduced into the US dairy industry. Thermal pasteurization of milk was quickly expanded in the industry which led to decreases in milk-borne illnesses, including substantial reductions in the number of cases of tuberculosis and Q fever. Pasteurization became the dairy industry's primary safeguard against foodborne illness, and sanitation practices from the certified milk approach became the foundation for hygienic standards in the dairy industry. The first version of the Standard Milk Ordinance (the predecessor to the Grade A Pasteurized-Milk Ordinance) was proposed in 1924 and finalized by the Food and Drug Administration (FDA) in 1927, thus providing individual states with standards for industry practices to achieve the targeted microbial reduction in fluid-milk products (Knutson et al., 2010). Widespread implementation of pasteurization of fluid milk began in the United States in the 1930s.

15.2.3 Divergent Opinions—The Beginnings of the Advocating of Raw Milk

In the 1920s and 1930s, a debate was occurring between two subsets of scientific professionals: the biochemists and physiologists that were primarily concerned with human nutrition and the bacteriologists and public health workers that were more concerned with controlling the spread of infectious diseases. The physiologists and biochemists were concerned that pasteurization could cause thermal destruction of critical nutrients in milk and downplayed the contribution of milk to foodborne illnesses. At the same time, the bacteriologists and public health workers were proponents of mandatory thermal treatments citing that there was no convincing evidence that pasteurization damaged the nutritive value of milk (Wilson, 1938).

Dairy producers and processors joined in the debate by marketing the value of their respective raw or pasteurized milk in newspaper advertisements. These advertisements ranged in size from single line classified statements to full page displays to communicate the relative benefits and/ or to discredit the value of the alternative product. Below are selected statements from such advertisements published in the 1930s in Oregon:

Pasteurized-milk advertisements:

Dr. McCallum, the man who discovered vitamins in milk, says in his book on nutrition that all city milk supplies should be pasteurized. Mayo Brothers, world famous physicians and surgeons in Rochester, MN, pasteurize all milk from their two herds of pure bred cows.

"Mothers, would it not be best to take the advice of such authorities as quoted above and see that your loved ones use only pasteurized milk? Milk to be pasteurized by Sunny Brook Dairy is produced exclusively on two of the finest dairies in this locality, having fine, healthy Jersey and Guernsey cattle. Sunny Brook Pasteurized Milk costs no more than ordinary raw milk."—advertisement for Sunny Brook Dairy in The Corvallis Gazette-Times, September 6, 1934

Raw-milk advertisements:

"Pasteurization does not remove contamination, but it only an abortive attempt to destroy bacteria. There is no argument, and it is granted that Pasteurization will make milk reasonably safe for human consumption, that might otherwise be unfit."—advertisement for Superior Quality Raw Milk Group in The Corvallis Gazette-Times, February 16, 1934

The pasteurization of milk takes none of the filth out of it but it does destroy some of the bacteria. The excessive amount of liquidized filth which it contains is cooked or heated and you're having it served to you cooked instead of raw.

We have read volume after volume, numerous pamphlets published by high-powered individuals and advertising concerns and distributed by firms or individuals who sell pasteurized milk. And we have yet to read one article or hear one lecture, or even a quotation from purported eminent professors or doctors who sponsor the cause of pasteurization, which tells the actual facts about milk relative to sanitary production and proper handling which alone means good, pure milk.

"When properly pasteurized the usually called harmful bacteria are killed. But the dead carcasses remain in such number that they will and do cause milk when pasteurized to decay or rot before souring. Putrification will begin much sooner than in raw milk. You have often noticed a bad smell in pasteurized milk after it has become a little old. It is then starting to decay. Who wants to use milk full of dead carcasses of bacteria so prevalent and so inevitable in practically all pasteurized milk, when it is possible to get a good or even fairly good raw milk."—advertisement for Clover Leaf Dairy in The Corvallis Gazette-Times, April 27, 1934

Protect your growing children's teeth by giving them plenty of wholesome, tasteful raw milk, in which the normal chemical relationship is not disturbed. Calcium and Phosphorus are important in the prevention of tooth decay, be sure they are not affected by pasteurization.

"My dairy is open to the public at any and all times, and it is suggested that you pay this dairy a visit Sunday, April 29, and observe for yourself the conditions under which this milk is produced, then visit the other dairies and permit your own personal judgment to dictate to your conscience where best to secure your milk supply."—advertisement for Mt. View Dairy in The Corvallis Gazette-Times, April 28, 1934

Research studies on the influence of pasteurization on nutrient degradation occurred throughout the 1930s and 1940s. Studies demonstrated measurable changes in a number of nutrients (lactalbumin coagulation, rennin coagulation time, casein clot texture, soluble calcium and phosphate concentrations, iodine, vitamin B1, vitamin C) between raw and pasteurized milk; however, these changes were determined to be minimal or negligible with animal feeding studies demonstrating no significant differences between the two types of milk (Wilson, 1938). The growing body of scientific evidence supported pasteurization as an effective means to reduce milk-borne illnesses with little to no risk of having a negative impact on the nutritional needs of the population.

Despite these findings, criticism of pasteurization continued, including the publication of *"The Case Against Pasteurization of Milk: A Statistical Examination of the Claim that Pasteurization of Milk Saves Lives."* The main thesis of this book was that the consumption of raw milk contaminated with low levels of *Mycobacterium tuberculosis* served as a benefit to public health as a form of vaccination of children that would prevent more serious tuberculosis cases in adults (Kay, 1945).

15.2.4 Increasing Requirements for Pasteurization at the National Level

Michigan became the first state to require pasteurization of fluid milk in 1947 with most states implementing similar regulations by the 1950s (Katafiasz and Bartett, 2012); however, federal regulation of milk in inter-state commerce was not attempted until the 1970s. Interstate sale of raw milk was effectively prohibited in the United States by the FDA as of December 10, 1973 (Food and Drug Administration, 1973). In response to the new rules, The Association of Medical Milk Commissions, the Certified Milk Producers Association of America, and two of the three operating certified-milk dairies filed a formal objection of the pasteurization requirement. FDA issued a stay on enforcement of the pasteurization requirement for certified raw milk (Food and Drug Administration, 1974).

Throughout the 1970s, FDA worked with CDC to investigate milk-borne illnesses associated with raw milk and raw-milk products, including products coming from certified dairies. From 1971 to 1975, a number of invasive salmonellosis cases were associated with the consumption of certified raw milk from a single dairy in California. The *Salmonella* Dublin strain associated with the outbreak was the particularly invasive, leading to a high percentage of hospitalizations and several deaths. Many of the consumers had underlying health issues and had purchased raw milk as a "health food" (Currier, 1981). A second outbreak of *Salmonella* Dublin associated with certified raw milk from the same dairy occurred in 1977–78. Despite significant efforts on the part of the dairy and strict adherence to the requirements for certified-milk production, the dairy was unable to produce milk that was consistently free of *Salmonella* contamination (Currier, 1981). The California Department of Health Services calculated that an individual that consumes certified-milk from Alta-Dena dairy is 51 times more likely to become ill from *Salmonella* Dublin than an individual consuming pasteurized milk.

Despite these outbreaks and the very small number (2 in 1985) of certified dairies operating in the United States, FDA's stay on the pasteurization requirement for certified raw milk remained in effect until 1987. The change in regulation was prompted by a petition written by nonprofit public health groups, Public Citizen Health Research Group ("Public Citizen"), and the American Public Health Association, requesting FDA to ban all domestic sales of raw milk and raw-milk products. Further legal action compels FDA to hold an informal public hearing to collect information on "whether the consumption of raw milk, including certified raw milk, and raw-milk products is of public health concern" (Food and Drug Administration, 1984). The October 1984 hearing results in a 330-page transcript with >300 comments for a total docket size of 4000 pages. The primary arguments against mandatory pasteurization included (1) unequal regulation compared to other "dangerous" foods, (2) the absence of a case-control study, (3) a lack of information on nutritional benefits and sensory studies, and (4) labeling as an appropriate alternative.

In January 1985, FDA drafted a proposed rule requiring pasteurization of all milk and milk products moving in interstate commerce; however, the Secretary of Health and Human Services (Margaret Heckler) did not believe that a federal ban would an appropriate mechanism to significantly mitigate the risks associated with certified raw milk. In response, Public Citizen filed an additional lawsuit seeking a judicial review of FDA's action. Upon review of the administrative record, the court found FDA was regulating in a manner that was arbitrary and capricious by effectively stating that all raw milk posed a known health risk but refused to ban all types of raw milk. The court forced FDA to ban the interstate sales of raw milk and raw-milk products, both certified and noncertified and mandates that rulemaking be completed in haste. The FDA issued the proposed rule in June 1987 (Food and Drug Administration, 1987a). Few comments were received that opposed the proposal. The first was from a certified-milk producer arguing that individuals should have the right to freely choose whether the benefits of certified raw milk outweigh the potential risks. A second argument was submitted by US Representative Dannemeyer (R-California) which stressed the nutritional and immunological benefits of raw milk. In August 1987, FDA published the final rule requiring that all milk and milk products in final package for human consumption in interstate commerce be pasteurized (Food and Drug Administration, 1987b). The pasteurization requirement for milk in interstate commerce remains in effect today; however, individual states maintain the power to regulate intrastate raw-milk sales as they choose.

15.2.5 Decreasing Pasteurization Requirements at the State Level

Relative to federal regulators, the states were progressive in their dairy lawmaking and began to require mandatory pasteurization of fluid-milk products in the 1940s. Strict pasteurization requirements existed in most states; however, there were loopholes in the regulations that allowed consumers to gain access to raw milk through less-regulated mechanisms. Regulations at the state level continue to evolve as public health officials attempt to close loopholes while consumers are demanding additional legal access to raw milk. Some states, such as Montana and Iowa, have no legal mechanism for consumers to purchase raw milk. Other states, like Washington and California, allow for full retail sales (in-store). The most common legal statuses for raw-milk access are via on-farm sales or as a member of a herd-share. Regardless of the legal strategy within the state, none of these regulatory approaches have eliminated milk-borne illnesses (Table 15.1) (Knutson et al., 2010).

Some public health officials believe that providing a mechanism for legal access offers a practical way to deal with an unsafe product. Legal pathways provide opportunity for oversight that may help reduce risk via labeling, inspection, and testing programs. Without a legal path, consumers are likely to seek out riskier sources for raw milk (Beecher, 2016). The counter-argument to this stance is that by providing a legal channel for retail sales will encourage higher rates of consumption due to access to a wider consumer base.

Washington state regulators were forced to confront this conundrum in 2006. An 18-case outbreak of *Escherichia coli* O157:H7 was linked to a dairy herd-share operation, and the state had to decide whether to penalize farms involved in raw-milk production or to provide them with a legal pathway that would allow for licensing and include inspection and testing programs. The state opted for the latter as the best option to support public health efforts by providing raw milk that is the safest it can be and promote confidence in the dairy industry as a whole. Consumer demand for raw milk in Washington state is high and is continuing to grow (Beecher, 2016).

As consumer demand and legal market access has increased, the number of raw-milk producers has also increased. In Pennsylvania, the number of farms permitted to sell raw milk jumped form 20 in 2003 to 57 in 2006 and to 71 in 2016 (Pennsylvania Department of Agriculture, 2016). Similarly, the number of licensed Grade A raw-milk dairies in Washington state has been steadily increasing from 6 in 2006, 18 in 2013, and to 39 in January 2016 (Beecher, 2016). Because of the premium price that raw milk can demand in the marketplace, smaller dairy farms can be profitable.

Table 15.1 Legal status of raw-milk sales, consumption rates, and number of outbreaks in selected states in the United States

State	Legal status of intrastate sale of raw milk[a]	Consumption of unpasteurized milk[b]	Number of outbreaks linked to raw milk (2007−12)[a]
Alaska	Illegal	NR[c]	1
Arizona	Retail legal	NR	1
California	Retail legal	3.0%; 3.2%[d]	3
Colorado	Cow shares permitted	2.4%	3
Connecticut	Retail legal	2.7%	1
Georgia	Illegal (pet food legal)	3.8%	1
Idaho	Retail legal	NR	1
Indiana	Illegal	NR	1
Iowa	Illegal	NR	1
Kansas	Farm sales legal	NR	2
Maryland	Illegal (pet food legal)	3.0%	0
Massachusetts	Farm sales legal	NR	1
Michigan	Illegal	NR	4
Minnesota	Farm sales legal	2.3%	6
Missouri	Farm sales legal	NR	2
Montana	Illegal	NR	0
Nebraska	Farm sales legal	NR	1
New Mexico	Retail sales legal	3.4%	0
New York	Farm sales legal	3.5%	6
North Dakota	Illegal	NR	2
Ohio	Illegal	NR	4
Oregon	Minimal sales legal	2.8%	0
Pennsylvania	Retail legal	NR	17
South Carolina	Retail legal	NR	5
Tennessee	Illegal (herd shares)	3.5%	1
Utah	Retail legal	NR	5
Vermont	Farm sales legal	7.4%[e]	4
Washington	Retail legal	NR	5
Wisconsin	Farm sales legal	NR	3

[a]Legal status and outbreak information reported by the Centers for Disease Control and Prevention (2015).
[b]Consumption data from FoodNet surveys conducted in 2006−07; reported as consumed within the previous 7 days (Centers for Disease Control and Prevention, 2007).
[c]Not reported.
[d]Consumption data from 1994 telephone survey in California as reported by Headrick et al. (1994); reported as consumed in the past year.
[e]Consumption data from 2013 telephone survey in Vermont as reported by Leamy et al. (2014); reported as consumed in the past month.

15.3 RAW-MILK CONSUMERS

15.3.1 How Many Raw-Milk Consumers Are in the United States?

While an overwhelming majority ($>78\%$) of the US population consumes dairy products, a small portion ($\sim3\%$) consumes raw milk (2006–07 FoodNet Survey). This represents a doubling in the rate of raw-milk consumption from a decade earlier (1.5%; 1996–97 FoodNet Survey) (Shiferaw et al., 2000). Estimates on the number of consumers is difficult to estimate and may vary widely in different regions in the country due to types of allowable retail access and proximity to farms; however, the percentage of raw-milk consumers does not seem to correspond to legal access. For example, California and Maryland have estimated consumption rates of 3% of their populations, despite California having full retail access and Maryland allowing raw-milk sales for pets only (Table 15.1). It should be noted that these rates are based on the most recent FoodNet survey; however, this data is almost 10 years old. Changing state regulations that increase access may be having a significant influence on consumption patterns. For example, Vermont relaxed the ban on raw milk in 2009 to allow for on-farm sales. A survey conducted in Vermont in 2013 found a consumption rate of 11.6% in the previous year and approximately 7.4% in the previous month (Leamy et al., 2014). Relying on the 2006–07 FoodNet Survey data, a very rough, but likely conservative, estimate (3%) of the number of weekly raw-milk consumers in the United States would be 7.4 million adults.

15.3.2 Who Are Raw Milk Consumers?

The most comprehensive sociodemographic evaluation of raw-milk consumption in the United States is a compilation of the 1996–97, 2002–03, and 2006–07 FoodNet surveys by Buzby et al. (Food and Drug Administration, 1987a). Ethnicity, income, education, and area of residence were significantly different between raw-milk consumers and those that do not consume raw milk. Overall, raw-milk consumers were more likely to be Hispanic, earn incomes <$25,000, and have a high school education or less. Raw-milk drinkers are more likely to live on a farm, in rural areas, or in a city, but more unlikely to live in a suburban area than those who do not drink raw milk (Katafiasz and Bartett, 2012; Leamy et al., 2014; Bigouette et al., 2018; Buzby et al., 2013). Age and gender distributions were similar among raw-milk consumers and nonconsumers; however, it is important to note that 26.7% of raw-milk consumers are under the age of 18 years old and are likely have very limited control of purchasing decisions in their household (Buzby et al., 2013). Similar demographics of raw-milk consumers were reported from a survey conducted in California in 1994 (Headrick et al., 1994); however, more recent surveys have indicated alternate demographics associated with raw-milk consumption. Most notable is a seeming shift towards a larger number of raw-milk consumers being white, more highly educated (college degree), and higher income earners ($>$\$50,000) in the Pacific Northwest, Vermont, and Michigan (Katafiasz and Bartett, 2012; Leamy et al., 2014; Bigouette et al., 2018).

Raw-milk consumers can be characterized by a number of traditional demographics; however, there is very limited and dated information available for analyses. This is particularly problematic when the consumption patterns are low and are likely to be influenced by the changing regulatory environment that is influencing access and price.

15.3.3 Farmers and Farm Employees as Consumers

Farmers and their employees represent a unique category of raw-milk consumers. While they are a minority of the population of consumers, these people are immersed in the workings of the dairy and are serve an important role in the marketing and distribution of their product. Between 35% and 60% of dairy farmers consume raw-milk from their farm (Jayarao et al., 2006; Jayarao and Henning, 2001; Rohrbach et al., 1992). Most dairy farmers (68.5% in Pennsylvania) were aware that raw milk can cause foodborne illness; however, most (58.1%) continued to consume raw milk. Dairy farmers that weren't aware of the disease risk were twofold more likely to consume raw milk than those that were aware of the risk (Jayarao et al., 2006). Many farmers may allow employees to take home raw milk (Jayarao et al., 2006), thus encouraging consumption of raw milk by improving access and lowering price. Farmers as influencers will be further discussed later in this chapter.

15.3.4 Where Do Raw Milk Consumers Buy Their Milk?

Due to the huge differences in access to raw milk and a lack of data collection, it is difficult to characterize the efficacy of various distribution channels. In California (a state with full retail access), most consumers (39%) purchase their raw milk from retail stores. On-farm sales are also a very important purchasing option, comprising 30% of sales. Raw-milk purchases are also made in homes and from dairies (Headrick et al., 1994). A survey in Michigan (herd-share only) found that raw-milk consumers acquire milk an average of four times per month (Katafiasz and Bartett, 2012). In states with limited availability, dedicated raw-milk consumers drive long distances to get their raw milk. Raw-milk consumers in Michigan drive an average of 24.2 mi out of their way to pick up raw milk (Katafiasz and Bartett, 2012).

15.3.5 How Often Do Consumers Drink Raw Milk and How Much Raw Milk Do They Drink?

Consumption patterns of raw milk are very difficult to estimate as there is very limited data available; however, there is no evidence to demonstrate that raw-milk consumption patterns would be different than pasteurized-milk consumption patterns in the broader population. The USDA estimates that the average daily fluid-milk consumption by adults in the United States at slightly over 3/4 of a cup, on average children (2−11 years old) consume twice as much fluid milk (Sebastian et al., 2010). Raw-milk drinkers in California reportedly drank <4 glasses per month (59%), 4−8 glasses per month (12%) or >8 glasses per month (27%) (Headrick et al., 1994). A large percentage (47%) of raw-milk consumers in Vermont purchased at least a gallon of milk in the previous month and 16% had purchased >5 gal in the previous month (Leamy et al., 2014). Coupled with consumption statistics, it would seem unlikely that these consumers are exclusively drinking raw milk. Surveys in Michigan and the Pacific Northwest have demonstrated differences in the exclusivity of raw-milk consumers. The majority of consumers in Michigan drank raw milk exclusively, which is likely driven by their participation in a herd-share arrangement (Katafiasz and Bartett, 2012). In the Pacific Northwest, 47% of current consumers exclusively drink raw milk, while 53% are nonexclusive; however, raw-milk drinkers in this region are likely to drink raw milk daily (47%) (Bigouette et al., 2018). It is unknown how much raw milk is consumed in the United States every year, and due to the varied distribution channels, it would be difficult to accurately estimate. In 1994, California had an annual estimated production volume of raw milk at 1.5 million gallons. Production has significantly increased in over 20 years (Headrick et al., 1994). A highly conservative estimate of raw-milk consumption in the United States would be 2.5 million servings per day.

15.3.6 How Much Are Raw-Milk Consumers Willing to Pay?

Raw-milk consumers are willing to pay a premium price for raw milk, likely due to perception that raw milk is a better product. Typically, consumers will base at least part of their purchasing decision related to the difference in price between a comparable product. This concept is referred to as "anchor pricing." Conventional pasteurized milk is viewed as the anchor for pricing organic milk, and organic milk would serve as an appropriate anchor for raw milk in the marketplace. In 2010, consumers were willing to pay between 78% and 103% more for pasteurized organic milk ($5.78–$7.62/gal) than pasteurized conventional milk ($2.89–$3.69). Raw milk demanded an additional 57% higher price ($7.59–$10.50) than pasteurized organic milk (Knutson et al., 2010). Raw-milk prices have continued to increase with reports of consumers being willing to pay up to $24/gal in Oregon, a state with very restricted production and sales limits (Gumpert, 2015).

15.4 CONSUMER ATTITUDES: WHY ARE CONSUMERS CHOOSING RAW MILK?

In the United States, consumers view milk with a near "sacred image of wholesomeness" (Currier, 1981). This coupled with the restricted legal access has created a passionate and loyal consumer base.

As early as the 1890s, raw-milk consumers and certified milk producers began to promote the perceived benefits of raw milk over pasteurized milk. The certified milk medical commissions outwardly denounced pasteurization and claimed that it caused nutrient deficiencies, destroyed natural flavors, and allowed for the production and sale of sterilized filthy milk (Potter et al., 1984). Interestingly, these claims of the superiority of raw milk over pasteurized milk remain the basis of raw milk preferences over 100 years later. For the purpose of this chapter, the perceived value to the consumer will be divided into the broad categories of taste, health/nutrition, social, and values. Raw-milk consumers are likely making their purchasing decision due to a combination of these factors and likely many others that will not be discussed in this chapter.

15.4.1 Taste

A segment of virtually any population will consume "risky" food products because the food tastes better (Knutson et al., 2010). While raw milk is the focus of this chapter, it is certainly not the only food that falls in to this category. Most raw products, including oysters and spinach, carry high risks of foodborne illness; however, people continue to purchase and consume these products.

In every survey conducted, taste is identified as a driving factor for consumer selection of raw milk. Almost all raw-milk consumers consider raw milk to taste better than pasteurized milk (Beecher, 2016). Taste was the driving factor for raw-milk consumption in California in 1994 (Headrick et al., 1994). 72% of raw-milk consumers in the Pacific Northwest and 83.9% of raw-milk consumers in Michigan cite taste as a primary reason for consuming raw milk (Katafiasz and Bartett, 2012; Bigouette et al., 2018) Consumers in Vermont indicated liking the flavor of raw milk as a primary reason for their consumption. Secondary uses of raw milk, such as homemade cheese or yogurt production, are also taste-related motivations for purchasing raw milk (Leamy et al., 2014). While taste is the primary motivator for most raw-milk consumers, raw milk advocates believe that the benefits of raw-milk consumption extend far beyond sensory attributes (Knutson et al., 2010).

15.4.2 Health and Nutrition

Health and nutritional benefits of raw milk are typically identified as the secondary reason driving raw-milk purchases (Katafiasz and Bartett, 2012; Leamy et al., 2014; Bigouette et al., 2018). An overwhelming majority (91.1%) of Michigan raw-milk consumers believe that raw milk is healthier than pasteurized milk (Katafiasz and Bartett, 2012). During the 1980s, perceived health benefits associated with raw-milk consumption were considered the principal drivers in consumer choice (Potter et al., 1984; Fierer, 1983). Raw milk has been proposed to provide health benefits through a variety of mechanisms; however, few have been adequately investigated and even fewer have been proven. Regardless, consumers continue to perceive that raw-milk consumption will provide health and nutritional benefits.

Higher nutritive value. Raw-milk consumers believe that pasteurization destroys nutrients; therefore, they perceive raw milk as being more nutritious (Katafiasz and Bartett, 2012). Studies have demonstrated that pasteurization causes insignificant decreases in thiamine, vitamin B12, and vitamin C. Changes in the bioavailability of other milk constituents due to pasteurization have not been demonstrated (Potter et al., 1984).

Holistic health. A majority (67%) of current raw-milk consumers in the Pacific Northwest consider perceived holistic health benefits contributing to their decisions to drink raw milk. Almost all exclusive raw-milk consumers (93% vs 45% of nonexclusive raw-milk drinkers) indicated holistic health benefits as a primary reason that they consume raw milk (Bigouette et al., 2018). 76.8% of raw-milk consumers in Michigan indicate holistic health benefits as a primary reason for raw-milk preference (Katafiasz and Bartett, 2012).

Disease treatment and prevention. Some consumers of raw milk belief that raw milk can cure disease and/or prevent diseases, including arthritis and cancer (Beecher, 2016). Fifty percent of raw-milk consumers in the Pacific Northwest report disease prevention as a reason for consuming raw milk with 35% reporting that raw-milk consumption improved intestinal disease (Bigouette et al., 2018). 60.7% of raw-milk consumers in Michigan indicate immune-related disease prevention as a primary reason for raw-milk preference (Katafiasz and Bartett, 2012). Raw-milk consumers in Michigan think that psoriasis (19.6%), intestinal diseases (64.3%), cold and flu (44.6%), tooth decay (35.7%), and orthopedic disease (32.1%) are helped or prevented by raw-milk consumption (Katafiasz and Bartett, 2012). Consumers in Michigan also volunteered raw milk as being beneficial for heart disease, neurological disease, acne, and cancer (Katafiasz and Bartett, 2012).

Allergy relief. Forty-one percent of raw-milk consumers in the Pacific Northwest believe that raw-milk consumption reduced their allergies (Bigouette et al., 2018). 69.6% of raw-milk consumers in Michigan think that allergies are helped or prevented by raw-milk consumption (Katafiasz and Bartett, 2012).

Some raw-milk consumers feel that they have allergic reactions to pasteurized milk but do not experience symptoms when they drink raw milk (Beecher, 2016).

Digestive issues. Many raw-milk consumers state that drinking pasteurized milk causes them to experience bloating and other digestive problems; however, they can consume raw milk without any adverse symptoms (Beecher, 2016). Almost 59% of raw-milk consumers in the Pacific Northwest believe that raw-milk consumption alleviated digestive problems (Bigouette et al., 2018). 83.9% of raw-milk consumers in Michigan think that digestive issues are helped or prevented by raw-milk consumption, including alleviating symptoms associated with lactose intolerance (Katafiasz and Bartett, 2012). Raw-milk consumers also tend to think that pasteurization destroys enzymes that are important for diges-tion (Katafiasz and Bartett, 2012).

Probiotic/Inoculation. Many raw-milk consumers consider it to be "alive" and believe that the natural microbiota in raw milk contributes to health. Raw-milk consumers believe that the lactic acid bacteria present in raw milk have probiotic properties and can contribute to intestinal health (Ferguson, 2010). Some consumers also believe that the low level pathogenic bacteria are beneficial by providing a mechanism for inocula-tion that leads to immunization (Schmidt and Davidson, 2008).

Safety. A large percentage of raw-milk consumers in the Pacific Northwest feel that processed or pasteurized milk is not safe. Significantly more exclusive raw-milk consumers (59%) citing increased safety as a rea-son for consuming raw milk as compared to 19% of nonexclusive consu-mers (Bigouette et al., 2018). Similarly, 57.1% of raw-milk consumers in Michigan do not feel that processed milk is as safe as raw milk (Katafiasz and Bartett, 2012).

Nearly all raw-milk consumers (96%) in the Pacific Northwest do not believe that raw milk increases the risk of foodborne illness (Bigouette et al., 2018). Similarly, only 10.7% of raw-milk consumers in Michigan believe that consumption of raw milk increases risk of getting foodborne illness, and many consumers believe that milk from pasture-raised cows is less likely to be contaminated with foodborne pathogens (Katafiasz and Bartett, 2012).

15.4.3 Social

Social factors significantly influence individual consumer choices, includ-ing constraining or facilitating food purchasing decisions (Sobal and Bisogni, 2009). Past and current relationships have a complicated influ-ence on individual food consumption decisions.

Previous exposure/family experience. Food choices for adults are influ-enced and often guided by those available during childhood. For those who grew up on a dairy farm or in a family that consumed raw milk, it is likely that raw milk would be seen as an acceptable food choice as these children mature into adults even as they potentially relocate into more urban settings (Knutson et al., 2010). A small percentage (2.3%) of raw-milk consumers in Vermont reported that they consumed raw milk because they drank it when they were growing up (Leamy et al., 2014).

Farmer relationship. Raw milk drinkers indicated that a primary reason for their purchase (17.2%) was because they knew the farmer (Leamy et al., 2014). In states with legal access limited to herd-shares, raw-milk consumers have almost always (98.2%) visited the dairy farm in which they acquire their milk and have at least a contractual relationship with the farmer (Katafiasz and Bartett, 2012). Visits to the farm instill confidence in the health and care of the dairy animals as well as the cleanliness standards of the farm (Katafiasz and Bartett, 2012)

Other influential relationships. Other influential social groups can have a significant influence on raw-milk consumption habits. Family, friends, and neighbors are known to influence purchasing behaviors. Grocery cooperatives and farmers' markets may also influence raw milk purchase decisions (Knutson et al., 2010).

15.4.4 Values

Consumers make at least some of their food decisions through a series of conscious value negotiations. These values are highly personalized and can include considerations presented in earlier categories, such as health, but are often associated with other more abstract systems (e.g., environmental or economic). In addition to those listed below, values may be assigned to organic farming, sustainability, slow food, etc.

Local, family farms. Pasteurization requirements forced dairy farms to contract with milk processing facilities which led to further commoditization of milk and depressed milk prices. This favored larger farms and retailer systems and negatively impacted the profitability of rural dairies as well as distanced the farmer–consumer relationship (Newsholme, 1935). Many raw-milk consumers prefer to use their food budget to support family farms as opposed to large-scale "factory farms" (Beecher, 2016). Sixty percent of Pacific Northwest raw-milk consumers indicate that supporting local farms is part of their reason for consuming raw milk (Bigouette et al., 2018). A small percentage (1%) of Vermont raw-milk consumers indicated supporting local farms as the reason for purchasing raw milk (Leamy et al., 2014). 85.7% of raw-milk consumers in Michigan indicate supporting local farms as a primary reason for raw-milk preference (Katafiasz and Bartett, 2012). Consumers also perceive that purchases made on farm or through farmers' markets are safer (Knutson et al., 2010).

The desire to support local, family farms may also stem from distrust of larger social constructs. A segment of the US population has a general mistrust of the food industry. This subset seeks wholesome, natural, fresh products with the preference to purchase products directly from the producer. A majority of the US population does not have confidence nor trust in the government's ability to regulate the food industry (Knutson et al., 2010). A majority (68%) of current raw-milk consumers in the Pacific Northwest do not trust state health officials' recommendations on the safety of foods (Bigouette et al., 2018). A smaller percentage (7.1%) of raw-milk consumers in Michigan distrusted public health officials' recommendations (Katafiasz and Bartett, 2012). Americans are also losing confidence in science and medical professionals (Knutson et al., 2010).

Animal husbandry and traditional farming. Many raw-milk dairies follow more traditional animal husbandry practices and comply with requirements for organic production, including pasturing. Raw-milk dairies also tend to have single breed herds of traditional dairy breeds, such as Jersey or Brown Swiss, and promote their superior milk (e.g., butterfat) (Knutson et al., 2010).

15.5 MESSAGING AND CONSUMER PERCEPTIONS

Given the multitude of reasons for raw-milk consumption decisions, it is clear that raw-milk purchase decisions are individualized and multifaceted. Understanding the consumer perception of messaging is important to identify strategies to improve communication to enhance informed consumer decisions and potentially affect changes in individual behaviors.

15.5.1 What is the Goal of the Messaging?

The intent of any messaging is skewed towards the objective of the group providing the message. In the case of raw milk, public health officials would like to eliminate or minimize raw-milk consumption, whereas raw milk advocates would like to promote consumption. Public health officials perceive that there are no substantiated benefits that would make the consumption of raw milk an acceptable risk. Raw milk advocates promote belief in numerous benefits and disbelief in disease risk. There exists a continuum between these extremes that includes the perceptions of the majority of the population, including dairy industry professionals, consumers, and medical professionals.

15.5.2 Is Current Food Safety Messaging Effective?

Food safety messaging discourages the consumption of raw milk and clearly seeks to further restrict or completely prohibit access (Table 15.2). Very little information is available on whether current consumer messaging related to the risks of raw milk is "working." Based on the low rates of consumption ($\sim$3%), it is likely that government and public health messaging is achieving the goal of keeping raw-milk consumption to a minimum. A recent survey in the Pacific Northwest found that consumers that had never consumed raw milk identified health risks as the most common reason (48.3%) for not consuming raw milk. Convenience (33.6%), cost (10.4%), and taste (9.5%) were also major reasons that consumers had never consumed raw milk (Bigouette et al., 2018).

In contrast, raw-milk consumption rates seem to be increasing, and raw milk advocates are actively working to improve and expand access to raw milk in various states. Recent surveys of raw-milk consumers in the Pacific Northwest and Vermont indicated the lack of access and/or inconvenience (34%—40%) as the primary reason for not recently purchasing raw milk. Health and safety concerns also contributed to the lack of raw-milk purchases (19%—21%) (Leamy et al., 2014; Bigouette et al., 2018). This would seem to indicate that risk communication is having the intended negative impact on consumption; however, the lack of access is a more effective deterrent than current messaging. Based on this information, it is likely that increased access will lead increased consumption which is likely to contribute to increased rates of foodborne illness. It would be very helpful to know what health and safety messaging influenced former consumers to discontinue drinking raw milk.

Nearly all raw-milk consumers (96%) in the Pacific Northwest do not believe that consumption of raw milk increases the risk of foodborne illness, with a majority (68%) of current consumers indicating that they do not trust state health officials' recommendations on the safety of foods (Bigouette et al., 2018). This is a troubling statistic and requires consideration of alternative delivery of food safety messages. Effective messaging would need to originate from sources that influence raw-milk producers and consumers. Extension and outreach programs may be effective strategies; however, personal interactions with dairy farmers, family, and friends are likely to be more influential (Leamy et al., 2014; Jayarao et al., 2006).

	Authors	Message
AAP	Physicians	"The AAP supports the position of FDA ... endorsing the consumption of only pasteurized milk and milk products for pregnant women, infants, and children. The AAP also endorses a ban on the sale of raw or unpasteurized milk and milk products throughout the United States, including the sale of certain raw milk cheeses ...." (American Academy of Pediatrics, 2014)
AAPHV	Veterinarians	"The Public Health Veterinarian Coalition Committee recommends that only pasteurized milk/products be consumed or sold." (American Association of Public Health Veterinarians, 2000)
AMA	Physicians	"The AMA reaffirms its policy that all milk sold for human consumption should be required to be pasteurized." (American Medical Association, 2015)
AFDO	Government officials (regulatory)	"AFDO supports mandatory pasteurization for all milk and milk products intended for direct human consumption except where alternative procedures to pasteurization are provided (i.e., curing of certain cheese varieties) to ensure the safety of finished products." (Association for Food and Drug Officials, 2005)
CDC	Public health government officials (nonregulatory)	"To protect the health of the public, state regulators should continue to support pasteurization and consider further restricting or prohibiting the sale and distribution of raw milk and other unpasteurized dairy products in their states." (Public Citizen vs. Heckler, 1987)
Cornell University Food Science Department	University staff, extension and research faculty	"We recommend pasteurization of milk intended for consumption by humans. Specifically, we strongly recommend that raw milk not be served to infants, toddlers, or pregnant women, or any person suffering from a chronic disease, or a suppressed immune system. In addition, we strongly recommend that raw milk not be provided to the general public at farms or at retail ...." (Cornell University Food Science Department, n.d.)

(Continued)

Table 15.2 (Continued)

Organization	Authors	Message
Dairy Processors of Canada	Dairy processors	"Dairy processors support government actions that maintain prohibitions on the sale of raw milk anywhere in Canada." (Dairy Processors Association of Canada, 2010)
FDA	Government officials (regulatory)	"Raw milk, no matter how carefully produced, may be unsafe." (Food and Drug Administration, 1987b) "The U.S. Food and Drug Administration strongly advises against the consumption of raw milk." (Food and Drug Administration, 2003)
Health Canada	Government officials (regulatory)	"Because of health concerns, Food and Drug Regulations require that all milk available for sale in Canada be pasteurized …." (Health Canada, 2005)
International Association for Food Protection	Research faculty	"…it is the position of IAFP that: consumption of unpasteurized milk will lead to increased risk of serious milkborne illness and even death, especially among at risk populations; and allowing the sale of unpasteurized milk for direct consumption, as a public health policy, would place many consumers at risk and should be prohibited." (Schmidt and Davidson, 2008)
International Dairy Food Association & National Milk Federation	Producer and processing consortia	"While consumer choice is an important value, it should not pre-empt public health and well-being. Legalizing the sale of raw milk and raw-milk products to consumers, either through direct sale or through cow-share programs, represents an unnecessary risk to consumer safety." (National milk producers federation and International Dairy Foods Association, 2012)

AAP, American Academy of Pediatrics; *AAPHV*, American Association of Public Health Veterinarians; *AMA*, American Medical Association; *AFDO*, Association for Food and Drug Officials; *CDC*, Centers for Disease Control and Prevention; *FDA*, Food and Drug Administration.

15.5.3 Why Is Raw-Milk Consumption Messaging Effective?

Potential raw-milk consumers are often provided with incorrect or incomplete information about the potential benefits associated with raw-milk consumption; however, raw–milk consumers tend to favor these messages over risk-based messages (Katafiasz and Bartett, 2012). Evaluation of the efficacy of these messages or message-delivery mechanisms may provide insight into new strategies for food safety messaging.

Messages about the benefits of raw-milk consumption typically come from personal interactions with a variety of individuals that are perceived to be trustworthy by the consumer. Primary sources of information on raw milk are typically in-person conversations with dairy farmers, friends, family, and coworkers; however, online resources (i.e., producer websites, social media, advocate websites) and printed materials were also identified as effective communication tools (Leamy et al., 2014).

15.5.4 Dairy Farmers and the Personal Touch

Raw-milk consumers in Vermont identified dairy farmers as their primary source (38.9%) of information on raw milk (Leamy et al., 2014). Since the 1930s, raw-milk producers have been consistent in consumer messaging that emphasizes the nutritional superiority of raw milk (Currier, 1981). Raw-milk dairies, along with other farm-direct sellers, are working to become increasingly connected to their consumers. In recent years, raw-milk dairy farmers have embraced the digital age and promote their business through websites. Interestingly, most raw-milk websites do not seem to promote their product as much as their farm. While they often provide information or links to information on the benefits of raw-milk consumption, the websites are often more focused on communicating the history, goals, and culture of their farm and how they make decisions related to animal care and selection and their choices on herd management. There are often pictures of the owners and important employees as well as pictures of the cows on pasture in ideal weather.

Social media and blogs are providing producers with a tool to rapidly and efficiently communicate their thoughts and test results in directly to their consumers. The transparency of these messages strengthens the producer—consumer relationship and instills confidence in future purchases. As an example, in August 2016, raw milk produced by a family run dairy in Midland, Utah was identified as the cause of an outbreak of

Salmonella Saintpaul. Heber Valley Milk used their Facebook page to communicate recent negative test results and emphasize food safety as a priority of their company and their family (Siegner, 2016).

15.5.5 The Power of Constantly Varied Messaging

Unlike food safety messaging from public health officials, messaging promoting raw milk are diverse in approach and interesting in content. Due to the constantly varying messages, the consumer is less likely to become dismissive. In addition to messaging described in the consumer attitudes section of this chapter, new marketing messages are beginning to appear on producer websites. New messages include agrotourism, sustainability, nonorganic (with a justification for disagreement with requirements), non-Genetically Modified Organisms (GMO), and breed-specific advantages.

15.5.6 The Power of Allied Messaging

Due to the advocate culture amongst a subset of raw-milk consumers, raw-milk farmers have allies in marketing that attack and undermine messages from public health agencies. These advocates, including groups such as the Weston A. Price Foundation, spin food safety messages from public health agencies into absurdities. Their messages are effective in causing the consumer to distrust government regulation and the dairy industry as well as appeal to value-based decisions. Examples of these messages are listed below:

> *"Never in the annals of health and nutrition has there been a food so maligned, lied about and conspired against as raw milk."*—blog post from Alton Eliason

> *"The US FDA would like us all to believe that raw milk is a flaming health hazard with the potential to cause a national disaster. What could be more toxic than raw food, right? That must be what is making our nation sick — not the over-consumption of genetically-modified, pesticide-laden foodstuffs."*—blog post from Angel4Light777

> *"The national effort to prevent people from obtaining raw milk has become so absurd that state and local governments around the country are willing to sick SWAT teams on US citizens to protect us from the potential harm in consuming raw milk which has been a dietary staple for generations."*—blog post from Kougar Kisses

15.5.7 Time to Consider Tolerant and Respectful Food Safety Messaging

Attempts to discourage raw-milk consumption of exclusive or frequent raw-milk drinkers are unlikely to be effective. This population is likely to be aware of the risks and have determined that the risk is acceptable or their personal experience seems to contrast the message being delivered. Based on the definitive and intolerant tone of current food safety messages (Table 15.2), it is likely that the latter is the reason for the raw–milk consumer's disregard. Perhaps it is time to consider food safety messaging that is more tolerant and respectful of current consumers while being firm, accurate, and intentional. An example of this type of message was previously proposed by a former physician representative from a certified milk operation: "Raw milk and raw milk products should be avoided, unless the consumer believes that the improved taste of the product warrants the risk" (Knutson et al., 2010; Leedom, 2006).

Results from these surveys suggest that current food safety warning messages are most influential to consumers that have never consumed raw milk. This would seem to indicate that this type of messaging would be most effective prior to the implementation of increased access in individual states as opposed to elevated messaging at the federal level. Point-of-purchase warning labeling may also serve as a deterrent for first-time buyers but would likely be ineffective for repeat purchasers (Knutson et al., 2010).

15.6 REGIONAL DIFFERENCES IN RAW-MILK ACCESS AND CONSUMER ATTITUDES

The culture of raw-milk consumption and consumer attitudes in the United States is complicated by a long history with considerable controversy. However, the United States is certainly not unique in this struggle to manage public health risk and consumer demand. Inconsistent messaging in the global marketplace further confuses the issues and can undermine public health goals. Data on consumer attitudes is limited in the United States and is even less available for other countries. The global similarities and differences highlighted below are included to demonstrate consistencies and inconsistencies across cultures.

15.6.1 Restricting Access: Canada, Australia, and Brazil

Canada and Australia prohibit the sale of raw milk at the federal level; however, unlike the United States, the federal regulation has forced the creation of provincial and state laws to further restrict raw-milk access. Certain provinces in Canada prohibit a farmer from giving away raw milk to a neighbor. Farmers illegally providing raw milk in both countries have been subjected to raids and numerous lawsuits for continuing to supply raw milk to consumers (this has also happened in the United States) (Ijaz, 2014). The New South Wales Food Authority recently approved high pressure processing as an alternative to thermal pasteurization and may allow for the pressurized milk to be marketed as "raw milk" (New South Wales Food Authority, 2016). Retail sales of raw milk are not permitted in Brazil. Nevertheless, the frequency of raw–milk consumption has been documented as high as 25% in certain regions. Not surprisingly, high consumption of raw milk appears to coincide with lack of knowledge of risks associated with such consumption (Pieri et al., 2014).

15.6.2 Increasing Access: Europe

Europe took a similar approach to United States by requiring pasteurization of fluid milk to achieve public health goals in the 1900s; however, most of Europe has significantly relaxed these requirements and is increasing consumer access to raw milk. Similar to the United States, falling milk prices in the larger dairy industry have forced farmers to reevaluate their revenue streams to remain in business. Raw–milk vending machines are becoming increasingly popular on-farm and in the cities. The raw-milk market is likely to increase as awareness of health benefits increases. Three companies currently produce vending machines specifically for raw milk; however, they intend to adapt the machines to be able to market other products (i.e., buttermilk, yogurt, cheese). In 2015, the raw-milk vending machine market was worth $6.45 million and is projected to almost triple in value by 2024.

Europe is the only part of the world that is actively engaged in long-term research related to raw-milk consumption. PASTURE is a cohort of researchers, doctors, and other medical professionals that have been investigating the effects of raw milk, boiled farm-fresh milk, and commercially pasteurized milk on pregnant women (living on and off-farm) and their offspring to evaluate the impacts of environment and milk consumption on various health outcomes. A growing body of evidence is demonstrating that raw-milk consumption may protect children from certain infectious diseases (Baars, 2013).

15.7 RAW-MILK CHEESES AND OTHER PRODUCTS

There are obvious differences in food safety risks associated with raw fluid milk and manufactured raw-milk products because pathogens that thrive in raw milk are less likely to survive in manufactured raw-milk products. Therefore, the second part of this chapter focuses on manufactured dairy products such as cheese and yogurt. The issue of safety of raw-milk cheeses is of tremendous importance to consumers' attitudes towards pasteurized and raw-milk cheese. Likewise, regulations regarding sale of raw-milk dairy products also impact consumers' attitudes. Consumers, from countries with regulations limiting sale of raw-milk cheeses, will likely be concerned about consuming such cheeses for safety reasons, while this would be less likely to influence consumers' attitudes in countries that do not limit sale of raw-milk cheese.

15.7.1 Safety of Raw-Milk Cheeses

It is not possible to make the blanket statement that all pathogens can't survive within the cheese environment. Rather it depends on the pathogen and on the cheese type. Nevertheless, the general trend is that pathogens do not survive in cheese due to the harsh environment of low pH, low water activity, high salt levels, and high populations of lactic acid bacteria. Therefore, less outbreaks are associated with raw-milk cheeses than with raw fluid milk, and many countries do allow the production and sale of raw-milk cheese (Table 15.3).

15.7.2 Regulation of Production and Sale of Raw-Milk Cheeses

Although sale of raw-milk cheeses is currently permitted in multiple countries, the regulations can change. For example, in the United States, the FDA, which is responsible for regulating production and sale of dairy products in interstate commerce, is frequently evaluating whether to forbid the sale of raw-milk cheeses. As part of this ongoing assessment, the FDA initiated, in 2014, a 2-year study that aggressively sampled domestic and imported raw-milk cheeses to determine prevalence of three pathogens. The results were released in August of 2016 (Food and Drug Administration, 2016). A total of 1606 cheeses were tested for *Salmonella*, *Listeria monocytogenes*, and pathogenic Shiga toxin-producing *E. coli* (STEC). Pathogens were detected in 14 samples: 10 with *L. monocytogenes*, 3 with *Salmonella*, and 1 with STEC. Thus, the prevalence for each pathogen was well below 1%. In spite of the low prevalence, FDA concludes "Taking into account the prevalence found and known pathogenicity, the FDA continues to be concerned about the presence of *Listeria* in raw-milk cheese, which is a ready to eat food, and we will take action as necessary." Besides regulatory

Table 15.3 Regulations relating to commercial production and sale of raw-milk cheeses in select countries

Country	Permits sale of raw-milk cheese	Restrictions	Food safety agency	Reference
United States	Yes	Cheese must be aged for at least 60 days at a temperature at or above 1.7°C prior to sale	FDA	Code of Federal Regulations
France	Yes	The production of raw-milk cheeses is allowed, as long as certain minimum requirements are met. The label (packaging, document, placard, label, ring, or band) that accompanies products made from raw milk must clearly indicate "made with raw milk"	EU and ANSES	European Commission
Norway	Yes	Products must be registered or approved by the FSA and products manufactured with raw milk and where the manufacturing process does not include any heat treatment or other physical or chemical treatment shall be labeled with the words "made from raw milk"	The Norwegian Food Safety Authority	Norwegian Food Safety Authority
England	Yes	The production of raw-milk cheeses is allowed, as long as certain minimum requirements are met. The label (packaging, document, placard, label, ring, or band) that accompanies products made from raw milk must clearly indicate "made with raw milk"	Food Standards Agency	Food Law Code of Practice
India	Yes	Needs conform to the microbiological requirements prescribed in Appendix B and the product standards of the Food Safety and Standards	Food Safety and Standards Authority of India	Food Safety and Standards (Food Products Standards and Food Additives) Regulations

research, academic studies have reported ambivalent results regarding safety of raw-milk products. For example, for washed rind soft cheeses, that are considered among the highest risk cheeses, data confirms that the prevalence of *L. monocytogenes* for raw and pasteurized versions of the cheeses is similar (Rudolf and Scherer, 2001). Ironically, the FDA's 60-day aging requirement would contribute to increased pathogen content when applied to raw-milk soft cheeses as these cheeses likely support growth of multiple pathogens during aging. Recently, Waldman and Kerr (2015) examined if the FDA's policy regarding artisan cheese is consistent with consumers' preferences. Indeed, this is not the case. The conclusions of the study are "artisan cheese consumers make purchasing decisions based on taste, not their attitude toward food safety." Furthermore, consumers are not willing to pay more for pasteurized-milk cheese even if it's considered more safe.

Nevertheless, there is broad agreement that one specific consumer group, pregnant women, should avoid raw milk and certain cheeses. Pregnant women and their fetuses are especially vulnerable to infection by *L. monocytogenes*. Athearn et al. (2004) examined pregnant women's awareness and acceptance of food safety advice during their pregnancies. In general, women were very reluctant to change their dietary habits even after receiving information about safety concerns. The women generally were open to advise such as not eating raw seafood and not handling pets when preparing foods. They were also receptive to advice on avoiding consumption of raw milk and raw-milk products. However, they did not find it necessary to avoid soft milk cheeses, such as queso fresco, and cold deli salads. This indicates that even consumers, with an increased motivation to prioritize safety, are skeptical of experts' food safety advice.

15.7.3 Risks Associated With Raw-Milk Cheeses

The concept of controlling risks associated with food consumption is challenging. Food scientists typically agree that there is an inherent risk associated with foods. Food safety is therefore an issue of controlling risk. Food scientists are trained to strive to minimize risk. In contrast, there are value-based stake holders who support raw-milk cheeses, promote wooden boards for aging of cheeses, and scorn industrialized production in closed cheese vats. These value-based stakeholders balance risk against cultural and social contexts (Nestle, 2003). The discussion on safety is ongoing and impacts consumers globally. Sociologists have investigated the divergent messages originating from scientists associated with regulatory agencies and raw-milk cheese proponents such as the American Cheese Society (ACS). West (2008) examined the debate in "Food fears and raw-milk cheese." West states that there are multiple stakeholders in this debate including regulatory agencies, scientists, large scale pasteurized cheese producers, artisans, and their consumers. Not surprisingly, regulatory agencies are driven by risk aversion supported by scientific experiments that don't necessarily replicate real-life scenarios. Large scale pasteurized-milk cheese processors have an interest in producing pasteurized-milk cheeses due to increased predictability and consistency along with decreased waste. In addition, these processors would have an interest in promoting an end to raw-milk cheese production by artisans due to potential harm a raw-milk cheese outbreak could have on consumer perception of all cheese categories. In contrast, artisans and their supporters emphasize the value of authentic cheese characteristics, terroir, and bio diversity. West concludes that the pressures to halt raw-milk cheese production are prevalent, and raw-milk cheese producers and their consumers must remain vigilant to ensure the continued permission to produce these products.

A study by Colonna et al. (2011) explored consumers' attitudes toward safety of raw vs pasteurized-milk cheeses along with food safety messaging. Interestingly, when asked if raw-milk cheeses are less safe than pasteurized-milk cheeses, only one third of the 891 consumers stated that raw-milk cheeses are less safe. However, when informed that raw-milk cheeses are made by an FDA-approved method (aging for at least 60 days at a temperature above 1.7°C), two thirds of these skeptical consumers changed their opinion. Thus producers of raw-milk cheeses would likely benefit from communicating that the raw-milk cheese process is approved by local food safety authorities. There are multiple different ways to accomplish this; for example, by printing a small message directly on the cheese package or by placing a message at the point of sale. The finding that the majority of consumers are not concerned about safety of raw-milk cheeses is consistent with the findings by Waldman and Kerr (2015). It is important to note that these two recent studies focusing on specialty cheese consumers in Oregon, Michigan, New York, and Vermont both conclude that consumers generally trust the safety of raw-milk cheeses. Yet, the US culinary culture has often been accused of promoting bland and sterile food. These two studies illustrate that if this was ever the case, then the United States has moved well beyond that, and US consumers are ready to embrace foods that contain bacteria.

15.7.4 Promoting Raw-Milk Cheeses

In the United States, multiple organizations have promoted raw-milk cheeses. Chief among them is the ACS. ACS represents specialty cheese producers, retailers, and general cheese enthusiasts. As such, the organization works with the FDA to promote a regulatory environment favorable to production and sale of raw-milk cheeses. Thus, the cheese makers and retailers are organized on a national level to promote raw-milk cheeses. This work also involves direct lobbying and encouraging members to contact local legislatures to prevent legislation prohibiting sale of raw-milk cheeses. Support for raw-milk cheeses can also be found among activists promoting social justice. For example, Halweil (2000, 2002) connected opposition to raw-milk cheeses with commodity cheese makers protecting their markets. Halweil also encourages new age food consumers to take an active role in promoting locally produced food. Nevertheless, the argument that commodity cheese makers are concerned to lose market share to artisans is difficult to defend. Today in the United States, artisan cheeses make up less than 1% of the cheese market. This is likely due to the price of these cheeses that are often 10 times more expensive than commodity cheeses. A more probably cause would be that commodity dairy processors, that produce pasteurized products, are concerned that an outbreak linked to raw-milk products could reflect negatively on the wholesome image of all dairy products.

Along with the regulatory work, the ACS directs an outreach program to inform US consumers about benefits of specialty cheeses whether made from raw or pasteurized milk. Thanks to the ACS campaign and multiple high profile cheese advocates, there is now a general perception in the US that raw-milk cheeses are often more complex and superior to pasteurized-milk cheeses. For example, one study found that cheese consumers associate raw-milk cheeses with a more complex flavor profile, while pasteurized-milk cheeses are associated with a less complex flavor (Colonna et al., 2011). Unfortunately, complex flavor was not further defined in the study. Although the term complex could be considered both as a positive and negative adjective, the assumption is that complex flavor is a positive attribute. Consumers correctly connected raw-milk cheese production with small scale production and pasteurized-milk cheeses with industrial scale production (Table 15.4). While some artisans produce pasteurized-milk products, very few large scale processors manufacture raw-milk products. Large dairy companies produce pasteurized-milk products to limit

Table 15.4 Terms that US Consumers associate with specialty raw and pasteurized-milk cheeses

	Terms associated with raw-milk cheese	Terms associated with pasteurized-milk cheese
Primary terms (> 15% of respondents)	Small production/ farmstead/artisan, more complex flavor profile, less safe, higher price per pound, higher quality product, positive health attributes	More safe, large industrial production, less complex flavor profile, positive health attributes, lower price per pound, higher quality product, lower quality product
Secondary terms (<15% of respondents)	Negative health attributes, lower quality products, less complex flavor profile, lower price per pound, more safe, large industrial production	More complex flavor profile, negative health attributes, higher price per pound, small production/farmstead artisan, less safe

Source: Data rearranged from Colonna et al. (2011).

risk and liability, improve consistency, and extend product shelf-life. Interestingly, optimizing product flavor quality is not on the list. This has provided a niche market for artisan producers who primarily focus on producing the best quality product. It is worth noting that consumers listed positive health attributes for both raw and pasteurized-milk cheeses. This is likely because consumers have different ideas about the meaning of health attributes. Some may consider raw-milk cheese as having beneficial nutritional or bioactive properties. This attitude has found widespread support among emerging consumer groups who believe that minimally processed foods are superior. In contrast, others may associate positive health attributes with safety and therefore decide that a pasteurized-milk cheese is safer and consequently healthier. In fact, some US cheese companies produce heat-shocked-milk cheese and do not state this on the label to avoid rejection from consumers who might find this less safe and therefore less attractive. Heat-shock is a treatment that is less intense than pasteurization. It is sufficient to destroy most pathogens while retaining significant enzyme activity and thereby promoting flavor development (Johnson et al., 1990). Based on US regulations, heat-shocked milk is considered raw, while in France, heat-shocked milk cannot be considered raw. This means that a

US cheese producer making cheese from heat-shocked milk could label the cheese as a raw-milk cheese, while the opposite goes for French cheese made with heat-shocked milk.

15.7.5 Consumer Preferences for Raw-Milk vs Pasteurized Dairy Products

Norway. Consumer perspectives vary among countries. For example, in Norway, raw-milk cheeses were not allowed in the market place until recently. Thus, Norwegian consumers don't have a tradition of appreciating and consuming these products. Norwegians are prolific cheese consumers (approximately 17 kg/year,) but basically all local cheeses are produced from pasteurized milk (Canadian Dairy Information Centre, 2010). Recently regulations changed and the sale of raw-milk cheeses is now permitted. Nevertheless, a population that is used to viewing pasteurization as a positive factor is not likely to quickly embrace raw-milk products. In a recent study by Almli et al. (2011), Norwegian consumers expressed a preference for pasteurized-milk cheeses. When questioned about positive attributes associated with cheese innovations, pasteurization was considered an advantage, while raw-milk cheeses were perceived negatively and actively rejected. The authors of the study speculate that the preference for pasteurized cheese was linked to the decades of regulations outlawing raw milk that likely led consumers to consider such cheeses as unsafe. However, a subgroup of Norwegian consumers was indifferent to milk heat treatment and was willing to embrace raw-milk cheese. Not surprisingly, these consumers were also more willing to buy new and different foods and were characterized as having a higher education and income. It seems likely that this population group has traveled more extensively and therefore been exposed to diverse foods including raw-milk cheeses. Thus, they have a history of being willing to try different products. If raw-milk cheeses will ever return to the Norwegian market place, this is the consumer group that will likely drive the change. However, it's reasonable to expect the reintroduction of raw-milk cheeses to Norway to be slow and raw-milk cheeses to remain a niche product.

France. Raw-milk cheeses are often associated with French dairy products. Around the world, people believe that most French cheeses are produced with raw milk. There is nothing more authentically French than a raw-milk camembert. Yet, today only approximately 10% of French cheeses are made from raw milk. Moreover, 25% of French raw-milk cheeses are Comté; a cheese type fabricated with a cook step that basically mimics the heat treatment experienced during batch pasteurization. Nevertheless, French consumers overwhelmingly favor raw-milk cheeses and are significantly more willing to buy raw-milk cheeses than pasteurized-milk cheeses (Almli et al., 2011). The same was observed in Italy, where a study by Pasta et al. (2009) revealed an overwhelming support for raw-milk cheese among 78% of the consumers surveyed. In 2007–08, two major French cheese companies requested to modify the traditional Appellation d'Origine Controle regulation for camembert to allow for usage of pasteurized milk. The attempt was met with significant opposition and the initiative failed. This is obviously in complete contrast to the actual market situation. If consumers overwhelmingly support raw-milk cheeses, why do these cheeses have such a low-market share? One problem is that they tend to be more expensive. As stated previously, large cheese manufacturers prefer to produce pasteurized-milk cheeses. Thus, it's left to the small scale producers to focus on raw-milk cheeses. As these producers don't benefit from economies of scale, their cheeses will be more expensive. It is also possible that this difference in French consumers' preferences and actual purchase decisions is due to the need for convenience. Consumption of shredded, sliced, and conveniently packaged cheeses is growing around the world, and these products tend to be made from pasteurized milk. The most popular French cheeses such as Emmental and fromage frais are made from pasteurized milk, and it is possible that French consumers do not realize that such a high percentage of their cheeses are made from pasteurized milk. Although the study demonstrates a preference for raw-milk cheeses in France and pasteurized-milk cheeses in Norway, the authors argue that in both cases, this expresses a preference for the cultural norm. In both countries, consumers prefer the products that their culinary culture deem superior, thus consumers are creatures of habit and will select what they have been exposed to.

United States. Preferences for raw vs pasteurized-milk cheeses in the United States were explored in the study by Colonna et al. (2011). They found that artisan cheese makers have an interest in producing raw-milk cheeses because specialty cheese consumers apparently prefer these cheeses. However, it's important to note that they obtained data from consumers who attended a so-called foodie festival which generally attract high income consumers. In their study, 891 specialty consumers tasted pairs of cheeses produced by local cheese makers. Each cheese maker produced two cheeses by similar processes except that one was made from raw milk and the other by pasteurized milk. The cheeses had very different flavor profiles. Consumers were served the pairs of raw and pasteurized-milk cheeses and asked for their preferences. Half the consumers received cheese pairs labeled by three digit codes, while the other half received cheeses labeled as pasteurized and nonpasteurized cheese. When asked which cheese they preferred, consumers who tasted cheeses labeled with three digit codes had no overall preference. Approximately half of the consumers preferred the raw-milk cheese sample, and the other half preferred the pasteurized-milk sample. In contrast, the consumers who knew in advance which cheeses were made with raw and pasteurized milk articulated a strong preference for raw-milk cheese. This demonstrates that people believe raw-milk cheese is superior to pasteurized-milk cheese. Therefore, the conclusion of the study is that artisan cheese makers in the United States have an interest in producing raw-milk cheese, and they should label their cheese as being made from raw milk. Nevertheless, it's important to note the limitations to this study, including the type of consumers participating in this study. The consumers were not average American consumers, but rather people expected to have a strong interest in specialty foods since they attended a local food festival. On the other hand, it could be argued that this is the target consumer group for artisan cheese makers, and the recommendation to label raw-milk cheese is therefore valid. The data in Table 15.4 demonstrates that these consumers appear to have a good understanding of the overall differences between raw and pasteurized-milk cheeses.

Ireland. There is limited information available about cheese preferences by Irish consumers. Murphy et al. (2004) investigated preferences for farmhouse (artisan) cheese consumers. They found that different consumer groups preferred either raw or pasteurized-milk cheeses or both. More importantly, Irish artisan cheese consumers ranked packaging as being more than twice as important as pasteurization or absence thereof. In fact, the study found that factors such as packaging, flavor, texture, nutrition, color, and price were all of higher relative importance than the thermal treatment of cheese milk. And for those who had an interest in this factor, pasteurization was considered an advantage over raw-milk cheese. The authors expressed surprise by this result as the Irish artisan cheese movement has worked diligently to preserve raw-milk cheeses (Murphy et al., 2004). Interestingly, there was a smaller cluster of consumers who preferred raw-milk cheeses. These consumers also placed most value on cheese flavor, while ranking packaging much lower. The two consumer groups outlined characteristics for their ideal cheeses. Not surprisingly, the groups preferred very different cheeses. The pasteurized-milk cheese group (139 consumers) characterized their ideal cheese as being mass-produced pasteurized-milk white Cheddar, and their least favorite being a farmhouse raw-milk cheese. The raw-milk cheese group (117 consumers) preferred a strong flavored white raw-milk cheese. This latter group was less price sensitive and was willing to pay more for their ideal cheese. Thus, similar to the subgroup of Norwegian consumers, it is clear that consumers in higher income groups are more likely to embrace raw-milk cheeses—at least in countries where raw-milk cheese is not the norm. Colonna et al. (2011) explored the connection between income and purchase intent in a slightly different manner. They found that higher income consumers are more likely to purchase expensive cheeses such as bloomy rind and other soft cheeses. This is not surprising and is not directly linked to pasteurized vs raw-milk cheese. Although they did find that higher income consumers have a preference for pungent flavored cheeses, a characteristic linked to raw-milk cheeses (Chambers et al., 2010).

Turkey. The studies summarized above for raw or pasteurized milk specialty cheeses have focused on higher income population segments within developed countries, with wealthier consumers being more willing to purchase the more expensive raw-milk cheeses. However, in developing countries, raw-milk dairy products may be preferred due to lower cost. Ates and Ceylan (2010) investigated preferences among urban and rural populations in Turkey with the urban population being significant better educated and wealthier. In Turkey, yogurt consumption is important with urban households consuming an average of 14.06 kg/month and rural households consuming 34.26 kg/month. While urban consumers primarily purchase pasteurized-milk yogurt, rural consumers prefer producing the yogurt at home from raw milk. Even among rural consumers, there are differences, and the lower the income the more yogurt being consumed, and the more likely it is that the yogurt is homemade from raw milk. The study concludes that high income consumers purchase pasteurized dairy products based on freshness and packaging, while low income consumers depend on raw-milk products derived from milk produced by animals belonging to the individual household.

It is apparent from the studies summarized above that consumers in different countries have very different views on raw-milk vs pasteurized-milk dairy products. The studies are also summarized in Table 15.5.

Table 15.5 Consumer preferences for raw and pasteurized-milk cheeses and yogurt produced in select countries

Country	Consumers	Preferences for raw or pasteurized-milk cheeses	Year	Study
Italy	Cheese consumers	Strong preference for raw-milk cheeses (73%)	2009	Pasta et al. (2009)
France	Like and consume Epoisses cheese at least twice a year	Strong preference for raw-milk cheese and rejection of pasteurized-milk cheese	2011	Almli et al. (2011)
Norway	Like and consume Jarlsberg cheese at least once a month	Preference for pasteurized-milk cheese with a minority preferring raw-milk cheese	2011	Almli et al. (2011)
Ireland	Cheese consumers with 50% consuming Irish farmhouse cheeses (artisan cheeses)	Preference for pasteurized-milk cheese with a minority preferring raw-milk cheese	2004	Murphy et al. (2004)
Turkey	Two distinct socioeconomic consumer groups: wealthy urban and lower income rural populations	Wealthy urban consumers prefer pasteurized-milk yogurt while low income urban consumers prefer raw-milk yogurt	2010	Ates and Ceylan (2010)
United States	Attendees at specialty food festival	Apparent preference for raw-milk cheese	2011	Colonna et al. (2011)

So are raw-milk cheeses better than pasteurized-milk cheeses? The answer would have to be that "it depends." Numerous studies have attempted to answer this question, and the results are not conclusive. However, it's clearly beyond the scope of this chapter to attempt to answer the question based on a review of scientific studies. Instead it's important to consider some of the shortcomings of such studies. For example, in many studies that compare raw vs pasteurized-milk cheeses, the only parameter that's modified is the heat treatment. Yet cheese professionals know that to obtain a good quality pasteurized-milk cheese, a cheese maker will likely need to add adjunct cultures and perhaps change fermentation time and other cheese-making parameters. Thus, in studies of cheeses that differ only in heat treatment, the pasteurized-milk cheeses are likely to score less favorably than the corresponding raw-milk cheeses. This means that there are inherent problems with a number of academic studies that try to answer the question of which cheese is best. In addition, some preference testing studies utilize consumers, while others use trained panelists or cheese professionals. Clearly, results will vary based on who taste the cheeses (Barcenas et al., 2004) which makes comparisons difficult. Finally, the impact of pasteurization appears to depend on the cheese type. Retiveau et al. (2005) evaluated 22 different French cheeses and could not draw conclusions across all cheese types. Even if we could turn to science to determine if raw-milk cheeses are better or worse than pasteurized-milk cheeses, the result wouldn't be important. As demonstrated by the study of Colonna et al. (2011), it's perception that matters. Consumers who believe that raw-milk cheeses are best will likely find confirmation in their beliefs. In contrast, consumers who believe that pasteurized-milk cheeses are superior—as found for Norwegian consumers (Almli et al., 2011)—will find evidence to support their beliefs.

This overview of consumer preferences in regard to pasteurized vs raw-milk cheeses and yogurt has revealed great differences among nationalities which are likely to be deeply rooted in cultural differences in our relationship with the food we eat. Only a few trends emerge such as the preferences for raw-milk cheeses in Southern Europe that is contrasted by the preference for pasteurized-milk cheeses in Northern Europe. Preferences also appear to align with a certain price dependency with raw-milk products being more expensive in developed countries and less expensive in developing countries compared to the pasteurized alternatives.

REFERENCES

Almli, V., Nas, R., Enderli, G., Sulmont-Rosse, C., Issanchou, S., Hersleth, M., 2011. Consumers' acceptance of innovations in traditional cheese. A comparative study in France and Norway. Appetite 57, 110–120.

American Academy of Pediatrics (AAP), 2014. Consumption of raw or unpasteurized milk and milk products by pregnant women and children. Pediatrics 133, 175–179.

American Association of Medical Milk Commissions (AAMMC), 1912. Methods and Standards for the Production and Distribution of "Certified Milk". Washington Government Printing Office, Washington, DC, Reprint from Public Health Reports No. 85.

American Association of Public Health Veterinarians (AAPHV), 2000. Position statement on raw (unpasteurized) milk/products. Available from: <https://marlerclark.com/images/uploads/about_ecoli/PUBLIC_HEALTH_VETERINARIAN_COALITION_COMMITTEE.pdf>.

American Medical Association (AMA), 2015. H-150.980 Milk and human health. Available at: <https://policysearch.ama-assn.org/policyfinder>.

Association for Food and Drug Officials (AFDO), 2005. Presenting information and position statement to state legislative officials considering changing food laws regarding sale of raw milk and raw milk products. Resolution Number 1. Available at: <https://marlerclark.com/pdfs/AFDOrawmilkres.pdf>.

Ates, H., Ceylan, M., 2010. Effects of socio-economic factors on the consumption of milk, yoghurt, and cheese. Insights from Turkey. Br. Food J. 3, 234–250.

Athearn, P., Kendall, P., Hillers, V., Schroeder, M., Bergmann, M., Chen, G., et al., 2004. Awareness and acceptance of current food safety recommendations during pregnancy. Matern. Child Health J. 8, 149–162.

Baars, T., 2013. Milk consumption, raw and general, in the discussion on health or hazard. J. Nutr. Ecol. Food Res. 1, 91–107.

Barcenas, P., Perez Elortondo, F., Albisu, M., 2004. Projective mapping in sensory analysis of ewes milk cheeses: a study on consumers and trained panel performance. Food Res. Int. 37, 723–772.

Beecher, C., 2016. Raw milk's "explosive growth" comes with costs to the state. Food Saf. News. Available from: http://www.foodsafetynews.com/2016/01/raw-milks-explosive-growth-comes-with-costs-to-the-state/#.V28QSGOtS7Y.

Bigouette, J.P., Bethel, J.W., Bovbjerg, M.L., Waite-Cusic, J.G., Häse, C.C., Poulsen, K. P., 2018. Knowledge, attitudes and practices regarding raw milk consumption in the Pacific Northwest. Food Protect Trends 38 (2), 104–110.

Buzby, J.C., Gould, L.H., Kendall, M.E., Jones, T.F., Robinson, T., Blayney, D.O.N.P., 2013. Characteristics of consumers of unpasteurized milk in the United States. J. Consum. Aff. 47, 153–166.

Canadian Dairy Information Centre, 2010. World cheese production. Canadian Dairy Information Center. Government of Canada, Ottawa. Available from: https://www.canada.ca/en/health-canada/services/food-nutrition/food-safety/information-product/statement-about-drinking-milk.html.

Centers for Disease Control and Prevention (CDC), 2007. Foodborne active surveillance network (FoodNet) population survey Atlas of exposures. U.S. Dep. Heal. Hum. Serv. Centers Dis. Control Prev. 1, 1–28.

Centers for Disease Control and Prevention (CDC), 2014. Letter to state and territorial epidemiologists and state public health veterinarians – the ongoing public health hazard of consuming raw milk. Available at: <https://www.cdc.gov/foodsafety/pdfs/raw-milk-letter-to-states-2014-508c.pdf>.

Centers for Disease Control and Prevention (CDC), 2015. Legal Status of the Sale of Raw Milk and Outbreaks Linked to Raw Milk, by State, 2007–2012. Available at: https://www.cdc.gov/foodsafety/pdfs/legal-status-of-raw-milk-sales-and-outbreaks-map-508c.pdf.

Chambers, D., Retiveau, A., Esteve, E., 2010. Effect of milk pasteurization on flavor properties of seven commercially available French cheese types. J. Sens. Stud. 25, 494–511.

Colonna, A., Durham, C., Meunier-Goddik, L., 2011. Factors affecting consumers' preferences for and purchasing decisions regarding pasteurized and raw milk specialty cheeses. J. Dairy Sci. 94, 5217–5226.

Cornell University Food Science Department, n.d. Cornell University Food Science Department position statement on raw milk sales and consumption. Available at: <http://www.milkfacts.info/CurrentEvents/PositionStatementRawMilk.pdf>.

Currier, R.W., 1981. Raw milk and human gastrointestinal disease: problems resulting from legalized sale of "certified raw milk. J. Public Health Policy 3, 226–234.

Dairy Processors Association of Canada (DPAC), 2010. Dairy processors support government actions to ban the sale of raw milk. Available at: <http://www.newswire.ca/news-releases/dairy-processors-support-government-actions-to-ban-the-sale-of-raw-milk-539704312.html>.

Ferguson, A., 2010. Who benefits from raw milk? Food Saf. News. Available from: http://www.foodsafetynews.com/2010/02/who-benefits-from-raw-milk/#.WCnQXztEzww.

Fierer, J., 1983. Invasive *Salmonella* Dublin infections associated with drinking raw milk. West. J. Med. 138, 665–669.

Food and Drug Administration, 1973. Part 18—milk and cream. 38 FR. Fed. Regist. 38, 27924.

Food and Drug Administration, 1974. Identity Standards for Milk and Cream: Order Staying Certain Provisions. 39 FR.

Food and Drug Administration, 1984. Notice of public hearing to receive information on whether milk and milk products sold for human consumption should be pasteurized. Fed. Reg 49, 31065.

Food and Drug Administration, 1987a. Final rule: requirements affecting raw milk for human consumption in interstate commerce. Fed. Regist. 52, 29509.

Food and Drug Administration, 1987b. Requirements affecting raw milk for human consumption in interstate commerce. Fed. Reg 52 (1987), 22340.

Food and Drug Administration (FDA), 2003. M-I-03-4: Sale/consumption of raw milk—position statement. Available at: <http://www.fda.gov/food/guidanceregulation/guidancedocumentsregulatoryinformation/milk/ucm079103.htm>.

Food and Drug Administration (FDA), 2016. FY 2014-2016 Microbiological Sampling Assignment Summary Report: Raw Milk Cheese Aged 60 Days. Available at: https://www.fda.gov/downloads/Food/ComplianceEnforcement/Sampling/UCM512217.pdf.

Gumpert, D., 2015. Who Says You Can't Succeed By Selling Raw Milk at $24 Per Gallon?. Available at: http://www.davidgumpert.com/who-says-you-cant-succeed-by-selling-raw-milk-at-24-per-gallon.

Halweil, B., 2000. Setting the cheez whiz standard. World Watch 163, 5–58.

Halweil, B., 2002. Home grown. The case for local food in a global market. World Watch.

Headrick, M.L., Timbo, B., Klontz, K.C., Werner, S.B., 1994. Profile of raw milk consumers in California. Public Health Rep. 112, 418–422.

Health Canada, 2005. Statement from health Canada about drinking raw milk. Available from: <http://www.hc-sc.gc.ca/fn-an/securit/facts-faits/rawmilk-laitcru-eng.php>.

Ijaz, N., 2014. Canada's "other" illegal white substance: evidence, economics and raw milk policy. Health Law Rev 22, 26–39.

Jayarao, B.M., Henning, D.R., 2001. Prevalence of foodborne pathogens in bulk tank milk, J. Dairy Sci., 84. pp. 2157–2162.

Jayarao, B.M., Donaldson, S.C., Straley, B.A., Sawant, A.A., Hegde, N.V., Brown, J.L., 2006. A survey of foodborne pathogens in bulk tank milk and raw milk consumption among farm families in Pennsylvania, J. Dairy Sci., 89. pp. 2451–2458.

Johnson, E., Nelson, J., Johnson, M., 1990. Microbiological safety of cheese made from heat-treated milk. Part II. Microbiology. J. Food Prot. 53, 519–540.

Katafiasz, A.R., Bartett, P., 2012. Motivation for unpasteurized milk consumption in Michigan, 2011. Food Prot. Trends 32, 124–128.

Kay, H.D., 1945. A critique of pasteurization. The case against pasteurization of milk: a statistical examination of the claim that pasteurization of milk saves lives. Nature 33.

Knutson, R.D., Currier, R.W., Ribera, L., Goeringer, P., 2010. Asymmetry in Raw Milk Safety Perceptions and Information: Implications for Risk in Fresh Produce Marketing and Policy. The Economics of Food, Food Choice and Health, Freising, Germany.

Leamy, R.J., Heiss, S.N., Roche, E., 2014. The impact of consumer motivations and sources of information on unpasteurized milk consumption in Vermont, 2013. Food Prot. Trends 34, 216−225.

Leedom, J., 2006. Milk of nonhuman origin and infectious diseases in humans. Clin. Infect. Dis. 43, 610−615.

Murphy, M., Cowan, C., Meehan, H., 2004. A conjoint analysis of Irish consumer preferences for farmhouse cheese. Br. Food J. 106, 288−300.

National Milk Producers Federation (NMPF) and International Dairy Foods Association (IDFA), 2012. Oppose Sen. Rand Paul's (R-KY) amendment No. 2180 permitting the interstate sale of raw milk. Available at: < http://www.realrawmilkfacts.com/PDFs/NMPF-IDFA-Letter-Sen-Rand-Amendment-060812.pdf >.

Nestle, M., 2003. Safe Food: Bacteria, Biotechnology, and Bioterrorism. University of California Press, Berkeley, CA.

New South Wales Food Authority, 2016. Approval of High Pressure Processing (HPP) of Milk. Available at: http://www.foodauthority.nsw.gov.au/news/newsandmedia/departmental/2016-06-03-HPP-milk.

Newsholme, A., 1935. Pasteurization of Milk. Nature 136, 1−3.

Pasta, C., Cortese, G., Campo, P., Licitra, G., 2009. Do biodiversity factors really affect consumer preferences? Prog. Nutr. 11, 3−11.

Pennsylvania Department of Agriculture, 2016. Raw Milk Bottlers. Available at: http://www.agriculture.pa.gov/Protect/FoodSafety/DairyandDairyProductManufacturing/Documents/ListingofPAPermittedRawMilkBottlers.pdf.

Pieri, F.A., Colombo, M., Merhi, C.M., Juliati, V.A., Ferreira, M.S., Nero, M.A., et al., 2014. Risky consumption habits and safety of fluid milk Available in retail sales outlets in Viçosa, Minas Gerais State, Brazil. Foodborne Pathog. Dis. 11, 490−496.

Potter, M.E., Kaufmann, A.F., Blake, P.A., Feldman, R.A., 1984. Unpasteurized milk: the hazards of a health fetish. JAMA 252, 2048−2052.

Public Citizen v. Heckler. 1987. 653 F. Suppl.1229. Civ. A. No. 85-1395. United States District Court, District of Columbia (March 11, 1987).

Retiveau, A., Chambers, D., Esteve, E., 2005. Developing a lexicon for the flavor description of French cheeses. Food Qual. Prefer. 16, 517−527.

Rohrbach, B.W., Draughon, F.A.N.N., Davidson, P.M., Oliver, S.P., 1992. Prevalence of *Listeria monocytogenes*, *Campylobacter jejuni*, *Yersinia enterocolitica*, and *Salmonella* in bulk tank milk: risk factors and risk of human exposure. J. Food Prot. 55, 93−97.

Rudolf, M., Scherer, S., 2001. High incidence of Listeria monocytogenes in European red smear cheese. Int. J. Food Microbiol. 63, 91−98.

Schmidt, R.H., Davidson, P.M., 2008. International association for food protection (IAFP) position statement: milk pasteurization and the consumption of raw milk in the United States. Food Prot. Trends 45−47. Available from: https://dairy.nv.gov/safety/International_Association_for_Food_Protection/.

Sebastian, R.S., Goldman, J.D., Enns, C.W., Randy, P. 2010. Fluid Milk Consumption in the United States. U.S. Department Of Agriculture Agricultural Research Service Beltsville Human Nutrition Research Center Food Surveys Research Group. Available at: https://www.ars.usda.gov/ARSUserFiles/80400530/pdf/DBrief/3_milk_consumption_0506.pdf.

Shiferaw, B., Yang, S., Cieslak, P., Vugia, D.U.C., Marcus, R., Koehler, J., et al.,. 2000. Prevalence of high-risk food consumption and food-handling practices among adults: a multistate survey, 1996 to 1997. The Foodnet Working Group. J. Food Prot. 63, 1538−1543.

Siegner, C., 2016. Nine *Salmonella* illnesses linked to raw milk from Utah dairy. Food Saf. News. Available from: http://www.foodsafetynews.com/2016/08/nine-cases-of-salmonella-infection-linked-to-raw-milk-from-utah-dairy/#.WvSx1y_MxsM.

Sobal, J., Bisogni, C.A., 2009. Constructing food choice decisions. Ann. Behav. Med. 38 (Suppl. 1), S37–S46.

Waldman, K., Kerr, J., 2015. Is Food and Drug Administration policy governing artisan cheese consistent with consumers' preferences? Food Policy 55, 71–80.

West, H.G., 2008. Food fears and raw-milk cheese. Appetite 51, 25–29.

Wilson, G.S., 1938. Pasteurization of milk. Nature 141, 579–581.

CHAPTER 16

Challenges for Production and Consumption of Raw Milk and Raw Milk Products

Luís A. Nero[1] and Antonio F. de Carvalho[2]
[1]Departamento de Veterinária, Universidade Federal de Viçosa, Viçosa, Brazil
[2]Departamento de Tecnologia de Alimentos, Universidade Federal de Viçosa, Viçosa, Brazil

16.1 INTRODUCTION

The consumption of raw milk and raw milk products, such as cheeses and fermented milks, has long been a controversial issue. Animal domestication for food purposes led to consumption of animal milks as an alternative source of nutrition. This has ultimately developed into a complex production chain that continues to grow and improve. There can be little doubt today of the importance of milk and dairy products in the human diet.

Once dairy cattle began to be bred for milk production, contact between humans and the domesticated animals increased. The benefits of this new nutrition source (milk) were clear, but they carried with them certain negative aspects that arose from closer contact with the producing animals. As people began to suffer from diseases with similar characteristics to the animal's diseases, questions arose about the disease origins. The belief that raw milk consumption could be one of the disease causes, above and beyond direct contact with the producing animals spurred development of new technologies to eliminate potential disease hazards. Increasingly, evidence showed that new milk treatment technologies were not enough to ensure the complete safety of milk and dairy products; hygiene controls were essential from the outset of production. The technological advances improved the dairy production chain by guaranteeing the safety and quality of raw milk and dairy products when procedures are applied correctly.

Despite the technologies developed to eliminate hazards and control contamination during the various milk production steps, there remains a

351

strong demand for raw milk and raw milk products which are tied to both cultural and health-oriented choices. Numerous scientific studies have demonstrated the beneficial aspects of raw milk, drawing on the identification of bacteria with beneficial/probiotic traits that can improve health. Other studies have focused on the technological potential of raw milk, namely its use in obtaining adjunct cultures that help control microbial contamination and starter cultures that can be used in the dairy industry. Lastly, many consumers around the world accept and overlook potential raw milk risks when it comes to specific artisanal products, such as cheeses and fermented milks when they are part of a dietary and cultural heritage.

Both the positive and negative aspects related to raw milk and raw milk products and their consumption need to be taken into consideration to form a well-founded opinion of the subject. These issues have been detailed and addressed in the past chapters of this book to provide a deeper understanding of the paradoxical role that raw milk and raw milk products play in food and food production.

16.2 NEGATIVE ASPECTS

The presence of potential hazards in raw milk is a given (Becker-Algeri et al., 2016; van Asselt et al., 2017; Verraes et al., 2014, 2015; Zastempowska et al., 2016). During production, animals are exposed to a wide range of biological, chemical, and physical risks, which can directly interfere with production (Claeys et al., 2013). Dairy cattle are exposed to a variety of biological agents right from the start of the milk production chain, which can sometimes lead to contamination (Can et al., 2015; Cavirani, 2008; Franco et al., 2013; Garcia et al., 2010; Hurtado et al., 2017; Michel et al., 2015; Oliver et al., 2005; Widgren et al., 2013). In addition to biological agents that can cause diseases, environmental contamination must also be taken into consideration. Various biological contaminants, such as utensils and equipment present in the producing environment, can act as contamination vehicles to the end product (Knowlton and Cobb, 2006; Liu and Haynes, 2011; Oliver et al., 2005; Rychen et al., 2008; Saegerman et al., 2006; Santorum et al., 2012). In this sense, transmission hazardous biological agent transmission can come both not only from the animals but also from their natural presence in the milk production environment. Then, there is the human element: dairy farm employees can be hosts of biological contamination as well

(Barkema et al., 2015; Delgado-Pertinez et al., 2003; Devendra, 2001; Gran et al., 2002; Guerreiro et al., 2005; Kijlstra et al., 2009; Vallin et al., 2009; Ventura et al., 2016). This multifaceted scenario highlights the need for critical and extensive contamination control at all stages of dairy production, beginning with raw milk. Yes, new technologies and equipment can improve conditions considerably, but it must be emphasized that as the number of equipment/processes used for milk production increases, so must the contamination controls, with increasing attention paid to the adoption of reliable and effective hygienic procedures throughout the dairy chain.

Chemical hazards also play an important role in milk production (Mitchell et al., 1998; Pacheco-Silva et al., 2014). During production, animals can undergo diverse clinical treatments using antibiotic, antiviral, and antiparasitic drugs. These treatments must be conducted under proper veterinary supervision, and strict recommendations must be given for not making milk from treated animals available for consumption. The residual presence of such drugs in milk can pose major health issues, due to possible individual sensitivity to specific molecules, development of antimicrobial resistance, and intoxications (Mitchell et al., 1998; Oliver et al., 2011; Pacheco-Silva et al., 2014; Straley et al., 2006). Moreover, the presence of drug residues in milk can jeopardize the proper growth of starter cultures or the survival of probiotic strains in fermented milks and cheeses in dairy industries (Mitchell et al., 1998). Chemical hazards are not limited to drugs employed for animal treatments, either. A variety of chemicals can be present in the production environment as a result of pollution, pasture and crop treatment, and chemical contamination in water sources, to name a few factors (Bilandzic et al., 2011; Miclean et al., 2011; Perween, 2015; Zhao et al., 2012). Producing animals are exposed to all these chemical contaminants throughout their life, and the milk they produce can be contaminated by substances from diverse origins.

The current state of dairy regulation for raw milk and raw milk products presents another negative aspect that must be addressed. When a country/state has established that sale and consumption of raw milk are forbidden but consumer demand for raw milk persists, unofficial sales take place and taxes cannot be applied. This sets off a chain of events where official agents identify illegal raw milk sales and apply penalties and fees, but the sale cycle comes full circle and the raw milk or raw milk products pop up in another area for another group of consumers. Policing an illegal raw milk market requires time and resources which would be better spent focusing on how to improve the quality and safety of the raw milk produced. Ultimately, the time and resources are wasted as raw milk continues to be sold, and no taxes are collected.

These negative aspects clearly demonstrate the concerns related to consumption of raw milk and raw milk products. The issues cited, inherent to raw milk consumption, require proper control throughout production as well as regulatory procedures that adequately oversee the dairy chain. But the outlook is not all negative; there are positive aspects to raw milk consumption as well.

16.3 POSITIVE ASPECTS

Yes, raw milk and raw milk products can carry many risks, and the absence of proper taxes when their sale is forbidden is a concern. And yes, the frequency of diseases and deaths decreased substantially after the development and adoption of industrial procedures that assure the safety of milk products. But humans have consumed raw milk and raw milk products since the inception of dairy breeding and there remains a real and growing demand for producing and consuming raw milk and raw milk products (Lucey, 2015). Though many of the reasons for raw milk consumption may not always be scientifically sound, they are worth taking into account.

While raw milk and raw milk products may potentially carry pathogenic bacteria, they can also harbor beneficial bacteria that can, and must, be exploited by the dairy industry (Fernandez et al., 2015; Montel et al., 2014; Quigley et al., 2013). Many autochthonous bacteria from raw milk present strong probiotic potential and could play an important role in human health and well-being (Abushelaibi et al., 2017; Aloglu et al., 2016; Ayyash et al., 2018; De Sant'Anna et al., 2017; del Rio et al., 2016; Vimont et al., 2017; Zhang et al., 2016, 2017). In addition to this probiotic potential, some raw milk bacteria can produce antimicrobial compounds that may in some way play an effective role in controlling the growth of undesirable bacteria, such as pathogens and spoilage bacteria (de Souza and Dias, 2017; Furtado et al., 2015; Gaaloul et al., 2015; Macaluso et al., 2016; Mirkovic et al., 2016; Perin et al., 2016, 2017; Perin and Nero, 2014; Portilla-Vazquez et al., 2016; Ribeiro et al., 2014; Sobrino-Lopez and Martin-Belloso, 2008; Tulini et al., 2016; Vimont et al., 2017; Ziarno, 2006). Various studies have already demonstrated the antagonistic role of autochthonous microbiota on raw milk, which can interfere in the establishment of certain foodborne pathogens (Cavicchioli et al., 2015; Nero et al., 2008; Ortolani et al., 2010; Valero et al., 2014; Yoon et al., 2016). Finally, many autochthonous bacteria in raw milk can produce substances that may be of technological interest to the dairy industry. These substances play a key role in the production of fermented milks and ripened cheeses, because they ensure distinctive taste, texture, and aromas that improve the added value of the final products (Banwo et al., 2013; Bendimerad et al., 2012; de Souza and Dias, 2017; Fguiri et al., 2016; Perin et al., 2017; Tulini et al., 2016).

The positive technological aspects related to raw milk microbiota lead to another important element: artisanal food production. Artisanal foods are part of our cultural heritage and should be remembered, preserved, and celebrated. Artisanal cheeses play an important role in this context, as they represent iconic foods for a number of cultures worldwide (Alichanidis and Polychroniadou, 2008; Luiz et al., 2016; von Dentz, 2017). Maintaining traditional artisanal cheese production procedures has a historical relevance as well which must be preserved and respected. In France, Italy, Spain, Greece, and even Brazil (to name just a few), there is a current trend to venerate and restore artisanal cheese production in order to preserve the history of these countries to its fullest.

Now that the potential hazards and consumer demands for raw milk and raw milk products have been covered, there's another positive aspect to address: the development of alternative and new technologies to improve the safety of raw milk (Aguero et al., 2017; Amaral et al., 2017; Kumar et al., 2013; Meena et al., 2017; Ng et al., 2017; Odueke et al., 2016). This is the natural evolution of the raw milk and raw milk product market where supply rises to meet demand and product safety has to be ensured. The result has been the introduction of different and alternative technologies used to promote proper cleaning of equipment and utensils, and the development of new milk treatment procedures (beyond heat treatments, like pasteurization and ultrahigh temperature) (Aguero et al., 2017; Kumar et al., 2013; Meena et al., 2017). Thus, thanks to the increasing demand for raw milk, scientific activities around dairy processing are improving, resulting in significant scientific advances in the field.

These positive aspects, along with others that were addressed in different chapters of this book, further demonstrate the beneficial potential of raw milk and its products. Because raw milk and raw milk products present both positive and negative aspects, production and consumption must be conducted with care and explained in full to consumers and regulatory agencies.

16.4 RAW MILK: GOOD OR BAD?

There is no right or wrong answer to this question. As has been addressed in this final chapter, both the positives and negatives for raw milk production and consumption must be evaluated in order to determine what it is needed to improve and adapt the dairy production chain to include the age-old tradition of consuming raw milk. There is no doubt that milk and raw milk products, especially cheeses, are, and will continue to be, consumed by mankind. There is also no doubt that in certain situations, raw milk and raw milk products can pose real dangers to consumers. It is up to regulatory agencies to ensure product safety in order to avoid the transmission of potential hazards to consumers.

This brings us to the relevance of regulatory agencies. Regulatory agencies play an important role in defining strict and reliable guidelines for raw milk production and overseeing rigorous control of animal diseases and disease treatments in producing animals. Mandatory registration of authorized farms, disease surveillance, and production hygiene condition monitoring are all essential. All of the above require proper training and resources to be implemented in full.

Then, there are taxes: only by regulating the production and sale of raw milk and raw milk products can adequate and reliable taxes be collected. Given the current scenario of sale and consumption of raw milk and raw milk products, taxing the products could generate resources that can then be earmarked for improving their quality and safety. Monitoring key points of raw milk production and predicting direct human consumption must come with strict guidelines and implementation, both of which require substantial financial investment. That investment is in turn justified by the proposed taxes. Farmers must also unite in cooperatives and associations to promote clear organization practices and establish objectives to preserve and improve raw milk production. Many of these steps have been implemented by European raw milk cheese producers and the corresponding authorities, resulting in a vast improvement in the quality and safety of traditional European cheeses, along with preservation the countries' cultural heritage.

Education is vital to the production and consumption of raw milk and raw milk products. Consumers must be informed of any and all hazards that can be associated with raw milk and raw milk products. This in turn will drive them to ensure producers follow strict production procedures and hold regulatory agencies accountable for reliable monitoring of purchased and consumed products. Correct, scientific-based information is key: consumers must have access to unbiased information regarding the quality, safety, and risks related to raw milk and raw milk products. They must also know how monitoring and surveillance programs are conducted by regulatory agencies. In addition, special educational programs must be developed for at-risk populations, like the elderly, pregnant, and lactating women, newborns, children, and immunocompromised patients.

These key elements proposed for assessing the real impact of raw milk and raw milk products demonstrate the relevance of risk analysis to measure the possible impacts of these products on human health (De Roever, 1998; Nesbitt et al., 2014; Papademas and Bintsis, 2010; Young et al., 2017a,b). Continuous surveillance and monitoring to ensure the quality and safety of raw milk and raw milk products, reliable policies from regulatory agencies, and consumer education based on scientific, unbiased information are paramount for future determination of whether raw milk can be considered a good or bad food.

ACKNOWLEDGMENTS

CNPq, CAPES, and FAPEMIG.

REFERENCES

Abushelaibi, A., Al-Mahadin, S., El-Tarabily, K., Shah, N.P., Ayyash, M., 2017. Characterization of potential probiotic lactic acid bacteria isolated from camel milk. LWT—Food Sci. Technol. 79, 316–325.

Aguero, R., Bringas, E., San Roman, M.F., Ortiz, I., Ibanez, R., 2017. Membrane processes for whey proteins separation and purification. A review. Curr. Org. Chem. 21, 1740–1752.

Alichanidis, E., Polychroniadou, A., 2008. Characteristics of major traditional regional cheese varieties of East-Mediterranean countries: a review. Dairy Sci. Technol. 88, 495–510.

Aloglu, H.S., Ozer, E.D., Oner, Z., 2016. Assimilation of cholesterol and probiotic characterisation of yeast strains isolated from raw milk and fermented foods. Int. J. Dairy Technol. 69, 63–70.

Amaral, G.V., Silva, E.K., Cavalcanti, R.N., Cappato, L.P., Guimaraes, J.T., Alvarenga, V.O., et al., 2017. Dairy processing using supercritical carbon dioxide technology: theoretical fundamentals, quality and safety aspects. Trends Food Sci. Technol. 64, 94–101.

Ayyash, M., Abushelaibi, A., Al-Mahadin, S., Enan, M., El-Tarabily, K., Shah, N., 2018. In-vitro investigation into probiotic characterisation of *Streptococcus* and *Enterococcus* isolated from camel milk. LWT—Food Sci. Technol. 87, 478–487.

Banwo, K., Sanni, A., Tan, H., 2013. Technological properties and probiotic potential of *Enterococcus faecium* strains isolated from cow milk. J. Appl. Microbiol. 114, 229–241.

Barkema, H.W., von Keyserlingk, M.A.G., Kastelic, J.P., Lam, T., Luby, C., Roy, J.P., et al., 2015. Invited review: changes in the dairy industry affecting dairy cattle health and welfare. J. Dairy Sci. 98, 7426—7445.

Becker-Algeri, T.A., Castagnaro, D., de Bortoli, K., de Souza, C., Drunkler, D.A., Badiale-Furlong, E., 2016. Mycotoxins in bovine milk and dairy products: a review. J. Food Sci. 81, R544—R552.

Bendimerad, N., Kihal, M., Berthier, F., 2012. Isolation, identification, and technological characterization of wild leuconostocs and lactococci for traditional Raib type milk fermentation. Dairy Sci. Technol. 92, 249—264.

Bilandzic, N., Dokic, M., Sedak, M., Solomun, B., Varenina, I., Knezevic, Z., et al., 2011. Trace element levels in raw milk from northern and southern regions of Croatia. Food Chem. 127, 63—66.

Can, H.Y., Elmali, M., Karagoz, A., 2015. Detection of Coxiella burnetii in cows', goats', and ewes' bulk milk samples using polymerase chain reaction (PCR). Mljekarstvo 65, 26—31.

Cavicchioli, V.Q., Dornellas, W.D., Perin, L.M., Pieri, F.A., Franco, B., Todorov, S.D., et al., 2015. Genetic diversity and some aspects of antimicrobial activity of lactic acid bacteria isolated from goat milk. Appl. Biochem. Biotechnol. 175, 2806—2822.

Cavirani, S., 2008. Cattle industry and zoonotic risk. Vet. Res. Commun. 32, S19—S24.

Claeys, W.L., Cardoen, S., Daube, G., De Block, J., Dewettinck, K., Dierick, K., et al., 2013. Raw or heated cow milk consumption: review of risks and benefits. Food Control 31, 251—262.

De Roever, C., 1998. Microbiological safety evaluations and recommendations on fresh produce. Food Control 9, 321—347.

De Sant'Anna, F.M., Acurcio, L.B., Alvim, L.B., De Castro, R.D., De Oliveira, L.G., Da Silva, A.M., et al., 2017. Assessment of the probiotic potential of lactic acid bacteria isolated from Minas artisanal cheese produced in the Campo das Vertentes region, Brazil. Int. J. Dairy Technol. 70, 592—601.

de Souza, J.V., Dias, F.S., 2017. Protective, technological, and functional properties of select autochthonous lactic acid bacteria from goat dairy products. Curr. Opin. Food Sci. 13, 1—9.

del Rio, M.D.S., Andrighetto, C., Dalmasso, A., Lombardi, A., Civera, T., Bottero, M.T., 2016. Isolation and characterisation of lactic acid bacteria from donkey milk. J. Dairy Res. 83, 383—386.

Delgado-Pertinez, M., Alcalde, M.J., Guzman-Guerrero, J.L., Castel, J.M., Mena, Y., Caravaca, F., 2003. Effect of hygiene-sanitary management on goat milk quality in semi-extensive systems in Spain. Small Ruminant Res. 47, 51—61.

Devendra, C., 2001. Smallholder dairy production systems in developing countries: characteristics, potential and opportunities for improvement—review. Asian-Australas. J. Anim. Sci. 14, 104—113.

Fernandez, M., Hudson, J.A., Korpela, R., de los Reyes-Gavilsn, C.G., 2015. Impact on human health of microorganisms present in fermented dairy products: an overview. Biomed. Res. Int. 2015, 13.

Fguiri, I., Ziadi, M., Atigui, M., Ayeb, N., Arroum, S., Assadi, M., et al., 2016. Isolation and characterisation of lactic acid bacteria strains from raw camel milk for potential use in the production of fermented Tunisian dairy products. Int. J. Dairy Technol. 69, 103—113.

Franco, M.M.J., Paes, A.C., Ribeiro, M.G., Pantoja, J.C.D., Santos, A.C.B., Miyata, M., et al., 2013. Occurrence of mycobacteria in bovine milk samples from both individual and collective bulk tanks at farms and informal markets in the southeast region of Sao Paulo, Brazil. BMC Vet. Res. 9, 85.

Furtado, D.N., Todorov, S.D., Landgraf, M., Destro, M.T., Franco, B., 2015. Bacteriocinogenic *Lactococcus lactis* subsp lactis DF04Mi isolated from goat milk: application in the control of *Listeria monocytogenes* in fresh Minas-type goat cheese. Braz. J. Microbiol. 46, 201–206.

Gaaloul, N., ben Braiek, O., Hani, K., Volski, A., Chikindas, M.L., Ghrairi, T., 2015. Isolation and characterization of large spectrum and multiple bacteriocin-producing *Enterococcus faecium* strain from raw bovine milk. J. Appl. Microbiol. 118, 343–355.

Garcia, A., Fox, J.G., Besser, T.E., 2010. Zoonotic enterohemorrhagic *Escherichia coli*: a one health perspective. ILAR J. 51, 221–232.

Gran, H.M., Mutukumira, A.N., Wetlesen, A., Narvhus, J.A., 2002. Smallholder dairy processing in Zimbabwe: hygienic practices during milking and the microbiological quality of the milk at the farm and on delivery. Food Control 13, 41–47.

Guerreiro, P.K., Machado, M.R.F., Braga, G.C., Gasparino, E., Franzener, A.D.M., 2005. Microbiological quality of milk through preventive techniques in the handling of production. Cienc. Agrotecnol. 29, 216–222.

Hurtado, A., Ocejo, M., Oporto, B., 2017. *Salmonella* spp. and *Listeria monocytogenes* shedding in domestic ruminants and characterization of potentially pathogenic strains. Vet. Microbiol. 210, 71–76.

Kijlstra, A., Meerburg, B.G., Bos, A.P., 2009. Food safety in free-range and organic livestock systems: risk management and responsibility. J. Food Prot. 72, 2629–2637.

Knowlton, K.F., Cobb, T.D., 2006. ADSA foundation scholar award: implementing waste solutions for dairy and livestock farms. J. Dairy Sci. 89, 1372–1383.

Kumar, P., Sharma, N., Ranjan, R., Kumar, S., Bhat, Z.F., Jeong, D.K., 2013. Perspective of membrane technology in dairy industry: a review. Asian-Australas. J. Anim. Sci. 26, 1347–1358.

Liu, Y.Y., Haynes, R.J., 2011. Origin, nature, and treatment of effluents from dairy and meat processing factories and the effects of their irrigation on the quality of agricultural soils. Crit. Rev. Environ. Sci. Technol. 41, 1531–1599.

Lucey, J.A., 2015. Raw milk consumption: risks and benefits. Nutr. Today 50, 189–193.

Luiz, L.M.P., Chuat, V., Madec, M.N., Araujo, E.A., de Carvalho, A.F., Valence, F., 2016. Mesophilic lactic acid bacteria diversity encountered in Brazilian farms producing milk with particular interest in *Lactococcus lactis* strains. Curr. Microbiol. 73, 503–511.

Macaluso, G., Fiorenza, G., Gagho, R., Mancuso, I., Scatassa, M.L., 2016. In vitro evaluation of bacteriocin-like inhibitory substances produced by lactic acid bacteria isolated during traditional Sicilian cheese making. Ital. J. Food Saf. 5, 5503.

Meena, G.S., Singh, A.K., Panjagari, N.R., Arora, S., 2017. Milk protein concentrates: opportunities and challenges. J. Food Sci. Technol. 54, 3010–3024.

Michel, A.L., Geoghegan, C., Hlokwe, T., Raseleka, K., Getz, W.M., Marcotty, T., 2015. Longevity of *Mycobacterium bovis* in raw and traditional souring milk as a function of storage temperature and dose. PLoS ONE 10, e0129926.

Miclean, M., Cadar, O., Roman, C., Tanaselia, C., Stefanescu, L., Stezar, C.I., et al., 2011. The influence of environmental contamination on heavy metals and organochlorine compounds levels in milk. Environ. Eng. Manage. J. 10, 37–42.

Mirkovic, N., Polovic, N., Vukotic, G., Jovcic, B., Miljkovic, M., Radulovic, Z., et al., 2016. *Lactococcus lactis* LMG2081 produces two bacteriocins, a nonlantibiotic and a novel lantibiotic. Appl. Environ. Microbiol. 82, 2555–2562.

Mitchell, J.M., Griffiths, M.W., McEwen, S.A., McNab, W.B., Yee, A.J., 1998. Antimicrobial drug residues in milk and meat: causes, concerns, prevalence, regulations, tests, and test performance. J. Food Prot. 61, 742–756.

Montel, M.-C., Buchin, S., Mallet, A., Delbes-Paus, C., Vuitton, D.A., Desmasures, N., et al., 2014. Traditional cheeses: rich and diverse microbiota with associated benefits. Int. J. Food Microbiol. 177, 136–154.

Nero, L.A., de Mattos, M.R., Barros, M.D.F., Ortolani, M.B.T., Beloti, V., Franco, B., 2008. *Listeria monocytogenes* and *Salmonella* spp. in raw milk produced in Brazil: occurrence and interference of indigenous microbiota in their isolation and development. Zoonoses Public Health 55, 299–305.

Nesbitt, A., Thomas, M.K., Marshall, B., Snedeker, K., Meleta, K., Watson, B., et al., 2014. Baseline for consumer food safety knowledge and behaviour in Canada. Food Control 38, 157–173.

Ng, K.S.Y., Haribabu, M., Harvie, D.J.E., Dunstan, D.E., Martins, G.J.O., 2017. Mechanisms of flux decline in skim milk ultrafiltration: a review. J. Membr. Sci. 523, 144–162.

Odueke, O.B., Farag, K.W., Baines, R.N., Chadd, S.A., 2016. Irradiation applications in dairy products: a review. Food Bioprocess Technol. 9, 751–767.

Oliver, S.P., Jayarao, B.M., Almeida, R.A., 2005. Foodborne pathogens in milk and the dairy farm environment: food safety and public health implications. Foodborne Pathog. Dis. 2, 115–129.

Oliver, S.P., Murinda, S.E., Jayarao, B.M., 2011. Impact of antibiotic use in adult dairy cows on antimicrobial resistance of veterinary and human pathogens: a comprehensive review. Foodborne Pathog. Dis. 8, 337–355.

Ortolani, M.B.T., Yamazi, A.K., Moraes, P.M., Vicosa, G.N., Nero, L.A., 2010. Microbiological quality and safety of raw milk and soft cheese and detection of autochthonous lactic acid bacteria with antagonistic activity against *Listeria monocytogenes*, *Salmonella* spp., and *Staphylococcus aureus*. Foodborne Pathog. Dis. 7, 175–180.

Pacheco-Silva, E., de Souza, J.R., Caldas, E.D., 2014. Veterinary drug residues in milk and eggs. Quim. Nova 37, 111–122.

Papademas, P., Bintsis, T., 2010. Food safety management systems (FSMS) in the dairy industry: a review. Int. J. Dairy Technol. 63, 489–503.

Perin, L.M., Belviso, S., dal Bello, B., Nero, L.A., Cocolin, L., 2017. Technological properties and biogenic amines production by bacteriocinogenic lactococci and enterococci strains isolated from raw goat's milk. J. Food Prot. 80, 151–157.

Perin, L.M., Nero, L.A., 2014. Antagonistic lactic acid bacteria isolated from goat milk and identification of a novel nisin variant *Lactococcus lactis*. BMC Microbiol. 14, 36.

Perin, L.M., Todorov, S.D., Nero, L.A., 2016. Investigation of genes involved in nisin production in *Enterococcus* spp. strains isolated from raw goat milk. Antonie Van Leeuwenhoek 109, 1271–1280.

Perween, R., 2015. Factors involving in fluctuation of trace metals concentrations in bovine milk. Pak. J. Pharm. Sci. 28, 1033–1038.

Portilla-Vazquez, S., Rodriguez, A., Ramirez-Lepe, M., Mendoza-Garcia, P.G., Martinez, B., 2016. Biodiversity of bacteriocin-producing lactic acid bacteria from Mexican regional cheeses and their contribution to milk fermentation. Food Biotechnol. 30, 155–172.

Quigley, L., O'Sullivan, O., Stanton, C., Beresford, T.P., Ross, R.P., Fitzgerald, G.F., et al., 2013. The complex microbiota of raw milk. FEMS Microbiol. Rev. 37, 664–698.

Ribeiro, S.C., Coelho, M.C., Todorov, S.D., Franco, B., Dapkevicius, M.L.E., Silva, C.C.G., 2014. Technological properties of bacteriocin-producing lactic acid bacteria isolated from Pico cheese an artisanal cow's milk cheese. J. Appl. Microbiol. 116, 573–585.

Rychen, G., Jurjanz, S., Toussaint, H., Feidt, C., 2008. Dairy ruminant exposure to persistent organic pollutants and excretion to milk. Animal 2, 312–323.

Saegerman, C., Pussemier, L., Huyghebaert, A., Scippo, M.L., Berkvens, D., 2006. On-farm contamination of animals with chemical contaminants. Rev. Sci. Tech. 25, 655–673.

Santorum, P., Garcia, R., Lopez, V., Martinez-Suarez, J.V., 2012. Review. Dairy farm management and production practices associated with the presence of *Listeria monocytogenes* in raw milk and beef. Span. J. Agric. Res. 10, 360–371.

Sobrino-Lopez, A., Martin-Belloso, O., 2008. Use of nisin and other bacteriocins for preservation of dairy products. Int. Dairy J. 18, 329–343.

Straley, B.A., Donaldson, S.C., Hedge, N.V., Sawant, A.A., Srinivasan, V., Oliver, S.P., et al., 2006. Public health significance of antimicrobial-resistant Gram-negative bacteria in raw bulk tank milk. Foodborne Pathog. Dis. 3, 222–233.

Tulini, F.L., Hymery, N., Haertle, T., Le Blay, G., De Martinis, E.C.P., 2016. Screening for antimicrobial and proteolytic activities of lactic acid bacteria isolated from cow, buffalo and goat milk and cheeses marketed in the southeast region of Brazil. J. Dairy Res. 83, 115–124.

Valero, A., Hernandez, M., De Cesare, A., Manfreda, G., Gonzalez-Garcia, P., Rodriguez-Lazaro, D., 2014. Survival kinetics of *Listeria monocytogenes* on raw sheep milk cured cheese under different storage temperatures. Int. J. Food Microbiol. 184, 39–44.

Vallin, V.M., Beloti, V., Battaglini, A.P.P., Tamanini, R., Fagnani, R., da Angela, H.L., et al., 2009. Milk quality improvement after implantation of good manufacturing practices in milking in 19 cities of the central region of Parana. Semina Cienc. Agrar. 30, 181–188.

van Asselt, E.D., van der Fels-Klerx, H.J., Marvin, H.J.P., van Bokhorst-van de Veen, H., Groot, M.N., 2017. Overview of food safety hazards in the European dairy supply chain. Compr. Rev. Food Sci. Food Saf. 16, 59–75.

Ventura, B.A., von Keyserlingk, M.A.G., Wittman, H., Weary, D.M., 2016. What difference does a visit make? Changes in animal welfare perceptions after interested citizens tour a dairy farm. PLoS ONE 11, e0154733.

Verraes, C., Claeys, W., Cardoen, S., Daube, G., De Zutter, L., Imberechts, H., et al., 2014. A review of the microbiological hazards of raw milk from animal species other than cows. Int. Dairy J. 39, 121–130.

Verraes, C., Vlaemynck, G., Van Weyenberg, S., De Zutter, L., Daube, G., Sindic, M., et al., 2015. A review of the microbiological hazards of dairy products made from raw milk. Int. Dairy J. 50, 32–44.

Vimont, A., Fernandez, B., Hammami, R., Ababsa, A., Daba, H., Fliss, I., 2017. Bacteriocin-producing *Enterococcus faecium* LCW 44: a high potential probiotic candidate from raw camel milk. Front. Microbiol. 8, 865.

von Dentz, B.G.Z., 2017. Artisan production of traditional food as an intangible patrimony: prospects and possibilities. *RIVAR* 4, 92–115.

Widgren, S., Eriksson, E., Aspan, A., Emanuelson, U., Alenius, S., Lindberg, A., 2013. Environmental sampling for evaluating verotoxigenic *Escherichia coli* O157:H7 status in dairy cattle herds. J. Vet. Diagn. Invest. 25, 189–198.

Yoon, Y., Lee, S., Choi, K.H., 2016. Microbial benefits and risks of raw milk cheese. Food Control 63, 201–215.

Young, I., Reimer, D., Greig, J., Meldrum, R., Turgeon, P., Waddell, L., 2017a. Explaining consumer safe food handling through behavior-change theories: a systematic review. Foodborne Pathog. Dis. 14, 609–622.

Young, I., Thaivalappil, A., Reimer, D., Greig, J., 2017b. Food safety at farmers' markets: a knowledge synthesis of published research. J. Food Prot. 80, 2033–2047.

Zastempowska, E., Grajewski, J., Twaruzek, M., 2016. Food-borne pathogens and contaminants in raw milk—a review. Ann. Anim. Sci. 16, 623–639.

Zhang, B., Wang, Y.P., Tan, Z.F., Li, Z.W., Jiao, Z., Huang, Q.C., 2016. Screening of probiotic activities of lactobacilli strains isolated from traditional Tibetan Qula, a raw yak milk cheese. Asian-Australas. J. Anim. Sci. 29, 1490–1499.

Zhang, F.X., Wang, Z.X., Lei, F.Y., Wang, B.N., Jiang, S.M., Peng, Q.N., et al., 2017. Bacterial diversity in goat milk from the Guanzhong area of China. J. Dairy Sci. 100, 7812—7824.

Zhao, X.H., Bo, L.Y., Wang, J., Li, T.J., 2012. Survey of seven organophosphorus pesticides in drinking water, feedstuffs and raw milk from dairy farms in the Province Heilongjiang during 2008—2009. Milchwissenschaft 67, 293—296.

Ziarno, M., 2006. Bacteria of *Enterococcus* genus in milk and dairy products. Med. Weter. 62, 145—148.

INDEX

Note: Page numbers followed by "*f*," "*t*," and "*b*" refer to figures, tables, and boxes, respectively.